D1255703

BODY AND MIND

BBF

BODY AND MIND

READINGS IN PHILOSOPHY

René Descartes   F. H. Bradley
Benedict Spinoza   James Ward
G. W. Leibniz   V. I. Lenin
Nicolas Malebranche   G. E. Moore
John Locke   Samuel Alexander
George Berkeley   G. F. Stout
David Hume   Bertrand Russell
Immanuel Kant   C. D. Broad
Thomas Reid   Moritz Schlick
Arthur Schopenhauer   A. M. Maciver
Shadworth Hodgson   C. S. Sherrington
T. H. Huxley   C. I. Lewis
Franz Brentano   Gilbert Ryle
G. H. Lewes   J. N. Findlay
W. K. Clifford   John Wisdom
Ernst Mach   C. A. Campbell
G. J. Romanes   D. M. Mackay
Morton Prince   P. F. Strawson
William James   J. J. C. Smart
Karl Pearson   G. N. A. Vesey
Jerome Shaffer

BBFAL

EDITED BY

G. N. A. VESEY

M.A., M.Litt. (Cantab)
Lecturer in Philosophy, King's College, University of London

LONDON. GEORGE ALLEN AND UNWIN LTD

0189103
65177

FIRST PUBLISHED IN 1964
SECOND IMPRESSION 1970

*This book is copyright under the Berne Convention. All
rights are reserved. Apart from any fair dealing for the
purpose of private study, research, criticism or review, as
permitted under the Copyright Act, 1956, no part of this
publication may be reproduced, stored in a retrieval system,
or transmitted, in any form or by any means, electronic,
electrical, chemical, mechanical, optical, photocopying re-
cording or otherwise, without the prior permission of the
copyright owner. Enquiries should be addressed to the
publishers.*

© *George Allen & Unwin Ltd., 1964*

SBN 04 130010 6 *cloth*
SBN 04 130014 9 *paper*

PRINTED IN GREAT BRITAIN
BY PHOTOLITHOGRAPHY BY BILLING & SONS LTD.
GUILDFORD AND LONDON

CONTENTS

0189103   ~~65177~~

PREFACE

(i) *Questions*

Is the mind merely a product of the working of the brain? Is it 'as completely without any power of modifying that working as the steam-whistle which accompanies the working of a locomotive engine is without influence upon its machinery'?[1] Or has it an independent existence, a life of its own? And do events in that life—our thoughts, feelings, desires—actually cause the brain to work in the way it does?

On either hypothesis it is assumed that it makes sense to talk of a causal relation between bodily and mental events. Is this assumption justified? Ought we, rather, to think of there being *one* process with two 'sides' to it—a physical, public, outer side, and a mental, private, inner side?

But to talk of 'sides', here, is to talk in metaphors. What is the literal significance of such talk? What empirical difference is there between there being one process with two sides, mental and physical, and there being two kinds of events inexplicably associated with one another? Should we avoid such questions by asserting that mind-events and brain-events are in some sense identical? But in what sense? Or is the whole endeavour—to try to understand the place of mind in nature—misconceived?

These questions are *one* expression of a problem—the problem of the relation of body and mind—which has been to the forefront in the investigations and speculations of philosophers for over 300 years. It is a problem which is coming to have a new significance with increasing awareness of the possibility of explaining differences in human behaviour in terms of the functioning of a material organ, the brain, and of constructing machines which simulate man's most treasured possession, intelligence. What was a paradox in 1874, T. H. Huxley's dictum that man is a conscious automaton, is little short of a platitude among the spiritual heirs of Watson, Pavlov, and Weiner, in 1964.

The roots of the problem lie in our concepts—the concepts of mind, of matter, and of causation. The history of the problem is the history of the development of these concepts. This volume of *Readings in Philosophy* is a source-book for the study of that history from the time of Descartes to the present day.

[1] T. H. Huxley.

(ii) A Pattern in the Development of our Concept of Mind

A pattern can be traced in the development of our concept of mind. It is a complex pattern, comprising, in addition to variations on one central theme, a number of 'counter-themes', and variations on them. The one central theme is provided by the Cartesian notion of substance.

The notion of substance is one with a long and varied history. Aristotle, in his *Metaphysics*, carried out what was virtually an elimination-contest for the true meaning of the word, finally settling on there being two kinds of substance, or, rather, 'substance in two senses'. These were the senses which he had distinguished in the *Categories*: 'primary substance', the individual thing, defined negatively so as to exclude such dependent 'individuals' as items of information in people's heads; and 'secondary substance', the 'forms' or 'essences' of things. It is easy to over-simplify Aristotle's concept of 'form'. The form of a brass vase is said to be its shape, as distinct from its matter, brass. More to the point, the form of the eye is eyesight, the form of an axe what might be called its 'axeity'. An eye, by itself, does not see; it is lifeless. If it had life (that is, if it were itself responsible for its changes), as has the body to which it belongs, it would be capable of sight, and this capacity would then be its 'soul'. This, in fact, is how Aristotle explains what he means by the word 'soul' in the *De Anima*. The soul is the first grade of actuality (corresponding to the possession, not to the exercise, of a capacity) of a natural body (as distinct from an artefact) having life potentially in it. Roughly, it is the 'form' of the body, and as such can be considered under different headings (nutritive, sensitive, etc.).

Although Descartes paid some lip-service to the Aristotelian notion of the soul as the form of the body, his definition of substance was based, not on Aristotle's 'secondary' sense of substance, but on his 'primary' sense. Substance, for him, was 'nothing other than a thing existing in such a manner that it has need of no other thing in order to exist'.

This definition, in itself, is clearly not such as to entail that minds and bodies are distinct substances. In the absence of any indication as to the meaning of the phrase 'needing another thing in order to exist' nothing is entailed about what sort of things substances are, or how many of them there are. It seemed that Descartes might be providing a meaning for the phrase when he wrote of our being able to think of one thing without thinking of another. At one point in his *Meditations*, it seemed that he might be advancing this as the *criterion* for two things being distinct substances. But it later became evident that our being able to think of one thing without thinking of another was, for him, merely a *sign* that they were distinct substances. 'Because I know that all things which I apprehend clearly and distinctly can be created by God as I apprehend them, it suffices that I am able to apprehend one thing apart from another clearly and distinctly in order to be certain that the one is different from the other, since they may be made to exist in separation at least by the omnipotence of God.'

The question to which this gave rise was: How can one be sure that one's apprehension of something is sufficiently 'clear and distinct'? It could hardly be maintained that two things, which we can think of independently, could be made to exist in separation by God, if we can think of them independently only because our thought misses some aspect of their essential nature. How can one be sure that one's notion of mind, or of matter, is *adequate*?

This question, raised by Arnauld, in the *Objections and Replies*, received an answer of sorts at the hands of Locke, nearly fifty years later. 'We have the ideas of matter and thinking, but possibly shall never be able to know whether any mere material being thinks or no; it being impossible for us, by the contemplation of our own ideas without revelation, to discover whether Omnipotency has not given to some systems of matter, fitly disposed, a power to perceive and think, or else joined and fixed to matter, so disposed, a thinking immaterial substance.' This was the inevitable outcome of the indeterminacy of the notion of substance.

The central theme for the Cartesians was provided by the notion of substance. But whereas Descartes was a Dualist, Spinoza was a Monist, and Leibniz a Pluralist. The philosophies of both Spinoza and Leibniz can be viewed as attempts, within a framework of ideas dominated by the notion of substance, to show that the contingency of the body-mind relation is only apparent. Spinoza sought to remove the appearance of contingency by making body and mind two attributes of one substance. Leibniz sought to remove it by making changes in body and mind equally dependent on one master-plan; his doctrine was one of a 'harmony' between body and mind. The harmony was provided by God, and, in this respect, Leibniz's system resembled that of Malebranche. The difference was that whereas for Leibniz the harmony was 'pre-established', for Malebranche it was the result of God, on the occasion of a bodily or mental event, *willing* the appropriate mental or bodily event to accompany it ('occasionalism').

The 'counter-themes' are provided by concepts of mind deliberately put forward as alternatives to Descartes' notion of mind as one of two kinds of substances. Two such concepts deserve special mention.

One of them is the concept of mind as *subject*, as opposed to what is the *object* of its activities. This is a concept which is associated particularly with Brentano, who defined mentality in terms of 'intentionality', directedness to an object; but it can be seen at work in Reid and Kant. In this connection it is interesting to compare the writings of Reid with those of Moore (*Subject-matter of Psychology*) and Ryle (*Dilemmas*). Moore was not the first 'common sense' philosopher, nor Ryle the first to deny that the concept of seeing is the concept of an effect of stimulation of the eye.

A second concept of mind deserving special mention is that of the mental as being what is 'private', as opposed to what is 'public'. This concept can be regarded as arising out of a limitation in the scope of the subject-object distinction. To the object of a subject's act of consciousness there may not correspond anything real. Thus if one hallucinates a snake, the snake exists as an object of one's awareness, but not as a constituent of the real world. The question of the existence, or non-existence, of something real corresponding to the object of one's act of consciousness is a question neither about acts of consciousness nor about their objects. But it is a question which cannot be avoided for long. It was natural, therefore, to progress to a concept of mind which was such that what is mental could be opposed to what exists not merely as an object of one person's awareness, but as a possible object of anyone's consciousness. This was the concept of the mental as the private. Perhaps the most articulate expression of this concept of mind, in this volume, is that contained in the contribution by Wisdom. 'The peculiarity of the soul is not that it is visible to none but that it is visible only to one.'

A variation on the theme of the mental as the private is that of the mental as what is known 'directly', or 'without inference'. Here the mental is opposed neither to the object of an act of consciousness, nor to what is 'public', but to whatever scientists discover to be the real nature of things.

(iii) Concepts of Mind, and the Body-Mind Problem

There is one expression of the body-mind problem which, historically, has precedence in the period under survey in this volume. It is this. In this world, at any rate, body and mind would appear to be intimately related. Yet there is nothing in their nature to explain this relation, for they are distinct substances, the essence of one of them being spatial extension, that of the other, thought. Hence their relation, if they are indeed related, can only be an 'external', causal, one. But even this possibility seems unintelligible, for how can what is non-extended move, or be moved by, what is extended?

It is not hard to see the relevance of the development of our concept of mind to this problem. If mind is conceived as one term of a reciprocal relation (subject—object) then there is, *in the nature of mind*, an explanation of its intimate relation with at least one thing, the object of its acts. Mind is essentially a *minding*. It is this 'internal' relation which gives the mind, so conceived, its relation with body; and there is no call for an external, causal, relation to do the same thing.

Alternatively, if the mental is thought of as being what is private, as opposed to what is public, then again the problem does not arise in the old form. It becomes a problem in epistemology; the problem, perhaps, as to how, on the basis of what is private, we can make judgments about what is public, or how, on the basis of what is known without inference, we can infer what we cannot know otherwise than by inference.

If the relation of body and mind, when body and mind are thought of in terms of what is public and what is private, is still thought of as a causal relation, then it will be in an emasculated sense of 'cause'. No more will be meant than that one can correlate private and public happenings. Bertrand Russell, in the second extract from his works contained in this volume, holds body and mind to be causally connected in this sense. So does A. J. Ayer, in a paper too short for inclusion in this volume (his contribution to *The Physical Basis of Mind*, Ed. Peter Laslett, Basil Blackwell, 1950). Philosophers who hold that this is all that is meant by talk of a causal relation between body and mind strenuously deny that there is any mystery about the relation. Thus Ayer writes:

It seems to me that when it is asserted that the two events in question—the mental and the physical—are causally connected, that the pattern of nerve impulses 'produces' the sensation, or that the thought 'decides' what nerve cells are to operate, all that is meant, or at least all that can properly be meant, is that these two sets of observations are correlated in the way that I have described. But if this is so, where is the difficulty? There is nothing especially mysterious about the fact that two different sets of observations are correlated; that, given the appropriate conditions, they habitually accompany one another.

(iv) The Embodied Mind

It might be objected, to the foregoing attempts to remove the traditional body-mind problem by replacing the concept of mind as non-extended substance by some other concept, that they succeed only by taking 'the intimate relation of body and mind' to refer to the relation of mind to body (matter) in general, and not to the relation of a mind to the one body which it 'animates'. What force has this objection?

G. F. Stout remarks that each of us has experience of his own body in a way essentially different from the way in which any one else can have experience of it. Each of us apprehends his own body 'as entering into the being of himself'. 'What we know or seem to know in ordinary self-consciousness,' he writes, 'is a concrete whole within which mind and body are only abstractly distinguishable as partial factors.' What is apprehended in ordinary experience is 'the unity of mind and body'. (It is interesting to compare with this what Descartes says on the same topic in his correspondence with Princess Elizabeth, and also to compare what Descartes says, in this correspondence, about the priority of the concept of 'person', with what P. F. Strawson says in his paper, 'Persons'.)

Stout calls this unity 'the unity of the embodied self'; and he says that 'this experience of the self as embodied ought either to be shown to be illusory, or to be taken as a fundamental datum in any attempt to determine the relation of body and mind'.

The two features of our experience which would seem to contribute most to the concept of the mind as embodied are:

(a) our experience of moving our own bodies in a manner in which we cannot move anything other than our own bodies, and

(b) our experience of having feelings (aches, tickles, etc.) which we locate in our bodies, and which it is hard, if not impossible, to imagine locating anywhere else.

Under the influence of the concept of mind as non-extended substance, certain 'theories' of these experiences were for a long time accepted by psychologists (see the extract from the works of William James) and, in one form or another, would appear still to attract some philosophers (for instance, C. A. Campbell). They are:

(α) the Ideo-motor theory of voluntary movement, and

(β) the Local Sign theory of the location of bodily sensations.

According to the Ideo-motor theory, we *cause* the movements of our bodies by having ideas—ideas of what it would be like either to see, or to feel, the movement occurring. According to the Local Sign theory, feelings only *appear* to be in our bodies: really they have some 'quality' which we have learnt to interpret as meaning that the *cause* of the sensation has a certain location in the body. On both the theories there is an association of something bodily with something mental. In the case of the Ideo-motor theory it is the association of an idea of a movement occurring with a certain part of the body being in motion. In the case of the Local Sign theory it is the association of a certain part of the body being stimulated with a sensation having a certain quality. That there are these associations has just to be accepted as a brute fact. There is no intrinsic connection between the associated items. This is obviously so in the case of the Local Sign theory. It is so, also, in the case of the Ideo-motor theory. Moreover, there is no hope of the association ever being explained, for the associated items are attributed to distinct substances, between which there can be no middle term.

My own view is that if we are to escape from the traditional body-mind problem then accounts must be given of the experiences which contribute to our concept of mind as embodied, which do not leave us having to accept associations of body and mind as brute facts. Perhaps it is a mistake to dislike brute facts. If so, it is a mistake without which there would be neither philosophy nor science.

(v) Contents and Acknowledgments

1. RENÉ DESCARTES. (i) Extracts from the First, Second and Sixth of the *Meditations on First Philosophy*, 1641; (ii) Extracts from the Third, Fourth and Fifth sets of *Objections* (by Hobbes, Arnauld and Gassendi, respectively) *and Replies*, 1642; (iii) Extracts from *The Principles of Philosophy*, 1644 (Principles 40, 41, 48, 51–54, 60); (iv) Extracts from *The Passions of the Soul*, 1649 (Articles 23, 24, 30–34); (v) Extracts from Descartes' Correspondence with Princess Elizabeth, 1643. (i), (ii), (iii), and (iv) are reprinted from *The Philosophical Works of Descartes*, rendered into English by E. S. Haldane and G. T. R. Ross, 2 vols., Cambridge University Press, 1911–12, by kind permission of the publishers. (v) is reprinted from *Descartes: Philosophical Writings*, a selection translated and edited by E. Anscombe and P. T. Geach, London: Nelson, 1954, by kind permission of the publishers.

2. BENEDICT SPINOZA. Extracts from *The Ethics*, 1677 (First Part, Definitions 3–6, Propositions, 14, 15; Second Part, Definition 1, Propositions 1, 2, 6, 7; Third Part, Proposition 2; Fifth Part, Preface), reprinted from *The Ethics of Benedict de Spinoza*, New York: Van Nostrand, 1876.

3. G. W. LEIBNIZ. (i) Extracts from *The Discourse on Metaphysics*, written 1685–86 (Articles 8, 9, 12, 14, 28, 33); (ii) Extracts from *Correspondence relating to the Metaphysics*, 1686. (i) is reprinted from *Leibniz: Discourse on Metaphysics*, translated by P. G. Lucas and L. Grint, Manchester University Press, 1953, by kind permission of the publishers. (ii) is reprinted from *Leibniz: Discourse on Metaphysics, Correspondence with Arnauld, and Monadology*, translated by G. R. Montgomery, Chicago: Open Court, 1908, by kind permission of the publishers.

4. NICOLAS MALEBRANCHE. Extracts from *Dialogues on Metaphysics and Religion*, 1688, reprinted from *Malebranche: Dialogues on Metaphysics and Religion*, translated by M. Ginsberg, London: Allen & Unwin, 1923, by kind permission of the publishers.

5. JOHN LOCKE. Extracts from *An Essay concerning Human Understanding*, 1690 (Book 2, Ch. 13, Sections 18, 19, Ch. 23, Sections 1–5, 15–20, 29, 30; Book 4, Ch. 3, Section 6).

6. GEORGE BERKELEY. Extracts from *The Principles of Human Knowledge*, 1710 (Sections 1, 2, 25, 27, 135, 137–140, 142).

7. DAVID HUME. Extracts from *Enquiry concerning the Human Understanding*, 1748 (Part 1, Section 7).

8. IMMANUEL KANT. Extracts from *The Critique of Pure Reason*, 1st Ed., 1781 (Fourth Paralogism of Pure Reason), reprinted from *Immanuel Kant's Critique of Pure Reason*, translated by N. K. Smith, London: Macmillan, 1929; New York: St Martin's Press, Inc., by kind permission of the publishers.

9. THOMAS REID. Extracts from *Essays on the Intellectual Powers of Man*, 1785 (Essay 1, Ch. 1; Essay 2, Ch. 4).

10. ARTHUR SCHOPENHAUER. (i) Extracts from *The World as Will and Idea*, 1818 (Vol. 1, Book 2); (ii) Extracts from *On the Will in Nature*, 1835. (i) is reprinted from *Schopenhauer: The World as Will and Idea*, translated by R. B. Haldane and J. Kemp, London: Routledge & Kegan Paul, 1883, by kind permission of the publishers. (ii) is reprinted from *On the Fourfold Root of the Principle of Sufficient Reason and On the Will in Nature*, translated by Mme. K. Hillebrand, Bohn's Library, London: George Bell & Sons, 1889, by kind permission of the publishers.

11. SHADWORTH HODGSON. Extracts from *The Theory of Practice*, London: Longmans, Green, Reader & Dyer, 1870 (Book 1, Ch. 3, Sections 49, 57).

12. T. H. HUXLEY. Extracts from *On the Hypothesis that Animals are Automata, and its History* (Address, British Association for the Advancement of Science, Belfast), 1874, reprinted from T. H. Huxley, *Collected Essays*, London: Macmillan, 1898, Vol. 1.

13. FRANZ BRENTANO. Extracts from *Psychologie vom Empirischen Standpunkt*, 1874, Hamburg: Felix Meiner, 1955 (Book 2, Ch. 1), translated by D. B. Terrell, and reprinted by kind permission of the Trustees, the Franz Brentano Foundation.

14. G. H. LEWES. Extracts from *The Physical Basis of Mind*, London: Trubner & Co., 1877 (Problem 3, Chs. 3, 7).

15. W. K. CLIFFORD. Extracts from 'On the Nature of Things-in-Themselves', *Mind*, 1878.

16. ERNST MACH. Extracts from *Contributions to the Analysis of Sensations*, 1886 (Ch. 1), reprinted from *Ernst Mach: Contributions to the Analysis of Sensations*, translated by C. M. Williams, Chicago: Open Court, 1897, by kind permission of the publishers.

17. G. J. ROMANES. Extracts from *Mind and Motion*, Rede Lecture, 1885, reprinted from G. J. Romanes, *Mind and Motion and Monism*, London: Longmans Green & Co., 1896.

18. MORTON PRINCE. Extracts from *The Nature of Mind and Human Automatism*, Philadelphia: J. B. Lippincott, 1885 (Part 1, Chs. 1–3).

19. WILLIAM JAMES. (i) Extracts from *The Principles of Psychology*, Macmillan, 1891 (Chs. 20, 26); (ii) Extracts from 'Does "consciousness" exist?', *Journal of Philosophy, Psychology and Scientific Methods*, Vol. 1, 1904 (reprinted in William James, *Essays in Radical Empiricism*, London: Longmans Green & Co., 1912).

20. KARL PEARSON. Extracts from *The Grammar of Science*, London: A. & C. Black, 1892 (Ch. 2), reprinted by kind permission of the publishers.

21. F. H. BRADLEY. 'On the Supposed Uselessness of the Soul', *Mind*, N.S. Vol. 4, 1895, reprinted by kind permission of the Editor, *Mind*.

22. JAMES WARD. Extracts from *Naturalism and Agnosticism*, Gifford Lectures, 1896–98, London: A. & C. Black, 1899 (Part 4), reprinted by kind permission of the publishers.

23. V. I. LENIN. Extracts from *Materialism and Empirio-Criticism*, 1908, translated by A. Fineberg, London: Lawrence & Wishart, 1948, reprinted by kind permission of the publishers.

24. G. E. MOORE. (i) Extracts from 'The Subject-matter of Psychology', *Proc. Arist. Soc.*, 1909–10; (ii) Extracts from *Some Main Problems of Philosophy*, lectures delivered in 1910–11, London: Allen & Unwin, 1953 (Ch. 8). (i) is reprinted by kind permission of the Editor, *Proc. Arist. Soc.* (ii) is reprinted by kind permission of the publishers.

25. SAMUEL ALEXANDER. Extracts from *Space, Time and Deity*, Gifford Lectures, 1916–18, London: Macmillan, 1920 (Book 3, Ch. 1), reprinted by kind permission of the publishers and of the University of Manchester.

26. G. F. STOUT. Extracts from *Mind and Matter*, Gifford Lectures, 1919–21, Cambridge University Press, 1931 (Book 2, Chs. 1, 8; Book 4, Ch. 7), reprinted by kind permission of the publishers.

27. BERTRAND RUSSELL. (i) Extracts from *The Analysis of Mind*, London: Allen & Unwin, 1921 (Lecture 1); (ii) Extracts from *Human Knowledge: Its Scope and Limits*, London: Allen & Unwin, 1948 (Part 1, Ch. 5; Part 3, Chs. 4, 7). (i) and (ii) are reprinted by kind permission of the publishers.

28. C. D. BROAD. Extracts from *The Mind and its Place in Nature*, Tarner Lectures, 1923, London: Routledge & Kegan Paul, 1925 (Ch. 3), reprinted by kind permission of the publishers.

29. MORITZ SCHLICK. Extracts from *Allgemeine Erkenntnislehre*, Leipzig: Springer Verlag, 1925 (Section 32), translated for this volume by Gillian Brown, and reprinted by kind permission of the publishers.

30. A. M. MACIVER. Extracts from 'Is there Mind-Body Interaction?', *Proc. Arist. Soc.*, 1935–6, reprinted by kind permission of the Editor, *Proc. Arist. Soc.*

31. C. S. SHERRINGTON. Extracts from *Man on his Nature*, Gifford Lectures, 1937–8, Cambridge University Press, 1940 (Lectures 8–11), reprinted by kind permission of the publishers.

32. C. I. LEWIS. 'Some Logical Considerations concerning the Mental', *Journal of Philosophy*, Vol. 38, 1941, reprinted by kind permission of the author, and of the Directors, *Journal of Philosophy*.

33. GILBERT RYLE. (i) Extracts from *The Concept of Mind*, Hutchinson's University Library, London: Hutchinson, 1949 (Ch. 1); (ii) Extracts from *Dilemmas*, Tarner Lectures, 1953, Cambridge University Press, 1954 (Ch. 7). (i) and (ii) are reprinted by kind permission of the respective publishers.

34. J. N. FINDLAY. 'Linguistic Approach to Psycho-Physics', *Proc. Arist. Soc.*, 1949–50 (reprinted in J. N. Findlay, *Language, Mind and Value*, London: Allen & Unwin, 1963), reprinted by kind permission of the Editor, *Proc. Arist. Soc.*

35. JOHN WISDOM. Extracts from 'The Concept of Mind', *Proc. Arist. Soc.*, 1950–51 (reprinted in John Wisdom, *Other Minds*, Blackwell, 1952), reprinted by kind permission of the Editor, *Proc. Arist. Soc.*

C189103

36. C. A. CAMPBELL. Extracts from *On Selfhood and Godhood*, Gifford Lectures, 1953–5, London: Allen & Unwin, 1957 (Lectures 6, 8), reprinted by kind permission of the publishers.

37. D. M. MACKAY. 'Brain and Will', *Listener*, May 9th, 16th, 1957 (reprinted in *Faith and Thought*, Vol. 90, 1958), reprinted by kind permission of the author.

38. P. F. STRAWSON. 'Persons', *Minnesota Studies in the Philosophy of Science*, Vol. 2, Concepts, Theories, and the Mind-Body Problem, ed. Herbert Feigl, Michael Scriven, and Grover Maxwell, University of Minnesota Press, Minneapolis, copyright 1958 by the University of Minnesota, reprinted by kind permission of the publishers.

39. J. J. C. SMART. 'Sensations and Brain Processes', *Phil. Review*, Vol. 68, 1959, reprinted by kind permission of the author, and of the Editorial Board, *Phil. Review*.

40. G. N. A. VESEY. 'Volition', *Philosophy*, Vol. 36, 1961, reprinted by kind permission of the Editor, *Philosophy*.

41. JEROME SHAFFER. 'Could mental states be brain processes?', *Journal of Philosophy*, Vol. 58, 1961, reprinted by kind permission of the author and of the Directors, *Journal of Philosophy*.

I

RENÉ DESCARTES

I. MEDITATIONS ON FIRST PHILOSOPHY (1641)

It is now some years since I detected how many were the false beliefs that I had from my earliest youth admitted as true, and how doubtful was everything I had since constructed on this basis; and from that time I was convinced that I must once for all seriously undertake to rid myself of all the opinions which I had formerly accepted, and commence to build anew from the foundation, if I wanted to establish any firm and permanent structure in the sciences. But as this enterprise appeared to be a very great one, I waited until I had attained an age so mature that I could not hope that at any later date I should be better fitted to execute my design. This reason caused me to delay so long that I should feel that I was doing wrong were I to occupy in deliberation the time that yet remains to me for action. Today, then, since very opportunely for the plan I have in view I have delivered my mind from every care (and I am happily agitated by no passions) and since I have procured for myself an assured leisure in a peaceable retirement, I shall at last seriously and freely address myself to the general upheaval of all my former opinions. . . . I shall proceed by setting aside all that in which the least doubt could be supposed to exist, just as if I had discovered that it was absolutely false; and I shall ever follow in this road until I have met with something which is certain, or at least, if I can do nothing else, until I have learned for certain that there is nothing in the world that is certain. Archimedes, in order that he might draw the terrestrial globe out of its place, and transport it elsewhere, demanded only that one point should be fixed and immovable; in the same way I shall have the right to conceive high hopes if I am happy enough to discover one thing only which is certain and indubitable.

I suppose, then, that all the things that I see are false; I persuade myself that nothing has ever existed of all that my fallacious memory represents to me. I consider that I possess no senses; I imagine that body, figure, extension, movement and place are but the fictions of my mind. What, then, can be esteemed as true? Perhaps nothing at all, unless that there is nothing in the world that is certain.

But how can I know there is not something different from those things that I have just considered, of which one cannot have the slightest doubt? Is there not some God, or some other being by whatever name we call it, who puts these reflections into my mind? That is not necessary, for is it not possible that I am capable of producing them myself? I myself, am I not at least something? But I have already denied that I had senses and body. Yet I hesitate, for what follows from that? Am I so dependent on body and senses that I cannot exist without these? But I was persuaded that there was nothing in all the world, that there was no heaven, no earth, that there were no minds, nor any bodies; was I not then likewise persuaded that I did not exist? Not at all; of a surety I myself did exist since I persuaded myself of something (or merely because I thought of something). But there is some deceiver or other, very powerful and very cunning, who ever employs his ingenuity in deceiving me. Then without doubt I exist also if he deceives me, and let him deceive me as much as he will, he can never cause me to be nothing so long as I think that I am something. So that after having reflected well and carefully examined all things, we must come to the definite conclusion that this proposition: I am, I exist, is necessarily true each time that I pronounce it, or that I mentally conceive it.

But I do not yet know clearly enough what I am, I who am certain that I am; and hence I must be careful to see that I do not imprudently take some other object in place of myself, and thus that I do not go astray in respect of this knowledge that I hold to be the most certain and most evident of all that I have formerly learned. That is why I shall now consider anew what I believed myself to be before I embarked upon these last reflections; and of my former opinions I shall withdraw all that might even in a small degree be invalidated by the reasons which I have just brought forward, in order that there may be nothing at all left beyond what is absolutely certain and indubitable.

When then did I formerly believe myself to be? Undoubtedly I believed myself to be a man. But what is a man? Shall I say a reasonable animal? Certainly not; for then I should have to inquire what an animal is, and what is reasonable; and thus from a single question I should insensibly fall into an infinitude of others more difficult; and I should not wish to waste the little time and leisure remaining to me in trying to unravel subtleties like these. But I shall rather stop here to consider the thoughts which of themselves spring up in my mind, and which were not inspired by anything beyond my own nature alone when I applied myself to the consideration of my being. In the first place, then, I considered myself as having a face, hands, arms, and all that system of members composed of bones and flesh as seen in a corpse which I designated by the name of body. In addition to this I considered that I was nourished, that I walked, that I felt, and that I thought, and I referred all these actions to the soul: but I did not stop to consider what the soul was, or if I did stop, I imagined that it was something extremely rare and subtle like a wind, a flame, or an ether, which was spread throughout my grosser parts. As to body I had no manner of doubt about its nature, but thought I had a very clear knowledge of it; and if I had desired to explain it according to the notions that I had then formed of it, I should have described it thus: By the body I understand all that which can be defined by a certain figure: something which can be confined in a certain place, and which can fill a given space in such a way that every other body will be excluded from it; which can be perceived either by touch, or by sight, or by hearing, or by taste, or by smell; which can be moved in many ways not, in truth, by itself, but by something which is foreign to it, by which it is touched (and from which it receives impressions): for to have the power of self-movement, as also of feeling or of thinking, I did not consider to appertain to the nature of body; on the contrary, I was rather astonished to find that faculties similar to them existed in some bodies.

But what am I, now that I suppose that there is a certain genius which is extremely powerful, and, if I may say so, malicious, who employs all his powers in deceiving me? Can I affirm that I possess the least of all those things which I have just said pertain to the nature of body? I pause to consider, I revolve all these things in my mind, and I find none of which I can say that it pertains to me. It would be tedious to stop to enumerate them. Let us pass to the attributes of soul and see if there is any one which is in me? What of nutrition or walking (the first mentioned)? But if it is so that I have no body it is also true that I can neither walk nor take nourishment. Another attribute is sensation. But one cannot feel without body, and besides I have thought I perceived many things during sleep that I recognized in my waking moments as not having been experienced at all. What of thinking? I find here that thought is an attribute that belongs to me; it alone cannot be separated from me. I am, I exist, that is certain. But how often? Just when I think; for it might possibly be the case if I ceased entirely to think, that I should likewise cease altogether to exist. I do not now admit anything which is not necessarily true: to speak accurately I am not more than a thing which thinks, that is to say a mind or a soul, or an understanding, or a reason, which are terms whose significance was formerly unknown to me. I am, however, a real thing and really exist; but what thing? I have answered: a thing which thinks.

And what more? I shall exercise my imagination (in order to see if I am not something more). I am not a collection of members which we call the human body: I am not a subtle air distributed through these members, I am not a wind, a fire, a vapour, a breath, nor anything at all which I can imagine or conceive; because I have assumed that all these were nothing. Without changing that supposition I find that I only leave myself certain of the fact that I am somewhat. But perhaps it is true that these same things which I supposed were non-existent because they are unknown to me, are really not different from the self which I know. I am not sure about this, I shall not dispute about it now; I can only give judgment on things that are known to me. I know that I exist, and I inquire what I am, I whom I know to exist. But it is very certain that the knowledge of my existence taken in its precise significance does not depend on things whose existence is not yet known to me; consequently it does not depend on those which I can feign in imagination. And indeed the very term *feign* in imagination proves to me my error, for I really do this if I image myself a something, since to imagine is nothing else than to contemplate the figure or image of a corporeal thing. But I already know for certain that I am, and that it may be that all these images and, speaking generally, all things that relate to the nature of body are nothing but dreams (and chimeras). For this reason I see clearly that I have as little reason to say, 'I shall stimulate my imagination in order to know more distinctly what I am,' than if I were to say, 'I am now awake, and I perceive somewhat that is real and true: but because I do not yet perceive it distinctly enough, I shall go to sleep of express purpose, so that my dreams may represent the perception with greatest truth and evidence.' And, thus, I know for certain that nothing of all that I can understand by means of my imagination belongs to this knowledge which I have of myself, and that it is necessary to recall the mind from this mode of thought with the utmost diligence in order that it may be able to know its own nature with perfect distinctness.

But what then am I? A thing which thinks. What is a thing which thinks? It is a thing which doubts, understands, (conceives), affirms, denies, wills, refuses, which also imagines and feels.

Certainly it is no small matter if all these things pertain to my nature. But why should they not so pertain? Am I not that being who now doubts nearly everything, who nevertheless understands certain things, who affirms that one only is true, who denies all the others, who desires to know more, is averse from being deceived, who imagines many things, sometimes indeed despite his will, and who perceives many likewise, as by the intervention of the bodily organs? Is there nothing in all this which is as true as it is certain that I exist, even though I should always sleep and though he who has given me being employed all his ingenuity in deceiving me? Is there likewise any one of these attributes which can be distinguished from my thought, or which might be said to be separated from myself?

For it is so evident of itself that it is I who doubts, who understands, and who desires, that there is no reason here to add anything to explain it. And I have certainly the power of imagining likewise; for although it may happen (as I formerly supposed) that none of the things which I imagine are true, nevertheless this power of imagining does not cease to be really in use, and it forms part of my thought. Finally, I am the same who feels, that is to say, who perceives certain things, as by the organs of sense, since in truth I see light, I hear noise, I feel heat. But it will be said that these phenomena are false and that I am dreaming. Let it be so; still it is at least quite certain that it seems to me that I see light, that I hear noise and that I feel heat. That cannot be false; properly speaking it is what is in me called feeling; and used in this precise sense that is no other thing than thinking. . . .

First of all I shall recall to my memory those matters which I hitherto held to be true, as having perceived them through the senses, and the foundations on which my belief has rested; in the next place I shall examine the reasons which have since obliged me to place them in doubt; in the last place I shall consider which of them I must now believe.

First of all, then, I perceived that I had a head, hands, feet, and all other members of which this body—which I considered as a part, or possibly even as the whole, of myself—is composed. Further I was sensible that this body was placed amidst many others, from which it was capable of being affected in many different ways, beneficial and hurtful, and I remarked that a certain feeling of pleasure accompanied those that were beneficial, and pain those which were harmful. And in addition to this pleasure and pain, I also experienced hunger, thirst, and other similar appetites, as also certain corporeal inclinations towards joy, sadness, anger, and other similar passions. And outside myself, in addition to extension, figure, and motions of bodies, I remarked in them hardness, heat, and all other tactile qualities, and, further, light and colour, and scents and sounds, the variety of which gave me the means of distinguishing the sky, the earth, the sea, and generally all the other bodies, one from the other. And certainly, considering the ideas of all these qualities which presented themselves to my mind, and which alone I perceived properly or immediately, it was not without reason that I believed myself to perceive objects quite different from my thought, to wit, bodies from which those ideas proceeded; for I found by experience that these ideas presented themselves to me without my consent being requisite, so that I could not perceive any object, however desirous I might be, unless it were present to the organs of sense; and it was not in my power not to perceive it, when it was present. And because the ideas which I received through the senses were much more lively, more clear, and even, in their own way, more distinct than any of those which I could of myself frame in meditation, or than those I found impressed on my memory, it appeared as though they could not have proceeded from my mind, so that they must necessarily have been produced in me by some other things. And having no knowledge of those objects, excepting the knowledge which the ideas themselves gave me, nothing was more likely to occur to my mind than that the objects were similar to the ideas which were caused. And because I likewise remembered that I had formerly made use of my senses rather than my reason, and recognized that the ideas which I formed of myself were not so distinct as those which I perceived through the senses, and that they were most frequently even composed of portions of these last, I persuaded myself easily that I had no idea in my mind which had not formerly come to me through the senses. Nor was it without some reason that I believed that this body (which by a certain special right I call my own) belonged to me more properly and more strictly than any other; for in fact I could never be separated from it as from other bodies; I experienced in it and on account of it all my appetites and affections, and finally I was touched by the feeling of pain and the titillation of pleasure in its parts, and not in the parts of other bodies which were separated from it. But when I inquired, why, from some, I know not what, painful sensation, there follows sadness of mind, and from the pleasurable sensation there arises joy, or why this mysterious pinching of the stomach which I call hunger causes me to desire to eat, and dryness of throat causes a desire to drink, and so on, I could give no reason excepting that nature taught me so; for there is certainly no affinity (that I at least can understand) between the craving of the stomach and the desire to eat, any more than between the perception of whatever causes pain and the thought of sadness which arises from this perception. And in the same way it appeared to me that I had learned from nature all the other judgments which I formed regarding the objects of my senses, since I remarked that these judgments were formed in me before I had the leisure to weigh and consider any reasons which might oblige me to make them.

But afterwards many experiences little by little destroyed all the faith which I had rested in my senses; for I from time to time observed that those towers which from afar appeared to me to be round, more closely observed seemed square, and that colossal statues raised on the summit of these towers, appeared as quite tiny statues when viewed from the bottom; and so in an infinitude of other cases I found error in judgments founded on the external senses. And not only in those founded on the external senses but even in those founded on the internal as well; for is there anything more intimate or more internal than pain? And yet I have learned from some persons whose arms or legs have been cut off, that they sometimes seemed to feel pain in the part which had been amputated, which made me think that I could not be quite certain that it was a certain member which pained me, even although I felt pain in it. And to those grounds of doubt I have lately added two others, which are very general; the first is that I never have believed myself to feel anything in waking moments which I cannot also sometimes believe myself to feel when I sleep, and as I do not think that these things which I seem to feel in sleep, proceed from objects outside of me, I do not see any reason why I should have this belief regarding objects which I seem to perceive while awake. The other was that being still ignorant, or rather supposing myself to be ignorant, of the author of my being, I saw nothing to prevent me from having been so constituted by nature that I might be deceived even in matters which seemed to me to be most certain. And as to the grounds on which I was formerly persuaded of the truth of sensible objects, I had not much trouble in replying to them. For since nature seemed to cause me to lean towards many things from which reason repelled me, I did not believe that I should trust much to the teachings of nature. And although the ideas which I receive by the senses do not depend on my will, I did not think that one should for that reason conclude that they proceeded from things different from myself, since possibly some faculty might be discovered in me—though hitherto unknown to me—which produced them.

But now that I begin to know myself better, and to discover more clearly the author of my being, I do not in truth think that I should rashly admit all the matters which the senses seem to teach us, but, on the other hand, I do not think that I should doubt them all universally.

And first of all, because I know that all things which I apprehend clearly and distinctly can be created by God as I apprehend them, it suffices that I am able to apprehend one thing apart from another clearly and distinctly in order to be certain that the one is different from the other, since they may be made to exist in separation at least by the omnipotence of God; and it does not signify by what power this separation is made in order to compel me to judge them to be different: and, therefore, just because I know certainly that I exist, and that meanwhile I do not remark that any other thing necessarily pertains to my nature or essence, excepting that I am a thinking thing, I rightly conclude that my essence consists solely in the fact that I am a thinking thing (or a substance whose whole essence or nature is to think). And although possibly (or rather certainly, as I shall say in a moment) I possess a body with which I am very intimately conjoined, yet because, on the one side, I have a clear and distinct idea of myself inasmuch as I am only a thinking and unextended thing, and as, on the other, I possess a distinct idea of body, inasmuch as it is only an extended and unthinking thing, it is certain that this I (that is to say, my soul by which I am what I am), is entirely and absolutely distinct from my body, and can exist without it.

I further find in myself faculties employing modes of thinking peculiar to themselves, to wit, the faculties of imagination and feeling, without which I can easily conceive myself clearly and distinctly as a complete being; while, on the other hand, they cannot be so conceived apart from me, that is without an intelligent substance in which they reside for (in the notion we have of these faculties, or, to use the language of the Schools) in their formal concept, some kind of intellection is comprised, from which I infer that they are distinct from me as its modes are from a thing. I observe also in me some other faculties such as that of change of position, the assumption of different figures and such like, which cannot be conceived, any more than can the preceding, apart from some substance to which they are attached, and consequently cannot exist without it; but it is very clear that these faculties, if it be true that they exist, must be attached to some corporeal or extended substance, and not to an intelligent substance, since in the clear and distinct conception of these there is some sort of extension found to be present, but no intellection at all. There is certainly further in me a certain passive faculty of perception, that is, of receiving and recognizing the ideas of sensible things, but this would be useless to me (and I could in no way avail myself of it), if there were not either in me or in some other thing another active faculty capable of forming and producing these ideas. But this active faculty cannot exist in me (inasmuch as I am a thing that thinks) seeing that it does not presuppose thought, and also that those ideas are often produced in me without my contributing in any way to the same, and often even against my will; it is thus necessarily the case that the faculty resides in some substance different from me in which all the reality which is objectively in the ideas that are produced by this faculty is formally or eminently contained, as I remarked before. And this substance is either a body, that is, a corporeal nature in which there is contained formally (and really) all that which is objectively (and by representation) in those ideas, or it is God Himself, or some other creature more noble than body in which that same is contained eminently. But, since God is no deceiver, it is very manifest that He does not communicate to me these ideas immediately and by Himself nor yet by the intervention of some creature in which their reality is not formally, but only eminently, contained. For since He has given me no faculty to recognize that this is the case, but, on the other hand, a very great inclination to believe (that they are sent to me or) that they are conveyed to me by corporeal objects, I do not see how He could be defended from the accusation of deceit if these ideas were produced by causes other than corporeal objects. Hence we must allow that corporeal things exist. However, they are perhaps not exactly what we perceive by the senses, since this comprehension by the senses is in many instances very obscure and confused; but we must at least admit that all things which I conceive in them clearly and distinctly, that is to say, all things which, speaking generally, are comprehended in the object of pure mathematics, are truly to be recognized as external objects.

As to other things, however, which are either particular only, as for example, that the sun is of such and such a figure, etc., or which are less clearly and distinctly conceived, such as light, sound, pain and the like, it is certain that although they are very dubious and uncertain, yet on the sole ground that God is not a deceiver, and that consequently He has not permitted any falsity to exist in my opinion which He has not likewise given me the faculty of correcting, I may assuredly hope to conclude that I have within me the means of arriving at the truth even here. And first of all there is no doubt that in all things which nature teaches me there is some truth contained; for by nature, considered in general, I now understand no other thing than either God Himself or else the order and disposition which God has established in created things; and by my nature in particular I understand no other thing than the complexus of all the things which God has given me.

But there is nothing which this nature teaches me more expressly (nor more sensibly) than that I have a body which is adversely affected when I feel pain, which has need of food or drink when I experience the feelings of hunger and thirst, and so on; nor can I doubt there being some truth in all this.

Nature also teaches me by these sensations of pain, hunger, thirst, etc., that I am not only lodged in my body as a pilot in a vessel, but that I am very closely united to it, and so to speak so intermingled with it that I seem to compose with it one whole. For if that were not the case, when my body is hurt, I, who am merely a thinking thing, should not feel pain, for I should perceive this wound by the understanding only, just as the sailor perceives by sight when something is damaged in his vessel; and when my body has need of drink or food, I should clearly understand the fact without being warned of it by confused feelings of hunger and thirst. For all these sensations of hunger, thirst, pain, etc. are in truth none other than certain confused modes of thought which are produced by the union and apparent intermingling of mind and body.

Moreover, nature teaches me that many other bodies exist around mine, of which some are to be avoided, and others sought after. And certainly from the fact that I am sensible of different sorts of colours, sounds, scents, tastes, heat, hardness, etc., I very easily conclude that there are in the bodies from which all these diverse sense-perceptions proceed certain variations which answer to them, although possibly these are not really at all similar to them. And also from the fact that amongst these different sense-perceptions some are very agreeable to me and others disagreeable, it is quite certain that my body (or rather myself in my entirety, inasmuch as I am formed of body and soul) may receive different impressions agreeable and disagreeable from the other bodies which surround it.

But there are many other things which nature seems to have taught me, but which at the same time I have never really received from her, but which have been brought about in my mind by a certain habit which I have of forming inconsiderate judgments on things; and thus it may easily happen that these judgments contain some error. Take, for example, the opinion which I hold that all space in which there is nothing that affects (or makes an impression on) my senses is void; that in a body which is warm there is something entirely similar to the idea of heat which is in me; that in a white or green body there is the same whiteness or greenness that I perceive; that in a bitter or sweet body there is the same taste, and so on in other instances; that the stars, the towers, and all other distant bodies are of the same figure and size as they appear from far off to our eyes, etc. But in order that in this there should be nothing which I do not conceive distinctly, I should define exactly what I really understand when I say that I am taught somewhat by nature. For here I take nature in a more limited signification than when I term it the sum of all the things given me by God, since in this sum many things are comprehended which only pertain to mind (and to these I do not refer in speaking of nature) such as the notion which I have of the fact that what has once been done cannot ever be undone and an infinitude of such things which I know by the light of nature (without the help of the body); and seeing that it comprehends many other matters besides which only pertain to body, and are no longer here contained under the name of nature, such as the quality of weight which it possesses and the like, with which I also do not deal; for in talking of nature I only treat of those things given by God to me as a being composed of mind and body. But the nature here described truly teaches me to flee from things which cause the sensation of pain, and seek after the things which communicate to me the sentiment of pleasure and so forth; but I do not see that beyond this it teaches me that from those diverse sense-perceptions we should ever form any conclusion regarding things outside of us, without having (carefully and maturely) mentally examined them beforehand. For it seems to me that it is mind alone, and not mind and body in conjunction, that is requisite to a knowledge of the truth in regard to such things. Thus, although a star makes no larger an impression on my eye than the flame of a little candle there is yet in me no real or positive propensity impelling me to believe that it is not greater than that flame; but I have judged it to be so from my earliest years, without any rational foundation. And although in approaching fire I feel heat, and in approaching it a little too near I even feel pain, there is at the same time no reason in this which could persuade me that there is in the fire something resembling this heat any more than there is in it something resembling the pain; all that I have any reason to believe from this is, that there is something in it, whatever it may be, which excites in me these sensations of heat or of pain. So also, although there are spaces in which I find nothing which excites my senses, I must not from that conclude that these spaces contain no body; for I see in this, as in other similar things, that I have been in the habit of perverting the order of nature, because these perceptions of sense have been placed within me by nature merely for the purpose of signifying to my mind what things are beneficial or hurtful to the composite whole of which it forms a part, and being up to that point sufficiently clear and distinct, I yet avail myself of them as though they were absolute rules by which I might immediately determine the essence of the bodies which are outside me, as to which, in fact, they can teach me nothing but what is most obscure and confused.

But I have already sufficiently considered how, notwithstanding the supreme goodness of God, falsity enters into the judgments I make. Only here a new difficulty is presented—one respecting those things the pursuit or avoidance of which is taught me by nature, and also respecting the internal sensations which I possess, and in which I seem to have sometimes detected error (and thus to be directly deceived by my own nature). To take an example, the agreeable taste of some food in which poison has been intermingled may induce me to partake of the poison, and thus deceive me. It is true, at the same time, that in this case nature may be excused, for it only induces me to desire food in which I find a pleasant taste, and not to desire the poison which is unknown to it; and thus I can infer nothing from this fact, except that my nature is not omniscient, at which there is certainly no reason to be astonished, since man, being finite in nature, can only have knowledge the perfectness of which is limited.

But we not unfrequently deceive ourselves even in those things to which we are directly impelled by nature, as happens with those who when they are sick desire to drink or eat things hurtful to them. It will perhaps be said here that the cause of their deceptiveness is that their nature is corrupt, but that does not remove the difficulty, because a sick man is none the less truly God's creature than he who is in health; and it is therefore as repugant to God's goodness for the one to have a deceitful nature as it is for the other. And as a clock composed of wheels and counter-weights no less exactly observes the laws of nature when it is badly made, and does not show the time properly, than when it entirely satisfies the wishes of its maker, and as, if I consider the body of a man as being a sort of machine so built up and composed of nerves, muscles, veins, blood and skin, that though there were no mind in it at all, it would not cease to have the same motions as at present, exception being made of those movements which are due to the direction of the will, and in consequence depend upon the mind (as opposed to whose which operate by the disposition of its organs), I easily recognize that it would be as natural to this body, supposing it to be, for example, dropsical, to suffer the parchedness of the throat, which usually signifies to the mind the feeling of thirst, and to be disposed by this parched feeling to move the nerves and other parts in the way requisite for drinking, and thus to augment its malady and do harm to itself, as it is natural to it, when it has no indisposition, to be impelled to drink for its good by a similar cause. And although, considering the use to which the clock has been destined by its maker, I may say that it deflects from the order of its nature when it does not indicate the hours correctly; and as, in the same way, considering the machine of the human body as having been formed by God in order to have in itself all the movements usually manifested there, I have reason for thinking that it does not follow the order of nature when, if the throat is dry, drinking does harm to the conservation of health, nevertheless I recognize at the same time that this last mode of explaining nature is very different from the other. For this is but a purely verbal characterization depending entirely on my thought, which compares a sick man and a badly constructed clock with the idea which I have of a healthy man and a well made clock, and it is hence extrinsic to the things to which it is applied; but according to the other interpretation of the term nature I understand something which is truly found in things and which is therefore not without some truth.

But certainly although in regard to the dropsical body it is only so to speak to apply an extrinsic term when we say that its nature is corrupted, inasmuch as apart from the need to drink, the throat is parched; yet in regard to the composite whole, that is to say, to the mind or soul united to this body, it is not a purely verbal predicate, but a real error of nature, for it to have thirst when drinking would be hurtful to it. And thus it still remains to inquire how the goodness of God does not prevent the nature of man so regarded from being fallacious.

In order to begin this examination, then, I here say, in the first place, that there is a great difference between mind and body, inasmuch as body is by nature always divisible, and the mind is entirely indivisible. For, as a matter of fact, when I consider the mind, that is to say, myself inasmuch as I am only a thinking thing, I cannot distinguish in myself any parts, but apprehend myself to be clearly one and entire; and although the

B

whole mind seems to be united to the whole body, yet if a foot, or an arm, or some other part is separated from my body, I am aware that nothing has been taken away from my mind. And the faculties of willing, feeling, conceiving, etc. cannot be properly speaking said to be its parts, for it is one and the same mind which employs itself in willing and in feeling and understanding. But it is quite otherwise with corporeal or extended objects, for there is not one of these imaginable by me which my mind cannot easily divide into parts, and which consequently I do not recognize as being divisible; this would be sufficient to teach me that the mind or soul of man is entirely different from the body, if I had not already learned it from other sources.

I further notice that the mind does not receive the impressions from all parts of the body immediately, but only from the brain, or perhaps even from one of its smallest parts, to wit, from that in which the common sense is said to reside, which, whenever it is disposed in the same particular way, conveys the same thing to the mind, although meanwhile the other portions of the body may be differently disposed, as is testified by innumerable experiments which it is unnecessary here to recount.

I notice, also, that the nature of body is such that none of its parts can be moved by another part a little way off which cannot also be moved in the same way by each one of the parts which are between the two, although this more remote part does not act at all. As, for example, in the cord ABCD (which is in tension) if we pull the last part D, the first part A will not be moved in any way differently from what would be the case if one of the intervening parts B or C were pulled, and the last part D were to remain unmoved. And in the same way, when I feel pain in my foot, my knowledge of physics teaches me that this sensation is communicated by means of nerves dispersed through the foot, which, being extended like cords from there to the brain, when they are contracted in the foot, at the same time contract the inmost portions of the brain which is their extremity and place of origin, and then excite a certain movement which nature has established in order to cause the mind to be affected by a sensation of pain represented as existing in the foot. But because these nerves must pass through the tibia, the thigh, the loins, the back and the neck, in order to reach from the leg to the brain, it may happen that although their extremities which are in the foot are not affected, but only certain ones of their intervening parts (which pass by the loins or the neck), this action will excite the same movement in the brain that might have been excited there by a hurt received in the foot, in consequence of which the mind will necessarily feel in the foot the same pain as if it had received a hurt. And the same holds good of all the other perceptions of our senses.

I notice finally that since each of the movements which are in the portion of the brain by which the mind is immediately affected brings about one particular sensation only, we cannot under the circumstances imagine anything more likely than that this movement, amongst all the sensations which it is capable of impressing on it, causes mind to be affected by that one which is best fitted and most generally useful for the conservation of the human body when it is in health. But experience makes us aware that all the feelings with which nature inspires us are such as I have just spoken of; and there is therefore nothing in them which does not give testimony to the power and goodness of the God (who has produced them). Thus, for example, when the nerves which are in the feet are violently or more than usually moved, their movement, passing through the medulla of the spine to the inmost parts of the brain, gives a sign to the mind which makes it feel somewhat, to wit, pain, as though in the foot, by which the mind is excited to do its utmost to remove the cause of the evil as dangerous and hurtful to the foot. It is true that God could have constituted the nature of man in such a way that this same movement in the brain would have conveyed something quite different to the mind; for example, it might have produced consciousness of itself either in so far as it is in the brain, or as it is in the foot, or as it is in some other place between the foot and the brain, or it might finally have produced consciousness of anything else whatsoever; but none of all this would have contributed so well to the conservation of the body. Similarly, when we desire to drink, a certain dryness of the throat is produced which moves its nerves, and by their means the internal portions of the brain; and this movement causes in the mind the sensation of thirst, because in this case there is nothing more useful to us than to become aware that we have need to drink for the conservation of our health; and the same holds good in other instances.

From this it is quite clear that, notwithstanding the supreme goodness of God, the nature of man, inasmuch as it is composed of mind and body, cannot be otherwise than sometimes a source of deception. For if there is any cause which excites, not in the foot but in some part of the nerves which are extended between the foot and the brain, or even in the brain itself, the same movement which usually is produced when the foot is detrimentally affected, pain will be experienced as though it were in the foot, and the sense will thus naturally be deceived; for since the same movement in the brain is capable of causing but one sensation in the mind and this sensation is much more frequently excited by a cause which hurts the foot than by another existing in some other quarter, it is reasonable that it should convey to the mind pain in the foot rather than in any other part of the body. And although the parchedness of the throat does not always proceed, as it usually does, from the fact that drinking is necessary for the health of the body, but sometimes comes from quite a different cause, as is the case with dropsical patients, it is yet much better that it should mislead on this occasion than if, on the other hand, it were always to deceive us when the body is in good health; and so on in similar cases.

II. OBJECTIONS AND REPLIES (1642)

Hobbes. 'I am a thing that thinks'; quite correct. From the fact that I think, or have an image, whether sleeping or waking, it is inferred that I am exercising thought; for 'I think' and 'I am exercising thought' mean the same thing. From the fact that I am exercising thought it follows that 'I am', since that which thinks is not nothing. But, where it is added, 'this is the mind, the spirit, the understanding, the reason', a doubt arises. For it does not seem to be good reasoning to say: 'I am exercising thought, *hence* I am thought'; or 'I am using my intellect, *hence* I am intellect'. For in the same way I might say, 'I am walking; *hence* I am the walking'. It is hence an assumption on the part of M. Descartes that that which understands is the same as the exercise of understanding which is an act of that which understands, or, at least, that that which understands is the same as the understanding, which is a power possessed by that which thinks. Yet all Philosophers distinguish a subject from its faculties and activities, i.e. from its properties and essences; for the *entity* itself is one thing, its *essence* another. Hence it is possible for a thing that thinks to be the subject of the mind, reason, or understanding, and hence to be something corporeal and the opposite of this has been assumed, not proved. Yet this inference is the basis of the conclusion that M. Descartes seems to wish to establish.

Descartes. It is certain that no thought can exist apart from a thing that thinks; no activity, no accident can be without a substance in which to exist. Moreover, since we do not apprehend the substance itself immediately through itself, but by means only of the fact that it is the subject of certain activities, it is highly rational, and a requirement forced on us by custom, to give diverse names to those substances that we recognize to be the subjects of clearly diverse activities or accidents, and afterwards to inquire whether those diverse names refer to one and the same or to diverse things. But there are *certain* activities, which we call *corporeal*, e.g. magnitude, figure, motion, and all those that cannot be thought of apart from extension in space; and the substance in which they exist is called *body*. It cannot be pretended that the substance that is the subject of figure is different from that which is the subject of spatial motion, etc., since all these activities agree in presupposing extension. Further, there are other activities, which we call *thinking* activities, e.g. understanding, willing, imagining, feeling, etc., which agree in falling under the description of thought, perception, or consciousness. The substance in which they reside we call a *thinking thing* or *the mind*, or any other name we care, provided only we do not confound it with corporeal substance, since thinking activities have no affinity with corporeal activities, and thought, which is the common nature in which the former agree, is totally different from extension, the common term for describing the latter.

But after we have formed two distinct concepts of those two substances, it is easy, from what has been said in the sixth Meditation, to determine whether they are one and the same or distinct.

Arnauld. The problem is: *how it follows, from the fact that one is unaware that anything else (except the fact of being a thinking thing) belongs to one's essence, that nothing else really belongs to one's essence.* But, not to conceal my dullness, I have been unable to discover in the whole of Meditation II where he has shown this. Yet so far as I can conjecture, he attempts this proof in Meditation VI, because he believes that it is dependent on the possession of the clear knowledge of God to which in Meditation II he has not yet attained. Here is his proof:

'Because I know that all the things I clearly and distinctly understand can be created by God just as I conceive them to exist, it is sufficient for me to be able to comprehend one thing clearly and distinctly apart from another, in order to be sure that the one is diverse from the other, because at least God can isolate them; and it does not matter by what power that isolation is effected, in order that I may be obliged to think them different from one another. Hence because, on the one hand, I have a clear and distinct idea of myself in so far as I am a thinking being, and not extended, and on the other hand, a distinct idea of body, in so far as it is only an extended thing, not one that thinks, it is certain that I am in reality distinct from my body and can exist apart from it.'

Here we must halt awhile; for on these few words the whole of the difficulty seems to hinge.

Firstly, in order to be true, the major premiss of that syllogism must be held to refer to the adequate notion of a thing (i.e. the notion which comprises everything which may be known of the thing), not to any notion, even a clear and distinct one. For M. Descartes in his reply to his theological critic admits that it is sufficient to have a 'formal' distinction 'and that a real' one is not required, 'to cause one thing to be conceived separately and as distinct from another by the abstracting action of the mind when it conceives a thing inadequately'. Whence in the same passage he draws the conclusion which he adds:— 'But still I understand in a complete manner what body is (i.e. I conceive body as a complete thing), merely by thinking that it is extended, has figure, can move, etc., and by denying of it everything which belongs to the nature of mind. Conversely also, I understand that mind is something complete, which doubts, knows, wishes, etc., although I deny that anything belongs to it which is contained in the idea of body. Hence there is a real distinction between mind and body.'

But, if anyone casts doubt on the (minor) premiss here assumed, and contends that it is merely that your conception is inadequate when you conceive yourself (i.e., your mind) as being a thinking but not an extended thing, and similarly when you conceive yourself (i.e. your body) as being an extended and not a thinking thing, we must look to its proof in the previous part of the argument. For I do not reckon a matter like this to be so clear as to warrant us in assuming it as an indemonstrable first principle and in dispensing with proof.

Now as to the first part of the statement, namely, 'that you completely understand what body is, merely by thinking that it is extended, has figure, can move, etc., and by denying of it everything which belongs to the nature of mind', this is of little value. For one who contends that the human mind is corporeal does not on that account believe that every body is a mind. Hence body would be so related to mind as genus is to species. But the genus can be conceived without the species, even although one deny of it whatsoever is proper and peculiar to the species; whence comes the common dictum of Logicians, 'the negation of the species does not negate the genus.' Thus, I can conceive figure without conceiving any of the attributes proper to the circle. Therefore, we must prove over and above this that the mind can be completely and adequately conceived apart from the body.

I can discover no passage in the whole work capable of effecting this proof, save the proposition laid down at the outset: 'I can deny that there is any body or that any extended thing exists, but yet it is certain that I exist, so long as I make this denial, or think; hence I am a thing that thinks and, not a body, and the body does not pertain to the knowledge of myself.'

But the only result that I can see this to give, is that a certain knowledge of myself be obtained without a knowledge of the body. But it is not yet quite clear to me that this knowledge is complete and adequate, so as to make me sure that I am not in error in excluding the body from my essence. I shall explain by means of an example:—

Let us assume that a certain man is quite sure that the angle in a semi-circle is a right angle and that hence the triangle made by this angle and the diameter is right-angled; but suppose he questions and has not yet firmly apprehended, nay, let us imagine that, misled by some fallacy, he denies that the square on its base is equal to the squares on the sides of the right-angle triangle. Now, according to our author's reasoning, he will see himself confirmed in his false belief. 'For,' he will argue, 'while I clearly and distinctly perceive that this triangle is right-angled I yet doubt whether the square on its base is equal to the squares on its sides. Hence the equality of the square on the base to those on the sides does not belong to its essence.'

Further, even though I deny that the square on its base is equal to the squares on its sides, I yet remain certain that it is right-angled, and the knowledge that one of its angles is a right angle remains clear and distinct in my mind; and this remaining so, not God himself could cause it not to be right-angled.

Hence, that of which I doubt, or the removal of which leaves me with the idea still, cannot belong to its essence.

Besides, 'since I know that all things I clearly and distinctly understand can be created by God just as I conceive them to exist, it is sufficient for me, in order to be sure that one thing is distinct from another, to be able to comprehend the one clearly and distinctly apart from the other, because it can be isolated by God'. But I clearly and distinctly understand that this triangle is right-angled, without comprehending that the square on its base is equal to the squares on its sides. Hence God at least can create a right-angled triangle, the square on the base of which is not equal to the squares on its sides.

I do not see what reply can here be made, except that the man in question does not perceive clearly that the triangle is right-angled. But whence do I obtain any perception of the nature of my mind clearer than that which he has of the nature of the triangle? He is as sure that the triangle in a semi-circle has one right angle (which is the notion of a right-angled triangle) as I am in believing that I exist because I think.

Hence, just as a man errs in not believing that the equality of the square on its base to the squares on its sides belongs to the nature of that triangle, which he clearly and distinctly knows to be right-angled, so why am I not perhaps in the wrong in thinking that nothing else belongs to my nature, which I clearly and distinctly know to be something that thinks, except the fact that I am this thinking being? Perhaps it also belongs to my essence to be something extended.

And certainly, some one will say it is no marvel if, in deducing my existence from the fact that I think, the idea that I form of the self, which is in this way an object of thought, represent me to my mind as merely a thinking being, since it has been derived from my thinking alone. And hence from this idea, no argument can be drawn to prove that nothing more belongs to my essence than what the idea contains.

Descartes. I must explain how it is that, 'from the mere fact that I apprehend one substance clearly and distinctly apart from another, I am sure that the one excludes the other'.

Really the notion of *substance* is just this—that which can exist by itself, without the aid of any other substance. No one who perceives two instances by means of two diverse concepts ever doubts that they are really distinct.

Consequently, if I had not been in search of a certitude greater than the vulgar, I should have been satisfied with showing in the Second Meditation that *Mind* was apprehended as a thing that subsists, although nothing belonging to the body be ascribed to it, and conversely that *Body* was understood to be something subsistent without anything being attributed to it that pertains to the mind. And I should have added nothing more in order to prove that there was a real distinction between mind and body: because commonly we judge that all things stand to each other in respect to their actual relations in the same way as they are related in our consciousness. But, since one of those hyperbolical doubts adduced in the First Meditation went so far as to prevent me from being sure of this very fact (viz. that things are in their true nature exactly as we perceive them to be), so long as I supposed that I had no knowledge of the author of my being, all that I have said about God and about truth in the Third, Fourth and Fifth Meditations serves to further the conclusion as to the real distinction between *mind* and *body*, which is finally completed in Meditation VI.

My opponent, however, says, 'I apprehend the triangle inscribed in the semicircle without knowing that the square on its base is equal to the squares on the sides'. True, that triangle may indeed be apprehended although there is no thought of the ratio prevailing between the squares on the base and sides; but we can never think that this ratio must be denied. It is quite otherwise in the case of the mind where, not only do we understand that it exists apart from the body, but also that all the attributes of body may be denied of it; for reciprocal exclusion of one another belongs to the nature of substances.

There is no conflict between my theory and the point M. Arnauld next brings up, 'that it is no marvel if, in deducing my existence from the fact that I think, the idea I thus form of myself represents me merely as a thinking being'. For, similarly, when I examine the nature of body I find nothing at all in it that savours of thought; and there is no better proof of the distinctness of two things than if, when we study each separately, we find nothing in the one that does not differ from what we find in the other.

Gassendi. You investigate whether, 'the existence of a deceiving agent being up to this point supposed, you can affirm that any of the things which you judged to belong to the nature of body exist in you'. You say that 'after the most careful scrutiny nothing of such a sort can be found in you'. Already at this point you consider yourself not as a complete human being, but as that inner and more hidden part, such as you deemed the soul to be. Wherefore I ask thee, O soul, or whatever the name be by which you choose to be addressed, have you by this time corrected that notion in virtue of which you previously imagined that you were something similar to wind, or a like substance, diffused throughout the members of the body? You certainly have not. Why then, cannot you be a wind, or rather a very subtle spirit, which, by means of the heat of the heart, is distilled from the purest of the blood or from some other source; or may there not be some other cause by which you are evoked and preserved; and may you not, being diffused throughout the members, attribute life to them, and see with the eye, hear with the ear, think by means of the brain and discharge the other functions which by common consent are ascribed to you?

At length you come to the conclusion that thought belongs to you. True, that is not to be denied; but you still have to prove that the power of thinking is so much superior to the nature of body, that neither breath nor any other mobile, pure, and rarefied body, can by any means be so adapted as to be capable of exercising thought. . . .

You must prove that this solid body contributes absolutely nothing to your thinking (though you have never existed without it nor have ever hitherto had any thought in isolation from it), and that your thinking is hence independent of it.

Descartes. I corrected it (the notion that that which thinks is like wind or some similar body) when I showed that it could be supposed that no wind or other body existed, and that nevertheless everything by means of which I recognize myself as a thinking being remains. Hence your subsequent questions as to why I cannot therefore be still a wind, and why I cannot occupy space, and why I cannot be subject to many motions, etc., are so devoid of sense as to require no reply. . . .

In philosophizing correctly, there is no need for us to prove the falsity of all those things which we do not admit because we do not know whether they are true. We have merely to take the greatest care not to admit as true what we cannot prove to be true. Thus when I find that I am a thinking substance, and form a clear and distinct concept of that substance, in which there is none of those attributes which belong to the concept of corporeal substance, this is quite sufficient to let me affirm that I, in so far as I know myself, am nothing but a thing which thinks, which statement alone I have affirmed in the second meditation—that with which we are at present occupied. Neither was I bound to admit that this thinking substance was some mobile, simple, and rarified body, when I found no reason inducing me to believe that. But it is for you, it is your duty, to expound the reason, if you have one; you have no right to demand that I shall prove that false which I refused to entertain only for the reason that I had no knowledge about it. You act as if, when I asserted that I now lived in Holland, you were to deny that that was to be believed, unless I proved that I was neither in China nor in any other part of the world, because it is perchance possible that the same body should, owing to the action of the divine power, exist in two different places.

III. THE PRINCIPLES OF PHILOSOPHY (1644)

That we likewise know certainly that everything is pre-ordained of God
But because that which we have already learnt about God proves to us that His power is so immense that it would be a crime for us to think ourselves ever capable of doing anything which He had not already pre-ordained, we should soon be involved in great difficulties if we undertook to make His pre-ordinances harmonize with the freedom of our will, and if we tried to comprehend them both at one time.

How the freedom of the will may be reconciled with Divine pre-ordination
Instead of this, we shall have no trouble at all if we recollect that our thought is finite, and that the omnipotence of God, whereby He has not only known from all eternity that which is or can be, but also willed and pre-ordained it, is infinite. In this way we may have intelligence enough to come clearly and distinctly to know that this power in in God, but not enough to comprehend how He leaves the free action of man indeterminate; and, on the other hand, we are so conscious of the liberty and indifference which exists in us, that there is nothing that we comprehend more clearly and perfectly. For it would be absurd to doubt that of which we inwardly experience and perceive as existing within ourselves, just because we do not comprehend a matter which from its nature we know to be incomprehensible.

That all the objects of our perceptions are to be considered either as things or the affectious of things, or else as eternal truths; and the enumeration of things
I distinguish all the objects of our knowledge either into things or the affections of things, or as eternal truths having no existence outside our

thought. Of the things we consider as real, the most general are substance, duration, order, number, and possibly such other similar matters as range through all the classes of real things. I do not however observe more than two ultimate classes of real things—the one is intellectual things, or those of the intelligence that is, pertaining to the mind or to thinking substance, the other is material things, or that pertaining to extended substance, i.e., to body. Perception, volition, and every mode of knowing and willing, pertain to thinking substance; while to extended substance pertain magnitude or extension in length, breadth and depth, figure, movement, situation, divisibility into parts themselves divisible, and such like. Besides these, there are, however, certain things which we experience in ourselves and which should be attributed neither to mind nor body alone, but to the close and intimate union that exists between the body and mind as I shall later on explain in the proper place. Such are the appetites of hunger, thirst, etc., and also the emotions or passions of the mind which do not subsist in mind or thought alone, as the emotions of anger, joy, sadness, love, etc.; and, finally all the sensations such as pain, pleasure, light and colour, sounds, odours, tastes, heat, hardness, and all other tactile qualities.

What substance is, and that it is a name which we cannot attribute in the same sense to God and to His creatures

As regards these matters which we consider as being things or modes of things, it is necessary that we should examine them here one by one. By substance, we can understand nothing else than a thing which so exists that it needs no other thing in order to exist. And in fact only one single substance can be understood which clearly needs nothing else, namely, God. That is why the word substance does not pertain *univoce* to God and to other things, as they say in the Schools, that is, no common signification for this appellation which will apply equally to God and to them can be distinctly understood.

That it may be attributed univocally to the soul and to body, and how we know substance

Created substances, however, whether corporeal or thinking, may be conceived under this common concept; for they are things which need only the concurrence of God in order to exist. But yet substance cannot be first discovered merely from the fact that it is a thing that exists, for that fact alone is not observed by us. We may, however, easily discover it by means of any one of its attributes because it is a common notion that nothing is possessed of no attributes, properties, or qualities. For this reason, when we perceive any attribute, we therefore conclude that some existing thing or substance to which it may be attributed, is necessarily present.

That each substance has a principal attribute, and that the attribute of the mind is thought, while that of body is extension

But although any one attribute is sufficient to give us a knowledge of substance, there is always one principal property of substance which constitutes its nature and essence, and on which all the others depend. Thus extension in length, breadth and depth, constitutes the nature of corporeal substance; and thought constitutes the nature of thinking substance. For all else that may be attributed to body presupposes extension, and is but a mode of this extended thing; as everything that we find in mind is but so many diverse forms of thinking. Thus, for example, we cannot conceive figure but as an extended thing, nor movement but as in an extended space; so imagination, feeling, and will, only exist in a thinking thing. But, on the other hand, we can conceive extension without figure or action, and thinking without imagination or sensation, and so on with the rest; as is quite clear to anyone who attends to the matter.

How we may have clear and distinct notions of thinking substance, of corporeal substance, and of God

We may thus easily have two clear and distinct notions or ideas, the one of created substance which thinks, the other of corporeal substance, provided we carefully separate all the attributes of thought from those of extension. We can also have a clear and distinct idea of an uncreated and independent thinking substance, that is to say, of God, provided that we do not suppose that this idea represents to us all that is exhibited in God, and that we do not mingle anything fictitious with it, but simply attend to what is evidently contained in the notion, and which we are aware pertains to the nature of an absolutely perfect Being. For no one can deny that such an idea of God exists in us, unless he groundlessly asserts that the mind of man cannot attain to a knowledge of God.

Of distinctions, and firstly of real distinction

But as to the number in things themselves, this proceeds from the distinction which exists between them; and *distinction* is of three sorts, viz. *real*, *modal*, and *of reason*. The *real* is properly speaking found between two or more substances; and we can conclude that two substances are really distinct one from the other from the sole fact that we can conceive the one clearly and distinctly without the other. For in accordance with the knowledge which we have of God, we are certain that He can carry into effect all that of which we have a distinct idea. That is why from the fact that we now have, e.g. the idea of an extended or corporeal substance, although we do not yet know certainly whether such really exists at all, we may yet conclude that it may exist; and if it does exist, any one portion of it which we can demarcate in our thought must be distinct from every other part of the same substance. Similarly because each one of us is conscious that he thinks, and that in thinking he can shut off from himself all other substance, either thinking or extended, we may conclude that each of us, similarly regarded, is really distinct from every other thinking substance and from every corporeal substance. And even if we suppose that God had united a body to a soul so closely that it was impossible to bring them together more closely, and made a single thing out of the two, they would yet remain really distinct one from the other notwithstanding the union; because however closely God connected them He could not set aside the power which He possessed of separating them, or conserving them one apart from the other, and those things which God can separate, or conceive in separation, are really distinct.

IV. THE PASSIONS OF THE SOUL (1649)

Of the perceptions which we relate to objects which are without us

Those which we relate to the things which are without us, to wit to the objects of our senses, are caused, at least when our opinion is not false, by these objects which, exciting certain movements in the organs of the external senses, excite them also in the brain by the intermission of the nerves, which cause the soul to perceive them. Thus when we see the light of a torch, and hear the sound of a bell, this sound and this light are two different actions which, simply by the fact that they excite two different movements in certain of our nerves, and by these means in the brain, giving two different sensations to the soul, which sensations we relate to the subjects which we suppose to be their causes in such a way that we think we see the torch itself and hear the bell, and do not perceive just the movements which proceed from them.

Of the perceptions which we relate to our body

The perceptions which we relate to our body, or to some of its parts, are those which we have of hunger, thirst, and other natural appetites, to which we may unite pain, heat and the other affections which we perceive as though they were in our members, and not as in objects which are outside us; we may thus perceive at the same time and by the inter-mission of the same nerves, the cold of our hand and the heat of the flame to which it approaches; or, on the other hand, the heat of the hand and the cold of the air to which it is exposed, without there being any difference between the actions which cause us to feel the heat or the cold which is in our hand, and those which make us perceive that which is without us, excepting that from the one of these actions following upon the other, we judge that the first is already in us, and what supervenes is not so yet, but is in the object which causes it.

That the soul is united to all the portions of the body conjointly

But in order to understand all these things more perfectly, we must know that the soul is really joined to the whole body, and that we cannot, properly speaking, say that it exists in any one of its parts to the exclusion of the others, because it is one and in some manner indivisible, owing to the disposition of its organs, which are so related to one another that when any one of them is removed, that renders the whole body defective; and because it is of a nature which has no relation to extension, or dimensions, nor other properties of the matter of which the body is composed, but only to the whole conglomerate of its organs, as appears from the fact that we could not in any way conceive of the half or the third of a soul, nor of the space it occupies, and because it does not become smaller owing to the cutting off of some portion of the body, but separates itself from it entirely when the union of its assembled organs is dissolved.

That there is a small gland in the brain in which the soul exercises its functions more particularly than in the other parts

It is likewise necessary to know that although the soul is joined to the whole body, there is yet in that a certain part in which it exercises its functions more particularly than in all the others; and it is usually believed that this part is the brain, or possibly the heart: the brain, because it is with it that the organs of sense are connected, and the heart because it is apparently in it that we experience the passions. But, in examining the matter with care, it seems as though I had clearly ascertained that the part of the body in which the soul exercises its functions immediately is in nowise the heart, nor the whole of the brain, but merely the most inward of all its parts, to wit, a certain very small gland which is situated in the middle of its substance and so suspended above the duct whereby the animal spirits in its anterior cavities have communication with those in the posterior, that the slightest movements which take place in it may alter very greatly the course of these spirits; and reciprocally that the smallest changes which occur in the course of the spirits may do much to change the movements of this gland.

How we know that this gland is the main seat of the soul

The reason which persuades me that the soul cannot have any other seat in all the body than this gland wherein to exercise its functions immediately, is that I reflect that the other parts of our brain are all of them double, just as we have two eyes, two hands, two ears, and finally all the organs of our outside senses are double; and inasmuch as we have but one solitary and simple thought of one particular thing at one and the same moment, it must necessarily be the case that there must somewhere be a place where the two images which come to us by the two eyes, where the two other impressions which proceed from a single object by means of the double organs of the other senses, can unite before arriving at the soul, in order that they may not represent to it two objects instead of one. And it is easy to apprehend how these images or other impressions might unite in this gland by the intermission of the spirits which fill the cavities of the brain; but there is no other place in the body where they can be thus united unless they are so in this gland.

That the seat of the passions is not in the heart

As to the opinion of those who think that the soul receives its passions in the heart, it is not of much consideration, for it is only founded on the fact that the passions cause us to feel some change taking place there; and it is easy to see that this change is not felt in the heart excepting through the medium of a small nerve which descends from the brain towards it, just as pain is felt as in the foot by means of the nerves of the foot, and the stars are perceived as in the heavens by means of their light and of the optic nerves; so that it is not more necessary that our soul should exercise its functions immediately in the heart, in order to feel its passions there, than it is necessary for the soul to be in the heavens in order to see the stars there.

How the soul and the body act on one another

Let us then conceive here that the soul has its principal seat in the little gland which exists in the middle of the brain, from whence it radiates forth through all the remainder of the body by means of the animal spirits, nerves, and even the blood, which, participating in the impressions of the spirits, can carry them by the arteries into all the members. And recollecting what has been said above about the machine of our body, i.e. that the little filaments of our nerves are so distributed in all its parts, that on the occasion of the diverse movements which are there excited by sensible objects, they open in diverse ways the pores of the brain, which causes the animal spirits contained in these cavities to enter in diverse ways into the muscles, by which means they can move the members in all the different ways in which they are capable of being moved; and also that all the other causes which are capable of moving the spirits in diverse ways suffice to conduct them into diverse muscles; let us here add that the small gland which is the main seat of the soul is so suspended between the cavities which contain the spirits that it can be moved by them in as many different ways as there are sensible diversities in the object, but that it may also be moved in diverse ways by the soul, whose nature is such that it receives in itself as many divine impressions, that is to say, that it possesses as many diverse perceptions as there are divine movements in this gland. Reciprocally, likewise, the machine of the body is so formed that from the simple fact that this gland is diversely moved by the soul, or by such other cause, whatever it is, it thrusts the spirits which surround it towards the pores of the brain, which conduct them by the nerves into the muscles, by which means it causes them to move the limbs.

V. CORRESPONDENCE WITH PRINCESS ELIZABETH (1643)

Princess Elizabeth to Descartes, May 6–16, 1643

. . . I beg of you to tell me how the human soul can determine the movement of the animal spirits in the body so as to perform voluntary acts— being as it is merely a conscious (*pensante*) substance. For the determination of movement seems always to come about from the moving body's being propelled—to depend on the kind of impulse it gets from what sets it in motion, or again, on the nature and shape of this latter thing's surface. Now the first two conditions involve contact, and the third involves that the impelling thing has extension; but you utterly exclude extension from your notion of soul, and contact seems to me incompatible with a thing's being immaterial.

I therefore ask you for a more specific definition of the soul than you give in your metaphysics: a definition of its substance, as distinct from its activity, consciousness (*pensée*). Even if we supposed these to be in fact inseparable—a matter hard to prove in regard to children in their mother's womb and severe fainting-fits—to be inseparable as the divine attributes are: nevertheless we may get a more perfect idea of them by considering them apart.

Descartes to Princess Elizabeth, May 21, 1643

. . . I may truly say that what your Highness is propounding seems to me to be the question people have most right to ask me in view of my published works. For there are two facts about the human soul on which there depends any knowledge we may have as to its nature: first, that it is conscious; secondly, that, being united to a body, it is able to act and suffer along with it. Of the second fact I said almost nothing; my aim was simply to make the first properly understood; for my main object was to prove the distinction of soul and body; and to this end only the first was serviceable, the second might have been prejudicial. But since your Highness sees too clearly for dissimulation to be possible, I will here try to explain how I conceive the union of soul and body and how the soul has the power of moving the body.

My first observation is that there are in us certain primitive notions—the originals, so to say, on the pattern of which we form all other knowledge. These notions are very few in number. First, there are the most general ones, existence, number, duration, etc., which apply to everything we can conceive. As regards body in particular, we have merely the notion of extension and the consequent notions of shape and movement. As regards the soul taken by itself, we have merely the notion of consciousness which comprises the conceptions (*perceptions*) of the intellect and the inclinations of the will. Finally, as regards the soul and body together, we have merely the notion of their union; and on this there depend our notions of the soul's power to move the body, and of the body's power to act on the soul and cause sensations and emotions.

I would also observe that all human knowledge consists just in properly distinguishing these notions and attaching each of them only to the objects that it applies to. If we try to explain some problem by means of a notion that does not apply, we cannot help making mistakes; we are just as wrong if we try to explain one of these notions in terms of another, since, being primitive, each such notion has to be understood in itself. The use of our senses has made us much more familiar with notions of extension, shape, and movement than with others; thus the chief cause of our errors is that ordinarily we try to use these notions to explain matters to which they do not apply; e.g. we try to use our imagination in conceiving the nature of the soul, or to conceive the way the soul moves the body in terms of the way that one body is moved by another body.

In the meditations that your Highness condescended to read, I tried to bring before the mind the notions that apply to the soul taken by itself, and to distinguish them from those that apply to the body taken by itself. Accordingly, the next thing I have to explain is how we are to form the notions that apply to the union of the soul with the body, as opposed to those that apply to the body taken by itself or the mind taken by itself. . . . These simple notions are to be sought only within the soul, which is naturally endowed with all of them, but does not always adequately distinguish between them, or again, does not always attach them to the right objects.

So I think people have hitherto confused the notions of the soul's power to act within the body and the power one body has to act within another; and they have ascribed both powers not to soul, whose nature was so far unknown, but to various qualities of bodies—gravity, heat, etc. These qualities were imagined to be real, i.e. to have an existence distinct from the existence of bodies; consequently, they are imagined to be substances, although they were called qualities. In order to conceive of them, people have used sometimes notions that we have for the purpose of knowing body, and sometimes those that we have for the purpose of knowing the soul, according as they were ascribing to them a material or an immaterial nature. For example, on the supposition that gravity is a real quality, about which we know no more than its power of moving the body in which it occurs towards the centre of the Earth, we find no difficulty in conceiving how it moves the body or how it is united to it; and we do not think of this as taking place by means of real mutual contact between two surfaces; our inner experience shows (*nous expérimentons*) that that notion is a specific one. Now I hold that we misuse this notion by applying it to gravity (which, as I hope to show in my *Physics*, is nothing really distinct from body), but that it has been given to us in order that we may conceive of the way that the soul moves the body.

Princess Elizabeth to Descartes, June 10–20, 1643

... [I cannot] understand the idea by means of which we are to judge of the way that the soul, unextended and immaterial, moves the body, in terms of the idea you used to have about gravity. You used falsely to ascribe to gravity, under the style of a 'quality', the power of carrying bodies towards the centre of the Earth. But I cannot see why this should convince us that a body may be impelled by something immaterial; why we should not rather be confirmed in the view that this is impossible, by the demonstration of a true [view of gravity], opposed [to this], which you promise us in your *Physics*; especially as the idea [that a body may be so impelled] cannot claim the same degree of perfection and representative reality (*réalité objective*) as the idea of God, and may be a figment resulting from ignorance of what really moves bodies towards the centre. Since no material cause was apparent to the senses, people may well have ascribed this to the opposite cause, the immaterial; but I have never been able to conceive *that*, except as a negation of matter, which can have no communication with matter.

And I must confess that I could more readily allow that the soul has matter and extension than that an immaterial being has the capacity of moving a body and being affected by it. If the first, [the soul's moving the body], took place by [the soul's giving] information [to the body], then the [animal] spirits, which carry out the movement, would have to be intelligent; but you do not allow intelligence to anything corporeal. You do indeed show the possibility of the second thing [the body's affecting the soul], in your Metaphysical Meditations; but it is very hard to see how a soul such as you describe, after possessing the power and the habit of correct reasoning, may lose all that because of some vapours [in the brain]; or why the soul is so much governed by the body, when it can subsist separately, and has nothing in common with it. . . .

Descartes to Princess Elizabeth, June 28, 1643

I am most deeply obliged to your Highness for condescending, after experience of my previous ill success in explaining the problem you were pleased to propound to me, to be patient enough to listen to me once more on the same subject, and to give me an opportunity of making remarks on matters I had passed over. My chief omissions seem to be the following. I began by distinguishing three kinds of primitive ideas or notions, each of which is known in a specific way and not by comparison to another kind; viz., the notion of soul, the notion of body, and the notion of the union between soul and body. I still had to explain the difference between these three kinds of notions, and again between the operations of the soul by means of which we get them, and to show the means of becoming readily familiar with each kind. Further, I had to explain why I used the comparison of gravity. Next, I had to show that even if we try to conceive of the soul as material (which means, properly speaking, to conceive of its union with the body), we cannot help going on to recognize that it is separable from the body. This, I think, is the sum of the task your Highness has set me.

In the first place, then, I discern this great difference between the three kinds of notions: the soul is conceived only by pure intellect; body (i.e. extension, shape, and movement) can likewise be known by pure intellect, but is known much better when intellect is aided by imagination; finally, what belongs to the union of soul and body can be understood only in an obscure way either by pure intellect or even when the intellect is aided by imagination, but is understood very clearly by means of the senses. Consequently, those who never do philosophize and make use only of their senses have no doubt that the soul moves the body and the body acts on the soul; indeed, they consider the two as a single thing, i.e. they conceive of their union; for to conceive of the union between two things is to conceive of them as a single thing. Metaphysical reflections, which exercise the pure intellect, are what make us familiar with the notion of the soul; the study of mathematics, which chiefly exercises the imagination in considering figures and movements, accustoms us to form very distinct notions of body; finally, it is just by means of ordinary life and conversation, by abstaining from meditating and from studying things that exercise the imagination, that one learns to conceive the union of soul and body.

I am half afraid that your Highness may think I am not speaking seriously here; but that would be contrary to the respect that I owe to your Highness and will never fail to pay. I can truly say that the chief rule I have always observed in my studies, and the one I think has been most serviceable to me in acquiring some measure of knowledge, has been never to spend more than a few hours a day in thoughts that demand imagination, or more than a few hours a year in thoughts that demand pure intellect; I have given all the rest of my time to the relaxation of my senses and the repose of my mind. I here count among exercises of imagination all serious conversations, and everything that demands attention. This is what made me retire to the country; it is true that in the busiest city in the world I might have as many hours to myself as I now spend in study, but I could not employ them so usefully when my mind was wearied by the attention that the troubles of life demand.

I take the liberty of writing thus to your Highness, to express my sincere admiration of your Highness's ability, among all the business and cares that are never lacking to persons who combine high intelligence and high birth, to find leisure for the meditations that are necessary for proper understanding of the distinction between soul and body. I formed the opinion that it was these meditations, rather than thoughts demanding less attention, that made your Highness find some obscurity in our notion of their union. It seems to me that the human mind is incapable of distinctly conceiving both the distinction between body and soul and their union, at one and the same time; for that requires our conceiving them as a single thing and simultaneously conceiving them as two things, which is self-contradictory. I supposed that your Highness still had very much in mind the arguments proving the distinction of soul and body; and I did not wish to ask you to lay them aside, in order to represent to yourself that notion of their union which everybody always has in himself without doing philosophy—viz., that there is one single person who has at once body and consciousness, so that this consciousness can move the body and be aware of the events that happen to it. Accordingly, I used in my previous letter the simile of gravity and other qualities, which we imagine to be united to bodies as consciousness is united to ours. I did not worry over the fact that this simile is lame, because these qualities are not, as one imagines, realities; for I thought your Highness was already fully convinced that the soul is a substance distinct from the body.

Your Highness, however, makes the remark that it is easier to ascribe matter and extension to the soul than to ascribe to it the power of moving a body and being moved by it without having any matter. Now I would ask your Highness to hold yourself free to ascribe 'matter and extension' to the soul; for this is nothing else than to conceive the soul as united to the body. After forming a proper conception of this, and experiencing it in your own case, your Highness will find it easy to reflect that the matter you thus ascribe to your consciousness (*pensée*) is not the consciousness itself; again, the extension of the matter is essentially different from the extension of the consciousness, for the first extension is determined to a certain place, and excludes any other corporeal extension from that place, whereas the second does not. In this way your Highness will assuredly find it easy to come back to a realization of the distinction between soul and body, in spite of having conceived of them as united.

Finally, I think it is very necessary to have got a good understanding, for once in one's life, of the principles of metaphysics, because it is from these that we have knowledge of God and of our soul. But I also think it would be very harmful to occupy one's intellect often with meditating on them, for it would be the less able to find leisure for the functioning of the imagination and the senses; the best thing is to be content with retaining in memory and in belief the conclusions one has drawn once for all, and to spend the rest of one's time for study in reflections in which the intellect co-operates with the imagination and the senses. . . .

2

BENEDICT SPINOZA

THE ETHICS (1677)

First part: of God

Definitions

III. I understand by *Substance* that which exists of itself, and is conceived by and through itself; that is to say, that of which the conception can be formed without having need of the conception of any other thing as its cause.

IV. I understand by *attribute* that which the understanding perceives in substance as constituting its essence.

V. I understand by *mode* an affection of substance, or that which is in some other thing, by or through which it is also conceived.

VI. I understand by GOD the Absolutely Infinite Being; that is to say, substance constituted by an infinity of attributes, each of which expresses an eternal and infinite essence.

Propositions

XIV. There cannot be, nor be conceived to be, any other substance besides God.

XV. Whatever is, is in God; and nothing can be, nor be conceived to be, without God.

Second part: of the nature and origin of the mind or soul

Definition

I. By *body* I understand a mode which in a certain determinate way expresses the essence of God, in so far considered as God is extended being.

Propositions

I. Thought is an attribute of God, or God is Thinking Being.

II. Extension is an attribute of God, or God is Extended Being.

VI. The modes of any attribute whatever have God for their cause in so far only as God is considered under that particular attribute of which they are the modes, and not under any other attribute.

VII. The order and connection of ideas is the same as the order and connection of things.

Note: Before going further it will be well to recall to mind what has been already said, viz., that all that can be perceived by the infinite intelligence as constituting the essence of substance belongs to the one substance only; and consequently that thinking substance and extended substance are only one and the same substance, which is conceived now under this attribute, and now under that. So also a mode of extension, and the idea of that mode, are only one and the same thing expressed in two ways. And this is what appears to have been perceived dimly as through a cloud by certain Hebrews, who maintain that God, the intelligence of God, and the things understood of God, are one and the same thing. For example: a circle which exists in nature, and the idea of an existing circle, which is also in God, are one and the same thing expressed by different attributes; and consequently, whether we conceive nature under the attribute of extension, or under the attribute of thought, or under any other attribute whatever, we shall always find one and the same order and connection of causes; that is, the same things will be found following one after another. And if I have said that God is the cause of the idea of the circle for example, in so far only as God is thinking Being, and cause of the circle itself in so far only as God is extended Being, I have said it for no other reason than this: that the formal being of the idea of the circle can only be perceived by another mode of thought as its proximate cause, this again by another, and so on to infinity; so that, so long as things are considered as modes of thought, we must explain the entire order of nature or the connection of causes by the attribute of thought alone; and if they are considered as modes of extension then by the attribute of extension alone; and in the same way for other attributes. Wherefore we conclude that of things considered in themselves, God, as constituted by an infinity of attributes, is the true cause; but I cannot at present explain this more clearly.

Third part: of the origin and nature of the affections or passions

Proposition

II. The body cannot determine the soul to thought, nor can the soul determine the body to motion or rest, or to anything else (if there be anything else).

Proof: All modes of thought have God for their cause in so far as God is considered as the Thing Thinking, and not as God is revealed or explained by some other attribute; that, therefore, which determines the soul to think is a mode of thought, and not a mode of extension; in other words, it is not the body. This is the first point. Again, the motion or rest of the body must proceed from another body, which was itself determined to motion or rest by another body; and absolutely whatever is produced in the body must proceed from God in so far considered as affected by some mode of extension, and not by some mode of thought; in other words, motion and rest cannot proceed from the mind or soul, which is a mode of thought. This is the second point. Therefore the body cannot determine, etc. Q.E.D.

Note: This will be more clearly understood by what has been said in the Note to Prop. 7, Part II, viz. that the soul and body are one and the same thing, conceived now under the attribute of thought, and now under that of extension. Whence it comes that the order or concatenation of things is one and the same under whatever attribute nature is conceived; and consequently that the order of the actions and passions of the body, and the order of the actions and passions of the soul, are simultaneous in nature.

But however strong these proofs may be, and although there should remain no reason to doubt them, yet I can scarcely believe that men will be induced to ponder them carefully unless I confirm them by experience, so firmly are they persuaded that it is by the will of the soul alone that the body is put now in motion and now at rest, and, in short, that it does a great many things which depend strictly upon the volitions of the soul and its power of thinking. No one, however, has as yet shown by experiment what the body can do solely by the laws of corporeal nature, and so far as the body only is considered; and what it cannot do without being determined thereto by the soul. For no one has yet acquired such an accurate knowledge of the structure of the human body as to be able to explain all its functions—and here I say nothing of the many things observed in the lower animals and which far exceed human sagacity, nor of the things somnambulists do in their sleep which they would not dare to attempt when awake, and which show plainly enough that the body by the laws of its nature alone can do many things which are a matter of astonishment to the soul. Moreover, no one yet knows in what way and by what means the soul moves the body, nor how many degrees of motion it can give to it, nor with what rapidity it can move it. Whence it follows that when men say that this or that action is produced by the soul which has dominion over the body, they really do not know what they are talking about, and are only confessing in terms flattering to their vanity, that they are ignorant of the true cause of the bodily actions which surprise and astonish them. But they may say, that whether they do or do not know by what means the soul moves the body, they nevertheless know by experience that unless the human soul was capable of thinking the body would be inert; and further, that experience teaches them also that it is in the power of the soul alone to speak or to be silent, and to do or abstain from doing many other things which, consequently, they believe must depend entirely on decisions of the soul.

But, as regards the first point, I ask whether experience does not also teach that the mind or soul is powerless to think when the body is in a state of inertia? For when the body lies sunk in sleep the mind slumbers at the same time, and has not the power of thinking which it has when awake. Further, I believe that all experience teaches us that the mind is not at all times equally apt or fit for thinking on the same subject, but that in the degree that the mind is more or less apt to have images of this or that object excited in it, so is it more or less apt for the contemplation of this or that subject.

But it may be said that, in so far as the body only is considered, it would be impossible to deduce solely from the laws of corporeal nature the causes of edifices, paintings, and all things of the kind which are the work of human art alone; and that the human body, unless it was moved and determined by the soul, would be incapable of constructing a temple, or any other edifice. But I have already shown that they who speak thus, do not know of what the body is capable, nor what can be deduced from the consideration of its nature alone; and that they themselves must have had experience of many things accomplished solely by the laws of nature, which they would not have believed possible unless done under the direction of the mind—such as the actions which somnambulists perform while sleeping and which are subjects of wonder to themselves when awake. I add, finally, that from the structure of the human body itself, which is fabricated with an art that infinitely surpasses human ingenuity and skill—and leaving out of the question all that I have just shown—I say that from the structure of the human body, and from its nature, under whatever attribute it is considered, there must follow from it an infinity of capabilities.

As regards the second point, I willingly admit that human affairs would go on much better if it were equally in the power of men to speak or to be silent. But experience more than sufficiently teaches us that there is nothing which men control less than the tongue, and that they are no less incapable of moderating or governing their appetites; whence it happens that many persons believe that we act freely only in respect of those things which we desire slightly or feebly, because then the appetite for those things can be easily controlled by the recollection of other things which our memory frequently recalls; but that we by no means act freely in respect of those things which we eagerly or strongly desire, and which the recollection of other things cannot make us cease to desire. But indeed nothing would prevent these persons from believing that our actions are always free, if they did not know by experience that we do many acts of which we afterwards repent, and that we often, when agitated by contending passions, see what is best and yet do what is worst. It is thus the infant would believe that it freely desires the breast—the angered boy that he freely seeks revenge—the timid that he is free to fly. It is thus also that an intoxicated man would believe that he speaks by the free will of his soul the words which when again sober he wishes he had not spoken—and it is even thus that the delirious, the garrulous, children, and many others, would believe that they speak by a free decision of the soul, when, nevertheless, they cannot restrain the impulse to speak. Thus, then, experience no less clearly than reason sufficiently teaches that men believe themselves free solely because they are conscious of their actions, but ignorant of the causes which determine them; and that, moreover, the decisions of the soul are nothing else than its appetites, which vary in accordance with the variable dispositions or states of the body. For every one, indeed, would control all things according to his own desires; and they, moreover, who are agitated by conflicting passions scarcely know what they desire; whilst they who are passive or have no desire, are easily led this way or that.

Now it clearly results from all that has been said, that the decision of the soul as well as the appetites and determinations of the body are simultaneous in nature, or rather that they are one and the same thing, which when considered under the attribute of *thought* and explained by it, we call a *decision*; and when considered under the attribute of *extension* and deduced from the laws of motion and rest, we call a *determination*—but all this will appear still more clearly in the course of this treatise. There is another point, however, to which I would here ask particular attention—namely: that we are unable to do anything by a decision of the soul without the aid of the memory. For example: we cannot speak a single word unless we remember it. Further, it evidently does not depend upon the free power of the soul either to remember or to forget anything. Wherefore, we believe that it is only in the power of the soul, by its sole decision, to speak or to be silent on a thing which is remembered. But when in sleep we dream that we speak, we believe we speak by virtue of the free decision of the soul; and yet we either do not speak at all, or if we do, it is by a spontaneous movement of the body. And if, further, we dream that we keep certain things secret, this is in virtue of a like decision of the soul as that whereby when awake we keep silent on things we know. Lastly, do we dream that by a decision of the soul we do certain things which awake we would not dare to do—I would then wish to know whether there are two kinds of decisions of the soul—one fantastical, another free? And if we are not disposed to be so irrational as to admit that there are, then it is necessary to concede that this decision of the soul which is believed to be free, is really not distinguishable from imagination or memory itself; and that it is, in fact, nothing but the affirmation which an idea, in so far as it is an idea, necessarily involves. Consequently, these decisions arise in the soul by the same necessity as the ideas of things actually existing arise in it. They, therefore, who believe that they speak, or are silent, or do anything whatsoever by the free decisions of the soul, dream with their eyes open.

Fifth part: of man's freedom, or the power of the understanding

Preface

I come at last to that other part of Ethics which relates to the mode or course of life that leads to Freedom. In this Part, therefore, I shall speak of the Power of the Understanding, and show what reason of itself can do in respect of the passions, and, afterwards, wherein freedom of the soul or beatitude consists. We shall then see how much the wise excel the ignorant. In what way, however, the understanding or reason is to be perfected, and how the body is to be cared for so that it may be most capable of performing its functions, does not belong to my subject, the former pertaining more properly to Logic, and the latter to Medicine. Here, therefore, as I have said, I shall treat of the power of the understanding, or of reason alone, and, above all, shall show the nature and extent of the empire it possesses to restrain and moderate the passions; for that we have no absolute dominion over these has been already demonstrated. The Stoics, indeed, held that our passions were entirely dependent upon our *will*, and that we could govern or control them absolutely. But experience loudly contradicted their principles, and they were constrained to admit that it required long habit and careful study to restrain and moderate them; a truth which (if I remember correctly) they sought to illustrate by the example of two dogs—one, a house or watch-dog, and the other a hunting dog, which by careful training were at length so changed in character that the watch-dog became a hunter, whilst, on the other hand, the hunting dog, which had been accustomed to the chase, ceased to pursue game. These views of the Stoics are not a little favoured by Descartes. For he thinks that the mind or soul is especially united with a certain part of the brain called the pineal gland, by means of which the soul is made sensible of every motion that is excited in the body and perceives external objects;

and that the soul by *willing* alone can effect numberless movements of this gland. This gland, moreover, he thinks, is suspended in the middle of the brain in such a way that it can be put in motion by the slightest movements of the animal spirits, and is so hung or suspended that it can be moved in as many different ways as there are different ways in which the animal spirits impinge upon it, and that as many various impressions are made upon it as there are various external objects that propel the animal spirits towards it; whence it results that if this gland has communicated to it by the will of the soul a motion similar to that which it had before received when acted upon by the animal spirits impelled towards it, then this gland itself propels and determines the animal spirits in the same manner as they had before been repelled when they impinged upon it similarly suspended. He thought, besides, that every volition of the soul is by nature united with a certain movement of this pineal gland. For example, if any one *wills* to look at a distant object, this *will* would have the effect to dilate the pupil of his eye; but if he merely thought to dilate the pupil and nothing more, that effect would not be produced by the volition, because nature has not united that motion of the pineal gland which serves to impel the spirits towards the optic nerve for the purpose of dilating or contracting the pupil of the eye with the will of merely dilating or contracting it and nothing more, but has united it with the will to look at objects distant or near. Finally, Descartes is of the opinion that although each particular motion of the pineal gland seems to be connected by nature from the beginning of our lives with some particular thought, still these motions may by force of habit be joined with other thoughts; and this is what he endeavours to establish in his treatise on the *Passions of the Soul*, Article 50, Part 1. He concludes from this, that there is no soul so imbecile that it cannot, if well directed, acquire absolute control over its passions. For the passions, according to his definition of them, are *perceptions, sensations, or commotions of the soul, which are specially referred to it, and produced, maintained, and strengthened by certain movements of the spirits*. (*Vide* Art. 27, Part I, *Passiones Animae*.) Now, since if any one could unite with his volitions such or such a movement of the pineal gland, and consequently of the spirits, and if the determination of our will depends entirely upon our own power, then our will being surely and firmly fixed and the desired actions of our life and the determination and movement of our passions being joined to it, it would follow that we could acquire an absolute empire over our passions. Such (in so far as I can understand him) is the opinion of this distinguished man; and if it had been less ingenious, less subtile, I must confess that I could scarcely have believed that it emanated from him. I cannot, indeed, sufficiently express my wonder that this great Philosopher, who has so broadly and firmly laid down the rule that nothing is to be inferred except from self-evident truths, and nothing to be affirmed save that which is clearly and distinctly understood or perceived, and who has so often reprehended the scholastics for having wished or attempted to explain obscure things by occult qualities—that he, I say, should assume an hypothesis more occult than the most occult quality. What, I ask, does he understand by the union of soul and body? What clear and distinct conception has he of thought most closely united with even the smallest particle of any quantitative thing? I would wish, indeed, that he had explained this union by its proximate cause. But he had conceived the soul as so distinct from the body that he could neither assign any particular cause for this union nor for the soul itself, but was necessarily constrained to have recourse to the cause of the universe at large, that is, to God. I would also wish to know how many degrees of motion the soul can give to this pineal gland, and with what degree of force it can hold it suspended? For I know not whether this gland moves about more quickly or more slowly when acted upon by the soul than by the animal spirits, and whether the movements of the passions which are so closely connected with our decisions cannot be dissevered from them by corporeal causes, so that it might follow that although the soul had firmly resolved to meet a certain danger and with this decision had joined the motion producing courage, nevertheless, in presence of the danger the gland might not be so suspended that the soul could think of nothing but flight. And, indeed, as there is no ratio given between the will and motion, so there can be no comparison made between the power or force of the soul and that of the body, and consequently the power of the one can in nowise be determined by the power of the other. Add to this, that neither is the pineal gland ascertained to be so situated in the middle of the brain that it can be easily acted upon and moved in so many different ways, nor are all the nerves produced or extended to the cavities of the brain.

I omit saying anything in reference to the assertions of Descartes as regards the will and its freedom, inasmuch as I have more than sufficiently shown the error of his views on this subject. Therefore, inasmuch as the power of the soul, as I have shown, is defined by the understanding alone, the remedies against the affections or passions which all experience, but which, as I believe, all do not accurately observe nor distinctly understand, are only to be determined by the *knowledge of the soul*; and it is from this that we shall deduce whatsoever bears upon man's true happiness or beatitude.

3

G. W. LEIBNIZ

I. THE DISCOURSE ON METAPHYSICS (1685-6)

In order to distinguish the actions of God and of creatures we explain in what the notion of an individual substance consists

It is difficult enough to distinguish the actions of God from those of creatures; for there are some[1] who believe that God does every thing, and others[2] imagine that all he does is to conserve the force which he has given to creatures: the sequel will show how far the one or the other can be said. Now since actions and passions properly belong to individual substances, it will be necessary to explain what such a substance is.

It is indeed true that when several predicates are attributed to the same subject and this subject is not attributed to any other, it is called an individual substance; but that is not enough, and such an explanation is only nominal. We must therefore consider what it is to be truly attributed to a certain subject.

Now it is a fact that all true predication has some foundation in the nature of things, and when a proposition is not identical, that is to say when the predicate is not expressly comprised in the subject, it must be comprised in it virtually, and that is what the Philosophers call *in-esse* when they say that the predicate is in the subject. Thus the term of the subject must always include that of the predicate, so that whoever understood perfectly the notion of the subject would also judge that the predicate belongs to it.

This being so, we can say that the nature of an individual substance or of a complete being is to have a notion so complete that it is sufficient to comprise and to allow the deduction from it of all the predicates of the subject to which this notion is attributed. Whereas an accident is a being the notion of which does not include all that can be attributed to the subject to which this notion is attributed. Thus the quality of King which belongs to Alexander the Great, in abstraction from the subject, is not sufficiently determined for an individual, and does not include the other

---

[1] The occasionalists, following Malebranch, *De la recherche de la vérité*, 1674.
[2] The Cartesians.

qualities of the same subject, nor all that the notion of this Prince comprises; whereas God seeing the individual notion or hæccity[1] of Alexander sees in it at the same time the foundation and reason of all the predicates that can be truly said of him, as for example that he would conquer Darius and Porus, even to the point of knowing from it *a priori* (and not by experience) whether he dies a natural death or by poison, which we can only know by history. Also, when we consider well the connection of things, we can say that there are at all times in the soul of Alexander vestiges of all that has happened to him and the marks of all that will happen to him, and even traces of all that happens in the universe, although it belongs only to God to recognize them all.

That each single substance expresses the whole universe after its own manner, and that in its notion all its events are comprised with all their circumstances and all the sequence of external things

... Every substance is like a whole world and like a mirror of God or of all the universe, which each expresses after its own fashion, much as the same town is variously represented according to the different situations of the man who is looking at it. Thus the universe is in some sort multiplied as many times as there are substances, and the glory of God is also redoubled by the same number of wholly different representations of his work. One can even say that every substance bears in some sort the character of God's infinite wisdom and omnipotence, and imitates him as far as it is capable. For it expresses, albeit confusedly, all that happens in the universe, past, present or future, and this has some resemblance to an infinite perception or knowledge; and as all other substances express this one in their turn and accommodate themselves to it, one can say that it extends its power over all the others in imitation of the omnipotence of the Creator.

That the notions which consist in extension contain something imaginary and cannot constitute the substance of body

But to take up again the thread of our considerations, I believe that anyone who meditates on the nature of substance, which I have explained above, will find that the whole nature of body does not consist solely in extension, that is to say in size, figure and motion, but that there must necessarily be recognized in it something which is related to souls and which is commonly called substantial form, though it brings about no changes in phenomena, no more than does the soul of beasts, if they have one. It can even be demonstrated that the notion of size, figure and motion is not so distinct as is imagined, and that it includes something imaginary and

[1] 'thisness'.

relative to our perceptions, as are also (although much more so) colour, heat and other similar qualities, of which it can be doubted whether they are truly present in the nature of things outside us. That is why these kinds of qualities cannot constitute any substance. And if there were no other principle of identity in bodies than what we have just said, a body would never subsist for more than a moment.

Yet the souls and substantial forms of other bodies are very different from intelligent souls, which alone know their actions, and which not only do not perish naturally, but also retain for ever the foundation of their knowledge of what they are; which makes them alone susceptible of punishment and reward and makes them citizens of the republic of the universe, of which God is the monarch; whence it follows that all other creatures must serve them, of which we shall speak at greater length presently.

God produces different substances according to the different views which he has of the universe, and by the intervention of God the nature proper to each substance carries with it that what happens to one corresponds to what happens to all the others, without their acting immediately on one another

Having come to know in some fashion in what the nature of substance consists, we must next try to explain the dependence which they have on one another, and their actions and passions. Now in the first place it is very obvious that created substances depend on God who conserves them and also produces them continually by a kind of emanation, as we produce our thoughts. For God turning so to say on all sides and in every fashion the general system of phenomena which he finds it good to produce to manifest his glory, and looking at all the faces of the world in all possible ways since there is no bearing on it which escapes his omniscience, the result of each view of the universe, as looked at from a certain place, is a substance which expresses the universe conformably with this view, if God finds it good to make his thought effective and to produce this substance. And as God's view is always true, our perceptions are true also, but it is our judgments which are of ourselves and which deceive us.

Now we have said above and it follows from what we have just said, that each substance is like a world apart, independent of any other thing save God; thus all our phenomena, that is to say all that can ever happen to us, are only consequences of our being. These phenomena maintain a certain order in conformity with our nature, or so to say with the world which is in us, and this enables us to make observations which are useful for regulating our conduct and are justified by the success of future phenomena, and thus often to judge the future by the past without making mistakes. This would therefore suffice for saying that these phenomena are true, without troubling ourselves about whether they are outside us and whether others perceive them also. Yet it is very true that the perceptions or expressions of all substances mutually correspond, so that each carefully following certain reasons or laws which it has observed agrees with the other doing the same, as when several people, having agreed to meet at a certain place on a certain prearranged day, are able to do so effectively if they wish. Now although all express the same phenomena, their expressions do not therefore have to be perfectly alike, but it is enough that they should be proportional; as several spectators believe that they are seeing the same thing, and in fact understand each other, although each sees and speaks according to the measure of his view.

Now there is none but God (from whom all individuals emanate continually and who sees the universe not only as they see it but also quite differently from all of them) to be the cause of this correspondence of their phenomena, and to make what is private to one public to all; otherwise there would be no communication.[1] It could therefore be said in some sort, and in a good sense, although remote from ordinary usage, that a particular substance never acts on another particular substance, nor is acted on by it, if we consider that what happens to each one is only a consequence of its idea or complete notion alone, since this idea already includes all predicates or events and expresses the whole universe. In fact nothing can happen to us but thoughts and perceptions, and all our future thoughts and perceptions are only consequences, albeit contingent, of our preceding thoughts and perceptions, such that if I were capable of considering distinctly everything that is happening or appearing to me at this moment, I should be able to see therein everything that will happen or appear to me for ever after; nor would it fail but would happen to me in the very same way, though everything outside me were destroyed, provided that there remained only God and myself.

God alone is the immediate object of our perceptions which exist outside us, and he alone is our light

Now in rigorous metaphysical truth there is no external cause which acts on us except God alone and he alone communicates himself to us immediately by virtue of our continual dependence. From which it follows that there is no other external object which affects our soul and which immediately excites our perception. Hence we have in our souls ideas of everything only by virtue of the continual action of God on us, that is to say because every effect expresses its cause and thus the essence of our soul is a certain expression, imitation or image of the divine essence, thought

[1] 'liaison'.

and will, and of all the ideas which are comprised therein. It can be said then that God alone is our immediate object outside us and that we see all things by him; for example when we see the sun and the stars it is God who has given to us and conserves for us the ideas of them and who determines us to think of them effectively by his ordinary concourse at the time at which our senses are disposed in a certain manner, according to the laws which he has established.

Explanation of the commerce of the soul and the body, which has passed for inexplicable or for miraculous, and of the origin of confused perceptions

We also see the unexpected elucidation of the great mystery of the union of the soul and of the body, that is to say how it happens that the passions and actions of the one are accompanied by actions and passions, or by suitable phenomena, of the other. For it is impossible to conceive that the one should have influence on the other, and it is not reasonable simply to have recourse to the extraordinary operation of the universal cause in an ordinary and particular matter. But here is the true reason of it: we have said that everything that happens to the soul and to each substance is a consequence of its notion; hence the idea itself or essence of the soul carries with it that all its appearances or perceptions must be born (*sponte*) from its own nature, and precisely in such a way that they correspond of themselves to what happens in the whole universe, but more particularly and more perfectly to what happens in the body which is assigned to it, because, in some fashion and for a time, it is according to the relation of other bodies to its own that the soul expresses the state of the universe. Which also makes known how our body belongs to us, but without being attached to our essence. And I believe that people who can meditate will judge favourably of our principles for this reason, that they will be able to see easily in what the connection which there is between the soul and the body consists, which seems inexplicable by any other way.

II. CORRESPONDENCE WITH ARNAULD (1686)

Leibniz to Arnauld, July 14, 1686

When the question of the union of the soul and the body, or of action and of passion of one spirit with regard to another created thing, comes into question, many have felt obliged to grant that their immediate influence one upon another is inconceivable. Nevertheless, the hypothesis of occasional causes is not satisfactory, it seems to me, to a philosopher, because it introduces a sort of continuous miracle as though God at every moment was changing the laws of bodies on the occasions when minds had thoughts, or was changing the regular course of the thinking of the soul by exciting in it other thoughts on the occasion of a bodily movement; and in general as though God was interfering otherwise for the ordinary events of life than in preserving each substance in its course and in the laws established for it. Only the hypothesis of the concomitance or the agreement of substances among themselves therefore is able to explain these things in a manner wholly conceivable and worthy of God. And as this hypothesis alone is demonstrative and inevitable in my opinion, according to the proposition which we have just established, it seems also that it agrees better with the freedom of reasonable creatures than the hypothesis of impressions or of occasional causes. God created the soul from the very start in such a manner that for the ordinary events it has no need of these interventions, and whatever happens to the soul comes from its own being, without any necessity, on its part, of accommodation in the sequence of events to the body, any more than there is of the body's accommodating itself to the soul. Each one follows its laws, the one acts freely, the other without choice, and they accord with one another in the same phenomena.

Arnauld to Leibniz, September 28, 1686

What do you mean by 'the hypothesis of the concomitance and of the agreement of substances among themselves'? You claim that by this means, that which happens in the union of the soul and the body and in the action or the passion of a mind with respect to any other created thing, can be explained. I cannot understand what you say in explaining this thought, which, according to you, agrees neither with those who think that the soul acts physically upon the body and the body upon the soul, nor with those who think that God alone is the physical cause of these effects, and that the soul and the body are only the occasional causes. You say, 'God created the soul in such a way that for the ordinary events it has no need of these changes, and that which happens to the soul arises from its own being without its having to agree with the body in what results, any more than the body does with the soul. Each one follows its laws. The one acting with freedom, and the other without choice, they fit in together, one with another, in the same phenomenon.' Examples will enable you to make your thought clearer: some one wounds my arm. With regard to my body, this is only a bodily motion but my soul at once has a feeling of pain which it would not have if this had not happened to my arm. The question is, what is the cause of this pain? You deny that my body has acted upon my soul, and that God, on the occasion of this which happened to my arm, immediately produced in my soul the feeling of pain. It must be, therefore, that you think that it is the soul which has formed this feeling in itself and this must be what you mean when you say that, 'What happens in the soul on the occasioning of the body arises from its own being'. St Augustine was of this opinion because he thought that bodily pain was nothing else than the grief which the soul had when its body was ill-affected. But what reply can be made to those who object that the soul must therefore have known that its body was ill-affected before it could become sorrowful, while in fact it seems to be the pain which informs the soul that the body is injured?

Let us take another example where the body has some movement on the occasioning of the soul. If I wish to take off my hat, I lift my arm to my head. This movement of my arm upward is not at all in line with the ordinary laws of motion. What then is its cause? It is because the spirits, having entered into certain nerves, have stimulated them. But these spirits have not been through their own power determined to enter into these nerves. They had not given to themselves the movements which cause them to enter into these nerves. What has given it to them then? Is it God, who has done it on the occasion of my wishing to lift my arm? This is what the partisans of occasional causes say. It seems to me that you do not approve of their position. It must, therefore, be our soul itself, but this again it seems that you will not grant, for this would be to act physically upon the body; and you appear to deny that a substance can act physically upon another.

Draft of the letter from Leibniz to Arnauld, November 28–December 8, 1686
The hypothesis of the concomitance or of the agreement of substances among themselves, follows from what I have said regarding each individual substance: that it involves, forever, all the accidents that will happen to it and that it expresses the whole universe in its manner. Thus whatever is expressed in the body by a movement or by a change of position, is perhaps expressed in the soul by a sense of pain. Since pains are only thoughts, we must not be surprised if they are the consequences of a substance whose nature it is to think. If it happens constantly that certain thoughts are joined to certain movements, this is because God has created from the very start all substances in such a way that in the sequence, all their phenomena shall correspond without any need for a mutual physical influence. This latter does not even appear explicable. Perhaps M. Descartes would rather have accepted this concomitance than the hypothesis of occasional causes, for so far as I know, he has never expressed himself upon the matter. I am pleasantly surprised, M., that St Augustine, as you say, already held some such view, when he maintained that pain is nothing else than the grief which the soul has when its body is ill disposed. This great man surely thought far into things. The soul, however, feels

that its body is ill disposed, not through an influence of the body upon the soul, nor by a particular intervention of God who carries the information, but because it is the nature of the soul to express whatever happens in the body, having been created from the start in such a way that the sequence of its thoughts will agree with the sequence of the movements.

4

NICOLAS MALEBRANCHE

Theodore. Nothing or Non-being has no qualities. I think, therefore I am. But what am I, I that think during the time that I am thinking? Am I a body, a mind, a man? As yet I know nothing of all this. I know only that during the time in which I think I am something that thinks. Now let us see. Can a body think? Can a piece of extension whether of length, width or depth, reason, desire, feel? No, beyond a doubt, for all the modifications of such an extension consist only in certain relations of distance; and it is obvious that such relations are not perceptions, reasonings, pleasures, desires, feelings, in a word, thoughts. This 'I' that thinks, then, my own substance, is not a body, since my perceptions, which certainly belong to me, are entirely different things from these relations of distance.

Aristes. It is clear to me that modifications of extension can only be relations of distance, and that, therefore, extension cannot know, will or feel. But perhaps my body is something else besides extension. For, it seems to me, it is my finger that feels the pain of a prick, my heart which desires, my brain which reasons. The inner feeling I have of all that goes on within me teaches me what I am saying to you. Prove to me that my body is nothing but extension, and I will admit that my mind, or that in me which thinks, wills and reasons, is not material or corporeal.

Theodore. What, Aristes! Do you believe that your body consists of some substance other than extension? Do you not understand that it suffices alone to have extension to form out of it a brain, a heart, arms, hands, all the veins, the arteries, the nerves, and whatever else the body is composed of? If God were to destroy the extension of your body would you still have a brain, veins, arteries, etc? Do you believe, then, that a body can be reduced to a mathematical point? That God can form all that there is in the universe out of the extension of a grain of sand, I do not doubt. But, assuredly, when there is no extension (I say *no* extension), there is no corporeal substance. Think it over seriously, and in order to become convinced of it, pay attention to this.

All that is or has being can either be conceived by itself, or it cannot. There is no middle course, for these two propositions are contradictories.

Now, all that can be conceived by itself and without the thought of anything else, all, I say, that can be conceived by itself as existing independently of every other thing, and without the idea which we have of it representing any other thing, is assuredly a being or a substance, and all that cannot be conceived by itself and without the thought of anything else is a mode of Being or a modification of Substance.

For example. We cannot think of roundness without thinking of extension. Roundness, then, is not a being or substance, but a mode of being. We can think of extension without thinking of any other thing in particular. Therefore, extension is not a mode of being. It is itself a being. Since the modification of a substance is only the substance itself determined in a particular way, it is evident that the idea of a modification necessarily involves the idea of the substance of which it is a modification. Again, since a substance is that which subsists by itself, the idea of a substance does not necessarily involve the idea of any other being. We have no other way of distinguishing substances or beings, modifications or modes of being, than by the different ways in which we think of them. Now, consider. Is it not true that you can think of extension without thinking of any other thing? Is it not true that you can become aware of extension by itself? Extension, therefore, is a substance and not a mode of substance. Accordingly, extension and matter are one and the same substance. But I can think of thought, desires, pleasures, without thinking of extension, and even if I suppose that there is no extension. Hence all these are not modes of extension, but modes of a substance which thinks, which feels, which desires, and which is quite different from extension.

All the modifications of extension consist in nothing but relations of distance. But it is evident that my pleasures, my desires, my thoughts, are not relations of distance. All relations of distance can be compared, measured, determined, in an exact manner by the principles of geometry, but we cannot compare or measure our perceptions or our feelings in this way. Therefore, my soul is not material. It is not a modification of my body. It is a substance which thinks and which has no resemblance to the extended substance of which my body is made up.

Aristes. That seems to me demonstrated. But what conclusions can you draw from it?

Theodore. I can deduce an infinite number of truths from it. For the distinction of body and soul is the basis of the main tenets of philosophy, and among others of the immortality of the soul. For, let me say this in passing, if the soul is a substance distinguished from the body, it is clear that, even if death were to annihilate our body (which it does not do), it would not follow from that that our soul was also annihilated.

Aristes. As soon as you left me, Theodore, I fell into deep meditation in order to consult reason, and I recognized far better than when you were speaking to me and I was yielding to your arguments that the ideas of created beings are eternal, that God has made all bodies in accordance with the idea of extension, that this idea must, therefore, represent their nature, and that I must consequently consider it carefully in order to discover their properties. . . .

It was in following this principle that I realized that light is neither in the sun nor in the air where we see it; that colours are not on the surface of bodies; that the sun could perhaps set in motion the fine particles of the air, and these latter could communicate the same impression of movement to the optic nerve, and thence to that part of the brain where the soul resides, and that these small bodies in movement when encountering solid objects might be reflected differently according to the diversity in the surfaces which were causing them to rebound. So much for their boasted light and variety of colours.

I have understood likewise that the heat which I feel is not in the fire, nor the cold in the ice, nor even pain in my own body, in which I have often felt it so cruelly acute. Neither is sweetness in the sugar, nor bitterness in the aloes, nor acidity in sour grapes, nor sourness in vinegar, nor that sweetness and strength in wine which deceives and stupefies so many drunkards. I see all this, by the same reason which enabled me to see that sound must be regarded as not in the air and that there is an infinite difference between the vibrations of strings and the sounds which they yield, between the proportions of their vibrations and the variety of the consonances.

It would take me too long, Theodore, if I were to give you in detail all the proofs which have convinced me that bodies have no other qualities than those which result from their figures, not any other activity than their various movements. But I cannot conceal from you a difficulty which, despite all my efforts, I was unable to surmount. I follow, for instance, without misgiving, the action of the sun through all the space which separates it from me. For, granted that there is no empty space, I can understand that the sun can make no impression in the places it occupies without the impression being transmitted to the place which I occupy or to my eyes, and by my eyes to my brain. But, in following the clear idea of movement, I could not understand whence there came to me the sensation of light. I see quite well that the movement of the optic nerve is alone sufficient to produce the sensation in me. For, pressing the corner of my eye with my finger on a spot behind which I know the optic nerve is located, I saw a bright light in a place otherwise dark on the side opposite to that on which my eye was pressed. Yet this change from movement to light seemed to me then and seems to me still altogether incomprehensible. What a strange metamorphosis, from a pressure on the eye to a brilliant light! And this is all the more astounding because I do not see this radiance of light in my soul of which it is the modification, nor in my brain, where the disturbance ends, nor in the eye where the pressure takes place, nor on the side on which I press my eye, but in the air—in the air which surely is incapable of such a modification, and on the side opposite to the eye which I press. What a marvellous thing!

At first I thought that my soul, on being warned of the disturbance that had taken place in my body, was the cause of the sensations which it had of the things around it. But a little reflection undeceived me. For it is not true, it seems to me, that the soul knows anything of the disturbance caused by the sun in the fibres of the brain. I saw light before I knew of this disturbance. For children who do not even know that they have a brain are struck by the brilliance of light just as much as philosophers are. Again, what relation is there between the vibrations of a corporeal thing and the different sensations which follow such vibrations? How can I see light in bodies if it is a modification of my soul, how see it in bodies around me, if the disturbance takes place in my body alone? I press the corner of my eye on the right side, why do I see the light on the left side, notwithstanding the fact that I am well aware that it is not on that side that I am pressing?

From all this, and from a number of other things which it would take me too long to tell you, I concluded that the sensations were in myself, that I was in no wise their cause, and that if corporeal things were capable of acting on me and of making themselves felt in the way I feel them, it would be necessary that they should be of a nature more excellent than my body, endowed with a terrible power, and some of them even with a wisdom truly marvellous, always uniform in their behaviour, always effective in their action, always incomprehensible in the astounding results of their power. All this appeared to me tremendous and terrible to think of, though my senses encouraged the madness and quite accommodated themselves to it. But, Theodore, will you kindly clear this matter up for me?

Theodore. There is no time to resolve your difficulties unless you desire that we should leave the general truths of metaphysics and enter upon an explanation of the principles of physics and of the laws of the conjunction of soul and body.

Aristes. Say a few words, please, on this point. It will give me much pleasure to meditate upon the matter. My mind is quite prepared for it.

Theodore. Listen, then; but remember to meditate upon what I have already told you. When we seek to find the reason of certain effects, and in following the chain of causes and effects arrive at last at a general cause or at a cause that we can quite well see has no relation to the effect which it produces or rather appears to produce, then instead of being satisfied with chimeras, we ought to have recourse to the author of the laws of nature. For example, if you were to ask me what is the cause of the pain which one feels when one is pricked, I should be wrong to tell you forthwith that it is one of the laws of the author of nature that a prick should be followed by pain. I ought to tell you that the prick cannot separate the fibres of my flesh without disturbing the nerves which propagate stimulation to the brain, and without disturbing the brain itself. But if you wish to know how it is that when a certain part of my brain is disturbed in a given way, I feel the pain of a prick, this question concerns a general effect; and, as one cannot by tracing the matter further, find a natural or particular cause, one must have recourse to a general cause. For this amounts to a question as to who is the author of the general laws of the conjunction of soul and body. Now, since admittedly, there can be no relation or necessary connection between a disturbance in the brain and certain sensations, it is evident that we must have recourse to a power which is not to be met with in either of these entities. It is not sufficient to say that as the prick wounds the body, the soul must be warned of the fact by pain, so that it may go to its assistance. For this would be to substitute a final for an efficient cause, and the difficulty would remain; for we should still have to ascertain the cause which brings it about, that, on the occasion of the body being wounded, the soul suffers in consequence, and experiences a particular kind of pain for a particular kind of wound.

Further, to say, with certain philosophers, that the soul is the cause of the pain, because the pain is but the sadness which the soul feels when there takes place in the body which it loves some disturbance of which it is warned by the difficulty which it has in the exercise of its functions, is to neglect the inner feeling which we experience of what takes place in us. For every one feels unmistakably, when he is being bled, for example, or when he burns himself, that he is not the cause of the pain. He feels it against his own will, and he cannot doubt that it comes to him from an external cause. Again, the soul does not feel pain and a particular kind of pain because it has learnt that a disturbance is taking place in the brain, and a particular kind of disturbance. Nothing is more certain than this. Finally, pain and sadness are entirely different. Pain precedes the awareness of the evil, sadness follows it. Pain is not agreeable, but sadness sometimes pleases us so much that those who wish to banish it from our mind, without freeing us at the same time from the evil which causes it, grieve and irritate us just as if they disturbed our joy, because sadness is, in fact, a state of the soul which is most suitable for us when we suffer some evil or are deprived of some good, and the feeling which accompanies this state of mind is the most suitable we can have under the circumstances. Pain, then, is entirely different from sadness. Moreover, I think that the soul is not the cause of its sadness; and that the thought which we have of the loss of some good only produces this feeling in us in consequence of the natural and necessary movement which God unceasingly impresses upon us for our welfare. But let us return to the difficulties which you have regarding the action and the qualities of light.

Firstly, there is no metamorphosis. The disturbance that takes place in the brain cannot change into light or into colours. For as modifications of bodies are nothing but these bodies themselves determined in a particular manner, they cannot be transformed into modifications of mind. That is evident.

Secondly, you press the corner of your eye and you have a certain sensation. That is so because He who alone can act upon minds has established certain laws owing to which body and soul operate and suffer in reciprocal determination.

Thirdly, when you press your eye you have a sensation of light, though there is present no luminous body, because it is by a pressure similar to that which your finger exerts upon your eye, and from there on your brain, that bodies which we call luminous operate upon those around them, and through the latter upon our eyes and our brains. All this takes place in consequence of natural laws. For it is one of the laws of the conjunction of soul and body in accordance with which God acts incessantly upon those two substances, that a particular pressure or a particular disturbance should be followed by a particular sensation.

Fourthly, you see the light which is a modification of your mind and which, therefore, can exist in it alone; for there is a contradiction in the thought of a modification of a being existing where that being is not. You see it, I say, in the vast spaces which your mind does not fill, for the mind does not occupy space. Those spaces which you see are only intelligible spaces which do not occupy any place. For the spaces which you see are quite different from the material spaces which you survey. One must not confuse the ideas of things with the things themselves. Remember, that we do not see bodies in themselves, and that it is only through their ideas that they are visible. Often we can see what does not actually exist, a proof positive that those things which we see are intelligible and quite different from those which we look at.

Fifthly and lastly, you see the light not on the side on which you press your eye but on the opposite side, because, the nerve being constructed and adapted to receive impressions from luminous bodies through the pupil of the eye and not otherwise, the pressure of your finger on the left produces the same effect on your eye as a luminous body on the right, whose rays were to pass the pupil and the transparent part of the eye, would produce. For in pressing the eye from without you are pressing the optic nerve from within against what is called the vitreous humour, which in turn offers some resistance. Thus, God makes you experience the light on the side on which you see it because He always follows the laws which He has established in order to keep His procedure perfectly uniform. . . .

There is no necessary relation between the two substances of which we are composed. The modifications of our bodies cannot, by their own activity, change those of our minds. Nevertheless, the modifications of a certain part of the brain which I will not further determine are always followed by modifications or feelings of our soul; and this solely in consequence of the continual exercise of the laws of the union of these two substances—that is to say, to speak more clearly, in consequence of the constant and ever effective will of the author of our being. There is no relation of causality between a body and a mind. What am I saying? That there is no relation between a mind and a body. I am saying more. There is no real relation between one body and another, between one mind and another. In a word, no created thing can act upon another by an activity which is its own. This I will prove to you presently. But, at least, it is evident that a body, that extension, a purely passive substance, cannot operate by its own activity upon a mind, upon a being of another nature and infinitely more excellent than it. Thus, it is clear that, in the union of soul and body, there is no other bond than the efficacy of divine and immutable decrees, an efficacy never without its effects. God has then willed, and wills without ceasing that the various disturbances of the brain shall always be followed by the various thoughts of the mind with which it is in union. And it is this constant and efficient will of the Creator which causes the union of these two substances. For there is no other nature, I mean no other natural laws, than the efficient volitions of the Omnipotent.

Do not ask, Aristes, why God wills to unite minds to bodies. The fact is unquestionable, but the principal reasons for it hitherto have remained unknown to philosophy, and perhaps even religion does not teach us.

Theodore. If we had to examine all the relations which the bodies of our environment have to a given position of our own, in order to discover whether and how and to what extent we ought to have commerce with them, that would take up a good deal of our time, indeed, it would entirely usurp the capacity of the mind. And, assuredly, our body would not be the better for it. It would soon be destroyed in some unforeseen manner; for our wants change so often and sometimes so quickly that it would require a vigilance of which we are incapable not to be overtaken by some fatal accident. When would one think of eating, for example, or of what to eat or when to cease eating? How busy would a mind which guides and exercises its body be if it had to know at every step which the body is made to take, that it is moving in a fluid air which cannot wound it or trouble it with cold or heat, wind or rain, or with some malignant or corrupt vapour; that there is not at each spot where the person wishes to place his foot a sharp or hard body capable of hurting him; that he must lower the head promptly to avoid a stone, and look after his equilibrium to prevent himself from falling! A man always occupied in this way with the whole mechanism of his body and with an infinity of objects in his environment could never think of the true goods, or at any rate could not think of the true goods as much as they demand or consequently as much as is their due, seeing that our mind is made and can only be made for the purpose of occupying itself with those goods which can illumine it or make it happy.

Thus, it is evident that God, willing to conjoin minds with bodies, had to establish for an occasional cause of the confused awareness we have of the presence of objects and of their properties as in relation to us, not our attention which deserves clear and distinct knowledge, but the various disturbances in these same bodies. He had to give us distinct proofs not of the nature or properties of the things around us but of the relation in which they stand to us, so that we should be able to work successfully for the preservation of life without having to pay incessant attention to our needs. He had, so to speak, to undertake the task of warning us at the proper time and place, by means of anticipatory feelings, of all that concerns the good of the body, so as to give us full opportunity to occupy ourselves in the pursuit of the true goods. He had to give us curt warnings of all that concerns the body, so as to convince us promptly, vivid proofs so as to determine us effectively, certain and irrefutable proofs so as to preserve us more surely; yet proofs which are confused, although indubitable, not of the relations which subsist between the objects themselves, in which relations the evidence of truth consists, but of the relations in which they stand to our body situated as it is at the time. I make the latter reservation because we find, for example, or ought to find, tepid water warm if we touch it with a cold hand, and cold if we touch it with a warm hand. We find it, or ought to find it, pleasant when thirsty; but when our thirst is quenched we find it tasteless and unpleasant. Let us admire, then,

Aristes, the wisdom of the laws of the conjunction of soul and body; and, though all our senses should tell us that sense qualities are in the objects, let us attribute to corporeal things only what we see clearly belongs to them, after having consulted the ideas which represent them. For since the senses give us different accounts of the same things according to the interest which they have in them, since they invariably contradict themselves when the welfare of the body requires, we must regard them as false witnesses with reference to truth, but as faithful monitors so far as the preservation and the conveniences of life are concerned.

Aristes. We have no need of a revelation to teach us that we have a body; when we are pricked, we feel it quite sufficiently.

Theodore. Yes, no doubt we feel it. But the feeling of pain which we have is a kind of revelation. This expression is a striking one. But it is precisely for that reason that I make use of it. For you always forget that it is God alone who produces in your soul all those different feelings which it experiences, on the occasion of the changes which take place in your body, in consequence of the general laws of the conjunction of the two natures of which man is constituted; laws which are nothing but the efficient and constant volitions of the Creator, as I shall explain in the sequel. The point through which our hand is pricked does not cause the pain through the hole which it makes in the body. Neither is it the soul which produces this uncomfortable feeling, since it suffers the pain despite itself. It is produced assuredly by a superior power. It is God Himself, who through the feelings with which He affects us reveals to us all that takes place outside us, I mean in our body and in the bodies of our environment. Remember, please, what I have already said so many times.

Aristes. It seems to me, Theodore, that there is nothing to which I am more intimately united than my own body. For it cannot be touched without disturbing me. As soon as it is wounded I feel that I am injured, that I am hurt. There is nothing more insignificant than the proboscis of those importunate gnats that attack us on our evening walk; and, nevertheless, however slightly they bury the imperceptible point of their venomous proboscis into my skin, my soul feels pain. The mere noise which they make in my ears alarms me—a sure indication that I am more closely united to my body than to anything else. Yes, Theodore, this is so true that it is really only through our body that we are united to the objects of our environment. If the sun did not disturb my eyes it would be invisible so far as I am concerned, and if, unfortunately for myself, I were to become deaf, I should no longer find so much delight in the intercourse I have with my friends. In fact, it is through my body that I hold to my religion. It is through my ears and my eyes that faith has entered into my mind and heart. Thus it is through my body that I have everything. I am therefore united to my body more intimately than to any other thing.

Theodore. Have you meditated long, my dear Aristes, in order to make this great discovery?

Theotimus. All that may quite well be maintained, Theodore.

Theodore. Yes, Theotimus, by people who consult only their senses. Whom are you taking Aristes for if you approve in his mouth that which any peasant might utter? I do not recognize Aristes in this reply.

Aristes. I see that I have made a very bad beginning.

Theodore. Very bad indeed. I did not expect this sort of beginning. For I did not believe that you would forget today what you knew yesterday. But prejudices will always return to the attack and deprive us of our conquests, if we do not know how to maintain our position by our vigilance and good intrenchments. Oh well! I submit to you that we are not united to our body at all, much less are we more intimately united to it than to anything else. I am using somewhat extreme expressions so that they shall leave a vivid impression and that you may not forget what I am saying. No, Aristes, to speak accurately and in all strictness, your mind is not and cannot be united to your body, for it can be united only to that which can act upon it. How do you think that your body can act upon your mind? Do you think it is through your body that you are rational, happy or unhappy, and so on? Is it your body which unites you to God, to the Reason which enlightens you, or is it God who unites you to your body and through your body to everything in your environment?

Aristes. Of course, Theodore, it is God who has joined my body to my mind. But can we not say . . .

Theodore. What? That it is your mind which now acts upon your body and your body upon your mind? I understand you. God has instituted this union of mind and body. But as a result your body, and through it all objects, are capable of acting upon the mind. That union once established, your mind can act upon your body, and through it upon all things in your environment. Can we not put the matter thus?

Aristes. There is something here that I do not quite understand. How is all this accomplished? I speak to you now as though I had forgotten the best part of what you have told me through neglecting to meditate upon it.

Theodore. I have my doubts about that. You want me to prove to you more exactly and with greater detail the principles concerning which I have spoken hitherto. I must try to satisfy you. But I ask you to give me your attention, and you, Theotimus, to watch us both.

Do you think, Aristes, that matter, which, I take it, you do not believe to be capable of moving itself or of modifying itself, can ever modify a mind, make it happy or unhappy, represent ideas to it, or give to it various feelings? Think this over and answer me.

Aristes. That does not seem to me possible.

Theodore. Once again, think it over. Consult the idea of extension, and judge by means of the idea which represents all bodies, if anything represents them, whether they can have any other property but the passive faculty of receiving various figures and various movements. Is it not absolutely evident that the properties of extension can consist in nothing but relations of distance?

Aristes. That is clear, and I have already granted you all that.

Theodore. Hence it is not possible that bodies should act on minds.

Aristes. Not in themselves or by means of their own force, one might reply. But why should they not be able to do so by means of a power which is the result of their union with minds?

Theodore. Why do you say by means of a power which is the result of their union? These general terms convey nothing to my mind. Remember, Aristes, the principle of clear ideas. If you abandon it, you will at once be enveloped in obscurity. At the first step you will fall over the precipice. I can understand quite well that bodies, in consequence of certain natural laws, can act upon our mind in the sense that their modifications determine the activity of the divine volitions or of the general laws of the conjunction of body and soul, all of which I will explain to you soon. But that bodies should in themselves be capable of receiving a certain power by the efficacy of which they can act upon the mind I cannot understand. For what would this power be? Would it be a substance or a mode? If a substance, then the bodies do not act, but only this substance in bodies. If this power is a mode, then there is a mode in bodies which will be neither movement nor figure. Extension, therefore, will have modes other than relations of distance. But really, why should I dwell on this point? It is for you, Aristes, to give me some idea of the power which you conceive to be the effect of the conjunction of body and soul.

Aristes. We do not know, one might reply, what this power is. But what can you infer from this confession of our ignorance?

Theodore. That it is better to say nothing than not to know what one is saying.

Aristes. Agreed. But one is saying only what one knows when one maintains that bodies act on minds, for nothing is more certain. Experience does not permit us to doubt that.

Theodore. I doubt it very much, nevertheless, or rather I do not believe it at all. Experience teaches me that I feel pain, for example, when a pin pricks me. That is certain. But here let us stop, for experience does not teach us that a pin can act on our mind nor that it has any power. Let us believe none of this, I advise you.

Aristes. I do not believe, Theodore, that a pin can act upon my mind. But it might be said perhaps that it can act upon my body and through my body upon my mind in consequence of their conjunction, for I admit that matter cannot act immediately on a mind. Note the word, *immediately*.

Theodore. But your body, is it not matter?

Aristes. Yes, certainly.

Theodore. Your body, then, cannot act *immediately* upon your mind. Thus, if your finger be pricked by a pin, though your brain be disturbed by its action, neither the one nor the other can act upon your soul or cause it to feel pain; for neither the one nor the other can act immediately upon the mind, since your brain and your finger are nothing but matter.

Aristes. Neither is it my soul which produces in itself this feeling of pain which afflicts it, for it suffers pain despite itself; I am obviously aware that the pain comes from some external cause. Thus your reasoning proves too much. I see quite well that you are going to say that it is God who causes my pain in me, and I agree; but He causes it only in consequence of the general laws of the conjunction of body and soul.

Theodore. What do you mean, Aristes? All that is true. Explain your meaning more distinctly.

Aristes. I believe, Theodore, that God has united my mind to my body so that in consequence of this union my mind and my body can act reciprocally upon one another, in virtue of the natural laws which God always follows very closely. That is all I have to say.

Theodore. You do not explain yourself, Aristes. It is a sufficiently good indication that you do not understand. Union, general laws—what kind of reality do you understand by these terms?

Theotimus. Apparently, Aristes believes that these terms are clear and without ambiguity because custom has made them very common, for when one often repeats an obscure or false thing without having even examined it one finds it difficult to believe that it is not true. This word 'union' is one of the most ambiguous of words. But it is so common and convenient that it passes everywhere without hindrance on the part of anyone, without anyone examining whether it calls up within the mind any distinct idea; for nothing that is familiar receives that attention without which it is impossible to understand; and all that affects the imagination pleasantly seems very clear to the mind which mistrusts nothing when it is paid in cash.

Aristes. What, Theotimus, are you quite of the same opinion as Theodore? Can one be in doubt as to whether the soul and the body are united in the closest way conceivable? I would willingly believe that you have conspired to confuse my mind and to amuse yourself at my expense if I were not convinced that you are too good to have so uncharitable a design.

Theotimus. You are a little too prejudiced, Aristes. Theodore maintains part of the truth, and if he exaggerates a little, it is in order to set us right. He sees that the weight of our prejudices drags us down, and his violence is meant only to hold us back. Let us listen to him, I beg of you.

Theodore. You maintain, Aristes, that your soul is joined to your body more closely than to any other thing. Well, for the moment I agree; but I do so on condition that you on your part will undertake for a day or two not to account for certain effects by means of principles which neither you nor I understand. Is not that quite reasonable?

Aristes. Only too reasonable. But what do you mean?

Theodore. This. There is the closest union in the world between your mind and your body. Eh! How can we doubt it? But you cannot say what precisely this union is. Let us not use it, therefore, as a principle for explaining the effects of the causes for which we are in search.

Aristes. But what if these effects depend upon it necessarily?

Theodore. If they depend upon it we shall be obliged to come back to it. But let us not assume this. If I asked you, Aristes, how it is that when I merely draw the arm of this chair all the remaining parts follow, would you believe that you had sufficiently explained the effect to me by replying that this is due to the union between the arm of this chair and the other parts which compose it? Assuredly, Theotimus would not be satisfied with such a reply. Children may be permitted to answer thus, but not philosophers, unless on occasions when they are not philosophizing. In order to satisfy Theotimus on this question, it would be necessary to get back to the physical cause of that union of the parts which constitute hard bodies, and to demonstrate to him that the hardness of bodies can come only from the compression of an invisible matter which surrounds them. This word 'union', then, explains nothing. It is itself in need of explanation. Thus, Aristes, you may like to take vague and general words for reasons. But do not think you can pay us in this coin, for though many people accept it and are satisfied with it, we are not so easily dealt with, owing to the fear which we have of being deceived.

Aristes. What do you want me to do? I am paying you in a coin which I have accepted as good. I have no better. And since it has currency in the world, you might be satisfied with it. But let us just see in what way you yourself pay people. Prove to me by good arguments that bodies and minds mutually act on one another without having recourse to their union.

Theodore. Let us not assume, Aristes, that they mutually act upon one another, but only that their modifications are reciprocal. Assume precisely nothing but what experience teaches you, and try to be attentive to what I am going to say. . . .

Let us suppose that God wills that there shall be a certain body upon this floor, say a ball; forthwith this is accomplished. Nothing is more movable than a sphere upon a plane, but all the powers imaginable could not disturb it so long as God does not intervene; for, once again, so long as God wills to create or keep this ball at the point A, or at any other point you please, and of necessity He must place it somewhere, no force could make it leave that point. Do not forget this; it is the basal principle.

Aristes. I hold it in mind, this principle. The Creator alone can be the mover, only He who gives being to bodies can put them in the places which they occupy. . . .

Theodore. We are accordingly, agreed upon the principle. Let us pursue it a little further. You cannot, then, Aristes, of yourself move your arm or alter your position, situation, posture, do to other men good or evil, or effect the least change in the world. You find yourself in the world, without any power, immovable as a rock, stupid, so to speak, as a log of wood. Let your soul be united to your body as closely as you please, let there come about a union between it and all the bodies of your environment. What advantage would you derive from this imaginary union? What would you do in order merely to move the tip of your finger, or to utter even a monosyllable? Alas! unless God came to your aid, your efforts would be vain, the desires which you formed impotent; for just think, do you know what is necessary for the pronunciation of your best friend's name, or for bending or holding up that particular finger which you use most? But let us suppose that you know quite well what no one knows, about which even some scientists are not agreed, namely, that the arm can be moved only by means of the animal spirits, which flowing along the nerves to the muscles make them contract and draw towards themselves the bones to which they are attached. Let us suppose that you are acquainted with the anatomy and the action of your mechanism as well as a clockmaker is acquainted with his handiwork. But, at any rate, remember the principle that no one but the Creator of bodies can be their mover. This principle is sufficient to bind, indeed to annihilate, all your boasted faculties; for, after all, the animal spirits are bodies, however small they may be. They are, indeed, nothing but the subtlest parts of the blood and the humours. God alone, then, is able to move these small bodies. He alone knows how to make them flow from the brain along the nerves, from the nerves through the muscles, from one muscle to its antagonist—all of which is necessary for the movement of our limbs. It follows that, notwithstanding the conjunction of soul and body in whatever way it may please you to imagine it, you would be dead and inert if it were not for the fact that God wills to adapt His volitions to yours—His volitions, which are always effective, to your desires, which are always impotent. This then, my dear Aristes, is the solution of the mystery. All creatures are united to God alone in an immediate union. They depend essentially and directly upon Him. Being all alike equally impotent, they cannot be in reciprocal dependence upon one another. One may, indeed, say that they are united to one another and that they depend upon one another. I grant this, provided it is not understood in the ordinary and vulgar sense of the term, provided that one agrees that they are so only in consequence of the immutable and ever effective will of the Creator, only in consequence of the general laws which He has established, and by means of which He regulates the ordinary course of His providence. God has willed that my arm shall be set in motion at the instant that I will it myself (given the necessary conditions). His will is efficacious, His will is immutable, it alone is the source of my power and faculties. He has willed that I should experience certain feelings, certain emotions, whenever there are present in my brain certain traces, or whenever a certain disturbance takes place therein. In a word, He has willed—He wills incessantly—that the modifications of the mind and those of the body shall be reciprocal. This is the conjunction and the natural dependence of the two parts of which we are constituted. It is but the mutual and reciprocal dependence of our modifications based on the unshakable foundation of the divine decrees—decrees which through their efficacy endow me with the power which I have over my body, and through it over certain other bodies—decrees which through their immutability unite me with my body, and through it to my friends, my possessions, my whole environment. I derive nothing whatever from my own nature, nothing from the nature imagined by the philosophers—all comes from God and His decrees. God has linked together all His works, though He has not on that account produced in them entities charged with the function of union. He has subordinated them to one another without endowing them with active qualities. The latter are but the vain pretensions of human pride, the chimerical productions of the philosophers' ignorance. Men's senses being affected by the presence of objects, their minds being moved by the inner feeling which they have of their own movements, they have not recognized the invisible operations of the Creator, the uniformity of His mode of action, the fruitfulness of His laws, the ever-present efficacy of His volitions, the infinite wisdom of His providence. Do not say any more, my dear Aristes, that your soul is united to your body more intimately than to anything else; since its immediate union is with God alone, since the divine decrees are the indissoluble bonds of union between the various parts of the universe and of the marvellous network of all the subordinate causes.

Aristes. Ah, Theodore, how clear, how sound and how Christian your principles are! Moreover, how estimable and affecting! I am deeply moved by them. What! It is then God himself who is present in the midst of us, not as a mere spectator nor as an observer of our good and bad actions, but as the principle of our society, the bond of our friendship, the soul, so to speak, of the intercourse and communication which we have with one another. I can speak to you only through the efficacy of His powers, touch you or disturb you only by means of the movement which He communicates to me. I do not even know what arrangement of organs is necessary in order to make my voice utter what I am saying to you without any hesitation. The play of these organs is beyond me. The variety of words, tones, modulations, is almost infinite in detail. God knows this detail, He alone regulates the movement at the very instant of my desire. Yes, He alone drives back the air which He has Himself made me breathe. He alone produces by means of my organs the vibrations and disturbances which are necessary. He alone diffuses them and makes out of them the words by the air of which I can reach your mind and pour into your heart what mine can no longer keep within itself. In truth, it is not I who breathe; I breathe despite myself. It is not I who speak to you; I merely wish to speak to you. But suppose my breath did depend upon myself, suppose I knew exactly what to do in order to explain myself, suppose I could form words and give them utterance, how would they reach you, how strike your ears, how disturb your brain or affect your heart, were it not for the efficacy of the divine power which links together all the parts of the universe? Yes, Theodore, all this is a necessary consequence of the laws of the conjunction of soul and body and of the communication of motion. All this depends upon these two principles, of which I am convinced, that none but the Creator of bodies can be their mover, and that God communicates His power to us only through the establishment of certain general laws, the realization of which we determine through our various modifications.

Aristes. I believe, Theodore, that God is present in the world in the way in which you believe your soul is present in your body. For I know well that you do not think that the soul is diffused through all the parts of the body. It is in the head, because there it reasons. It is also in our arms and feet, because it sets them in motion. In the same way, God is in the world, because He conserves and governs it.

Theodore. What a mass of prejudices and obscurities there is in your comparison! The soul is not in the body, nor is the body in the soul, though their modifications are reciprocal in consequence of the general laws of their union. But both are in God, who is the true cause of the mutual adaptation of their modifications. Minds are in the divine Reason and bodies in His immensity, but neither can be in the other, for mind and body have no essential relation to one another. It is with God alone that they have necessary relation. The mind can think without the body, but it can know nothing save in the divine Reason. Body can be extended without mind, but it cannot exist except in the immensity of God. The qualities of body have nothing in common with those of mind, for body cannot think, nor mind be extended. But the one, no less than the other, participates in the divine Being. God, who gives them their reality, possesses that reality, for He possesses all the perfections of all created things without their limitations. He knows, as minds do. He is extended, as bodies are, but all this in a way entirely different from theirs. Thus God is everywhere in the world beyond. But the soul is not present anywhere in bodies. It does not know in the brain as you imagine. It knows only in the intelligible substance of the divine Word, though it knows in God only in virtue of what takes place in a certain portion of matter called the brain. Neither does it set the limbs of the body in motion by the application of a force which belongs to its nature. It moves them only because He who is everywhere in His immensity executes by His power the impotent desires of His creatures. Do not say then, Aristes, that God is in the world which He produces as the soul is in the body which it animates, for there is no truth in your comparison; not only because the soul cannot be in the body, nor the body in the soul, but still more because as minds cannot operate in the bodies which they animate, they cannot be diffused in them through their operation in the way in which you maintain the divine operation is present in the world, through which operation alone, according to you, God is present everywhere.

Theodore. You know, Aristes, that man is composed of two substances, soul and body, the modifications of which are reciprocal as a result of the general laws, which are the causes of the conjunction of these two natures; and you are not ignorant of the fact that these laws are nothing but the constant and ever effective volitions of the Creator. Let us just glance at the wisdom of these laws.

At the moment a torch is lighted, or the sun rises, it sheds light in all directions, or rather it pushes the matter of its environment in all directions. The surfaces of bodies being variously situated, they reflect the light in different ways, or rather, they modify in different ways the pressure which the sun causes. (Picture this to yourself in any way you please, it matters not at present. For my part I believe that these modifications of pressure consist merely in vibrations or disturbances which the subtle matter receives from that which touches it lightly in gliding incessantly over the surface of the bodies between it and these same bodies.) All these vibrations or modes of pressure, alternatively more or less strong, spread out and are communicated in circular fashion from all sides, and in an instant because there is no void. Thus, so soon as one opens one's eyes, all the rays of light reflected from the surface of bodies, and entering through the apple of the eye, disperse in the humours of the eye in order to become united again in the optic nerve. The optic nerve is thus affected in several different ways by the diverse vibrations of matter which freely come into contact with it, the affections of this nerve are communicated to that part of the brain with which the soul is closely united. Whence it happens, in consequence of the laws of conjunction of soul and body:—

1. That we are given warning of the presence of objects. For, though bodies are in themselves invisible, the sensations of colour which we have in ourselves, and even despite ourselves on the occasion of their presence, make us believe that we see them as they are, because the operation of God upon us has nothing sensuous in it. And since colours affect us lightly, we attribute them to objects, instead of looking upon them as sensations which belong to us. In this way we judge that objects exist, and that they are white and black, red and blue—in a word, such as we see them.

2. Although the different kinds of the reflected light of objects consist merely in vibrations of pressure more or less rapid, nevertheless the sensations of colour which correspond to these vibrations or modifications of light have essential differences, in order that by this means we may distinguish objects from one another the more easily.

3. Thus, through the sensible different kinds of colours which determine in an exact manner the intelligible parts which we find in the idea of space or extension, we discern in one glance an infinity of different objects, their magnitude, figure, situation, movement or rest; all this with great exactness so far as the preservation of life is concerned, but otherwise confusedly and very imperfectly; for we must always remember that the senses are not given to us in order to reveal to us the truth, or to indicate the exact relations subsisting amongst things, but in order to preserve our body and everything that may be of use to it. As everything that we see is not, for example, always either good or bad for our health, and as often two different objects may reflect the light in the same way (for are not many objects equally white or black?), the sensations that we have of colour hardly touch or affect us. They are of use to us in distinguishing objects rather than in uniting ourselves to or separating ourselves from them. It

is to the objects that we refer these sensations, and not to the eyes which receive the impression of light. For we always refer our sensations to that a reference to which is conducive to the good of the body. We refer the pain of a pin-prick, not to the pin, but to the pricked finger. We refer heat, smell, taste, both to the organs and to objects. As to colour, it is referred to objects alone. It is clear that all this must be for the good of the body, and it is not necessary for me to explain it to you.

Aristes. I admit that an infinite wisdom is necessary in order to effect within our soul, as soon as we open our eyes, that distribution of colours which partially reveals to us how the world is made. But I would that our senses never deceived us, at least in matters of importance, and not in so palpable a way. The other day, as I was walking quickly down by the river, it appeared to me as though the trees on the shore were moving, and I have a friend who often sees things turning in front of him so that he cannot keep upright. These are very palpable and troublesome illusions.

Theodore. God was unable, Aristes, to contrive things better if He willed to act upon us by means of certain general laws; for you must remember the principle which I have been indicating to you. The occasional causes of that which is to take place in the soul are to be found only in what takes place in the body, since it is the soul and the body which God has willed to join together. Thus, God can be determined to act upon our soul in any particular manner only by the different changes which occur in the body. He must not act upon it as though He knew what is taking place outside us, but as though He knew of all the things of our environment only through the knowledge which He has of what is taking place in our organs. Once again, Aristes, this is the principle. Imagine that your soul knows exactly of everything new that is taking place in its body and that it gives itself all those feelings or sensations which are best adapted to further the preservation of life; that will be exactly what God does in it.

You are walking, let us say, and your soul has an inner feeling of the movements which are taking place at the moment in your body. Accordingly, though the traces of the objects within your eyes shift their position, your soul sees those objects as immobile. But supposing you are in a ship. You do not feel that you are being moved, since the movement of the ship effects no change in your body which could serve as an indication to you. The whole shore ought, therefore, to appear to you to be moving, since the images of the objects within your eyes keep on changing their position continually.

Similarly, if you bend your head, or turn your eyes, or look at a clock from between your legs, you ought not to see it turned upside down; for, though the image of the clock be inverted in your eyes, or rather in your brain, since the images of objects within the eyes are always inverted, your soul, being aware of the position of your body through the changes effected by this position in your brain, must conclude that the clock is upright.

Now, once more, God in consequence of the laws of the conjunction of soul and body gives us sensations of objects in the same way as our own soul would give them, if it could reason in an exact manner about the knowledge which it should have of what takes place in the body or in the principal part of the brain. But note that the knowledge we have of the magnitude or situation of objects does not help us at all in rectifying our sensations, unless this knowledge is sensuous and is acquired at the moment through some change then taking place in the brain; for, though I know that the sun is not larger in the evening or morning than at noon, it appears to me larger all the same; though I know the shore is not moving, it nevertheless seems to me to be moving; though I know that a certain medicine is good for me, I nevertheless find it unpleasant; and so on with the other feelings or sensations, because God regulates the sensations which He gives to us only by the activity of the occasional cause which He has established for that purpose, that is to say, only by the changes of that principal part of our body to which our soul is immediately united. Now, it happens occasionally that the flow of the animal spirits is so impetuous and irregular that it prevents the present change in the arrangement of the nerves and muscles from being communicated to this principal part of the brain, and then everything is upside down, one sees two objects instead of one, one can no longer maintain one's equilibrium in order to remain upright, and this is perhaps what happens to your friend. Yet what would you have? The laws of the union of body and soul are infinitely wise and always exactly followed; but the occasional cause which determines the efficacy of those laws often fails at the moment of need because the laws of the communication of movements are not in submission to our wills.

Aristes. What order and wisdom there is in the laws the conjunction of soul and body! As soon as we open our eyes we see an infinity of different objects and their different relations without any effort on our part. Assuredly, nothing is more marvellous, though no one reflects upon the matter.

5

JOHN LOCKE

Names made at pleasure neither alter the nature of things, nor make us understand them but as they are signs of and stand for determined ideas. And I desire those who lay so much stress on the sound of these two syllables, *substance*, to consider whether, applying it as they do to the infinite incomprehensible God, to finite spirits, and to body, it be in the same sense; and whether it stands for the same idea, when each of those three so different beings are called substances? If so, whether it will not thence follow, that God, spirits, and body, agreeing in the same common nature of substance, differ not any otherwise than in a bare different modification of that substance; as a tree and a pebble, being in the same sense body, and agreeing in the common nature of body, differ only in a bare modification of that common matter; which will be a very harsh doctrine. If they say that they apply it to God, finite spirits, and matter, in three different significations, and that it stands for one idea when God is said to be a substance, for another when the soul is called substance, and for a third when a body is called so—if the name substance stands for three several distinct ideas, they would do well to make known those distinct ideas, or at least to give three distinct names to them, to prevent, in so important a notion, the confusion and errors that will naturally follow from the promiscuous use of so doubtful a term; which is so far from being suspected to have three distinct, that in ordinary use it has scarce one clear distinct signification; and if they can thus make three distinct ideas of substance, what hinders why another may not make a fourth?

They who first ran into the notion of *accidents*, as a sort of real beings that needed something to inhere in, were forced to find out the word *substance* to support them. Had the poor Indian philosopher (who imagined that the earth also wanted something to bear it up) but thought of this word substance, he needed not to have been at the trouble to find an elephant to support it, and a tortoise to support his elephant: the word substance would have done it effectually. And he that inquired, might have taken it for as good an answer from an Indian philosopher, that substance, without knowing what it is, is that which supports the earth, as we take it for a sufficient answer and good doctrine from our European philosophers, that substance, without knowing what it is, is that which supports accidents. So that of substance we have no idea of what it is, but only a confused obscure one of what it does.

The mind being, as I have declared, furnished with a great number of the simple ideas conveyed in by the seness, as they are found in exterior things, or by reflection on its own operations, takes notice also, that a certain number of these simple ideas go constantly together; which being presumed to belong to one thing, and words being suited to common apprehensions, and made use of for quick dispatch, are called, so united in one subject, by one name; which, by inadvertency, we are apt afterward to talk of and consider as one simple idea, which indeed is a complication of many ideas together: because, as I have said, not imagining how these simple ideas can subsist by themselves, we accustom ourselves to suppose some *substratum* wherein they do subsist, and from which they do result, which therefore we call *substance*.

So that if any one will examine himself concerning his notion of pure substance in general, he will find he has no other idea of it at all, but only a supposition of he knows not what support of such qualities which are capable of producing simple ideas in us; which qualities are commonly called accidents. If anyone should be asked, what is the subject wherein colour or weight inheres, he would have nothing to say, but the solid extended parts: and if he were demanded, what is it that that solidity and extension inhere in, he would not be in a much better case than the Indian before mentioned, who saying that the world was supported by a great elephant, was asked, what the elephant rested on; to which his answer was, a great tortoise: but being again pressed to know what gave support to the broad-backed tortoise, replied, something, he knew not what. And thus here, as in all other cases where we use words without having clear and distinct ideas, we talk like children; who being questioned what such a thing is which they know not, readily give this satisfactory answer, that it is *something*; which in truth signifies no more, when so used, either by children or men, but that they know not what; and that the thing they pretend to know, and talk of, is what they have no distinct idea of at all, and so are perfectly ignorant of it, and in the dark. The idea, then, we have, to which we give the general name substance, being nothing but the supposed, but unknown, support of those qualities we find existing, which we imagine cannot subsist *sine re substante*, without something to support them, we call that support *substantia*; which, according to the true import of the word, is, in plain English, standing under, or upholding.

An obscure and relative idea of substance in general being thus made, we come to have the ideas of *particular sorts of substances*, by collecting such combinations of simple ideas as are, by experience and observation of men's senses, taken notice of to exist together, and are therefore supposed to flow from the particular internal constitution or unknown essence of that substance. Thus we come to have the ideas of a man, horse, gold, water, etc., of which substances, whether any one has any other clear idea, farther than of certain simple ideas coexisting together, I appeal to every one's own experience. It is the ordinary qualities observable in iron or a diamond, put together, that make the true complex idea of those substances, which a smith or a jeweller commonly knows better than a philosopher; who, whatever substantial forms he may talk of, has no other idea of those substances than what is framed by a collection of those simple ideas which are to be found in them. Only we must take notice, that our complex ideas of substances, besides all these simple ideas they are made up of, have always the confused idea of something to which they belong and in which they subsist. And therefore, when we speak of any sort of substance, we say it is a thing having such or such qualities; as body is a thing that is extended, figured, and capable of motion; a spirit, a thing capable of thinking; and so hardness, friability, and power to draw iron, we say, are qualities to be found in a loadstone. These and the like fashions of speaking intimate that the substance is supposed always something besides the extension, figure, solidity, motion, thinking, or other observable ideas, though we know not what it is.

Hence, when we talk or think of any particular sort of corporeal substances, as horse, stone, etc., though the idea we have of either of them be but the complication or collection of those several simple ideas of sensible qualities which we used to find united in the thing called horse or stone; yet because we cannot conceive how they should subsist alone, nor one in another, we suppose them existing in, and supported by, some common subject; which support we denote by the name substance, though it be certain we have no clear or distinct idea of that thing we suppose a support.

The same happens concerning the operations of the mind, viz., thinking, reasoning, fearing, etc., which we concluding not to subsist of themselves, nor apprehending how they can belong to body, or be produced by it, we are apt to think these the actions of some other substance, which we call spirit; whereby yet it is evident, that having no other idea or notion of matter, but something wherein those many sensible qualities which affect our senses do subsist; by supposing a substance wherein thinking, knowing, doubting, and a power of moving, etc., do subsist; we have as clear a notion of the substance of spirit as we have of body; the one being supposed to be (without knowing what it is) the *substratum* to those simple ideas we have from without; and the other supposed (with a like ignorance of what it is) to be the *substratum* to those operations which we experiment in ourselves within.

Besides the complex ideas we have of material sensible substances, by the simple ideas we have taken from those operations of our own minds, which we experiment daily in ourselves, we are able to frame the *complex idea of an immaterial spirit*. For putting together the ideas of thinking and willing, or the power of moving or quieting corporeal motion, joined to substance, of which we have no distinct idea, we have the idea of an immaterial spirit; and by putting together the ideas of coherent solid parts, and a power of being moved, joined with substance, of which likewise we have no positive idea, we have the idea of matter. The one is as clear and distinct an idea as the other: the idea of thinking and moving a body being as clear and distinct ideas as the ideas of extension, solidity, and being moved. For our idea of substance is equally obscure, or none at all, in both; it is but a supposed I know not what, to support those ideas we call accidents.

By the complex idea of extended, figured, coloured, and all other sensible qualities which is all that we know of it, we are as far from the idea of the substance of body as if we knew nothing at all: nor, after all the acquaintance and familiarity which we imagine we have with matter, and the many qualities men assure themselves they perceive and know in bodies, will it, perhaps, upon examination, be found, that they have any more or clearer primary ideas belonging to body than they have belonging to immaterial spirit.

The primary ideas we have *peculiar to body*, as contra-distinguished to spirit, are *the cohesion of solid*, and consequently separable *parts, and a power of communicating motion by impulse*. These, I think, are the original ideas proper and peculiar to body; for figure is but the consequence of finite extension.

The ideas we have belonging and *peculiar to spirit* are *thinking*, and *will*, or a power of putting body into motion by thought, and, which is consequent to it, liberty. For as body cannot but communicate its motion by impulse to another body, which it meets with at rest; so the mind can put bodies into motion, or forbear to do so, as it pleases. The ideas of existence, duration, and mobility, are common to them both.

There is no reason why it should be thought strange that I make mobility belong to spirit: for having no other idea of motion but change of distance with other beings that are considered as at rest, and finding that spirits as well as bodies cannot operate but where they are, and that spirits do operate at several times in several places, I cannot but attribute change of place to all finite spirits; (for of the infinite Spirit I speak not here). For my soul, being a real being, as well as my body, is certainly as capable of changing distance with any other body or being as body itself, and so is capable of motion. And if a mathematician can consider a certain distance or a change of that distance between two points, one may certainly conceive a distance and a change of distance between two spirits; and so conceive their motion, their approach or removal, one from another.

Every one finds in himself, that his soul can think, will, and operate on his body, in the place where that is; but cannot operate in a body, or in a place, a hundred miles distant from it. Nobody can imagine, that his soul can think or move a body at Oxford, whilst he is at London; and cannot but know that, being united to his body, it constantly changes place all the whole journey between Oxford and London, as the coach or horse does that carries him; and I think may be said to be truly all that while in motion: or if that will not be allowed to afford us a clear idea enough of its motion, its being separated from the body in death, I think, will: for to consider it as going out of the body, or leaving it, and yet to have no idea of its motion, seems to me impossible.

To conclude: Sensation convinces us, that there are solid, extended substances; and reflection, that there are thinking ones: experience assures us of the existence of such beings; and that the one hath a power to move body by impulse, the other by thought; this we cannot doubt of. Experience, I say, every moment furnishes us with the clear ideas both of the one and the other. But beyond these ideas, as received from their proper sources, our faculties will not reach. If we would inquire farther into their nature, causes, and manner, we perceive not the nature of extension clearer than we do of thinking. If we would explain them any farther, one is as easy as the other; and there is no more difficulty to conceive how a substance we know not should by thought set body into motion, than how a substance we know not should by impulse set body into motion. So that we are no more able to discover wherein the ideas belonging to body consist, than those belonging to spirit. From whence it seems probable to me, that the simple ideas we receive from sensation and reflection are the boundaries of our thoughts; beyond which, the mind, whatever efforts it would make, is not able to advance one jot; nor can it make any discoveries when it would pry into the nature and hidden causes of those ideas.

So that, in short, the idea we have of spirit, compared with the idea we have of body, stands thus: The substance of spirit is unknown to us; and so is the substance of body equally unknown to us.

From all which it is evident, that the extent of our knowledge comes not only short of the reality of things, but even of the extent of our own ideas. We have the ideas of a square, a circle, and equality: and yet, perhaps, shall never be able to find a circle equal to a square, and certainly know that it is so. We have the ideas of matter and thinking, but possibly shall never be able to know whether any mere material being thinks or no; it being impossible for us, by the contemplation of our own ideas without revelation, to discover whether Omnipotency has not given to some systems of matter, fitly disposed, a power to perceive and think, or else joined and fixed to matter, so disposed, a thinking immaterial substance: it being, in respect of our notions, not much more remote from our comprehension to conceive that God can, if he pleases, superadd to matter a faculty of thinking, than that he should superadd to it another substance with a faculty of thinking; since we know not wherein thinking consists, nor to what sort of substances the Almighty has been pleased to give that power, which cannot be in any created being, but merely by the good pleasure and bounty of the Creator. What certainty of knowledge can anyone have that some perceptions, such as, e.g., pleasure and pain, should not be in some bodies themselves, after a certain manner modified and moved, as well as that they should be in an immaterial substance upon the motion of the parts of body? Body, as far as we can conceive, being able only to strike and affect body; and motion, according to the utmost reach of our ideas, being able to produce nothing but motion: so that when we allow it to produce pleasure or pain, or the idea of a colour or sound, we are fain to quit our reason, go beyond our ideas, and attribute it wholly to the good pleasure of our Maker. For since we must allow He has annexed effects to motion, which we can no way conceive motion able to produce, what reason have we to conclude that He could not order them as well to be produced in a subject we cannot conceive capable of them, as well as in a subject we cannot conceive the notion of matter can any way operate upon? I say not this that I would any way lessen the belief of the soul's immateriality: I am not here speaking of probability, but knowledge; and I think not only that it becomes the modesty of philosophy not to pronounce magisterially, where we want that evidence that can produce knowledge; but also, that it is of use to us to discern how far our knowledge does reach; for the state we are at present in, not being that of vision, we must, in many things, content ourselves with faith and probability: and in the present question about the immateriality of the soul, if our faculties cannot arrive at demonstrative certainty, we need not think it strange. All the great ends of morality and religion are well enough secured, without philosophical proofs of the soul's immateriality; since it is evident that He who made us at first begin to subsist here, sensible intelligent beings, and for several years continued us in such a state, can and will restore us to the like state of sensibility in another world, and make us capable there to receive the retribution He has designed to men according to their doings in this life.

6

GEORGE BERKELEY

It is evident to any one who takes a survey of the objects of human knowledge, that they are either *ideas* actually (1) imprinted on the senses, or else such as are (2) perceived by attending to the passions and operations of the mind, or lastly, ideas (3) formed by help of memory and imagination, either compounding, dividing, or barely representing those originally perceived in the aforesaid ways. By sight I have the ideas of light and colours with their several degrees and variations. By touch I perceive, for example, hard and soft, heat and cold, motion and resistance, and of all these more and less either as to quantity or degree. Smelling furnishes me with odours; the palate with tastes; and hearing conveys sounds to the mind in all their variety of tone and composition. And as several of these are observed to accompany each other, they come to be marked by one name, and so to be reputed as one thing. . . .

But besides all that endless variety of ideas or objects of knowledge, there is likewise something which knows or perceives them, and exercises divers operations, as willing, imagining, remembering about them. This perceiving, active being is what I call *mind*, *spirit*, *soul*, or *myself*. By which words I do not denote any one of my ideas, but a thing entirely distinct from them, *wherein they exist*, or, which is the same thing, whereby they are perceived; for the existence of an idea consists in being perceived. . . .

All our ideas, sensations, or the things which we perceive, by whatsoever names they may be distinguished, are visibly inactive; there is nothing of power or agency included in them. So that *one idea* or object of thought *cannot produce*, or make *any alteration in another*. To be satisfied of the truth of this, there is nothing else requisite but a bare observation of our ideas. For since they and every part of them exist only in the mind, it follows that there is nothing in them but what is perceived. But whoever shall attend to his ideas, whether of sense or reflection, will not perceive in them any power or activity; there is therefore no such thing contained in them.

Whence it plainly follows that extension, figure, and motion, cannot be the cause of our sensations. To say, therefore, that these are the effects of powers resulting from the configuration, number, motion, and size of corpuscles, must certainly be false. . . .

A spirit is one simple, undivided, active being: as it perceives ideas, it is called the *understanding*, and as it produces or otherwise operates about them, it is called the *will*. Hence there can be no idea formed of a soul or spirit: (for all ideas whatever, being passive and inert, they cannot represent unto us, by way of image or *likeness*, that which acts).

If any man shall doubt of the truth of what is here delivered, let him but reflect and try if he can frame the idea of any power or active being; and whether he hath ideas of two principal powers, marked by the names *will* and *understanding*, distinct from each other as well as from a third idea of substance or being in general, with a relative notion of its supporting or being the subject of the aforesaid powers, which is signified by the name *soul* or *spirit*. This is what some hold; but so far as I can see, the words *will, soul, spirit*, do not stand for different ideas, or in truth, for any idea at all, but for something which is very different from ideas, and which being an agent cannot be like unto, or represented by, any idea whatsoever. Though it must be owned at the same time, that we have some notion of soul, spirit, and the operations of the mind, such as willing, loving, hating, inasmuch as we know or understand the meaning of those words. . . .

The great reason that is assigned for our being thought ignorant of the nature of spirits, is, our not having an idea of it. But surely it ought not to be looked on as a defect in a human understanding, that it does not perceive the idea of *spirit*, if it is *manifestly impossible there should be any such idea*. . . .

That an *idea*, which is inactive, and the existence whereof consists in being perceived, should be the image or likeness of an agent subsisting by itself seems to need no other refutation, than barely attending to what is meant by those words.

For by the word *spirit* we mean only that which thinks, wills, and perceives; this, and this alone, constitutes the signification of that term. If, therefore, it is impossible that any degree of those powers should be represented in an idea, it is evident there can be no idea of a spirit. . . .

What I am myself, that which I denote by the term I, is the same with what is meant by *soul* or *spiritual substance*. If it be said that this is only quarrelling at a word, and that since the immediate significations of other

D

names are, by common consent, called *ideas*, no reason can be assigned, why that which is signified by the name *spirit* or *soul*, may not partake in the same appellation, I answer, all the unthinking objects of the mind agree, in that they are *entirely passive*, and their existence consists only in being perceived: whereas a soul or spirit is an active being, whose existence consists not in being perceived, but in *perceiving ideas* and thinking. It is therefore necessary, *in order to prevent equivocation*, and confounding natures perfectly disagreeing and unalike, that we distinguish between *spirit* and *idea*.

In a large sense indeed, we may be said to have an idea, or rather a notion of *spirit*, that is, (1) we understand the meaning of the word, otherwise we could not affirm or deny anything of it. Moreover, (2) we conceive the ideas that are in the minds of other spirits by means of our own, which we suppose to be *resemblances* of them: so we know other spirits by means of our own soul, which in that sense is the image or idea of them, it having a like respect to other spirits, that blueness or heat by me perceived hath to those ideas perceived by another. . . .

Spirits and *ideas* are things so wholly different, that when we say *they exist, they are known*, or the like, these words must not be thought to signify any thing common to both natures. There is nothing alike or common in them: and to expect that by any multiplication or enlargement of our faculties, we may be enabled to know a spirit as we do a triangle, seems as absurd as if we should hope to *see a sound*. This is inculcated because I imagine it may be of moment towards clearing several important questions, and preventing some very dangerous errors concerning the nature of the soul. We may not, I think, strictly be said to have an idea of an active being, or of an action, although we may be said to have a notion of them. I have some knowledge or notion of my mind, and its acts about ideas, inasmuch as I know or understand what is meant by those words. . . .

From what hath been said, it is plain that *we* cannot *know the existence of other spirits* otherwise than *by their operations*, or *the ideas by them excited in us*. I perceive several motions, changes, and combinations of ideas, that inform me there are certain particular agents *like myself*, which accompany them, and concur in their production. Hence the knowledge I have of other spirits is *not immediate*, as is the knowledge of my ideas; but depending on the intervention of ideas, by me referred to *agents or spirits* distinct from myself, as effects or concomitant signs.

But though there be some things which convince us human agents are concerned in producing them; yet it is evident to every one, that those things which are called the works of nature, that is, the far greater part of the ideas or sensations perceived by us, are not produced by, or dependent on, the wills of men. There is therefore some other spirit that causes them, since it is repugnant that they should subsist by themselves. But if we attentively consider the constant regularity, order, and concatenation of natural things, the surprising magnificence, beauty, and perfection of the larger, and the exquisite contrivance of the smaller parts of the creation, together with the exact harmony and correspondence of the whole, but, above all, the never enough admired laws of pain and pleasure, and the instincts or natural inclinations, appetites, and passions of animals; I say if we consider all these things, and at the same time attend to the meaning and import of the attributes, one, eternal, infinitely wise, good, and perfect, we shall clearly perceive that they belong to the aforesaid spirit, *who works all in all, and by whom all things consist.*

Hence it is evident, that God is known as certainly and immediately as any other mind or spirit whatsoever, distinct from ourselves. We may even assert, that the existence of God is far more evidently perceived than the existence of men; because the effects of nature are infinitely *more numerous and considerable* than those ascribed to human agents. There is not any one mark that denotes a man, or effect produced by him, which doth not more strongly evince the being of that Spirit who is the *Author of nature.* For it is evident that in affecting other persons, the will of man hath no other object than barely the *motion of the limbs of his body*; but that such a motion should be attended by, or excite *any idea in the mind of another*, depends wholly on the will of the Creator. He alone it is who, 'upholding all things by the word of his power', maintains that intercourse between spirits, whereby they are able to perceive the existence of each other.

It is therefore plain, that *nothing can be more evident* to any one that is capable of the least reflection *than the existence of God*, or a Spirit who is intimately present to our minds, producing in them all that variety of ideas or sensations, which continually affect us, on whom we have an absolute and entire dependence, in short, *in whom we live, and move, and have our being.* That the discovery of this great truth, which lies so near and obvious to the mind, should be attained to by the reason of so very few, is a sad instance of the stupidity and inattention of men, who, though they are surrounded with such clear manifestations of the Deity, are yet so little affected by them, that they seem as it were blinded with excess of light.

7

DAVID HUME

INQUIRY CONCERNING THE HUMAN UNDERSTANDING (1748)

There are no ideas, which occur in metaphysics, more obscure and uncertain, than those of *power, force, energy* or *necessary connection*, of which it is every moment necessary for us to treat in all our disquisitions. We shall, therefore, endeavour, in this section, to fix, if possible, the precise meaning of these terms, and thereby remove some part of that obscurity, which is so much complained of in this species of philosophy.

It seems a proposition, which will not admit of much dispute, that all our ideas are nothing but copies of our impressions, or, in other words, that it is impossible for us to *think* of anything, which we have not antecedently *felt*, either by our external or internal senses. . . .

To be fully acquainted, therefore, with the idea of power or necessary connection, let us examine its impression; and in order to find the impression with greater certainty, let us search for it in all the sources, from which it may possibly be derived.

When we look about us towards external objects, and consider the operation of causes, we are never able, in a single instance, to discover any power or necessary connection; any quality, which binds the effect to the cause, and renders the one an infallible consequence of the other. We only find, that the one does actually, in fact, follow the other. The impulse of one billiard-ball is attended with motion in the second. . . .

Since, therefore, external objects as they appear to the senses, give us no idea of power or necessary connection, by their operation in particular instances, let us see, whether this idea be derived from reflection on the operations of our own minds, and be copied from any internal impression. It may be said, that we are every moment conscious of internal power; while we feel, that, by the simple command of our will, we can move the organs of our body, or direct the faculties of our mind. An act of volition produces motion in our limbs, or raises a new idea in our imagination. This influence of the will we know by consciousness. Hence we acquire the idea of power or energy; and are certain, that we ourselves and all other intelligent beings are possessed of power. This idea, then, is an idea of reflection, since it arises from reflecting on the operations of our own mind, and on the command which is exercised by will, both over the organs of the body and faculties of the soul.

We shall proceed to examine this pretension; and first with regard to the influence of volition over the organs of the body. This influence, we may observe, is a fact, which, like all other natural events, can be known only by experience, and can never be foreseen from any apparent energy or power in the cause, which connects it with the effect, and renders the one an infallible consequence of the other. The motion of our body follows upon the command of our will. Of this we are every moment conscious. But the means, by which this is effected; the energy, by which the will performs so extraordinary an operation; of this we are so far from being immediately conscious, that it must for ever escape our most diligent inquiry.

For *first*; is there any principle in all nature more mysterious than the union of soul with body; by which a supposed spiritual substance acquires such an influence over a material one, that the most refined thought is able to actuate the grossest matter? Were we empowered, by a secret wish, to remove mountains, or control the planets in their orbit; this extensive authority would not be more extraordinary, nor more beyond our comprehension. But if by consciousness we perceived any power or energy in the will, we must know this power; we must know its connection with the effect; we must know the secret union of soul and body, and the nature of both these substances; by which the one is able to operate, in so many instances, upon the other.

Secondly, we are not able to move all the organs of the body with a like authority; though we cannot assign any reason besides experience, for so remarkable a difference between one and the other. Why has the will an influence over the tongue and fingers, not over the heart or liver? This question would never embarrass us, were we conscious of a power in the former case, not in the latter. We should then perceive, independent of experience, why the authority of will over the organs of the body is circumscribed within such particular limits. Being in that case fully acquainted with the power or force, by which it operates, we should also know, why its influence reaches precisely to such boundaries, and no farther.

A man, suddenly struck with palsy in the leg or arm, or who had newly lost those members, frequently endeavours, at first to move them, and employ them in their usual offices. Here he is as much conscious of power to command such limbs, as a man in perfect health is conscious of power to actuate any member which remains in its natural state and condition. But consciousness never deceives. Consequently, neither in the one case nor in the other, are we ever conscious of any power. We learn the influence of our will from experience alone. And experience only teaches us, how one event constantly follows another; without instructing us in the secret connection, which binds them together, and renders them inseparable.

Thirdly, we learn from anatomy, that the immediate object of power in voluntary motion, is not the member itself which is moved, but certain muscles, and nerves, and animal spirits, and, perhaps, something still more minute and more unknown, through which the motion is successively propagated, ere it reach the member itself whose motion is the immediate object of volition. Can there be a more certain proof, that the power, by which this whole operation is performed, so far from being directly and fully known by an inward sentiment or consciousness, is, to the last degree, mysterious and unintelligible? Here the mind wills a certain event: Immediately another event, unknown to ourselves, and totally different from the one intended, is produced: This event produces another, equally unknown: Till at last, through a long succession, the desired event is produced. But if the original power were felt, it must be known: Were it known, its effect also must be known; since all power is relative to its effect. And *vice versa*, if the effect be not known, the power cannot be known nor felt. How indeed can we be conscious of a power to move our limbs, when we have no such power; but only that to move certain animal spirits, which, though they produce at last the motion of our limbs, yet operate in such a manner as is wholly beyond our comprehension?

We may, therefore, conclude from the whole, I hope, without any temerity, though with assurance; that our idea of power is not copied from any sentiment or consciousness of power within ourselves, when we give rise to animal motion, or apply our limbs to their proper use and office. That their motion follows the command of the will is a matter of common experience, like other natural events: But the power or energy by which this is effected, like that in other natural events, is unknown and inconceivable.

8

IMMANUEL KANT

By *transcendental idealism* I mean the doctrine that appearances are to be regarded as being, one and all, representations only, not things in themselves, and that time and space are therefore only sensible forms of our intuition, not determinations given as existing by themselves, nor conditions of objects viewed as things in themselves. To this idealism there is opposed a *transcendental realism* which regards time and space as something given in themselves, independently of our sensibility. The transcendental realist thus interprets outer appearances (their reality being taken as granted) as things-in-themselves, which exist independently of us and of our sensibility, and which are therefore outside us—the phrase 'outside us' being interpreted in conformity with pure concepts of understanding. It is, in fact, this transcendental realist who afterwards plays the part of empirical idealist. After wrongly supposing that objects of the senses, if they are to be external, must have an existence by themselves, and independently of the senses, he finds that, judged from this point of view, all our sensuous representations are inadequate to establish their reality.

The transcendental idealist, on the other hand, may be an empirical realist or, as he is called, a *dualist*; that is, he may admit the existence of matter without going outside his mere self-consciousness, or assuming anything more than the certainty of his representations, that is, the *cogito, ergo sum*. For he considers this matter and even its inner possibility to be appearance merely; and appearance, if separated from our sensibility, is nothing. Matter is with him, therefore, only a species of representations (intuition), which are called external, not as standing in relation to objects *in themselves external*, but because they relate perceptions to the space in which all things are external to one another, while yet the space itself is in us.

From the start, we have declared ourselves in favour of this transcendental idealism; and our doctrine thus removes all difficulty in the way of accepting the existence of matter on the unaided testimony of our mere self-consciousness, or declaring it to be thereby proved in the same manner as the existence of myself as a thinking being is proved. There can be no question that I am conscious of my representations; these representations and I myself, who have the representations, therefore exist. External objects (bodies), however, are mere appearances, and are therefore nothing but a species of my representations, the objects of which are something only through these representations. Apart from them they are nothing. Thus external things exist as well as I myself, and both, indeed, upon the immediate witness of my self-consciousness. The only difference is that the representation of myself, as the thinking subject, belongs to inner sense only, while the representations which mark extended beings belong also to outer sense. In order to arrive at the reality of outer objects I have just as little need to resort to inference as I have in regard to the reality of the object of my inner sense, that is, in regard to the reality of my thoughts. For in both cases alike the objects are nothing but representations, the immediate perception (consciousness) of which is at the same time a sufficient proof of their reality. . . .

We can indeed admit that something, which may be (in the transcendental sense) outside us, is the cause of our outer intuitions, but this is not the object of which we are thinking in the representations of matter and of corporeal things; for these are merely appearances, that is, mere kinds of representation, which are never to be met with save in us, and the reality of which depends on immediate consciousness, just as does the consciousness of my own thoughts. The transcendental object is equally unknown in respect to inner and outer intuition. But it is not of this that we are here speaking, but of the empirical object, which is called an *external* object if it is represented *in space*, and an *inner* object if it is represented only *in its time-relations*. Neither space nor time, however, is to be found save *in us*.

The expression '*outside us*' is thus unavoidably ambiguous in meaning, sometimes signifying what *as thing in itself* exists apart from us, and sometimes what belongs solely to outer *appearance*. . . .

If we treat outer objects as things in themselves, it is quite impossible to understand how we could arrive at a knowledge of their reality outside us, since we have to rely merely on the representation which is in us. For we cannot be sentient (of what is) outside ourselves, but only (of what is) in us, and the whole of our self-consciousness therefore yields nothing save merely our own determinations. Sceptical idealism thus constrains us to have recourse to the only refuge still open, namely, the ideality of all appearances, a doctrine which has already been established in the Transcendental Aesthetic independently of these consequences, which we could not at that stage foresee. If then we ask, whether it follows that in the doctrine of the soul dualism alone is tenable, we must answer: 'Yes, certainly; but dualism only in the empirical sense'. That is to say, in the connection of experience matter, as substance in the (field of) appearance, is really given to outer sense, just as the thinking 'I', also as substance in the (field of) appearance, is given to inner sense. Further, appearances in both fields must be connected with each other according to the rules which this category introduces into that connection of our outer as well as of our inner perceptions whereby they constitute one experience. If, however, as commonly happens, we seek to extend the concept of dualism, and take it in the transcendental sense, neither it nor the two counter-alternatives—*pneumatism* on the one hand, *materialism* on the other— would have any sort of basis, since we should then have misapplied our concepts, taking the difference in the mode of representing objects, which as regards what they are in themselves, still remain unknown to us, as a difference in the things themselves. Though the 'I', as represented through inner sense in time, and objects in space outside me, are specifically quite distinct appearances, they are not for that reason thought as being different things. Neither the *transcendental object* which underlies outer appearances nor that which underlies inner intuition, is in itself either matter or a thinking being, but a ground (to us unknown) of the appearances which supply to us the empirical concept of the former as well as of the latter mode of existence. . . .

If we compare the *doctrine of the soul* as the physiology of inner sense, with the *doctrine of the body* as a physiology of the object of the outer senses, we find that while in both much can be learnt empirically, there is yet this notable difference. In the latter science much that is *a priori* can be synthetically known from the mere concept of an extended impenetrable being, but in the former nothing whatsoever that is *a priori* can be known synthetically from the concept of a thinking being. The cause is this. Although both are appearances, the appearance to outer sense has something fixed or abiding which supplies a substratum as the basis of its transitory determinations and therefore a synthetic concept, namely, that of space and of an appearance in space; whereas time, which is the sole form of our inner intuition, has nothing abiding, and therefore yields knowledge only of the change of determinations, not of any object that can be thereby determined. For in what we entitle 'soul', everything is in continual flux and there is nothing abiding except (if we must so express ourselves) the 'I', which is simple solely because its representation has no content, and therefore no manifold, and for this reason seems to represent, or (to use a more correct term), denote, a simple object. In order that it should be possible, by pure reason, to obtain knowledge of the nature of a thinking being in general, this 'I' would have to be an intuition which, in being presupposed in all thought (prior to all experience), might as intuition yield *a priori* synthetic propositions. This 'I' is, however, as little an intuition as it is a concept of any object; it is the mere form of consciousness, which can accompany the two kinds of representation and which is in a position to elevate them to the rank of knowledge only in so far as something else is given in intuition which provides material for a representation of an object. Thus the whole of rational psychology, as a science surpassing all powers of human reason, proves abortive, and nothing is left for us but to study our soul under the guidance of experience, and to confine ourselves to those questions which do not go beyond the limits within which a content can be provided for them by possible inner experience.

But although rational psychology cannot be used to extend knowledge, and when so employed is entirely made up of paralogisms, still we cannot deny it a considerable negative value, if it is taken as nothing more than a critical treatment of our dialectical inferences, those that arise from the common and natural reason of men.

Why do we have resort to a doctrine of the soul founded exclusively on pure principles of reason? Beyond all doubt, chiefly in order to secure our thinking self against the danger of materialism. This is achieved by means of the pure concept of our thinking self which we have just given. For by this teaching so completely are we freed from the fear that on the removal of matter all thought, and even the very existence of thinking beings, would be destroyed, that on the contrary it is clearly shown, that if I remove the thinking subject the whole corporeal world must at once vanish: it is nothing save an appearance in the sensibility of our subject and a mode of its representations.

I admit that this does not give me any further knowledge of the properties of this thinking self, nor does it enable me to determine its permanence or even that it exists independently of what we may conjecture to be the transcendental substratum of outer appearances; for the latter is just as unknown to me as is the thinking self. But it is nevertheless possible that I may find cause, on other than merely speculative grounds, to hope for an independent and continuing existence of my thinking nature, throughout all possible change of my state. In that case much will already have been gained if, while freely confessing my own ignorance, I am yet in a position to repel the dogmatic assaults of a speculative opponent, and to show him that he can never know more of the nature of the self in denying the possibility of my expectations than I can know in clinging to them.

Three other dialectical questions, constituting the real goal of rational psychology, are grounded on this transcendental illusion in our psychological concepts, and cannot be decided except by means of the above inquiries: namely (1) of the possibility of the communion of the soul with an organized body, i.e. concerning animality and the state of the soul in the life of man; (2) of the beginning of this communion, that is, of the soul in and before birth; (3) of the end of this communion, that is, of the soul in and after death (the question of immortality).

Now I maintain that all the difficulties commonly found in these questions, and by means of which, as dogmatic objections, men seek to gain credit for a deeper insight into the nature of things than any to which the ordinary understanding can properly lay claim, rest on a mere delusion by which they hypostatize what exists merely in thought, and take it as a real object existing, in the same character, outside the thinking subject. In other words, they regard extension, which is nothing but appearance, as a property of outer things that subsists even apart from our sensibility, and hold that motion is due to these things and really occurs in and by itself, apart from our senses. For matter, the communion of which with the soul arouses so much questioning, is nothing but a mere form, or a particular way of representing an unknown object by means of that intuition which is called outer sense. There may well be something outside us to which this appearance, which we call matter, corresponds; in its character of appearance it is not, however, outside us, but is only a thought in us, although this thought, owing to the above-mentioned outer sense, represents it as existing outside us. Matter, therefore, does not mean a kind of substance quite distinct and heterogeneous from the object of inner sense (the soul), but only the distinctive nature of those appearances of objects—in themselves unknown to us—the representations of which we call outer as compared with those which we count as belonging to inner sense, although like all other thoughts these outer representations belong only to the thinking object. They have, indeed, this deceptive property that, representing objects in space, they detach themselves as it were from the soul and appear to hover outside it. Yet the very space in which they are intuited is nothing but a representation, and no counterpart of the same quality is to be found outside the soul. Consequently, the question is no longer of the communion of the soul with other known substances of a different kind outside us, but only of the connection of the representations of inner sense with the modifications of our outer sensibility—as to how these can be so connected with each other according to settled laws that they exhibit the unity of a coherent experience.

As long as we take inner and outer appearances together as mere representations in experience, we find nothing absurd and strange in the association of the two kinds of senses. But as soon as we hypostatize outer appearances and come to regard them not as representations but *as things existing by themselves outside us, with the same quality as that with which they exist in us,* and as bringing to bear in our thinking subject the activities which they exhibit as appearances in relation to each other, then the efficient causes outside us assume a character which is irreconcilable with their effects in us. For the cause relates only to outer sense, the effect to inner sense—senses which, although combined in one subject, are extremely unlike each other. In outer sense we find no other outer effects save changes of place, and no forces except mere tendencies which issue in spatial relations as their effects. Within us, on the other hand, the effects are thoughts, among which is not to be found any relation of place, motion, shape, or other spatial determination, and we altogether lose the thread of the causes in the effects to which they are supposed to have given rise in inner sense. We ought, however, to bear in mind that bodies are not objects in themselves which are present to us, but a mere appearance of we know not what unknown object; that motion is not the effect of this unknown cause, but only the appearance of its influence on our senses. Neither bodies nor motions are anything outside us; both alike are mere representations in us; and it is not, therefore, the motion of matter that produces representations in us; the motion itself is representation only, as also is the matter which makes itself known in this way. Thus in the end the whole difficulty which we have made for ourselves comes to this, how and why the representations of our sensibility are so interconnected that those which we entitle outer intuitions can be represented according to empirical laws as objects outside us—a question which is not in any way bound up with the supposed difficulty of explaining the origin of our representations from quite heterogeneous efficient causes outside us. That difficulty has arisen from our taking the appearances of an unknown cause as being the cause itself outside us, a view which can result in nothing but confusion. In the case of judgments in which a misapprehension has taken deep root through long custom, it is impossible at once to give to their correction that clarity which can be achieved in other cases where no such inevitable illusion confuses the concept. Our freeing of reason from sophistical theories can hardly, therefore, at this stage have the clearness which is necessary for its complete success.

The following comments will, I think, be helpful as contributing towards this ultimate clarity.

All *objections* can be divided into *dogmatic, critical,* and *sceptical.* A dogmatic objection is directed against a proposition, a critical objection against the *proof* of a proposition. The former requires an insight into the nature of the object such that we can maintain the opposite of what the proposition has alleged in regard to this object. It is therefore itself dogmatic, claiming acquaintance with the constitution of the object fuller than that of the counter-assertion. A critical objection, since it leaves the validity or invalidity of the proposition unchallenged, and assails only the proof, does not presuppose fuller acquaintance with the object or oblige us to claim superior knowledge of its nature; it shows only that the assertion is unsupported, not that it is wrong. A sceptical objection sets assertion and counter-assertion in mutual opposition to each other as having equal weight, treating each in turn as dogma and the other as the objection thereto. And the conflict, as the being thus seemingly dogmatic on both the opposing sides, is taken as showing that all judgment in regard to the object is completely null and void. Thus dogmatic and sceptical objections alike lay claim to such insight into their object as is required to assert or to deny something in regard to it. A critical objection, on the other hand, confines itself to pointing out that in the making of the assertion something has been presupposed that is void and merely fictitious; and it thus overthrows the theory by removing its alleged foundation without claiming to establish anything that bears directly upon the constitution of the object.

So long as we hold to the ordinary concepts of our reason with regard to the communion in which our thinking subject stands with the things outside us, we are dogmatic, looking upon them as real objects existing independently of us, in accordance with a certain transcendental dualism which does not assign these outer appearances to the subject as representations, but sets them, just as they are given us in sensible intuition, as objects outside us, completely separating them from the thinking subject. This subreption is the basis of all theories in regard to the communion between soul and body. The objective reality thus assigned to appearances is never brought into question. On the contrary, it is taken for granted; the theorizing is merely as to the mode in which it has to be explained and understood. There are three usual systems devised on these lines, and they are indeed the only possible systems: that of *physical influence*, that of predetermined *harmony*, and that of *supernatural intervention*.

The two last methods of explaining the communion between the soul and matter are based on objections to the first view, which is that of common sense. It is argued, namely, that what appears as matter cannot by its immediate influence be the cause of representations, these being effects which are quite different in kind from matter. Now those who take this line cannot attach to what they understand by 'object of outer senses' the concept of a matter which is nothing but appearance, and so itself a mere representation produced by some sort of outer objects. For in that case they would be saying that the representations of outer objects (appearances) cannot be outer causes of the representations in our mind;

and this would be a quite meaningless objection, since no one could dream of holding that what he has once come to recognize as mere representation, is an outer cause. On our principles they can establish their theory only by showing that that which is the true (transcendental) object of our outer senses cannot be the cause of those representations (appearances) which we comprehend under the title 'matter'. No one, however, can have the right to claim that he knows anything in regard to the transcendental cause of our representations of the outer senses; and their assertion is therefore entirely groundless. If, on the other hand, those who profess to improve upon the doctrine of physical influence keep to the ordinary outlook of transcendental dualism, and suppose matter, as such, to be a thing-in-itself (not the mere appearance of an unknown thing), they will direct their objection to showing that such an outer object, which in itself exhibits no causality save that of movements, can never be the efficient cause of representations, but that a third entity must intervene to establish, if not reciprocal interaction, at least correspondence and harmony between the two. But in arguing in this way, they begin their refutation by admitting into their dualism the πρῶτον ψεῦδος of (a doctrine of) physical influence, and consequently their objection is not so much a disproof of natural influence as of their own dualistic presupposition. For the difficulties in regard to the connection of our thinking nature with matter have their origin, one and all, in the illicitly assumed dualistic view, that matter as such is not appearance, that is, a mere representation of the mind to which an unknown object corresponds, but is the object in itself as it exists outside us independently of all sensibility.

As against the commonly accepted doctrine of physical influence, an objection of the dogmatic type is not, therefore, practicable. For if the opponent of the doctrine accepts the view that matter and its motion are mere appearances and so themselves mere representations, his difficulty is then simply this, that it is impossible that the unknown object of our sensibility should be the cause of the representations in us. He cannot, however, have the least justification for any such contention, since no one is in a position to decide what an unknown object may or may not be able to do. And this transcendental idealism, as we have just proved, he cannot but concede. His only way of escape would be frankly to hypostatize representations, and to set them outside himself as real things.

The doctrine of physical influence, in its ordinary form, is, however, subject to a well-founded *critical* objection. The alleged communion between two kinds of substances, the thinking and the extended, rests on a crude dualism, and treats the extended substances, which are really nothing but mere representations of the thinking subject, as existing by themselves. This mistaken interpretation of physical influence can thus be effectively disposed of: we have shown that the proof of it is void and illicit.

The much-discussed question of the communion between the thinking and the extended, if we leave aside all that is merely fictitious, comes then simply to this: *how in a thinking subject outer intuition*, namely, that of space, with its filling-in of figure and motion, *is possible*. And this is a question which no human being can possibly answer. This gap in our knowledge can never be filled; all that can be done is to indicate it through the ascription of outer appearances to that transcendental object which is the cause of this species of representations, but of which we can have no knowledge whatsoever and of which we shall never acquire any concept. In all problems which may arise in the field of experience we treat these appearances as objects in themselves, without troubling ourselves about the primary ground of their possibility (as appearances). But to advance beyond these limits the concept of a transcendental object would be indispensably required.

The settlement of all disputes or objections which concern the state of the thinking nature prior to this communion (prior to life), or after the cessation of such communion (in death), rests upon these considerations regarding the communion between thinking beings and extended beings. The opinion that the thinking subject has been capable of thought prior to any communion with bodies would now appear as an assertion that, prior to the beginning of the species of sensibility in virtue of which something appears to us in space, those transcendental objects, which in our present state appears as bodies, could have been intuited in an entirely different manner. The opinion that the soul after the cessation of all communion with the corporeal world could still continue to think, would be formulated as the view that, if that species of sensibility in virtue of which transcendental objects, at present quite unknown to us, appear as a material world, should cease, all intuition of the transcendental objects would not for that reason be removed, and it would still be quite possible that those same unknown objects should continue to be known by the thinking subject, though no longer, indeed, in the quality of bodies.

Now on speculative principles no one can give the least ground for any such assertion. Even the possibility of what is asserted cannot be established; it can only be assumed. But it is equally impossible for anyone to bring any valid dogmatic objection against it. For whoever he may be, he knows just as little of the absolute, inner cause of outer corporeal appearances as I or anybody else. Since he cannot, therefore, offer any justification for claiming to know on what the outer appearances in our present state (that of life) really rest, neither can he know that the condition of all outer intuition, or the thinking subject itself, will cease with this state (in death).

Thus all controversy in regard to the nature of the thinking being and its connection with the corporeal world is merely a result of filling the gap where knowledge is wholly lacking to us with paralogisms of reason, treating our thoughts as things and hypostatizing them. Hence originates an imaginary science, imaginary both in the case of him who affirms and of him who denies, since all parties either suppose some knowledge of objects of which no human being has any concept, or treat their own representations as objects, and so revolve in a perpetual circle of ambiguities and contradictions. Nothing but the sobriety of a critique, at once strict and just, can free us from this dogmatic delusion, which through the lure of an imagined felicity keeps so many in bondage to theories and systems. Such a critique confines all our speculative claims rigidly to the field of possible experience; and it does this not by shallow scoffing at ever-repeated failures or pious sighs over the limits of our reason, but by an effective determining of these limits in accordance with established principles, inscribing its *nihil ulterius* on those Pillars of Hercules which nature herself has erected in order that the voyage of our reason may be extended no further than the continuous coastline of experience itself reaches—a coast we cannot leave without venturing upon a shoreless ocean which, after alluring us with ever-deceptive prospects, compels us in the end to abandon as hopeless all this vexatious and tedious endeavour.

9

THOMAS REID

———

ESSAYS ON THE INTELLECTUAL POWERS OF MAN (1785)

Most of the operations of the mind, from their very nature, must have objects to which they are directed and about which they are employed. He that perceives must perceive something; and that which he perceives is called the object of his perception. To perceive, without having any object of perception, is impossible. The mind that perceives, the object perceived, and the *operation* of perceiving that object, are distinct things, and are distinguished in the structure of all languages. In this sentence, 'I see, or perceive the moon', *I* is the person or *mind*, the active verb *see* denotes the operation of that mind, and the *moon* denotes the object. What we have said of perceiving is equally applicable to most operations of the mind. Such operations are, in all languages, expressed by active transitive verbs; and we know that, in all languages, such verbs require a thing or person, which is the agent, and a noun following in an oblique case, which is the object. Whence it is evident that all mankind, both those who have contrived language and those who use it with understanding, have distinguished these three things as different—to wit, the operations of the mind, which are expressed by active verbs; the mind itself, which is the nominative to those verbs; and the object, which is, in the oblique case, governed by them.

It would have been unnecessary to explain so obvious a distinction if some systems of philosophy had not confounded it. Mr Hume's system, in particular, confounds all distinction between the operations of the mind and their objects. When he speaks of the ideas of memory, the ideas of imagination, and the ideas of sense, it is often impossible, from the tenor of his discourse, to know whether by those ideas he means the operations of the mind or the objects about which they are employed. And indeed, according to his system, there is no distinction between the one and the other.

A philosopher is, no doubt, entitled to examine even those distinctions that are to be found in the structure of all languages; and, if he is able to show that there is no foundation for them in the nature of the things distinguished—if he can point out some prejudice common to mankind which has led them to distinguish things that are not really different—in that case, such a distinction may be imputed to a vulgar error which ought to be corrected in philosophy. But when, in his first setting out, he takes it for granted, without proof, that distinctions found in the structure of all languages have no foundation in nature, this, surely, is too fastidious a way of treating the common sense of mankind. When we come to be instructed by philosophers, we must bring the old light of common sense along with us, and by it judge of the new light which the philosopher communicates to us. But when we are required to put out the old light altogether that we may follow the new, we have reason to be on our guard. There may be distinctions that have a real foundation and which may be necessary in philosophy, which are not made in common language, because not necessary in the common business of life. But I believe no instance will be found of a distinction made in all languages which has not a just foundation in nature.

The word *idea* occurs so frequently in modern philosophical writings upon the mind, and is so ambiguous in its meaning, that it is necessary to make some observations upon it. There are chiefly two meanings of this word in modern authors—a popular and a philosophical.

First, in popular language *idea* signifies the same thing as conception, apprehension, notion. To have an idea of anything is to conceive it. To have a distinct idea is to conceive it distinctly. To have no idea of it is not to conceive it at all. It was before observed that conceiving or apprehending has always been considered by all men as an act or operation of the mind, and, on that account, has been expressed in all languages by an active verb. When, therefore, we use the phrase of having ideas, in the popular sense, we ought to attend to this, that it signifies precisely the same thing which we commonly express by the active verbs, conceiving or apprehending.

When the word idea is taken in this popular sense, no man can possibly doubt whether he has ideas. For he that doubts must think, and to think is to have ideas.

Secondly, according to the philosophical meaning of the word idea, it does not signify that act of the mind which we call thought or conception, but some object of thought. Ideas, according to Mr Locke (whose very frequent use of this word has probably been the occasion of its being adopted into common language), 'are nothing but the immediate objects of the mind in thinking'.[1]

Modern philosophers, as well as the Peripatetics and Epicureans of old, have conceived that external objects cannot be the immediate objects of our thought; that there must be some image of them in the mind itself in

[1] Cf. Essay, I. i. 8; IV. i. 1.

which, as in a mirror, they are seen. And the name *idea*, in the philosophical sense of it, is given to those internal and immediate objects of our thoughts. The external thing is the remote or mediate object; but the idea, or image of that object in the mind, is the immediate object without which we could have no perception, no remembrance, no conception of the mediate object.

When therefore, in common language, we speak of having an idea of anything, we mean no more by that expression but thinking of it. The vulgar allow that this expression implies a mind that thinks, an act of that which we call thinking, and an object about which we think. But besides these three, the philosopher conceives that there is a fourth—to wit, the *idea*, which is the immediate object. The idea is in the mind itself, and can have no existence but in a mind that thinks; but the remote or mediate object may be something external, as the sun or moon; it may be something past or future; it may be something which never existed. This is the philosophical meaning of the word *idea*; and we may observe that this meaning of that word is built upon a philosophical opinion: for, if philosophers had not believed that there are such immediate objects of all our thoughts in the mind, they would never have used the word idea to express them.

I shall only add, on this article, that although I may have occasion to use the word idea in this philosophical sense in explaining the opinions of others, I shall have no occasion to use it in expressing my own, because I believe *ideas*, taken in this sense, to be a mere fiction of philosophers. . . .

The word *impression* is used by Mr Hume, in speaking of the operations of the mind, almost as often as the word *idea* is by Mr Locke. What the latter calls ideas, the former divides into two classes; one of which he calls impressions, the other ideas. I shall make some observations upon Mr Hume's explication of *that* word, and then consider the proper meaning of it in the English language.

'We may divide', says Mr Hume, 'all the perceptions of the human mind into two classes or species, which are distinguished by their different degrees of force and vivacity. The less lively and forcible are commonly denominated thoughts or ideas. The other species want a name in our language, and in most others. Let us, therefore, use a little freedom and call them impressions. By the term *impression*, then, I mean all our more lively perceptions, when we hear, or see, or feel, or love, or hate, or desire, or will. Ideas are the less lively perceptions, of which we are conscious, when we reflect on any of those sensations or movements above mentioned.'

Disputes about words belong rather to grammarians than to philosophers; but philosophers ought not to escape censure when they corrupt a language, by using words in a way which the purity of the language will not admit. . . .

We may observe that this author, having given the general name of perception to all the operations of the mind, and distinguished them into two classes or species which differ only in degree of force and vivacity, tells us that he gives the name of impressions to all our more lively perceptions—to wit, when we hear, or see, or feel, or love, or hate, or desire, or will. There is great confusion in this account of the meaning of the word *impression*. When I see, this is an *impression*. But why has not the author told us whether he gives the name of *impression* to the object seen, or to that act of my mind by which I see it? When I see the full moon, the full moon is one thing, my perceiving it is another thing. Which of these two things does he call an impression? We are left to guess this; nor does all that this author writes about impressions clear this point. Everything he says tends to darken it, and to lead us to think that the full moon which I see, and my seeing it, are not two things, but one and the same thing. . . .

In the most extensive sense, an impression is a change produced in some passive subject by the operation of an external cause. If we suppose an active being to produce any change in itself by its own active power, this is never called an impression. It is the act or operation of the being itself, not an impression upon it. From this it appears that to give the name of an impression to any effect produced in the mind is to suppose that the mind does not act at all in the production of that effect. If seeing, hearing, desiring, willing, be operations of the mind, they cannot be impressions. If they be impressions, they cannot be operations of the mind. In the structure of all languages they are considered as acts or operations of the mind itself, and the names given them imply this. To call them impressions, therefore, is to trespass against the structure, not of a particular language only, but of all languages.

If the word *impression* be an improper word to signify the operations of the mind, it is at least as improper to signify their objects; for would any man be thought to speak with propriety who should say that the sun is an impression, that the earth and the sea are impressions?

It is commonly believed, and taken for granted, that every language, if it be sufficiently copious in words, is equally fit to express all opinions, whether they be true or false. I apprehend, however, that there is an exception to this general rule which deserves our notice. There are certain common opinions of mankind upon which the structure and grammar of all languages are founded. While these opinions are common to all men, there will be a great similarity in all languages that are to be found on the face of the earth. Such a similarity there really is; for we find in all languages the same parts of speech, the distinction of nouns and verbs, the distinction of nouns into adjective and substantive, of verbs into active and passive. In verbs we find like tenses, moods, persons, and numbers. There are general rules of grammar, the same in all languages. This similarity of structure in all languages shows a uniformity among men in those opinions upon which the structure of language is founded.

If, for instance, we should suppose that there was a nation who believed that the things which we call attributes might exist without a subject, there would be in their language no distinction between adjectives and substantives, nor would it be a rule with them that an adjective has no meaning unless when joined to a substantive. If there were any nation who did not distinguish between acting and being acted upon, there would in their language be no distinction between active and passive verbs; nor would it be a rule that the active verb must have an agent in the nominative case, but that, in the passive verb, the agent must be in an oblique case.

The structure of all languages is grounded upon common notions which Mr Hume's philosophy opposes and endeavours to overturn. This, no doubt, led him to warp the common language into a conformity with his principles; but we ought not to imitate him in this until we are satisfied that his principles are built on a solid foundation.

There is a figurative meaning of impressions on the mind which is well authorized, but this meaning applies only to objects that are interesting. To say that an object which I see with perfect indifference makes an impression upon my mind is not, as I apprehend, good English. If philosophers mean no more but that I see the object, why should they invent an improper phrase to express what every man knows how to express in plain English?

But it is evident, from the manner in which this phrase is used by modern philosophers, that they mean, not barely to express by it my perceiving an object, but to explain the manner of perception. They think that the object perceived acts upon the mind in some way similar to that in which one body acts upon another, by making an impression upon it. The impression upon the mind is conceived to be something wherein the mind is altogether passive, and has some effect produced in it by the object. But this is a hypothesis which contradicts the common sense of mankind, and which ought not to be admitted without proof.

When I look upon the wall of my room, the wall does not act at all, nor is capable of acting; the perceiving it is an act or operation in me. That this is the common apprehension of mankind with regard to perception is evident from the manner of expressing it in all languages.

The vulgar give themselves no trouble how they perceive the objects—

they express what they are conscious of, and they express it with propriety; but philosophers have an avidity to know how we perceive objects; and, conceiving some similitude between a body that is put in motion and a mind that is made to perceive, they are led to think that, as the body must receive some impulse to make it move, so the mind must receive some impulse or impression to make it perceive. This analogy seems to be confirmed, by observing that we perceive objects only when they make some impression upon the organs of sense, and upon the nerves and brain; but it ought to be observed that such is the nature of body that it cannot change its state but by some force impressed upon it. This is not the nature of mind. All that we know about it shows it to be in its nature living and active, and to have the power of perception in its constitution, but still within those limits to which it is confined by the laws of nature.

It appears, therefore, that this phrase of the mind's having impressions made upon it by corporeal objects in perception is either a phrase without any distinct meaning, and contrary to the propriety of the English language, or it is grounded upon an hypothesis which is destitute of proof. On that account, though we grant that in perception there is an impression made upon the organ of sense and upon the nerves and brain, we do not admit that the object makes any impression upon the mind.

There is another conclusion drawn from the impressions made upon the brain in perception, which I conceive to have no solid foundation, though it has been adopted very generally by philosophers. It is that, by the impressions made on the brain, images are formed of the object perceived; and that the mind, being seated in the brain as its chamber of presence, immediately perceives those images only, and has no perception of the external object but by them. This notion of our perceiving external objects, not immediately, but in certain images or species of them conveyed by the senses, seems to be the most ancient philosophical hypothesis we have on the subject of perception, and to have with small variations retained its authority to this day. . . .

With regard to this hypothesis, there are three things that deserve to be considered, because the hypothesis leans upon them; and, if any one of them fail, it must fall to the ground. The *first* is, that the soul has its seat, or, as Mr Locke calls it, its presence room in the brain. The *second*, that there are images formed in the brain of all the objects of sense. The *third*, that the mind or soul perceives these images in the brain; and that it perceives not external objects immediately, but only perceives them by means of those images.

As to the *first* point—that the soul has its seat in the brain—this, surely, is not so well established as that we can safely build other principles upon it. There have been various opinions and much disputation about the place of spirits: whether they have a place; and, if they have, how they occupy that place. After men had fought in the dark about those points for ages, the wiser part seem to have left off disputing about them, as matters beyond the reach of the human faculties.

As to the *second* point—that images of all the objects of sense are formed in the brain—we may venture to affirm that there is no proof nor probability of this, with regard to any of the objects of sense; and that, with regard to the greater part of them, it is words without any meaning.

We have not the least evidence that the image of any external object is formed in the brain. The brain has been dissected times innumerable by the nicest anatomists; every part of it examined by the naked eye, and with the help of microscopes; but no vestige of an image of any external object was ever found. The brain seems to be the most improper substance that can be imagined for receiving or retaining images, being a soft, moist, medullary substance.

But how are these images formed? or whence do they come? Says Mr Locke, the organs of sense and nerves convey them from without. This is just the Aristotelian hypothesis of sensible species which modern philosophers have been at great pains to refute, and which must be acknowledged to be one of the most unintelligible parts of the Peripatetic system. Those who consider species of colour, figure, sound, and smell, coming from the object, and entering by the organs of sense, as a part of the scholastic jargon long ago discarded from sound philosophy, ought to have discarded images in the brain along with them. There never was a shadow of argument brought by any author to show that an image of any external object ever entered by any of the organs of sense.

That external objects make some impression on the organs of sense, and by them on the nerves and brain, is granted; but that those impressions resemble the objects they are made by, so that they may be called images of the objects, is most improbable. Every hypothesis that has been contrived, shows that there can be no such resemblance; for neither the motions of animal spirits nor the vibrations of elastic chords, or of elastic ether, or of the infinitesimal particles of the nerves, can be supposed to resemble the objects by which they are excited.

The *third* point in this hypothesis is, that the mind perceives the images in the brain, and external objects only by means of them. This is as improbable as that there are such images to be perceived. If our powers of perception be not altogether fallacious, the objects we perceive are not in our brain but without us. We are so far from perceiving images in the brain that we do not perceive our brain at all; nor would any man ever have known that he had a brain if anatomy had not discovered, by dissection, that the brain is a constituent part of the human body.

To sum up what has been said with regard to the organs of perception, and the impressions made upon our nerves and brain. It is a law of our nature, established by the will of the Supreme Being, that we perceive no external object but by means of the organs given us for that purpose. But these organs do not perceive. The eye is the organ of sight, but it sees not. A telescope is an artificial organ of sight. The eye is a natural organ of sight, but it sees as little as the telescope. We know how the eye forms a picture of the visible object upon the retina; but how this picture makes us see the object we know not; and if experience had not informed us that such a picture is necessary to vision, we should never have known it. We can give no reason why the picture on the retina should be followed by vision, while a like picture on any other part of the body produces nothing like vision.

It is likewise a law of our nature that we perceive not external objects unless certain impressions be made by the object upon the organ, and by means of the organ upon the nerves and brain. But of the nature of those impressions we are perfectly ignorant; and though they are conjoined with perception by the will of our Maker, yet it does not appear that they have any necessary connection with it in their own nature, far less that they can be the proper efficient cause of it. We perceive, because God has given us the power of perceiving, and not because we have impressions from objects. We perceive nothing without those impressions, because our Maker has limited and circumscribed our powers of perception by such laws of nature as to his wisdom seemed meet, and such as suited our rank in his creation.

10

ARTHUR SCHOPENHAUER

I. THE WORLD AS WILL AND IDEA (1818)

We can never arrive at the real nature of things from without. However much we investigate, we can never reach anything but images and names. We are like a man who goes round a castle seeking in vain for an entrance, and sometimes sketching the façades. And yet this is the method that has been followed by all philosophers before me.

In fact, the meaning for which we seek of that world which is present to us only as our idea, or the transition from the world as mere idea of the knowing subject to whatever it may be besides this, would never be found if the investigator himself were nothing more than the pure knowing subject (a winged cherub without a body). But he is himself rooted in that world; he finds himself in it as an *individual*, that is to say, his knowledge, which is the necessary supporter of the whole world as idea, is yet always given through the medium of a body, whose affections are, as we have shown, the starting-point for the understanding in the perception of that world. His body is for the pure knowing subject, an idea like every other idea, an object among objects. Its movements and actions are so far known to him in precisely the same way as the changes of all other perceived objects, and would be just as strange and incomprehensible to him if their meaning were not explained for him in an entirely different way. Otherwise he would see his actions follow upon given motives with the constancy of a law of nature, just as the changes of other objects follow upon causes, stimuli, or motives. But he would not understand the influence of the motives any more than the connection between every other effect which he sees and its cause. He would then call the inner nature of these manifestations and actions of his body which he did not understand a force, a quality, or a character, as he pleased, but he would have no further insight into it. But all this is not the case; indeed the answer to the riddle is given to the subject of knowledge who appears as an individual, and the answer is *will*. This and this alone gives him the key to his own existence, reveals to him the significance, shows him the inner mechanism of his being, of his action, of his movements. The body is given in two entirely different ways to the subject of knowledge, who becomes an individual only through his identity with it. It is given as an idea in intelligent perception, as an object among objects and subject to the laws of objects. And it is also given in quite a different way as that which is immediately known to every one, and is signified by the word *will*. Every true act of his will is also at once and without exception a movement of his body. The act of will and the movement of the body are not two different things objectively known, which the bond of causality unites; they do not stand in the relation of cause and effect; they are one and the same, but they are given in entirely different ways—immediately, and again in perception for the understanding. The action of the body is nothing but the act of the will objectified, i.e., passed into perception. It will appear later that this is true of every movement of the body, not merely those which follow upon motives, but also involuntary movements which follow upon mere stimuli, and, indeed, that the whole body is nothing but objectified will, i.e. will become idea. All this will be proved and made quite clear in the course of this work. . . .

If every action of my body is the manifestation of an act of will in which my will itself in general, and as a whole, thus my character, expresses itself under given motives, manifestation of the will must be the inevitable condition and presupposition of every action. For the fact of its manifestation cannot depend upon something which does not exist directly and only through it, which consequently is for it merely accidental, and through which its manifestation itself would be merely accidental. Now that condition is just the whole body itself. Thus the body itself must be manifestation of the will, and it must be related to my will as a whole, that is, to my intelligible character, whose phenomenal appearance in time is my empirical character, as the particular action of the body is related to the particular act of the will. The whole body, then, must be simply my will become visible, must be my will itself, so far as this is object of perception. . . .

Whoever has gained from all these expositions a knowledge *in abstracto*, and therefore clear and certain, of what every one knows directly *in concreto*, i.e. as feeling, a knowledge that his will is the real inner nature of his phenomenal being, which manifests itself to him as idea . . . will find that of itself it affords him the key to the knowledge of the inmost being of the whole of nature; for he now transfers it to all those phenomena which are not given to him, like his own phenomenal existence, both in direct and indirect knowledge, but only in the latter, thus merely one-sidedly as *idea* alone. He will recognize this will of which we are speaking not only in those phenomenal existences which exactly resemble his own, in men and animals as their inmost nature, but the course of reflection will lead him to recognize the force which germinates and vegetates in the plant, and indeed the force through which the crystal is formed, that by which the magnet turns to the north pole, the force whose shock he experiences from the contact of two different kinds of metals, the force which appears in the elective affinities of matter as repulsion and attraction, decomposition and combination, and, lastly, even gravitation, which acts so powerfully throughout matter, draws the stone to the earth and the earth to the sun—all these, I say, he will recognize as different only in their phenomenal existence, but in their inner nature as identical, as that which is directly known to him so intimately and so much better than anything else, and which in its most distinct manifestation is called *will*. . . .

Hitherto it was not recognized that every kind of active and operating force in nature is essentially identical with will, and therefore the multifarious kinds of phenomena were not seen to be merely different species of the same genus, but were treated as heterogeneous. Consequently there could be no word to denote the concept of this genus. I therefore name the genus after its most important species, the direct knowledge of which lies nearer to us and guides us to the indirect knowledge of all other species. But whoever is incapable of carrying out the required extension of the concept will remain involved in a permanent misunderstanding. For by the word *will* he understands only that species of it which has hitherto been exclusively denoted by it, the will which is guided by knowledge, and whose manifestation follows only upon motives, and indeed merely abstract motives, and thus takes place under the guidance of the reason. This, we have said, is only the most prominent example of the manifestation of will. We must now distinctly separate in thought the inmost essence of this manifestation which is known to us directly, and then transfer it to all the weaker, less distinct manifestations of the same nature, and thus we shall accomplish the desired extension of the concept of will. From another point of view I should be equally misunderstood by any one who should think that it is all the same in the end whether we denote this inner nature of all phenomena by the word *will* or by any other. This would be the case if the thing-in-itself were something whose existence we merely *inferred*, and thus knew indirectly and only in the abstract. Then, indeed, we might call it what we pleased; the name would stand merely as the symbol of an unknown quantity. But the word *will*, which, like a magic spell, discloses to us the inmost being of everything in nature, is by no means an unknown quantity, something arrived at only by inference, but is fully and immediately comprehended, and is so familiar to us that we know and understand what will is far better than anything

else whatever. The concept of will has hitherto commonly been subordinated to that of force, but I reverse the matter entirely, and desire that every
force in nature should be thought as will. It must not be supposed that this
is mere verbal quibbling or of no consequence; rather, it is of the greatest
significance and importance. For at the foundation of the concept of force,
as of all other concepts, there ultimately lies the knowledge in sense-
perception of the objective world, that is to say, the phenomenon, the
idea; and the concept is constructed out of this. It is an abstraction from
the province in which cause and effect reign, i.e. from ideas of perception,
and means just the causal nature of causes at the point at which this causal
nature is no further etiologically explicable, but is the necessary presupposition of all etiological explanation. The concept will, on the other hand,
is of all possible concepts the only one which has its source *not* in the
phenomenal, *not* in the mere idea of perception, but comes from within,
and proceeds from the most immediate consciousness of each of us, in
which each of us knows his own individuality, according to its nature,
immediately, apart from all form, even that of subject and object, and
which at the same time is this individuality, for here the subject and the
object of knowledge are one. If, therefore, we refer the concept of *force* to
that of *will*, we have in fact referred the less known to what is infinitely
better known; indeed, to the one thing that is really immediately and fully
known to us, and have very greatly extended our knowledge. If, on the
contrary, we subsume the concept of will under that of force, as has hitherto always been done, we renounce the only immediate knowledge which
we have of the inner nature of the world for we allow it to disappear in a
concept which is abstracted from the phenomenal and with which we can
therefore never go beyond the phenomenal. . . .

If we observe the strong and unceasing impulse with which the waters
hurry to the ocean, the persistency with which the magnet turns ever to
the north pole, the readiness with which iron flies to the magnet, the
eagerness with which the electric poles seek to be reunited, and which,
just like human desire, is increased by obstacles; if we see the crystal
quickly and suddenly take form with such wonderful regularity of construction, which is clearly only a perfectly definite and accurately determined impulse in different directions, seized and retained by crystallization; if we observe the choice with which bodies repel and attract each
other, combine and separate, when they are set free in a fluid state, and
emancipated from the bonds of rigidness; lastly, if we feel directly how a
burden which hampers our body by its gravitation towards the earth,
unceasingly presses and strains upon it in pursuit of its one tendency; if we
observe all this, I say, it will require no great effort of the imagination to

recognize, even at so great a distance, our own nature. That which in us pursues its ends by the light of knowledge; but here, in the weakest of its manifestations, only strives blindly and dumbly in a one-sided and unchangeable manner, must yet in both cases come under the name of will, as it is everywhere one and the same—just as the first dim light of dawn must share the name of sunlight with the rays of the full midday. For the name *will* denotes that which is the inner nature of everything in the world, and the one kernel of every phenomenon.

II. ON THE WILL IN NATURE (1835)

I break silence after seventeen years, in order to point out to the few who, in advance of the age, may have given their attention to my philosophy, sundry corroborations which have been contributed to it by unbiased empiricists, unacquainted with my writings, who, in pursuing their own road in search of merely empirical knowledge, discovered at its extreme end what my doctrine has propounded as the Metaphysical (*das Metaphysische*), from which the explanation of experience as a whole must come. . . .

Now the extraneous and empirical corroborations I am about to bring forward, all concern the kernel and chief point of my doctrine, its Metaphysic proper. They concern, that is, the paradoxical fundamental truth,

that what Kant opposed as *thing in itself* to mere *phenomenon*—called more decidedly by me *representation*—and what he held to be absolutely unknowable, that this *thing in itself*, this substratum of all phenomena, and therefore of the whole of Nature, is nothing but what we know directly and intimately and find within ourselves as *the will*;

that accordingly, this *will*, far from being inseparable from, and even a mere result of, *knowledge*, differs radically and entirely from, and is quite independent of, knowledge, which is secondary and of later origin; and can consequently subsist and manifest itself without knowledge: a thing which actually takes place throughout the whole of Nature, from the animal kingdom downwards;

that this *will*, being the one and only thing in itself, the sole truly real, primary, metaphysical thing in a world in which everything else is only phenomenon—i.e. mere representation—gives all things, whatever they may be, the power to exist and to act;

that accordingly, not only the voluntary actions of animals, but the organic mechanism, nay even the shape and quality of their living body, the vegetation of plants and finally, even in inorganic Nature, crystallization, and in general every primary force which manifests itself in physical and chemical phenomena, not excepting Gravity—that all this, I say, in itself, i.e. independently of phenomenon (which only means, independently of our brain and its representations), is absolutely identical with the *will* we find within us and know as intimately as we can know anything;

that further, the individual manifestations of the will are set in motion by *motives* in beings gifted with an intellect, but no less by *stimuli* in the organic life of animals and of plants, and finally in all inorganic Nature, by *causes* in the narrowest sense of the word—these distinctions applying exclusively to phenomena;

that, on the other hand, knowledge with its substratum, the intellect, is a merely secondary phenomenon, differing completely from the will, only accompanying its higher degrees of objectification and not essential to it; which, as it depends upon the manifestations of the will in the animal organism, is therefore physical, and not, like the will, metaphysical;

that we are never able therefore to infer absence of will from absence of knowledge; for the will may be pointed out even in all phenomena of unconscious Nature, whether in plants or in inorganic bodies; in short,

that the will is not conditioned by knowledge, as has hitherto been universally assumed, although knowledge *is* conditioned by the will.

Before all things we must learn to distinguish will (*voluntas*) from free-will (*arbitrium*) and to understand that the former can subsist without the latter; this however presupposes my whole philosophy. The will is called free-will when it is illumined by knowledge, therefore when the causes which move it are motives: that is, representations. Objectively speaking this means: when the influence from outside which causes the act, has a *brain* for its mediator. A motive may be defined as an external stimulus, whose action first of all causes an *image* to arise in the *brain*, through the medium of which the will carries out the effect proper—an outward action of the body. Now, in the human species however, the place of such an image as this may be taken by a conception drawn from former images of this kind by dropping their differences, which conception consequently is no longer perceptible, but merely denoted and fixed by words. As the action of motives accordingly does not depend upon contact, they can try their power on the will against each other: in other words, they permit a certain choice which, in animals, is limited to the narrow sphere of that which has *perceptible* existence for them; whereas, in man, its range comprises the vast extent of all that is *thinkable*: that is, of his conceptions. Accordingly we designate as *voluntary* those movements which are occasioned, not by *causes* in the narrowest sense of the word, as in inorganic bodies, nor even by *mere stimuli*, as in plants, but by *motives*. These motives however presuppose an *intellect* as *their mediator*, through which causality here acts, without prejudice to its entire necessity in all other respects. Physiologically, the difference between stimulus and motive admits also of the following definition. The stimulus provokes *immediate* reaction, which proceeds from the very part on which the stimulus has acted; whereas the motive is a stimulus that has to go a roundabout way through the brain, where its action first causes an image to arise, which then, but not till then, provokes the consequent reaction, which is now called an act of volition, and *voluntary*. The distinction between voluntary and involuntary movement does not therefore concern what is essential and primary—for this is in both cases the will—but only what is secondary, the rousing of the will's manifestation: it has to do with the determination whether *causes* proper, *stimuli* or *motives* (i.e. causes having passed through the medium of knowledge) are the guidance under which that manifestation takes place. It is in human consciousness—differing from that of animals by not only containing perceptible representations but also abstract conceptions independent of time-distinctions, which act simultaneously and collaterally, whereby deliberation, i.e. a conflict of motives, becomes possible—it is in human consciousness, I say, that free-will (*arbitrium*) in its narrowest sense first makes its appearance; and this I have called elective decision. It nevertheless merely consists in the *strongest* motive for a given individual character overcoming the others and thus determining the act, just as an impact is overcome by a stronger counter-impact, the result thus ensuing with precisely the same necessity as the movement of a stone that has been struck. That all great thinkers in all ages were decided and at one on this point, is just as certain, as that the multitude will never understand, never grasp, the important truth, that the work of our freedom must not be sought in our individual actions, but in our very existence and nature itself. In my prize-essay on Freedom of the Will, I have shown this as clearly as possible. The *liberum arbitrium indifferentiae* which is assumed to be the distinctive characteristic of movements proceeding from *the will*, is accordingly quite inadmissible: for it asserts that effects are possible without causes.

As soon therefore as we have got so far as to distinguish *will* from *free-will*, and to consider the latter as a particular kind or particular phenomenon of the former, we shall find no difficulty in recognizing the will, even in unconscious processes. Thus the assertion, that all bodily movements, even those which are purely vegetative and organic, proceed from *the will*, by no means implies that they are voluntary. For that would mean that they were occasioned by motives; but motives are representations, and their seat is the brain: only those parts of our body which communicate with the brain by means of the nerves, can be put in movement by the brain, consequently by motives, and this movement alone is what is called voluntary. . . .

The progress made in Physiology since Haller has placed beyond doubt, that not only those actions which are consciously performed (*functiones animales*), but even vital processes that take place quite unconsciously (*functiones vitales et naturales*), are directed throughout by the *nervous system*. Likewise that their only difference, as far as our consciousness of them is concerned, consists in the former being directed by nerves proceeding from the brain, the latter by nerves that do not directly communicate with that chief centre of the nervous system—mainly directed towards the outside—but with subordinate, minor centres, with the nerve-knots, the ganglia and their net-work, which preside as it were like vice-regents over the various departments of the nervous system, directing those internal processes that follow upon internal stimuli, just as the brain directs the external actions that follow upon external motives, and thus receiving impressions from inside upon which they react correspondingly, just as the brain receives representations on the strength of which it forms resolutions; only each of these minor centres is confined to a narrower sphere of action. Upon this rests the *vita propria* of each system, in referring to which Van Helmont said that each organ has, as it were, its own *ego*. It accounts also for life continuing in parts which have been cut off the bodies of insects, reptiles, and other inferior animals, whose brain has no marked preponderance over the ganglia of single parts; and it likewise explains how many reptiles are able to live for weeks, nay even months, after their brain has been removed. Now, if our surest experience teaches us that *the will*, which is known to us in most immediate consciousness and in a totally different way from the outer world, is the real agent in actions attended by consciousness and directed by the chief centre of the nervous system; how can we help admitting that those other actions which, proceeding from that nervous system but obeying the direction of its subordinate centres, keep the vital processes constantly going, must also be manifestations of *the will*? Especially as we know perfectly well the cause of which they are not, like the others, attended by consciousness: we know, that is to say, that all consciousness resides in the brain and therefore is limited to such parts as have nerves which communicate directly with the brain; and we know also that, even in these, consciousness ceases when those nerves are severed. By this the difference between all that is conscious and unconscious and together with it the difference between all that is voluntary and involuntary in the movements of the body is perfectly explained, and no reason remains for assuming two entirely different primary sources of movement. . . .

There is moreover special evidence that the movements induced by stimuli (involuntary movements) proceed from the will just as well as those occasioned by motives (voluntary movements): for instance, when the same movement follows now upon a stimulus, now again upon a motive, as is the case when the pupil of the eye is contracted. This movement, when caused by increased light, follows upon a stimulus; whereas, when occasioned by the wish to examine a very small object minutely in close proximity, it follows upon a motive; because contracting the pupil enables us to see things distinctly even when quite near to us, and this distinctness may be increased by our looking through a hole pierced in a card with a pin; conversely, the pupil is dilated when we look at distant objects. Surely the same movement of the same organ is not likely to proceed alternately from two fundamentally different sources. . . .

The truth that the innermost mainspring of unconsciously performed vital and vegetative functions is the will, we find moreover confirmed by the consideration, that even the movement of a limb recognized as voluntary, is only the ultimate result of a multitude of preceding changes which have taken place inside that limb and which no more enter into our consciousness than those organic functions. Yet these changes are evidently that which was first set in motion by the will, the movement of the limb being merely their remote consequence; nevertheless this remains so foreign to our consciousness that physiologists try to reach it by means of such hypotheses as these: that the sinews and muscular fibre are contracted by a change in the cellular tissue wrought by a precipitation of the blood-vapour in that tissue to serum; but that this change is brought about by the nerve's action, and this—by *the will*. Thus, even here, it is not the change which proceeded originally from the will which comes into consciousness, but only its remote result; and even this, properly speaking, only through the special perception of the brain in which it presents itself together with the whole organism. Now by following the path of experimental research and hypotheses physiologists would never have arrived at the truth, that the last link in this ascending causal series is *the will*; it is known to them, on the contrary, in quite a different way. The solution of the enigma comes to them in a whisper from outside the investigation, owing to the fortunate circumstance that the investigator is in this case at the same time himself the object of the investigation and by this learns the secret of the inward process, his explanation of which would otherwise, like that of every other phenomenon, be brought to a standstill by an inscrutable force. And conversely, if we stood in the same inward relation towards every natural phenomenon as towards our own organism, the explanation of every natural phenomenon, as well as of all the properties of every body, would likewise ultimately be reduced to a

E

will manifesting itself in them. For the difference does not reside in the thing itself, but in our relation to the thing. Wherever explanation of the physical comes to an end, it is met by the metaphysical; and wherever this last is accessible to immediate knowledge, the result will be, as here, the will.

SHADWORTH HODGSON

THE THEORY OF PRACTICE (1870)

The immediate cause both of feeling and changes in feeling is found in the nervous organism alone. Feelings are not the causes of feelings; there is no causation between them; the series of feelings which constitutes a life can be arranged in a classified order, but the former members of the series do not contain the cause of the later members. Neither do feelings react upon, or contain the causes of, subsequent states of the nervous organism upon which other feelings depend. The sequences and combinations of feelings form, as it were, a kind of mosaic picture, the separate stones of which both support the picture and keep each other in their places; the stones are the states of the nervous organism, the colours on the stones the states of consciousness which are supported by the nerve states. The states of consciousness, the feelings, are effects of the nature, sequence, and combination, of the nerve states, without being themselves causes either of one another or of changes in the nerve states which support them. In inquiring, therefore, into the origin and laws of movement of feelings or states of consciousness, the nature and modes of action of the nervous organism and its various parts are the first object of investigation; and the origin and laws of movement of feeling will be so far only explained as we may succeed in attaching them to their proper causes in the nature and working of the nervous organism. . . .

It should not be thought surprising that causation is denied to states of consciousness. Causation exists, so far as scientific investigation has made out, only between objects of a single class, namely, objects or portions of matter which are visible and tangible. Atoms, molecules, and masses, which are such portions of visibility and tangibility combined, are the only things between which that action and reaction takes place which we call causation. Everything else is an effect of this action and reaction, without being in its turn a cause, or reacting upon it. Everything else is thought to be explained when it can be shown to be a case of the action and reaction of atoms, molecules, or masses. The various forces in nature are held to be cases of such action and reaction; the mechanical, the chemical, the physical, the vital, forces are all held to be modes of change in the relations of atoms, molecules, or masses, to each other. One kind of visible and tangible matter, nerve substance, which is one of the seats of vital forces, or the motions in which are some mode or modes of life, is also the seat of sensation or consciousness, and the motions in it are followed by consciousness. The more finely organized this nerve substance is, and the more minutely complex, interdependent, and individualized, its motions are, so much the more complex and organic is the system of states of consciousness which arises from them. And from our knowledge of this system we can reason back to the states of nerve substance upon which it depends; and it becomes in fact one kind of evidence or *causa cognoscendi* of the nature and working of nerve substance.

The relation, then, of nerve substance and its changes to consciousness and its changes is, that it is its *causa existendi*; while consciousness and its changes are the *causa cognoscendi* of the former. But consciousness is much more than this; it is the *causa cognoscendi* not only of nerve substance and its workings but of everything else, of all existing things. Let us suppose the whole world existing before consciousness arises in it; and then from the moment of consciousness arising we shall recognize in it, not a new existence, but the perception of the pre-existing world; the pre-existing world and no other, felt and known, that is, as it were, mirrored and reduplicated in a new character. There is no other content of consciousness but this pre-existing and simultaneously existing world. . . . If, then, we draw a distinction between consciousness and the world in which it arises, this distinction can be no other than that between the subjective and objective aspects of the world, or, what is the same thing, of consciousness; in other words, the whole series of causes, *causae existendi*, is contained in the one, and the whole series of evidences, *causae cognoscendi*, in the other. The two aspects, the two series, are actually inseparable and only logically distinguishable; in the separation supposed at the beginning of this paragraph, the world supposed to exist before consciousness arises is, and must be, the same world that we know, distinguished from ourself in reflection, and imagined separate from our knowledge of it by logical abstraction; and it is so for this reason, that our reasoning about the two series or aspects, or about any part of them, is itself a portion of that series of states of consciousness which has been said to be nothing but a mirror or reduplication of the pre-existing and simultaneously existing world.

The two series are exactly parallel and correspondent, the physical series being the *causa existendi*, or efficient cause, of the conscious series in all its minuteness of division, and the conscious series being the *causa cognoscendi*, or evidence, of the physical series with equal minuteness. And, of each pair of corresponding states, the efficient cause or nerve state is always previous in time to its evidence, the conscious state; a circumstance in which this correspondence differs from that between the objective and subjective aspects of phenomena, which aspects are simultaneous; every state of consciousness corresponding to its previously existing efficient cause, the supporting nerve state or nerve movement, and to its simultaneously existing objective aspect, the object which it perceives or represents.

12

T. H. HUXLEY

ON THE HYPOTHESIS THAT ANIMALS ARE AUTOMATA, AND ITS HISTORY (1874)

The first half of the seventeenth century is one of the great epochs of biological science. For though suggestions and indications of the conceptions which took definite shape, at that time, are to be met with in works of earlier date, they are little more than the shadows which coming truth casts forward; men's knowledge was neither extensive enough, nor exact enough, to show them the solid body of fact which threw these shadows.

But, in the seventeenth century, the idea that the physical processes of life are capable of being explained in the same way as other physical phenomena, and, therefore, that the living body is a mechanism, was proved to be true for certain classes of vital actions; and, having thus taken firm root in irrefragable fact, this conception has not only successfully repelled every assault which has been made upon it, but has steadily grown in force and extent of application, until it is now the expressed or implied fundamental proposition of the whole doctrine of scientific Physiology.

If we ask to whom mankind are indebted for this great service, the general voice will name William Harvey. For, by his discovery of the circulation of the blood in the higher animals, by his explanation of the nature of the mechanism by which that circulation is effected, and by his no less remarkable, though less known, investigation of the process of development, Harvey solidly laid the foundations of all those physical explanations of the functions of sustentation and reproduction which modern physiologists have achieved.

But the living body is not only sustained and reproduced: it adjusts itself to external and internal changes; it moves and feels. The attempt to reduce the endless complexities of animal motion and feeling to law and order is, at least, as important a part of the task of the physiologist as the elucidation of what are sometimes called the vegetative processes. Harvey did not make this attempt himself; but the influence of his work upon the man who did make it is patent and unquestionable. This man was René Descartes, who, though by many years Harvey's junior, died before him;

and yet in his short span of fifty-four years, took an undisputed place, not only among the chiefs of philosophy, but amongst the greatest and most original of mathematicians; while, in my belief, he is no less certainly entitled to the rank of a great and original physiologist; inasmuch as he did for the physiology of motion and sensation that which Harvey had done for the circulation of the blood, and opened up that road to the mechanical theory of these processes, which has been followed by all his successors.

Thus far, the propositions respecting the physiology of the nervous system which are stated by Descartes have simply been more clearly defined, more fully illustrated, and, for the most part, demonstrated, by modern physiological research. But there remains a doctrine to which Descartes attached great weight, so that full acceptance of it became a sort of note of a thoroughgoing Cartesian, but which, nevertheless, is so opposed to ordinary prepossessions that it attained more general notoriety, and gave rise to more discussion, than almost any other Cartesian hypothesis. It is the doctrine that brute animals are mere machines or automata, devoid not only of reason, but of any kind of consciousness, which is stated briefly in the *Discours de la Méthode*, and more fully in the *Réponses aux Quartièmes Objections*, and in the correspondence with Henry More.

The process of reasoning by which Descartes arrived at this startling conclusion is well shown in the following passage of the *Réponses:*—

But as regards the souls of beasts, although this is not the place for considering them, and though, without a general exposition of physics, I can say no more on this subject than I have already said in the fifth part of my Treatise on Method; yet, I will further state, here, that it appears to me to be a very remarkable circumstance that no movement can take place, either in the bodies of beasts, or even in our own, if these bodies have not in themselves all the organs and instruments by means of which the very same movements would be accomplished in a machine. So that, even in us, the spirit, or the soul, does not directly move the limbs, but only determines the course of that very subtle liquid which is called the animal spirits, which, running continually from the heart by the brain into the muscles, is the cause of all the movements of our limbs, and often may cause many different motions, one as easily as the other.

And it does not even always exert this determination; for among the movements which take place in us, there are many which do not depend on the mind at all, such as the beating of the heart, the digestion of food, the nutrition, the respiration of those who sleep; and even in those who are awake, walking, singing, and other similar actions, when they are performed without the mind thinking about them. And, when one who falls from a height throws his hands forward to save his head, it is in virtue of no ratiocination that he performs this action; it does not depend upon his mind, but takes place merely because his senses being affected by the present danger, some change arises in his brain which determines the animal spirits to pass thence into the nerves, in such a manner as is required to produce this motion, in the same way as in a machine, and without the mind being able to hinder it. Now since we observe this in ourselves, why should we be so much astonished if the light reflected from the body of a wolf into the eye of a sheep has the same force to excite in it the motion of flight?

After having observed this, if we wish to learn by reasoning, whether certain movements of beasts are comparable to those which are effected in us by the operation of the mind, or, on the contrary, to those which depend only on the animal spirits and the disposition of the organs, it is necessary to consider the difference between the two, which I have explained in the fifth part of the *Discourse on Method* (for I do not think that any others are discoverable), and then it will easily be seen, that all the actions of beasts are similar only to those which we perform without the help of our minds. For which reason we shall be forced to conclude, that we know of the existence in them of no other principal of motion than the disposition of their organs and the continual affluence of animal spirits produced by the heat of the heart, which attenuates and subtilizes the blood; and, at the same time, we shall acknowledge that we have had no reason for assuming any other principle, except that, not having distinguished these two principles of motion, and seeing that the one, which depends only on the animal spirits and the organs, exists in beasts as well as in us, we have hastily concluded that the other, which depends on mind and on thought, was also possessed by them.

Descartes' line of argument is perfectly clear. He starts from reflex action in man, from the unquestionable fact that, in ourselves, co-ordinate, purposive, actions may take place, without the intervention of consciousness or volition, or even contrary to the latter. As actions of a certain degree of complexity are brought about by mere mechanism, why may not actions of still greater complexity be the result of a more refined mechanism? What proof is there that brutes are other than a superior race of marionettes, which eat without pleasure, cry without pain, desire nothing, know nothing, and only simulate intelligence as a bee simulates a mathematician?

Suppose that the anterior division of the brain of a frog—so much of it as lies in front of the 'optic lobes'—is removed. If that operation is

performed quickly and skilfully, the frog may be kept in a state of full
bodily vigour for months, or it may be for years; but it will sit unmoved.
It sees nothing: it hears nothing. It will starve sooner than feed itself,
although food put into its mouth is swallowed. On irritation, it jumps or
walks; if thrown into the water it swims. If it be put on the hand, it sits
there, crouched, perfectly quiet, and would sit there for ever. If the hand
be inclined very gently and slowly, so that the frog would naturally tend
to slip off, the creature's fore paws are shifted on to the edge of the hand,
until he can just prevent himself from falling. If the turning of the hand
be slowly continued, he mounts up with great care and deliberation,
putting first one leg forward and then another, until he balances himself
with perfect precision upon the edge; and if the turning of the hand is
continued, he goes through the needful set of muscular operations, until
he comes to be seated in security, upon the back of the hand. The doing
of all this requires a delicacy of co-ordination, and a precision of adjustment of the muscular apparatus of the body, which are only comparable
to those of a rope-dancer. To the ordinary influences of light, the frog,
deprived of its cerebral hemispheres, appears to be blind. Nevertheless, if
the animal be put upon a table, with a book at some little distance between
it and the light, and the skin of the hinder part of its body is then irritated,
it will jump forward, avoiding the book by passing to the right or left of
it. Therefore, although the frog appears to have no sensation of light,
visible objects act through its brain upon the motor mechanisms of its
body.[1]

It is obvious, that had Descartes been acquainted with these remarkable
results of modern research, they would have furnished him with far more
powerful arguments than he possessed in favour of his view of the
automatism of brutes. The habits of a frog, leading its natural life, involve
such simple adaptations to surrounding conditions, that the machinery
which is competent to do so much without the intervention of consciousness, might well do all. And this argument is vastly strengthened by what
has been learned in recent times of the marvellously complex operations
which are performed mechanically, and to all appearance without consciousness, by men, when, in consequence of injury or disease, they are
reduced to a condition more or less comparable to that of a frog, in which
the anterior part of the brain has been removed.

If such facts as these had come under the knowledge of Descartes, would
they not have formed an apt commentary upon that remarkable passage

---

[1] See the remarkable essay of Göltz, *Beiträge zur Lehre von den Functionen der Nervencentren
des Frosches*, published in 1869. I have repeated Göltz's experiments, and obtained the same
results.

in the *Traité de l'Homme*, which I have quoted elsewhere, but which is worth repetition?:—

All the functions which I have attributed to this machine (the body), as the digestion of food, the pulsation of the heart and of the arteries; the nutrition and the growth of the limbs; respiration, wakefulness, and sleep; the reception of light, sounds, odours, flavours, heat, and such like qualities, in the organs of the external senses; the impression of the ideas of these in the organ of common sensation and in the imagination; the retention or the impression of these ideas on the memory; the internal movements of the appetites and the passions; and lastly the external movements of all the limbs, which follow so aptly, as well the action of the objects which are presented to the senses, as the impressions which meet in the memory, that they imitate as nearly as possible those of a real man; I desire, I say, that you should consider that these functions in the machine naturally proceed from the mere arrangement of its organs, neither more nor less than do the movements of a clock, or other automaton, from that of its weights and its wheels; so that, so far as these are concerned, it is not necessary to conceive any other vegetative or sensitive soul, nor any other principle of motion or of life, than the blood and the spirits agitated by the fire which burns continually in the heart, and which is no wise essentially different from all the fires which exist in inanimate bodies.

And would Descartes not have been justified in asking why we need deny that animals are machines, when men, in a state of unconsciousness, perform, mechanically, actions as complicated and as seemingly rational as those of any animals?

But though I do not think that Descartes' hypothesis can be positively refuted, I am not disposed to accept it. The doctrine of continuity is too well established for it to be permissible to me to suppose that any complex natural phenomenon comes into existence suddenly, and without being preceded by simpler modifications; and very strong arguments would be needed to prove that such complex phenomena as those of consciousness, first make their appearance in man. We know, that, in the individual man, consciousness grows from a dim glimmer to its full light, whether we consider the infant advancing in years, or the adult emerging from slumber and swoon. We know, further, that the lower animals possess, though less developed, that part of the brain which we have every reason to believe to be the organ of consciousness in man; and, as in other cases, function and organ are proportional, so we have a right to conclude it is with the brain; and that the brutes, though they may not possess our intensity of consciousness, and though, from the absence of language, they can have no trains of thoughts, but only trains of feelings, yet have a consciousness which, more or less distinctly, foreshadows our own.

I confess that, in view of the struggle for existence which goes on in the animal world, and of the frightful quantity of pain with which it must be accompanied, I should be glad if the probabilities were in favour of Descartes' hypothesis; but, on the other hand, considering the terrible practical consequences to domestic animals which might ensue from any error on our part, it is as well to err on the right side, if we err at all, and deal with them as weaker brethren, who are bound, like the rest of us, to pay their toll for living, and suffer what is needful for the general good. As Hartley finely says, 'We seem to be in the place of God to them'; and we may justly follow the precedents He sets in nature in our dealings with them.

But though we may see reason to disagree with Descartes' hypothesis that brutes are unconscious machines, it does not follow that he was wrong in regarding them as automata. They may be more or less conscious, sensitive, automata; and the view that they are such conscious machines is that which is implicitly, or explicitly, adopted by most persons. When we speak of the actions of the lower animals being guided by instinct and not by reason, what we really mean is that, though they feel as we do, yet their actions are the results of their physical organization. We believe, in short, that they are machines, one part of which (the nervous system) not only sets the rest in motion, and co-ordinates its movements in relation with changes in surrounding bodies, but is provided with special apparatus, the function of which is the calling into existence of those states of consciousness which are termed sensations, emotions and ideas. I believe that this generally accepted view is the best expression of the facts at present known.

It is experimentally demonstrable—any one who cares to run a pin into himself may perform a sufficient demonstration of the fact—that a mode of motion of the nervous system is the immediate antecedent of a state of consciousness. All but the adherents of 'Occasionalism', or of the doctrine of 'Pre-established Harmony' (if any such now exist), must admit that we have as much reason for regarding the mode of motion of the nervous system as the cause of the state of consciousness, as we have for regarding any event as the cause of another. How the one phenomenon causes the other we know, as much or as little, as in any other case of causation; but we have as much right to believe that the sensation is an effect of the molecular change, as we have to believe that motion is an effect of impact; and there is as much propriety in saying that the brain evolves sensation, as there is in saying that an iron rod, when hammered, evolves heat.

As I have endeavoured to show, we are justified in supposing that something analogous to what happens in ourselves takes place in the brutes, and that the affections of their sensory nerves give rise to molecular changes in the brain, which again give rise to, or evolve, the corresponding states of consciousness. Nor can there be any reasonable doubt that the emotions of brutes, and such ideas as they possess, are similarly dependent upon molecular brain changes. Each sensory impression leaves behind a record in the structure of the brain—an 'ideagenous' molecule, so to speak, which is competent, under certain conditions, to reproduce, in a fainter condition, the state of consciousness which corresponds with that sensory impression; and it is these 'ideagenous molecules' which are the physical basis of memory.

It may be assumed, then, that molecular changes in the brain are the causes of all the states of consciousness of brutes. Is there any evidence that these states of consciousness may, conversely, cause those molecular changes which give rise to muscular motion? I see no such evidence. The frog walks, hops, swims, and goes through his gymnastic performances quite as well without consciousness, and consequently without volition, as with it; and, if a frog, in his natural state, possesses anything corresponding with what we call volition, there is no reason to think that it is anything but a concomitant of the molecular changes in the brain which form part of the series involved in the production of motion.

The consciousness of brutes would appear to be related to the mechanism of their body simply as a collateral product of its working, and to be as completely without any power of modifying that working as the steam-whistle which accompanies the working of a locomotive engine is without influence upon its machinery. Their volition, if they have any, is an emotion indicative of physical changes, not a cause of such changes.

This conception of the relations of states of consciousness with molecular changes in the brain—of *psychoses* with *neuroses*—does not prevent us from ascribing free will to brutes. For an agent is free when there is nothing to prevent him from doing that which he desires to do. If a greyhound chases a hare, he is a free agent, because his action is in entire accordance with his strong desire to catch the hare; while so long as he is held back by the leash he is not free, being prevented by external force from following his inclination. And the ascription of freedom to the greyhound under the former circumstances is by no means inconsistent with the other aspect of the facts of the case—that he is a machine impelled to the chase, and caused, at the same time, to have the desire to catch the game by the impression which the rays of light proceeding from the hare make upon his eyes, and through them upon his brain.

Much ingenious argument has at various times been bestowed upon the question: How is it possible to imagine that volition, which is a state of consciousness, and, as such, has not the slightest community of nature with matter in motion, can act upon the moving matter of which the body is composed, as it is assumed to do in voluntary acts? But if, as is here suggested, the voluntary acts of brutes—or, in other words, the acts which they desire to perform—are as purely mechanical as the rest of their actions, and are simply accompanied by the state of consciousness called volition, the inquiry, so far as they are concerned, becomes superfluous. Their volitions do not enter into the chain of causation of their actions at all.

The hypothesis that brutes are conscious automata is perfectly consistent with any view that may be held respecting the often discussed and curious question whether they have souls or not; and, if they have souls, whether those souls are immortal or not. It is obviously harmonious with the most literal adherence to the text of Scripture concerning 'the beast that perisheth'; but it is not inconsistent with the amiable conviction ascribed by Pope to his 'untutored savage', that when he passes to the happy hunting-grounds in the sky, 'his faithful dog shall bear him company'. If the brutes have consciousness and no souls, then it is clear that, in them, consciousness is a direct function of material changes; while, if they possess immaterial subjects of consciousness, or souls, then, as consciousness is brought into existence only as the consequence of molecular motion of the brain, it follows that it is an indirect product of material changes. The soul stands related to the body as the bell of a clock to the works, and consciousness answers to the sound which the bell gives out when it is struck.

Thus far I have strictly confined myself to the problem with which I proposed to deal at starting—the automatism of brutes. The question is, I believe, a perfectly open one, and I feel happy in running no risk of either Papal or Presbyterian condemnation for the views which I have ventured to put forward. And there are so very few interesting questions which one is, at present, allowed to think out scientifically—to go as far as reason leads, and stop where evidence comes to an end—without speedily being deafened by the tattoo of 'the drum ecclesiastic'—that I have luxuriated in my rare freedom, and would now willingly bring this disquisition to an end if I could hope that other people would go no farther. Unfortunately, past experience debars me from entertaining any such hope, even if

> '. . . that drum's discordant sound
> Parading round and round and round,'

were not, at present, as audible to me as it was to the mild poet who ventured to express his hatred of drums in general, in that well-known couplet.

It will be said, that I mean that the conclusions deduced from the study of the brutes are applicable to man, and that the logical consequences of such application are fatalism, materialism, and atheism—whereupon the drums will beat the *pas de charge*.

One does not do battle with drummers; but I venture to offer a few remarks for the calm consideration of thoughtful persons, untrammelled by foregone conclusions, unpledged to shore-up tottering dogmas, and anxious only to know the true bearings of the case.

It is quite true that, to the best of my judgment, the argumentation which applies to brutes holds equally good of men; and, therefore, that all states of consciousness in us, as in them, are immediately caused by molecular changes of the brain substance. It seems to me that in men, as in brutes, there is no proof that any state of consciousness is the cause of change in the motion of the matter of the organism. If these positions are well based, it follows that our mental conditions are simply the symbols in consciousness of the changes which take place automatically in the organism; and that, to take an extreme illustration, the feeling we call volition is not the cause of a voluntary act, but the symbol of that state of the brain which is the immediate cause of that act. We are conscious automata, endowed with free will in the only intelligible sense of that much-abused term—inasmuch as in many respects we are able to do as we like—but none the less parts of the great series of causes and effects which, in unbroken continuity, composes that which is, and has been, and shall be—the sum of existence.

As to the logical consequences of this conviction of mine, I may be permitted to remark that logical consequences are the scarecrows of fools and the beacons of wise men. The only question which any wise man can ask himself, and which any honest man will ask himself, is whether a doctrine is true or false. Consequences will take care of themselves; at most their importance can only justify us in testing with extra care the reasoning process from which they result.

So that if the view I have taken did really and logically lead to fatalism, materialism, and atheism, I should profess myself a fatalist, materialist, and atheist; and I should look upon those who, while they believed in my honesty of purpose and intellectual competency, should raise a hue and cry against me, as people who by their own admission preferred lying to truth, and whose opinions therefore were unworthy of the smallest attention.

But, as I have endeavoured to explain on other occasions, I really have no claim to rank myself among fatalistic, materialistic, or atheistic philosophers. Not among fatalists, for I take the conception of necessity to have a logical, and not a physical foundation; not among materialists, for I am utterly incapable of conceiving the existence of matter if there is no mind in which to picture that existence; not among atheists, for the problem of the ultimate cause of existence is one which seems to me to be hopelessly out of reach of my poor powers. Of all the senseless babble I have ever had occasion to read, the demonstrations of these philosophers who undertake to tell us all about the nature of God would be the worst, if they were not surpassed by the still greater absurdities of the philosophers who try to prove that there is no God.

13

FRANZ BRENTANO

The data of our consciousness make up a world which, taken in its entirety, falls into two great classes, the class of *physical* and the class of *mental* phenomena. We spoke of this distinction much earlier, in the course of defining the concept of psychology, and we returned to it again in our investigation of method. But what was said is still insufficient; what was then only suggested in passing we must now delineate more firmly and rigorously. . . .

Let us start with an attempt to make our concepts clear by way of examples.

Every presentation (*Vorstellung*) of sensation or imagination offers an example of the mental phenomenon; and here I understand by presentation not that which is presented, but the act of presentation. Thus, hearing a sound, seeing a coloured object, sensing warm or cold, and the comparable states of imagination as well, are examples of what I mean; but thinking of a general concept, provided such a thing does actually occur, is equally so. Furthermore, every judgment, every recollection, every expectation, every inference, every conviction or opinion, every doubt, is a mental phenomenon. And again, every emotion, joy, sorrow, fear, hope, courage, despair, anger, love, hate, desire, choice, intention, astonishment, wonder, contempt, etc., is such a phenomenon.

Examples of physical phenomena, on the other hand, are a colour, a shape, a landscape, which I see; a musical chord, which I hear; heat, cold, odour, which I sense; as well as comparable images, which appear to me in my imagination.

These examples may suffice as concrete illustration of the distinction between the two classes.

Nevertheless, we will attempt to give a definition of the mental phenomenon in another, more unified way. For this, there is available a definition we have used before, when we said that by the term, mental phenomena, we designate presentations and, likewise, all those phenomena which are based on presentations. It scarcely requires notice that, once

---

[1] Interpretative notes, referring to passages in the text indicated by letters, are on pages 153-4.

again, by presentation we understand here not what is presented but the presenting of it. This presentation forms the basis not merely of judgments, but also of desires, as well as of every other mental act. We cannot judge of anything, cannot desire anything, cannot hope for anything, or fear anything, if it is not presented. Hence, the definition which we gave embraces all of the examples just introduced and, in general, all of the phenomena belonging to this domain.

It is a sign of the immature state in which psychology finds itself that one can scarcely utter a single sentence about mental phenomena which would not be disputed by many. Still, the great majority agree with what we just said; presentations are the basis for the other mental phenomena. Thus, Herbart is quite correct in saying: 'In every case of emotion, something, no matter how diversified and complicated, must be in consciousness as something presented; so that this particular presentation is included in this particular feeling. And every time we have a desire . . . (we) also have in our thoughts that which we desire. . . .'[1]

Still, we may surely find that, as regards some kinds of sensual feelings of pleasure and displeasure, someone does actually hold the opinion that there is no presentation, even in our sense, on which they are based. We cannot deny a certain temptation in that direction, at least. This holds, for example, in regard to feelings which are caused by a cut or a burn. If someone is cut, then for the most part he has no further perception of touch; if he is burned, no further perception of heat; but pain alone seems to be present in the one case and the other.

Nonetheless, there is no doubt that even here the feeling is based on a presentation. In such cases we always have the presentation of a definite spatial location, which we ordinarily specify in relation to one or the other of the visible and palpable parts of our body. We say that our foot hurts, or our hand hurts, this or the other place on our body is in pain. In the first place, then, those who look on such a spatial presentation as something originally given by means of the neural stimulation itself will therefore be unable to deny that a presentation is the basis of this feeling. But others, too, cannot avoid making the same assumption. For we have within us not merely the presentation of a definite spatial location, but also that of a particular sensory quality, analogous to colour, sound, and other so-called sensory qualities, a quality which belongs among the physical phenomena and which is definitely to be distinguished from the accompanying feeling. If we hear a pleasant, mild sound or a shrill one, a harmonious chord or a discord, it will occur to no one to identify the sound with the accompanying feeling of pleasure or pain. But, likewise,

---

[1] *Psych. als Wissensch*, Part II, Sec. 1, chap. i, S103. Cf. also Drobisch, *Empir. Psychol.*, pp. 38 and 348, and others of Herbart's school.

when a cut, a burn, or a tickle arouses a feeling of pain or pleasure in us, we must maintain in a similar manner the distinction between a physical phenomenon, which enters in as the object of outer perception, and a mental phenomenon of feeling, which accompanies its appearance, even though the superficial observer is rather inclined to confusion here.

The principal basis of the illusion is probably the following. It is well known that our sensations are mediated by the so-called afferent (*sensibeln*) nerves. It was believed earlier that specialized nerves served exclusively as conductors for each class of sensory qualities, colour, sound, and so on. Recently, physiology has inclined more and more to the opposite point of view.[1] Particularly, it teaches almost universally that the nerves for tactile sensations, when stimulated in one way, produce in us the sensations of heat and cold, and when stimulated in another way, produce the so-called sensations of pain and pleasure. In fact, however, something similar holds for all nerves, insofar as a sensory phenomenon of the kind just mentioned can be aroused in us by way of every nerve. If they are very strongly stimulated, all nerves arouse painful phenomena, which are not distinguished in kind one from another. If a nerve serves as the medium of diverse classes of sensations, it often happens that it serves as the medium of several at the same time, as, for example, looking at an electric light results simultaneously in a 'beautiful' sensation of colour, i.e., one that is pleasant to us, and a painful phenomenon of another class. The nerves of the tactile sense frequently communicate at the same time a so-called sensation of touch, a sensation of heat or cold, and a so-called sensation of pain or pleasure. Now it is manifest that when several sensory phenomena appear together, it is not seldom the case that they are regarded as being *one*. This has been demonstrated in a striking way in connection with the sensations of taste and smell. It is established that almost all of the differences which we are accustomed to look upon as differences of taste are, in fact, only differences in simultaneously occurring phenomena of smell. It is a similar matter when we eat a food cold or warm; we often believe ourselves to have differences in taste which are in fact only differences in phenomena of temperature. It is not to be wondered at, then, if we do not always maintain a strict distinction between what is a phenomenon of temperature and what is a tactile phenomenon. Indeed, we would perhaps not distinguish them at all if they did not ordinarily appear independently of each other. But if now we consider the sensations of feeling (*Gefühlsempfindungen*) we find that for the most part they are bound up with sensations of another class and that when the excitation is very strong these other sensations sink into insignificance beside them. It is very easy, then, to account for the fact that we should be deceived about

---

[1] Cf. especially Wundt, *Physiol. Psychol.*, pp. 345 ff.

the occurrence of a particular class of sensory qualities and believe ourselves to have a single sensation instead of two. Since the supervening presentation was accompanied by a relatively very strong feeling, incomparably stronger than the one which followed upon the first kind of quality, this mental phenomenon was regarded as the only one which had newly been experienced. And if the first kind of quality disappeared entirely, then we would believe that we possessed nothing besides a feeling, without any presentation on which it was based.

A further basis of the illusion is that the quality on which the feeling ensues, and the feeling itself, do not bear two distinct names. We call the physical phenomenon, which occurs along with the feeling of pain, itself pain in this case. We do not say that this or that phenomenon in the foot is experienced with pain so much as we say that pain is experienced in the foot. To be sure, this is an equivocation such as we find elsewhere, whenever things stand in a close relationship to each other. We call the body healthy, and in connection with it, the air, food, facial colour, and so on, but plainly in different senses. In our case, a physical phenomenon itself is called pleasure or pain, after the feeling of pleasure or pain which accompanies its appearance, and here too the sense is modified. It is as if we should say of a harmonious sound that it is a pleasure to us, because we experience a feeling of pleasure on its occurrence; or that the loss of a friend is a great sorrow to us. Experience shows that equivocation is one of the foremost hindrances to our knowledge of distinctions. It must necessarily be very much so here, where a danger of being deluded exists in and of itself, and the transference of the term was perhaps itself the result of a confusion. Hence, many psychologists were deceived, and further errors were tied up with this one. Many arrived at the false conclusion that the experiencing subject must be present at the place of the injured limb in which a painful phenomenon is localized in perception. For, insofar as they identified the phenomenon with the accompanying feeling of pain, they regarded it as a mental, not as a physical, phenomenon. And for just that reason, they believed its perception in the limb to be an inner, and consequently, an evident and infallible perception.[1] But their opinion is contradicted by the fact that the same phenomena often appear in the same way after the limb has been amputated. Others accordingly argued rather to the opposite effect, sceptically opposing the self-evidence (*Evidenz*) of inner perception. This is all resolved, if one has learned to distinguish between the pain in the sense in which the term designates the apparent property of a part of our body and the feeling of pain which is tied up with sensing it. But if one has done this, then one is no longer

[1] This is the opinion of the Jesuit, Tongiorgi, in his very widely circulated philosophy textbook.

inclined to hold that the feeling of sensory pain which one experiences on being injured is not based on any presentation.

We may, accordingly, regard it as an indubitably correct definition of mental phenomena that they are either presentations or (in the sense which has been explained) rest on presentations as their basis. In this we would thus have a second definition of the concept (of mental phenomena) which breaks down into fewer terms. Yet it is not entirely unified, since it presents mental phenomena as divided into two groups.

The attempt has been made to give a perfectly unified definition which distinguishes all of the mental phenomena, as contrasted with the physical, by means of negation. All physical phenomena, it is said, manifest extension and definite spatial location, whether they are appearances to sight or another sense, or products of the imagination, which presents similar objects to us. The opposite, however, is true of mental phenomena; thinking, willing, and so on appear as unextended and without a situation in space.

According to this view, we would be in a position to characterize the physical phenomena easily and rigorously in contrast to the mental, if we were to say that they are those which appear extended and spatial. And, with the same exactitude, the mental phenomena would then be definable, as contrasted with the physical, as those which exhibit no extension or definite spatial location. One could call on Descartes and Spinoza in support of such a differentiation, but particularly on Kant, who declares space to be the form of intuition of outer sensation.

A. Bain has recently given the same definition: 'The department of the Object, or Object-World,' he says, 'is exactly circumscribed by one property, Extension. The world of Subject-experience is devoid of this property.'

'A tree or a river is said to possess extended magnitude. A pleasure has no length, breadth, or thickness; it is in no respect an extended thing. A thought or idea may refer to extended magnitudes, but it cannot be said to have extension in itself. Neither can we say that an act of the will, a desire, a belief, occupy dimensions in space. Hence all that comes within the sphere of the Subject is spoken of as the Unextended.'

'Thus, if Mind, as commonly happens, is put for the sum total of Subject-experiences, we may define it negatively by a single fact—the absence of Extension.'[1]

So it appears that we have found, negatively at least, a unified definition for the sum-total of mental phenomena.

But here, too, unanimity does not prevail among the psychologists, and for diverse reasons we often hear it denied that extension and the absence

---

[1] *Mental Science*, Intro., chap. i.

of extension are differentiating characteristics distinguishing physical and mental phenomena.

Many believe that the definition is false because not only mental, but also many physical phenomena, appear without extension. Thus, a large number of not unimportant psychologists teach that the phenomena of certain senses, or even of the senses in general, originally manifest themselves free of all extension and definite spatial character. This is very generally believed (to be true) of sounds and of the phenomena of smell. According to Berkeley, the same holds true of colours, and according to Platner, of the phenomena of the sense of touch. According to Herbart and Lotze, as well as Hartley, Brown, the two Mills, H. Spencer, and others, (it is true) of the phenomena of all the external senses. To be sure, it appears to us as if the phenomena which the external senses, particularly vision and the sense of touch, manifest to us were all spatially extended. But the reason for this, it is said, is the fact that on the basis of prior experience we connect with them our gradually developed presentation of *space*; originally without definite spatial location, they are later localized by us. If this should really be the only way in which physical phenomena attain definite spatial location, then we could plainly no longer distinguish the two realms by reference to this property. (The possibility of such a distinction) is decreased still more by the fact that mental phenomena are also localized by us in such a way, as, for example, when we mistakenly place a phenomenon of anger in the irritable lion, and our own thoughts in the space that is filled by us.

So that would be one way, from the point of view of a large number of important psychologists, in which the stated definition must be contested. When all is said, even Bain, who seems to advance it, is to be counted among these thinkers; for he follows Hartley's line of thought completely. He is able to speak as he has spoken only because (even though without complete consistency) he has not included the phenomena of the external senses, in and for themselves, among the physical phenomena.

Others, as I have said, will reject the definition for contrary reasons. It is not so much the claim that all physical phenomena appear extended that arouses their opposition. It is the claim, rather, that all mental phenomena lack extension; according to them, certain mental phenomena also manifest themselves as extended. Aristotle appears to have been of this opinion when, in the first chapter of his treatise on sensation and the object of sense, he regards it as evident, immediately and without previous proof, that sense perception is the act of a physical organ.[1] Modern psychologists and physiologists express themselves similarly at times in connection with

---

[1] *De sens. et sens* 1, p. 436, b, 7. See also what he says in *De anim.* I. 1, p. 403, a, 16 about the affects, especially those of fear.

certain affects. They speak of feelings of pleasure and pain which appear in the external organs, sometimes, indeed, even after the amputation of the member; and surely, feeling, like perception is a mental phenomenon. Many also say of sensual desires that they appear localized; and the fact that poets speak, perhaps not of thought, but of bliss and yearning which suffuse the heart and all the parts of the body, is in accord with that view.

So we see that the stated distinction is assailed with regard to both physical and mental phenomena. Perhaps both points raised against it are equally unfounded.[1] Nevertheless, a further definition common to mental phenomena is still desirable in any case. For conflict over the question whether certain mental and physical phenomena appear extended or not shows at once that the alleged attribute does not suffice for a distinct differentiation; furthermore, for the mental phenomena it is negative only.

What positive attribute will we now be able to advance? Or is there, perhaps, no positive definition at all which holds true of all mental phenomena generally?

A. Bain says that in fact there is none.[2] Nonetheless, psychologists of an earlier period have already directed attention to a particular affinity and analogy which exists among all mental phenomena, while the physical do not share in it. Every mental phenomenon is characterized by what the scholastics of the Middle Ages called the intentional (and also mental)[3] inexistence (*Inexistenz*) of an object (*Gegenstand*), and what we could call, although in not entirely unambiguous terms, the reference to a content, a direction upon an object (by which we are not to understand a reality in this case),[a] or an immanent objectivity. Each one includes something as object within itself, although not always in the same way. In presentation something is presented, in judgment something is affirmed or denied, in love (something is) loved, in hate (something) hated, in desire (something) desired, etc.[4]

[1] The claim that even mental phenomena appear extended rests plainly on a confusion between physical and mental phenomena similar to the one we became convinced of above, when we established that even sensory feelings are necessarily based on a presentation.

[2] *The Senses and the Intellect*, Intro.

[3] They also use the expression 'to be in something objectively', which, if we should wish to make use of it now, could possibly be taken in just the opposite sense, as the designation of a real existence outside of the mind. Nevertheless, it reminds one of the expression 'to be immanently objective', which we sometimes use in a similar sense, and in which the 'immanently' is intended to exclude the misunderstanding that was to be feared.

[4] Aristotle has already spoken of this mental inherence. In his books on the soul he says that what is experienced, insofar as it is experienced, is in the one experiencing it, that sense contains what is experienced without its matter, that what is thought is in the thinking intellect. In Philo we likewise find the doctrine of mental existence and inexistence. In confusing this, however, with existence in the strict sense, he arrives at his doctrine of the Logos and Ideas, with its wealth of contradictions. The like holds true of the Neo-Platonists. Augustine touches on the same fact in his theory of the *Verbum mentis* and its internal origin. Anselm

This intentional inexistence is exclusively characteristic of mental phenomena. No physical phenomenon manifests anything similar. Consequently, we can define mental phenomena by saying that they are such phenomena as include an object intentionally within themselves. . . .[b]

It is a further general characteristic of all mental phenomena that they are perceived only in inner consciousness, while only outer perception is possible for the physical. Hamilton advances this distinguishing attribute.[1]

One could believe that such a definition says little, since it would seem more natural to take the opposite course, defining the act by reference to its object, and so defining inner perception of mental phenomena. But inner perception has still another characteristic, apart from the special nature of its object, which distinguishes it: namely, that immediate, infallible self-evidence, which pertains to it alone among all the cases in which we know objects of experience. Thus, if we say that mental phenomena are those which are grasped by means of inner perception, we have accordingly said that their perception is immediately evident.

Still more! Inner perception is not merely unique as immediately evident perception; it is really unique as perception (*Wahrnehmung*) in the strict sense of the word. We have seen that the phenomena of so-called outer perception can in no way be demonstrated to be true and real, even by means of indirect reasoning. Indeed, we have seen that anyone who placed confidence in them and took them to be what they presented themselves as being is misled by the way the phenomena hang together. Strictly speaking, so-called outer perception is thus not perception; and mental phenomena can accordingly be designated as the only ones of which perception in the strict sense of the word is possible.

Mental phenomena are also adequately characterized by means of this definition. It is not as if all mental phenomena are introspectively perceivable for everyone, and therefore that everything which a person cannot perceive he is to count among the physical phenomena. On the contrary, it is obvious, and was already expressly remarked by us earlier, that no mental phenomenon is perceived by more than a single individual; but on that occasion we also saw that every type of mental phenomenon is represented in the psychical life of every fully developed human being.

does so in his well-known ontological argument; and many have alleged the basis of his fallacy to be the fact that he regarded mental existence as if it were actual existence (see *Ueberweg, History of Philosophy*, Vol. II). Thomas Aquinas teaches that what is thought is intentionally in the one thinking, the object of love in the person loving, what is desired in the person desiring, and uses this for theological purposes. When the scripture speaks of an indwelling of the Holy Ghost, he explains this as an intentional indwelling by way of love. And he also seeks to find in intentional inexistence, in the cases of thinking and loving, a certain analogy for the mystery of the Trinity and the procession of the Word and Spirit.

[1] *Lect. on Metaphysics.*

For this reason, reference to the phenomena which constitute the realm of inner perception serves our purpose satisfactorily.

We said that mental phenomena are the only ones of which a perception in the strict sense is possible. We could just as well say that they are the only phenomena to which actual, as well as intentional, existence pertains. Knowledge, joy, desire, exist actually; colour, sound, heat, only phenomenally and intentionally.

There are philosophers who go so far as to say that it is self-evident that no actuality *could* correspond to a phenomenon such as we call a physical one. They maintain that anyone who assumes this and ascribes to physical phenomena any existence other than mental holds a view which is self-contradictory in itself. Bain, for example, says that some people have attempted to explain the phenomena of outer perception by the hypothesis of a material world, 'in the first instance, detached from perception, and, afterwards, coming into perception, by operating upon the mind'. 'This view,' he says, 'involves a contradiction. The prevailing doctrine is that a tree is something in itself apart from all perception; that, by its luminous emanations, it impresses our mind and is then perceived; the perception being an effect, and the unperceived tree (i.e. the one which exists outside of perception) the cause. But the tree is known only through perception; what it may be anterior to, or independent of, perception, we cannot tell; we can think of it as perceived but not as unperceived. There is a manifest contradiction in the supposition; we are required at the same moment to perceive the thing and not to perceive it. We know the touch of iron, but we cannot know the touch apart from the touch.'[1]

I am not convinced of the correctness of this argument. . . . If what Bain says were correct: 'We can think of (a tree) as perceived, but not as unperceived. There is manifest contradiction in the supposition', then his further conclusion would surely no longer be subject to objection. But it is precisely this which is not to be granted. Bain explains his dictum by saying: 'We are required at the same moment to perceive the thing and not to perceive it.' But it is not true that this is required: For, in the first place, not every case of thinking is a perception; and further, even if this were the case, it would only follow that a person could only think of trees perceived by him, but not that he could only think of trees *as perceived by him*. To taste a white piece of sugar does not mean to taste a piece of sugar *as white*. The fallacy reveals itself quite distinctly when it is applied to mental phenomena. If one should say: 'I cannot think of a mental phenomenon without thinking of it; and so I can only think of mental phenomena as thought by me; hence no mental phenomena exists outside of my thinking', this mode of inference would be exactly like the one

[1] *Mental Science*, 3rd ed., p. 198.

Bain uses. Nonetheless, Bain himself will not deny that his individual mental life is not the only thing to which actual existence belongs. When Bain adds, 'We know the touch of iron, but it is not possible that we should know the touch apart from the touch', he uses the word 'touch', in the first place, obviously, in the sense of what is felt, and then in the sense of the feeling of it. These are different concepts even if they have the same name. Accordingly, only someone who permits himself to be deceived by the equivocation could make the concession of immediate evidence required by Bain.

It is not true, then, that the hypothesis that a physical phenomenon like those which exist intentionally in us exists outside of the mind, in actuality includes a contradiction.[c] It is only that, when we compare one with the other, conflicts are revealed, which show clearly that there is no actual existence in this case. And even though this holds true in the first instance only as far as our experience extends, we will, nevertheless, make no mistake if we quite generally deny to physical phenomena any existence other than intentional existence. . . .[d]

In conclusion, let us summarize the results of our comments on the distinction between physical and mental phenomena. First of all, we made ourselves concretely aware of the distinctive nature of the two classes by means of *examples*. We then defined mental phenomena as *presentations* and such phenomena which are *based upon presentations*; all the rest belong to the physical. We next spoke of the attribute of *extension*, which was taken by psychologists to be a distinctive characteristic of all physical phenomena; all mental phenomena were supposed to lack it. The contention had not remained uncontested, however, and only later investigations could decide the issue; that in fact mental phenomena do invariably appear unextended was all that could be confirmed now. We next found *intentional inexistence*, the reference to something as an object,[e] to be a distinguishing feature of all mental phenomena; no physical phenomenon manifests anything similar. We further defined mental phenomena as the exclusive *object of inner perception*; they alone are therefore perceived with immediate evidence; indeed, they alone are perceived in the strict sense of the word. And with this there was bound up the further definition, that they alone are phenomena which possess *actual* existence besides their intentional existence.[f]

INTERPRETATIVE NOTES

(Contributed by Dr George Katkov, St Antony's College, Oxford)

[Book II Chapter I of Brentano's *Psychologie vom empirischen Standpunkte* contains not only the first expression of his basic contribution to philosophy, but also the point of departure for many philosophical trends inaugurated by his numerous pupils. Unfortunately, they—in particular Husserl, Meinong and Stumpf—often misunderstood the unusual wording (for example, 'intentional inexistence of the object') of some of the passages. In his edition of the

Psychologie in 1924, Oscar Kraus (together with A. Kastil, the literary executor of Franz Brentano) supplied the text with a great number of notes indicating both these misunderstandings and the few but important points where Brentano later amended his views of 1874. The following six notes, relating to the passages indicated in the above extract, are based on some of Kraus' commentaries to the text.]

a Brentano later held the view, that we can relate ourselves to objects which, even if they existed, would not be things, i.e. real beings in the proper sense, but *'irrealia'* or *'entia rationis'*, such as 'possibilities', 'existences', 'non-existences', 'necessities', and also 'values', to be utterly mistaken. His new views on the matter are expressed in a number of papers published in the second volume of the Kraus edition of *Psychologie*, and in a collection of letters and articles published by Kraus under the title of *Wahreit und Evidenz*. See, also, O. Kraus, *Franz Brentano*, Beck, Munich, 1919.

Brentano's discarded conception has, however, lived on in the theories of his pupils, and has been developed by Husserl into the theory of Phenomenology and by Meinong into the so-called 'General Theory of Objects'.

b Brentano's attempt, here, to give an account of what consciousness is, leaning on the traditional Aristotelian notion of 'mental inexistence of the object', he later considered inadequate. The so-called 'inexistence of the object', the 'immanent objectivity', should not be taken for a special kind of existence of a thing inside consciousness but rather for a confused description of the fact that one has something, or is related mentally to something (a thing, a *res*, a being), as an object. See O. Kraus' introduction to *Psychologie*, Vol. I, 1924, and also the appendix to Vol. II of the same edition (F. Meiner's *Philosophische Bibliothek*, volumes 192 and 193).

c This means that coloured surfaces, tunes, and so on could very well exist, because their existence in no way implies a contradiction. A critical approach convinces us, however, that our belief in these objects of the outer senses is purely instinctive, and natural science convinces us of its errors. In this paragraph, Brentano uses the term 'experience' in the widest sense, making Alexander Bain's usage his own. We should not forget, however, that trees and landscapes cannot be 'experienced', if by 'experienced' we mean 'given to our senses'.

d It has been alleged, with reference to this passage, that Brentano was a phenomenalist. This is the opposite of the truth, for Brentano has always been a decided opponent of phenomenalism. What he wanted to say was merely that coloured things, tunes filling space, etc., are objects to which we are intentionally related, but that at the same time there is no proof of the existence of such qualities filling space, so that our assertion of them when we sense them is probably erroneous. We should not forget that even if three-dimensional bodies exist but have no colour, our assertion of coloured expanses is false, for any assertion claims the existence of the whole content of the concept, and our sensations are nothing but assertive beliefs in that which we are sensing. These beliefs, these compulsory assertions of sensual qualities, are blind, lack inner logical justification, and differ in this respect from self-evident beliefs. According to all rules of induction and probability, it appears furthermore that these beliefs are probably false. Locke's experiment and Aristotle's ball experiment with crossed fingers should convince us of that. And yet certain ambiguities of language might still favour naive realism, as happens when physicists speak of 'pressure' without referring to the sensual quality which we experience when we 'feel' pressure.

e The expression 'reference to something as an object' is the one which is least ambiguous, and Brentano retained it in the later stages of his philosophy, while the expression 'mental inexistence of the object' he recognised as an imperfect description. He also spoke sometimes of 'making something one's object' or of 'having it for an object'.

f This means that 'mental phenomena' are present in the mind and believed in with a belief which is correct and even self-evident; 'physical phenomena' (coloured spots, tunes, and so on) are, on the other hand, believed in with an instinctive, uncontrollable urge. They are merely intentional, that is, merely objects for the mind, which only means that one senses them or imagines them, not that they actually exist.

14

G. H. LEWES

What I know as Myself is a Body, in one aspect, and a Soul, in the other. What I call my Body is a persistent aggregate of objective phenomena; and my Soul is a persistent aggregate of subjective phenomena: the one is an individualized group of experiences expressible in terms of Matter and Motion, and therefore designated *physical*; the other an individualized group of experiences expressible in terms of Feeling, and therefore designated *psychical*. But, however contrasted, they are both simply embodiments of Experience, that is to say, are Modes of Feeling. All Existence— as known to us—is the Felt. . . .

Whatever Philosophy may discover, it cannot displace the fact that I know I am a Soul, *in every sense in which that phrase represents Experience*: I know the Soul in knowing its concretes (feelings), and in knowing it as an abstraction which condenses those concretes in a symbol. The secondary question is, Whether this abstraction represents one Existent, and the abstraction Body another and wholly different Existent, or the two abstractions represent only two different Aspects? This may be debated, and must be answered according to theoretic probabilities.

What are the probabilities? We are all agreed that Consciousness is the final arbiter. Its primary deliverance is simply that of *a* radical distinction. It is silent on the nature of the distinction—says nothing as to whether the distinction is one of agents or of aspects. It says, 'I am a Soul'. With equal clearness it says, 'I am a Body'. It does *not* say, 'I am two things'. Nor does the fact of a radical distinction imply more than a contrast of aspects, such as that of convex and concave. The curve has at every point this contrast of convex and concave, and yet is the identical line throughout. A mental process is at every point contrasted with the physical process assumed to be its correlate; and this contrast demands equivalent expression in the terms of each. The identity underlying the two aspects of the curve is evident to Sense. The identity underlying the mental and physical process is not evident to Sense, but may be made eminently *probable* to Speculation, especially when we have explained the grounds of the difference, namely, that they are apprehended through different modes. But although I admit that the conclusion is only one of probability, it is one which greatly transcends the probability of any counter-hypothesis. Let us see how this can be made out.

We start from the position that a broad line of demarcation must be drawn between the mental and the physical aspect of a process, supposing them to be identical in reality. Nothing can be more *unlike* a logical proposition than the physical process which is its correlate; so that Philosophy has hitherto been forced to forego every attempt at an explanation of how the two can be causally connected: referring the connection to a mystery, or invoking two different agents, spiritual and material, moving on parallel lines, like two clocks regulated to work simultaneously. But having recognized this difference, can we not also discern fundamental resemblances? First and foremost, we note that there is common to both the basis in Feeling: they are both modes of Consciousness. The Mind thinking the logical proposition is not, indeed, in the same *state* as the Mind picturing the physical process which is the correlate of that logical proposition—no more than I, who see you move on being struck, have the same feelings as you who are struck. But the Mind which pictures the logical proposition as a process, and pictures the physical process as a bodily change, is contemplating one and the same event under its subjective and objective aspects; just as when I picture to myself the feelings you experience on being struck I separate the subjective aspect of the blow from its objective aspect. . . .

Let us approach the question on a more accessible side. Sensation avowedly lies at the basis of mental manifestations. Now, rightly or wrongly, Sensation is viewed alternately as a purely subjective fact—a psychological process—and as a purely objective fact—the physiological reaction of a sense-organ. It is so conspicuously a physiological process that many writers exclude it from the domain of Mind, assign it to the material organism, and believe that it is explicable on purely mechanical principles. This seems to me eminently disputable; but the point is noticed in proof of the well-marked objective character which the phenomenon assumes. In this aspect a sensation is simply the reaction of a bodily organ. The physiologist describes how a stimulus excites the organ, and declares its reaction to be the sensation. Thus viewed, and expressed in terms of Matter and Motion, there is absolutely nothing of that subjective quality which characterizes sensation. Yet without this quality the objective process cannot be a sensation. Exclude Feeling, and the excitation of the auditory organ will no more yield the sensation of Sound by its reaction, than the strings and sounding-board of a piano when the keys are struck will yield music to a deaf spectator. Hence the natural inference has been that inside the organism there is a *listener*: the Soul is said to listen, transforming excitation into sensation. . . .

Having recognized the distinction between the two processes objective and subjective, physical and mental, we have recognized the vanity of attempting to assign their limits, and to say where Motion ends and Feeling begins, or how Feeling again changes into Motion. The one does *not* begin where the other ends. According to the two-clock theory of Dualism, the two *agents* move on parallel lines. On the theory of Monism the two *aspects* are throughout opposed. Both theories explain the facts; which explanation is the most congruous with experience? Against the first we may object that the hypothesis of two Agents utterly unallied in nature wants the cardinal character of a fertile hypothesis in its unverifiableness: it may be true, we can never know that it is true. By the very terms of its definition, the Spirit—if that mean *more* than an abstract expression of sentient states—is beyond all sensible experience. This is indeed admitted by the dualists, for they postulate a Spirit merely because they cannot otherwise explain the phenomena of Consciousness. Herein they fail to see that even their postulate brings no explanation, it merely restates the old problem in other terms.

Up to the present time these same objections might have been urged with equal force against Monism. Indeed, although many philosophers have rejected the two-clock theory of Leibniz, they have gained a very hesitating acceptance of their own hypothesis of identity. To most minds the difficulty of imagining how a physical process could *also* be a psychical process, a movement also be a feeling, seemed not less than that of imagining how two such distinct Agents as Matter and Mind could co-operate, and react on each other, or move simultaneously on parallel lines. Although for many years I have accepted the hypothesis of Monism, I have always recognized its want of an adequate reply to such objections. Unless I greatly deceive myself, I have now found a solution of the main difficulty; and found it in psychological considerations which are perfectly intelligible. But knowing how easily one may deceive onself in such matters, I will only ask the reader to meditate with open-mindedness the considerations now to be laid before him, and see if he can feel the same confidence in their validity. . . .

Psychological investigation shows that the objects supposed to *have* forms, colours, and positions within an external hemisphere, have these only in virtue of the very feelings from which they are supposed to be separated. The *visible* universe exists only *as seen*: the objects are Reals conditioned by the laws of Sensibility. The space in which we see them, their geometrical relations, the light and shadows which reveal them, the forms they affect, the lines of their changing directions, the qualities which distinguish them—all these are but the externally projected signs of feelings. They are signs which we interpret according to organized laws of experience; each sign being itself a feeling connected with other feelings. . . .

One and the same object will necessarily present very different aspects under different subjective conditions, since it is *these* which determine the aspect. The object cannot be to Sight what it is to Hearing, to Touch what it is to Smell. The vibrations of a tuning-fork are seen as movements, heard as sounds. In current language the vibrations are said to cause the sounds. Misled by this, philosophers puzzle themselves as to how a material process (vibration) can be transformed into a mental process (sensation), how such a cause can have so utterly different an effect. But I have formerly[1] argued at some length that there is no transformation or causation of the kind supposed. The tuning-fork—or that Real which in relation to Sense is the particular object thus named—will, by one of its modes of acting on my Sensibility through my optical apparatus, determine the response known as *vibrations*; but it is not this response of the optical organ which is transformed into, or causes the response of the auditory organ, known as *sound*. The auditory organ knows nothing of vibrations, the optical nothing of sounds. The responses are both modes of Feeling determined by organic conditions, and represent the two different relations in which the Real is apprehended. The Real *is* alternately the one and the other. And if the one mode of Feeling has a physical significance, while the other has a mental significance, so that we regard the vibrations as objective facts, belonging to the external world, and the sounds as subjective facts, exclusively belonging to the internal world, this is due to certain psychological influences presently to be expounded. Meanwhile let us fix clearly in our minds that both vibrations and sounds are modes of Feeling. . . .

Assuming that a mental process is only another aspect of a physical process—and this we shall find the more probable hypothesis—we have to explain by what influences these diametrically opposite aspects are determined. From all that has just been said we must seek these in the modes of apprehension. There can be no doubt that we express the fact in very different terms; the question is, What do these terms *signify*? Why do we express one aspect in terms of Matter and Motion, assigning the process to the objective world; and the other aspect in terms of Feeling, assigning the process to the subjective world?

Let the example chosen be a logical process as the mental aspect, and a neural process as its physical correlate. The particular proposition may be viewed logically, as a grouping of experiences, or physiologically, as a grouping of neural tremors. Here we have the twofold aspect of one and the same reality; and these different aspects are expressed in different

[1] *Problems of Life and Mind*, vol. ii, pp. 417 and 466.

terms. We cannot be too rigorous in our separation of the terms; for every attentive student must have noted how frequently discussions are made turbid by the unconscious *shifting of terms* in the course of the argumentation. This is not only the mistake of opponents who are unaware of the shifting which has occurred in each other's minds, so that practically the adversaries do not meet on common ground, but cross and recross each other; it is also the mistake of the solitary thinker losing himself in the maze of interlacing conceptions instead of keeping steadily to one path. Only by such shifting of terms can the notion of the physical process causing, or being transformed into, the mental process for a moment gain credit; and this also greatly sustains the hypothesis of Dualism with its formidable objections: How can Matter think? How can Mind act on Matter causing Motion?

Those who recognized that the terms Matter and Mind were abstractions mutually exclusive, saw at once that these questions, instead of being formidable, were in truth irrational. To ask if Matter could think, or Mind move Matter, was a confusion of symbols equivalent to speaking of a yard of Hope, and a ton of Terror. Although Measure and Weight are symbols of Feeling, and in *this* respect are on a par with Hope and Terror, yet because they are objective symbols they cannot be applied to subjective states, without violation of the very significance they were invented to express. No one ever asks whether a sensation of Sound can be a sensation of Colour; nor whether Colour can move a machine, although Heat can, yet the one is no less a sensation than the other. On similar grounds no one should ask whether Matter can think, or Mind move Matter. The only rational question is one preserving the integrity of the terms, namely, whether the living, thinking organism presents itself to apprehension under the twofold aspect—now under the modes of Feeling classified as objective or physical; now under the modes classified as subjective or mental.

We are told that it is 'impossible to imagine Matter thinking', which is very true; only by a gross *confusion* of terms can Thought be called a property of cerebral tissue, or of Matter at all. We may, indeed, penetrate beneath the terms which relate to aspects, and recognize in the underlying reality not two existences, but one. Our conceptions of this reality, however, are expressed in symbols representing different classes of feelings, objective and subjective; and to employ the terms of one class to designate the conceptions of the other is to frustrate the very purposes of language. . . .

It is because we do know what Matter is, that we know it is *not* Mind: they are symbols of two different modes of Feeling. . . . In my Feeling, that which is not Me is Matter, the objective aspect of the Felt, as Mind is the subjective aspect. . . .

When we refer feelings to material conditions, we follow the natural tendency to translate the little known in terms of the better known, and employ the symbols Matter and Motion, because these furnish the intellect with images, i.e., definite and exact elements to operate with. In hearing a sound, there is nothing at all like 'vibrations', nothing like 'aerial waves' and 'neural processes', given in that feeling; but on attempting to *explain* it, we remove it from the sphere of Sensation to carry it into the sphere of Intellect, and we must change our symbols in changing our problem; here our only recourse is to translate the subjective state into an *imaginable* objective process, which can only be expressed in terms of Matter and Motion. What we *heard* as Sound is then *seen* as Vibration. When we are optically or mentally contemplating vibrations and neural processes, we are supplanting one source of feeling by another, translating an event in another set of symbols. But we can no more hear the sound in seeing the vibrations, than a blind man can see the fly in the amber which he feels with his fingers, or than we can feel the amber he holds, while we are only looking at it. The phrase 'material conditions of Feeling' sometimes designates the objective aspect of the subjective process, and sometimes the agencies in the external medium which co-operate with the organism in the production of the feelings. In each case there is an attempt to explain a feeling by intelligible symbols. . . .

'I see an elephant.' In other words, I am affected in a certain way, and interpret my affection by previous similar experiences, expressing these in verbal symbols. But I want an explanation, and this the philosopher vouchsafes to me by translating my affection into his terms. He takes me into another sphere—tells me of an undulating Ether, the waves of which beat upon my retina—of lines of Light refracted by media and converged by lenses according to geometric laws—of the formation thereby of a tiny image of the gigantic elephant on my retina as on the plate of a camera-obscura—this, and much more, is what *he* sees in *my* visual feeling, and he bids me see it also. Grateful for the novel instruction, I am compelled to say that it does not alter my vision of the elephant, does not make the fact a whit clearer, does not indeed correspond with what I feel. It is outside knowledge, valuable, as all knowledge is, but supplementary. It is translation into another language. And when I come to examine the translation, I find it very imperfect. I ask my instructor: Is it the tiny image on my retina which I see, and not the big elephant on the grass? And how do I see this retinal image, which you explain to be upside down?—how is it carried from my retina to my mind? I have no consciousness of tiny reversed image, none of my retina, only of a fact of feeling, which I call 'seeing an elephant'. The camera-obscura has no such feeling—it reflects the image, it does not see the object. Here my instructor, having reached the limit of his science, hands me over to the physiologist, who will translate the fact for me in terms not of Geometry, but of Anatomy and Physiology. The laws of Dioptrics cease at this point: the image they help to form on the retina is ruthlessly dispersed, and all its beautiful geometric construction is lost in a neural excitation, which is transmitted through semi-fluid channels of an optic tract to a semi-fluid ganglion, whence a thrill is shot through the whole brain, and is there *transformed* into a visual sensation. Again I fancy I have gained novel instruction of a valuable kind; but it does not affect my original experience that I am enabled to translate it into different terms; the less so because I cannot help the conviction that the translation is imperfect, leaving out the essential points. If a phrase be translated for me into French or German I gain thereby an addition to my linguistic knowledge, but the experience thus variously expressed remains unaffected. When the fact is expressed in geometrical or physiological terms, the *psychical process* finds no adequate expression. Neither in the details, nor in the totals, do I recognize any of the qualities of my state of feeling in seeing the elephant. I do not see the geometrical process, I do not see the anatomical mechanism, I see the elephant, and am conscious only of that feeling. You may consider my organism geometrically or anatomically, and bring it thus within the circle of objective knowledge; but my subjective experience, my spiritual existence, that of which I am most deeply assured, demands another expression. Nay more, on closely scrutinizing your objective explanations, it is evident that a psychical process is *implied* throughout—such terms as undulations, refractions, media, lenses, retina, neural excitation, overtly refer, indeed, to the material objective aspect of the facts, but they are themselves the modes of Feeling by which the facts are apprehended, and would not exist *as such* without the 'greeting of the spirit'.

What, then, is our conclusion? It is, that to make an adequate explanation of psychical processes by material conditions we must first establish an equivalence between the subjective and objective aspects; and, having taken this step, we must complete it by showing wherein the difference exists; having established this identity and diversity, we have solved the problem.

Let us attempt this solution. . . . In thinking a proposition, we are logically grouping verbal symbols representative of sensible experiences; and this is a quite peculiar state of Consciousness, wholly unlike what would arise in the mental or visual contemplation of the neural grouping, which is its physiological equivalent. But this diversity does not discredit the idea of their identity; and although some of my readers will protest against such an idea, and will affirm that the logical process is not a process taking place in the organism at all, but in a spirit which uses the organism

F

as its instrument, I must be allowed in this exposition to consider the identity established, my purpose being to explain the diversity necessarily accompanying it. Therefore, I say, that although a logical process is identical with a neural process, it must appear differently when the modes of apprehending it are different. While you are thinking a logical proposition, grouping your verbal symbols, I, who mentally *see* the process, am grouping a totally different set of symbols: to you the proposition is a subjective state, i.e., a *state* of feeling, not an *object* of feeling: to become an object, it must be apprehended by objective modes: and this it can become to you as to me, when we see it as a process, or imagine it as a process. But obviously your state in seeing or imagining the process must be different from your state when the process itself is passing, since the modes of apprehension are so different. There may be every ground for concluding that a logical process has its correlative physical process, and that the two processes are merely two aspects of one event; but because we cannot apprehend the one aspect as we apprehend the other, cannot *see* the logical sequence as we *see* the physical sequence, this difference in our modes of apprehension compels us to separate the two, assigning one to the subjective, the other to the objective class. . . .

Our intelligible universe is constructed out of the elements of Feeling according to certain classifications, the broadest of which is that into external and internal, object and subject. The abstractions Matter and Mind once formed and fixed in representative symbols, are easily accredited as two different Reals. But the separation is ideal, and is really a distinction of Aspects. We know ourselves as Body-Mind; we do not know ourselves as Body *and* Mind, if by that be meant two coexistent independent Existents.

Let us now pass to another consideration, namely, whether Consciousness —however interpreted—is legitimately conceived as a factor in the so-called conscious and voluntary actions; or is it merely a *collateral result* of certain organic activities? To answer this, we must first remember that Consciousness is a purely subjective process; although we may believe it to be objectively a neural process, we are nevertheless passing out of the region of Physiology when we speak of Feeling determining Action. Motion may determine Motion; but Feeling can only determine Feeling. Yet we do so speak, and are justified. For thereby we implicitly declare, what Psychology explicitly teaches, namely, that these two widely different aspects, objective and subjective, are but the two faces of one and the same reality. It is thus indifferent whether we say a sensation is a neural process, or a mental process: a molecular change in the nervous system or a change in Feeling. It is either, and it is both, as I have elsewhere explained.[1] There it was argued that the current hypothesis of a neural process *causing* the mental process— molecular movement being in some mysterious way transformed into sensation—is not only inconceivable, but altogether unnecessary; whereas the hypothesis that the two aspects of the one phenomenon are simply two different expressions, now in terms of Matter and Motion, and now in terms of Consciousness, is in harmony with all the inductive evidence.

'It may be assumed,' says Professor Huxley, 'that molecular changes in the brain are the causes of all the states of consciousness of brutes. Is there any evidence that these states of consciousness may conversely cause those molecular changes which give rise to muscular motion? I see no such evidence. The frog walks, hops, swims, and goes through his gymnastic performances, quite as well without consciousness, and consequently without volition, as with it; and if a frog in his natural state possesses anything corresponding with what we call volition, there is no reason to think that *it is anything but a concomitant of the molecular changes in the brain, which form part of the series involved in the production of motion.* The consciousness of brutes would appear to be related to the mechanism of their body simply as a collateral product of its working, and to be *as completely without any power of modifying that working as the steam-whistle which accompanies the work of a locomotive engine is without influence upon its machinery.* Their volition, if they have any, is an emotion *indicative* of physical changes, not a *cause* of such changes.' Particular attention is called to the passages in italics. In the first is expressed a view which seems not unlike the one I am advocating, but which is contradicted by the second. Let us consider what is implied.

When Consciousness is regarded solely under its subjective aspect there is obviously no place for it among material agencies, regarded as objective. So long as we have the material mechanism in view we have nothing but material changes. This applies to the frog, with or without its brain; to man, supposed to be moved by volition, or supposed to move automatically. The introduction of Consciousness is not the introduction of another agent in the series, but of a new aspect; the neural process drops out of sight, the mental process replaces it. The question whether we have any ground for inferring that in the series there is included the particular neural state which subjectively is a state of Consciousness, must be answered according to the evidence. Well, the evidence shows that the actions do involve the co-operation; and this Professor Huxley expresses when he says that the molecular changes in the brain form part of the series involved in the production of motion. Whether we regard the process objectively as a series of molecular changes, or subjectively as a

[1] *Problems*, vol. ii, p. 457, *sq.*

succession of sentient changes, the sum of which is on the one side a motor impulse, on the other a state of consciousness, we must declare Consciousness to be an agent, *in the same sense that we declare one change in the organism to be an agent in some other change.* The facts are the same, whether we express them in physiological or in psychological terms.

15

W. K. CLIFFORD

ON THE NATURE OF THINGS-IN-THEMSELVES (1878)

Meaning of the Individual Object

My feelings arrange and order themselves in two distinct ways. There is the internal or subjective order, in which sorrow succeeds the hearing of bad news, or the abstraction 'dog' symbolizes the perception of many different dogs. And there is the external or objective order, in which the sensation of letting go is followed by the sight of a falling object and the sound of its fall. The objective order, *qua* order, is treated by physical science, which investigates the uniform relations of *objects* in time and space. Here the word *object* (or *phenomenon*) is taken merely to mean a group of my feelings, which persists as a group in a certain manner; for I am at present considering only the objective order cf my feelings. The object, then, is a set of changes *in* my consciousness, and not anything out of it. Here is as yet no metaphysical doctrine, but only a fixing of the meaning of a word. We may subsequently find reason to infer that there is something which is not object, but which corresponds in a certain way with the object; this will be a metaphysical doctrine, and neither it nor its denial is involved in the present determination of meaning. But the determination must be taken as extending to all those inferences which are made by science in the objective order. If I hold that there is hydrogen in the sun, I mean that if I could get some of it in a bottle, and explode it with half its volume of oxygen, I should get that group of possible sensations which we call 'water'. The inferences of physical science are all inferences of my real or possible feelings; inferences of something actually or potentially in my consciousness, not of anything outside it.

Distinction of Object and Eject

There are, however, some inferences which are profoundly different from those of physical science. When I come to the conclusion that *you* are conscious, and that there are objects in your consciousness similar to those in mine, I am not inferring any actual or possible feelings of my own, but *your* feelings, which are not, and cannot by any possibility become objects in my consciousness. The complicated processes of your body and the motions of your brain and nervous system, inferred from evidence of anatomical researches, are all inferred as things possibly visible to me. However remote the inference of physical science, the thing inferred is always a part of me, a possible set of changes in my consciousness bound up in the objective order with other known changes. But the inferred existence of your feelings, of objective groupings among them similar to those among my feelings, and of a subjective order in many respects analogous to my own—these inferred existences are in the very act of inference *thrown out* of my consciousness, recognized as outside of it, as *not* being a part of me. I propose, accordingly, to call these inferred existences *ejects*, things thrown out of my consciousness, to distinguish them from *objects*, things presented in my consciousness, phenomena. It is to be noticed that there is a set of changes of my consciousness symbolic of the eject, which may be called my conception of you; it is (I think) a rough picture of the whole aggregate of my consciousness, under imagined circumstances like yours; *qua* group of my feelings, this conception is like the object in substance and constitution, but differs from it in implying the existence of something that is not itself, but corresponds to it, namely, of the eject. The existence of the object, whether perceived or inferred, carries with it a group of beliefs; these are always beliefs in the future sequence of certain of my feelings. The existence of this table, for example, as an object in my consciousness carries with it the belief that if I climb up on it I shall be able to walk about on it as if it were the ground. But the existence of my conception of you in my consciousness carries with it a belief in the existence of you outside of my consciousness, a belief which can never be expressed in terms of the future sequence of my feelings. How this inference is justified, how consciousness can testify to the existence of anything outside of itself, I do not pretend to say; I need not untie a knot which the world has cut for me long ago. It may very well be that I myself am the only existence, but it is simply ridiculous to suppose that anybody else is. The position of absolute idealism may, therefore, be left out of count, although each individual may be unable to justify his dissent from it.

Formation of the Social Object

The belief, however, in the existence of other men's consciousness, in the existence of ejects, dominates every thought and every action of our lives. In the first place, it profoundly modifies the object. This room, the table, the chairs, your bodies, are all objects in my consciousness; as simple objects, they are parts of me. But I, somehow, infer the existence of similar objects in your consciousness, and these are not objects to me, nor can they ever be made so; they are ejects. This being so, I bind up with each object as it exists in my mind the thought of similar objects existing in other men's minds; and I thus form the complex conception, 'this table, as an object in the minds of men'—or, as Mr Shadworth Hodgson puts it, an object of consciousness in general. This conception symbolizes an indefinite number of ejects, together with one object which the conception of each eject more or less resembles. Its character is therefore mainly ejective in respect of what it symbolizes, but mainly objective in respect of its nature. I shall call this complex conception the *social object*; it is a symbol of one thing (the *individual object*, it may be called for distinction's sake) which is in my consciousness, and of an indefinite number of other things which are ejects and out of my consciousness. . . .

Difference between Mind and Body

Your body is an object in my consciousness; your mind is not, and never can be. Being an object, your body follows the laws of physical science, which deals with the objective order of my feelings. . . . Every question about your body is a question about the physical laws of matter, and about nothing else. To say: 'Up to this point science can explain; here the soul steps in', is not to say what is untrue, but to talk nonsense. If evidence were found that the matter constituting the brain behaved otherwise than ordinary matter, or if it were impossible to describe vital actions as particular examples of general physical rules, this would be a fact in physics, a fact relating to the motion of matter; and it must either be explained by further elaboration of physical science, or else our conception of the objective order of our feelings would have to be changed. The question, 'Is the mind a force?' is condemned by similar considerations. A certain variable quality of matter (the rates of change of its motion) is found to be invariably connected with the position relatively to it of other matter; considered as expressed in terms of this position, the quality is called Force. Force is thus an abstraction relating to *objective* facts; it is a mode of grouping of my feelings, and cannot possibly be the same thing as an eject, another man's consciousness. But the question: 'Do the changes in a man's consciousness *run parallel* with the changes of motion, and therefore with the forces in his brain?' is a real question, and not *prima facie* nonsense. . . .

Correspondence of Elements of Mind and Brain-Action

The parallelism here meant is a parallelism of complexity, an analogy of structure. . . . I need not set down here the evidence which shows that the complexity of consciousness is paralleled by complexity of action in the brain. It is only necessary to point out what appears to me to be a consequence of the discoveries of Müller and Helmholtz in regard to sensation: that at least those distinct feelings which can be remembered and examined by reflection are paralleled by changes in a portion of the brain only. In the case of sight, for example, there is a message taken from things outside to the retina, and therefrom sent in somewhither by the optic nerve; now we can tap this telegraph at any point and produce the sensation of sight, without any impression on the retina. It seems to follow that what is known *directly* is what takes place at the inner end of this nerve, or that the consciousness of sight is simultaneous and parallel in complexity with the changes in the grey matter at the internal extremity, and not with the changes in the nerve itself, or in the retina. So also a pain in a particular part of the body may be mimicked by neuralgia due to lesion of another part.

We come, finally, to say then that as your consciousness is made up of elementary feelings grouped together in various ways (ejective facts), so a part of the action in your brain is made up of more elementary actions in parts of it, grouped together *in the same ways* (objective facts). The knowledge of this correspondence is a help to the analysis of both sets of facts; but it teaches us in particular that any feeling, however apparently simple, which can be retained and examined by reflection, is already itself a most complex structure. We may, however, conclude that this correspondence extends to the elements, and that each simple feeling corresponds to a special comparatively simple change of nerve-matter.

The Elementary Feeling is a Thing-in-itself

The conclusion that elementary feeling co-exists with elementary brain-motion in the same way as consciousness co-exists with complex brain-motion, involves more important consequences than might at first sight appear. We have regarded consciousness as a complex of feelings, and explained the fact that the complex is conscious, as depending on the mode of complication. But does not the elementary feeling itself imply a consciousness in which alone it can exist, and of which it is a modification? Can a feeling exist by itself, without forming part of a consciousness? I shall say *no* to the first question, and *yes* to the second, and it seems to me that these answers are required by the doctrine of evolution. For if that doctrine be true, we shall have along the line of the human pedigree a series of imperceptible steps connecting inorganic matter with ourselves. To the later members of that series we must undoubtedly ascribe consciousness, although it must, of course, have been simpler than our own. But where are we to stop? In the case of organisms of a certain complexity, consciousness is inferred. As we go back along the line, the complexity of the organism and of its nerve-action insensibly diminishes; and for the first part of our course, we see reason to think that the complexity of consciousness insensibly diminishes also. But if we make a jump, say to the tunicate molluscs, we see no reason there to infer the existence of consciousness at all. Yet not only is it impossible to point out a place where any sudden break takes place, but it is contrary to all the natural training of our minds to suppose a breach of continuity so great. All this imagined line of organisms is a series of objects in my consciousness; they form an insensible gradation, and yet there is a certain unknown point at which I am at liberty to infer facts *out* of my consciousness corresponding to them! There is only one way out of the difficulty, and to that we are driven. Consciousness is a complex of ejective facts—of elementary feelings, or rather of those remoter elements which cannot even be felt, but of which the simplest feeling is built up. Such elementary ejective facts go along with the action of every organism, however simple; but it is only when the material organism has reached a certain complexity of nervous structure (not now to be specified) that the complex of ejective facts reaches that mode of complication which is called Consciousness. But as the line of ascent is unbroken, and must end at last in inorganic matter, we have no choice but to admit that every motion of matter is simultaneous with some ejective fact or event which might be part of a consciousness. From this follow two important corollaries.

1. A feeling can exist by itself, without forming part of a consciousness. It does not depend for its existence on the consciousness of which it may form a part. Hence a feeling (or an eject-element) is *Ding-an-sich*, an absolute, whose existence is not relative to anything else. *Sentitur* is all that can be said.

2. These eject-elements, which correspond to motions of matter, are connected together in their sequence and co-existence by counterparts of the physical laws of matter. For otherwise the correspondence could not be kept up.

Mind-stuff is the reality which we perceive as Matter

That element of which, as we have seen, even the simplest feeling is a complex, I shall call *Mind-stuff*. A moving molecule of inorganic matter does not possess mind, or consciousness; but it possesses a small piece of mind-stuff. When molecules are so combined together as to form the film on the under side of a jelly-fish, the elements of mind-stuff which go along with them are so combined as to form the faint beginnings of Sentience. When the molecules are so combined as to form the brain and nervous system of a vertebrate, the corresponding elements of mind-stuff are so combined as to form some kind of consciousness; that is to say, changes in the complex which take place at the same time get so linked together that the repetition of one implies the repetition of the other. When matter takes the complex form of a living human brain, the corresponding mind-stuff takes the form of a human consciousness, having intelligence and volition.

Suppose that I see a man looking at a candlestick. Both of these are objects, or phenomena, in my mind. An *image* of the candlestick, in the optical sense, is formed upon his retina, and nerve messages go from all parts of this to form what we may call a *cerebral image* somewhere in the neighbourhood of the optic thalami in the inside of his brain. This cerebral image is a certain complex of disturbances in the matter of these organs; it is a material or physical fact, therefore a group of my possible sensations, just as the candlestick is. The cerebral image is an imperfect representation of the candlestick, corresponding to it point for point in a certain way. Both the candlestick and the cerebral image are matter; but one material complex *represents* the other material complex in an imperfect way.

Now the candlestick is not the external reality whose existence is represented in the man's mind; for the candlestick is mere perception in *my* mind. Nor is the cerebral image the man's perception of the candle-stick; for the cerebral image is merely an idea of a possible perception in my mind. But there *is* a perception in the man's mind, which we may call the *mental image*; and this corresponds to some external reality. *The external reality bears the same relation to the mental image that the (phenomenal) candle-stick bears to the cerebral image.* Now the candlestick and the cerebral image are both matter; they are made of the same stuff. Therefore the external reality is made of the same stuff as the man's perception or mental image, that is, it is made of mind-stuff. And as the cerebral image represents imperfectly the candlestick, in the same way and to the same extent the mental image represents the reality external to his consciousness. Thus in order to find the thing-in-itself which is represented by any object in my consciousness, such as a candlestick, I have to solve this question in pro-portion, or rule of three:

As the physical configuration of my cerebral image of the object
   is to the physical configuration of the object,
   so is my perception of the object (the object regarded as complex of my feelings)
   to the thing-in-itself.

Hence we are obliged to identify the thing-in-itself with that complex of elementary mind-stuff which on other grounds we have seen reason to think of as going along with the material object. Or, to say the same thing in other words, the reality external to our minds which is represented in our minds as matter, is in itself mind-stuff.

The universe, then, consists entirely of mind-stuff. Some of this is woven into the complex form of human minds, containing imperfect representations also, as a mirror reflects its own image in another mirror, *ad infinitum*. Such an imperfect representation is called a material universe. It is a picture in a man's mind of the real universe of mind-stuff.

The two chief points of this doctrine may be thus summed up:

Matter is a mental picture in which mind-stuff is the thing represented.

Reason, intelligence, and volition are properties of a complex which is made up of elements themselves not rational, not intelligent, not conscious.

Note. The doctrine here expounded appears to have been arrived at independently by many persons; as was natural, seeing that it is (or seems to me) a necessary consequence of recent advances in the theory of perception. Kant threw out a suggestion that the *Ding-an-sich* might be of the nature of mind; but the first statement of the doctrine in its true connection that I know of, is by Wundt. Since it dawned on me, some time ago, I have supposed myself to find it more or less plainly hinted at in many writings; but the question is one in which it is peculiarly difficult to make out precisely what another man means, and even what one means oneself.

Some writers (e.g. Dr Tyndall) have used the word *matter* to mean the phenomenon *plus* the reality represented; and there are many reasons in favour of such usage in general. But for the purposes of the present discussion I have thought it clearer to use the word for the phenomenon as distinguished from the thing-in-itself.

16

ERNST MACH

Colours, sounds, temperatures, pressures, spaces, times, and so forth, are connected with one another in manifold ways; and with them are associated moods of mind, feelings, and volitions. Out of this fabric, that which is relatively more fixed and permanent stands prominently forth, engraves itself in the memory, and expresses itself in language. Relatively greater permanency exhibit, first, certain *complexes* of colours, sounds, pressures, and so forth, connected in time and space, which therefore receive special names, and are designated *bodies*. Absolutely permanent such complexes are not.

My table is now brightly, now dimly lighted. Its temperature varies. It may receive an ink stain. One of its legs may be broken. It may be repaired, polished, and replaced part for part. But for me, amid all its changes, it remains the table at which I daily write.

My friend may put on a different coat. His countenance may assume a serious or a cheerful expression. His complexion, under the effects of light or emotion, may change. His shape may be altered by motion, or be definitely changed. Yet the number of the permanent features presented, compared with the number of the gradual alterations, is always so great, that the latter may be overlooked. It is the same friend with whom I take my daily walk.

My coat may receive a stain, a tear. My very manner of expression shows that we are concerned here with a sum-total of permanency, to which the new element is added and from which that which is lacking is subsequently taken away.

Our greater intimacy with this sum-total of permanency, and its preponderance as contrasted with the changeable, impel us to the partly instinctive, partly voluntary and conscious economy of mental representation and designation, as expressed in ordinary thought and speech. That which is perceptually represented in a single image receives a *single* designation, a *single* name.

As relatively permanent, is exhibited, further, that complex of memories, moods, and feelings, joined to a particular body (the human body), which is denominated the 'I' or 'Ego'. I may be engaged upon this or that subject, I may be quiet or animated, excited or ill-humoured. Yet, pathological cases apart, enough durable features remain to identify the ego. Of course, the ego also is only of relative permanency. . . .

The useful habit of designating such relatively permanent compounds by *single* names, and of apprehending them by *single* thoughts, without going to the trouble each time of an analysis of their component parts, is apt to come into strange conflict with the tendency to isolate the component parts. The vague image which we have of a given permanent complex, being an image which does not perceptibly change when one or another of the component parts is taken away, gradually establishes itself as something which exists *by itself*. Inasmuch as it is possible to take away *singly* every constituent part without destroying the capacity of the image to *stand for* the totality and of being recognized again, it is imagined that it is possible to subtract *all* the parts and to have something still remaining. Thus arises the monstrous notion of a *thing in itself*, unknowable and different from its 'phenomenal' existence.

Thing, body, matter, are nothing apart from their complexes of colours, sounds, and so forth—nothing apart from their so-called attributes. That Protean, supposititious problem, which springs up so much in philosophy, of a *single* thing with *many* attributes, arises wholly from a mistaking of the fact, that summary comprehension and precise analysis, although both are provisionally justifiable and for many purposes profitable, cannot and must not be carried on *simultaneously*. . . .

The ego, and the relation of bodies to the ego, give rise to similar pseudo-problems, the character of which may be briefly indicated as follows:

Let those complexes of colours, sounds, and so forth, commonly called bodies, be designated, for the sake of simplicity, by ABC; the complex, known as our own body, which constitutes a part of the former, may be called KLM; the complex composed of volitions, memory-images, and the rest, we shall represent by $\alpha\beta\gamma$. Usually, now, the complex $\alpha\beta\gamma$, KLM, as making up the ego, is opposed to the complex ABC, as making up the world of substance; sometimes, also, $\alpha\beta\gamma$ is viewed as ego, and KLM, ABC, as world of substance. Now, at first blush, ABC appears independent of the ego, and opposed to it as a separate existence. But this independence is only relative, and gives way upon closer inspection. Much, it is true, may change in the complex $\alpha\beta\gamma$ without a perceptible change being induced in ABC; and *vice versa*. But many changes in $\alpha\beta\gamma$ do pass, by way of changes in KLM, to ABC; and *vice versa*. (As, for example, when powerful ideas burst forth into acts, or our environment induces noticeable changes in our body.) At the same time the group KLM, appears to be more intimately connected with $\alpha\beta\gamma$ and with ABC, than the latter do with one another; relations which find their expression in common thought and speech.

Precisely viewed, however, it appears that the group ABC is *always* codetermined by KLM. A cube of wood when seen close at hand, looks large; when seen at a distance, small; it looks different with the right eye from what it does with the left; sometimes it appears double; with closed eyes it is invisible. The properties of the same body, therefore, appear modified by our own body; they appear conditioned by it. But where, now, is that *same* body, which to the appearance is so *different*? All that can be said is, that with different KLM different ABC are associated.

We see an object having a point S. If we touch S, that is, bring it into connection with our body, we receive a prick. We can see S, without feeling the prick. But as soon as we feel the prick we find S. The visible point, therefore, is a *permanent fact* or *nucleus*, to which the prick is annexed, according to circumstances, as something accidental. From the frequency of such occurrences we ultimately accustom ourselves to regard *all* properties of bodies as 'effects' proceeding from permanent nuclei and conveyed to the ego through the medium of the body; which effects we call *sensations*. By this operation, however, our imagined nuclei are deprived of their entire sensory contents, and converted into mere mental symbols. The assertion, then, is correct that the world consists only of our sensations. In which case we have knowledge *only* of sensations, and the assumption of the nuclei referred to, or of a reciprocal action between them, from which sensations proceed, turns out to be quite idle and superfluous. Such a view can only suit with a half-hearted realism or a half-hearted philosophical criticism.

Ordinarily the complex $\alpha\beta\gamma$ KLM is contrasted as ego with the complex ABC. Those elements only of ABC that more strongly alter $\alpha\beta\gamma$, as a prick, a pain, are wont to be comprised in the ego. Afterwards, however, through observations of the kind just referred to, it appears that the right to annex ABC to the ego nowhere ceases. In conformity with this view the ego can be so extended as ultimately to embrace the entire world. The ego is not sharply marked off, its limits are very indefinite and arbitrarily displaceable. Only by failing to observe this fact, and by unconsciously narrowing those limits, while at the same time we enlarge them, arise, in the conflict of points of view, the metaphysical difficulties met with in this connection.

As soon as we have perceived that the supposed unities 'body' and 'ego' are only makeshifts, designed for provisional survey and for certain practical ends (so that we may take hold of bodies, protect *ourselves* against pain, and so forth) we find ourselves obliged, in many profound scientific investigations, to abandon them as insufficient and inappropriate. The antithesis of ego and world, sensation (phenomenon) and thing, then vanishes, and we have simply to deal with the *connection* of the *elements* $\alpha\beta\gamma$, ABC, KLM, of which this antithesis was only a partially appropriate and imperfect expression. This connection is nothing more nor less than the combination of the above-mentioned elements with other similar elements (time and space). Science has simply to *accept* this connection, and to set itself aright (get its bearings) in the intellectual environment which is thereby furnished, without attempting to explain its existence.

On a superficial examination the complex $\alpha\beta\gamma$ appears to be made up of much more evanescent elements than ABC and KLM in which last the elements seem to be connected with greater *stability* and *in a more permanent manner* (being joined to solid nuclei as it were). Although on closer inspection the elements of all complexes prove to be *homogeneous*, yet in spite of the knowledge of this fact, the early notion of an antithesis of body and spirit easily regains the ascendancy in the mind. The philosophical spiritualist is often sensible of the difficulty of imparting the needed solidity to his mind-created world of bodies; the materialist is at a loss when required to endow the world of matter with sensation. The *monistic* point of view, which artificial reflection has evolved, is easily clouded by our older and more powerful instinctive notions.

The difficulty referred to is particularly felt in the following case. In the complex ABC, which we have called the world of matter, we find as parts, not only our own body KLM, but also the bodies of other persons (or animals) $K'L'M'$, $K''L''M''$, to which, on analogy, we imagine other $\alpha'\beta'\gamma'$, $\alpha''\beta''\gamma''$, annexed, similar to $\alpha\beta\gamma$. So long as we deal with $K'L'M'$, we find ourselves in a thoroughly familiar province at every point sensorially accessible to us. When, however, we inquire after the sensations or feelings appurtenant to the body $K'L'M'$, we no longer find the elements we seek in the province of sense: *we add them in thought*. Not only is the domain which we now enter far less familiar to us, but the transition into it is also relatively unsafe. We have the feeling as if we were plunging into an abyss. Persons who adopt this method only, will never thoroughly rid themselves of this sense of insecurity, which is a frequent source of illusive problems.

But we are not restricted to this course. Let us consider, first, the reciprocal relations of the elements of the complex ABC, without regarding KLM (our body). All physical investigations are of this sort. A white bullet falls upon a bell; a sound is heard. The bullet turns yellow before a sodium lamp, red before a lithium lamp. Here the elements (ABC) appear to be connected only *with one another* and to be independent of our body (KLM). But if we take santonine, the bullet again turns yellow. If we press one eye to the side, we see two bullets. If we close our eyes entirely, we see none at all. If we sever the auditory nerve, no sound is heard. The elements ABC, therefore, are not only connected among one another, but also with KLM. To this extent, and to this extent *only*, do we call ABC *sensations*, and regard ABC as belonging to the ego. In this way, accordingly, we do not find the gap between bodies and sensations above described, between what is without and what is within, between the material world and the spiritual world. All elements ABC, KLM constitute a *single* coherent mass only, in which, when any one element is disturbed, *all* is put in motion; except that a disturbance in KLM has a more extensive and profound action than in ABC. A magnet in our neighbourhood disturbs the particles of iron near it; a falling boulder shakes the earth; but the severing of a nerve sets in motion the *whole* system of elements.

That traditional gulf between physical and psychological research, accordingly, exists only for the habitual stereotyped method of observation. A colour is a physical object so long as we consider its dependence upon its luminous source, upon other colours, upon heat, upon space, and so forth. Regarding, however, its dependence upon the retina (the elements KLM), it becomes a psychological object, a sensation. Not the subject, but the direction of our investigation, is different in the two domains.

Both in reasoning from the observation of the bodies of other men or animals, to the sensations which they possess, as well as in investigating the influence of our own body upon our own sensations, we must complete observed facts by analogy. This is accomplished with much greater readiness and certainty, when it relates, say, only to nervous processes, which cannot be fully observed in our own bodies—that is, when it is carried out in the more familiar physical domain—than when it is made in connection with psychical processes. Otherwise there is no essential difference. . . .

Reference has already been made to the different character of the groups of elements designated by ABC and αβγ. As a matter of fact, when we *see* a green tree before us, or *remember* a green tree, that is, represent a green tree to ourselves, we are perfectly aware of the difference of the two cases. The represented tree has a much less determinate, a much more changeable form; its green is much paler and more evanescent; and, what is of especial note, it is plainly situate in a *different* domain. A movement that we *propose* to execute is never more than a represented movement, and appears in a different sphere from that of the executed movement, which always takes place when the image is vivid enough. The statement that the elements A and α appear in different spheres, means, if we go to the bottom of it, simply this, that these elements are united with different other elements. Thus far, therefore, the fundamental constituents of ABC, $\alpha\beta\gamma$, would seem to be *the same* (colours, sounds, spaces, times, motor sensations), and only the character of their connection different.

Ordinarily pleasure and pain are regarded as different from sensations. Yet not only tactile sensations, but all other kinds of sensations, may pass gradually into pleasure and pain. Pleasure and pain also may be justly termed sensations. Only they are not so well analysed and so familiar as the common sensations. In fact, sensations of pleasure and pain, however faint they may be, really make up the contents of all so-called emotions. Thus, perceptions, ideas, volition, and emotion, in short the whole inner and outer world, are composed of a small number of homogeneous elements connected in relations of varying evanescence or permanence. Usually, these elements are called sensations. But as vestiges of a one-sided theory inhere in that term, we prefer to speak simply of *elements*, as we have already done. The aim of all research is to ascertain the mode of connection of these elements.

That in this complex of elements, which fundamentally is *one*, the boundaries of bodies and of the ego do not admit of being established in a manner definite and sufficient for all cases, has already been remarked. The comprehending of the elements that are most intimately connected with pleasure and pain, under one ideal mental-economical unity, the ego, is a work of the highest significance for the intellect in the functions which it performs for the pain-avoiding, pleasure-seeking will. The delimitation of the ego, therefore, is instinctively effected, is rendered familiar, and possibly becomes fixed through heredity. Owing to their high practical value, not only for the individual, but for the entire species, the composites 'ego' and 'body' assert instinctively their claims, and operate with all the power of natural elements. In special cases, however, in which practical ends are not concerned, but where knowledge is an object in itself, the delimitation in question may prove to be insufficient, obstructive, and untenable.

The primary fact is not the I, the ego, but the elements (sensations). The elements *constitute* the *I*. I have the sensation green, signifies that the element green occurs in a given complex of other elements (sensations, memories). When *I* cease to have the sensation green, when *I* die, then the elements no longer occur in their ordinary, familiar way of association. That is all. Only an ideal mental-economical unity, not a real unity, has ceased to exist.

If a knowledge of the connection of the elements (sensations) does not suffice us, and we ask, *Who* possessed this connection of sensations, *Who* experiences the sensations? then we have succumbed to the habit of subsuming every element (every sensation) under some *unanalysed* complex, and we are falling back imperceptibly upon an older, lower, and more limited point of view.[1]

The so-called unity of consciousness is not an argument in point. Since the apparent antithesis of *real* world and *perceived* world is due entirely to our mode of view, and no actual gulf exists between them, a rich and variously interconnected content of consciousness is in no respect more difficult to understand than a rich and diversified interconnection of the world.

If we regard the ego as a *real* unity, we become involved in the following dilemma: either we must set over against the ego a world of unknowable entities (which would be quite idle and purposeless), or we must regard the whole world, the egos of other people included, as comprised in our own ego (a proposition to which it is difficult to yield serious assent).

But if we take the ego simply as a *practical* unity, put together for purposes of provisional survey, or simply as a more strongly coherent group of elements, less strongly connected with other groups of this kind, questions like those above discussed will not arise and research will have an unobstructed future.

In his philosophical notes Lichtenberg says: 'We become conscious of certain percepts that are not dependent upon us; of others that we at least think are dependent upon us. Where is the border-line? We know only the existence of our sensations, percepts, and thoughts. We should say, *It thinks*, just as we say, *It lightens*. It is going too far to say, *cogito*, if we translate *cogito* by *I think*. The assumption, or postulation, of the ego is a mere practical necessity.' Though the method by which Lichtenberg arrived at this result is somewhat different from ours, we must nevertheless give our full assent to his conclusion.

[1] The habit of treating the unanalysed ego-complex as an indiscerptible unity frequently assumes in science remarkable forms. First, the nervous system is separated from the body as the seat of the sensations. In the nervous system again, the brain is selected as the organ best fitted for this end, and finally, to save the supposed psychical unity, a *point* is sought in the brain as the seat of the soul. But such crude conceptions are hardly fit even to foreshadow the roughest outlines of what future research will do for the connection of the physical and the psychical. The fact that the different organs of sensation and memory are physically *connected* with, and can be readily *excited* by, one another, is probably the foundation of the 'psychical unity'.

I once heard the question seriously discussed, 'How the precept of a large tree could find room in the little head of a man?' Now, although this 'problem' is no problem, yet it renders us vividly sensible of the absurdity that can be committed by thinking sensations spatially into the brain. When I speak of the sensations of *another* person, those sensations are, of course, not exhibited in my optical or physical space; they are mentally added, and I conceive them *causally*, not spatially, annexed to the brain observed or represented. When I speak of *my own* sensations, these sensations do not exist spatially in my head, but rather my 'head' *shares* with them the same spatial field.

Bodies do not produce sensations, but complexes of sensations (complexes of elements) make up bodies. If, to the physicist, bodies appear the real, abiding existences, whilst sensations are regarded merely as their evanescent, transitory show, the physicist forgets, in the assumption of such a view, that all bodies are but thought-symbols for complexes of sensations (complexes of elements). Here, too, the *elements* form the real, immediate, and ultimate foundation, which it is the task of physiological research to investigate. By the recognition of this fact, many points of psychology and physics assume more distinct and more economical forms, and many spurious problems are disposed of.

For us, therefore, the world does not consist of mysterious entities, which by their interaction with another, equally mysterious entity, the ego, produce sensations, which alone are accessible. For us, colours, sounds, spaces, times, are the ultimate elements, whose given connection it is our business to investigate. In this investigation we must not allow ourselves to be impeded by such intellectual abridgments and delimitations as body, ego, matter, mind, etc., which have been formed for special, practical purposes and with wholly provisional and limited ends in view. On the contrary, the fittest forms of thought must be created in and by that research *itself*, just as is done in every special science. In place of the traditional, instinctive ways of thought, a freer, fresher view, conforming to developed experience, must be substituted.

17

G. J. ROMANES

MIND AND MOTION (1885)

Although we are still very far from understanding the operations of the brain in thought, there can be no longer any question that in these operations of the brain we have what I may term the objective machinery of thought. 'Not every thought to every thought succeeds indifferently', said Hobbes. Starting from this fact, modern physiology has clearly shown why it is a fact; and looking to the astonishing rate at which the science of physiology is now advancing, I think we may fairly expect that within a time less remote than the two centuries which now separate us from Hobbes, the course of ideas in a given train of thought will admit of having its footsteps tracked in the corresponding pathways of the brain. Be this, however, as it may, even now we know enough to say that, whether or not these footsteps will ever admit of being thus tracked in detail, they are all certainly present in the cerebral structures of each one of us. What we know on the side of mind as logical sequence, is on the side of the nervous system nothing more than a passage of nervous energy through one series of cells and fibres rather than through another: what we recognize as truth is merely the fact of the brain vibrating in tune with Nature.

Such being the intimate relation between nerve-action and mind-action, it has become the scientifically orthodox teaching that the two stand to one another in the relation of cause to effect. One of the most distinguished of my predecessors in this place, the President of the Royal Society, has said in one of the most celebrated of his lectures: 'We have as much reason for regarding the mode of motion of the nervous system as the cause of the state of consciousness, as we have for regarding any event as the cause of another.' And, by way of perfectly logical deduction from this statement, Professor Huxley argues that thought and feeling have nothing whatever to do with determining action: they are merely the bye-products of cerebration, or, as he expresses it, the indices of changes which are going on in the brain. Under this view we are all what he terms conscious automata, or machines which happen, as it were by chance, to be conscious of some of their own movements. But the consciousness is altogether adventitious, and bears the same ineffectual relation to the activity of the brain as a steam-whistle bears to the activity of a locomotive, or the striking of a clock to the time-keeping adjustments of the clock-work. . . .

Now, this theory of conscious automatism is not merely a legitimate outcome of the theory that nervous changes are the causes of mental changes, but it is logically the only possible outcome. Nor do I see any way in which this theory can be fought on the grounds of physiology. If we persist in regarding the association between brain and thought exclusively from a physiological point of view, we must of necessity be materialists. Further, so far as we are physiologists our materialism can do us no harm. On the contrary, it is to us of the utmost service, as at once the simplest physiological explanation of facts already known, and the best working hypothesis to guide us in our further researches. But it does not follow from this that the theory of materialism is true. The bells of St Mary's over the way always ring for a quarter of an hour before the University sermon; yet the ringing of the bells is not the cause of the sermon, although, as long as the association remains constant, there would be no harm in assuming, for any practical purposes, that it is so. But just as we should be wrong in concluding, if we did not happen to know so much about the matter as we do, that the University sermon is produced by the vibration of bells in the tower of St Mary's Church, so we may be similarly wrong if we were definitely to conclude that the sermon is produced by the vibration of a number of little nerve-cells in the brain of the preacher. . . .

Hobbes was perfectly right in saying that with respect to its movements the animal body resembles an engine or a watch; and if he had been acquainted with the products of higher evolution in watch-making, he might with full propriety have argued, for instance, that in the compensating balance, whereby a watch adjusts its own movements in adaptation to external changes of temperature, a watch is exhibiting the mechanical aspect of volition. And, similarly, it is perhaps possible to conceive that the principles of mechanism might be more and more extended in their effects, until, in so marvellously perfected a structure as the human brain, all the voluntary movements of the body might be originated in the same mechanical manner as are the compensating movements of a watch; for this, indeed, as we have seen, is no more than happens in the case of all the nerve-centres other than the cerebral hemispheres. If this were so, motion would be producing nothing but motion, and upon the subject of brain action there would be nothing further to say. Without consciousness I should be delivering this lecture; without consciousness you would be hearing it; and all the busy brains in this University would be conducting their researches, or preparing for their examinations, mindlessly. Strange as such a state of things might be, still motion would be producing nothing but motion; and, therefore, if there were any mind to contemplate the facts, it would encounter no philosophical paradox: it would merely have to conclude that such were the astonishing possibilities of mechanism. But, as the facts actually stand, we find that this is not the case. We find, indeed, that up to a certain level of complexity mechanism alone is able to perform all the compensations or adjustments which are performed by the animal body; but we also find that beyond this level such compensations or adjustments are never performed without the intervention of consciousness. . . .

Is it not in itself a strikingly suggestive fact that consciousness only, yet always, appears upon the scene when the adjustive actions of any animal body rise above the certain level of intricacy to which I have alluded? Surely this large and general fact points with irresistible force to the conclusion, that in the performance of these more complex adjustments, consciousness—or the power of feeling and the power of willing—is of some *use*. Assuredly on the principles of evolution, which materialists at all events cannot afford to disregard, it would be a wholly anomalous fact that so wide and important a class of faculties as those of mind should have become developed in constantly ascending degrees throughout the animal kingdom, if they were entirely without use to animals. And, be it observed, this consideration holds good whatever views we may happen to entertain upon the special theory of natural selection. For the consideration stands upon the general fact that all the organs and functions of animals are of use to animals: we never meet, on any large or general scale, with organs and functions which are wholly adventitious. Is it to be supposed that this general principle fails just where its presence is most required, and that the highest functions of the highest organs of the highest animals stand out of analogy with all other functions in being themselves functionless? To this question I, for one, can only answer, and answer unequivocally, No. As a rational being who wants to take a wider view of the facts than that which is open to the one line of research pursued by the physiologist, I am forced to conclude that not without a reason does mind exist in the frame of things; and that apart from the activity of mind, whereby motion is related to that which is not motion, this planet could never have held the wonderful being, who in multiplying has replenished the earth and subdued it—holding dominion over the fish of the sea, and over the fowl of the air, and over every living thing that moveth.

What, then, shall we say touching this mysterious union of mind and motion? Having found it physically impossible that there should be a causal connection proceeding from motion to mind, shall we try to reverse the terms, and suppose a causal connection proceeding from mind to motion? This is the oldest and still the most popular theory—the theory of spiritualism. And, no doubt, in one important respect it is less un-philosophical than the opposite theory of materialism. For spiritualism supposes the causation to proceed from that which is the source of our idea of causality—the mind: not from that into which this idea has been read —the brain. . . . Nevertheless, it is opposed to the whole momentum of science. For if mind is supposed, on no matter how small a scale, to be a cause of motion, the fundamental axiom of science is impugned. This fundamental axiom is that energy can neither be created nor destroyed— that just as motion can produce nothing but motion, so, conversely, motion can be produced by nothing but motion. Regarded, therefore, from the standpoint of physical science, the theory of spiritualism is in precisely the same case as the theory of materialism: that is to say, if the supposed causation takes place, it can only be supposed to do so by way of miracle.

And this is a conclusion which the more clear-sighted of the idealists have expressly recognized. That subtle and most entertaining thinker, for example, the late Professor Green of Oxford, has said that the self-conscious volition of man 'does not consist in a series of natural events, . . . is not natural in the ordinary sense of that term; not natural at any rate in any sense in which naturalness would imply its determination by antecedent events, or by conditions of which it is not itself the source'.

Thus the theory of spiritualism, although not directly refutable by any process of logic, is certainly enfeebled by its collision with the instincts of physical science. In necessarily holding the facts of consciousness and volition super-natural, extra-natural, or non-natural, the theory is opposed to the principle of continuity.

Spiritualism being thus unsatisfactory, and materialism impossible, is there yet any third hypothesis in which we may hope to find intellectual rest? In my opinion there is. If we unite in a higher synthesis the elements both of spiritualism and of materialism, we obtain a product which satisfies every fact of feeling on the one hand, and of observation on the other. The manner in which this synthesis may be effected is perfectly simple. We have only to suppose that the antithesis between mind and motion—subject and object—is itself phenomenal or apparent: not abso-lute or real. We have only to suppose that the seeming duality is relative to our modes of apprehension; and, therefore, that any change taking place in the mind, and any corresponding change taking place in the brain, are really not two changes, but one change. When a violin is played upon we hear a musical sound, and at the same time we see a vibration of the strings. Relatively to our consciousness, therefore, we have here two sets of changes, which appear to be very different in kind; yet we know that in an absolute sense they are one and the same: we know that the diversity in consciousness is created only by the difference in our modes of perceiving the same event—whether we see or whether we hear the vibration of the strings. Similarly, we may suppose that a vibration of nerve-strings and a process of thought are really one and the same event, which is dual or diverse only in relation to our modes of perceiving it.

The great advantage of this theory is that it supposes only one stream of causation, in which both mind and motion are simultaneously concerned. The theory, therefore, escapes all the difficulties and contradictions with which both spiritualism and materialism are beset. Thus, motion is supposed to be producing nothing but motion; mind-changes nothing but mind-changes: both producing both simultaneously, neither could be what it is without the other, because without the other neither could be the cause which in fact it is. Impossible, therefore, is the supposition of the materialist that consciousness is adventitious, or that in the absence of mind changes of brain could be what they are; for it belongs to the very causation of these changes that they should have a mental side. The use of mind to animals is thus rendered apparent; for intelligent volition is thus shown to be a true cause of adjustive movement, in that the cerebration which it involves could not otherwise be possible: the causation would not otherwise be complete.

A simple illustration may serve at once to render this doctrine more easily intelligible, and to show that, if accepted, the doctrine, as it appears to me, terminates the otherwise interminable controversy on the freedom of the will.

In an Edison lamp the light which is emitted from the burner may be said indifferently to be caused by the number of vibrations per second going on in the carbon, or by the temperature of the carbon; for this rate of vibration could not take place in the carbon without constituting that degree of temperature which affects our eyes as luminous. Similarly a train of thought may be said indifferently to be caused by brain-action or by mind-action; for, *ex hypothesi*, the one could not take place without the other. Now, when we contemplate the phenomena of volition by themselves, it is as though we were contemplating the phenomena of light by themselves: volition is produced by mind in brain, just as light is produced by temperature in carbon. And just as we may correctly speak of light as the cause, say, of a photograph, so we may correctly speak of volition as the cause of bodily movement. That particular kind of physical activity which takes place in the carbon could not take place without the light which causes a photograph; and, similarly, that particular kind of physical activity which takes place in the brain could not take place without the volition which causes a bodily movement. So that volition is as truly a cause of bodily movement as is the physical activity of the brain;

seeing that, in an absolute sense, the cause is one and the same. But if we once clearly perceive that what in a relative sense we know as volition is, in a similar sense, the cause of bodily movement, we terminate the question touching the freedom of the will. For this question in its last resort— and apart from the ambiguity which has been thrown around it by some of our metaphysicians—is merely the question whether the will is to be regarded as a cause of Nature. And the theory which we have now before us sanctions the doctrine that it may be so regarded, if only we remember that its causal activity depends upon its identity with the obverse aspect known as cerebration, without which identity in apparent duality neither volition nor cerebration could be the cause which in fact they are. It thus becomes a mere matter of phraseology whether we speak of the will determining, or being determined by, changes going on in the external world; just as it is but a matter of phraseology whether we speak of temperature determining, or being determined by, molecular vibration. All the requirements alike of the free-will and of the bond-will hypotheses are thus satisfied by a synthesis which comprises them both. On the one hand, it would be as impossible for an *un*conscious automaton to do the work or to perform the adjustments of a conscious agent, as it would be for an Edison lamp to give out light and cause a photograph when not heated by an electric current. On the other hand, it would be as impossible for the will to originate bodily movement without the occurrence of a strictly physical process of cerebration, as it would be for light to shine in an Edison lamp which had been deprived of its carbon-burner.

It may be said of this theory that it is highly speculative, not verifiable by any possible experiment, and therefore at best is but a mere guess. All which is, no doubt, perfectly true; but, on the other hand, we must remember that this theory comes to us as the only one which is logically possible, and at the same time competent to satisfy the facts alike of the outer and of the inner world. It is a speculation in the sense of not being verifiable by experiment; but it has much more value than ordinarily attaches to an unverifiable speculation, in that there is really no alternative hypothesis to be considered: if we choose to call it a guess, we must at the same time remember it is a guess where it does not appear that any other is open. Once more to quote Hobbes, who, as we have seen, was himself a remarkable instance of what he here says: 'The best prophet naturally is the best guesser; and the best guesser, he that is most versed and studied in the matters he guesses at'. In this case, therefore, the best prophet is not the physiologist, whose guess ends in materialism; nor the purely mental philosopher, whose guess ends in spiritualism; but rather the man who, being 'versed and studied' in all the facts appertaining to both sides of the matter, ends in the only alternative guess which remains open. And if that most troublesome individual, the 'plain man' of Locke, should say it seems at least opposed to common sense to suppose that there is anything in a burning candle or a rolling billiard-ball substantially the same as mind, the answer is that if he could look into my brain at this moment he would see nothing there but motion of molecules, or motion of masses; and apart from the accident of my being able to tell him so, his 'common sense' could never have divined that these motions in my brain are concerned in the genesis of my spoken thoughts.

18

MORTON PRINCE

THE NATURE OF MIND AND HUMAN AUTOMATISM (1885)

The time has not yet arrived when we can hope to thoroughly understand the relations of the mental to the physical world. Nevertheless, as the merchant from time to time stops in the midst of his transactions to 'take account of stock', so in the progress of science, it is well to occasionally pause, and cast our eyes over what has been done, to sum up the evidence that has been accumulated, and see whither we are drifting. Accordingly, the writer has ventured in these pages to call attention to that explanation of the problem which seems most in accordance with the present condition of science. . . .

A man is sitting in his library quietly reading. The rays of light from his book fall upon his retina and excite the terminal filaments of the optic nerve; from here the impression is carried as a neural current to the brain, and excites the molecules of the cells. Along with this excitement of the cerebral molecules there arises the image called the book, and all the various thoughts corresponding to the printed words of the page. These thoughts are said to occur side by side with the molecular agitation. Suddenly the cry of 'fire' is raised. The man throws down his book, jumps from his chair, and runs downstairs in answer to the alarm. Now what has occurred in his nervous apparatus? The pulsations of the atmosphere corresponding to the sound 'fire' have struck upon his auditory apparatus; from there they have been conveyed as a neural undulation or current along the auditory nerve to his brain and there aroused a new set of molecular motions; and with them a new set of thoughts has arisen, embracing perhaps a mental picture of the house in flames and of danger to the inmates. But not stopping here, the cerebral motion has been transmitted along the outgoing nerves to the muscles, and resulted in the actions just described; we have here, from a physical point of view, what is called a nervous circuit. On the one hand we have a series of molecular motions beginning with irritations of sensory nerves, and passing as cerebral motions through the brain, ending in muscular action; and on the other hand we have states of consciousness correlated with a portion of that circuit, the cerebral portion. In this or in some modified form of this consists all nervous and mental action. On this fact is based the doctrine of the physical basis of mind, which recognizes the association and inter-dependence of molecular motions and consciousness. Underneath, then, every mental act there flows a physical current. With every thought, sensation, or emotion is associated a physical change in a material sub-stance—the brain. No mental act can take place without a corresponding physical change; no physical change without a corresponding mental act. Such is the usually accepted doctrine of the present day.

According to this view we have two sets of phenomena, two classes of facts, a mental act and a physical change, invariably associated together. But this is very far from explaining the nature of mental processes. The further question is here presented to us, What is the nature of this associa-tion? Is it to be looked upon, as many think, as a mere *coexistence* of dis-similar phenomena, rather than as one in which any dependency of the one upon the other can be traced? And are we here to place a limit to our inquiries, and consider that the problem has been reduced to its lowest terms? If we are content to do so, very little progress can be said to have been made towards understanding the relationship between mind and matter. Unless some causal or interdependent relation between the two can be established, we shall be very little better off than we were before physiological science undertook to solve the problem.

But, in truth, physiological science does pretend to go further, though a careful study of the teachings of the exponents of the modern school will reveal two different interpretations of the facts, however unanimous they may appear at first sight. These two interpretations may be termed the Theory of Functions and the Theory of Aspects. Both theories I hope to be able to show are neither a sufficient nor correct explanation of the facts.

The basis of both doctrines is a physical substance underlying both series of facts—the physical disturbances, and consciousness—but the relation which the two series bear to this substance differs in the two theories. First, as to the Theory of Functions.

After a careful study of the reasoning by which this conclusion has been reached, as well as of the general meaning which seems to underlie the writings of the principal authorities on the subject, I am convinced that there is only one intelligible meaning with which this doctrine can be invested, and that is this: there is one underlying matter or substance; this substance has two properties—one of these properties is known as those disturbances we call nerve-motions, the other is consciousness; that is, our idea, sensations, and emotions. When nerve-motions, the one 'property' of this matter, is present, consciousness, the other 'property', appears simultaneously. Both come and both go side by side together; but *why* when one appears the other should do so also we do not know....

According to this doctrine we may be said to have to do with a unity of substance and a duality of properties.

The Theory of Aspects differs considerably from this, though the two are sometimes confused and regarded as identical. There is certainly often lacking that precision of language which is essential to a clear understanding of the problem.

According to the Theory of Aspects, consciousness and nerve motions (vibrations) are only different aspects of one and the same underlying substance, which is unknown. This view has perhaps been as clearly expressed by Bain, as by any one else, when he says, 'the one substance with two sets of properties, two sides (the physical and the mental), a double-faced unity, would seem to comply with all the exigencies of the case'.[1]

The same notion has thus been described by Lewes: 'There may be every ground for concluding that a logical process has its correlative physical process, and that the two processes are merely two aspects of one event.'[2] And again: 'The two processes are equivalent, and the difference arises from the difference in the mode of apprehension.' . . .[3]

The inadequacy of the above explanations, however simple and satisfactory they may appear at first sight, is recognized on all sides, and is the same whether it be approached on the physical or on the subjective side. They simply avoid the difficulty, they do not remove it. This difficulty is, as I have said, in explaining *how we come to have two aspects*, and how these two 'aspects' are related; how physical changes become translated into the subjective feeling. That the two are correlated in time, that is, that the two occur simultaneously, side by side, is plain enough and easily understood, but it is confessedly not so easy to understand how the one becomes 'transformed' (?) into the other; how, in fact, a feeling insures the presence of a physical motion, and a physical motion, of a feeling. Thus, Mr Spencer, who, as a psychologist, has treated the matter in a masterly manner, maintains this view of different aspects. 'For what,' he says, 'is objectively a change in a superior nerve-centre is subjectively a feeling, and the duration under the one aspect measures the duration of it under the other.'[4] And the same thing is repeated in other passages. But this is no explanation, as Mr Spencer himself tacitly recognizes when he later adds, 'though accumulated observations and experiments have led us by a very indirect series of inferences to the belief that mind and nervous action are the subjective and objective faces of the same thing, *we remain utterly incapable of seeing and even of imagining how the two are related*. Mind still continues to us a something without any kinship to other things; and

---

[1] *Mind and Body*, p. 196.   [2] *Physical Basis of Mind*, p. 395.
[3] Ibid.   [4] *Principles of Psychology*, 2nd ed., ii, p. 107.

from the science which discovers by introspection the laws of this something, there is no passage by transitional steps to the sciences which discover the laws of these other things'.[1] Here is a mystery which he recognizes in common even with his spiritualistic opponents.

Professor Tyndall, as a physicist and avowed materialist, as one who
finds in the properties of matter alone sufficient to account for everything
in the universe, both for the objective phenomena about us, and for the
subjective world of consciousness within, 'bows his head in the dust before
that mystery of the mind, which has hitherto defied its own penetrative
power, and which may ultimately resolve itself into a demonstrable
impossibility of self-penetration'.[2] While Professor Tyndall finds in matter
alone sufficient to account for the existence of mind, he still recognizes the
difficulty whereof we speak. 'The passage,' he says, 'from the physics of
the brain to the corresponding facts of consciousness is unthinkable.
Granted that a definite thought, and a definite molecular action of the
brain, occur simultaneously: we do not possess the intellectual organ, nor
apparently any rudiment of the organs which would enable us to pass, by a
process of reasoning, from one to the other. They appear together, but we
do not know why. Were our minds and senses so expanded, strengthened,
and illuminated as to enable us to see and feel the very molecules of the
brain; were we capable of following all their motions, all their groupings,
all their electrical discharges, if such there be; and were we intimately
acquainted with the corresponding states of thought and feeling, we should
be as far as ever from the solution of the problem: How are these physical
processes connected with the facts of consciousness? The chasm between
the two classes of phenomena would still remain intellectually impassable.'[3]
'We may think over the subject again and again; it eludes all intellectual
presentation; we stand at length face to face with the incomprehensible.'[4]

Having now become familiar with that doctrine which has been most
generally accepted by those best qualified to judge, and having seen how
far short it falls of explaining the connection between those activities we
call mental and those activities we call physical; nay, having seen that it
has even been declared that 'the task of transcending or abolishing the
radical antithesis between the phenomena of mind and the phenomena of
motions of matter must always remain an impractical task. For in order
to transcend or abolish this radical antithesis, we must be prepared to show
how a given quantity of molecular motion in nerve-tissue can become

---

[1] *Principles of Psychology*, 2nd ed., p. 140. The italics not in original .
[2] Apology for the Belfast Address.
[3] Scientific Materialism in Fragments of Science, p. 420.
[4] Apology for the Belfast Address. Same, p. 560.

transformed into a definable amount of ideation or feeling. But this, it is quite safe to say, can never be done'[1]; having become conversant with all this, we shall now proceed, refusing to accept this verdict, to attempt the task; with what success we shall leave to the reader to determine.

I shall state at the outset that theorem which I conceive will answer all the requirements of the case and which it shall be my effort to prove.

It is this: instead of there being one substance with *two properties* or 'aspects'—mind and motion—*there is one substance, mind*; and the other *apparent* property, motion, is only the way in which this real substance, mind, is apprehended by a *second organism*: only the sensations of, or effect upon, the second organism, when acted upon (ideally) by the real substance, mind.

This may, at first sight, appear to the reader as practically the same thing, only expressed in different terms. But it is not so. There is a radical difference in the conception. The one recognizes one substance with duality of 'properties' or 'aspects'; the other, one substance with one aspect only. If the meaning of this, at this time, be not clear or be not admitted, I must ask the reader to suspend his judgment, and to follow me with open-mindedness through the next chapter. If it shall then be found that this theorem both explains all the difficulties we have encountered and does not lead to conclusions inconsistent with the facts, I shall consider that I am justified in my reasoning.

In this problem we have to do with the relationship between two worlds which are considered to be radically antithetical in their nature—the world of thought and feeling, and the world of things. The former is called subjective, the latter objective. It will be necessary before going further to inquire more intimately into what we mean by each. This inquiry will necessarily involve what will probably be judged by those learned in the matter a tedious restatement of first principles, but it is absolutely necessary for a proper appreciation of the argument for those not well versed in philosophic matters. Therefore no apology will be offered for the digression.

The subjective world is well known to every one. We all know what a thought is, or an emotion of fear, or anger, or a sensation of pain or sweetness. No definition can make the knowledge any more definite. But the objective world about us is not so well known to us. He who imagines that the things about him in the room—the chairs, the table, the pictures —are really what they seem, is grievously mistaken. He who picks up a book, and perceiving something which has a certain shape, size, hardness and colour, say redness, and thinks that these qualities reside as such in the something he calls a book, does not know what perceiving a thing consists

[1] Fiske's *Cosmic Philosophy*, ii, p. 442.

in. Physiology teaches us that the qualities of any object, as the book, are only a number of sensations, and accordingly states of our own consciousness. These sensations we are in the habit of projecting outside of us, and then imagining they exist as such independent of our own consciousness; but as a matter of fact they do not exist as such. When these sensations occur grouped together in a particular way, we call the group, after being thus imagined to exist outside our minds, an object. Each sensation then becomes a quality of the object which is the whole group.

The object, then, does not exist as such outside of us, but is only a bundle of our sensations. Undoubtedly something exists outside of us which is the cause of these sensations in us. This something has been called the thing-in-itself, but its nature is unknown to us. . . .

The only thing we know is our sensations. The material world is thus resolved into certain unknown activities and certain groups of sensations, which latter constitute our perception of the former.

That these activities, constituting the thing-in-itself, exist at all is an inference, but an inference of such irresistible force that we cannot resist it. Thus, the properties of objects are all sensations dependent on unknown activities outside of us. When these activities exist grouped together in a particular way, so as to produce a particular group of sensations, we call this group a book, or table, or chair, and artificially locate the sensations in the external matter as its qualities. These activities in matter, which may be said to constitute matter, are unknown, and should be denominated simply by X.

The application of all this will soon become apparent, if it is not so already. That which we call the subjective world is composed of our thoughts and feelings; that which we call the objective world is a mass of activities unknown to us, but conventionally designated by subjective terms of sensation, as red, hard, sweet, etc.; and these *sensations are the reaction of the organism to these external unknown activities.* . . .

When we talk about matter, then, what do we mean? We may have four different notions, each radically distinct, and unless we bear constantly in mind to which we refer we are liable to be led into confusion of thought.

1st. There is the notion we may have of our own conscious states as such, without reference to anything beyond them, and consisting of groups of sensations, as of the notion of two points (which points may again be resolved into sensations—colour, shape, etc.). This notion may be called *subjective matter.*

2nd. The notion of the unknown reality, or thing-in-itself, existing outside of us, and corresponding to these sensations—the unknown X. This may be called *actual matter.*

3rd. The double notion of both of these two classes of facts and the relation between them. This embraces the other two, and is the one which should be particularly kept in view when inquiring into the ultimate nature of things.

4th. The common idea of matter as employed in ordinary discourse and in the physical sciences. In this sense, matter is made to include our conscious states (1st notion) after being projected outside of us, and artificially made to have an active existence as phenomena or objects. This may be called *phenomenal matter*. This, as has already been explained, is philosophically an erroneous notion, being only an artifice, but nevertheless one that is necessary for the ordinary purposes of social life and the pursuit of the physical sciences. Here it is of inestimable value, and, in fact, we could not do without it. It would be ridiculous, not only in our everyday use of language, but in our conceptions employed to carry on the ordinary affairs of life, to bear any other notion in mind. . . .

Now in these different notions embraced by 'matter' lies the gist of the whole question under consideration. . . .

It is evident that in speaking of the molecular motions occurring in your brain I may refer either to the motion proper, which is my state of consciousness, or I may have reference to the reality occurring outside of me and belonging to you, and a part of you. If I refer to the former, I know what it is; it is my sensation. If I refer to the latter, the Reality, the question arises, What is it? Is it unknown, and if not, what is its nature? We will approach this question in another way, which will make its meaning clearer.

Let us consider these physical cerebral activities, and ask from a purely physical point of view what kind of activities they are. We have reference, of course, only to those activities which are supposed to constitute nerve-force and to underlie all conscious states. Suppose that by a suitable device we could have them presented to us *objectively*, so that we could actually recognize them, how would they appear to us? That would depend upon the sense we employed in perceiving them. We might ideally (as we do when thinking of them) or actually *see* them; they would then appear as motions, oscillations, undulations, or some such movement. We might, by the suitable microphone, *hear* them; they would then appear as musical notes. If our tactile sense were sufficiently developed we might *feel* them; they might then appear as heat. But none of these sensations represent these activities as they really *are*.

Now, to put another hypothetical question, suppose, for a moment, that what they really *are* is consciousness—that is, a thought or sensation of pain—how would this sensation of pain *appear* to us if we could apprehend it through our senses, and through the sense of sight in par-

G

ticular (either, of course, ideally or in the brain of another)? The answer is, Only as all other activities in matter appear to us, namely, as motions, undulations, etc. *If, then, these hypothetical conditions were the facts*, it would be easy to understand how mental states can become 'transformed' into physical disturbances, and *vice versa*, because there is no *transformation* about it. *There would be in this case only one thing, mental states, which would appear as physical activities when viewed (ideally) through the senses, as tremors if viewed through sight.* . . .

In other words, *a mental state and those physical changes which are known in the objective world as neural undulations are one and the same thing*, BUT THE FORMER IS THE ACTUALITY, THE LATTER A MODE BY WHICH IT IS PRESENTED TO THE CONSCIOUSNESS OF A SECOND PERSON,[1] i.e., to the non-possessor of it. . . .

It may at first sight appear impossible that these physical phenomena, with which we are familiar, as motion, undulations, or what you will, can also appear as states of consciousness. But this is because in our daily experience we are apt to overlook the well-known fact, which has been sufficiently explained in the preceding chapter, that all those properties with which we endow matter have no objective existence, but are only subjective states called sensations, and hence forms of consciousness, and these are symbolic only of the unknown changes occurring in matter. Just as the words written on this page are symbolic of the ideas they represent, but are as unlike as possible the ideas themselves. Any sensation, such as light, is a representation in consciousness of physical changes in matter outside the brain, but gives us no idea what those changes are. A sensation is related to its physical external cause as the dent in the hot iron is to the blow of the blacksmith's hammer that fashions it. The true nature of a physical change in a foreign body—a piece of iron, for example —is absolutely beyond our range of comprehension. A physical change in my brain is an idea, my idea. To you, could you in some way become conscious of it, it would appear only like other physical phenomenon—as, for instance, a vibration—being only symbolized in your consciousness; and when you ideally conceive it, it is not the idea itself which you are conscious of, but the disturbance in your brain in the form of a sensation, and this you characterize as a physical phenomenon, and locate in mine. So that a disturbance in my brain which I experience as an idea of an orange, you *ideally* experience as a physical phenomenon in the form of a neural undulation or some similar (objective) sensation.

Let us take a concrete example. We will imagine that you have a sensation of pain presented to your mind; we will also picture to ourselves a

---

[1] It is not sufficiently exact to say that *both* are different modes of apprehending one and the same thing, for that implies that neither is the actuality.

physical process in your brain in the form of neural vibrations. Now these two—the mental and physical—are usually described as two processes, both of which occur somehow in you. They are said to take place synchronously, and one is the correlate of the other. But this is not the correct way of putting it. We will suppose now, further, I could apply a microscope to your brain and watch the cells (as I can *ideally*) when this pain is felt by you. What now would happen? At the moment when *you* have the sensation of *pain I* become conscious of *neural vibrations*, which I locate as such (but erroneously) in your brain-cells. The real activities in you are pain, not neural vibrations. The reason for this is this: your mental process, the pain, acting upon my retina, sets up a process in me, and as this process of mine is excited through my organ of vision, I am affected according to the physiological laws of this organ and become conscious of neural vibrations. These neural vibrations I erroneously locate in you while they really are parts of my consciousness, and the only thing which occurs in you is the feeling of *pain*. The reaction of my brain to your feeling is a sensation of vibrations. The only way in which these activities could be apprehended by me is objectively as neural vibrations. The only way in which they can be brought into your consciousness is as the sensation of pain. But, in fact, it is one process in you, the sensation of pain, which is the real activity. Here, then, lies the parallelism of the phenomena: *your* consciousness or pain is the correlate of *my* apprehension of this consciousness as neural vibration. *The parallelism is between your consciousness and my consciousness of your consciousness, or, what is the same thing, between the consciousness in you and the picture in my mind of neural vibrations.* The former is the reality, the latter the symbol of it. There is an invariable concomitance of these facts.

Again, under the hypothetical conditions stated above, I cannot become conscious of your physical changes or process in its true form, the sensation of pain, for that which I become conscious of is the *effect* which this physical process produces in my brain, the reaction of my brain to it, as a sensation of neural vibrations. To be sure, I can conjure up the sensation of pain by allowing my mind to dwell on it, and produce in this way a so-called imaginary pain; but this is an entirely different thing. In that case there would be no relation between *my* mental state of pain and *your* mental state, which I am endeavouring to become conscious of. So you can picture to yourself neural vibrations as well as I, and perceive them as objective phenomena. But here, too, the conditions are altered, and we have to do not with a mental process and its correlated neural process, but with a physical process ideally projected outside of your cerebrum, and a symbolic representation of it as neural vibrations in your mind.

It is no objection to this statement of the nature of the parallelism to say that there is something more than a parallelism between your consciousness and my mode of becoming conscious of your consciousness, because you can have both consciousness as pain and a picture of neural vibrations supposed to occur side by side with the former, for this amounts to the same thing. For when you conceive of correlated neural processes in your brain you in reality have gone through the following logical process: you first have perceived hypothetical physical disturbances in someone else's brain, and these you have recognized as neural vibrations. Then you have inferred that they occur invariably side by side with the consciousness of the individual. Having determined this, you ideally abstract them, transfer them to your own brain, and infer that they occur there under similar conditions. This is the same thing as if a second individual had been the object of your study. Then it follows that when you think of physical changes in the protoplasm of your brain you ideally abstract and project them outside of you, and then ideally become conscious of the *effect* which they produce on your mind, namely, the sensation of vibrations; but this *effect* is entirely distinct in character from, though correlative with, the ideas which are the realities.

Physical changes occurring in a foreign body, as a piece of iron, though giving us our experience of it, must be absolutely unknown to us. Physical changes occurring in our brains are clearly known to us; they are our thoughts, our sensations, and our emotions.

19

WILLIAM JAMES

I. THE PRINCIPLES OF PSYCHOLOGY (1891)

The Meaning of Localization

Confining ourselves to the problem of locality for the present, let us begin with the simple case of a sensitive surface, only two points of which receive stimulation from without. How, first, are these two points felt as alongside of each other with an interval of space between them? We must be conscious of two things for this: of the duality of the excited points, and of the extensiveness of the unexcited interval. The duality alone, although a necessary, is not a sufficient condition of the spatial separation. We may, for instance, discern two sounds in the same place, sweet and sour in the same lemonade, warm and cold, round and pointed contact in the same place on the skin, etc. In all discrimination the recognition of the duality of two feelings by the mind is the easier the more strongly the feelings are contrasted in quality. If our two excited points awaken identical qualities of sensation, they must, perforce, appear to the mind as one; and, not distinguished at all, they are, *a fortiori*, not localized apart. Spots four centimetres distant on the back have no qualitative contrast at all, and fuse into a single sensation. Points less than three thousandths of a millimetre apart awaken on the retina sensations so contrasted that we apprehend them immediately as two. Now these unlikenesses which arise so slowly when we pass from one point to another in the back, so much faster on the tongue and finger-tips, but with such inconceivable rapidity on the retina, what are they? Can we discover anything about their intrinsic nature?

The most natural and immediate answer to make is that they are unlikenesses of *place* pure and simple. In the words of a German physiologist,[1] to whom psychophysics owes much:

'The sensations are from the outset (*von vornherein*) localized ... Every sensation as such is from the very beginning affected with the spatial quality, so that this quality is nothing like an external attribute coming to

---

[1] Vierordt, *Grundriss der Physiologie*, 5te Auflage (1877), pp. 326, 436.

the sensation from a higher faculty, but must be regarded as something immanently residing in the sensation itself.'

And yet the moment we reflect on this answer an insuperable logical difficulty seems to present itself. No single *quale* of sensation can, by itself, amount to a consciousness of *position*. Suppose no feeling but that of a single point ever to be awakened. Could that possibly be the feeling of any special *whereness* or *thereness*? Certainly not. *Only when a second point is felt to arise can the first one acquire a determination of up, down, right or left, and these determinations are all relative to that second point.* Each point, so far as it is *placed*, is there only by virtue of what it *is not*, namely, by virtue of another point. This is as much as to say that position has nothing *intrinsic* about it; and that, although a feeling of absolute bigness may, *a feeling of place cannot, possibly form an immanent element in any single isolated sensation.* The very writer we have quoted has given heed to this objection, for he continues (p. 335) by saying that the sensations thus originally localized 'are only so *in themselves*, but not in the representation of consciousness, which is not yet present. They are, in the first instance, devoid of all mutual relations with each other'. But such a localization of the sensation 'in itself' would seem to mean nothing more than the susceptibility or *potentiality* of being distinctly localized when the time came and other conditions became fulfilled. Can we now discover anything about such susceptibility in itself before it has borne its ulterior fruits in the developed consciousness?

'Local Signs'

To begin with, every sensation of the skin and every visceral sensation seems to derive from its topographic seat a peculiar shade of feeling, which it would not have in another place. And this feeling *per se* seems quite another thing from the perception of the place. Says Wundt[1]:

'If with the finger we touch first the cheek and then the palm, exerting each time precisely the same pressure, the sensation shows notwithstanding a distinctly marked difference in the two cases. Similarly, when we compare the palm with the back of the hand, the nape of the neck with its anterior surface, the breast with the back; in short, any two distant parts of the skin with each other. And moreover, we easily remark, by attentively observing, that spots even tolerably close together differ in respect of the quality of their feeling. If we pass from one point of our cutaneous surface to another, we find a perfectly gradual and continuous alteration in our feeling, notwithstanding the objective nature of the

---

[1] *Vorlesungen üb. Menschen-u. Thierseale* (Leipzig, 1863), I. 214.

contact has remained the same. Even the sensations of corresponding points on opposite sides of the body, though similar, are not identical. If, for instance, we touch first the back of one hand, and then of the other, we remark a qualitative unlikeness of sensation. It must not be thought that such differences are mere matters of imagination, and that we take the sensations to be different because we represent each of them to ourselves as occupying a different place. With sufficient sharpening of the attention, we may, confining ourselves to the quality of the feelings alone, entirely abstract from their locality, and yet notice the differences quite as markedly.'

Whether these local contrasts shade into each other with absolutely continuous gradations, we cannot say. But we know (continues Wundt) that

'they change, when we pass from one point of the skin to its neighbour, with very different degrees of rapidity. On delicately-feeling parts, used principally for touching, such as the finger-tips, the difference of sensation between two closely approximate points is already strongly pronounced; whilst in parts of lesser delicacy, as the arm, the back, the legs, the disparities of sensation are observable only between distant spots.'

The internal organs, too, have their specific *qualia* of sensation. An inflammation of the kidney is different from one of the liver; pains in joints and muscular insertions are distinguished. Pain in the dental nerves is wholly unlike the pain of a burn. But very important and curious similarities prevail throughout these differences. Internal pains, whose seat we cannot see, and have no means of knowing unless the character of the pain itself reveal it, are felt *where* they belong. Diseases of the stomach, kidney, liver, rectum, prostate, etc., of the bones, of the brain and its membranes, are referred to their proper position. Nerve-pains describe the length of the nerve. Such localizations as those of vertical, frontal, or occipital headache of intracranial origin force us to conclude that parts which are neighbours, whether inner or outer, may possess by mere virtue of that fact a common peculiarity of feeling, a respect in which their sensations agree, and which serves as a token of their proximity. These *local* colourings are, moreover, so strong that we cognize them as the same, throughout all contrasts of sensible quality in the accompanying perception. Cold and heat are wide as the poles asunder; yet if both fall on the cheek, there mixes with them something that makes them in *that respect* identical; just as, contrariwise, despite the identity of cold with itself wherever found, when we get it first on the palm and then on the cheek, some difference comes, which keeps the two experiences for ever asunder.

And now let us revert to the query propounded a moment since: *Can these differences of mere quality in feeling, varying according to locality yet having each sensibly and intrinsically and by itself nothing to do with position, constitute the 'susceptibilities' we mentioned, the conditions of being perceived in position, of the localities to which they belong?* The numbers on a row of houses, the initial letters of a set of words, have no intrinsic kinship with points of space, and yet they are the conditions of our knowledge of where any house is in the row, or any word in the dictionary. Can the modifications of feeling in question be tags or labels of this kind which in no wise originally reveal the position of the spot to which they are attached, but guide us to it by what Berkeley would call a 'customary tie'? Many authors have unhesitatingly replied in the affirmative; Lotze, who in his Medizinische Psychologie first described the sensations in this way, designating them, thus conceived, as *local signs.* This term has obtained wide currency in Germany, and *in speaking of the 'LOCAL-SIGN THEORY' hereafter, I shall always mean the theory which denies that there can be in a sensation any element of actual locality, of inherent spatial order,* any tone as it were which cries to us immediately and without further ado, 'I am *here*', or 'I am *there*'.

If, as may well be the case we by this time find ourselves tempted to accept the Local-sign theory in a general way, we have to clear up several further matters. If a sign is to lead us to *the thing* it means, we must have some other source of knowledge of that thing. Either the thing has been given in a previous experience of which the sign also formed part—they are *associated;* or it is what Reid calls a 'natural' sign, that is, a feeling which, the first time it enters the mind, evokes from the native powers thereof a cognition of the thing that hitherto had lain dormant. In both cases, however, the sign is one thing, and the thing another. In the instance that now concerns us, *the sign is a quality of feeling and the thing is a position.* Now we have seen that the position of a point is not only revealed, but created, by the existence of other points to which it stands in determinate *relations. If the sign can by any machinery which it sets in motion evoke a consciousness either of the other points, or of the relations, or of both, it would seem to fulfil its function, and reveal to us the position we seek.*

But such a machinery is already familiar to us. It is neither more nor less than the law of habit in the nervous system. When any point of the sensitive surface has been frequently excited simultaneously with, or immediately before or after, other points, and afterwards comes to be excited alone, there will be a tendency for its perceptive nerve-centre to irradiate into the nerve-centres of the other points. Subjectively considered, this is the same as if we said that *the peculiar feeling of the first point* SUGGESTS *the feeling of the entire region with whose stimulation its own excitement has been habitually* ASSOCIATED.

Ideo-Motor Action

The question is this: *Is the bare idea of a movement's sensible effects its sufficient mental cue, or must there be an additional mental antecedent, in the shape of a fiat, decision, consent, volitional mandate, or other synonymous phenomenon of consciousness, before the movement can follow?*

I answer: Sometimes the bare idea is sufficient, but sometimes an additional conscious element, in the shape of a fiat, mandate, or express consent, has to intervene and precede the movement. The cases without a fiat constitute the more fundamental, because the more simple, variety. The others involve a special complication, which must be fully discussed at the proper time. For the present let us turn to *ideo-motor action*, as it has been termed, or the sequence of movement upon the mere thought of it, as the type of the process of volition. ...

We know what it is to get out of bed on a freezing morning in a room without a fire, and how the very vital principle within us protests against the ordeal. Probably most persons have lain on certain mornings for an hour at a time unable to brace themselves to the resolve. We think how late we shall be, how the duties of the day will suffer; we say, 'I *must* get up, this is ignominious', etc.; but still the warm couch feels too delicious, the cold outside too cruel, and resolution faints away and postpones itself again and again just as it seemed on the verge of bursting the resistance and passing over into the decisive act. Now how do we *ever* get up under such circumstances? If I may generalize from my own experience, we more often than not get up without any struggle or decision at all. We suddenly find that we *have* got up. A fortunate lapse of consciousness occurs; we forget both the warmth and the cold; we fall into some reverie connected with the day's life, in the course of which the idea flashes across us, 'Hullo! I must lie here no longer'. —an idea which at that lucky instant awakens no contradictory or paralysing suggestions, and consequently produces immediately its appropriate motor effects. It was our acute consciousness of both the warmth and the cold during the period of struggle, which paralysed our activity then and kept our idea of rising in the condition of *wish* and not *will*. The moment these inhibitory ideas ceased, the original idea exerted its effects.

This case seems to me to contain in miniature form the data for an entire psychology of volition. It was in fact through meditating on the phenomenon in my own person that I first became convinced of the truth of the doctrine which these pages present, and which I need here illustrate by no further examples. The reason why that doctrine is not a self-evident truth is that we have so many ideas which *do not* result in action. But it will be seen that in every such case, without exception, that is because other ideas simultaneously present rob them of their impulsive power. But even here, and when a movement is inhibited from *completely* taking place by contrary ideas, it will *incipiently* take place. To quote Lotze once more:

'The spectator accompanies the throwing of a billiard-ball, or the thrust of the swordsman, with slight movements of his arm; the untaught narrator tells his story with many gesticulations; the reader while absorbed in the perusal of a battle-scene feels a slight tension run through his muscular system, keeping time as it were with the actions he is reading of. These results become the more marked the more we are absorbed in thinking of the movements which suggest them; they grow fainter exactly in proportion as a complex consciousness, under the dominion of a crowd of other representations, withstands the passing over of mental contemplation into outward action.'

The 'willing-game', the exhibitions of so-called 'mind-reading', or more properly muscle-reading, which have lately grown so fashionable, are based on this incipient obedience of muscular contraction to idea, even when the deliberate intention is that no contraction shall occur.

We may then lay it down for certain that *every representation of a movement awakens in some degree the actual movement which is its object; and awakens it in a maximum degree whenever it is not kept from so doing by an antagonistic representation present simultaneously to the mind.*

II. DOES 'CONSCIOUSNESS' EXIST? (1904)

'Thoughts' and 'things' are names for two sorts of object, which common sense will always find contrasted and will always practically oppose to each other. Philosophy, reflecting on the contrast, has varied in the past in her explanations of it, and may be expected to vary in the future. At first, 'spirit and matter', 'soul and body', stood for a pair of equipollent substances quite on a par in weight and interest. But one day Kant undermined the soul and brought in the transcendental ego, and ever since then the bipolar relation has been very much off its balance. The transcendental ego seems nowadays in rationalist quarters to stand for everything, in empiricist quarters for almost nothing. In the hands of such writers as Schuppe, Rehmke, Natorp, Münsterberg—at any rate in his earlier writings, Schubert-Soldern and others, the spiritual principle attenuates itself to a thoroughly ghostly condition, being only a name for the fact that the 'content' of experience *is known*. It loses personal form and activity—these passing over to the content—and becomes a bare *Bewusstheit* or

Bewusstsein überhaupt, of which in its own right absolutely nothing can be said.

I believe that 'consciousness', when once it has evaporated to this estate of pure diaphaneity, is on the point of disappearing altogether. It is the name of a nonentity, and has no right to a place among first principles. Those who still cling to it are clinging to a mere echo, the faint rumour left behind by the disappearing 'soul' upon the air of philosophy. During the past year, I have read a number of articles whose authors seemed just on the point of abandoning the notion of consciousness,[1] and substituting for it that of an absolute experience not due to two factors. But they were not quite radical enough, not quite daring enough in their negations. For twenty years past I have mistrusted 'consciousness' as an entity; for seven or eight years past I have suggested its non-existence to my students, and tried to give them its pragmatic equivalent in realities of experience. It seems to me that the hour is ripe for it to be openly and universally discarded.

To deny plumply that 'consciousness' exists seems so absurd on the face of it—for undeniably 'thoughts' do exist—that I fear some readers will follow me no farther. Let me then immediately explain that I mean only to deny that the word stands for an entity, but to insist most emphatically that it does stand for a function. There is, I mean, no aboriginal stuff or quality of being, contrasted with that of which material objects are made, out of which our thoughts of them are made; but there is a function in experience which thoughts perform, and for the performance of which this quality of being is invoked. That function is *knowing*. 'Consciousness' is supposed necessary to explain the fact that things not only are, but get reported, are known. Whoever blots out the notion of consciousness from his list of first principles must still provide in some way for that function's being carried on.

My thesis is that if we start with the supposition that there is only one primal stuff or material in the world, a stuff of which everything is composed, and if we call that stuff 'pure experience', then knowing can easily be explained as a particular sort of relation towards one another into which portions of pure experience may enter. The relation itself is a part of pure experience; one of its 'terms' becomes the subject or bearer of the knowledge, the knower,[2] the other becomes the object known. This will need much explanation before it can be understood. The best way to get it understood is to contrast it with the alternative view; and for that we may

---

[1] Articles by Baldwin, Ward, Bawden, King, Alexander and others. Dr Perry is frankly over the border.

[2] In my *Psychology* I have tried to show that we need no knower other than the 'passing thought'. (*Principles of Psychology*, vol. I, pp. 38 ff.).

take the recentest alternative, that in which the evaporation of the definite soul-substance has proceeded as far as it can go without being yet complete. If neo-Kantism has expelled earlier forms of dualism, we shall have expelled all forms if we are able to expel neo-Kantism in its turn.

For the thinkers I call neo-Kantian, the word 'consciousness' today does no more than signalize the fact that experience is indefeasibly dualistic in structure. It means that not subject, not object, but object-plus-subject is the minimum that can actually be. The subject-object distinction meanwhile is entirely different from that between mind and matter, from that between body and soul. Souls were detachable, had separate destinies; things could happen to them. To consciousness as such nothing can happen, for, timeless itself, it is only a witness of happenings in time, in which it plays no part. It is, in a word, but the logical correlative of 'content' in an Experience of which the peculiarity is that *fact comes to light* in it, that *awareness of content* takes place. Consciousness as such is entirely impersonal —'self' and its activities belong to the content. To say that I am self-conscious, or conscious of putting forth volition, means only that certain contents, for which 'self' and 'effort of will' are the names, are not without witness as they occur.

Thus, for these belated drinkers at the Kantian spring, we should have to admit consciousness as an 'epistemological' necessity, even if we had no direct evidence of its being there.

But in addition to this, we are supposed by almost every one to have an immediate consciousness of consciousness itself. When the world of outer fact ceases to be materially present, and we merely recall it in memory, or fancy it, the consciousness is believed to stand out and to be felt as a kind of impalpable inner flowing, which, once known in this sort of experience, may equally be detected in presentations of the outer world. 'The moment we try to fix our attention upon consciousness and to see *what*, distinctly, it is,' says a recent writer, 'it seems to vanish. It seems as if we had before us a mere emptiness. When we try to introspect the sensation of blue, all we can see is the blue; the other element is as if it were diaphanous. Yet it *can* be distinguished, if we look attentively enough, and know that there is something to look for.'[1] 'Consciousness' (Bewusstheit), says another philosopher, 'is inexplicable and hardly describable, yet all conscious experiences have this in common that what we call their content has this peculiar reference to a centre for which 'self' is the name, in virtue of which reference alone the content is subjectively given, or appears.... While in this way consciousness, or reference to a self, is the only thing which distinguishes a conscious content from any sort of being that might be there with no one conscious of it, yet this only ground of the distinction

[1] G. E. Moore: *Mind*, vol. XII, N.S., (1903), p. 450.

defies all closer explanations. The existence of consciousness, although it is the fundamental fact of psychology, can indeed be laid down as certain, can be brought out by analysis, but can neither be defined nor deduced from anything but itself.'[1]

'Can be brought out by analysis', this author says. This supposes that the consciousness is one element, moment, factor—call it what you like— of an experience of essentially dualistic inner constitution, from which, if you abstract the content, the consciousness will remain revealed to its own eye. Experience, at this rate, would be much like a paint of which the world pictures were made. Paint has a dual constitution, involving, as it does, a menstruum[2] (oil, size or what not) and a mass of content in the form of pigment suspended therein. We can get the pure menstruum by letting the pigment settle, and the pure pigment by pouring off the size and oil. We operate here by physical subtraction; and the usual view is, that by mental subtraction we can separate the two factors of experience in an analogous way—not isolating them entirely, but distinguishing them enough to know that they are two.

Now my contention is exactly the reverse of this. *Experience, I believe, has no such inner duplicity; and the separation of it into consciousness and content comes, not by way of subtraction, but by way of addition*—the addition, to a given concrete piece of it, of other sets of experiences, in connection with which severally its use or function may be of two different kinds. The paint will also serve here as an illustration. In a pot in a paint-shop, along with other paints, it serves in its entirety as so much saleable matter. Spread on a canvas, with other paints around it, it represents, on the contrary, a feature in a picture and performs a spiritual function. Just so, I maintain, does a given undivided portion of experience, taken in one context of associates, play the part of a knower, of a state of mind, of 'consciousness'; while in a different context the same undivided bit of experience plays the part of a thing known, of an objective 'content'. In a word, in one group it figures as a thought, in another group as a thing. And, since it can figure in both groups simultaneously we have every right to speak of it as subjective and objective both at once. The dualism connoted by such double-barrelled terms as 'experience', 'phenomenon', 'datum', *'Vorfindung'*—terms which, in philosophy at any rate, tend more to replace the single-barrelled terms of 'thought' and 'thing'—that dualism, I say, is still preserved in this account, but reinterpreted, so that, instead of being mysterious and elusive, it becomes verifiable and concrete.

[1] Paul Natorp: *Einleitung in die Psychologie*, 1888, pp. 14, 112.

[2] 'Figuratively speaking, consciousness may be said to be the one universal solvent, or menstruum, in which the different concrete kinds of psychic acts and facts are contained, whether in concealed or in obvious form.' G. T. Ladd: *Psychology, Descriptive and Explanatory*, 1894, p. 30.

It is an affair of relations, it falls outside, not inside, the single experience considered, and can always be particularized and defined.

The entering wedge for this more concrete way of understanding the dualism was fashioned by Locke when he made the word 'idea' stand indifferently for thing and thought, and by Berkeley when he said that what common sense means by realities is exactly what the philosopher means by ideas. Neither Locke nor Berkeley thought his truth out into perfect clearness, but it seems to me that the conception I am defending does little more than consistently carry out the 'pragmatic' method which they were the first to use.

If the reader will take his own experiences, he will see what I mean. Let him begin with a perceptual experience, the 'presentation', so called, of a physical object, his actual field of vision, the room he sits in, with the book he is reading as its centre; and let him for the present treat this complex object in the commonsense way as being 'really' what it seems to be, namely, a collection of physical things cut out from an environing world of other physical things with which these physical things have actual or potential relations. Now at the same time it is just *those self-same things* which his mind, as we say, perceives; and the whole philosophy of perception from Democritus's time downwards has been just one long wrangle over the paradox that what is evidently one reality should be in two places at once, both in outer space and in a person's mind. 'Representative' theories of perception avoid the logical paradox, but on the other hand they violate the reader's sense of life, which knows no intervening mental image but seems to see the room and the book immediately just as they physically exist.

The puzzle of how the one identical room can be in two places is at bottom just the puzzle of how one identical point can be on two lines. It can, if it be situated at their intersection; and similarly, if the 'pure experience' of the room were a place of intersection of two processes, which connected it with different groups of associates respectively, it could be counted twice over, as belonging to either group, and spoken of loosely as existing in two places, although it would remain all the time a numerically single thing.

Well, the experience is a member of diverse processes that can be followed away from it along entirely different lines. The one self-identical thing has so many relations to the rest of experience that you can take it in disparate systems of association, and treat it as belonging with opposite contexts. In one of these contexts it is your 'field of consciousness'; in another it is 'the room in which you sit', and it enters both contexts in its wholeness, giving no pretext for being said to attach itself to consciousness by one of its parts or aspects, and to outer reality by another. What are the two processes, now, into which the room-experience simultaneously enters in this way?

One of them is the reader's personal biography, the other is the history of the house of which the room is part. The presentation, the experience, the *that* in short (for until we have decided *what* it is it must be a mere *that*) is the last term of a train of sensations, emotions, decisions, movements, classifications, expectations, etc., ending in the present, and the first term of a series of similar 'inner' operations extending into the future, on the reader's part. On the other hand, the very same *that* is the *terminus ad quem* of a lot of previous physical operations, carpentering, papering, furnishing, warming, etc., and the *terminus a quo* of a lot of future ones, in which it will be concerned when undergoing the destiny of a physical room. The physical and the mental operations form curiously incompatible groups. As a room, the experience has occupied that spot and had that environment for thirty years. As your field of consciousness it may never have existed until now. As a room, attention will go on to discover endless new details in it. As your mental state merely, few new ones will emerge under attention's eye. As a room, it will take an earthquake, or a gang of men, and in any case a certain amount of time, to destroy it. As your subjective state, the closing of your eyes, or any instantaneous play of your fancy will suffice. In the real world, fire will consume it. In your mind, you can let fire play over it without effect. As an outer object, you must pay so much a month to inhabit it. As an inner content, you may occupy it for any length of time rent-free. If, in short, you follow it in the mental direction, taking it along with events of personal biography solely, all sorts of things are true of it which are false, and false of it which are true if you treat it as a real thing experienced, follow it in the physical direction, and relate it to associates in the outer world. . . .

As 'subjective' we say that the experience represents; as 'objective' it is represented. What represents and what is represented is here numerically the same; but we must remember that no dualism of being represented and representing resides in the experience *per se*. In its pure state, or when isolated, there is no self-splitting of it into consciousness and what the consciousness is 'of'. Its subjectivity and objectivity are functional attributes solely, realized only when the experience is 'taken', *i.e.*, talked-of, twice, considered along with its two differing contexts respectively, by a new retrospective experience, of which that whole past complication now forms the fresh content.

The instant field of the present is at all times what I call the 'pure' experience. It is only virtually or potentially either object or subject as yet. For the time being, it is plain, unqualified actuality, or existence, a simple *that*. . . .

I think I may now claim to have made my thesis clear. Consciousness connotes a kind of external relation, and does not denote a special stuff or way of being. *The peculiarity of your experiences, that they not only are, but are known, which their 'conscious' quality is invoked to explain, is better explained by their relations—these relations themselves being experiences—to one another.* . . .

But a last cry of *non possumus* will probably go up from many readers. 'All very pretty as a piece of ingenuity,' they will say, 'but our consciousness itself intuitively contradicts you. We, for our part, *know* that we are conscious. We *feel* our thought, flowing as a life within us, in absolute contrast with the objects which it so unremittingly escorts. We can not be faithless to this immediate intuition. The dualism is a fundamental *datum*: Let no man join what God has put asunder.'

My reply to this is my last word, and I greatly grieve that to many it will sound materialistic. I cannot help that, however, for I, too, have my intuitions and I must obey them. Let the case be what it may in others, I am as confident as I am of anything that, in myself, the stream of thinking (which I recognize emphatically as a phenomenon) is only a careless name for what, when scrutinized, reveals itself to consist chiefly of the stream of my breathing. The 'I think' which Kant said must be able to accompany all my objects, is the 'I breathe' which actually does accompany them. There are other internal facts besides breathing (intracephalic muscular adjustments, etc., of which I have said a word in my larger Psychology), and these increase the assets of 'consciousness', so far as the latter is subject to immediate perception; but breath, which was ever the original of 'spirit', breath moving outwards, between the glottis and the nostrils, is, I am persuaded, the essence out of which philosophers have constructed the entity known to them as consciousness. *That entity is fictitious, while thoughts in the concrete are fully real. But thoughts in the concrete are made of the same stuff as things are.*

20

KARL PEARSON

THE GRAMMAR OF SCIENCE (1892)

1. *The Reality of Things*

Let us start our investigation with some 'external object', and as apparent simplicity will be satisfied by taking a familiar requisite of the author's calling, namely, a blackboard, let us take it. We find an outer rectangular frame of brownish-yellow colour, which on closer inspection we presume to be wood, surrounding an inner fairly smooth surface painted black. We can measure a certain height, thickness, and breadth, we notice a certain degree of hardness, weight, resistance to breaking, and, if we examine further, a certain temperature, for the board feels to us cold or warm. Now although the blackboard at first sight appears a very simple object, we see that it at once leads us up to a very complex group of properties. In common talk we attribute all these properties to the blackboard, but when we begin to think over the matter carefully we shall find that the real link between them is by no means so simple as it seems to be. To begin with, I receive certain impressions of size and shape and colour by means of my organs of sight, and these enable me to pronounce with very considerable certainty that the object is a blackboard made of wood and coated with paint, even before I have touched or measured it. I *infer* that I shall find it hard and heavy, that I could if I pleased saw it up, and that I should find it to possess various other properties which I have learnt to *associate* with wood and paint. These inferences and associations are something which I *add* to the sight-impressions, and which I myself contribute from my past experience and put into the object—blackboard. I might have reached my conception of the blackboard by impressions of touch and not by those of sight. Blindfolded I might have judged of its size and shape, of its hardness and surface texture, and then have inferred its probable use and appearance, and associated with it all blackboard characteristics. In both cases it must be noted that a *sine qua non* of the existence of an *actual* blackboard is some immediate sense-impression to start with. The sense-impressions which determine the reality of the external object may be very few indeed, the object may be largely constructed by inferences and associations, but *some* sense-impressions there must be if I am to term the object real, and not a product merely of my imagination. The existence of a certain number of sense-impressions leads me to infer the possibility of my receiving others, and this possibility I can, if I please, put to the test.

I have heard of the Capitol at Washington and although I have never been to America, I am convinced of the reality of America and the Capitol —that is, I believe certain sense-impressions would be experienced by me if I put myself in the proper circumstances. In this case I have had indirect sense-impressions, contact with Americans, and with ships and chattels coming from America, which lead me to believe in the 'reality' of America and of what my eyes or ears have told me of its contents. In constructing the Capitol it is clear that past experience of a variety of kinds is largely drawn upon. But it must be noted that this past experience is itself based upon sense-impressions of one kind or another. These sense-impressions have been as it were stored in the memory. A sense-impression, if sufficiently strong, leaves in our brain some more or less permanent trace of itself, which is rendered manifest in the form of association whenever an immediate sense-impression of a like kind recurs. The stored effects of past sense-impressions form to a great extent what we are accustomed to speak of as an 'external object'. On this account such an object must be recognized as largely constructed by ourselves; we add to a greater or less number of immediate sense-impressions an associated group of stored sense-impressions. The proportion of the two contributions will depend largely on the keenness of our organs of sense and on the length and variety of our experience. Owing to the large amount we ourselves contribute to most external objects, Professor Lloyd Morgan, in the able discussion of this matter in his *Animal Life and Intelligence* (p. 312), proposes to use the term *construct* for the external object. For our present purpose, it is very needful to bear in mind that an external object is in general a construct—that is, a combination of immediate with past or stored sense-impressions. The reality of a thing depends upon the possibility of its occurring in whole or part as a group of immediate sense-impressions.

2. *Sense-Impressions and Consciousness*

This conception of reality as based upon sense-impressions requires careful consideration and some reservations and modifications. Let us examine a little more closely what we are to understand by the word sense-impression. In turning round quickly in my chair, I knock my knee against a sharp edge of the table. Without any thought of what I am doing my hand moves down and rubs the bruised part, or the knee may cause me so much discomfort that I get up, think of what I shall do, and settle to apply some arnica. Now the two actions on my part appear of totally different character—at least on first examination. In both cases physiologists tell us that as a primary stage a message is carried from the affected part by what is termed a *sensory nerve* to the brain. The manner in which this nerve conveys its message is without doubt physical, although its exact *modus operandi* is still unknown. At the brain what we term the sense-impression is formed, and there most probably some physical change takes place which remains with a greater or less degree of persistence in the case of those stored sense-impressions which we term memories. Everything up to the receipt of the sense-impression by the brain is what we are accustomed to term physical or mechanical, it is a legitimate inference to suppose that what from the psychical aspect we term memory has also a physical side, that the brain takes for every memory a permanent physical impress, whether by change in the molecular constitution or in the elementary motions of the brain-substance, and that such physical impress is the source of our stored sense-impression. These physical impresses play an important part in the manner in which future sense-impressions of a like character are received. If these immediate sense-impressions be of sufficient strength, or amplitude as we might perhaps venture to say, they will call into some sort of activity a number of physical impresses due to past sense-impressions allied, or, to use a more suggestive word, *attuned* to the immediate sense-impression. The immediate sense-impression is conditioned by the physical impresses of the past, and the general result is that complex of present and stored sense-impressions which we have termed a 'construct'.

Besides the *sensory* nerves which convey the messages to the brain, there are other nerves which proceed from the brain and control the muscles, termed *motor nerves*. Through these motor nerves a message is sent to my hand bidding it rub my bruised knee. This message may be sent immediately or after my fingers have been dipped in arnica. In the latter case a very complex process has been gone through. I have realized that the sense-impression corresponds to a bruised knee, that arnica is good for a bruise, that a bottle of arnica is to be found in a certain cupboard, and so forth. Clearly the sense-impression has been conditioned by a number of past impresses before the motor nerve of the arm is called into play to rub the knee. The process is described as thinking, and as a variety of past experiences may come into play, the ultimate message to the motor nerves appears to us voluntary, and we call it an act of *will*, however much it is really conditioned by the stored sense-impressions of the past. On the other hand, when, without apparently exciting any past sense-impressions, the message from the sensory nerve no sooner reaches the brain than a command is sent along the motor nerve for the hand to rub the knee, I am said to act involuntarily, from instinct or habit. The whole process may be so rapid, I may be so absorbed in my work, that I never realized the message from the sensory nerve at all. I do not even say to myself, 'I have knocked my knee and rubbed it'. Only a spectator, perhaps has been conscious of the whole process of knee-knocking and rubbing. Now this is in many respects an important result. I can receive a sense-impression without recognizing it, or a sense-impression does not involve conscious-ness. In this case there is no exciting of a group of stored sense-impressions, no chain of what we term thoughts intervening between the immediate sense-impression and the message to the motor nerve. Thus what we term consciousness is largely, if not wholly, due to the stock of stored impresses, and to the manner in which these condition the messages given to the motor nerves when a sensory nerve has conveyed a message to the brain. The measure of consciousness will thus largely depend on (1) the extent and variety of past sense-impressions, and (2) the degree to which the brain can permanently preserve the impress of these sense-impressions, or what might be termed the complexity and plasticity of the brain.

3. The Brain as a Central Telephone Exchange

The view of brain activity here discussed may perhaps be elucidated by comparing the brain to the central office of a telephone exchange, from which wires radiate to the subscribers A, B, C, D, E, F, etc., who are senders, and to W, X, Y, Z, etc., who are receivers of messages. A, having notified to the company that he never intends to correspond with anybody but W, his wire is joined to W's, and the clerk remains unconscious of the arrival of the message from A and its despatch to W, although it passes through his office.[1] There is indeed no call-bell. This corresponds to an instinctive exertion following unconsciously on a sense-impression. Next the clerk finds by experience that B invariably desires to correspond with X, and consequently, whenever he hears B's call-bell he links him mechanically to X, without stopping for a moment his perusal of *Tit-Bits*. This corresponds to a habitual exertion following unconsciously on a sense-impression. Lastly, C, D, E, and F may set their bells ringing for a variety of purposes; the clerk has in each case to answer their demands, but this may require him to listen to the special communications of these subscribers, to examine his lists, his post-office directory, or any other source of information stored in his office. Finally, he shunts their wires so as to bring them in circuit with those of Y and Z, which seems to best suit

---

[1] If these wires were connected *outside* the office, we should have an analogy to certain possibilities of reflex action, which arise from sensory and motor nerves being linked before reaching the brain—e.g. a frog's leg will be moved so as to rub an irritated point on its back even after the removal of the brain.

the nature of the demands. This corresponds to an exertion following consciously on the receipt of a sense-impression. In all cases the activity of the exchange arises from the receipt of a message from one of a possibly great but still finite number of senders, A, B, C, D, etc.; the originality of the clerk is confined to immediately following their behests or to satisfying their demands to the best of his ability by the information stored in his office. The analogy, of course, must not be pressed too far—in particular, senders and receivers must be considered distinct, for sensory and motor nerves do not appear to interchange functions. But the conception of the brain as a central exchange certainly casts considerable light not only on the action of sensory and motor nerves, but also on thought and consciousness. Without sense-impressions there would be nothing to store; without the faculty of receiving permanent impress, without memory, there would be no possibility of thought; and without this thought, this period of hesitation between sense-impression and exertion, there would be no consciousness. When an exertion follows immediately on a sense-impression we speak of the exertion as involuntary, our action as subject to the mechanical control of the 'external object' to which we attribute the sense-impression. On the other hand, when the exertion is conditioned by stored sense-impresses we term our action voluntary. We speak of it as determined from 'within ourselves', and assert the 'freedom of our will'. In the former case the exertion is conditioned solely by the immediate sense-impression; in the latter it is conditioned by a complex of impressions partly immediate and partly stored. The past training, the past history and experience which mould character and determine the will, are really based on sense-impressions received at one time or another, and hence we may say that exertion, whether immediate or deferred, is to a large extent the product, directly or indirectly, of sense-impressions.

4. The Nature of Thought

There are still one or two points to be noted here. In the first place, the immediate sense-impression is to be looked upon as the spark which kindles thought, which brings into play the still remaining impresses of past sense-impressions. But the complexity of the human brain is such, its stored sense-impressions are linked together in so many and diverse ways —partly by continual thinking, partly by immediate sense-impressions occurring in proximity and so linking together apparently discordant groups of past impressions—that we are not always able to recognize the relation between an immediate sense-impression and the resulting train of thought. Nor, on the other hand, can we always trace back a train of thought to the immediate sense-impression from which it started. Yet we may take it for certain that elements of thought are ultimately the permanent impresses of past sense-impressions, and that thought itself is started by immediate sense-impressions.[1]

This statement must not be in any way supposed to narrow the material of thought to those combinations of 'external objects' which we associate with immediate sense-impressions. Thought once excited, the mind passes with wonderful activity from one stored impression to another, it classifies these impressions, analyses or simplifies their characteristics, and forms general notions of properties and modes. It proceeds from the direct—what might perhaps be termed the physical—association of memory, to the indirect or mental association; it passes from *perceiving* to *conceiving*. The mental association or recognition of relation between the impresses of past sense-impressions has probably, if we could follow it, as definite a physical side as the physical association of immediate sense-impressions with past impresses. But the physical side of the impress is only a reasonable inference from the physical nature of the immediate sense-impression, and we must therefore content ourselves at present by considering it highly probable that every process of thought has a physical aspect, even if we are very far as yet from being able to trace it out.

This process of mental association we can only recognize as certainly occurring in our individual selves. The reason why we infer it in others we shall consider later. The amount of it, however, in our individual selves must largely depend on the variety and extent of our store of impresses, and further on the individual capacity for thinking, or on the form and development of the physical organ wherein the process of thinking takes place, i.e. on the brain. The brain in the individual man is probably considerably influenced by heredity, by health, by exercise, and by other factors, but speaking generally the physical instruments of thought in two normal human beings are machines of the same type, varying indeed in efficiency, but not in kind or function. For the same two normal human beings the organs of sense are also machines of the same type and thus within limits only capable of conveying the same sense-impressions to the brain. Herein consists the similarity of the universe for all normal human beings. The same type of physical organ receives the same sense-impressions and forms the same 'constructs'. Two normal perceptive faculties construct practically the same universe. Were this not true, the results of thinking in one mind would have no validity for a second mind. The universal validity of science depends upon the similarity of the perceptive and reasoning faculties in normal civilized men.

---

[1] The exact train of thought which follows an immediate sense-impression depends largely on the physical condition of the brain at the time of its receipt, and is further largely conditioned by the mode in which stored sense-impressions have been previously excited, i.e. the extent to which memory has been exercised in the past.

The above discussion of the nature of thought is of course incomplete; it offers no real explanation of the psychical side of thought. It is merely intended to suggest the manner in which we may consider thought to be associated with its physical accompaniments. What the actual relations between the psychical and physical aspects of thought are, we do not know, and, as in all such cases, it is best to directly confess our ignorance. It is no use, indeed only dangerous, in the present state of our knowledge with regard to psychology and the physics of the brain, to fill the void of ignorance by hypotheses which can neither be proven nor refuted. Thus if we say that thought and motion are the same thing seen from different sides, we make no real progress in our analysis for we can form no conception whatever as to what the nature in itself of this thing may be. Indeed, if we go further and compare thought and motion to the concave and convex sides of the same surface, we may do positive harm rather than good; for convexity and concavity when accurately defined by the mathematician are not different qualities, but only degrees of the same quantity, curvature, passing the one into the other through zero-curvature or flatness. On the other hand, the distinction between the psychical and physical aspects of brain activity seems to be essentially one of quality, not of degree. It is better to content ourselves in the present state of our knowledge by remarking that in all probability sense-impressions lead to certain physical (including under this term possible chemical) activities of the brain, and that these activities are recognized by each individual *for himself only* under the form of thought. Each individual recognizes his own consciousness, perceives that the interval between sensation and exertion is occupied by a certain psychical process. We recognize consciousness in out individual selves, we *assume* it to exist in others.

5. Other-Consciousness as an Eject

The assumption just referred to is by no means of the same nature as that which we make every moment in the formation of what we have termed constructs from a limited group of immediate sense-impressions. I see the shape, size, and colour of the blackboard, and I *assume* that I shall find it hard and heavy. But here the assumed properties are capable of being put to the direct test of immediate sense-impression. I can touch and lift the blackboard and complete my analysis of its properties. Even the Capitol in Washington, of which I have had no direct sense-impression, is capable of being put to the same sort of direct test. Another man's consciousness, however, can never, it is said, be directly perceived by sense-impression, I can only *infer* its existence from the apparent similarity of our nervous systems, from observing the same hesitation in his case as in my own between sense-impression and exertion, and from the similarity between his activities and my own. The inference is really not so great as the metaphysicians would wish us to believe. It is an inference ultimately based on the physical fact of the interval between sense-impression and exertion; and though we cannot as yet physically demonstrate another person's consciousness, neither can we demonstrate physically that earth-grown apples would fall at the surface of the planet of a fixed star, nor that atoms really are component parts in the structure of matter. It may be suggested that if our organs of sense were finer, or our means of locomotion more complete, we might be able to see atoms or to carry earth-grown apples to a fixed star—in other words, to test physically, or by immediate sense-impression, these inferences. But:—

'When I come to the conclusion that *you* are conscious, and that there are objects in your consciousness similar to those in mind, I am not inferring any actual or possible feelings of my own, but *your* feelings, which are not, and cannot by any possibility become, objects in my consciousness.'[1]

To this it may be replied, that, were our physiological knowledge and surgical manipulation sufficiently complete, it is conceivable that it would be possible for me to be conscious of your feelings, to recognize your consciousness as a direct sense-impression; let us say, for example, by connecting the *cortex* of your brain with that of mine through a suitable commissure of nerve-substance. The possibility of this physical verification of other-consciousness does not seem more remote than that of a journey to a fixed star. Indeed, there are some who think that without this hypothetical nerve-connection the processes popularly termed 'anticipating another person's wishes', 'reading his thoughts', etc., have in them the elements of a sense-impression of other-consciousness, and are not entirely indirect inferences from practical experience.

Clifford has given the name *eject* to existences which, like other-consciousness, are only inferred, and the name is a convenient one. At the same time it seems to me doubtful whether the distinction between *object* (what might possibly come to my consciousness as a direct sense-impression) and *eject* is so marked as he would have us to believe. The complicated physical motions of another person's brain, it is admitted, might possibly be objective realities to me; but, on the other hand, might not the hypothetical brain commissure render me just as certain of the workings of another person's consciousness as I am of my own? In this respect, therefore, it does not seem necessary to assert that consciousness lies outside the field of science, or must perforce escape the methods of

[1] W. K. Clifford, 'On the Nature of Things-in-Themselves', *Lectures and Essays*, vol. ii, p. 72.

physical experiment and research. We may be far enough removed from knowledge at the present time, but I see no logical hindrance to our asserting that in the dim future we might possibly obtain objective acquaintance with what at present appears merely as an eject. We may say this indeed without any dogmatic assumption that psychical effects can all be *reduced* to physical motion. Psychical effects are without doubt excited by and accompanied by physical action, and our only assumption is the not unreasonable one, that a suitable physical link might transfer an appreciation of psychical activity from one psychical centre to another.

6. *Attitude of Science towards Ejects*

Indeed in some respects other-consciousness appears less beyond our reach than many inferred existences. Some physicists infer the existence of atoms, although they have had no experience of any individual atom, because the hypothesis of their existence enables them to briefly resume a number of sense-impressions. We infer the existence of other-consciousness for a precisely similar reason; but in this case we have the advantage of knowing at least one individual consciousness, namely, our own. We see in ourselves how it links sense-impression and deferred exertion. While the atom, like other-consciousness, might possibly some day attain to objective reality, there are certain conceptions dealt with by science for which this is impossible. For example, our geometrical ideas of curves and surfaces are of this character. None the less, although they might with greater logic be termed *ejects*, than, perhaps, other-consciousness, there are few who would deny that they have their ultimate origin in sense-impressions, from which they have been extracted or isolated by the process of mental generalization. A still more marked class of conceptions, which we are incapable of verifying directly by any form of immediate sense-impression, is that of historical facts. We believe that King John really signed *Magna Charta*, and that there was a period when snow-fields and glaciers covered the greater part of England, yet these conceptions can never have come to our consciousness as direct sense-impressions, nor can they be verified in like manner. They are conclusions we have reached by a long chain of inferences, starting in direct sense-impressions and ending in that which, unlike atom and other-consciousness, can by no possibility be verified directly by immediate sense-impression.

9. *The Limits to Other-Consciousness*

We cannot better illustrate the limits of legitimate inference than by considering the example we have dealt with in Section 5, and asking how far we may infer the existence of consciousness and of thought. We have seen that consciousness is associated with the process which *may* intervene between the receipt of a sense-impression from a sensory nerve and the dispatch of a stimulus to action through a motor nerve. Consciousness is thus associated with physiological machinery of a certain character, which we sum up under brain and nerves. Further, it depends upon the lapse of an interval between sense-impression and exertion, this interval being filled, as it were, with the mutual resonance and cling-clang of stored sense-impressions and the conceptions drawn from them. Where no like machinery, no like interval can be observed, there we have no right to infer any consciousness. In our fellow-men 'we observe this same machinery and the like interval, and we infer consciousness, it may be as an eject, but as an eject which, as we have seen, might not inconceivably, however improbably, become some day an object. In the lower forms of life we observe machinery approximately like our own, and a shorter and shorter interval between sense-impression and exertion; we may reasonably infer consciousness, if in reduced intensity. We cannot, indeed, put our finger on a definite type of life and say here consciousness ends, but it is completely illogical to infer its existence where we can find no interval between sense-impression and exertion, or where we can find no nervous system. Because we cannot point to the exact form of material life at which consciousness ceases, we have no more right to infer that consciousness is associated with all life, still less with all forms of matter, than we have to infer that there must always be wine mixed with water, because so little wine can be mixed with water that we are unable to detect its presence. Will, too, as we have seen, is closely connected with consciousness; it is the feeling in our individual selves when exertion flows from the store of past sense-impresses 'within us', and not from the immediate sense-impression which we term 'without us'. We are justified, therefore, in inferring the feeling of will as well as consciousness in nervous systems more or less akin to our own; we may throw them out from ourselves, *eject* them into certain forms of material life. But those who eject them into matter, where no nervous system can be found, or even into existences which they postulate as immaterial, are not only exceeding enormously the bounds of scientific inference, but forming conceptions which, like that of the centaur, are inconsistent in themselves. From will and consciousness associated with material machinery we can infer nothing whatever as to will and consciousness without that machinery. We are passing by the trick of a common-name to things of which we can postulate absolutely nothing, and of which we are only unable to deny the existence when we give to that term a meaning wholly opposed to the customary one.

21

F. H. BRADLEY

ON THE SUPPOSED USELESSNESS OF THE SOUL (1895)

The following considerations must not be taken as quite expressing my own beliefs, nor again are they offered as original. But they will perhaps bring some thoughts together in a way which may be useful.

There is a view as to the connection between body and soul which seems to grow every day more in fashion. On this view the bodily sequence is wholly independent of mind. It goes on as it would go on if nothing psychical were there. The soul is somehow an adjective which makes no difference to its substantive. It is the whistle of a steam-engine which has no effect on the engine's movement; for the soul is somehow that kind of whistle which expends no steam.

Now, though this view is respectable, it seems none the less ridiculous, but my first object is rather to show its connection with another prevailing doctrine. I refer to what we may perhaps call Darwinian teleology. Everything which on a certain scale persists must be taken as useful. It was not made to be useful, but, if not useful, it would by now have been unmade. So that whatever on a certain scale has arisen and has persisted must certainly be useful. Now, if this doctrine is good, I do not see why we should not apply it to the soul, unless we are prepared everywhere to make the soul an exception to everything except disadvantage; and no one, I believe, has as yet openly contended for that principle. But, when the Darwinian view is applied to the soul, the soul apparently must be of service. Pleasure and pain, volition and thought must after all be there for something. For otherwise by this time they would surely be no longer there at all, since, if so, they would be varieties useless and yet persisting.

The above reflection is obvious and, I presume, must be answered as follows. The soul is useless, but on the other side the soul costs nothing. To be pleased or pained brings no good but brings also no harm. And thus the soul, being something which with regard to advantage or hindrance is nothing, falls wholly outside the Darwinian doctrine. But this answer can hardly stand unless we are ready to accept the old wives' story of the whistle blown and blown by nothing.[1] And if we hold to the belief that

[1] Surely we have not got to take *this* as one of 'the fairy tales of science'.

something comes from something, and that from nothing nothing comes, we shall have to seek for a less irrational proof that the soul may be useless.

If we consider that, on any view, the soul covers a large area of fact, if we decline to believe that this mass of existence is produced from and costs nothing, if we reflect further that fruitless expenditure is disadvantage which (it seems) must eventually destroy itself—we shall find it impossible to take the soul as being of no service at all. The soul must be useful, but it may be useful perhaps in a qualified sense. It may afford an advantage perhaps which is but conditional, provisional and temporary. The soul in other words, though of service now, in the end may become useless. And in the end (we must add) having become useless the soul will cease. We can find also some further reason to expect such a supersession of the soul.

Every organism, we may anticipate, will become perfect. They will all in the end be adapted to their environments, and will be internally free from defect and jolting. But, if the soul is consciousness, the soul in its essence seems to involve imperfection. For consciousness consists in a process of distinction and relation and it implies some collision. That which later we know as choice between incompatibles is at first certainly not present, but at the very dawn of consciousness we have some struggle between suggestion and fact. And if it were not so, and if we felt nothing of a baulked attempt, we never, it would appear, should become conscious at all. But consciousness, so living through friction, through delay and wavering, tends, as defects are removed, itself to pass away. Thus habits of action and of perception, acquired haltingly and with painful prominence of each struggling detail, become automatic more and more and with that unconscious. From which we conclude that, when on the whole adaptation has grown perfect, consciousness will have become superseded wholly.

This conclusion, if correct, seems the solution of our difficulty. Consciousness, though useless (we may say) both in principle and in prospect, will none the less be at present of service. Or at the least it will be the necessary accompaniment of what is useful. It will be that crying of an imperfect machine which arises from friction. This friction is expensive to the machine, and in principle it is not useless merely but positively injurious. But because inseparable from the machine at a certain stage of its development, the friction must be taken as an advantage to what owns it. But when by Evolution machines grow perfect and friction gradually is reduced to nothing, consciousness then will meet the destiny assigned to it by principle. It will have become useless wholly, and, with that, will cease to exist. And, with that, the world will have become perfect and purely physical.

There are, however, some objections which this view perhaps too much ignores. (i) For it has assumed first that the soul is the same as conscious-ness. But consciousness, with its distinction of subject from object and of objects from each other, is perhaps after all not so wide as sentience. But if the unconscious may be psychical, perfection after all need not be physical merely, but may be a sentient whole in which the oppositions of consciousness are transcended. And this psychical fact cannot be proved as above to be useless even in the end. (ii) Further, even if the principle were not unsound, the detail seems refractory. Without a process in time it is hard to see how any machine is to work and go. But with a process the door seems opened to accidents and jars, and so to outbreaks of consciousness. And since new machines have, I presume, to grow, and since old machines will, I suppose, wear out, perhaps after all perpetually there must be infantile and senile relapses into soul. And in short the Evanescence of Imperfection seems little better than the craze of a theory-monger. The facts rebel, and the principle seems mainly prejudice. The sentient machine of the Universe, though perfect, may by its essence involve collisions and friction between its parts, together with an outcry of consciousness. And what is above consciousness may still contain it as a necessary factor, while consciousness thus always, and yet never is superseded.

The view of the soul as the result of friction seems in every way unten-able, and to be oneself the self-awareness of jolts in a half-finished machine would be too stupid altogether. The distinction we draw between friction and work depends after all, I suppose, on a selected point of view. And if we wish to insist that the harmonious movement of a physical machine is by itself the one work, and that all beyond this is injurious or at least superfluous—perhaps we might begin by asking whether our point of view is rational or arbitrary.

Living once near a quarry on a hill I was persecuted by a strange noise. It came from a wooden brake screwed against the wheels of descending and loaded carts. And listening to this noise I fancied it the cry of some soul forced at intervals out of matter by too rude motion. And I tried to imagine the thoughts of such a soul and the views which it might take of its own meaning and destiny. It would perhaps at first feel sure that its own feeling was an end in itself, and that except for the sake of that or some-thing like it nothing existed. But after many vagaries this soul might come to very different results. It might reflect perhaps how its self was engen-dered by accident and defect, and how a perfect cart would admit no friction nor be liable to any soul. A perfect cart would be motion un-hindered, harmonious and silent. Or this soul might think itself in any case but parallel to the physical motion. It might consider itself to be certainly in a sense dependent on the cart's movement, yet not so as to be produced at its expense, or as in any way to make any difference to it. But it struck me then that this last view was perhaps the most foolish of all. For that something could come from nothing and lead to nothing, or that something could happen with no expense to anything, remains always irrational. And I should dare to repeat this though I had thrown at my head some word longer even that 'psycho-physical'.

22

JAMES WARD

NATURALISM AND AGNOSTICISM (1896–98)

The function of philosophy, we are often told, is to organize and unify knowledge. To this end it is before all things necessary to make knowledge itself an object of reflection and study. This science does not do, and—what is worse—the dogmatic metaphysics of Descartes, on which the whole fabric of modern knowledge long rested, did not do it either. As a consequence, the dualism of things mental and things material, *res cogitantes* and *res extensae*, has been a problem for the critic of knowledge ever since. It ought not to be thought presumptuous if philosophers claim that during these two centuries of reflection on that problem they have made some progress.

Psychology and the natural sciences advancing independently on the basis of this dualism have, as we have seen, only widened the breach. For natural science the question was how to get from matter to mind; the attempted solution by the hypothesis of psychophysical parallelism we have found defective and unsatisfactory. For psychology the question was how to get from mind to matter, the problem, in other words, of external perception. The result, again, I am bound to say, is defective and unsatisfactory. Shut in within a circle of ideas, how could the mind know the things beyond, which this very circle shut out; how could it trust the copies if the originals were forever beyond reach, nay, how know that there are any originals at all? Such were the questions raised in particular by British thinkers, from Locke to Reid. These were the questions which Locke slyly remarked 'seem not to to want difficulty', and which Hume boldly declared hopelessly insoluble; while to resolve them Berkeley denied Descartes' outer circle of things and Reid his inner circle of ideas.[1]

Meanwhile the rationalistic thinkers of the Continent, setting aside sense-impressions as too obscure and confused to afford immediate knowledge, looked to clear, distinct, and orderly thinking as the one method by which knowledge was to be educed. This procedure too proved futile and disclosed its essentially formal character, when Wolff at length made the law of contradiction the cardinal principle of his philosophy. Then

[1] Cf. Fraser, *Life and Letters of Berkeley*, p. 386.

came Kant, and the question of external perception was taken up into the wider one of the nature of experience. . . .

It was his problem, taking experience as a fact, to render it intelligible, and he entered upon this, not by assuming a dualism of matter and mind, but by insisting on the duality in unity of subject and object. And with this we too must start.

Let no one hastily conclude that between this duality and that dualism there is only the faintest verbal difference, that subject and object are but mind and matter over again. According to the Cartesian philosophy, of course, mind and matter were not only distinct and disparate, but absolutely separate and mutually independent. Their union in fact was a miracle, and so, for science, a stumbling-block; and one, too, which the various hypotheses of occasionalism, pre-established harmony, psychophysical parallelism, have severally failed to surmount. But at any rate there cannot be this great gulf fixed dividing one part of experience from another. We may ask how such conceptions can have arisen and discuss their validity, but we cannot set out from them as a fact.

There is for each but one experience, his own; and an experience that is not owned is a contradiction. We can assign no *fixed boundary* to our experience except by extending it in thought, and thought itself involves experience. Hence the phrase, 'content of experience', or 'content of consciousness', is apt to be misleading. The experience of one is not limited by the experience of another as one portion of time or space is limited by another portion of time or space. The continuity of experience is not then imposed from without. Experience is rather an organic unity that we always regard as self-maintained. In a word it is life, βίος—life as it is for the living individual, not life, or ζωή, the interaction of organism and environment, with which the so-called biologist is exclusively concerned, and where both organism and environment are objects for a distinct observer. It behoves us therefore to take all possible pains to keep these two very different standpoints distinct. Psychology, as I have already remarked earlier in these lectures, has been most seriously hampered by confusing them.

We start then with this duality of subject and object in the unity of experience. What a subject without objects, or what objects without a subject, would be, is indeed, as we are often told, unknowable; for in truth the knowledge of either apart is a contradiction. It is their unity that specially interests us, for we look to this to free us from the perplexities of dualism. . . .

As regards the bare fact of presentation there is nothing to be said; it is that relation of subject to object and of object to subject, in virtue of which they are severally subject and object. As the absolutely ultimate relation within experience we can say either that it is inexplicable, or that it needs no explanation, or we may entertain the notion of an Absolute, in whom the unity of experience outlasts the duality. But one thing, I think, we must not do: we must not attempt to bring this relation of subject and object under the category of cause and effect. I do not mean to deny that there are causal relations between subject and object, object and subject—quite the contrary. Without meddling with any of the many vexed questions concerning causation, it is at least clear that causes must be real before they can be causes: an effect or consequent cannot give rise to its own cause or antecedent. Causality logically presupposes reality, not reality causality. But subject and object in the unity of experience is the real. . . .

The subject, no doubt, is active in thought and volition, for example; but thinking and willing presuppose objects: of a subject that either by thought or will posits its own perceptions *we* at least know nothing. Also it is true that one object, or rather one change in the objective continuum, may prove the cause of the presentation of another; so to relate change with change is indeed the special function of the category of cause. But this, like any other relation of particular object to particular object, leaves the more fundamental relation of subject to object just where it was.[1]

The fundamental and ultimate character of this relation is, in fact, the whole difficulty. Experience is far advanced before even the rudest reflection about it can begin. Imperfect analysis and deceptive analogies are the first result of such reflections; and as these become embodied in common thought and language they count for part of the facts, though really fictions that belie them. Thus, the subject being identified with the organism which is but a special object among others, the whole objective continuum is said to be an affection of the subject, because the physical environment affects the body. So we get the notion of sensations as subjective affections, whose causes are still to seek. Then come the metaphysical travesties of inner and outer, which refer originally and literally to space divided into two compartments by a man's skin. But presently, since it is said there is nothing in the intellect but what first came through sense, 'inner' comes to mean the whole of each one's experience as it is for him, the psychical side of his particular brain; inner is then the equivalent of subjective. Outer, on the other hand, is the brain side of this particular subject *plus* all the rest of the external world; in this all sentients alike are supposed to participate. Imagine a dozen genii, each one hermetically sealed in a bottle, but all collectively roaming at large, and you have a fair parallel to this figure of inner and outer. Again, look for a moment at another line, where reflection shows itself equally confused and incom-

---

[1] Cf. J. S. Mill, *Examination of Sir W. Hamilton's Philosophy*, third edition, p. 231.

H

plete. The sense of touch, from its intimate connection with muscular activity, is held to present the actual; while sight, in spite of its preeminence in cognition, being a fruitful source of illusion, is found often to present things as they 'appear', not as they actually, i.e. tangibly, palpably, are. So by an easy step *all* our sensible intuitions come to be regarded as phenomenal, the things *per se*, which are held to be their cause, and by which we might test them, being now out of reach. But how then, we are led to ask, can we speak of such things *per se* at all? And yet the answer is easy, once we are committed to the notion that sensations are subjectively affections, and objectively appearances or phenomena. For, the validity of these notions being taken for granted, Kant argues with perfect cogency when he says 'that we must have something to correspond to the receptivity of the sensibility'.[1] And again that 'it follows naturally that something must correspond to it that is not itself phenomenon'; also 'that the very word 'phenomenon' indicates a relation to something, the immediate presentation of which is indeed sensible, but which in itself apart from this condition of sensibility, must still be Something, namely, an object independent of sensibility.'[2] But the prime question is not what the notions of receptivity and phenomenality implicate; but what warrant these notions themselves possess in experience. And here we can only follow suit and, like the great body of Kant's critics, preach to Kant from himself. Let what may be outside experience, if there can be anything, and the supposition is not nonsense, at least there cannot be bare subjects lying in wait for objects, nor objects that by definition never are positively objects. If the categories of substance and cause are only valid *within* experience, they cannot be applied to experience as a whole. Whatever implications experience may involve, it surely cannot involve that of transcending itself. Such miscalled transcendence, if it have any validity, must really be immanence at bottom.

If this duality in unity of subject and object be indeed the fundamental fact of experience, present alike in cognition, in feeling, and in volition, then, so far at any rate, there can be nothing to explain. The demand for explanation may be taken as evidence that we have misconceived the facts. On this ground therefore we must suspect and avoid all statements of experience that introduce conceptions of relations narrower and more special than itself. Such, for example, is the reference to organs of sense excited by external stimuli. Such again is the contrast of perceptual experience with experience as modified by intersubjective intercourse, a contrast which leads us first to picture each individual as confined strictly to his own inside, and then with Mr Spencer and others to exclaim about 'the mysteriousness of the consciousness of something that is yet out of

[1] *Kritik der reinen Vernunft*, Kehrbach's edition, p. 403.   [2] Op. cit., p. 233.

consciousness, which nevertheless', they say, 'we are obliged to think'.[1] I am well aware that this is the region of controversy and that dogmatism is here peculiarly unbecoming. But there is another side to the situation. The very failures that have overtaken the old watchwords make it fitting to ask, whether it be not possible to take a little less for granted, and to be charier of metaphors; whether it is not time to treat as futile all attempts to *explain* experience, at any rate all attempts to explain it by what falls short of it on the one hand, or goes beyond it on the other. To enounce that experience is a whole, or more precisely a continuity, that it consists in the correlation of subject and object as its universal factors, is a statement that seems to tamper with no facts and to involve no hypotheses.

'When ten men look at the sun or moon', said Reid, 'they all see the same individual object'. But not so, Hamilton replies: 'the truth is that each of these persons sees a different object'.[2] With these diametrically opposite statements of the two chieftains of the Scottish philosophy, we may begin our inquiry. It is obvious that they are here at different standpoints: Reid at that of universal, Hamilton at that of individual, experience. In Hamilton's sense not one of the ten sees *the* sun; in Reid's 'the same individual object', which all mean, is not equivalent to the immediate experience of any one. Hamilton is right in so far as each concrete experience has its own concrete object; Reid in so far as common experience relates all these concrete objects to one phenomenon. . . .

Our first question is to get clear ideas as to the relation of the ten different (actual) objects of Hamilton's statement to the one identical (phenomenal) object of Reid's. The question naturally presents itself in the form: How does the one sun become an object to ten different men? Yet the proper form rather is: How, and in what sense, do the ten come to know that the actual object of each is the same individual object for all? For except on the basis of individual experience communication is impossible. Yet obvious as this admission is, it carries consequences that are usually forgotten, so dominant has the universalistic standpoint become. Now if the several subjects, L, M, N, . . . could, so to say, change places and the presentations of one become accessible in their actual entirety to the others, then it might be possible to ascertain directly how far the object of one was comparable or identical with that of another. But it is superfluous to say that this is just the most impossible thing in the world. Individuality consists precisely in this impossibility. So, when we speak of the totality of a given experience as Ego and non-Ego, we regard such totality not merely as a logical, but as an actual concrete, universe. In this wise,

---

[1] Cf. Spencer, *Principles of Psychology*, vol. ii, p. 452.
[2] *Lectures on Metaphysics and Logic*, vol. ii, p. 153.

Leibniz, for example, conceived each of his monads as mirroring the universe from a unique standpoint of its own. Thus when in place of the Ego L we have M or N, so too in place of the non-Ego non-L we have non-M or non-N. The most, then, that L can indicate or communicate to M of any part of his own experience, is so much of it as is common to the experience of both. We may be sure the earliest intercourse fell very far short of this, and even now the maximum is probably never attained. The process apparently begins with simple indications: we point to a particular thing as this or that, and then—if it be 'something more than phantasy'— each has 'the sensible and true avouch of his own eyes' that such particular is numerically identical in their several experiences.[1] And even the description of this particular must, it would seem, rest ultimately on indications. We point to other particulars that we find resembling it—other shining, moving, round objects; and so, by suggesting its likeness to these, take the chance that parallel relations or comparisons will be verified by our fellow-men. . . . So far as reality consists in particulars, so far it pertains to each experience for itself alone; and so far the solipsist in theory and the egoist, the solipsist in conduct, are logically unassailable; even though the proper place to put them be, as Schopenhauer said, the madhouse. All communication begins and ends in establishing relations between these primary *realia* of the communicants; so far as this is achieved they are said to understand each other. Language, soon superseding mere gesture and exclamation, becomes the medium of such understanding, and the two mutually advance together.

Without this intersubjective intercourse mankind would remain a herd; with it they become a society. The common knowledge that results might be roughly distinguished as practical, historical, and theoretical, including under the last both science and philosophy. . . .

It is not on the practical or historical side that common knowledge conflicts with individual experience, for there the reference to individual subjects is still present and essential. But intersubjective intercourse on what we may call the theoretical side leads almost inevitably to the omission of this reference; and so for the living green we have the sombre grey and Man at least 'and Nature are at strife'. Let us now try to see how this comes about.

It seems to depend upon three elements or conditions which are consequences of intersubjective intercourse: the notion of the trans-subjective, the hypothesis of introjection, and the reification of abstractions. The meaning of this somewhat novel terminology will, I hope, become clear as we go along. We shall be mainly concerned with the first two and

[1] In the case of ten hungry men and a loaf, for example, this object-lesson would be impressive.

with the third chiefly as it is implicated in these. The term 'trans-subjective'[1] has been devised to obviate the confusion of what is objective from the standpoint of universal Experience, the one individual object of Reid's ten men, with what is objective for an individual experience, the different objects of Hamilton's ten. *The* sun as trans-subjective objective is not L's sun or M's sun or N's sun,—if I may so say,—but rather what is common to them all, neglecting what is peculiar to each—neglecting, in particular, that direct and immediate relation to L, M, and N severally, which constitutes for each his own non-Ego. Apart from L or M their respective non-Egos,—non-L, non-M,—are non-existent, and their respective suns in like manner. Not so *the* sun as a trans-subjective object. If we ask: Since this object is not the peculiar object of any given consciousness, for what consciousness is it an object?, we have at once Kant's answer: *für Bewusstsein überhaupt*, for consciousness in general. Following out this answer, we might presently see that this conceptual consciousness,—absolute consciousness we may (in this context) fairly call it—presupposes and is inseparable from the individual consciousness of immediate experience; in this respect resembling the conceptual or absolute space and time already discussed. But we want first to be clear about the rise of dualism. To that end it will be sufficient here to note that ordinary thought does not raise Kant's question. It proceeds rather in this wise. Regarding *the* sun as independent of L and M and N *severally*, it concludes that it is and remains an object, independently of them all *collectively*. Such reasoning is about on a par with maintaining that the British House of Commons is an estate of the realm independent of each individual member and that therefore it might be addressed from the throne, for instance, though there were no members. This fallacy of naive realism is one step towards dualism; the hypothesis of introjection supplies the other.

The term 'introjection' we owe to a brilliant thinker but recently taken from us, the late Richard Avenarius of Zurich. The hypothesis to which it refers is familiar enough and as old apparently as human speech; it is substantially what Professor Tylor has called animism. But to Avenarius belongs the merit of making the epistemological bearings of this primitive doctrine clearer than they were before. The essence of introjection consists in applying to the immediate experience of my fellow creatures conceptions which have no counterpart in my own. I find myself in direct relation with my environment and only what I find for myself can I logically assume for another. But of another, common thought and language lead me to assume not merely that his experience is distinct from mine, but that it is *in* him in the form of sensations, perceptions and other 'internal states'. Of the sun in my environment I say there is a perception

---

[1] Cf. Volkelt, *Erfahrung und Denken*, p. 42.

in him. Thus while my environment is an external world for me, his experience is for me an internal world in him. This is introjection. And since I am led to apply this conception to all my fellow-creatures and it is applied by all my fellow-men to me I naturally apply it also to myself. Thus it comes about that instead of construing others' experience exactly and precisely on the lines of our own,—the duality of subject and object,— we are induced to misconstrue our own experience on the lines of a false but highly plausible assumption as to others' experience, which actually contradicts our own. To this contradiction, latent in common thought and language, we may fairly attribute the *impasse* to which the problem of external perception has been reduced. With this contradiction and the fallacy of naive realism just now referred to, dualism is essentially complete.

But, so long as the problem of external perception does not obtrude, the inconsistencies of these two positions, to which social thinking has led, remain latent and unheeded. Psychology and the natural sciences which work on the level of this uncritical thinking take each their own half of what—if they think about it at all—they suppose to be a consistent and complete whole. The one regarding 'the trans-subjective' as a real world devoid of all subjective implications, and the other accepting introjection as a fact, they go their several ways, till in the end they have not a single term in common—not even time, which Kant imagined belonged alike to both. So complete is the dualism that when philosophy essays to heal the breach, it has no adequate language in which to express itself; for its new wine there are only the old bottles. To the plain man its teaching is a stumbling-block; to the man of science it is foolishness. Not merely are familiar words used in what seems an unusual and non-natural sense, but a position is challenged which the several sciences have long held to be impregnable. For what is true, men say, if it be not true that mind and matter are disparate realities, if 'what takes place in the mind' cannot be at once and always distinguished from 'what takes place without it'. Well, it is not unfrequently a sure sign of radical disease, when the patient maintains that he is in perfect health and wants no physician. Science and common thought are, I make bold to say, in this plight as regards dualism, when they refuse the ministrations of philosophy. We can only prescribe reflection; and happily the reflection is sure sooner or later to come, and cannot in the end fail of its result. But it is the practice of too many philosophers in our day to defer this advice till the mischief has reached an advanced stage, and the difficulties of a thoroughgoing reflection are proportionally increased.

23

V. I. LENIN

MATERIALISM AND EMPIRIO-CRITICISM (1908)

Let us turn to empirio-criticism. Not only does Avenarius *dispute* the materialist thesis, but invents a whole 'theory' in order to refute it.

'The brain,' says Avenarius in *Der menschliche Weltbegriff*, 'is not the habitation, the seat, the creator, it is not the instrument or organ, the supporter or substratum, etc., of thought' (p. 76—approvingly quoted by Mach in the *Analyse der Empfindungen*, p. 22, note). 'Thought is not an indweller, or commander, or the other half, or side, etc., nor is it a product or even a physiological function, or a state in general of the brain' (ibid).

And Avenarius expresses himself no less emphatically in his *Bemerkungen*: 'presentations' are 'not functions (physiological, psychical, or psychophysical) of the brain' (op. cit. S115). Sensations are not 'psychical functions of the brain' (S116).

Thus, according to Avenarius, the brain is not the organ of thought, and thought is not a function of the brain. Take Engels, and we immediately find directly contrary, frankly materialist formulations.

'Thought and consciousness', says Engels in *Anti-Dühring*, 'are products of the human brain'. This idea is often repeated in that work. In *Ludwig Fuerbach* we have the following exposition of the views of Fuerbach and Engels:

'... the material (*stofflich*), sensuously perceptible world to which we ourselves belong is the only reality ... our consciousness and thinking, however supra-sensuous they may seem, are the product (*Erzeugnis*) of a material, bodily organ, the brain. Matter is not a product of mind, but mind itself is merely the highest product of matter. This is, of course, pure materialism' (4th German ed., p. 18).

Or on p. 4, where he speaks of the reflection of the processes of nature in 'the thinking brain', etc., etc.

Avenarius rejects this materialist standpoint, and says that 'the thinking brain' is a 'fetish of natural science' (*Der menschliche Weltbegriff*, 2. Aufl.,

S. 70). Hence, Avenarius cherishes no illusions concerning his absolute disagreement with natural science on this point. He admits, as do Mach and all the immanentists, that natural science holds an instinctive and unconscious materialist point of view. He admits and explicitly declares that he *absolutely differs from the 'prevailing psychology'* (*Bemerkungen*, S.150, etc.). This prevailing psychology is guilty of an inadmissible 'introjection' —such is the new term contrived by our philosopher—i.e., the insertion of thought into the brain, or of sensations into us. These 'two words' (into us—*in uns*), Avenarius goes on to say, contain the assumption (*Annahme*), that empirio-criticism disputes. 'This *insertion* (*Hineinverlegung*) of the visible, etc., into man is what we call *introjection*' (p. 153, S.45).

Introjection deviates 'in principle' from the 'natural conception of the world' (*natürlicher Weltbegriff*) by substituting 'into me' for 'before me' (*vor mir*, p. 154) 'by turning a component part of the (real) environment into a component part of (ideal) thought' (ibid).

'Out of the *amechanical* (a new word in place of 'psychical') which manifests itself freely and clearly in the experienced (or, in what is found—*im Vorgefundenen*), introjection makes something which hides itself (*Latitierendes*, says Avenarius—another new word) mysteriously in the central nervous system' (ibid).

The doctrine of introjection is a muddle; it smuggles in idealistic rubbish and is contradictory to natural science, which inflexibly holds that thought is a function of the brain, that sensations, i.e., the images of the *external world*, exist *within us*, produced by the action of things on our sense-organs. The materialist elimination of the 'dualism of spirit and body' (i.e. materialist monism) consists in the assertion that the spirit does not exist independently of the body, that spirit is secondary, a function of the brain, a reflection of the external world. The idealist elimination of the 'dualism of spirit and body' (i.e., idealist monism) consists in the assertion that spirit is *not* a function of the body, that, consequently, spirit is primary, that the 'environment' and the 'self' exist only in an inseparable connection of one and the same 'complexes of elements'. Apart from these two diametrically opposed methods of eliminating 'the dualism of spirit and body', there can be no third method, unless it be eclecticism, which is a senseless jumble of materialism and idealism. And it was this jumble of Avenarius' that seemed to Bogdanov and Co. 'the truth transcending materialism and idealism'.

But the professional philosophers are not as naive and credulous as are the Russian Machians. True, each of these professors-in-ordinary advocates his '*own*' system of refuting materialism, or, at any rate, of 'reconciling' materialism and idealism. But when it comes to a competitor they unceremoniously expose the unconnected fragments of materialism and idealism that are contained in all the 'recent' and 'original' systems. And if a few young intellectuals swallowed Avenarius' bait, that old bird Wundt was not to be enticed so easily. The idealist Wundt tore the mask from the poseur Avenarius very unceremoniously *when he praised him for the anti-materialist tendency of the theory of introjection.*

'If empirio-criticism', Wundt wrote, 'reproaches vulgar materialism because by such expressions as the brain "has" thought, or the brain "produces" thought, it expresses a relation which generally cannot be established by factual observation and description (evidently, for Wundt it is a "fact" that a person thinks without the help of a brain!) . . . this reproach, of course, is well founded'.

Nor is it surprising that the theory of introjection approved by Wundt appeals to the sympathy of the outspoken spiritualist, James Ward,[1] who wages systematic war on 'naturalism and agnosticism,' and especially on Huxley (not because he was an insufficiently outspoken and determined materialist, for which Engels reproached him, but) because his agnosticism served in fact to conceal materialism.

Let us note that Karl Pearson, the English Machian, who avoids all philosophical artifices, and who recognizes neither introjection, nor co-ordination, nor yet 'the discovery of the world-elements', arrives at the inevitable outcome of Machism when it is stripped of such 'disguises', namely, pure subjective idealism. Pearson knows no 'elements'; 'sense impressions' are his alpha and omega. He never doubts that man thinks with the help of the brain. And the contradiction between this thesis (which alone conforms with science) and the basis of his philosophy remains naked and obvious. Pearson spares no effort in combating the concept that matter exists independently of our sense-impressions (*The Grammar of Science*, Chap. VII). Repeating all Berkeley's arguments, Pearson declares that matter is a nonentity. But when he comes to speak of the relation of the brain to thought, Pearson emphatically declares:

'From will and consciousness associated with material machinery we can infer nothing whatever as to will and consciousness without that machinery'.[2]

What is matter? What is experience?

The first of these questions is constantly being put by the idealists and agnostics, including the Machians, to the materialists; the second question

---

[1] James Ward, *Naturalism and Agnosticism*, London, 1906, Vol. II, pp. 171–72.
[2] Karl Pearson, *The Grammar of Science*, 2nd ed., London, 1900, p. 58.

by the materialists to the Machians. Let us try to make the point at issue clear.

Avenarius says on the subject of matter:

'Within the purified, "complete experience" there is nothing "physical" —"matter" in the metaphysical absolute conception—for "matter" according to this conception is only an abstraction; it would be the total of the counter-terms abstracted from every central term. Just as in the "principal co-ordination", that is, "complete experience", a counter-term is inconceivable (*undenkbar*) without a central term, so matter in the absolute metaphysical conception is a complete chimera (*Unding*)' (Bemerkungen, S.119).

In all this gibberish one thing is evident, namely, that Avenarius designates the physical or matter by the terms absolute and metaphysical, for, according to his theory of the principal co-ordination (or, in the new way, 'complete experience'), the counter-term is inseparable from the central term, the environment from the self; the non-self is inseparable from the self (as J. G. Fichte said). That this theory is disguised subjective idealism we have already shown, and the nature of Avenarius' attacks on 'matter' is quite obvious: the idealist denies physical being that is independent of the psychical and therefore rejects the concept elaborated by philosophy for such being. That matter is 'physical' (i.e., that which is most familiar and immediately given to man, and the existence of which no one save an inmate of a lunatic asylum can doubt) is not denied by Avenarius; he only insists on the acceptance of '*his*' theory of the indissoluble connection between the environment and the self.

Mach expresses the same thought more simply, without philosophical flourishes:

'What we call matter is a certain systematic combination of the *elements* (sensations)' (*Analyse der Empfindungen*, S.270).

Mach thinks that by this assertion he is effecting a 'radical change' in the usual world outlook. In reality this is the old, old subjective idealism, the nakedness of which is concealed by the word 'element'.

And lastly, the English Machian, Pearson, a rabid antagonist of materialism, says:

'Now there can be no scientific objection to our classifying certain more or less permanent groups of sense-impressions together and terming them matter—to do so indeed leads us very near to John Stuart Mill's definition of matter as a "permanent possibility of sensation"—but this definition of matter then leads us entirely away from matter as the thing which moves' (*The Grammar of Science*, 2nd ed., 1900, p. 249).

Here there is not even the fig-leaf of the 'elements', and the idealist openly stretches out a hand to the agnostic.

As the reader sees, all these arguments of the founders of empirio-criticism entirely and exclusively revolve around the old epistemological question of the relation of thinking to being, of sensation to the physical. It required the extreme naiveté of the Russian Machians to discern anything here that is evenly remotely related to 'recent science', or 'recent positivism'. All the philosophers mentioned by us, some frankly, others surreptitiously, replace the fundamental philosophical line of materialism (from being to thinking, from matter to sensation) by the reverse line of idealism. Their denial of matter is the old answer to epistemological problems, which consists in denying the existence of an external, objective source of our sensations, of an objective reality corresponding to our sensations.

24

G. E. MOORE

I. THE SUBJECT-MATTER OF PSYCHOLOGY (1909-10)

It seems to me that Psychology has a special subject-matter of its own; and that this special subject-matter may be defined by saying that it consists of all those among the contents of the Universe, and those only, which are 'mental' or 'psychical' in their nature. And the chief thing which I wish to do in this paper is to consider which among the contents of the Universe *are* 'mental' or 'psychical' in their nature, and how these are distinguished from those which are not. It seems to me that the Universe contains an immense variety of different kinds of entities. For instance: My mind, any particular thought or perception of mine, the quality which distinguishes an act of volition from a mere act of perception, the Battle of Waterloo, the process of baking, the year 1908, the moon, the number 2, the distance between London and Paris, the relation of similarity—all these are contents of the Universe, all of them are or were contained in it. And I wish to ask with regard to them all which of them are 'mental' or 'psychical' in their nature and which are not. For this purpose, I wish to have some common name, which I can apply to any one of them without implying anything more, with regard to that to which I apply it, than simply that it is or was *something*, that it is or was a content of the Universe. And I propose to use the word I have already used—the word 'entity'—in this extremely wide sense. When I speak of an 'entity' I shall mean to imply absolutely nothing more with regard to that which I so call, than that it *is* or *was*—that it is or was contained in the Universe; and of anything whatever which *is* or *was*, I shall take the liberty to say that it is an 'entity'. It is by no means clear to me that all 'entities'— all the contents of the Universe—can rightly be said to 'exist' or to be 'phenomena'; and though all of them are, no doubt (in certain senses of these words), 'objects' and 'realities' and 'things', yet there are other senses of these words in which many of them are not 'objects', not 'real', not 'things'. It is for this reason that I prefer the word 'entities' to any of these words which are, I think, sometimes used as its equivalents; the words 'existents', 'phenomena', 'objects', 'realities', 'things'. And I may, therefore, put the main question of my paper in the following form: What kinds of 'entities' are 'mental' or 'psychical' entities? And how are those which *are* 'mental' entities distinguished from those which are not?

I shall divide my treatment of this question into two parts. I shall, first of all, (1) try to classify those kinds of entities which seem to me to be undoubtedly 'mental', and to consider what it is that distinguishes these from all the other contents of the Universe. And I shall then (2) consider certain entities or supposed entities, with regard to which it seems to me doubtful whether they are 'mental' entities or not, and shall inquire in what sense, if any, these could properly be said to be 'mental'.

1. Entities which are undoubtedly Mental

I wish here to define as clearly as I can those kinds of entities which seem to me to be undoubtedly mental, and to consider how they differ from those which are not mental.

To begin with, then: I see, I hear, I smell, I taste, etc.; I sometimes feel pains; I sometimes observe my own mental acts; I sometimes remember entities which I have formerly seen or heard, etc.; I sometimes imagine and I sometimes dream; I think of all sorts of different entities; I believe some propositions, and think of others, without believing them; I take pleasure in certain events, and am displeased at others; and I sometimes resolve that certain actions shall be done. All these things I do; and there is nothing more certain to me than that I do them all. And because, in a wide sense, they are all of them things which I do, I propose to call them all 'mental *acts*'. By calling them 'acts' I do not wish to imply that I am always particularly active when I do them. No doubt, I must be active in a sense, whenever I do any of them. But certainly, when I do some of them, I am sometimes very passive.

Now I think we may say that, whenever I do any of these things, I am always 'conscious of' something or other. Each of these mental acts consists, at least in part, in my being conscious of something. I do not mean to say that, in the case of each of them, I am conscious of something in one and the same sense. For instance, when I actually see a colour, I am certainly conscious of that colour in a very different sense from that in which I am conscious of it when I remember it half an hour afterwards and do not any longer see it. And I am not sure that there is anything whatever in common to these two senses of 'consciousness'. But still I think the name can certainly be rightly applied to what occurs in both these cases; and that similarly we are, in *some* proper sense of the word, conscious of something whenever we do any of the acts I have named. And I do not know how to explain what I mean by 'consciousness' except by saying that each of these acts I have named is an act of consciousness. But still I hope that this is a sufficient indication of what I mean. And I think it is at least sufficient to enable us to say with certainty that certain other acts, which I have not named, resemble these in being acts of consciousness.

'Consciousness', then, for all I know, may be a name for several very different kinds of entities. But in all the cases I have named there is, I think, one thing clear about it: namely, that in every case there is always a distinction between that *of* which we are conscious and our consciousness of it. I do not mean to say that the two are always 'separable'; nor yet do I mean to say anything with regard to the relation in which they stand to one another; I only mean to say that they are always *distinct* entities: and that they are so seems to me to be certain for the following reason. Let us consider any one of the mental acts I have named—seeing, for example. There is nothing more certain to me than that I do constantly see one colour at one time, and a different colour at a different time, and that, though the colours are different, I am conscious of them both in exactly the same sense. It follows, then, that since the colours are different in the two cases, whereas what I mean by my consciousness of them is in both cases the same, my consciousness of a colour must be something different from any of the colours of which I am conscious. And the same result follows, whichever of the mental acts I have named be considered. I am quite certain that I do at different times remember different events, will different actions, etc., and though *what* I remember, *what* I will, etc., may be in each case different, yet what I mean by 'remembering' or 'willing' may be in each case exactly the same. There is, therefore, always a distinction between *what* I am conscious of and *my consciousness* of it. And the latter of these two distinct entities is the first kind of entity which seems to me to be undoubtedly mental. Whenever anybody is conscious of anything in the sense or senses which I have tried to indicate, then his consciousness, as distinguished from that *of* which he is conscious, is, I think, undoubtedly a mental entity.

'Consciousness', then, is undoubtedly a name for a mental entity or for several different kinds of mental entities. Every act of consciousness is a mental entity. But what exactly do we mean by saying that it is 'mental'?

The first and most important thing we mean by this is, I think, just simply that it is an act of consciousness. 'Mental', in one of its senses and its most fundamental sense, is, I think, merely another way of saying that the entity said to be mental *is* an act of consciousness. So that, in this sense of the word, that which distinguishes mental entities from those which are not mental would be simply the fact that the former are acts of consciousness, whereas the latter are not. And, in this sense, it is quite plain that many entities are not mental. A red colour, for example, is certainly not an act of consciousness in the sense in which my seeing of it is. It may, indeed (as some people seem to think), be an 'appearance' of an act of consciousness; but, if so, then certainly the appearance is very different from the reality. This sense in which to be a mental entity is to be an act of consciousness is, I think, the most fundamental sense of the word 'mental': it is the one from which all others are derived. Had we not noticed the difference between acts of consciousness and entities which either are not or do not seem to be such, no one would ever have thought of dividing entities into mental or non-mental, or of speaking of 'mind' at all. But though this is the most fundamental sense of the word 'mental', there certainly are others derived from it, and important ones too, which might allow us to say that entities, which are not acts of consciousness, nevertheless are mental. And I must go on to speak of these.

The first of these is a property which might be thought to belong to *all* mental acts, and to be a further characteristic, in addition to the fact that all of them are acts of consciousness, which distinguishes them from entities which are not mental. And this characteristic is one which is, I think, certainly very often meant by the word 'mental'; when it is said that an entity is 'mental' or 'in the mind', it is, I think, very often meant that it has this characteristic. The characteristic I mean is the one which we express by saying that a given mental act is an act *of the same person* or *of the same mind* as another mental act. All the mental acts, of the existence of which we are most certain, do seem to have this characteristic. Each of them is the act of some one mind, and is related to a certain number of other acts by the fact that they are all of them acts of the same mind. In fact, all the mental acts we know best seem to be divided into groups, each group having the characteristic that all its members are acts of the same mind. Thus, for example, a certain number of the mental acts in the Universe have been mental acts of mine, a certain number have been the mental acts of King Edward VII, and so on in millions of other instances. That many mental acts have this characteristic, and that it is a most important characteristic, seems to me as certain as anything can be. Thus, for example, I am quite certain that a certain number of mental acts really have been mental acts of 'mine'; that what I mean by saying that they are all 'mine' is a most important characteristic that they have; and that it is one which distinguishes them from the mental acts of other people. That this is so we all of us constantly assume, and no philosopher has, I think, ever succeeded in avoiding the implication that it is so. The language we use constantly implies that one respect in which two mental acts may differ from one another is by the fact that one of them is the mental act of one person and the other the mental act of another person; and that one respect in which two mental acts may resemble one another is by the fact that both of them are mental acts of the same person. And that something important is meant by this language seems to me to be quite certain. As to *what* exactly is meant I confess I cannot be sure; and I shall presently have to say what I can about the matter. For the present, I wish only to insist that *something* true is meant when it is said that two mental acts are mental acts of the same person; that, for instance, there is *some* sense in which *my* mental acts are all *mine*. And hence that, if it is said to be a characteristic of all mental acts that they are the mental acts of somebody or other—that they all belong to *some* mind, though different ones to different minds— these words would express a characteristic which *might* belong to all mental acts, and which, if it did, would be a characteristic in addition to, and distinct from, that which is expressed by saying that they all *are* acts of consciousness. This characteristic, it seems to me, is one which is often meant when it is said that a given entity is 'mental' or 'in the mind': it is meant that the entity in question is related to some mind in the same way in which his mental acts are related to him—by that relation which is expressed by saying that they are all *his*. And if this be used as a *positive* criterion of what is mental, I can find no objection to it. That is to say, if it be said that any entity which *has* this relation to any person or to any mind is 'mental', I shall be prepared to admit it. It does seem to me, for example, that if any entity were related to me or to my mind in just that way in which my mental acts are related to me, we might quite properly say that such an entity was 'mental', and was 'in my mind' in the same sense in which my mental acts are 'in my mind'. Whether any entities, except mental acts, are or can be related to me in this way, is a question which I shall presently consider. But, *if* any are related to any mind in this manner, then, I should say we might properly call them 'mental'. Here, therefore, we have a sense of the word 'mental' which might possibly include other entities besides acts of consciousness. But if this characteristic be also proposed as a negative criterion of what is 'mental'—if, beside saying that anything which *does* possess it is 'mental', it be also said that nothing which does *not* possess it, is so—then, the assertion seems to me to be very doubtful. For it seems to me possible that there may be acts of consciousness which are *not* the acts of any mind— which are not related to any other acts, in the peculiar way in which the mental acts of any one person are related to one another. That there might be acts of consciousness, isolated in this way, seems to me possible; and if there were, then certainly they would be 'mental' entities, simply because they were acts of consciousness. That there are any such I don't feel at all sure; but the mere possibility that there should be seems to me a sufficient objection to saying that nothing can be 'mental' except what belongs to some mind in the sense in which my mental acts belong to mine.

The second characteristic I wish to mention is one which cannot, I think, be said to be a 'meaning' of the term 'mental', but which may be and has been proposed as a *criterion* of what is 'mental', and which is certainly a very important characteristic. It has been suggested, namely, that any entity which *can be directly known by one mind only* is a mental entity, and is 'in the mind' of the person in question, and also, conversely, that all mental entities can be directly known only by a single mind. By 'direct knowledge' is here meant the kind of relation which we have to a colour, when we actually see it, or to a sound when we actually hear it. And the suggestion that all mental entities have the characteristic that they can be directly known, in this sense, only by one single mind, is, I think, certainly plausible for the following reason. It certainly is a very remarkable difference between my own mental acts and those of other people, that my own are the only ones that I ever know directly. I certainly never have been conscious of anybody else's thoughts or feelings or perceptions in that direct manner in which I am conscious of a colour when I actually see it; but of my own mental acts I am very often conscious in this direct manner. I am, of course, conscious, in a sense, of the mental acts of other people; I do know some of them, in a very real sense, and know a great deal about them; but certainly I am never *directly* conscious of them, I do not know them *directly*, in the sense in which I often know my own. This is, I think, certainly a very remarkable distinction between my mental acts and those of other people. And the rule seems to be a nearly universal one: it seems to be nearly universally true that each of us can only know directly *his own* mental acts—never those of any other person. No one, for instance, that I know of, except myself, has ever known directly any mental act of mine. There is, therefore, plausibility in the suggestion that this may be a universal characteristic of mental acts: it certainly belongs to all of those which we know best, and know most about. But yet I think it is doubtful whether it belongs to *all* mental acts. There seems to be no reason why it should: no reason why one person should not *ever* be able to know directly the mental acts of any other person; at best, it seems only to be a fact that no one ever does. And, moreover, there seems to be a certain amount of evidence that it does actually occur in very rare cases. Dr Morton Prince's 'Sally' seems to have claimed that she knew directly some of the mental acts of B I; and if we admit her claim, and if also we admit (and for this also there is much to be said) that Sally was a different person from B I, this would be an instance of the direct knowledge by one person of the mental acts of another. I think, therefore, that it is doubtful whether it really is a characteristic of all mental acts, that they can be directly known by one mind only. And as for the converse proposition— the proposition that any entity which can be directly known by one person only must be mental, and must be 'in' that person's 'mind', it seems to be more doubtful still. Even if it were true that all undoubtedly mental entities can only be known by one person, namely the person 'in' whose 'mind' they are, there would seem to be no reason whatever why some non-mental entities should not possess the same characteristic. And, supposing any entities, except mental acts, do possess it, we should, I think, certainly need other and independent evidence that they were 'mental', in order to be entitled to call them so. On this ground alone, we certainly should not be so entitled.

So far, then, my conclusions have been as follows: I started with mental acts—acts of consciousness—as being undoubtedly mental entities. And I considered three characteritsics, which might be held to distinguish them from entities which are not mental. The first was the mere fact that they *were* acts of consciousness; and this is a characteristic which, of course, does belong *ex hypothesi* to all of them; but also it is a characteristic which can, *ex hypothesi*, belong to no entity except an act of consciousness. This, I said, seemed to me to be the most fundamental sense of the word 'mental', but I admitted that there were others. The second characteristic was one which does seem to belong to most mental acts, namely, the characteristic that they are all of them acts of some person or other—all of them belong to some mind; and I admitted that any entity which did belong to a mind, in this peculiar sense in which my mental acts belong to mine, would be mental. I admitted this, then, as a second sense of 'mental'; but I urged that possibly some mental acts were not mental in this sense— were not the acts of anybody: so that there might be entities which were undoubtedly 'mental' in the first fundamental sense, and yet not 'mental' in this second one. The third characteristic was also one which does seem to belong to most mental acts and does *perhaps* belong to all; namely, that they are entities which can be *directly known* by one person only. But in the case of this characteristic I urged that there seems no reason why it *should* belong to all mental acts—no reason why one person should not sometimes be able to know directly the mental acts of another; and also that there is a certain amount of evidence for believing that this actually does sometimes occur. And as for the contention that *every* entity which possesses this characteristic is 'mental', I urged that, if this is true, we certainly must have some *other* reason for saying that all such entities are mental beside the mere fact that they possess this characteristic. This characteristic alone would not entitle us to call them so; for it certainly is not one of the characteristics which we *mean* by 'mental', even if it should turn out to be a criterion of what is mental.

I have, therefore, so far recognized two different senses of 'mental', and only one sort of entities—namely, acts of consciousness—which are undoubtedly mental. All acts of consciousness are mental in the first sense, and nothing else can be. Whereas in the second sense it is not quite certain that all acts of consciousness are; and also it is abstractly possible that some entities, which are not acts of consciousness, should be.

2. *Doubtful mental entities*

The first entity I wish to consider under this head is *the mind itself.* It might be thought that, if any entity deserves to be called 'mental', the mind itself undoubtedly does deserve it; and that, so far from being reckoned among doubtful mental entities, it ought to be reckoned as the clearest and most undoubted case of a mental entity. And, in fact, I do not doubt that the mind is a mental entity. I do not doubt, for instance, that I have a mind; that there is such a thing as my mind; and that it is a mental entity. But all that I mean when I say this, is that I am quite sure that when I or other people talk about 'my mind', we are talking about something which really is and which is mental; that 'my mind' is the name of some entity or other, and that a mental one. What I do doubt about, in the case of my mind, is what sort of an entity it is: in particular, whether it is an entity of one of the kinds which I have already described; or whether it is a new kind of entity different from any of these, and which is also 'mental' in a different sense from that in which any of them are 'mental'.

There is a view (and I think Hume held it, for one) that my mind merely consists in the sum of all those mental acts, which are related to one another in the way which we describe by calling them all 'mine'; including, of course, any other entities (if there are any), beside mental acts, which may be related to my mental acts in this same way in which they are related to one another. And I cannot be sure that this view is not a true one. I am, in fact, much more sure that there are such things as my mental acts, than that there is an entity distinct from these, which could be called my mind. And if this view *were* a true one, if my mind does consist merely in the sum of my mental acts, it would, of course, merely be an instance of the third kind of entity, which I recognized as un-doubtedly mental; it would be a collection of acts of consciousness, having some kind of unity.

In favour of this view I have to urge the difficulty that I find in dis-covering any entity, other than my mental acts, which could be my mind. And, also, it alone seems to me to allow any proper sense to the phrase we are tempted to use when we say that such and such an entity, such and such a mental act, for instance, is 'in the mind'. If my mind is merely the collection of all my mental acts (and perhaps some other entities), each of them could be properly said to be 'in' it, in the sense of being one among the collection. Whereas, on any other view, I do not see how any mental act, or anything else, could be properly said to be 'in' the mind at all.

But, on the other hand, there seem to me to be certain arguments against this view. We certainly talk, also, as if it were my mind which hears, my mind which thinks, my mind which wills; as if, in short, my mind were some entity, *of* which my mental acts are acts; as if it were identical with the Ego, the 'me', the subject which is conscious whenever I am conscious. And though a meaning can be given to these expressions on Hume's view of the mind, it does not seem to me to be the meaning which they actually have. On Hume's view, we should have to hold that, when I say that *I*, or my mind, am seeing this paper or thinking these thoughts, what I mean is simply that my seeing and my thinking are, each of them, one among the mental acts which constitute me or my mind. And it does not seem to me that this is what I do mean. It seems to me that, when I say that *I* am seeing this room now, and saw another yesterday (and I am sure that I really am and really did), I mean to assert quite a different sort of relation between me and my seeing, than that the latter is *a part* of me—one member of a collection of acts which constitutes me.

Moreover, even on Hume's view, there still remains the difficulty of saying what kind of relation it is that all my mental acts have to one another, which constitutes them 'mine'. They most certainly have some relation to one another, which we express by saying that they are all 'mine', some relation which distinguishes them from the mental acts of other people. And, if we consider what this relation can be, this considera- tion also seems to me to point to the falsity of Hume's view. What I seem to know, when I know that all my mental acts are mental acts of *mine*, is that they all have a peculiar relation to some other entity which is me. I seem to know that their relation to one another consists in the fact that they all have the same relation to this other entity: I do not seem to be directly aware of any other relation which they all have to one another.

I think, therefore, there is something to be said for the view that *I* am an entity, distinct from every one of my mental acts and from all of them put together: an entity, whose acts they are; which is that which is conscious when I am conscious; and that what I mean by calling them all 'mine', is that they all of them are acts of this same entity. But even if I am such an entity, it does not follow that it is a mental entity. There is still another hypothesis, against which I can find no conclusive arguments: namely, that this entity which hears and sees and feels and thinks is some part of *my body*. I cannot see anything conclusive against Locke's view that matter may be capable of being conscious; and hence that it may be my body which is conscious whenever I am conscious. If this were so, then, I should say we could not identify myself with 'my mind'. I myself should not, then, be a mental entity: I should be my body. Whereas anything that is properly to be called 'my mind' must, I think, be allowed to be 'mental'. But we might combine this with Hume's view by saying that 'my mind' was the collection of my mental acts; and that what made them all 'mine' was not any direct relation they had to one another, but the fact that they all had a common relation to my body.

The view, therefore, that 'my mind' is a mental entity, distinct from any one of my mental acts and from all of them, seems to me to be only one among several possible alternatives, against none of which I have ever seen or can find conclusive arguments. But it does seem to me to be one possible alternative and if it were true, then, we should have to admit that there is another mental entity, distinct from any of those I have hitherto recognized and 'mental' in a different sense from any of them. Every mind would, then, be a mental entity of a new sort; and it would be 'mental' in the sense that it was something, *not* the body, *of* which certain mental acts were the acts—that it was that which is conscious whenever anyone is conscious.

II. SOME MAIN PROBLEMS OF PHILOSOPHY (1910)

I wish now to consider an entirely new and different argument to prove that material objects cannot exist. . . . The argument I mean, is drawn from considering the relation of our own minds to our bodies. It is roughly this. It is argued, in the first place, that our own minds do manifestly act upon our bodies, and our bodies on our minds. It is argued, in the second place, that our bodies, whatever they may be, are manifestly things of a sort which *can* be acted upon by, and *can* act upon, all the other kinds of objects which we commonly suppose to be material objects. *But*, it is said, it is not possible that a mind should either act upon or be acted upon *by*, anything whatever except what is itself a mind or of the nature of a mind. And hence, it is argued, in the first place, that since our own bodies and minds obviously do interact upon one another, our bodies must be minds or of the nature of minds. And, in the second place, that since our bodies *can* interact with all other supposed material objects, and since our bodies have already been proved to be mental in their nature, all other supposed material objects must also really be mental in their nature.

And both steps in this argument have, I think, seemed plausible to great numbers of people. The essential steps are two.

The first is that our minds do really act upon our bodies, and are acted upon by them. And, as regards this step, there is hardly anything which seems more obvious to Common Sense, or is more constantly assumed by all of us. We all of us know, for instance, or suppose that we know, that the drinking of alcohol, in large quantities, does produce, very often, very marked effects upon the mind of the person who drinks it. A person who

is drunk neither thinks, nor feels, nor perceives, nor wills in exactly the
same way as when he is sober. The alcohol, which he has drunk, produces
an effect upon his body, and the changes produced in his body cause
changes in his thoughts and feelings and perceptions and volitions. So too,
we all know, or think we know, that the taking of some drugs into the
body will produce a temporary cessation of consciousness, or at least a
very complete change in its nature: opiates will send a man to sleep—will
make his mind cease, for a time, to be conscious at all; and various
anaesthetics also will make his consciousness cease for a time, or will produce dreams, which are very different in nature from the perceptions which
he would have had, if he had not taken the anaesthetic. All these we should
commonly set down as obvious instances of an action by the body upon
the mind. And, of course, there are commoner instances still. We commonly suppose that our visual perceptions—that direct apprehension of
patches of colour, for instance, which we call the actual seeing of them, is
caused by changes which take place in our eyes; and our direct apprehension of sounds is caused by changes which take place in our ears. We know,
or suppose we know, that a blind man, who has lost his eyes, or whose
eyes are in a certain state, is no longer able actually to see colours, as we
see them; and we should take this as proof that the state of our eyes does
produce effects upon our minds. In fact, it seems nearly as certain as
anything can be that our bodies do constantly act upon our minds. And
so too, it seems equally certain that our minds do very often act upon our
bodies. For instance, I now make a movement with my arm. And this
movement, it seems to me quite certain, was caused by the fact that I
chose to move it. I should not have made it just then, unless I had chosen
to do so. We all constantly distinguish between voluntary movements of
our bodies, and involuntary ones: voluntary movements being those
which are caused by our willing to make them, and involuntary ones
those which are not caused by our own volitions. There are a certain
number of changes in our bodies, which we can, it seems, most of us,
almost at any moment, produce by willing them; whereas there are
others, which we cannot so produce. I cannot, now, by an act of volition
cause my hair to stand up on end, whereas I can move my arm as I did just
now. And the influence of our wills upon our bodies, is by no means the
only instance of the action of our minds upon them. Mere perceptions and
thoughts also seem often to have a marked effect upon them. For instance,
the mere fact that he sees a certain sight, may cause a man's body to
tremble. The fact that he hears certain words and the thoughts which they
suggest, may produce that change in the circulation of the blood, which
we call blushing, or may cause him to shed tears—in both cases quite
involuntarily. In cases like these it certainly does seem obvious that our

thoughts and feelings and perceptions do cause changes in our bodies. It does, therefore, seem obvious to Common Sense both that our bodies do often act upon our minds, and that our minds do often act upon our bodies. And for my part I do not see how to dispute this. If these instances which I have given are not instances of the *action* of one thing upon another, are not instances of *causation*, it seems to me we have no better reason to say that any other instances that can be given *are* instances of action and causation. I have no better reason for saying that that light, when I look upon it, is acting upon my eyes and causing changes in them, than for saying that these changes in my eyes are acting upon my mind, and causing me to see what I do see. I have no better reason for saying that my hand is acting upon this paper, now when I push it, and causing it, the paper, to move; than for saying that my *wish* to push it (in order to give you an instance of the action of mind upon body) was what acted upon my hand and caused *it*, my hand, to move.

If, therefore, we are to reject this argument at all, we must, I think find objections to the second step in it, *not* to this first step. This first step which merely asserts that our minds and bodies do interact, seems to me as certain as that anything does act upon or cause anything at all. If we use the words 'action' and 'cause' in their ordinary sense, it is as certain that our minds and bodies act upon and cause changes in one another, as that anything acts upon anything or causes any changes at all.

But the second step in the argument is also capable of seeming extremely plausible. This second step consists in the assertion that nothing that is a mind, or belongs to a mind—nothing that is *mental*—can possibly act upon or be acted upon by anything which is *not* mental. And the best proof how plausible this assertion may seem is that very many philosophers have been led, on the ground that it is true, to deny that our minds and bodies ever do act upon one another. They have believed that our bodies are material objects, in the sense which I defined—that is to say that they are *not* mental in their nature. And they have been so certain that material objects, in this sense, cannot act upon a mind or upon anything mental, nor anything mental upon them, that they have concluded that our minds and bodies do *not* really act upon one another, in spite of the fact that they so obviously seem to do so. This second step in the argument, has, then, been very often held to be true, *both* by those who do believe in the existence of purely material objects, and that our bodies are such objects, *and* by those who do not. Those who hold the first view are, of course, because they hold this also, bound to deny that our bodies and minds do ever interact; whereas those who hold the second view very often regard this second step, together with the plain fact that our bodies and minds do interact, as proof that their view is true—namely that our bodies are not material objects. The view, therefore, that a material object—an object which is not a mind—cannot possibly be acted upon or act upon a mind, has been held by very many philosophers, both of those who do believe in the existence of material objects and of those who do not. This view was held almost immediately after the beginning of modern philosophy among the disciples of Descartes. Some of his disciples, who never thought of questioning the existence of material objects, yet thought it so impossible that these should act upon our minds that they invented a theory which has been called 'Occasionalism': namely that, whenever certain changes occurred in our bodies, *God caused* certain corresponding changes to occur in our minds; they held, that is, that those bodily changes were not *causes* of the changes in our minds, but that they were merely *occasions*, on the occurrence of which God had arranged permanently, or definitely willed in each instance, that the mental changes should occur. And, of course, the same view, that minds and material objects cannot interact, is implied by the common modern view, that mental phenomena are events which merely happen to accompany certain material phenomena, without being either caused by or causing any. The view for instance that the mind is a mere 'epiphenomenon' attached to certain material phenomena, but incapable of influencing their course; or the view that there exists a parallelism, but no interaction, between mental and material phenomena—the view, that is, that mental phenomena regularly occur (to speak metaphorically) side by side with or parallel to material ones, but without being causally connected with them.

Let us consider this view that minds and material objects cannot interact, in relation to one quite definite theory as to their relation—a theory which is, I think, the one now commonly held, and which is, in fact, the one which I myself suppose to be true. According to this modern theory, absolutely every change which ever takes place in our minds, is accompanied by—absolutely simultaneous with—some definite change which takes place in the matter of the brain. Every different act of consciousness which you ever perform is accompanied by a different spatial arrangement of the material particles in some part of your brain; and whenever you perform a precisely similar act of consciousness, on two different occasions —if, for instance, you see a bright yellow colour on one day, and see a precisely similar bright yellow colour on the next day, or if on one day you think that twice two are four, and think the same again some other day—then, whenever this precisely similar act of consciousness recurs, it is accompanied by an arrangement of molecules in your brain precisely similar to that which accompanied it on the former occasion. There is therefore, on this view, for every different act of consciousness some configuration of the matter in a part of your brain, which occurs at absolutely the same time. And it is held too that each of these states of the matter in your brain is *caused* by some previous state of the matter in your brain, or in the nerves connected with it; and moreover that each of them has for its effect *some* subsequent state of the matter in your brain or in the nerves connected with it. It is agreed, then, according to this theory, which is, I believe, the one commonly held, that every state of consciousness is *accompanied* by some state of the brain, and that each of these accompanying brain-states is caused by and does cause some other brain-state or nerve-state. And it is worth while insisting that the brain and nerves and all their parts, are, on this view, material objects in precisely the sense I have been explaining. They are not merely collections of sense-data or possibilities of sense-data; they do actually exist, when no one is directly apprehending them—for instance, in my brain now; they are conceived as having position in space; and certainly they are not commonly conceived as being themselves minds or acts of consciousness—though the question whether they must really be so, is what we are now to consider.

Well, then, what must be asserted, on the view that minds and material objects cannot interact, is, as follows. We have it supposed, on the theory stated, that every mental act is *accompanied* by some particular brain-state. And there can be no question as to whether the mental acts are caused by the brain-states which accompany them: because, in the ordinary meaning of cause, we certainly mean by *a cause*, something which *precedes* in time, and is not simultaneous with the thing which is its effect. Our mental acts, therefore, are certainly not caused by the brain-states which *accompany* them. The only question can be as to whether that other nerve-state or brain-state, which, on this theory, *causes* the brain-state which accompanies the mental act, cannot *also* cause the mental act itself; and whether the nerve-state or brain-state which is *caused by* the brain-state which accompanies the mental act, cannot *also* be caused by the mental act itself. The view that minds and material objects cannot interact must deny this, if it denies anything. Unless it can be proved that *this* particular theory cannot be the truth, the whole argument to prove that minds and material objects cannot interact must fail. If they *can* interact in this case, they might in any.

What arguments, then, can be used to prove that a brain-state which *causes* the brain-state which accompanies a mental act, cannot also *cause* the mental act itself? and that a brain-state which is caused by the brain-state which accompanies a mental act, cannot be caused by the mental act itself?

So far as I know, there are two which are commonly used. The first is this. It is urged that a state of the brain, considered merely as a spatial arrangement of material particles, is something so utterly different in kind from a mental act, that we cannot conceive *how* the one should cause or be caused by the other. This argument, you see, if it is to be used as an argument to prove that what really causes the mental act, cannot be a brain-state, but must be another mental act, supposes that we *can* see how one mental act can cause another, though we cannot see how a brain-state should cause a mental act. And this is why it seems to me so unconvincing. I cannot see any difference between the two cases. Let us consider a case where one mental act undoubtedly does cause another. I am quite certain that, in many cases, the seeing of certain letters printed in a book, has caused me to have certain ideas of the incidents related in the book—ideas which I should not have had, if I had not seen those letters. Here, then, is an instance of the causation of one mental act by another. The seeing of printed letters in a copy of *Waverley*, has *caused* me to have ideas of the incidents which Scott meant to describe. The one mental act, the having of these ideas, is certainly an effect of the other mental act—the seeing of the printed sentences: I should not have had the ideas, had I not seen the sentences. But is it, in fact, any more easy to conceive, how that one mental act, the seeing of certain printed letters, should have caused the entirely different mental act, the imagination of certain incidents in the life of Waverley, than how either of them should have been caused by a state of my brain? It seems to me quite as easy to conceive the latter, as the former. I no more understand, in the last resort, how or why the one mental act, the seeing of certain letters, should cause the imagination of certain incidents, than how or why a state of my brain should cause the seeing of the letters. All that I can be certain of in any case of mental causation—that is, of the causation of one mental act by another—seems to me to be simply that the one mental act, the effect, certainly would not have occurred, under the circumstances, unless the other had preceded it: all I can be certain of is that this is so, as a matter of fact. As to why it should be so—if by this be meant, that the fact that it must be so, can be deduced from some self-evident principle—I am in every case quite ignorant. And if the question is thus merely a question as to what is, as a matter of fact, caused by what, I can quite well conceive that it should also be true, as a matter of fact, that no mental acts would ever occur unless certain states of the brain preceded them. I cannot see why the world should not be so constituted that this should be so.

The second argument, which may be used to show that mind and matter cannot possibly interact, is one which depends upon a different meaning of the word 'cause'—a sense, in which by a 'cause' we mean something upon the occurrence of which the effect always necessarily follows; so that, from the existence of the cause by itself it would be possible to predict with certainty that the effect must follow. Let us call a cause, of which this is true, a 'sufficient' cause—meaning by that that the mere existence of the cause is by itself a *sufficient* datum to enable us to infer the effect—that we do not need any other premises besides. Now it is widely held that *every* event in the material world has, in this sense, a *sufficient* cause in previous material events: that there is some set of previous material events from which any material event, which ever occurs, could, if we had sufficient knowledge, have been inferred with certainty. And, granted that this is so, it follows of course that every event in any one's body—in his nerves or in his brain—could have been inferred from previous material events by themselves: it follows that no knowledge of any mental events would have been necessary to enable an omniscient person to infer them. And it is, I think, often inferred from this that no mental event could have been *necessary* to produce them: that, even supposing that mental events did in fact accompany some of the material events which constitute the sufficient cause, they must yet have been something entirely superfluous and without influence on the result. But does this, in fact, follow? It seems to me quite plain, if we consider the case a little more carefully, that it does not. Granted we have a set of events from the existence of which, by themselves, it follows with absolute certainly that a certain result will follow, it by no means follows that some other event may not also be *necessary* to produce the result. The world may quite well be so constituted, that a cause which is sufficient to enable us to predict a result, should nevertheless not be sufficient to *produce* that result; it may be so constituted that the cause, which *is* sufficient for prediction, must nevertheless also, as a matter of fact, be always accompanied by some other cause, which is truly a cause, in the sense that the result would not have occurred *unless* it had existed also. Even, therefore, if we grant that every material event has a sufficient cause in previous material events, in the sense that from them alone its existence could be *predicted;* it by no means follows that in some cases mental events may not also be necessary for the *production* of the effect. And I do not see how it can possibly be proved that this is not, in fact, the case.

It seems to me, then, that both these arguments to prove that minds and material objects could not possibly interact, are inconclusive. And I know no better arguments to prove it. I conclude, then, that this particular argument to prove that material objects cannot exist, namely the argument which starts from the Common Sense fact that our minds and bodies do interact, and hence concludes that our bodies cannot be material objects, but must themselves be minds or composed of minds, is inconclusive also.

25

SAMUEL ALEXANDER

SPACE, TIME AND DEITY (1916–1918)

Our mind is experienced by us as a set of connected processes which have the character of being mental, possessing the quality of 'mentality', or as I shall most frequently say, the character of consciousness. Whether there is any department of mind, which, remaining mind, may be said to be unconscious, and in what sense this is true, is a question I shall defer for the present. Any one who wishes can substitute for the quality of consciousness the quality of being mind, and can, if he pleases, continue to think of mentality as something less specified than consciousness. A mind, then, is for immediate experience a thing or organization of processes with this distinctive property of being mind, and, however much interrupted it may be, it is normally linked up by memory in its various forms. Under consciousness I include without further ado those vague and indistinct mental processes on the extreme margin of consciousness which are sometimes described as subconscious, such as, in general, the tone of the organic sensations when we are occupied with external events. Such then is mind as we experience it. But we experience also our bodies, and, moreover, in the organic and motor sensations, such as hunger and breathing and the like, we experience our bodies as alive, while they are also experienced by touch and sight, etc., as being physical things of the order of external things. And, as we have seen in a previous chapter, experience leads us on to connect our mental processes with our body, and in particular with our central nervous system, and more specifically still with a certain part of our brain, and to localize our mental processes in the same places and times as certain neural processes. We thus become aware, partly by experience, partly by reflection, that a process with the distinctive quality of mind or consciousness is in the same place and time with a neural process, that is, with a highly differentiated and complex process of our living body. We are forced, therefore, to go beyond the mere correlation of the mental with these neural processes and to identify them. There is but one process which, being of a specific complexity, has the quality of consciousness; the term complexity being used to include not merely complexity in structure or constitution of the various motions engaged, but also intensity, and above all unimpeded outlet, that is, connection with the other processes or structures with which the process in question is organized. For failure in intensity may mean failure of an otherwise sufficiently complex process to be conscious, and so may any cause which disconnects it from the rest of the neural processes which in their connection give us mind. Correlation is therefore an inadequate and misleading word to describe the relation of the mental to the corresponding neural process, and is only used provisionally so long as the two are separated from one another. In truth, according to our conception, they are not two but one. That which as experienced from the inside or enjoyed is a conscious process, is as experienced from the outside or contemplated a neural one. When we speak of them separately it is that we consider the same process first in respect of the character which allies it with simpler vital processes, and second in respect of the new quality which emerges at this higher stage of vital complexity. It has then to be accepted as an empirical fact that neural process of a certain level of development possesses the quality of consciousness and is thereby a mental process; and, alternately, a mental process is *also* a vital one of a certain order.

Now it is not the character of being vital that gives the mental process its individuality, but its new quality of mentality or consciousness. Let us take as examples of vitality such operations as digestion or breathing or secretion. There is no reason that I know for not reckoning with them physiological reflex action or any neural process not attended with consciousness or mind. But while mental process is *also* neural, it is not *merely* neural, and therefore also not merely vital. For, that mind should emerge, there is required a constellation of neural or other vital conditions not found in vital actions which are not mental. To use the word which Mill has made familiar, mind requires, as a fact of experience, a collocation of conditions which constitutes something new. What that collocation is, might be very difficult for any one but a physiologist to say, and perhaps not possible completely for him. I take it that in the main what determines the difference of the psychical from the merely physiological process is its locality in the nervous system, implying as this does the special structure of the living nervous elements in that locality. It may still be open for discussion at what level in the brain-structure consciousness is found, whether it may attend processes in some of the higher ganglia or whether it belongs exclusively to the cerebral cortex, or whether, again, it is not different if it belongs to a lower and a higher level in the cortex itself. But assuming that the conception of localization of mental functions in specific regions of the brain is physiologically correct, we may safely regard locality of the mental process as what chiefly makes it mental as distinct from merely neural, or what distinguishes the different sorts of mental processes from one another. This is, however, a subsidiary matter for our purposes. What counts is, that without the specific physiological or vital constellation there is no mind. All less complex vital constellations remain purely vital. Thus not all vital processes are mental. There is not, or not necessarily, to each neurosis a corresponding psychosis. The equivalent proposition is, that while all psychoses are neuroses, the psychoses imply the emergence of a new feature, that of mind. It would follow that mental process may be expressible completely in physiological terms but is not *merely* physiological but *also* mental. Its resolution into physiological terms may be infinitely difficult, and even if it can be performed it remains that the statement of these conditions only means mental action because we are already acquainted with the fact of their mentality. To put the matter in different terms: suppose we regard the description of mind as a chapter of physiology; it would still be the physiology of mental action; we should still be attending to this kind of physiological constellation because it is the basis of mind, and should be directed to it from psychology. Nor, as we shall see later, could any physiological knowledge of the physiological constellation implied in a mental action enable us to predict that it would have the mental quality.

Mental process is therefore something new, a fresh creation, which, despite the possibility of resolving it into physiological terms, means the presence of so specific a physiological constitution as to separate it from simpler vital processes. I do not mean, to take a particular and interesting case, that the foresight of ends as distinguished from mere vital purposiveness, is not also vital. Every idea of an end to be gained, every thought of a universal, or of a combination to be made executive by some invention, I shall assume to be also a physiological process. I mean that such processes though they may be reduced to the class of vital processes *are* so distinct from the remainder of the class that they hold a privileged position in it. Precisely in the same way the king is a man and belongs to the same class with his subjects. But he is not one of his subjects. Abt Vogler in Browning's poem declares of the musician 'that out of three sounds he frames not a fourth sound but a star'. Out of certain physiological conditions nature has framed a new quality mind, which is therefore not itself physiological though it lives and moves and has its being in physiological conditions. Hence it is that there can be and is an independent science of psychology, and that the translation of mental processes into their physiological counterparts follows the lead of the more primary description of mind. Mind is thus at once new and old. No physiological constellation explains for us why it should be mind. But at the same time, being thus new, mind is through its physiological character continuous with the neural processes which are not mental. It is not something distinct and broken off from them, but it has its roots or foundations in all the rest of the nervous system. It is in this sense that mind and mental process are vital but not merely vital.

Hence it follows that we are entitled summarily to dismiss the conception that mind is but an inert accompaniment of neural process, a kind of aura which surrounds that process but plays no effective part of its own: the doctrine that mind is an epiphenomenon of nervous process, which nervous process would continue to work equally well if mind were absent. The doctrine is not simply to be rejected because it supposes something to exist in nature which has nothing to do, no purpose to serve, a species of *noblesse* which depends on the work of its inferiors, but is kept for show and might as well, and undoubtedly would in time be abolished. It is to be rejected because it is false to empirical facts. The mental state is the epiphenomenon of the neural process. But of what neural process? Of its own neural process. But that process possesses the mental character, and there is no evidence to show that it would possess its specific neural character if it were not also mental. On the contrary, we find that neural processes which are not mental are not of the same neural order as those which are. A neural process does not cease to be mental and remain in all respects the same neural process as before. Even if it remains in the same place, its connection with the rest of the brain is in some way disturbed, and it cannot proceed freely on its course. The neural process which carries thought becomes changed into a different one when it ceases to carry thought. All the available evidence of fact leads to the conclusion that the mental element is essential to the neural process which it is said to accompany by way of embellishment, and is not accidental to it, nor it in turn indifferent to the mental feature. Epiphenomenalism is a mere fallacy of observation.

It is otherwise with the other well-known doctrines of the relation of body and mind. The statement which has been given above is by no means new in principle nor for that matter in its particular form. It is a species of the identity doctrine of mind and body, maintaining that there are not two processes, one neural, the other mental, but one. We shall do well to deal shortly with these other doctrines, not in order to treat the subject with thoroughness but to defend it sufficiently for our objects against the rival conceptions, or at least to exhibit the contrast between it and these conceptions.

The mental process and its neural process are one and the same existence, not two existences. As mental it is in my language enjoyed by the experient; as neural it is contemplated by an outsider or may be contemplated in thought by the experient himself. There can therefore be no parallelism between the series of mental and the series of neural or physiological events, such as is postulated by the strict theory of so-called psychological parallelism. That theory was devised to give expression to the complete disparity of the merely physiological and the mental, and the reason for it disappears so soon as it is recognized that what corresponds to the mental is not merely physiological but the bearer of a new quality. It solved or evaded the problem by regarding the mental series as entirely independent of the neural and yet in precise correspondence therewith. The difficulties of establishing such precise correspondence in detail may be neglected here, and they are probably not insuperable. But it is evident that an exact correspondence of two completely disconnected series, which do not influence each other, is no more than a restatement of the problem. The only solution it offers is that the problem must be left unsolved. It could therefore at most be accepted for psychological purposes as a compendious statement of the fact that every psychosis has its corresponding neurosis. There still remains the metaphysical question whether the mind whose processes are mental is not a being which interacts with the brain, or whether, as I have urged, the mind is not itself identical with the totality of certain neural processes as they are enjoyed.

But even as a psychological convenience, the theory is without justification and superfluous, and moreover false in what it suggests. Psychology is concerned with a parallelism between the mental series and another series of a different order, the series of physical objects of which the mental processes are aware. One of the drawbacks of the order of exposition I am adopting is that I must take for granted what will only be fully clear hereafter, that the object of the mind in any mental process is something non-mental, which is contemplated, while the mental process is enjoyed. To each non-mental object (and there is no mental process which is without its non-mental object, even if it be only a sensum which is the object of sensing, even if it be only the internal condition of the percipient's body as in organic sensation) there corresponds a mental process which has the quality of conscious awareness. As the object varies, so does the neural process or the mental process vary. But there is no parallelism of the neural and the mental series of which psychology should take account. They are one. Psychology considers the series from the point of view of the experient or enjoyer; physiology from the point of view of the onlooker, or, if of the experient himself, not in his character of experiencing the mental process but of reflecting on its basis in neural process.

I can only account for the admission of a metaphysical miracle as a convenient psychological fiction, by supposing that mental processes were believed to have not merely the quality of consciousness, but other qualities disguised under the name of 'content' which varied with the object. If the sensory object blue or the image of a table is in some way contained in the apprehension of it, doubtless there is an unbridged chasm between the neural process which clearly has no such 'content' and the mental process which has. No one has indeed imagined that a mental process was itself blue or tabular. Yet these processes are supposed to be qualified correspondingly, or at least to have before them presentations or ideas which are not themselves merely external or a selection from what is external. The lingering tradition of representationism provides a mental process (hence called a mental state) with a mental object. But once we recognize that mental processes have no character, beyond the quality of being mental, other than such as all processes present, intensity or locality or velocity and the like, that is to say, empirical forms of categorial characters, all reason is removed for supposing the mental process to be a different existent from the neural one. That neural process differs with every difference in the object which stimulates it to activity, or upon which it is directed. The neurosis of green occurs for instance in a different place from that of sweet. The neuroses all possess the vital quality but are different configurations of categorial characters. In like manner the psychoses present, corresponding to the qualities of the object, differences in the process-features of the psychosis; but there is nothing to indicate the difference of quality of the object but these process-features. The separation of the mental process from the neural one is therefore superfluous, for it is the same process-features which are in the one case enjoyed and in the other contemplated. Ultimately this separation depends upon failing to recognize the distinctness of the mental process from its non-mental object. It is therefore not only superfluous but founded in error.

26

G. F. STOUT

MIND AND MATTER (1919–21)

The Scientific View of the Body

Each of us has experience of his own body in a way essentially different from the way in which any one else can have experience of it. This is especially obvious in organic sensations such as thirst, hunger, fatigue, sexual excitement, and, in general, the bodily excitement inseparable from emotion; also in motor sensations such as are involved in the actions of looking, listening, handling, lifting a weight, eating, walking, strenuous thinking. For each of us his body as thus privately experienced forms an integral part of what he means by himself when he uses the word 'I', and says for instance: 'I am or feel hungry'; 'I am in love'; 'I think hard'; 'I lift a weight'. It is not however as merely bodily occurrences that such bodily states and processes are apprehended as entering into the being of the self. They are included in self-consciousness only inasmuch as they are experienced as one with the experiencing individual. But an experiencing individual as such is a mind. What we know or seem to know in ordinary self-consciousness is therefore a concrete whole within which mind and body are only abstractly distinguishable as partial factors. It is, however, the mental factor which gives the whole the character of being a self or 'I'. Hence the unity of mind and body as apprehended in ordinary experience may properly be called the unity of the embodied self.

This experience of the self as embodied ought either to be shown to be illusory, or to be taken as a fundamental datum in any attempt to determine the relation of body and mind.

Inadequacy of the Scientific Standpoint

There are two radical defects in the view of the relation of body and mind which is reached by approaching the problem from the standpoint of physical science. In the first place we part company with the animism of Common Sense. Hence the existence of mind or 'mental phenomena' appears an exceptional or sporadic occurrence incongruous with the general order of nature. In the second place, we fail, from this point of view, to find any communion of body and mind. We find no single concrete experience into which both enter as intrinsically inseparable and essentially correlated factors. Yet unless such communion is assumed, both interaction and parallelism remain unintelligible. This difficulty is the more fundamental, and we have here to inquire whether there is any satisfactory way of meeting it. There is certainly none so long as we assume that the body, like other material objects, is known only through external perception, whereas self-consciousness reveals only mind.

As against this view, which is historically traceable to Descartes, I maintain that there are two fundamentally distinct ways in which the experiencing individual apprehends his own body. Each individual feels his own body, as it enters into his own subjective being, as contrasted with external objects. He is primarily aware of his own body in self-conscious-ness, and no one but himself can be thus aware of it. In this way and only in this way he knows, not by inference but immediately, the unity of body and mind as inseparably correlated factors within his own indivisible being as an embodied self. On the other hand, the individual is also cognisant of and interested in his own body in quite another manner, as one external object among others. He may by means of his own sense-organs observe his own body as he observes the bodies of other men, or as he observes trees and stones. He may accept the testimony of others for what he cannot thus observe himself. He may make inferences from the bodies of others to his own; e.g. that he has brains in his head because he discovers brains in other heads when the skull is split open. From this external point of view no unity of body and mind is discernible. On the contrary, they seem to fall apart as separate and mutually exclusive. Now it is only from the standpoint of external observation and experiment that physical science, including anatomy, physiology and biology, considers animal and human bodies. For the student of physical science as such, his own body is just one portion of the material world, and his aim is to bring it within the system of fundamental laws and concepts which hold for the material world in general. So long as he keeps within this his proper province he need not take account of mind at all, or officially recognize its existence. The psycho-physical problem is a strange and troublesome in-truder from outside. It emerges only with the reflection that physical science, even if it completely realized its ideal, would not cover the whole field.

There is a residuum which cannot be denied or explained away. The man of science cannot deny his own existence as a knowing, feeling, and willing individual. Otherwise he would be denying the existence of science itself and of the experience on which it depends. He is thus bound to recognize that in self-consciousness there is revealed something which falls outside the range of physical science. But he naturally assumes that whatever is knowable about the material world can be known from the scientific standpoint of external observation. Hence he naturally assumes that what self-consciousness or introspection reveals is mere mind, and is thus led to contrast purely mental phenomena with purely material phenomena. Thus the original unity of the embodied self is dissolved in such wise that body and mind appear as two separate existences which have no intrinsic connection with each other, but are merely found or inferred to be conjoined with each other as a brute matter of fact. The body as known to the physiologist, anatomist or chemist is simply substituted for the bodily coefficient in the whole experience of the self as embodied. For Common-Sense, mind is essentially embodied.

In the form in which it presents itself to the student of physical science, or to the philosopher who starts from science, the psycho-physical problem can hardly be said to exist for Common Sense. It is a technical problem which does not emerge in ordinary experience. Mind and body are not primarily apprehended as distinct *things*; mental processes are not taken apart from bodily in such wise as to raise questions concerning the way in which they are combined with each other. What we are primarily aware of is the individual unity of an embodied Self. It is this which is signified by the personal pronouns 'I', 'you' and 'he'. Consider the phrases: I see the moon, I heard a bird, I handle a knife, I walk from this place to that, I feel a wound, I am in prison. We cannot, at any rate without a radical change of meaning, substitute for the personal pronoun in these statements either 'my body' or 'my mind'. I cannot say 'My body sees a bird' or 'My mind sees a bird'. Such language does violence to Common Sense, though it may be appropriate to some materialistic or spiritualistic theory. I may indeed say 'My body walks' or 'My body handles a knife'. But if I do so it is because I intend to indicate that it is not I but only my body that is implicated. It is true also that there are cases in which 'I' and 'my body' may be used interchangeably. But when this is so, 'I' has no longer its proper and primary, but only a transferred and derivative meaning. I may say indifferently that 'I' or 'my body' will sometime be mouldering in the grave. But I readily recognize that the dead and buried body will not really be I. I continue to speak of it as 'I' or even as 'my body' only because it is thought of as connected by a continuous history with my present individual experience as an embodied self. The position of Common Sense is that there is no self or mind where there is no individual experience; and that individual experience includes body and mind in one.

Summary of Previous Results

The difficulties of the psycho-physical problem are due to the way in which it has been usually approached from the point of view of physical science. From this point of view the body of the individual self is regarded merely as one external object among others. So regarded, it is contrasted with the purely mental or immediately experienced process which is supposed to be all that is known in self-consciousness. Hence it becomes a question how mere mind and mere body can meet, in a unity so as to make possible either their interaction, or their uniform concomitance and co-variation, or the production of one by the other.

This question admits of no satisfactory answer because it is founded on a false assumption. What self-consciousness reveals is not mere mind or 'mental phenomena', but mind and body together in the inseparable unity of the embodied self. Thus the supposed contrast between merely bodily process and merely mental is in fact always, in part, a contrast between the body as external object and the same body as internal object. This contrast is indeed sharply marked, and becomes more and more so as physical science progresses in correlating perceptual data with each other, according to laws which hold for the physical world in general, including the bodies of experiencing individuals. Advance in this direction comes to depend more and more on such methods as measurement, in which the nature of external objects is determined indirectly by their relation to each other rather than directly by their perceptual appearance. The culmination of this development is found in modern theories of relativity. There is no such relativity in the primary awareness of the self as embodied. But however undeniable and important the distinction is between the body as external and as internal object, it neither is nor implies a severance of mind and body such as would make it a question how they can come together. It supplies no reason why their unity in self-consciousness should not be simply accepted as an ultimate datum.

How Body and Mind are united in Self-consciousness

We are now in a position to determine more precisely the nature of the unity of body and mind in the embodied self. We are enabled to do so by the outcome of our previous discussion of the way in which knowledge transcends immediate experience. This yields two results. We immediately know what we do not immediately experience only so far as what we do immediately experience, in the way of sense and active tendency, is so essentially incomplete that it cannot be known by itself. Hence whatever else is known is known as an extension of what we immediately experience in these two ways, and therefore as continuous with it in existence and fundamentally akin to it in nature. Active process in the individual is his distinctive share in world-process and has no separate existence. The sensory continuum of the individual is a partial extract from a world-continuum in which each of us has his own private share, though it also comprehends far more than what is immediately experienced by finite individuals.

Not only external objects but the individual himself is immediately known to himself in this way. The self of self-consciousness cannot be confined to what we immediately experience either in the way of sense or active tendency. On the side of sense it includes an extension of certain aspects of immediate sensation, which are relatively permanent, in contrast with those particular modifications in the sensory continuum which are perpetually coming and going, and are properly called sense-impressions. In like manner what we immediately experience in the way of active tendency is only a partial ingredient in what we perceive as our own action, incapable of existing or being known by itself, but only as one and continuous with a process which transcends and includes it. What we are thus immediately cognisant of in primary self-consciousness is our own body and bodily processes. If we mean by the term 'mental' only what strictly falls within immediate experience, body and mind are for self-consciousness in the most intimate and essential connection with each other. The connection is such that mental process is distinguishable from bodily only by an effort of introspective analysis. As it actually takes place mental process is also bodily; mental action is also bodily action, and mental passivity bodily passivity. There need be no interaction between them; indeed it is hard to see how the two can have the relative distinctness and independence required to make interaction possible. The question how it is that they regularly occur together and vary concomitantly answers itself from this point of view.

The Embodied Self and the Body as External Object

The same correlation of mental and bodily process will also be discoverable from the point of view of the external observer. This must be so because it is the same body which is known in private self-consciousness and also as an external object. In this respect it makes no difference whether we mean by mental only what is immediately experienced or take it loosely to include whatever the individual is aware of in self-consciousness. It is a besetting fallacy of those who approach the psycho-physical problem from the external point of view that they fail to distinguish this loose sense from the strict sense; they thus fail to see that what they call mental occurrences are not merely mental but bodily and mental in one. Having thus ignored the unity of body and mind where alone it is to be found, they vainly seek it elsewhere.

This fallacy is part of a wider one, the tendency to neglect and virtually to deny the unique distinctive nature of the subject-object relation, the relation of the experiencing individual to the world, as knowing it and interested in it.

On the other hand, the external point of view has great obvious advantages of its own. The scientific knowledge of the body, such as is attainable by the physiologist, though essentially abstract and schematic, is in its own way incomparably more exact and comprehensive than any which is possible through individual self-consciousness. Again, in self-consciousness each individual knows only his own body and other things as external to it. For physical science, on the contrary, the bodies of individual selves are known only as parts of the external world in general. Hence the scientific mode of approach leads to a sharp formulation of the fundamental problem, 'How is it that mental process arises in connection with certain external objects and not with others?' It is true that if it attempts to answer this question purely from its own standpoint, it encounters hopeless difficulties, which can be met only by taking account of the immediate unity of body and mind as revealed in self-consciousness. None the less, it is from the scientific standpoint that the speculative problem is first explicitly and comprehensively conceived.

The Range of Psycho-physical Correlation

It follows from my account of psycho-physical correlation that it ought to be found to exist between the body as external object and the bodily aspect of the embodied self. It ought also to include what is immediately experienced in the way of sensation and active tendency. So far, then, it is confined to that side of the nature of the individual which is common to him and to the rest of the world of which he is a member—in which he is a shareholder. Active process in him is the part which he plays in the world's process and in which he has his separate existence. His sensory continuum is a partial phase of the world-continuum. In thus exclusively considering the solidarity between the individual and the world to which he belongs, we have neglected that side of his nature which is peculiarly and distinctively his own as an individual subject capable of knowing and being interested in other things and himself. Knowledge can never be resolved into mere sensation. It essentially involves the thought of what is not immediately experienced. Apart from thought, active tendency is blind; it cannot take shape as will or desire; for this there must be some prenotion of what is sought before it is attained. Apart from thought, there can be no distinction between past, present and future, or between the real and the merely possible. Apart from thought, the individual cannot perceive either his own body or external objects. In short, he would not be an individual self at all if he were not a thinking being.

Has thought any psycho-physical correlate varying as its object varies? I answer that no separate correlate is discoverable, and none is needed over and above the correlate of immediate experience. Mere thought is an abstraction which cannot exist by itself as a process or state of the self. As

I have throughout maintained, it must always have a foothold in what is actually experienced, and vary as this varies. There is thus no difference in what is thought of which is not matched by a corresponding difference in what is actually experienced. It follows that thought does not require any distinctive correlate of its own.

An analogous question arises when we consider pleasure and pain. Active tendency and the content of sense-experience in experiencing individuals may be in their general nature fundamentally akin to, and continuous in existence with, the constitution of things which have no experience of their own. But this is not true of being pleased or the reverse. Pleasure and pain are inseparable from the individuality of the individual who feels them, and can have no counterpart or continuation in things which have no feelings. In this respect there seems to be a radical discontinuity between embodied selves and other parts of nature. But it does not follow that being pleased and the reverse require a physiological correlate peculiarly and distinctively belonging to them apart from active tendency and sensation. As I hold, they are the contrasted ways in which we immediately experience active tendency according as it is successful or unsuccessful, furthered or thwarted. Some psychologists deny that we can account in this way for sensuous pleasure and pain, e.g. the pain of a toothache or the pleasure of a sweet taste. They hold that these arise in connection with the quality, intensity and duration of sense-experiences, without being conditioned by active tendency. But even on this view, pleasure-pain need have no separate physiological correlate. The correlate of the connected sense-experience will serve for it also.

Ultimate Problems

In one way embodied selves are of a piece with the rest of the world of finite beings, within which they arise and disappear; in another, there is an abrupt breach of continuity between them and the parts of the same world which are devoid of sentience, feelings and thought. On the one hand, they have their being only as share-holders in a common stock, in which other things share also. On the other, they share in this common stock in an altogether peculiar way which constitutes their individuality. It is not only that what simply exists in other things is in them experienced. The being of an individual self essentially includes, besides immediate sense-experience, the thought which transcends it and makes it possible for him to know the world of which he is a member, and himself as a member of it. It involves also the feelings of pleasure and pain which make possible appreciation of values and the distinction between good and evil.

It has been a main contention of the present work that this inseparable intermingling of continuity and discontinuity between experiencing individuals and other parts of nature cannot be simply accepted as an ultimate fact concerning which there is nothing more to say. Those who adopt this attitude really mean that they are afraid of the question or not interested in it. But there is a question, and one that calls for an answer more imperatively than any other.

The direction in which an answer is to be sought may be gathered from what I have already said in the present work, more especially in the argument against Materialism. Mind, as I maintain, must be fundamental in the Universe of Being and not derivative from anything that is not mind. If we discard mind-stuff theories as failing to account for individual selves, and monadism as failing to account for anything else, we are bound to posit one universal and eternal Mind developing and expressing itself in the world of finite and changeable beings which we call Nature. But at this point there are two alternatives between which we have to decide. The universal Mind may be ascribed to Nature itself; this implies that Nature, in spite of the endless multiplicity of distinct existences which it comprehends, is a self-contained unity. Any such view seems to break down under intolerable difficulties. The alternative is to deny that Nature is the entire Universe of Being, and to recognize that it cannot exist at all or be what it is apart from a Being beyond it and distinct from it. This Being, whatever else it is, must be an eternal and universal Mind, giving to Nature, through and through, a character which is otherwise inexplicable.

27

BERTRAND RUSSELL

I. THE ANALYSIS OF MIND (1921)

In this lecture I shall be concerned to refute a theory which is widely held, and which I formerly held myself: the theory that the essence of every-thing mental is a certain quite peculiar something called 'consciousness', conceived either as a relation to objects, or as a pervading quality of psychical phenomena. . . .

Few things are more firmly established in popular philosophy than the distinction between mind and matter. Those who are not professional metaphysicians are willing to confess that they do not know what mind actually is, or how matter is constituted; but they remain convinced that there is an impassable gulf between the two, and that both belong to what actually exists in the world. Philosophers, on the other hand, have main-tained often that matter is a mere fiction imagined by mind, and some-times that mind is a mere property of a certain kind of matter. Those who maintain that mind is the reality and matter an evil dream are called 'idealists'—a word which has a different meaning in philosophy from that which it bears in ordinary life. Those who argue that matter is the reality and mind a mere property of protoplasm are called 'materialists'. They have been rare among philosophers, but common, at certain periods, among men of science. Idealists, materialists, and ordinary mortals have been in agreement on one point: that they knew sufficiently what they meant by the words 'mind' and 'matter' to be able to conduct their debate intelligently. Yet it was just in this point, as to which they were at one, that they seem to me to have been all alike in error.

The stuff of which the world of our experience is composed, is, in my belief, neither mind nor matter, but something more primitive than either. Both mind and matter seem to be composite, and the stuff of which they are compounded lies in a sense between the two, in a sense above them both, like a common ancestor. As regards matter, I have set forth my reasons for this view on former occasions, and I shall not now repeat them. But the question of mind is more difficult, and it is this question that I propose to discuss in these lectures. . . .

If there is one thing that may be said, in the popular estimation, to characterize mind, that one thing is 'consciousness'. We say that we are 'conscious' of what we see and hear, of what we remember, and of our own thoughts and feelings. . . .

There is one element which *seems* obviously in common among the different ways of being conscious, and that is, that they are all directed to *objects*. We are conscious 'of' something. The consciousness, it seems, is one thing, and that of which we are conscious is another thing. Unless we are to acquiesce in the view that we can never be conscious of anything outside our own minds, we must say that the object of consciousness need not be mental, though the consciousness must be. (I am speaking within the circle of conventional doctrines, not expressing my own beliefs.) This direction towards an object is commonly regarded as typical of every form of cognition, and sometimes of mental life altogether. We may distinguish two different tendencies in traditional psychology. There are those who take mental phenomena naively, just as they would physical phenomena. This school of psychologists tends not to emphasize the object. On the other hand, there are those whose primary interest is in the apparent fact that we have *knowledge*, that there is a world surrounding us of which we are aware. These men are interested in the mind because of its relation to the world, because knowledge, if it is a fact, is a very mysterious one. Their interest in psychology is naturally centred in the relation of consciousness to its object, a problem which, properly, belongs rather to theory of knowledge. We may take as one of the best and most typical representatives of this school the Austrian psychologist Brentano, whose *Psychology from the Empirical Standpoint*, though published in 1874, is still influential, and was the starting-point of a great deal of interesting work. He says (p. 115):

'Every psychical phenomenon is characterized by what the scholastics of the Middle Ages called the intentional (also the mental) inexistence of an object, and what we, although with not quite unambiguous expressions, would call relation to a content, direction towards an object (which is not here to be understood as a reality), or immanent objectivity. Each contains something in itself as an object, though not each in the same way. In presentation something is presented, in judgment something is acknowledged or rejected, in love, something is loved, in hatred hated, in desire desired, and so on.'

'This intentional inexistence is exclusively peculiar to psychical phenomena. No physical phenomenon shows anything similar. And so we can define psychical phenomena by saying that they are phenomena which intentionally contain an object in themselves.'

The view here expressed, that relation to an object is an ultimate irreducible characteristic of mental phenomena, is one which I shall be concerned to combat. Like Brentano, I am interested in psychology, not so much for its own sake, as for the light that it may throw on the problem of knowledge. Until very lately I believed, as he did, that mental pheno-mena have essential reference to objects, except possibly in the case of pleasure and pain. Now I no longer believe this, even in the case of knowledge. I shall try to make my reasons for this rejection clear as we proceed. . . .

The view expressed by Brentano has been held very generally, and developed by many writers. Among these we may take as an example his Austrian successor Meinong. According to him there are three elements involved in the thought of an object. These three he calls the act, the content and the object. The act is the same in any two cases of the same kind of consciousness; for instance, if I think of Smith or think of Brown, the act of thinking, in itself, is exactly similar on both occasions. But the content of my thought, the particular event that is happening in my mind, is different when I think of Smith and when I think of Brown. The content, Meinong argues, must not be confounded with the object, since the content must exist in my mind at the moment when I have the thought, whereas the object need not do so. The object may be something past or future; it may be physical, not mental; it may be something abstract, like equality for example; it may be something imaginary, like a golden mountain, or it may even be something self-contradictory, like a round square. But in all these cases, so he contends, the content exists when the thought exists, and is what distinguishes it, as an occurrence, from other thoughts. . . .

The above analysis of a thought, though I believe it to be mistaken, is very useful as affording a schema in terms of which other theories can be stated. In the remainder of the present lecture I shall state in outline the view which I advocate, and show how various other views out of which mine has grown result from modifications of the three-fold analysis into act, content and object.

The first criticism I have to make is that the *act* seems unnecessary and fictitious. The occurrence of the content of a thought constitutes the occurrence of the thought. Empirically, I cannot discover anything corresponding to the supposed act; and theoretically I cannot see that it is indispensable. We say: 'I think so-and-so', and this word 'I' suggests that thinking is the act of a person. . . . It would be better to say 'it thinks in me', like 'it rains here'; or better still, 'there is a thought in me'. This is simply on the ground that what Meinong calls the act in thinking is not empirically discoverable, or logically deducible from what we can observe.

The next point of criticism concerns the relation of content and object. . . .

Speaking in popular and unphilosophical terms, we may say that the content of a thought is supposed to be something in your head when you think the thought, while the object is usually something in the outer world. It is held that the knowledge of the outer world is constituted by the relation to the object, while the fact that knowledge is different from what it knows is due to the fact that knowledge comes by way of contents. We can begin to state the difference between realism and idealism in terms of this opposition of contents and objects. Speaking quite roughly and approximately, we may say that idealism tends to suppress the object, while realism tends to suppress the content.

There are two different kinds of realism, according as we make a thought consist of act and object, or of object alone. . . . It is especially sensation, I think, which is considered by those realists who retain only the object.[1] Their views, which are chiefly held in America, are in large measure derived from William James, and before going further it will be well to consider the revolutionary doctrine which he advocated. I believe this doctrine contains important new truth, and what I shall have to say will be in a considerable measure inspired by it.

William James's view was first set forth in an essay called 'Does "consciousness" exist?'[2] In this essay he explains how what used to be the soul has gradually been refined down to the 'transcendental ego', which, he says, 'attenuates itself to a thoroughly ghostly condition, being only a name for the fact that the "content" of experience *is known*'. . . .

James's view is that the raw material out of which the world is built up is not of two sorts, one matter and the other mind, but that it is arranged in different patterns by its inter-relations, and that some arrangements may be called mental, while others may be called physical.

'My thesis is,' he said, 'that if we start with the supposition that there is only one primal stuff or material in the world, a stuff of which everything is composed and if we call that stuff "pure experience", then knowing can easily be explained as a particular sort of relation towards one another into which portions of pure experience may enter. The relation itself is a part

[1] This is explicitly the case with Mach's *Analysis of Sensations*, a book of fundamental importance in the present connection. (Translation of fifth German edition, Open Court Co., 1914. First German edition, 1886.)

[2] *Journal of Philosophy, Psychology and Scientific Methods*, vol. i, 1904. Reprinted in *Essays in Radical Empiricism* (Longmans, Green & Co., 1912).

of pure experience; one of its "terms" becomes the subject or bearer of the knowledge, the knower, the other becomes the object known.' ...

My own belief is that James is right in rejecting consciousness as an entity, and that the American realists are partly right, though not wholly, in considering that both mind and matter are composed of a neutral-stuff which, in isolation, is neither mental nor material. I should admit this view as regards sensations: what is heard or seen belongs equally to psychology and to physics. But I should say that images belong only to the mental world, while those occurrences (if any) which do not form part of any 'experience' belong only to the physical world. There are, it seems to me, *prima facie* different kinds of causal laws, one belonging to physics and the other to psychology. The law of gravitation, for example, is a physical law, while the law of association is a psychological law. Sensations are subject to both kinds of laws, and are therefore truly 'neutral' in Holt's sense.[1] But entities subject only to physical laws, or only to psychological laws, are not neutral, and may be called respectively purely material and purely mental. ...

If, as we maintain, mind and matter are neither of them the actual stuff of reality, but different convenient groupings of an underlying material, then, clearly, the question whether, in regard to a given phenomenon, we are to seek a physical or a mental cause, is merely one to be decided by trial. Metaphysicians have argued endlessly as to the interaction of mind and matter. The followers of Descartes held that mind and matter are so different as to make any action of the one on the other impossible. When I will to move my arm, they said, it is not my will that operates on my arm, but God, who, by His omnipotence, moves my arm whenever I want it moved. The modern doctrine of psycho-physical parallelism is not appreciably different from this theory of the Cartesian school. Psycho-physical parallelism is the theory that mental and physical events each have causes in their own sphere, but run on side by side owing to the fact that every state of the brain co-exists with a definite state of the mind, and vice versa. This view of the reciprocal causal independence of mind and matter has no basis except in metaphysical theory. For us, there is no necessity to make any such assumption, which is very difficult to harmonize with obvious facts. I receive a letter inviting me to dinner: the letter is a physical fact, but my apprehension of its meaning is mental. Here we have an effect of matter on mind. In consequence of my apprehension of the meaning of the letter, I go to the right place at the right time; here we have an effect of mind on matter. I shall try to persuade you, in the course of these lectures, that matter is not so material and mind not so mental as is generally supposed. When we are speaking of matter, it will seem as if

---

[1] E. B. Holt, *The Concept of Consciousness* (George Allen and Unwin, 1914), p. 52.

we were inclining to idealism; when we are speaking of mind, it will seem as if we were inclining to materialism. Neither is the truth. Our world is to be constructed out of what the American realists call 'neutral' entities, which have neither the hardness and indestructibility of matter, nor the reference to objects which is supposed to characterize mind.

There is, it is true, one objection which might be felt, not indeed to the action of matter on mind, but to the action of mind on matter. The laws of physics, it may be urged, are apparently adequate to explain everything that happens to matter, even when it is matter in a man's brain. This, however, is only a hypothesis, not an established theory. There is no cogent empirical reason for supposing that the laws determining the motions of living bodies are exactly the same as those that apply to dead matter. Sometimes, of course, they are clearly the same. When a man falls from a precipice or slips on a piece of orange peel, his body behaves as if it were devoid of life. These are the occasions that make Bergson laugh. But when a man's bodily movement are what we call 'voluntary', they are, at any rate *prima facie*, very different in their laws from the movements of what is devoid of life. I do not wish to say dogmatically that the difference is irreducible; I think it highly probable that it is not. I say only that the study of the behaviour of living bodies, in the present state of our knowledge, is distinct from physics. The study of gases was originally quite distinct from that of rigid bodies, and would never have advanced to its present state if it had not been independently pursued. Nowadays both the gas and the rigid body are manufactured out of a more primitive and universal kind of matter. In like manner, as a question of methodology, the laws of living bodies are to be studied, in the first place, without any undue haste to subordinate them to the laws of physics. Boyle's law and the rest had to be discovered before the kinetic theory of gases became possible. But in psychology we are hardly yet at the stage of Boyle's law. Meanwhile we need not be held up by the bogey of the universal rigid exactness of physics. This is, as yet, a mere hypothesis, to be tested empirically without any preconceptions. It may be true, or it may not. So far, that is all we can say.

II. HUMAN KNOWLEDGE: ITS SCOPE AND LIMITS (1948)

From the standpoint of orthodox psychology, there are two boundaries between the mental and physical, namely sensation and volition. 'Sensation' may be defined as the first mental effect of a physical cause, 'volition' as the last mental cause of a physical effect. I am not maintaining that these definitions will prove ultimately satisfactory, but only that they may be adopted as a guide in our preliminary survey. In the present chapter I shall not be concerned with either sensation or volition themselves, since they belong to psychology; I shall be concerned only with the physiological antecedents and concomitants of sensation, and with the physiological concomitants and consequents of volition. Before considering what science has to say, it will be worth while to look at the matter first from a common-sense point of view.

Suppose something is said to you, and in consequence you take some action; for example, you may be a soldier obeying the word of command. Physics studies the sound waves that travel through the air until they reach the ear; physiology studies the consequent event in the ear and nerves and brain, up to the moment when you hear the sound; psychology studies the sensation of hearing and the consequent volition; physiology then resumes the study of the process, and considers the outgoing chain of events from the brain to the muscles and the bodily movement expressing the volition; from that point onward, what happens is again part of the subject-matter of physics. The problem of the relation of mind and matter, which is part of the stock in trade of philosophy, comes to a head in the transition from events in the brain to the sensation, and from the volition to other events in the brain. It is thus a two-fold problem; how does matter affect mind in sensation, and how does mind affect matter in volition? I do not propose to consider this problem at this stage; I mention it now only to show the relevance of certain parts of physiology to questions which philosophy must discuss. . . .

The most interesting question remains: what goes on in the brain between the arrival of a message by the afferent nerves and the departure of a message by the efferent nerves? Suppose you read a telegram saying 'all your property has been destroyed in an earthquake', and you exclaim 'heavens! I am ruined'. We feel, rightly or wrongly, that we know the psychological links, after a fashion, by introspection, but everybody is agreed that there must also be physiological links. The current brought into the vision centre by the optic nerve must pass thence to the speech centre, and then stimulate the muscles which produce your exclamation. How this happens is still obscure. But it seems clear that, from a physiological point of view, there is a unitary process from the physical stimulus to the muscular response. In man this process may be rendered exceedingly complex by the operation of acquired habits, especially language habits, but in some less highly organized animals the process is simpler and less difficult to study; the reason why the moth approaches the flame, for example, is fairly well understood in physiological terms.

This raises a question of great interest, namely: is the process in the brain, which connects the arrival of the sensory stimulus with the departure of the message to the muscles, completely explicable in physical terms? Or is it necessary to bring in 'mental' intermediaries, such as sensation, deliberation, and volition? Could a superhuman calculator, with sufficient knowledge of the structure of a given brain, predict the muscular response to a given stimulus by means of the laws of physics and chemistry? Or is the intervention of mind an essential link in connecting a physical antecedent (the stimulus) with a physical consequent (a bodily movement)?

Until more is known about the brain than is known at present, it will not be possible to answer this question confidently in either sense. But there are already some grounds, though not conclusive ones, for regarding what might be called the materialist answer as the more probable one. There are reflexes, where the response is automatic, and not controlled by volition. From unconditioned reflexes, by the law of habit, conditioned reflexes arise, and there is every reason to regard habit as physiologically explicable. Conditioned reflexes suffice to explain a great part of human behaviour; whether there is a residue that cannot be so explained must remain, for the present, an open question.

At a later stage I shall maintain that there is no such gulf between the mental and the physical as common sense supposes. I shall also maintain that, even if the physiological causal chain from sense-organ to muscle can be set forth in terms which ignore the psychological occurrences in the middle of the chain, that will not prove that volitions are not 'causes' in the only valid sense of the word 'cause'. But both of these contentions require considerable argument and elucidation. For the present, I will only add a few words from the standpoint of scientific common sense.

If—as seems likely—there is an uninterrupted chain of purely physical causation throughout the process from sense-organ to muscle, it follows that human actions are determined in the degree to which physics is deterministic. Now physics is only deterministic as regards macroscopic occurrences, and even in regard to them it asserts only very high probability, not certainty. It might be that, without infringing the laws of physics, intelligence could make improbable things happen, as Maxwell's demon would have defeated the second law of thermo-dynamics by opening the trap-door to fast-moving particles and closing it to slow-moving ones.

On these grounds it must be admitted that there is a bare possibility—no more—that, although occurrences in the brain do not infringe the laws of physics, nevertheless their outcome is not what it would be if no psychological factors were involved. I say there is no more than a bare possibility for several reasons. In the first place, the hypothesis supposes only the microscopic laws preserved, not the macroscopic laws. But the evidence for the macroscopic laws is better than the evidence for the microscopic laws, and very strong grounds would be needed to justify a belief that on some occasion they had failed. In the second place, all the occurrences which illustrate the connection of mind and matter are macroscopic: a volition, for example, results in a perceptible bodily movement, not in a mere atomic change. In the third place, the study of processes in the nerves and brain, so far, has shown physical causation wherever adequate observation was possible; the region as to which there is still ignorance is one where very minute phenomena are concerned, and where observation is very difficult. There is therefore, so far, not the smallest positive reason for supposing that there is anything about physical processes in the brain that involves different macroscopic laws from those of the physics of inanimate matter.

Nevertheless, for those who are anxious to assert the power of mind over matter it is possible to find a loophole. It may be maintained that one characteristic of living matter is a condition of unstable equilibrium, and that this condition is most highly developed in the brains of human beings. A rock weighing many tons might be so delicately poised on the summit of a conical mountain that a child could, by a gentle push, send it thundering down into any of the valleys below; here a tiny difference in the initial impulse makes an enormous difference to the result. Perhaps in the brain the unstable equilibrium is so delicate that the difference between two possible occurrences in one atom suffices to produce macroscopic differences in the movements of muscles. And since, according to quantum physics, there are no physical laws to determine which of several possible transitions a given atom will undergo, we may imagine that, in a brain, the choice between possible transitions is determined by a psychological cause called 'volition'. All this is *possible*, but no more than possible; there is not the faintest positive reason for supposing that anything of the sort actually takes place.

On the evidence as it exists the most probable hypothesis is that, in the chain of events from sense-organ to muscle, everything is determined by the laws of macroscopic physics. To return to our previous illustration of the man who reads a telegram and exclaims 'I am ruined': it seems probable that, if you had a sufficiently minute knowledge of his brain-structure, and if you were a sufficiently good mathematician, you could foretell that when the shapes making the message on the telegram came into his field of vision they would set up a process ending in certain movements in his mouth, to wit, those producing the sounds which we represent in writing as 'I am ruined'. It is here assumed that you could make this prophecy without knowing English; it should not be necessary for you to know the meaning either of the telegram or of his exclamation. The difference between a man knowing English and a man not knowing it should, on the physiological side, consist in the presence in one case, and absence in the other, of connections between the afferent nerves when stimulated by the hearing or reading of English words, and the efferent nerves producing the appropriate response. This difference we suppose visible to a hypothetical observer without his having to know the 'meaning' either of the stimulus or of the response.

This hypothesis, it must be admitted, does not seem very plausible, and I am far from asserting dogmatically that it is true. The most that can legitimately be asserted, in my opinion, is that it is the right working hypothesis for a man investigating the physiological concomitants of sensation and volition. In so far as it is true, it may help him to make discoveries; if, at some point, it is false, its falsehood is most likely to be discovered by means of experiments suggested by the assumption of its truth. In so far as the hypothesis is true, physiology is a science independent of psychology; if at any point it is false, physiology ceases to be autonomous. As a matter of practical policy, the physiologist does well to assume that his science is autonomous so long as no evidence to the contrary has been discovered.

There have, from the earliest times, been two types of theory as to perception, one empirical, the other idealist. According to the empirical theory, some continuous chain of causation leads from the object to the percipient, and what is called 'perceiving' the object is the last link in this chain, or rather the last before the chain begins to lead out of the percipient's body instead of into it. According to the idealist theory, when a percipient happens to be in the neighbourhood of an object a divine illumination causes the percipient's soul to have an experience which is like the object.

Each of these theories has its difficulties.

The idealist theory has its origin in Plato, but reaches its logical culmination in Leibniz, who held that the world consists of monads which never interact, but which all go through parallel developments, so that what happens to me at any instant has a similarity to what is happening to you at the same instant. When you think you move your arm, I think I see you moving it; thus we are both deceived, and no one before Leibniz was sufficiently acute to unmask the deception, which he regards as the best proof of God's goodness. This theory is fantastic, and has had few adherents; but in less logical forms portions of the idealistic theory of perception are to be found even among those who think themselves most remote from it.

Philosophy is an offshoot of theology, and most philosophers, like Malvolio, 'think nobly of the soul'. They are therefore predisposed to endow it with magical powers, and to suppose that the relation between perceiving and what is perceived must be something utterly different from physical causation. This view is reinforced by the belief that mind and matter are completely disparate, and that perceiving, which is a mental phenomenon, must be totally unlike an occurrence in the brain, which is all that can be attributed to physical causation.

The theory that perceiving depends upon a chain of physical causation is apt to be supplemented by a belief that to every state of the brain a certain state of the mind 'corresponds', and vice versa, so that, given either the state of the brain or the state of the mind, the other could be inferred by a person who sufficiently understood the correspondence. If it is held that there is no causal interaction between mind and brain, this is merely a new form of the pre-established harmony. But if causation is regarded— as it usually is by empiricists—as nothing but invariable sequence or concomitance, then the supposed correspondence of brain and mind tautologically involves causal interaction. The whole question of the dependence of mind on body or body on mind has been involved in quite needless obscurity owing to the emotions involved. The facts are quite plain. Certain observable occurrences are commonly called 'physical', certain others 'mental'; sometimes 'physical' occurrences appear as causes of 'mental' ones, sometimes vice versa. A blow causes me to feel pain, a volition causes me to move my arm. There is no reason to question either of these causal connections, or at any rate no reason which does not apply to all causal connections equally.

These considerations remove one set of difficulties that stand in the way of acceptance of the physical theory of perception. . . .

This brings us to the problem of the relation of mind and matter, since perception is commonly considered 'mental' while the object perceived and the stimulus to perceiving are considered 'physical'. My own belief is that there is no difficulty whatever about this problem. The supposed difficulties have their origin in bad metaphysics and bad ethics. Mind and matter, we are told, are two substances, and are utterly disparate. Mind is noble, matter is base. Sin consists in subjection of the mind to the body. Knowledge, being one of the noblest of mental activities, cannot depend upon sense, for sense marks a form of subjection to matter, and is therefore bad. Hence the Platonic objection to identifying knowledge with perception. All this, you may think, is antiquated, but it has left a trail of prejudices hard to overcome.

Nevertheless the distinction of mind and matter would hardly have arisen if it had not some foundation. We must seek, therefore, for one or more distinctions more or less analogous to the distinction between mind and matter. I should define a 'mental' occurrence as one which can be known without inference. But let us examine some more conventional definitions.

We cannot use the Cartesian distinction between thought and extension, if only on Leibniz's ground, that extension involves plurality and therefore cannot be an attribute of a single substance. But we might try a somewhat analogous distinction. Material things, we may say, have spatial relations, while mental things do not. The brain is in the head, but thoughts are not —so at least philosophers assure us. This point of view is due to a confusion between different meanings of the word 'space'. Among the things that I see at a given moment there are spatial relations which are a part of my percepts; if percepts are 'mental', as I should contend, then spatial relations which are ingredients of percepts are also 'mental'. Naive realism identifies my percepts with physical things; it assumes that the sun of the astronomers is what I see. This involves identifying the spatial relations of my percepts with those of physical things. Many people retain this aspect of naive realism although they have rejected all the rest.

But this identification is indefensible. The spatial relations of physics hold between electrons, protons, neutrons, etc., which we do not perceive; the spatial relations of visual percepts hold between things that we do perceive, and in the last analysis between coloured patches. There is a rough correlation between physical space and visual space, but it is very rough. First: depths become indistinguishable when they are great. Second: the timing is different; the place where the sun seems to be now corresponds to the place where the physical sun was eight minutes ago. Third: the percept is subject to changes which the physicist does not attribute to changes in the object, e.g. those brought about by clouds, telescopes, squinting, or closing the eyes. The correspondence between the percept and the physical object is therefore only approximate, and it is no more exact as regards spatial relations than it is in other respects. The sun of the physicist is not identical with the sun of my percepts, and the 93,000,000 miles that separate it from the moon are not identical with the spatial relation between the visual sun and the visual moon when I happen to see both at once.

When I say that something is 'outside' me, there are two different things that I may mean. I may mean that I have a percept which is outside the percept of my body in perceptual space, or I may mean that there is a physical object which is outside my body as a physical object in the space of physics. Generally there is a rough correspondence between these two. The table that I see is outside my body as I see it in perceptual space, and the physical table is outside my physical body in physical space. But sometimes the correspondence fails. I dream, say of a railway accident: I see the train falling down an embankment, and I hear the shrieks of the injured. These dream-objects are genuinely and truly 'outside' my dream body in my own perceptual space. But when I wake up I find that the whole dream was due to a noise in my ear. And when I say that the noise is in my ear, I mean that the physical source of the sound that I experience is 'in' my ear as a physical object in physical space. In another sense, we might say that all noises are in the ear, but if we confuse these two senses the result is an inextricable tangle.

Generalizing, we may say that my percept of anything other than my body is 'outside' the percept of my body in perceptual space, and if the perception is not misleading the physical object is 'outside' my physical body in physical space. It does not follow that my percept is outside my physical body. Indeed, such a hypothesis is *prima facie* meaningless, although, as we shall see, a meaning can be found for it, and it is then false.

We can now begin to tackle our central question, namely, what do we mean by a 'percept', and how can it be a source of knowledge as to something other than itself?

What is a percept? As I use the word, it is what happens when, in common-sense terms, I see something or hear something or otherwise believe myself to become aware of something through my senses. The sun, we believe, is always there, but I only sometimes see it: I do not see it at night, or in cloudy weather, or when I am otherwise occupied. But sometimes I see it. All the occasions on which I see the sun have a certain resemblance to each other, which enabled me in infancy to learn to use the word 'sun' on the right occasions. Some of the resemblances between different occasions when I see the sun are obviously in me; for example, I must have my eyes open and turn in the right direction. These, therefore, we do not regard as properties of the sun. But there are other resemblances which, so far as common sense can discover, do not depend upon us; when we see the sun, it is almost always round and bright and hot. The few occasions when it is not are easily explicable as due to fog or to an eclipse. Common sense therefore says: there is an object which is round and bright and hot; the kind of event called 'seeing the sun' consists in a relation between me and this object, and when this relation occurs I am 'perceiving' the object. . . .

The dualistic view of perception, as a relation of a subject to an object, is one which, following the leadership of William James, empiricists have now for the most part abandoned. The distinction between 'seeing the sun' as a mental event, and the immediate object of my seeing, is now generally rejected as invalid, and in this view I concur. But many of those who take the view that I take on this point nevertheless inconsistently adhere to some form of naive realism. If my seeing of the sun is identical with the sun that I see, then the sun that I see is not the astronomer's sun. For exactly the same reasons, the tables and chairs that I see, if they are identical with my seeing of them, are not located where physics says they are, but where my seeing is. You may say that my seeing, being mental, is not in space; if you do, I will not argue the point. But I shall none the less insist that there is one, and only one, region of space-time with which my seeing is always causally bound up, and that is my brain at the time of the seeing. And exactly the same is true of all objects of sense-perception.

We are now in a position to consider the relation between a physical occurrence and the subsequent occurrence popularly regarded as seeing it. Consider, say, a flash of lightning on a dark night. The flash, for the physicist, is an electrical discharge, which causes electromagnetic waves to travel outward from the region where it has taken place. These waves, if they meet no opaque matter, merely travel further and further; but when they meet opaque matter their energy undergoes transformations into new forms. When they happen to meet a human eye connected with a human brain, all sorts of complicated things happen, which can be studied by the physiologist. At the moment when this causal process reaches the brain, the person to whom the brain belongs 'sees' the flash. This person, if he is unacquainted with physics, thinks that the flash *is* what takes place when he 'sees' the flash; or rather, he thinks that what takes place is a relation between himself and the flash, calling 'perceiving' the flash. If he is acquainted with physics, he does not think this, but he still holds that the sort of thing that takes place when he 'sees' the flash gives an adequate basis for knowledge of the physical world.

We can now at last tackle the question: How, and to what extent, can percepts be a source of knowledge as to physical objects? . . .

Why, for example, when a number of people see the sun, should we believe that there is a sun outside their percepts, and not merely that there are laws determining the circumstances in which we shall have the experience called 'seeing the sun'?

Here we come up against a principle which is used both by science and by common sense, to the effect that, when a number of phenomena in separated parts of space-time are obviously causally interconnected, there must be some continuous process in the intervening regions which links them all together. This principle of spatio-temporal continuity needs to be re-examined after we have considered the inference from perceptual to physical space. In the meantime, it can be accepted as at least a first step towards formalizing inference from perceptual to physical objects.

Our main question was: If physics is true, how can it be known, and what, besides physics, must we know to infer physics? This problem arises through the physical causation of perception, which makes it probable that physical objects differ greatly from percepts; but if so, how can we infer physical objects from percepts? Moreover, since perceiving is considered to be 'mental' while its causes are 'physical', we are confronted with the old problem of the relation between mind and matter. My own belief is that the 'mental' and the 'physical' are not so disparate as is generally thought. I should define a 'mental' occurrence as one which some one knows otherwise than by inference; the distinction between 'mental' and 'physical' therefore belongs to theory of knowledge, not to metaphysics.

One of the difficulties which have led to confusion was failure to distinguish between perceptual and physical space. Perceptual space consists of perceptible relations between parts of percepts, whereas physical space consists of inferred relations between inferred physical things. What I see may be outside my percept of my body, but not outside my body as a physical thing.

Percepts, considered causally, are between events in afferent nerves (stimulus) and events in efferent nerves (reaction); their location in causal chains is the same as that of certain events in the brain. Percepts as a source of knowledge of physical objects can only serve their purpose in so far as there are separable, more or less independent, causal chains in the physical world. This only happens approximately, and therefore the inference from percepts to physical objects cannot be precise. Science consists largely of devices for overcoming this initial lack of precision on the assumption that perception gives a first approximation to the truth. . . .

The inferences from experiences to the physical world can, I think, all be justified by the assumption that there are causal chains, each member of which is a complex structure ordered by the spatio-temporal relation of compresence (or of contiguity); that all the members of such a chain are similar in structure; that each member is connected with each other by a series of contiguous structures; and that, when a number of such similar structures are found to be grouped about a centre earlier in time than any of them, it is probable that they all have their causal origin in a complex event which is at that centre and has a structure similar to the structure of the observed events. I shall, at a later stage, endeavour to give greater precision to this assumption, and to show reasons for accepting it. For the present, to avoid verbiage, I shall treat it as though it were unquestionably correct, and on this basis I shall return to the relations between mental and physical events.

When, on a common-sense basis, people talk of the gulf between mind and matter, what they really have in mind is the gulf between a visual or tactual percept and a 'thought'—e.g., a memory, a pleasure, or a volition. But this, as we have seen, is a division within the mental world; the percept is as mental as the 'thought'. Slightly more sophisticated people may think of matter as the unknown cause of sensation, the 'thing-in-itself' which certainly does not have the secondary qualities and perhaps does not have the primary qualities either. But however much they may emphasize the unknown character of the thing-in-itself, they still suppose themselves to know enough of it to be sure that it is very different from a mind. This comes, I think, of not having rid their imaginations of the conception of material things as something hard that you can bump into. You can bump into your friend's body, but not into his mind; therefore his body is different from his mind. This sort of argument persists imaginatively in many people who have rejected it intellectually.

Then, again, there is the argument about brain and mind. When a physiologist examines a brain, he does not see thoughts, therefore the brain is one thing and the mind which thinks is another. The fallacy in this argument consists in supposing that a man can see matter. Not even the ablest physiologist can perform this feat. His percept when he looks at a brain is an event in his own mind, and has only a causal connection with the brain that he fancies he is seeing. When, in a powerful telescope, he sees a tiny luminous dot, and interprets it as a vast nebula existing a million years ago, he realizes that what he sees is different from what he infers. The difference from the case of a brain looked at through a microscope is only one of degree; there is exactly the same need of inference, by means of the laws of physics, from the visual datum to its physical cause. And just as no one supposes that the nebula has any close resemblance to a luminous dot, so no one should suppose that the brain has any close resemblance to what the physiologist sees.

What then, do we know about the physical world? Let us first define more exactly what we mean by a 'physical' event. I should define it as an event which, if known to occur, is inferred, and which is not known to be mental. And I define a 'mental' event (to repeat) as one with which some one is acquainted otherwise than by inference. Thus a 'physical' event is one which is either totally unknown, or, if known at all, is not known to any one except by inference—or, perhaps we should say, is not known to be known to any one except by inference.

If physical events are to suffice as a basis for physics, and, indeed, if we are to have any reason for believing in them, they must not be *totally* unknown, like Kant's things-in-themselves. In fact, on the principle which we are assuming, they are known, though perhaps incompletely, so far as their space-time structure is concerned, for this must be similar to the space-time structure of their effects upon percipients. E.g. from the fact that the sun looks round in perceptual space we have a right to infer that it is round in physical space. We have no right to make a similar inference as regards brightness, because brightness is not a structural property.

We cannot however infer that the sun is *not* bright—meaning by 'brightness' the quality that we know in perception. The only legitimate inferences as regards the physical sun are structural; concerning a property which is not structural, such as brightness, we must remain completely agnostic. We may perhaps say that it is unlikely that the physical sun is bright, since we have no knowledge of the qualities of things that are not percepts, and therefore there seems to be an illimitable field of choice of possible qualities. But such an argument is so speculative that perhaps we ought not to attach much weight to it.

This brings us to the question: Is there any reason, and if so what, for supposing that physical events differ in quality from mental events?

Here we must, to begin with, distinguish events in a living brain from events elsewhere. I will begin with events in a living brain.

I assume that a small region of space-time is a collection of compresent events, and that space-time regions are ordered by means of causal relations. The former assumption has the consequence that there is no reason why thoughts should not be among the events of which the brain consists, and the latter assumption leads to the conclusion that, in physical space, thoughts are in the brain. Or, more exactly, each region of the brain is a class of events, and among the events constituting a region thoughts are included. It is to be observed that, if we say thoughts are in the brain, we are using an ellipsis. The correct statement is that thoughts are among the events which, as a class, constitute a region in the brain. A given thought, that is to say, is a member of a class, and the class is a region in the brain. In this sense, where events in brains are concerned, we have no reason to suppose that they are not thoughts, but, on the contrary, have strong reason to suppose that at least some of them are thoughts. I am using 'thoughts' as a generic term for mental events.

When we come to events in parts of physical space-time where there are no brains, we have still no positive argument to prove that they are not thoughts, except such as may be derived from observation of the differences between living and dead matter coupled with inferences based on analogy or its absence. We may contend, for instance, that habit is in the main confined to living matter, and that, since memory is a species of habit, it is unlikely that there is memory except where there is living matter. Extending this argument, we can observe that the behaviour of living matter, especially of its higher forms, is much more dependent on its past history than that of dead matter, and that, therefore, the whole of that large part of our mental life that depends upon habit is presumably only to be found where there is living matter. But such arguments are inconclusive and limited in scope. Just as we cannot be *sure* that the sun is not bright, so we cannot be *sure* that it is not intelligent. We may be right in thinking both improbable, but we are certainly wrong if we say they are impossible.

I conclude that, while mental events and their qualities can be known without inference, physical events are known only as regards their space-time structure. The qualities that compose such events are unknown—so completely unknown that we cannot say either that they are, or that they are not, different from the qualities that we know as belonging to mental events.

28

C. D. BROAD

There is a question which has been argued about for some centuries now under the name of 'Interaction'; this is the question whether minds really do act on the organisms which they animate, and whether organisms really do act on the minds which animate them. (I must point out at once that I imply no particular theory of mind or body by the word 'to animate'. I use it as a perfectly neutral name to express the fact that a certain mind is connected in some peculiarly intimate way with a certain body, and, under normal conditions with no other body. This is a fact even on a purely behaviouristic theory of mind; on such a view to say that the mind M animates the body B would mean that the body B, in so far as it behaves in certain ways, *is* the mind M. A body which did not act in these ways would be said not to be animated by a mind. And a different body B', which acted in the same general way as B, would be said to be animated by a different mind M'.)

The problem of Interaction is generally discussed at the level of enlightened common-sense; where it is assumed that we know pretty well what we mean by 'mind', by 'matter' and by 'causation'. Obviously no solution which is reached at that level can claim to be ultimate. If what we call 'matter' should turn out to be a collection of spirits of low intelligence, as Leibniz thought, the argument that mind and body are so unlike that their interaction is impossible would become irrelevant. Again, if causation be nothing but regular sequence and concomitance, as some philosophers have held, it is ridiculous to regard psychoneural parallelism and interaction as mutually exclusive alternatives. For interaction will mean no more than parallelism, and parallelism will mean no less than interaction. Nevertheless I am going to discuss the arguments here at the common-sense level, because they are so incredibly bad and yet have imposed upon so many learned men.

We start then by assuming a developed mind and a developed organism as two distinct things, and by admitting that the two are now intimately connected in some way or other which I express by saying that 'this mind *animates* this organism'. We assume that bodies are very much as enlight-

ened common-sense believes them to be; and that, even if we cannot define
'causation', we have some means of recognizing when it is present and
when it is absent. The question then is: 'Does a mind ever act on the body
which it animates, and does a body ever act on the mind which animates
it?' The answer which common-sense would give to both questions is:
'Yes, certainly'. On the face of it, my body acts on my mind whenever a
pin is stuck into the former and a painful sensation thereupon arises in the
latter. And, on the face of it, my mind acts on my body whenever a desire
to move my arm arises in the former and is followed by this movement in
the latter. Let us call this common-sense view 'Two-sided Interaction'.
Although it seems so obvious it has been denied by probably a majority
of philosophers and a majority of physiologists. So the question is: 'Why
should so many distinguished men, who have studied the subject, have
denied the apparently obvious fact of Two-sided Interaction?'

The arguments against Two-sided Interaction fall into two sets:—
Philosophical and Scientific. We will take the philosophical arguments
first: for we shall find that the professedly scientific arguments come back
in the end to the principles or prejudices which are made explicit in the
philosophical arguments.

Philosophical Arguments against Two-sided Interaction

No one can deny that there is a close correlation between certain bodily
events and certain mental events, and conversely. Therefore anyone who
denies that there is action of mind on body and of body on mind must
presumably hold:

(a) that the concomitant variation is not an adequate criterion of
    causal connection, and

(b) that the other feature which is essential for causal connection is
    absent in the case of body and mind.

Now the common philosophical argument is that minds and mental states
are so extremely unlike bodies and bodily states that it is inconceivable
that the two should be causally connected. It is certainly true that, if minds
and mental events are just what they seem to be to introspection and
nothing more, and if bodies and bodily events are just what enlightened
common-sense thinks them to be and nothing more, the two *are* extremely
unlike. And this fact is supposed to show that, however closely correlated
certain pairs of events in mind and body respectively may be, they cannot
be causally connected.

Evidently the assumption at the back of this argument is that concomitant variation, together with a high enough degree of likeness, is an
adequate test for causation; but that no amount of concomitant variation

can establish causation in the absence of a high enough degree of likeness. Now I am inclined to admit part of this assumption. I think it is practically certain that causation does not simply *mean* concomitant variation. (And, if it did, *cadit quaestio*.) Hence the existence of the latter is not *ipso facto* a proof of the presence of the former. Again, I think it is almost certain that concomitant variation between A and B is not in fact a sufficient sign of the presence of a *direct* causal relation between the two. (I think it may perhaps be a sufficient sign of *either* a direct causal relation between A and B *or* of several causal relations which indirectly unite A and B through the medium of other terms, C, D, etc.) So far I agree with the assumptions of the argument. But I cannot see the least reason to think that the other characteristic, which must be added to concomitant variation before we can be sure that A and B are causally connected, is a high degree of likeness between the two. One would like to know just how unlike two events may be before it becomes impossible to admit the existence of a causal relation between them. No one hesitates to hold that draughts and colds in the head are causally connected, although the two are extremely unlike each other. If the unlikeness of draughts and colds in the head does not prevent one from admitting a causal connection between the two, why should the unlikeness of volitions and voluntary movements prevent one from holding that they are causally connected? To sum up. I am willing to admit that an adequate criterion of causal connection needs some other relation between a pair of events beside concomitant variation; but I do not believe for a moment that this other relation is that of qualitative likeness.

This brings us to a rather more refined form of the argument against interaction. It is said that, whenever we admit the existence of a causal relation between two events, these two events (to put it crudely) must also form parts of a single substantial whole. E.g., all physical events are spatially related and form one great extended whole. And the mental events which would commonly be admitted to be causally connected are always events in a single mind. A mind is a substantial whole of a peculiar kind too. Now it is said that between bodily events and mental events there are no relations such as those which unite physical events in different parts of the same Space or mental events in the history of the same mind. In the absence of such relations, binding mind and body into a single substantial whole, we cannot admit that bodily and mental events can be causally connected with each other, no matter how closely correlated their variations may be.

This is a much better argument than the argument about qualitative likeness and unlikeness. If we accept the premise that causal relations can subsist only between terms which form parts of a single substantial whole must we deny that mental and bodily events can be causally connected? I do not think that we need.

(i) It is of course perfectly true that an organism and the mind which animates it do not form a physical whole, and that they do not form a mental whole; and these, no doubt, are the two kinds of substantial whole with which we are most familiar. But it does not follow that a mind and its organism do not form a substantial whole of *some* kind. There, plainly, is the extraordinary intimate union between the two which I have called 'animation' of the one by the other. Even if the mind be just what it seems to introspection, and the body be just what it seems to perception aided by the more precise methods of science, this seems to me to be enough to make a mind and its body a substantial whole. Even so extreme a dualist about Mind and Matter as Descartes occasionally suggests that a mind and its body together form a quasi-substance; and, although we may quarrel with the language of the very numerous philosophers who have said that the mind is 'the form' of its body, we must admit that such language would never have seemed plausible unless a mind and its body together had formed something very much like a single substantial whole.

(ii) We must, moreover, admit the possibility that minds and mental events have properties and relations which do not reveal themselves to introspection, and that bodies and bodily events may have properties and relations which do not reveal themselves to perception or to physical and chemical experiment. In virtue of these properties and relations the two together may well form a single substantial whole of the kind which is alleged to be needed for causal interaction. Thus, if we accept the premise of the argument, we have no right to assert that mind and body *cannot* interact; but only the much more modest proposition that introspection and perception do not suffice to assure us that mind and body are so interrelated that they *can* interact.

(iii) We must further remember that the Two-sided Interactionist is under no obligation to hold that the *complete* conditions of any bodily event are mental. He needs only to assert that some mental events include certain bodily events among their necessary conditions, and that some bodily events include certain mental events among their necessary conditions. If I am paralysed my volition may not move my arm; and, if I am hypnotized or intensely interested or frightened, a wound may not produce a painful sensation. Now, if the complete cause and the complete effect in all interaction include both a bodily and a mental factor, the two wholes will be related by the fact that the mental constituents belong to a single mind, that the bodily constituents belong to a single body, and that this mind animates this body. This amount of connection should surely be enough to allow of causal interaction.

This will be the most appropriate place to deal with the contention that, in voluntary action, and there only, we are immediately acquainted with an instance of causal connection. If this be true the controversy is of course settled at once in favour of the interactionist. It is generally supposed that this view was refuted once and for all by Mr Hume in his *Enquiry concerning Human Understanding* (Sect. VII, Part 1). I should not care to assert that the doctrine in question is true; but I do think that it is plausible, and I am quite sure that Mr Hume's arguments do not refute it. Mr Hume uses three closely connected arguments. (1) The connection between a successful volition and the resulting bodily movement is as mysterious and as little self-evident as the connection between any other event and its effect. (2) We have to learn from experience which of our volitions will be effective and which will not. E.g., we do not know, until we have tried, that we can voluntarily move our arms and cannot voluntarily move our livers. And again, if a man were suddenly paralysed, he would still expect to be able to move his arm voluntarily, and would be surprised when he found that it kept still in spite of his volition. (3) We have discovered that the immediate consequence of a volition is a change in our nerves and muscles, which most people know nothing about; and is not the movement of a limb, which most people believe to be its immediate and necessary consequence.

The second and third arguments are valid only against the contention that we know immediately that a volition to make a certain movement is the *sufficient* condition for the happening of that movement. They are quite irrelevant to the contention that we know immediately that the volition is a *necessary* condition for the happening of just that movement at just that time. No doubt many other conditions are also necessary, e.g., that our nerves and muscles shall be in the right state; and these other necessary conditions can be discovered only by special investigation. Since our volitions to move our limbs are in fact followed in the vast majority of cases by the willed movement, and since the other necessary conditions are not very obvious, it is natural enough that we should think that we know immediately that our volition is the *sufficient* condition of the movement of our limbs. If we think so, we are certainly wrong; and Mr Hume's arguments prove that we are. But they prove nothing else. It does not follow that we are wrong in thinking that we know, without having to wait for the result, that the volition is a *necessary* condition of the movement.

It remains to consider the first argument. Is the connection between cause and effect as mysterious and as little self-evident in the case of the voluntary production of bodily movement as in all other cases? If so, we must hold that the first time a baby wills to move its hand it is just as much surprised to find its hand moving as it would be to find its leg moving or its nurse bursting into flames. I do not profess to know anything about the infant mind; but it seems to me that this is a wildly paradoxical consequence, for which there is no evidence or likelihood. But there is no need to leave the matter there. It is perfectly plain that, in the case of volition and voluntary movement, there *is* a connection between the cause and the effect which is not present in other cases of causation, and which does make it plausible to hold that in this one case the nature of the effect can be foreseen by merely reflecting on the nature of the cause. The peculiarity of a volition as a cause-factor is that it involves as an essential part of it the idea of the effect. To say that a person has a volition to move his arm involves saying that he has an idea of his arm (and not of his leg or his liver) and an idea of the position in which he wants his arm to be. It is simply silly in view of this fact to say that there is no closer connection between the desire to move my arm and the movement of my arm than there is between this desire and the movement of my leg or my liver. We cannot detect any analogous connection between cause and effect in causal transactions which we view wholly from outside, such as the movement of a billiard-ball by a cue. It is therefore by no means unreasonable to suggest that, in the one case of our own voluntary movements, we can see without waiting for the result that such and such a volition is a necessary condition of such and such a bodily movement.

It seems to me that Mr Hume's arguments on this point are absolutely irrelevant, and that it may very well be true that in volition we positively know that our desire for such and such a bodily movement is a necessary (though not a sufficient) condition of the happening of just that movement at just that time. On the whole then I conclude that the philosophical arguments certainly do not disprove Two-sided Interaction, and that they do not even raise any strong presumption against it. And, while I am not prepared definitely to commit myself to the view that, in voluntary movement, we positively *know* that the mind acts on the body, I do think that this opinion is quite plausible when properly stated and that the arguments which have been brought against it are worthless. I pass therefore to the scientific arguments.

Scientific arguments against Two-sided Interaction

There are, so far as I know, two of these. One is supposed to be based on the physical principle of the Conservation of Energy, and on certain experiments which have been made on human bodies. The other is based on the close analogy which is said to exist between the structures of the physiological mechanism of reflex action and that of voluntary action. I will take them in turn.

K

(1) *The Argument from Energy*. It will first be needful to state clearly what is asserted by the principle of the Conservation of Energy. It is found that, if we take certain material systems, e.g., a gun, a cartridge, and a bullet, there is a certain magnitude which keeps approximately constant throughout all their changes. This is called 'Energy'. When the gun has not been fired it and the bullet have no motion, but the explosive in the cartridge has great chemical energy. When it has been fired the bullet is moving very fast and has great energy of movement. The gun, though not moving fast in its recoil, has also great energy of movement because it is very massive. The gases produced by the explosion have some energy of movement and some heat-energy, but much less chemical energy than the unexploded charge had. These various kinds of energy can be measured in common units according to certain conventions. To an innocent mind there seems to be a good deal of 'cooking' at this stage, i.e., the conventions seem to be chosen and various kinds and amounts of concealed energy seem to be postulated in order to make the principle come out right at the end. I do not propose to go into this in detail, for two reasons. In the first place, I think that the conventions adopted and the postulates made, though somewhat suggestive of the fraudulent company-promoter, can be justified by their coherence with certain experimental facts, and that they are not simply made *ad hoc*. Secondly, I shall show that the Conservation of Energy is absolutely irrelevant to the question at issue, so that it would be waste of time to treat it too seriously in the present connection. Now it is found that the total energy of all kinds in this system, when measured according to these conventions, is approximately the same in amount though very differently distributed after the explosion and before it. If we had confined our attention to a part of this system and *its* energy this would not have been true. The bullet, e.g., had no energy at all before the explosion and a great deal afterwards. A system like the bullet, the gun, and the charge, is called a 'Conservative System'; the bullet alone, or the gun and the charge, would be called 'Non-conservative Systems'. A conservative system might therefore be defined as one whose total energy is redistributed, but not altered in amount, by changes that happen within it. Of course a given system might be conservative for some kinds of change and not for others.

So far we have merely defined a 'Conservative System', and admitted that there are systems which, for some kinds of change at any rate, answer approximately to our definition. We can now state the Principle of the Conservation of Energy in terms of the conceptions just defined. The principle asserts that every material system is either itself conservative, or, if not, is part of a larger material system which is conservative. We may take it that there is good inductive evidence for this proposition.

The next thing to consider is the experiments on the human body. These tend to prove that a living body, with the air that it breathes and the food that it eats, forms a conservative system to a high degree of approximation. We can measure the chemical energy of the food given to a man, and that which enters his body in the form of Oxygen breathed in. We can also, with suitable apparatus, collect, measure and analyse the air breathed out, and thus find its chemical energy. Similarly, we can find the energy given out in bodily movement, in heat, and in excretion. It is alleged that, on the average, whatever the man may do, the energy of his bodily movements is exactly accounted for by the energy given to him in the form of food and of Oxygen. If you take the energy put in in food and Oxygen, and subtract the energy given out in waste-products, the balance is almost exactly equal to the energy put out in bodily movements. Such slight differences as are found are as often on one side as on the other, and are therefore probably due to unavoidable experimental errors. I do not propose to criticize the interpretation of these experiments in detail, because, as I shall show soon, they are completely irrelevant to the problem of whether mind and body interact. But there is just one point that I will make before passing on. It is perfectly clear that such experiments can tell us only what happens on the average over a long time. To know whether the balance was accurately kept at every moment we should have to kill the patient at each moment and analyse his body so as to find out the energy present then in the form of stored-up products. Obviously we cannot keep on killing the patient in order to analyse him, and then reviving him in order to go on with the experiment. Thus it would seem that the results of the experiment are perfectly compatible with the presence of quite large excesses or defects in the total bodily energy at certain moments, provided that these average out over longer periods. However, I do not want to press this criticism; I am quite ready to accept for our present purpose the traditional interpretation which has been put on the experiments.

We now understand the physical principle and the experimental facts. The two together are generally supposed to prove that mind and body cannot interact. What precisely is the argument, and is it valid? I imagine that the argument, when fully stated, would run somewhat as follows: 'I will to move my arm, and it moves. If the volition has anything to do with causing the movement we might expect energy to flow from my mind to my body. Thus the energy of my body ought to receive a measurable increase, not accounted for by the food that I eat and the Oxygen that I breathe. But no such physically unaccountable increases of bodily energy are found. Again, I tread on a tin-tack, and a painful sensation arises in my mind. If treading on the tack has anything to do with causing the sensation we might expect energy to flow from my body to my mind. Such energy would cease to be measurable. Thus there ought to be a noticeable decrease in my bodily energy, not balanced by increases anywhere in the physical system. But such unbalanced decreases of bodily energy are not found.' So it is concluded that the volition has nothing to do with causing my arm to move, and that treading on the tack has nothing to do with causing the painful sensation.

Is this argument valid? In the first place it is important to notice that the conclusion does not follow from the Conservation of Energy and the experimental facts alone. The real premise is a tacitly assumed proposition about causation; viz., that, if a change in A has anything to do with causing a change in B, energy must leave A and flow into B. This is neither asserted nor entailed by the Conservation of Energy. What *it* says is that, *if* energy leaves A, it must appear in something else, say B; so that A and B together form a conservative system. Since the Conservation of Energy is not itself the premise for the argument against Interaction, and since it does not entail that premise, the evidence for the Conservation of Energy is not evidence against Interaction. Is there any independent evidence for the premise? We may admit that it *is* true of many, though not of all, transactions within the physical realm. But there are cases where it is not true even of purely physical transactions; and, even if it were always true in the physical realm, it would not follow that it must also be true of trans-physical causation. Take the case of a weight swinging at the end of a string hung from a fixed point. The total energy of the weight is the same at all positions in its course. It is thus a conservative system. But at every moment the direction and velocity of the weight's motion are different, and the proportion between its kinetic and its potential energy is constantly changing. These changes are caused by the pull of the string, which acts in a different direction at each different moment. The string makes no difference to the total energy of the weight; but it makes all the difference in the world to the particular way in which the weight moves and the particular way in which the energy is distributed between the potential and the kinetic forms. This is evident when we remember that the weight would begin to move in an utterly different course if at any moment the string were cut.

Here, then, we have a clear case even in the physical realm where a system is conservative but is continually acted on by something which affects its movement and the distribution of its total energy. Why should not the mind act on the body in this way? If you say that you can see how a string can affect the movement of a weight, but cannot see how a volition could affect the movement of a material particle, you have deserted the scientific argument and have gone back to one of the philosophical arguments. Your real difficulty is either that volitions are so very unlike movements, or that the volition is in your mind whilst the movement belongs to the physical realm. And we have seen how little weight can be attached to these objections.

The fact is that, even in purely physical systems, the Conservation of Energy does not explain what changes will happen or when they will happen. It merely imposes a very general limiting condition on the changes that are possible. The fact that the system composed of bullet, charge, and gun, in our earlier example, is conservative does not tell us that the gun ever will be fired, or when it will be fired if at all or what will cause it to go off, or what forms of energy will appear if and when it does go off. The change in this case is determined by pulling the trigger. Likewise the mere fact that the human body and its neighbourhood form a conservative system does not explain any particular bodily movement; it does not explain why I ever move at all, or why I sometimes write, sometimes walk, and sometimes swim. To explain the happening of these particular movements at certain times it seems to be essential to take into account the volitions which happen from time to time in my mind; just as it is essential to take the string into account to explain the particular behaviour of the weight, and to take the trigger into account to explain the going off of the gun at a certain moment. The difference between the gun-system and the body-system is that a little energy does flow into the former when the trigger is pulled, whilst it is alleged that none does so when a volition starts a bodily movement. But there is not even this amount of difference between the body-system and the swinging weight.

Thus the argument from energy has no tendency to disprove Two-sided Interaction. It has gained a spurious authority from the august name of the Conservation of Energy. But this impressive principle proves to have nothing to do with the case. And the real premise of the argument is not self-evident, and is not universally true even in purely intra-physical transactions. In the end this scientific argument has to lean on the old philosophic arguments; and we have seen that these are but bruised reeds. Nevertheless, the facts brought forward by the argument from energy do throw some light on the *nature* of the interaction between mind and body, assuming this to happen. They do suggest that all the energy of our bodily actions comes out of and goes back into the physical world, and that minds neither add energy to nor abstract it from the latter. What they do, if they do anything, is to determine that at a given moment so much energy shall change from the chemical form to the form of bodily move-ment; and they determine this, so far as we can see, without altering the total amount of energy in the physical world.

(2) *The Argument from the Structure of the Nervous System.* There are purely reflex actions, like sneezing and blinking, in which there is no reason to suppose that the mind plays any essential part. Now we know the nervous structure which is used in such acts as these. A stimulus is given to the outer end of an afferent nerve; some change or other runs up this nerve, crosses a synapsis between this and an efferent nerve, travels down the latter to a muscle, causes the muscle to contract, and so produces a bodily movement. There seems no reason to believe that the mind plays any essential part in this process. The process may be irreducibly vital, and not merely physico-chemical; but there seems no need to assume anything more than this. Now it is said that the whole nervous system is simply an immense complication of interconnected nervous arcs. The result is that a change which travels inwards has an immense number of alternative paths by which it may travel outwards. Thus the reaction to a given stimulus is no longer one definite movement, as in the simple reflex. Almost any movement may follow any stimulus according to the path which the afferent disturbance happens to take. This path will depend on the relative resistance of the various synapses at the time. Now a variable response to the same stimulus is characteristic of deliberate as opposed to reflex action.

These are the facts. The argument based on them runs as follows. It is admitted that the mind has nothing to do with the causation of purely reflex actions. But the nervous structure and the nervous processes involved in deliberate action do not differ in kind from those involved in reflex action; they differ only in degree of complexity. The variability which characterizes deliberate action is fully explained by the variety of alternative paths and the variable resistances of the synapses. So it is unreasonable to suppose that the mind has any more to do with causing deliberate actions than it has to do with causing reflex actions.

I think that this argument is invalid. In the first place I am pretty sure that the persons who use it have before their imagination a kind of picture of how mind and body must interact if they interact at all. They find that the facts do not answer to this picture, and so they conclude that there is no interaction. The picture is of the following kind. They think of the mind as sitting somewhere in a hole in the brain, surrounded by telephones. And they think of the afferent disturbance as coming to an end at one of these telephones and there affecting the mind. The mind is then supposed to respond by sending an efferent impulse down another of these telephones. As no such hole, with afferent nerves stopping at its walls and efferent nerves starting from them, can be found, they conclude that the mind can play no part in the transaction. But another alternative is that this picture of how the mind must act if it acts at all is wrong. To put it shortly, the mistake is to confuse a gap in an explanation with a spatio-temporal gap, and to argue from the absence of the latter to the absence of the former.

The Interactionist's contention is simply that there is a gap in any purely physiological explanation of deliberate action; i.e., that all such explanations fail to account completely for the facts because they leave out one necessary condition. It does not follow in the least that there must be a spatio-temporal breach of continuity in the physiological conditions, and that the missing condition must fill this gap in the way in which the movement of a wire fills the spatio-temporal interval between the pulling of a bell-handle and the ringing of a distant bell. To assume this is to make the mind a kind of physical object, and to make its action a kind of mechanical action. Really, the mind and its actions are not literally in Space at all, and the time which is occupied by the mental event is no doubt *also* occupied by some part of the physiological process. Thus I am inclined to think that much of the force which this argument actually exercises on many people is simply due to the presupposition about the *modus operandi* of interaction, and that it is greatly weakened when this presupposition is shown to be a mere prejudice due to our limited power of envisaging unfamiliar alternative possibilities.

We can, however, make more detailed objections to the argument than this. There is a clear introspective difference between the mental accompaniment of voluntary action and that of reflex action. What goes on in our minds when we decide with difficulty to get out of a hot bath on a cold morning is obviously extremely different from what goes on in our minds when we sniff pepper and sneeze. And the difference is qualitative; it is not a mere difference of complexity. This difference has to be explained somehow; and the theory under discussion gives no plausible explanation of it. The ordinary view that, in the latter case, the mind is not acting on the body at all; whilst, in the former, it is acting on the body in a specific way, does at least make the introspective difference between the two intelligible.

Again, whilst it is true that deliberate action differs from reflex action in its greater variability of response to the same stimulus, this is certainly not the whole or the most important part of the difference between them. The really important difference is that, in deliberate action, the response is varied *appropriately* to meet the special circumstances which are supposed to exist at the time or are expected to arise later; whilst reflex action is not varied in this way, but is blind and almost mechanical. The complexity of the nervous system explains the *possibility* of variation; it does not in the least explain why the alternative which actually takes place should as a rule be appropriate and not merely haphazard. And so again it seems as if some factor were in operation in deliberate action which is not present in reflex action; and it is reasonable to suppose that this factor is the volition in the mind.

It seems to me that this second scientific argument has no tendency to disprove interaction; but that the facts which it brings forward do tend to suggest the particular form which interaction probably takes if it happens at all. They suggest that what the mind does to the body in voluntary action, if it does anything, is to lower the resistance of certain synapses and to raise that of others. The result is that the nervous current follows such a course as to produce the particular movement which the mind judges to be appropriate at the time. On such a view the difference between reflex, habitual, and deliberate actions for the present purpose becomes fairly plain. In pure reflexes the mind cannot voluntarily affect the resistance of the synapses concerned, and so the action takes place in spite of it. In habitual action it deliberately refrains from interfering with the resistance of the synapses, and so the action goes on like a complicated reflex. But it *can* affect these resistances if it wishes, though often only with difficulty; and it is ready to do so if it judges this to be expedient. Finally, it may lose the power altogether. This would be what happens when a person becomes a slave to some habit, such as drug-taking.

I conclude that, at the level of enlightened common-sense at which the ordinary discussion of Interaction moves, no good reason has been produced for doubting that the mind acts on the body in volition, and that the body acts on the mind in sensation. The philosophic arguments are quite inconclusive; and the scientific arguments, when properly understood, are quite compatible with Two-sided Interaction. At most they suggest certain conclusions as to the form which interaction probably takes if it happens at all.

29

MORITZ SCHLICK

ALLGEMEINE ERKENNTNISLEHRE (1925)

The problem which has been at the centre of all metaphysics in more modern philosophy, that is, since about the time of Descartes, is the question of the relationship of the spiritual to the physical, the 'soul' to the body. In my opinion it is one of those problems which owe their existence to a false formulation of the question. In fact, from the standpoint which we have reached in the foregoing investigations, a picture of the world unfolds before us without those dark nooks and crannies in which the peculiar difficulties which we fear, and call the psycho-physical problem, could hide. From that standpoint the problem is solved even before it can be stated. We are now going to prove this. But in order to reach complete satisfaction, we must also reveal the source of the error which was able to make the body-soul question into a worrying problem.

We have already firmly limited the concept of the mental: it meant what is 'absolutely known', which was identical with the 'contents of consciousness'; and the meaning of this expression surely needs no more detailed explanation now. Up to now, however, there was no real need to define the physical. We must now make up for this, and we shall see that in actual fact it is only necessary to give a clear presentation of the characteristics which constitute the concept of the physical in order to reach complete clarity on the supposed problem.

The universe appeared to us as an infinite multiplicity of qualities. Those among them which belong in the context of consciousness we called subjective; they are the given and the known. Opposite them stand the objective qualities, as not given and not known. The former are of course what we call *mental*, having already used this name for them. Should we now describe the latter, the objective qualities, as the physical? It would certainly be the term nearest at hand, but we could only use it if the concept thus defined meant exactly what we mean in ordinary speech by the expression 'physical'. But when we look more closely we see that this is not the case.

It is true that by the term 'physical' we usually mean everything (it may, incidentally, be a thing, quality, event, or something else) which cannot be ascribed to the inner world of a conscious being, and which, therefore, belongs neither in the context of one's own 'I', nor in that of another consciousness. Consequently the objective qualities (the qualities which are not given and not known) seem to come under this concept of the physical, at least if we disregard the doctrine of those philosophers who think that an 'unconscious mind' (which would be objective but not physical) has to be reckoned with. Yet everyone, in ordinary life as well as in the sciences, has counted other characteristics, too, in the concept of the physical, characteristics which in fact are considered to be the essential ones, but which, not sufficiently clarified, are put in quite the wrong place; one must blame them for the fact that the 'psycho-physical problem' has arisen at all: they are the characteristics of *spatiality*.

The physical and the extended are not only almost always considered as belonging inseparably together, but often enough as absolutely identical; this is known to be the case in Descartes. Spatial extension always belonged to the definition of the physical body; Kant actually used the sentence: 'all bodies have extension in space' as an example of an analytical judgment. This wrong sense completely ignores the difference upon which we should lay the greatest stress: that is, the difference between the spatial as visible reality and 'space' as a scheme of order in the objective world. We described the latter, for want of a better expression, as objective or transcendental space, but stressed at the same time that this introduced a figurative meaning of the word 'space', which cannot be distinguished carefully enough from the original meaning, where 'space' refers exclusively to something visible. But the important result of the investigations undertaken earlier was that it is this visible spatiality of the extra-mental world which does not belong among the objective qualities.

For we know that, in fact, imaginable *extension* is a characteristic of the *subjective* qualities; spatiality in this sense, therefore, possesses not an objective but, on the contrary, a psychic, subjective existence. In the popular concept of the physical, characteristics are supposed to be united which are in reality not compatible; the concept is supposed to be loaded with both the thing-in-itself (that is, no contents of consciousness), and also with the visible, perceptible characteristic of extension. Since the two are incompatible, this concept of the physical (corporeal, material) must give rise to contradictions; these contradictions are just what constitute the psychophysical problem.

All great philosophical problems rest in fact upon disturbing, tormenting contradictions, and they appear outwardly in certain antithetical concepts; if one can reconcile them one solves the philosophical problem. Such pairs of antithetical concepts are, for example, freedom-necessity, egoism-altruism, and essence-appearance; and our pair of concepts, physical-mental, or body-soul, or matter-mind, or whatever names may be given them, also belongs with them.

Therefore we have recognized that the traditional concept of the physical cannot be completed and is falsely formulated. Should we now, as in fact we ought to do, reject the use of the word entirely, and declare: there are no physical bodies at all? That would naturally not be right, for there must obviously be some sphere where the word can legitimately be used, since otherwise it could not have gained the eminently practical and methodical significance which it has actually developed. The subject of 'physical science' must somehow be able to be specified and limited. Up to now we have established, negatively at least, that we should fail in our object if we simply allowed the term 'physical' to describe all *non-psychic* qualities. The results of earlier investigations give us the means of solving the problem positively, too.

In order to establish the true sense of the word 'physical', there seems to me to be only *one* possible way. The question of the true significance of the word can only be a question of the significance which the word actually has, that is, which it has in that science which deals expressly with the physical as its specific subject—that is, in physical science. A solution of the problem which constructs a special concept of the physical deliberately contrived to avoid any conflict with the mental, cannot be satisfactory. The concept of the physical must be drawn from the individual science which found it in its crude form in prescientific thought and brought it to exactness and clarity.[1]

First and foremost, however, it is important to show proof that a body-soul problem cannot exist for us at all, that we need not fear a contradictory antithesis between body and mind if we persist in the view to which the investigations in the previous chapters have led us.

The world is a varied construction made of connected qualities; part of it is perceptible to my (or anyone else's) consciousness, and this I call subjective or mental; another part is not directly perceptible to our consciousness and this part I call objective or extra-mental—the concept of the physical does not enter into it at this stage. We must emphatically reject the misunderstanding which ascribes to each a different degree of reality, characterizing qualities of one type as mere 'manifestations' of qualities of the other. They should rather be considered as, so to speak, equivalent, one type belonging just as much to the general coherent pattern of the universe as the other. We cannot say that on principle a difference exists between the roles they play in the world. In that coherent whole every-

---

[1] For this reason R. Reininger's essay (*The Psychophysical Problem*, Vienna, 1916) in which a philosophical concept of the physical is specially created, does not seem to me to solve the actual question.

thing is interdependent, every happening is a function of all the other happenings, and it is irrelevant whether objective or subjective qualities are concerned. Whether I see red or experience joy will depend just as much upon my own earlier experiences, therefore on mental qualities, as on the presence of certain extra-mental qualities which can be perceived by me by the methods described earlier. And, conversely, the latter will also depend on the change of the former, they are for example certainly functions of my 'will' experiences, for objective events are without doubt influenced by my actions; for example, when I have the sensations produced by the firing of a revolver, and hear the report, then something definitely happens in the extra-mental world. Without question a universal interdependence, a 'reciprocal action' exists among the qualities of the universe, therefore also between those which belong to my consciousness and those extra-mental qualities which are described by the physical concept 'bodies outside my body.'

This is all quite natural and fits in without difficulty or force into the picture of the world which we have gained; there is no problem here, and no motive exists which would urge one to make any other assumption, for example to question whether perhaps instead of a universal and general cohesion of reality, a 'pre-established harmony' exists between consciousness and the 'external world'. Only from a completely false position can one ask a question formulated in this way.

It might therefore seem that we ought to take the part, in the body-soul question, of those philosophers who assert that there is psycho-physical reciprocal action. But in fact this is not so. It is obvious to us that we can assume a reciprocal action between the experiences of consciousness, and extra-mental events, that is, between 'inner world' and 'external world'. But whether this reciprocal action can be described as psycho-'physical' can only be decided when we have reached agreement on the concept of the physical. Up to now, at least, we have found no reason for calling the extra-mental world *as such* 'physical', and we must remember that even those people who pose the body-soul problem and try to solve it mean by 'physical' something *other* than these extra-mental qualities of ours; for they take as a basis the accepted notion of the visible body spatially extended. However, we have just established that this concept of the body is in itself contradictory. We must now see how we can express without contradiction *what* the traditional concept of the physical is really supposed to mean. If we do so we shall, at the same time, at last establish the meaning which we shall in future have to give to the word 'physical'.

To this end we need only look back at the developments of the previous section, which showed us how natural science builds up its purely quantitative picture of the world. In this picture of the world the concept of physical matter arose by eliminating 'the secondary qualities', a concept of matter without quality but with extension, which has dominated speculation in the field of natural philosophy from Democritus to Descartes, and up to and beyond Kant.

The modern development of physical science has radically altered and refined that picture of the world; the concept of extended 'substance' now no longer stands at the centre of physical science, but instead the more general concept of the space-time process. In that context, however, the concept of the physical can be deduced with both clarity and certainty: reality is *'physical'*, *insofar as it is described by the spatial-temporal-quantitative system of concepts of the natural sciences*. We perceived earlier that the scientific picture of the world is only a system of signs which we associate with the qualities, and complexes of qualities, which together as a coherent whole form the universe. Besides, the expression 'picture of the world' is not without dangers; we should rather say instead 'concept of the world', for the word 'picture' is better confined to something visible, imaginable, and the representation of the world given in physical science is in no way presentable, but a completely abstract structure, a mere scheme of order. Naturally the component parts of the physical concept of the world are, like all concepts, represented in our thought processes by intuitive images. And it is obvious that to illustrate objective spatial relationships mainly such images are used as belong to a visible space, for example to that of the sense of sight, (though the latter is by no means the sole possibility, just as indeed the objective temporal order is not always represented in our minds by intuitive happenings in time, but is illustrated just as well—in graphic representations—by, for example, visual space ideas).

Not only does unclear epistemological thought easily confuse the concept with the real object which it describes, but also with the intuitive images which represent the concept in our consciousness. When we think of the scientific concept of a certain body, we do so through images, for example visual pictures, which bear the intuitive characteristic of extension. The strict *concept* of the body, on the other hand, contains none of this, but only certain numbers which state the 'measurements', the 'shape' of the body. That does not mean—as shown in detail—an objective presence of spatial-visible qualities in the real object (these belong only to the perceptions and the images, not to something extra-mental), but it means instead that order which cannot be seen or represented, in which the objective qualities of the world follow each other.

We have therefore three kinds of realms to distinguish from each other, and it is by confusing them and mixing them up that the psycho-physical problem has actually been caused: (1) reality itself (the complexes of qualities, the things-in-themselves), (2) the quantitative concepts of natural science allied to reality, forming in their totality the concept of the world given by physical science, and (3) the intuitive images through which the quantities in (2) are represented in our consciousness. Naturally (3), here, is part of (1), that is, a subsidiary part of that part of reality which we call our consciousness.

Now in which of these three realms is the physical to be found? The answer is very easily, and it seems to me quite unequivocally, indicated. No one will argue with us when we say that we always mean something *real* when we talk of the physical, so the word refers without any doubt to objects in the *first* realm. But obviously not directly and unconditionally, for it only refers to those real objects which are associated, or, rather, can be associated, with concepts from the *second* realm. This is all that can be said at the outset, and then the question remains quite open as to whether *collectively* the objects in the first realm can be considered as described by the scientific system of concepts of the second realm, or whether this system is perhaps only possible for a *part* of reality—in other words, whether or not the *whole* world can be interpreted as being something physical. Therefore when we define the physical, the third realm and the psychic in general (which is after all a part of the first realm) do not enter into it at all. There is above all not the slightest reason for ascribing to this partial reality any distinctive role in regard to its capacity for being described by scientific concepts, for example for assuming that the boundary of the physical, therefore of the real, which can be described by space-time concepts—supposing such a boundary should exist—would coincide with the boundary between experienced and not-experienced reality, that is, between psychic and extra-psychic qualities.

But the simplest hypothesis, which is virtually forced on us by empirical findings to be mentioned immediately, is this: that a boundary of this kind does not exist at all, but rather that the space-time concepts are suited to describing any reality whatever, without exception, and therefore the realities of consciousness too. The fact that we also describe the latter as 'psychological' concepts offers no cause for intellectual difficulty, creates no kind of antithesis between physical and mental.

'Physical' consequently means not a special kind of reality, but a special way of describing reality, namely the scientific conception necessary for a knowledge of reality. 'Physical' should not be misunderstood as being an attribute which belongs to one part of reality and not to another: it is rather a word for a kind of abstract construction, just as 'geographical' or 'mathematical' do not describe any peculiar qualities of real things, but rather just describe one way of presenting them by means of concepts. Physical science is the system of exact concepts which allies our knowledge to everything real. To *everything* real, for, according to our hypothesis, in principle *the entire world* can be described by that system of concepts. Nature is everything, everything real is natural. Mind, the life of consciousness, is not antithetical to nature, but a piece cut out of the totality of the natural.

That we have found the right interpretation here, becomes clear subsequently, when we take a critical look at the other attempts to find a definition for the physical which cannot be disputed.

Modern philosophers who deal with the question try mainly to find the difference between the physical and the spiritual in a difference of points of view. Two philosophers so differently orientated as Mach and Wundt agree that physical science and psychology deal with the *same* objects, which they treat in different ways. If we pay attention, says Mach, to the dependence of an 'element' upon those elements which form my body, then it is a mental object, a sensation; if, however, we examine its dependence on other 'elements', then we are in physical science, and it is a physical object. 'Not the *subject*, but *the direction which the investigation takes* is different in both fields' (*Analysis of Sensations*, p. 14). Now in the last and earlier sections we have convinced ourselves that the essence of physical investigation is not correctly given by this definition. Elements directly known are never themselves included in physical theories, they are under all circumstances eliminated, and only what is substituted for them is called physical. But it is the quantity concepts which take the place of the known qualities. These stay in themselves, and from every point of view, mental. The yellow of this sunflower, the harmony of the sound of that bell are spiritual quantities, 'yellow' and 'sound' are psychological concepts; physical laws do not deal with them, but instead with frequencies of oscillation, amplitudes and other such quantities, and these are never made up of subjective qualities.

Wundt describes the standpoint of natural science as that of indirect experience in contrast to that of psychology as of direct experience, and stresses 'that the expressions external and inner experience indicate not different objects but different points of view which we use in the interpretation and scientific elaboration of experience, which is in itself unified'. (*Outline of Psychology*, p. 3.) But the concept of indirect experience is not suitable for defining the physical either. Wundt says it comes into being 'by means of the abstraction of the subjective factor contained in every real experience'; therefore natural science considers 'the *objects* of experience when seen as independent of the subject' ... the physical would therefore coincide with the objective, and a definition would be reached which we have already had to reject as unusable, and which after close consideration only makes sense if one presupposes that not only the points of view but also the *objects* are different.

So it seemed more promising when defining the physical to stress that in contrast to the spiritual it is not a reality directly experienced, but that in fact we only reach it by means of the mental, and it seems more promising to construe the expressions direct and indirect experience in this sense. But then one must note the fact that mental qualities can also be the objects of indirect experience, namely those which are part of someone else's consciousness, for we know that we are only able to reach them by drawing conclusions by analogy. The obvious answer was that the physical is that reality which *on principle* is *only* accessible through indirect experience. This is what Münsterberg is getting at in his attempt at definition (*Principles of Psychology*, I, p. 72, 1900) when he says 'mental' means 'what can be experienced by only one subject, physical what can be experienced in common by several subjects'. A. Messer supports him (*Introduction to Epistemology*, 1909, p. 121.) This definition could serve as an indisputable definition only if the words 'able to be experienced' here meant the same thing both times, if it were one and the same kind of experience through which both realms were made known to us. But this after all is not the case, for a spiritual quality is known absolutely and directly and always to only the one subject who experiences it; in the case of an extra-mental object, on the other hand, able to be experienced does not mean at the same time able to be lived, its connection with us is indirect, and it can be connected in the same way to many subjects at the same time. Again, however, the same is true of the mental life of other individuals: as many subjects as you like can possess indirect experience of it. Admittedly, this is quite a different kind of experience but this difference is the crux of the matter, and so long as it is not comprehended through the definition, then we have not reached a limit between the physical and spiritual. Consequently Münsterberg's formulation does not take us a step further.

E. Mach, too, (*Knowledge and Error*, 3rd ed., p. 6) attempted to define it: 'The totality of what is present in space for *everyone* may be described as the physical, and what is only perceptible to *one* person directly may be described as the mental.' But nothing exists which corresponds to this definition of the physical, for, as we convinced ourselves earlier, on principle the identical element is never known to two different individuals.

Nothing is achieved, either, by distinguishing two kinds of experience as 'inner' and 'external'; in fact this tends to lead to errors for the same reasons as those which we earlier considered in connection with 'inner perception'. Furthermore, if we count sensory perception as 'external' experience, as usually happens, then in this way the sensory qualities themselves are drawn into the realm of the physical; and that we have already recognized as inadmissible.

Even if these different attempts at defining the physical are corrected, by putting in place of the two kinds of experience or perception, by which people try to distinguish between physical and psychical, the indisputable antithesis of reality known and not known, we still have not obtained a usable definition of the concept of the physical. For the same reasons stand in our way as those which prevented us from simply describing the real qualities not known as physical: these transcendental qualities lack, as shown, all the characteristics which for both the scientific and the popular concept of the physical are in fact the essential ones.

As we have already remarked several times, quite definite experiences of extension prove that physical concepts can be applied to define reality directly experienced, that is, the mental; and in the previous section we already decided that the only possibility of a *complete* knowledge of the mental is to use the quantitative concepts of the natural sciences to describe mental qualities and the ideas associated with them. And empiricism shows with great clarity the way in which this must be done: it is the complex of concepts of certain 'cerebral processes' which must be associated with the world of consciousness. We know that the processes of our consciousness only take place undisturbed if certain parts of the brain are intact. Destruction of the occipital lobe destroys the faculty of sight, destruction of the temporal part of the brain removes the ability to form representations of words, and so on. All that we can learn from these discoveries is that an inner connection exists between the physical object 'brain' and the reality experienced, 'contents of consciousness'. If one wanted to interpret this connection only as reciprocal dependence, therefore as a causal connection, (as the dualistic teaching of reciprocal action between body and soul did) then the consciousness, the I, would be an object apart from the 'brain processes', and could not in principle be described by physical concepts. For since, according to this assumption, the concepts of cerebral processes are supposed to describe something else, and since concepts of processes outside the head certainly do not enter into the question, so no physical concepts *at all* could be associated with the contents of consciousness. Besides, it would then be impossible to make any cerebral processes physically intelligible, that is, to explain them by physical causes, for their causes would be found partly in mental causes which could not be represented by physical concepts—physical causality would have omissions, and this would have an absolutely destructive effect on the concept and formulation of natural laws.

But all these complications of the picture of the world are completely unnecessary and can easily be avoided if we introduce, in place of the dualistic assumption, the much simpler hypothesis that the scientific conception is suited to describe any reality whatever, and therefore reality directly experienced as well as any other. Then it is no longer causal interdependence which connects this reality and the physical brain processes, but absolute *identity*. It is one and the same reality, not 'considered somehow from two different sides', nor 'manifested in two different forms', but only described by two different systems of concepts, namely psychological and physical.

If we are talking of the brain and brain processes here, then the threefold distinction must be rigorously borne in mind: the words mean: (1) reality, the thing existing in itself, which is none other than the processes of consciousness experienced, (2) the physical concepts (ganglion cells, nervous excitement, etc.) which describe this reality, (3) the intuitive images which help us to represent the concepts just mentioned, and therefore the perceptions which we have if we contemplate the brain of a fellow man after the top of the skull has been opened, or when we examine a ganglion cell under a microscope. The gravest error which can be made in interpreting the psycho-physical problem, and which, incomprehensibly, is repeatedly being made, is the fact that, unnoticed, the perceptions or images of the brain processes are put in the place of the brain processes with which the mental processes are supposed to be identical. The perceptions are themselves reality experienced, are themselves mental processes, but they belong to another individual, that is to the man who contemplates the brain of the first individual, and they are naturally in no way identical with the experiences of the first individual; they are not 'parallel' with them, but rather are causally dependent upon them, for what I perceive in a man's brain will depend, on principle, upon what is happening in his consciousness.

In the present state of our knowledge we cannot say what specific brain processes must be associated with certain quite definite experiences, for research on the functions of the brain is still too little advanced. The possibility of a general link-up must be maintained, this postulate must be fulfilled if the psychical is to be *known* at all, that is, to be described in concepts reducible to each other. We cannot, on any account, consider *all* cerebral processes as signs of consciousness, for in a sleeping or unconscious brain there is no spiritual life as far as we know. But we do not even know *how* these physical processes, to which mental data, that is, subjective qualities cohering in a context, correspond, differ from those physical processes which are symbols of *objective* qualities, that is, those adhering to no consciousness.

Thus purely epistemological reasons lead us to the standpoint of psycho-physical parallelism. We want to be quite clear about the character of this parallelism: it is not metaphysical, does not mean a parallel movement of two kinds of being (as in Geulincx), or two attributes of a single substance (as in Spinoza), or two kinds of manifestation of one and the same 'being' (as in Kant), but instead it is an epistemological parallelism between on the one hand a psychological system of concepts and on the other a physical system of concepts. The 'physical world' *is* in fact the world described by the system of quantitative concepts of natural science.

30

A. M. MACIVER

IS THERE MIND-BODY INTERACTION? (1935-6)

The existence of a mind or soul, distinct from the body, is not an immediate datum of experience, or even (like the existence of bodies) a necessary postulate of ordinary practical life. If it were either, the distinction would be recognized in popular idiom, which it is not. If we accept the Platonic and Cartesian account of human nature, we ought strictly to say '*I* think' but '*My body* sits' and '*My body* walks', and if this account came natural to men, this (or something which made the same distinction) would be normal colloquial usage; but, in fact, ordinary language says equally '*I* think', '*I* sit', '*I* walk'—implying that *prima facie* the subject is in each case the same. That there are minds or souls attached to some bodies is simply a hypothesis, introduced to account for certain observed facts—the observed differences between living human bodies and various other bodies, including tables and chairs and mountains and also human corpses. Living human beings are capable of thought and voluntary action, of which tables and dead human beings apparently are not: this is the most that is directly observed, and this is all that we are obliged to recognize for the practical purposes of everyday life. But, for the theoretical purpose of explaining this difference, it is supposed that living human bodies have intimately attached to them immaterial entities, which perform the functions of thinking and willing, while tables, chairs, mountains and corpses have not. This may be a good hypothesis or it may be (as I think) a bad one, but it is nothing more than a hypothesis, and its value must be judged in the same way as that of other hypotheses, by its ability to account for the observed facts more simply and plausibly than any suggested alternative.

I am trying here to put forward such an alternative, which seems to account for the observed facts equally well and to conform better to the Principle of Parsimony by positing no unobserved entities, such as the substantial immaterial mind inevitably is. I suggest that the functions of thinking and willing belong to the sensible living human body itself; that (exactly as common language suggests) the 'I' which holds these opinions and attempts to justify them to you is the same 'I' which now occupies a particular place in this room, which walked into this room and will at some future time walk out of it, and which is moving in various ways in the meantime. The thinker is the extended human being as a whole—not only a part of him, such as the brain. The brain is an organ without which a man cannot think, and what in particular he thinks seems to depend much more on what happens in his brain than on what happens, say, in his big toe; but this is not enough to make the brain by itself the thinker. Thought is, in this respect like life. Some organs are essential to life, while others are not: a man can live without arms or legs, but not without a head. But it is not only the organs essential to life which are alive. There is a complication in the analogy, in that all the component cells of the body have a life of their own, which can be distinguished from the life of the body to which they belong (so that the body as a whole could be dead and all its component cells still alive): what I am talking about here is the life of the whole body. The whole body which has this life includes the organs which are not essential to it just as much as those which are; and in the same way I would argue that the thinking man is an extended whole which includes those organs (such as the big toe) which are not essential to his thinking just as much as the brain, which is.

This is so simple and obvious a theory that one has got to take serious notice of the fact that hardly anyone accepts it. It has not been merely overlooked: it has been rejected for what seemed good reasons. Actually, as we all know, 'the refutation of Materialism' is one of those things which every good student of philosophy is expected to be able to do in his sleep. There is no philosophical topic on which there is a greater stock of stale arguments. But I should like to review these arguments.

Descartes tried to prove demonstratively that what thinks in us must be unextended, starting from the *Cogito*. I know that I exist, because I think, and I know this with certainty; but, in knowing myself to exist, I do not know myself to be extended, because, while sure of my own existence, I can still be doubtful of the existence of all bodies; it is therefore concluded that the 'I' which is certainly known to exist is a thinking thing but not an extended thing—or in other words, an immaterial mind. This argument, with its professed conclusion, depends on the simple fallacy of supposing that, if we do not know with certainty that something is the case, we certainly know that it is not the case: if I know that I exist but do not know whether or not I am extended, I know that I am not extended. The most that is actually proved is that thought and extension are logically independent attributes, in the sense that from the fact that anything thinks it is not possible to conclude immediately that it is extended or from the fact that anything is extended that it thinks. And even the first part of this depends on the assumption that there is no self-contradiction in the notion of an unextended substance: if it were shown that there was, then it would follow, of course, at once that every thinking substance must be extended. But, even if it is proved quite conclusively that thought and extension are logically independent attributes, so that neither can be inferred *directly* from the other, it is always possible that *further* evidence should be forthcoming to show that some (or all) thinking things are, as a matter of fact, also extended, or even that all extended things think.

But this argument is largely eyewash. Descartes really believed that what thought in us was unextended for quite a different reason, and so did the people whom he convinced. He believed, and so did they, that all the behaviour of extended things could be explained mechanically; and it followed from this that thought could not be ascribed to the extended, because thought is obviously not a mechanical process. The assumption was entirely reasonable, given the state of the natural sciences in the seventeenth and eighteenth, and even the nineteenth, centuries; and this, I am sure, is the main reason (combined with the Platonic infection of Christian theology) why the belief in an independent immaterial mind has got so firm a hold on our popular philosophy. But now that the classical mechanics is no longer the accepted model of all the sciences—when biology is beginning to claim a separate hearing and even physics is having its doubts about 'physical causation'—it is time to wonder whether this argument still retains its old force.

I want to suggest that *teleological*, as opposed to mechanical, explanation can be applied to extended things just as well as to unextended. Admittedly there are great philosophical difficulties about teleological explanation. When we explain by final causes, we explain a present event by reference to a possible future event, which may even never actually occur. We say, for example, that a man is going down the road 'in order to post some letters'; and we may continue to say that this *was* why he was going down the road, even if the letters are never actually posted, either because the man forgets about them or changes his mind before he reaches the pillar-box or because he is run over by a motor-car on the way. Here the 'final cause' obviously does not 'explain' the event (the going down the road) in the same way in which an efficient cause explains its effect, for there is no necessary connection in this case, such as there is in the other, between the realization of the 'cause' and the realization of that of which it is the cause. But I cannot see that these difficulties are any greater if what is to be explained is the movement of an extended thing than if it is the act of an unextended thing. And it has got to be admitted that human behaviour is *somehow* purposive: even if the movements of the body are efficiently caused by acts of will of an unextended mind, those acts of will have got to be explained teleologically. Those who explain all the peculiar behaviour of living bodies by the action of minds upon them sometimes seem to forget that, if the intellect is to be satisfied, the behaviour of these minds has also got to be explained. As soon as this is recognized, teleology reappears, even if it has been banished as philosophically unsatisfactory. But, if it can explain the behaviour of the unextended, why not also that of the extended?

At the back of the refusal to admit that extended things can act purposively lingers the seventeenth-century conception, according to which bodies are only distinguishable from the places which they occupy by a persistent identity which makes the body that occupies a particular place at one time the same as a body which may have occupied a different place at another time, subject to the conditions that one body cannot occupy two different places, or two different bodies the same place, at the same time. From these principles it was deduced that bodies could only move from place to place, and be set in motion only by impact, one body moving out of a place when another moved into it. But, leaving out of account the problems raised by the behaviour of living bodies, we have known since the time of Newton and Leibniz that these principles will not even account for all the observed movements of such things as lead weights and bullets. All extended things must have some other characters as well as extension, and there is no reason for denying to them *a priori* any further characters that observation may suggest, of which purposiveness is one.

If in the light of these observations, we return to the traditional arguments against Materialism, we find that many of them are not arguments against Materialism at all but arguments against Mechanism, the reason for the confusion being that almost all Materialism since the seventeenth century has been, as a matter of fact, mechanistic. For example, it is argued that Materialism cannot account for thought, because a thinking thing must be a unity and Materialism can only offer an aggregate, whether it be the brain or the whole nervous system or the whole body. If this argument is valid at all, it is valid against any theory which makes the thinker an aggregate, whether it is material or immaterial: it is valid (as is generally recognized) against any theory, such as that of the Associationists, which makes of the mind an aggregate of immaterial 'ideas' acting upon one another in a mechanical fashion. But, if we understand by 'Materialism' simply the doctrine that every concrete existence must be extended, without taking it for granted that the activity of the extended must be determined mechanically, there is no reason why Materialism should not provide a thinker who is a unity just as well as Immaterialism. On mechanical principles, certainly, the only 'whole' is the aggregate, logically posterior to its parts; to explain mechanically the behaviour of a whole is just to explain severally the movements of all its parts and sum them together. But, where process is teleological, all the parts of a whole may be united by a common purpose and the whole logically prior to them, in the sense that the behaviour of the parts cannot be explained except by reference to it; to take Mr Joad's example, the development of the eye in the growing embryo is unintelligible so long as we consider only the particular cells which go to form the eye, but it is very intelligible considered with reference to the whole body. And the teleological unity is the same, whether the whole is extended or unextended.

31

C. S. SHERRINGTON

MAN ON HIS NATURE (1937–8)

Much as one special organ, the heart, maintains the flow of nutriment throughout the body; so one organ, the brain, is provider of mind for the whole individual. If we smile at so bald a statement we must yet agree that it states the practical situation with which the physician and the surgeon deal.

It shows us too the body in the grip of integration. Much of the body has no demonstrable mind. Of the rest most has mind only lent it, in the form of sensation by proxy. Such of it merely communicates with a certain restricted piece of the body, a particular part of a single organ, and there, so much of the body as feels, has its sensation done for it. There too the body's thinking seems to be done for it, namely, in the brain.

Of man we know even more confidently than of any other concrete life that his mind is correlated with his brain. But let us avoid the sophistication that for the mind to be in the brain is any self-evident proposition. 'Many men,' wrote Kant, 'fancy they feel their thought in their head, but that is a mistake. No experience tells me that I am shut up in some place in my brain.' We owe I suppose to medicine in the main the knowledge of where in the body the 'seat of the mind', as it is termed, is. But so far from its being a self-evident fact, one of the greatest of biologists, Aristotle, did not subscribe to it although it was accepted by physicians in his time. . . .

Between the study of the mind and that of the brain the gap is wider than between the studies of activity and of visible structure in most organs. Description of the action of a muscle could not dispense with reference to the muscle's visible structure. Reference to the brain at present affords little help to the study of the mind. Ignorance of the 'how' of the tie between the brain and the mind there makes itself felt. That is no fault of those who study the mind or of those who study the brain. It constitutes a disability common to both of them. A liaison between them is what each has been asking for. That there is a liaison neither of them doubts. The 'how' of it we must think remains for science as for philosophy a riddle pressing to be read.[1]

Knowledge, medical and other, allocates the 'seat' of the mind, as the phrase is, to the brain. That localization has importance for medicine. It may be asked, however, whether for the scope of what we have before us here, it has importance. It would seem to have importance and in this way.

The two concepts, mind and energy, which our experience finds, using the one where the other fails, cover all our experience, are both of course in themselves creations of thought. But what they respectively stand for still remains divided as having nothing in common except time and this curious one and only point of spatial relation, namely 'collocation in the brain'.

Medicine's localization of the mind in the brain is therefore not only in medicine itself the greatest of all the brain localizations. It is from the more general point of view a lonely datum correlating mind with place. In that respect the evidence it brings is of fundamental interest. It assures us that, as known to us at least, mind is always and without exception individual mind. That is to say, mind in the general and aggregate as known to us is always many contemporary minds. It tells us that the mental as we know it is always in actuality a limited and impermanent individual system.

In many of its bearings the relation between mind and energy seems, although touching life at countless points, too subtly elusive to be captured for examination. In this one instance, however, the elusiveness seems set aside; for the brain and the psyche lie together, so to say, on a knife's edge. Whatever the solution of the problem we can here feel this. That in the energy-pattern which is the brain, two sets of events happen such as, to human knowledge, happen nowhere else the perceptible universe over. In that universe, sampling it, standing where we do on our planet's side, ourselves compact of energy, nowhere does our glimpse detect in all the immensity of energy any relation of energy except to energy save in this one instance, the brain. There energy and mind seem in liaison as to place.

Mind, always, we know it, finite and individual, is individually insulated and devoid of direct liaison with other minds. These latter too are individual and each one finite and insulated. By means of the brain, liaison as it is between mind and energy, the finite mind obtains indirect liaison with other finite minds around it. Energy is the medium of this the indirect, but sole, liaison between mind and mind. The isolation of finite mind from finite mind is thus overcome, indirectly and by energy. Speech, to instance a detail, illustrates this indirect liaison by means of energy between finite mind and finite mind. I have seen the question asked

[1] Cf. Viscount Samuel, *Nature*, Feb. 1939; C. S. Myers, *Realm of Mind*, p. 112; W. McDougall, *Outline of Psychol.* (at end).

'why should mind have a body?' The answer may well run, 'to mediate between it and other mind'. Philosophical speculation might be tempted to suppose the main *raison d'être* for energy in the scheme of things to be this. Energy provided as a medium of communication between finite mind and finite mind. It might be objected that such a view is undiluted 'anthropism'. To that we might reply, anthropism seems the present aim of the planet, though presumably not its enduring aim. Man will, we may think, go; and anthropism cannot be when man is gone.

If we suppose the planet's programme be expression of an aim, then trying to read that programme to learn whither the aim would, surely we do well to draw what inference we can. It may be that the aim toward which what we observe as progress moves includes the human as step to a further stage, of which we may forecast it will be supra-human. If mind, as we experience it and argue it in others, seem to itself that which the programme of the planet has aimed at, and if 'more mind' seem what the planet would and the communication between mind and mind foster more mind, then to hesitate to read this message because it seem 'anthropic' is to be blind to our cause and to that of our planet, of which latter cause, it would seem for the moment, ours is a part.

For energy to be the only means of communication between finite mind and mind seems at least a significant fact in the economy of life. It is a special service rendered to life by energy. It is also yet one instance more of the unity of the complex of which energy and mind seem the two ultimate constituents, for unless mind have working contact—'*contact utile*'—with energy, how can energy serve it? . . .

The body is of cells and like the rest of the body the brain is of cells. Have then the cells of the brain mind and the body's other cells not? Supposing a cell to be sentient, surely we have little chance of knowing whether it be so. A well-versed observer of the one-celled animal world has said that were an amoeba as big as a dog we should all acknowledge its mind. We could then put many more questions to it, but, with all deference, I am not clear that mind would be recognizable in the answers given. Aristotle knew the exposed human brain insentient when touched or manipulated. For him to remark the fact it must have seemed to him noteworthy. Today the surgeon reports that he removes large areas of the cortex of the brain—the cortex is the region where brain and mind meet —from conscious patients without their noticing difference or change. This insentience of the brain may have conduced to Aristotle's view of the heart rather than the brain lodging the mind. But we can understand that the brain in order to feel may have to be approached in a right way. If the brain be mechanism and the mind be related mechanism then it will surely be so. The wireless set answers to turning the switch but not to shaking the box. The connection of the brain with mind seems to rest on the organization of the brain, and that organization is cell-organization. Does knowledge of that organization help us to understand the organization of the mind?

The organization might bring out by additive processes a cell-attribute too slight for detection in the single cell yet obvious when summed. What evidence is there in general of mind attaching to any single cell? . . .

A brain-cell is not unalterably from birth a brain-cell. In the embryo-frog the cells destined to be brain can be replaced by cells from the skin of the back, the back even of another embryo; these after transplantation become in their new host brain-cells and seem to serve the brain's purpose duly. But cells of the skin it is difficult to suppose as having a special germ of mind.

Moreover cells, like those of the brain in microscopic appearance, in chemical character, and in provenance, are elsewhere concerned with acts wholly devoid of mind, e.g. the knee-jerk, the light-reflex of the pupil. A knee-jerk 'kick' and a mathematical problem employ similar-looking cells. With the spine broken and the spinal cord so torn across as to disconnect the body below from the brain above, although the former retains the unharmed remainder of the spinal cord consisting of masses of nervous cells, and retains a number of its nervous reactions, it reveals no trace of recognizable mind.

That the brain derives its mind additively from a cumulative mental property of the individual cells composing it, has therefore no support from any facts of its cell-structure. For a class-room to exhibit an isolated brain-cell and label it large 'The organ of thought', may be dramatic pedagogy; it is certainly pedagogical over-statement. The cell-organization of the brain may be the key to the secret of its correlation with mind; but not, it would seem, by individual mental endowment of its constituent cells.

On the brain, it is true, devolves the managing of those of our acts of which we are directly aware. Looked at along the evolutionary series the brain it is with whose development has progressed the control of those acts which we most directly control. In it are carried to their highest pitch the nerve-actions which manage the individual as a whole. It integrates the individual as a system of motor acts, and the integrated act is the response to an integrated situation, integrated likewise by the brain, but especially by mind.

We are back at the close tie between motor act and mind. We saw it was primitive. We see it here still operative although no longer primitive.

Control of act and awareness of act meet. I cannot by any effort of my will evoke my knee-jerk. Likewise I do not directly experience it. When it is elicited I seem to look on at it, as I might at a motor-car moving. It is not so with my hand sketching; I do control its act and do directly experience it acting. My experience then is that it is 'I' doing the drawing. If I am told, as indeed science tells me, that I, as mind, have had nothing to do with this act of drawing except as an onlooker, I find that puzzling.

The dilemma goes further. The motor behaviour of the individual is our only contact with his individuality. Indirect indication of him though it be, we in that way interpret him and allow him 'values', moral, aesthetic, etc. We infer he will do a generous act because we have inferred of him a generous mind. We attribute his acts to his mental character which we have inferred from his acts. We even fancy that our mental opinion of him can influence our own motor behaviour toward him. I have come to regard my words as an outcome of such thought as I have. When I ask science to tell me how all this is so, science vouchsafes me no reply. If I ask again she tells me it is none of her business; that though spoken words are energy, thoughts are not. . . .

Activity of the brain involves great numbers, not to say, vast numbers, of nerve-cells co-operating. Yet the means of securing that co-operation is by impulses via the nerve-fibres connecting cells. A large and an essential part of even the highest brain activity must therefore consist of nerve-impulses.

We turn to the actual cells of the brain. They, if we pursue the simile of the telephone system, are not the mere wires but are the actual exchange; they do the re-transmitting. They too have now come under examination by electrical methods. Their changes of potential are of two kinds; the more usual fall and an opposed rise of potential. Since in these situations the neural process is known to be of two kinds, one activation, the other arrest of activation, these changes of opposed electrical sign suggest a significant fit into the physiological picture. And there are too, as we saw, the rhythmic electrical waves which can be picked up by pad-electrodes placed on the head. They come probably from the surface-sheet of the brain cells. The rhythm of the beat is not too quick to be easily distinguishable by us were it perceptible to our consciousness at all. But our consciousness knows nothing about it. Through all the ages no suspicion of it has dawned upon us. Not even when now told of it do we feel it. The seat of the rhythm is in the visual region of the brain; vision sees nothing of it. Yet with the shift of mind the beat is altered; to open the closed eyes immediately disturbs it. It is possible to upset the rhythm by trying, without opening the eyes, to see something. A flash of light on the eye and a whole series of waves can be picked up from the visual part of the brain.

Physiology has got so far therefore as examining the activity in the 'mental' part of the brain when activity there is in normal progress. The desideratum to carry observation into the telephone-exchange itself with that exchange normally at work seems thus at last fulfilled. But has it brought us to the 'mind'? It has brought us to the brain as a telephone-exchange. All the exchange consists of is switches. What we wanted really of the brain was it would seem, the subscribers using the exchange. The subscribers with their thoughts, their desires, their anticipations, their motives, their anxieties, their rejoicings. If it is a mind we are searching the brain for, then we are supposing the brain to be much more than a tele-phone-exchange. We are supposing it a telephone-exchange along with the subscribers as well. Does your admirably delicate electrical exploration vouchsafe us any word about them? Its finger is ultra-sensitive, but energy is all that it can feel. And is the mind energy?

The 'subject' whose eye opens and whose brain-waves then alter, ex-periences as the most significant fact of the moment the mental change that he now sees something whereas before he did not. Do the concurrent electrical potentials contribute anything at all to the conception of, or to the understanding of, this visual experience?

It is now some seventy years since the words of a great biological leader of his time to his hearers were 'the thoughts to which I am now giving utterance and your thoughts regarding them are the expression of mole-cular changes in that matter of life which is the source of our other vital phenomena' (Huxley). The terminology is a little 'dated', but is the main position thus set forth altered today? The concomitance in time and place between the 'molecular changes' and 'the thoughts' is still all we have correlating the two. Regarded as a paradox it has become more intriguing; regarded as a gap in knowledge more urgent. . . .

Our sixteenth-century physician Jean Fernel would have smiled at this difficulty which presents itself to us. For him there is no difference between thought and the rest of living. The cause of the brain's thinking was for him the life-spirit in it. That spirit has the brain for habitation, its tem-porary dwelling. He would tell us that what his boat is for the time being to the mariner, such the brain is for the time being to this spirit. That the brain should obey and do what the spirit would he finds no more remark-able than that the boat obeys the handling of him who sails it. But we recall a railway-coach attached to its locomotive solely by goodwill between guard and driver and it did not arrive.

For Fernel there was duality but that duality created a situation of no difficulty. Its members, matter and spirit, combined in perfectly satisfying co-operation. Matter was the servant. Spirit, mind, was the master. Perhaps that was from the Phaedo, where we remember the soul rules, the body obeys. Today the duality is there; and combination is there, but the footing on which the combination rests, so obvious to Fernel, is for our inquiry still to seek. Perhaps the 'servant and master' phrase had in view an assertion of free-will. But where in nature shall we find 'servant and master'? Where our knowledge halts our description will resort to metaphor. Long will man's fancy deal with the tie between body and mind by metaphor and often half forget the while that metaphor it is. Regarding this problem will a day come when metaphors can be dispensed with? . . .

The energy-concept, we saw, embraces and unifies much. The scheme seems coterminous with the perceptible. Therein lies its immensity and also its limitation. Immense as it is, and self-satisfying as it is, and self-contained as it is, it yet seems but an introduction to something else.

For instance a star which we perceive. The energy-scheme deals with it, describes the passing of radiation thence into the eye, the little light-image of it formed at the bottom of the eye, the ensuing photo-chemical action in the retina, the trains of action-potentials travelling along the nerve to the brain, the further electrical disturbance in the brain, the action-potentials streaming thence to the muscles of eye-balls and of the pupil, the contraction of them sharpening the light-image and placing the best seeing part of the retina under it. The best 'seeing'? That is where the energy-scheme forsakes it. It tells us nothing of any 'seeing'. Everything but that. Of the physical happenings, yes. A tiny patch of a particular radiant energy disturbing the surface of the body in a region specially reactive to it; it connects that patch with an energy-path entering the eye, then with one carrying brainward from it, a shower of repetitive electric potentials. It locates these in a certain region of the brain, which it therefore indicates as concerned with what occurs in us through the eye. It also accounts to us for all the manoeuvring of the eye-balls as they catch the photo-image and sharpen it and place the eye centrally under it, so too for our turning of the head to help the eyes.

But, as to our *seeing* the star it says nothing. That to our perception it is bright, has direction, has distance, that the image at the bottom of the eye-ball turns into a star overhead, a star moreover that does not move though we and our eyes as we move carry the image with us, and finally that it is the thing a star, endorsed by our cognition, about all this the energy-scheme has nothing to report. The energy-scheme deals with the star as one of the objects observable by us; as to the perceiving of it by the mind the scheme puts its finger to its lip and is silent. It may be said to bring us to the threshold of the act of perceiving, and there to bid us 'goodbye'. Its scheme seems to carry up to and through the very place and time which correlate with the mental experience, but to do so without one hint further. If the energy-scheme exhaust motion and embrace all 'doing' then the act of perceiving would seem not to be motion and it would seem, is not 'doing'. Otherwise it would be included. So with the whole of mental experience, the energy-scheme leaves it aside and does not touch it. Our mental experience is not open to observation through any sense-organ. All that the energy-scheme submits *is* thus open. The perceptible and the energy-scheme are co-extensive, for both are for us rooted in sense. Our mental experience has no such channel of entrance to the mind. It is already of the mind, mental. We can turn no sense-organ upon it. Such expressions as 'internal sense' mislead if they are taken literally. The mental act of 'knowing' we are aware of, but we cannot sensually observe it. It is experienced, not observed. . . .

The sense-organs are specifically fitted to pick up, i.e., to 'receive', stimuli which by their means the body can react to. But they do not all of them or at all times by so doing affect 'sense'. The energy-mind problem asks 'how can they affect sense?' Sense is an aspect of the mental; how then can the physical receptor affect sense? That the physical receptor, e.g. the eye, connects with the roof-brain does not remove the difficulty. How can a reaction in the brain condition a reaction in the mind? Yet what have we sense-organs for, if not for that? This difficulty with sense is the same difficulty, from the converse side, as besets the problem of the mind as influencing our motor acts.

I would submit that we have to accept the correlation, and to view it as interaction; body⇄mind. Macrocosm is a term with perhaps too mediæval connotations for use here; replacing it by 'surround', then we get surround⇄body⇄mind. The sun's energy is part of the closed energy-cycle. What leverage can it have on mind? Yet through my retina and brain it seems able to act on my mind. The theoretically impossible happens. In fine, I assert that it does act on my mind. Conversely my thinking 'self' thinks that it can bend my arm. Physics tells me that my arm cannot be bent without disturbing the sun. Physics tells me that unless my mind is energy it cannot disturb the sun. My mind then does not bend my arm. Or, the theoretically impossible happens. Let me prefer to think the theoretically impossible does happen. Despite the theoretical I take it my mind *does* bend my arm, and that it disturbs the sun.

Organic evolution, with its ways and means, appears to the biologist to treat and handle body and mind together as one concrete individual. To a human spectator it may well appear that the long series of animal creation has its *raison d'être* as a mechanism *for* evolving mind. He inclines to regard his own mind as the precious product which was the desideratum. But in that he may be suffering from 'anthropism'. The human mind is not a goal. Nature has started the bird's brain after already putting potentially the human on its way, that is, has started another and inferior mind after reaching the ground-plan of the human mind. Be that as it may, he regards his mind as associated with his brain which is also a part of him. He sees his brain so placed that certain nerve-paths reaching inward from specialized bits of the body, the eye, the ear, and so on, bring physical events, as it were by some natural magic, into such relation with the mind that they affect it. In other words, as we said, the theoretically impossible happens.

At the core of this difficulty is the attribute 'unextended' as applied to the finite mind. It is difficult to reconcile this attribution with certain facts. The mind of the individual, finite mind, as judged by an impressive concensus of opinion, has 'place'. It has 'whereness'; nor does it matter for our purpose of the moment what 'where' it has. It has a 'where'. Speaking for myself, although I can allow dialectically a Euclidean point and admit its artificiality to be a helpful convention, it is beyond me to conceive or figure or imagine even approximately a concrete anything as having whereness without magnitude. A thing without extension as descriptive of the mind, even though negatively descriptive, fails for me to be more than a conventional symbol. Kant seems, I would think, to have had something of a not dissimilar difficulty, when he wrote of the human soul that it 'resides in a place of a smallness impossible to describe'.

Accepting finite mind as having a 'where' and that 'where' within the brain, we find that the energy-system with which we correlate the mind has of course extension and parts and exhibits, moreover, marked spatial organization of those of its parts correlating in space and time with the finite mind. The roof-brain is a veritable labyrinth of spatial construction. With different parts of that labyrinth observational inference connects different mental actions. Thus, different ranges of memory are injured by brain-affections of different seat. There is a 'visual' part, an 'auditory' part, and so on. Again, in this 'mental' part of the brain 'touches' from different points of the skin are registered at separate brain-points, and each psychical 'touch' has according to its place its particular psychical 'local-sign'. Space relations of the brain seem then to count mentally. Different 'wheres' in the brain, in short, correlate with different mental actions. Nor is it that an 'unextended' mind simply jumps from one spot to another. Two or more different activities of mind correlating with different 'wheres' in the brain are commonly in action contemporaneously. It may be asked whether these separate regions are not mere separate channels of physiological approach to a mind-focus of Euclidean-point character. But their relation to mind is closer and more 'mental' than that. Witness such observations as those cited earlier from Dr Holmes. We have, I think, to accept that finite mind is in extended space.

Again, the change in living organisms which evolution produces is, as examination of them proves, a recollocation of the elemental parts. It is a rearrangement, a reshuffling, and often an addition of more such parts. The mind of the organism is embraced as well as the body by the evolutionary process. This would seem presumptive evidence that the mind has parts which can be reshuffled and amplified under evolution. But reshuffling, recollocation, implies extension in space. The mind to undergo it would seem to occupy extended space.

Again if 'things' through nerve can act on finite mind—and most of us would admit that to be the basis of perceiving—it then becomes difficult to suppose action between energy and mind is unilateral only, solely energy→mind. The action should be reaction. In that case mind influences energy. My mind seems to act on my 'material me' when at breakfast I lift my coffee cup with intent to drink. I infer a like situation in the chimpanzee when he peels his banana before eating it. Reversible interaction between the 'I' and the body seems to me an inference validly drawn from evidence.

The 'how' of it has the difficulty that finite mind is not an object of sense. There are at least two ways of being insensible, in other words, imperceptible. One way is to be quantitatively too little, i.e. below threshold. Another is to be inadequate to any sense-organ. Our sense-organs miss a number of the world's qualities and quantities of energy. Scientific devices help us partly out of this disability. Thus, nervous impulses in a fish's organ of smell may be insensible by our unaided sense-organs, but when Adrian to study them converts them into a noise like rattling rifle-fire, the roomful of us can hear them. By scientific means our powers of sense can in such ways be much extended. Yet the mental itself remains obstinately inaccessible to sense, and to all these extensions of it.

It may be so because it is not of the category of energy at all. Here we have of course to remember that in looking for mind as energy we are not looking for a form of energy then to translate it into mind. Of that we have abundant instances already. Thus, radiant energy via nerve into seeing, or into heat-sensation, or pain. That would be to look merely for forms of energy which nerve can transmute through sense into the mental. What we look for is an energy which *is* mind. In short we seek whether mind is energy; whether for instance seeing, feeling, pain, thinking, etc. are manifestations of energy—*are* energy. No evidence as yet assures us of this. No organism seems furnished with any sense-organ which takes into its purview even the place pertaining to its finite mind. We may perhaps take that as equivalent to saying that no advantage would accrue to the organism if its mind were an object of sense to itself and therefore it is not so. . . .

We have, it seems to me, to admit that energy and mind are phenomena of two categories. In that case the phasic appearance of a mental system alongside the energy-system of the developing body has the difficulty that the mental seems to spring suddenly out of nothing. But we have already dealt with instances in ourselves where mind is clearly inferable although not directly recognizable by us. If that be so in ourselves, still greater is the difficulty of observing mind objectively, that is as object, when, by its very nature, it is insensible, i.e. not accessible to 'sense'. Mind as attaching to any unicellular life would seem to me to be unrecognizable to observation; but I would not feel that permits me to affirm it is not there. Indeed, I would think, that since mind appears in the developing soma that amounts to showing that it is potential in the ovum (and sperm) from which the soma spring.

The appearance of recognizable mind in the soma would then be not a creation *de novo* but a development of mind from unrecognizable into recognizable. It is at this point therefore that on these admissions we become committed to dualism. But while accepting this duality we remember that Nature in instance after instance dealing with this duality treats it as a unity. Evolution evolves it as one. In this body-mind individual, with its two cohering systems, bodily and mental, even as the former component exhibits both inherited and acquired features, so too does the latter. . . .

Latterly our theme touched more than once the question of the relation between the two concepts 'energy' and 'mind'. I would venture here to turn specifically to that relation. To leave its argument, as that appears to me, merely tacit, might seem to invite mystery in a matter on which I would wish to arrive at clear expression. But over and above that there is an importance proper to the question. It has theoretical importance; that is perhaps generally admitted. But its claim to practical importance is apt to raise a smile. Yet the question surely touches the reading of man's situation in his world.

We need not think of it as an issue between idealism and materialism. Nor does it touch so-called 'reality'; our world is in any case an act of mind. It asks rather whether the world, as our mind apprehends it, is for one part of it known to us in one way, for its other part known to us in another, the two ways not of essential parity. One form in which the question states itself is how far the world as known to us is fundamentally of one kind throughout. We may then regard the question as that of dualism or monism in a limited scope, that is, with no reference to reality. To me what ultimate reality may be is one of those questions which rise to the mind, and that the mind of itself has not the means to answer.

We saw ground for thinking that in the evolution of mind a starting point for 'recognizable' mind, lay in its connection with motor acts. Motor behaviour would seem the cradle of recognizable mind. I incline to endorse the challenging remark, that, 'the most fundamental function of mind is to guide bodily movement so as to change our relation to objects about us'. Moreover the motor act is that which seems to clinch the distinction between self and non-self. The doer's doings affirm the self. Lotze's trodden worm contrasting itself with the world found of the two its trodden self the greater. We may wonder at such anthropoid reflection on the part of the worm, but we grant the statement expresses fairly the view native to the 'self'. The worm shares the impulse as motion though not as thought. And surely even as early as the 'suffering self' arose the 'doing self'. As far back in the evolutionary tree as intuitions go among them must be that of a subjective 'doing'.

The concept 'self' taken with all its connotations has become vastly far-reaching and intricate. Yet it would seem to have at its core an element relatively simply, germane to our question here. The awareness or consciousness of each of us, prominent in certain of our motor acts, relates the self to the act. The awareness is of course an example of what in the abstract is spoken of as mind. It seems a law of mind to connect its phenomena by relations. The awareness attaching to these motor acts relates the conscious 'self' to the acts as doing them.

In our awareness when doing these acts there would seem awareness both of the self and of its act, and a connection between them. This awareness-complex comes traceably from two sources. One source is sensual. The motor act in its bodily execution consists of changes in several bodily parts, for instance, changes of length and tension in muscles, etc. The muscles besides being motor instruments are sense-organs. The muscular act therefore affects sense. There is perception of the act. Sensual perception has, as always, spatial reference. Its awareness carries reference to the bodily parts operating the act, for instance to a limb, a finger, or what not. It is an awareness which, as the phrase goes, 'projects' spatial reference, in this case into the moving limb, finger or what not concerned in the act.

But there is in the conscious motor act an awareness also of the 'I-doing'. This latter awareness is not derived from sense. It is the 'I's' direct awareness of itself acting. A difference between it and the awareness derived from sense is that while that which derives from seense has, as we said, spatial projection, this which is not derived from sense has no spatial projection. It is awareness of the self 'doing' but it is not projected. . . .

In the complex of awareness belonging to a conscious motor act there is, along with the awareness of the 'I-doing' which is unprojected, the sense-derived awareness of the bodily act which is projected, for instance, referred to the moving limb. This latter is by spatial projection separated from the unprojected 'I'. The bodily movement is therefore distinguished from the 'I'. The mind, finding relations between phenomena, seeks also to couple some phenomena as cause and effect. This bent or tendency has served it well. Whatever it may mean, it has helped to sift events conjoined by sequence in time. The mind relates the 'I-doing' in the conscious motor act causally with the act. The unprojected 'I' is the 'cause' and the projected motor act is the 'effect'.

In this attribution we need not suppose that any conscious logical argument is at work. Rather it would be a naive unargued assumption. One of those unanalysable workings of the mind which are practically tantamount to inference but are drawn unconsciously and often so quickly that the conclusion is reached before there would seem time for full comprehension of the data. . . .

This 'I' which when I move my hand I experience as 'I-doing', how do I perceive it? I do not perceive it. If perception means awareness through sense I do not perceive the 'I'. My awareness and myself are one. I experience it. The 'I-doing' is my awareness of myself in the motor act. It is my mental experience in that phase of my activity. It is, if we prefer, my experience of 'self' explicit in action. In it my 'self' is not an object which I can examine through sense. As compared with the latter I am at the disadvantage that I cannot submit this to others besides myself to examine and report on. It is private to myself, but each of us can examine his own case. For examining it, all we can do is to attend to what we are aware of in it.

This may be felt too trustful of introspection. If introspection be our impressions of our own consciousness those impressions, although perforce individual, may yet be representative. However we have to be on our guard. The term introspection can, as is often insisted, be misleading. It might suppose that we can turn some perceptual process upon the 'I' and watch it and treat it as an object of perception, so to examine and analyse it. Kant was one of those who continued late to use the term 'inner sense', although he does not always make it clear with what meaning. The physiology of sense has advanced greatly since his time. The 'I' can never come into the plane of objects of sensual perception. It *is* 'awareness'. Even if the mind had a sense-organ which were turned inward, so to say upon the mind itself, what would it fulfil? Broadly taken, and briefly, and crudely put, if the purpose of sense be to translate events physical and chemical into mental, what use would it serve in application to the mind which is already mental? Besides the 'I', since it is awareness, would still remain not 'sensed'. The mind is no part of the perceptible.

But the mind does experience itself. Memory attaches to that experience. The self can remember and re-live at second-hand and reflect upon its experience of itself. It can think over what its experience in 'doing' was. That perhaps is more effective than the divided effort of trying to examine the awareness actually while the awareness is in process.

Of two components which can be traced in the awareness of a conscious motor act, one, we saw, is the immediate awareness belonging to the 'I-doing', the other the sensual awareness accompanying the bodily act. The second is in some instances, by disease or injury, stripped away. The dual complex of the conscious act is to that extent analysed. This happens when a limb though its motor power is retained is robbed of all sensation. The patient then does not sense his limb. He does not know where his limb is, unless he sees it. In bed he may 'lose' his arm. But the motor act is still evoked and consciously although there is no sensual perception of the limb. The 'I' still experiences itself in acting. The residual awareness in this insentient condition of the limb is therefore in so far not sensually given. It is the 'I's' direct awareness of itself in action.

It is true the motor act executed by the insentient limb is clumsy. That it is executed at all and consciously 'at will' is here the point. The launching of it as a conscious act although the sensory basis for it, and the sensual perception of it, are wanting, indicates that this 'I-acting' is not derived from sense perception but is directly given. . . .

These two concepts, (energy and mind) and they are two concepts of one mind, divide, and between them comprise, our world. One of them, the spatial, which we may call the energy-concept, derives by way of the senses. The other, as we saw, is not derived by way of any sense. We saw why. The mind has no sense which it can turn inwards so to say upon itself. The idea which mind forms of itself lacks extension in space, because sense is required for such extension as a datum, and mind does not derive its idea of itself through sense. . . .

How can the phenomena of the two (space-time energy and non-space mind) interact? The more the biologist studies life the less I fancy does it seem to him like life to have a loose wheel spinning. Yet how shall a spatial wheel cog into unextended mechanism or the non-spatial drive a spatial wheel? Spinoza, thinking of Descartes' interaction between the rational soul and the pineal gland, wrote, 'I would fain be told how many degrees of movement the mind can give to this little pineal gland, and with what force it can lift it. I feel surprise that so great a man and philosopher, one who has laid it down as his rule to draw conclusions only such as are self evident, and to assert nothing of which he has not a clear and distinct perception, he who so often has reproached scholasticism with explaining the obscure by qualities which are occult, allows himself an hypothesis more occult than all the occult qualities put together.' Actually the dilemma is now become for many acuter still, if that be possible. The pseudo-'go-betweens' have vanished. Not that they in truth, I think, ever existed for either Spinoza or Descartes; the latter likened the animal spirits to fine fire, i.e. they were physical.

'Energy' proves itself a closed system, shutting out 'mind'. They may be juxtaposed, but they do not blend. An instance where perhaps particularly they approximate is at the mental process and the cerebral process. There on one side electrical potentials with thermal and chemical action, compose a physiological entity held together by energy-relations; on the other a suite of mental experience, an activity no doubt; but in what, if any, relation to energy! A suggestion has been made that we must re-define 'energy' so as to bring 'mind' into it. We have not in our power to re-fashion a concept shaped by our sense-perception. Again, it has been ingeniously said that had in the development of Science biology preceded physical science, a concept reached by Science would have embraced 'mind' and 'energy' together, merging them without disparity. But who shall jockey 'space' out of its natural rights?

The puzzle might seem not altogether unlike that in regard to the physical interpretation of light, and indeed of 'matter' generally. The electron, following its discovery, acquired charge, mass, spin and a special dynamics of its own. But that was not enough to carry the observational data which accrued. Matter, like light, was found to possess both the properties of particles and the properties of waves. Louis de Broglie put forward an equation expressing the correlation of the particle-behaviour and the wave-behaviour of matter. This budded into a synthesis. It achieved success in accounting for, and even to the extent of predicting, many observed facts. But its basal assumption that a particle is associated with a system of waves is, I imagine, accepted as an assumption and left unaccounted for.

So our two concepts, space-time energy sensible, and insensible unextended mind, stand as in some way coupled together, but theory has nothing to submit as to how they can be so. Practical life assumes that they are so and on that assumption meets situation after situation; yet has no answer for the basal dilemma of how the two cohere. There is no more of course than mere analogy between this mind-energy complex which teases biology and that other the wave-particle dilemma which has been teasing physics. In the latter case both of its terms are at least assimilable in the measure that each is describable by space into time. Both are in short physical. The biological dilemma is of another order. In it the two terms are divergent to the degree that while the one is sensible the other is insensible. How then account for conjunction between two incommensurables? The physical dilemma however treated as parable does offer a certain pragmatic counsel. To carry on in biology as if the two terms, mind and energy, whose connection we cannot describe, are conjoined and to do so for the reason that to observation they act connectedly. With all humility, I imagine that physics argues 'wave and particle seem, although we do not know how they can do so, to go together as one. We accept that without understanding it.' Newton's essential modernity showed itself in no way more than in his acceptance of what he declared he could not account for. Our parable would preach acceptance of energy and mind as a working biological unity although we cannot describe the how of that unity.

Practical life regards, for instance, our thoughts as anaswerable for what we say. It proceeds as though qualities of mind, e.g. memory, courage, rightness of inference, and so on, affect the acts we do. Law proceeds on the same assumption, in its corrective system as elsewhere. Parent and schoolmaster regard well-bestowed praise as promotive of well-doing. Society in general regards mind as productive of acts. While our conception of the mind as unextended seems to preclude mind from interacting with any energy-system, the body inclusive, every-day life assumes there is interaction and that our mind shapes our conduct. Here ethics surely takes the same view as does daily life.

Of this dilemma Nature herself, if we may so apostrophise her, takes no notice. She proceeds as if no such dilemma existed. Nothing is clearer than that in her process of Evolution she evolves in living creatures characters which, largely as they spell advantage or disadvantage to the individual life, tend to survive or disappear. We have seen life *per se* to be a system of energy. Since life is a system of energy a character to be of advantage or disadvantage to that system must influence that system. Nothing is clearer than that mind has evolved. Mind therefore has had survival value. Mind it would seem then has an influence which Nature finds can count for advantage to the energy-system colligate with it, the body. Mind, as we know it, is never any other than embodied mind. Hence such properties as size, shape, movement, etc., are assessed by mind as being of account. Nature in her process Evolution, although we do not know her as ethical, proceeds as if believing in a working relation between mind and body as does our human ethics.

If the 'I-doing', which stands at some disadvantage, as we saw, for observing itself, had, instead of assuming that it was the 'cause' of its motor act, regarded itself simply as colligate with the act, a part with it of one event, the seeming inconsistency between the two concepts in this situation would disappear. There would then be no need to ask for interaction. Then, that Nature deals with both as one explains itself. The evolution of the one is of necessity the evolution of the other. There is no causal relation between them; they are both inseparably one. Their correlation is unity. The 'I' can accept itself as one aspect of the act. The 'I-perceiving' is not then a 'cause' within the spatial world. The 'I-experiencing' is just a part of the act it experiences. The relation is not as cause and effect but as parts of one event. So the relation between the 'I-doing' and what is done is not 'cause' and 'effect', but two colligate and concurrent components of one event. The 'I-doing' becomes thus in effect another aspect of its motor act. Its motor act and it are one. Its motor act can be called rightly a 'conscious motor act'. That is exactly what it is. Its awareness is part of it. It can also rightly be called a willed act, unless by that it is intended to say 'will' causes the motor act. This cannot be phrased more adequately I think than by some words in the De Anima, although their context is somewhat different from the present. 'We must add that to speak of the soul as feeling angry is no more appropriate than to speak of the soul as weaving or building. Perhaps, in fact, it is better to say not that the soul pities or learns or infers, but rather than the man does so through his soul.' The motor act and the 'I-doing' appear as two parts of one event, one fitting the spatial concept (energy), the other the non-sensual concept (mind). This is akin to regarding the finite mind as a sort of esoteric activity bound up with the cerebral activity, an inner phase of which the nervous activity is the outward phase.

32

C. I. LEWIS

SOME LOGICAL CONSIDERATIONS CONCERNING THE MENTAL
(1941)

It is a conception as old as Socrates and as modern as our current logical analyses that the central task in philosophic discussion of any topic is to arrive at and elucidate a definition. That, I take it, is what is properly meant by a philosophic 'theory'; a theory of X is a more or less elaborate definitive statement having 'X' as subject, together with such exposition as will remove difficulties of understanding and serve to show that this definition covers the phenomena to be taken into account.

I fear that what this occasion calls for is such a theory of mind. But if so, then I am unprepared for it. I am unable to present any statement of the form 'Mind is . . .' (where 'is' would express the relation of equivalence of meaning) which would satisfy me or which I should expect would satisfy you. I can only put forward certain statements intended to formulate attributes which are essential to mind; to point to phenomena of which we can say, 'Whatever else is or is not comprehended under "mind", at least it is intended to include *these*.' In particular, I shall wish to emphasize that whatever is called 'content of consciousness' is so included, and to consider certain consequences of that simple fact.

In so doing, however, I am aware of one danger. Confronted with problems of analysis which there is trouble to resolve, one may sometimes circumvent them by changing the subject. We find ourselves unprepared to formulate any sufficient criterion of X which precisely accords with what is comprehended under 'X' and what excluded. But we are—it may be—prepared to elaborate systematically and ingeniously some *other* definitive statement using the same term in a somewhat different signification, some definition of the *word* 'X' devised with a view to skirting what is dark to our insight and ruling out whatever we find unmanageable in current usage of the term. Theories are sometimes achieved in this way. But this fallacy of changing the subject, I would above all else avoid. I can not express precisely and clearly what you and I mean by 'mind'; but if anything I have to say should be found incompatible with that common meaning, then I should not wish to persist in maintaining it.

It is one such essential feature of what the word 'mind' means that minds are private; that one's own mind is something with which one is directly acquainted—nothing more so—but that the mind of another is something which one is unable directly to inspect.

If that is, in fact, a required feature of what we should call 'a mind', then indeed it must be admitted to be a question whether minds—anything having this character—exist. It must also be admitted that the statement itself, asserting the existence of mind in this sense, might contain some irremovable unclarity or some implicit inconsistency, rendering it a non-significant affirmation. However, any such possible doubts can, I think, be removed.

But first, let us observe that if the above statement is correct, when measured against the intended signification of 'mind', that of itself is sufficient to preclude certain prevalent theories. Whatever else such theories may be true of or false of, as statements about what is meant by 'mind' they are literally not pertinent. Behaviouristic interpretations of mind are thus not pertinent, nor is any identification of mind with brain states or brain functionings.

The point has been raised often enough and will not need to be elaborated here. All men are directly acquainted with their own minds, but no one is directly acquainted with the present state of his brain. We know nothing about our brain states except by complicated and more or less uncertain inferences. And if technical difficulties of observing our own brains should be overcome, still the man who should be suffering pain and at the same time observing his own brain, would be aware of two things, not one; and only by an inductive inference would he be led to suppose that the one of them had anything to do with the other.

Sometimes when such arguments as this are put forward however, it is not realized that they depend fundamentally upon what kind of thing is *meant* by 'mind'. That is the case: otherwise this type of objection to a behaviouristic or brain state interpretation of mind could be easily met. It could be observed, for example, that one may see a thing held in the hand and at the same time feel it with the fingers. And one who thus saw and felt the same object might not know that what he visually observed was the same thing that he tactually observed. An infant or a man who suddenly receives the sense of sight, must learn to make such identification of the visually with the tactually perceived; it requires to be inductively inferred. Nevertheless, identification in this case is valid. And it might be argued that identification of the mental with the behavioural or with brain states is similarly valid, in spite of the objection. However, in such a case as this, in which an identification which is valid requires to be established by inductive inference, there are also two things—or more than two—

whose *non*-identity is witnessed by the necessity of such learning. In our example, there is the tactually felt as such—the tactual datum—and there is the visually apprehended as such—the visual datum. There is also the object held in the hand; which is a different kind of entity from the other two. Thus in one signification of the phrases 'what is seen' and 'what is felt', they may denote the same thing, though this identity requires to be inferred from some course of experience. In another signification, what is seen is *not* identical with what is felt; and this non-identity is proved merely by the possibility of observing both without being able to identify them.

If, then, this kind of objection to behaviouristic and brain-state interpretations of mind is sound, it is so because of the meaning of terms referring to the mental; because these are so intended that if A is a present phenomenon of my mind, then anything I can not directly inspect is not identical with A, and anything I could observe without being able to identify it with A, would be in fact not identical with A.

This characteristic of the intended meaning of terms applied to the mental is not peculiar to them; nor is the kind of controversy which can arise on account of the type of ambiguity here illustrated. The question whether the sound of music is or is not correctly identified with certain harmonic motions, is a closely similar issue, which depends on the meaning of the language which is used, and upon appeal to criteria which are different according as it is one or another of two possible meanings which is intended.

Apparently there are two classifications of namable things; one of them such that 'A' and 'B' can denote the same entity only if a person who directly observes what 'A' names and what 'B' names will also be able to observe that they name the same thing; and the other classification such that what 'A' names can be identical with what 'B' names even though one may observe what 'A' names and what 'B' names without being able to make the identification. If I knew how to draw a sharp and clear line between these two classifications of namable things, I suspect that this distinction might be important for our present topic. But I do not know how to draw it in a manner at once comprehensive and faithful to our actual intentions in the use of language.

There is, however, one consideration which seems pertinent and clear. Some terms—or some terms in some uses—name what presents itself, or could present itself, as such; name appearances or data. The intent of this use of terms we may, for convenience, label 'phenomenal meaning'; and the language thus used may be called 'phenomenal language'. Other terms —or the same terms in a different and more frequent usage—name things which may appear but are in any case distinct from their appearances, that is, name something to which a given appearance may be attributable but something to which also more is attributable than could present itself to any single observer on one occasion. Physical objects are all of them included in this latter classification. And it is entities of this classification for which it may be true that A and B are identical, though one who observes what 'A' names and observes also what 'B' names may still be unable to make the identification. Phenomena of consciousness—it suggests itself—all of them belong in the former classification. They have universally the character here labelled 'datum'; and language used to name or apply to any conscious content as such, has phenomenal meaning. It denotes an appearance or appearances. Such data, when given, are entities whose identity and character it is impossible to mistake—though admittedly any language used to name them may be inappropriate or inadequate and fail to express just what is intended. An appearance or datum is just what it seems to be, and is nothing more than or other than what it appears to be.

If this is correct, then it may serve to explain the pertinence of the argument that mental facts can not be identified with brain facts or facts of physical behaviour because we directly inspect and are fully acquainted with the mental factuality but may be ignorant of the brain state or the behaviour; or if we should be also aware of these latter, may still be ignorant of any connection between them and what is mental. Admitting this phenomenal meaning of language used to denote the mental, such argument is entirely sound, and proves its point.

These considerations may also serve to locate more precisely one issue between those who interpret the mental in terms of behaviour or of brain states and those who would repudiate such interpretation. We who criticize these conceptions are talking about phenomenal entities as such when we use terms referring to the mental; they, by contrast, are in search of something belonging to the other classification; some entity to which these mental phenomena may be attributed, but a thing which by its nature transcends any possible phenomenal appearance which could be given at any one time. This thing is, on their account, a state of the physical brain or of the behaving organism.

If this does in fact correctly locate the issue—or *an* issue—then I think there is something further to be said about it which is obvious. It may well be that there are two kinds of namable entities to be talked about when the mental is under discussion; the directly given phenomena of consciousness, and a something—a substance, if you please—to which these are attributable. That there is such a thing or substance of which mental phenomena are attributes, and that this thing is the brain or the behaving organism, is one view, to be considered alongside others, including the dualistic conception of a non-physical substance as that to which mental states are attributable. But at least there are two things to be talked about: the substance of which the mental phenomena are attributes, and the directly given phenomena themselves which are to be attributed. There is a truth about these latter, and a kind of truth peculiarly patent, concerning which we can be mistaken only by some inadvertence. It is, moreover, this truth of the phenomenal which sets the problem in any search for that substance to which contents of consciousness are attributable. It is these phenomena which are to be accounted for, and the phenomenal facts about them which must be looked to in order to determine the correctness or incorrectness, or the plausibility, of any solution which may be offered for his problem which I have ventured to call the problem of substance.

In their preoccupation with this substance-problem, the proponents of behaviouristic and brain-state theories of mind sometimes speak as if there *were* no such entities as the directly inspected contents of consciousness; or appear to deny that there is any truth which can be told about them except in terms of those things—on their view, physical things—of which the mental are manifestations. By implication, they seem to accuse us, who would try first of all to state facts about these directly presented phenomena themselves, of talking nonsense or speaking of what does not exist. Such implication, intended or not, is certainly without justification. Whoever would deny that there are directly inspectable facts of the content of consciousness, would deny that which alone makes a theory of mind desirable and significant, and that which supplies the only final test of such a theory.

There is a second point which is pertinent to these issues, and can also be approached from grounds of analysis or logic. A definition, or a philosophic theory, should explicate the subject of it by specifying that criterion by which the thing in question could be selected from amongst all possible things which could be presented to us or imagined. It is not sufficient in a definition—and it should not be thought satisfactory in a theory—to characterize A by reference to XYZ, where XYZ are characters which, under conceivable circumstances, might be determined as present but leave us still in doubt whether what is presented is A. If we know what we mean by 'A' and if what we mean by 'A' is expressed by 'XYZ', then it could not conceivably happen that XYZ should be determined as present but there could be rational doubt whether what is presented is A.

Behaviouristic and brain-state interpretations of mind do not satisfy this prime requisite of definition and adequate theory. They do not satisfy it for the same reasons that the relation between mental phenomena and behaviour or brain states is something which can only be inferred inductively.

Let it be granted that there is some more or less complex character of behaviour such that whenever behaviour of just this character occurs there is consciousness, and whenever there is not behaviour of this sort there is no consciousness. Let it be further granted that for every qualitative specificity of consciousness there is some equally specific and correlated character of behaviour. Still the definitive explication of the mental in terms of the behavioural can not meet our requirement. First, because it would be possible, for example, to be in doubt whether the angle-worm on the fish-hook suffers pain; and we should be unable to dispel this doubt by observing its behaviour. The criterion of consciousness in terms of behaviour breaks down in such borderline cases, simply because nobody can specify this criterion except in some arbitrary fashion whose truth to what we mean by 'consciousness' he merely guesses at. Second, the various modes of one's own consciousness—suffering pain, hearing music, seeing green—are directly distinguishable by inspection. But no one could recognize these specificities of his own mentality in terms of behaviour, because neither he nor anyone else can state precisely what character of behaviour is unexceptionally present when there is pain or heard music or the seeing of green, and unexceptionably absent when there is not this specific mode of consciousness.

It is sufficiently evident that identification of the mental with the behavioural, or with brain states, represents a locution comparable to the physicist's statement that a specific pitch *is* a particular frequency of harmonic motion, and that sound *is* harmonic motion within a certain range of frequencies. Such locution represents first an empirically discovered correlation of two independently recognizable phenomena, a pitch and a rate of vibration. If 'middle C' did not *first* mean something identifiable without reference to vibration, and if 'vibration of 256 per second' did not *first* mean something identifiable without reference to sound, this correlation of the two could never have been empirically established and statement of it would be unintelligible verbiage. Eventually we may come to have a degree of inductive assurance of this correlation which exceeds our confidence in identifications of pitch by other means than physical determination of this frequency. That being the case, our most trusted criterion of pitch, and of the objectivity of sound, comes to be this criterion in terms of harmonic motion. To that extent and in that sense, it becomes understandable and even justifiable if the phenomena of sound are *defined* in terms of harmonic motion.

Such definition, which represents a type quite common in science, is of a peculiar sort which may be called 'definition by description' (definition by reference to some non-essential character but one uniformly found present in all actual cases of the thing in question and found absent in all other cases which are actual). A traditional example would be 'Man is the animal that laughs'. It is a distinguishing feature of such definition by description that the relation of definiens to definiendum which it states is one requiring to be established by induction and incapable of being established by logical analysis alone. Correlatively, the criterion of the definiendum which such a definition specifies is one (supposedly) sufficient for selecting what the definiendum denotes in all actual circumstances, but *not* sufficient to select what is defined under all thinkable circumstances or from amongst all imaginable things.

The behaviouristic or the brain-state theory of mind involves such definition of the mental by description. The principal difference of it from the example just discussed is that, whereas the correlation between sound and harmonic motion is well substantiated in all details, the correlation of mental phenomena with equally specific brain states or modes of behaviour is less well substantiated as a general thesis, and is quite undetermined in many of those specific details which the general truth of it requires. That being so, the definition of the utterly familiar specificities of the mental in terms of supposedly correlated brain functions or behaviour, is definition of the known in terms of the unknown.

There is also the consideration that whereas in natural science, which concerns itself exclusively with the existent, such definition by description has its pragmatic justification, such justification is lacking in philosophy, whose concern is not that of establishing synthetic *a posteriori* truths. From this point of view, the behaviouristic or the brain-state theory of mind substitutes an hypothesis which only the future development of natural science can corroborate or disprove for our more appropriate business of the analysis of meanings.

It has been regarded as a strong point in favour of interpreting the mental in terms of behaviour or of brain functions, and a strong point against any theory of the sort indicated by what has here been said, that minds other than our own, as anything distinguishable from certain physical phenomena, are unverifiable entities. And affirmations of what is unverifiable have sometimes been said to be meaningless. You will not expect me to attempt, in the space that remains, any adequate discussion of the questions here involved. But one or two considerations which are pertinent may be briefly indicated.

All of us who earlier were inclined to say that unverifiable statements are meaningless—and I include myself—have since learned to be more careful. This dictum is unclear; and in the most readily suggested interpretations of it, is too sweeping to be plausible. Also, the main point here does not have to do with verification at all. With empiricists in general and pragmatists in particular, such references to verifiability as essential to meaning is only a roundabout way of pointing out that unless you are somehow prepared to recognize the factuality you assert, in case that factuality should be, or could be, presented to you, your verbal expression is not a matter-of-fact statement because it affirms nothing intelligible. Any conditions of verification over and above this one requirement that a matter-of-fact assertion must have empirical sense—whether these further conditions be 'practical' or 'theoretical'—are irrelevant to the question of meaningfulness. And clearly the belief in other consciousness than one's own satisfies this one requirement of the meaningful; that there must be some criterion for recognition, some sense content indicative of what is meant. We can envisage the conscious experience of another, by empathy, in terms of our own. And we do. Any denial of that would be too egregious for consideration.

We significantly believe in other minds than our own, but we can not *know* that such exist. This belief is a postulate. At least I should have said this earlier; and did say it. But I now think this statement was a concession to an over-rigorous conception of what deserves the name of 'knowledge'. For empirical knowledge, in distinction from merely meaningful belief, verification is required. But there is what we call 'indirect verification' as well as 'direct'; and there is 'complete' or 'decisive verification' and also 'incomplete verification' or 'confirmation' as more or less probable. There are reasons to think that these two distinctions—direct or indirect and complete or incomplete—reduce to one: that in any distinctive sense of 'directly verifiable', that and that only is directly verifiable which is also completely and decisively verifiable. (The plausibility of this may be suggested by the thought that whatever is incompletely verified does not present itself in its full nature but is observed only in certain manifestations.) Most of what we call 'knowledge' is not only incompletely verified at any time but—when the matter is considered carefully—must remain so forever. (It may be completely verifiable, or completely confirmable, in the sense that there is nothing which the truth of it requires which could not, given the conditions of verification, be found true or found false; but it is not completely verifiable in the sense that verification of it can be completed—somewhat as there is no whole number which can not be counted, but counting of the whole numbers can not be completed.)

In view of these facts (if these suggestions indicate fact), it may be that there is no fundamental difference, by reference to its verifiability, between the belief in other minds and the belief, for example, in ultra-violet rays or in electrons. It might even be that the belief in other minds, though always incompletely verified and incapable of becoming otherwise, is supported by inductive evidence so extensive as to be better confirmed than some of the accepted theses of physical science.

33

GILBERT RYLE

I. THE CONCEPT OF MIND (1949)

The Official Doctrine

There is a doctrine about the nature and place of minds which is so prevalent among theorists and even among laymen that it deserves to be described as the official theory. Most philosophers, psychologists and religious teachers subscribe, with minor reservations, to its main articles and, although they admit certain theoretical difficulties in it, they tend to assume that these can be overcome without serious modifications being made to the architecture of the theory. It will be argued here that the central principles of the doctrine are unsound and conflict with the whole body of what we know about minds when we are not speculating about them.

The official doctrine, which hails chiefly from Descartes, is something like this. With the doubtful exceptions of idiots and infants in arms every human being has both a body and a mind. Some would prefer to say that every human being is both a body and a mind. His body and his mind are ordinarily harnessed together, but after the death of the body his mind may continue to exist and function.

Human bodies are in space and are subject to the mechanical laws which govern all other bodies in space. Bodily processes and states can be inspected by external observers. So a man's bodily life is as much a public affair as are the lives of animals and reptiles and even as the careers of trees, crystals and planets.

But minds are not in space, nor are their operations subject to mechanical laws. The workings of one mind are not witnessable by other observers; its career is private. Only I can take direct cognisance of the states and processes of my own mind. A person therefore lives through two collateral histories, one consisting of what happens in and to his body, the other consisting of what happens in and to his mind. The first is public, the second private. The events in the first history are events in the physical world, those in the second are events in the mental world.

It has been disputed whether a person does or can directly monitor all or only some of the episodes of his own private history; but, according to the official doctrine, of at least some of these episodes he has direct and unchallengeable cognisance. In consciousness, self-consciousness and introspection he is directly and authentically apprised of the present states and operations of his mind. He may have great or small uncertainties about concurrent and adjacent episodes in the physical world, but he can have none about at least part of what is momentarily occupying his mind.

It is customary to express the bifurcation of his two lives and of his two worlds by saying that the things and events which belong to the physical world, including his own body, are external, while the workings of his own mind are internal. This antithesis of outer and inner is of course meant to be construed as a metaphor, since minds, not being in space, could not be described as being spatially inside anything else, or as having things going on spatially inside themselves. But relapses from this good intention are common and theorists are found speculating how stimuli, the physical sources of which are yards or miles outside a person's skin, can generate mental responses inside his skull, or how decisions framed inside his cranium can set going movements of his extremities.

Even when 'inner' and 'outer' are construed as metaphors, the problem how a person's mind and body influence one another is notoriously charged with theoretical difficulties. What the mind wills, the legs, arms and the tongue execute; what affects the ear and the eye has something to do with what the mind perceives; grimaces and smiles betray the mind's moods and bodily castigations lead, it is hoped, to moral improvement. But the actual transactions between the episodes of the private history and those of the public history remain mysterious, since by definition they can belong to neither series. They could not be reported among the happenings described in a person's autobiography of his inner life, but nor could they be reported among those described in someone else's biography of that person's overt career. They can be inspected neither by introspection nor by laboratory experiment. They are theoretical shuttle-cocks which are forever being bandied from the physiologist back to the psychologist and from the psychologist back to the physiologist.

Underlying this partly metaphorical representation of the bifurcation of a person's two lives there is a seemingly more profound and philosophical assumption. It is assumed that there are two different kinds of existence or status. What exists or happens may have the status of physical existence, or it may have the status of mental existence. Somewhat as the faces of coins are either heads or tails, or somewhat as living creatures are either male or female, so, it is supposed, some existing is physical existing, other existing is mental existing. It is a necessary feature of what has physical existence that it is in space and time; it is a necessary feature of what has mental existence that it is in time but not in space. What has physical existence is composed of matter, or else is a function of matter; what has mental existence consists of consciousness, or else is a function of consciousness. . . .

The Absurdity of the Official Doctrine

Such in outline is the official theory. I shall often speak of it, with deliberate abusiveness, as 'the dogma of the Ghost in the Machine'. I hope to prove that it is entirely false, and false not in detail but in principle. It is not merely an assemblage of particular mistakes. It is one big mistake and a mistake of a special kind. It is, namely, a category-mistake. It represents the facts of mental life as if they belonged to one logical type or category (or range of types or categories), when they actually belong to another. The dogma is therefore a philosopher's myth. In attempting to explode the myth I shall probably be taken to be denying well-known facts about the mental life of human beings, and my plea that I aim at doing nothing more than rectify the logic of mental-conduct concepts will probably be disallowed as mere subterfuge.

I must first indicate what is meant by the phrase 'Category-mistake'. This I do in a series of illustrations.

A foreigner visiting Oxford or Cambridge for the first time is shown a number of colleges, libraries, playing fields, museums, scientific departments and administrative offices. He then asks 'But where is the University? I have seen where the members of the Colleges live, where the Registrar works, where the scientists experiment and the rest. But I have not yet seen the University in which reside and work the members of your University'. It has then to be explained to him that the University is not another collateral institution, some ulterior counterpart to the colleges, laboratories and offices which he has seen. The University is just the way in which all that he has already seen is organized. When they are seen and when their co-ordination is understood, the University has been seen. His mistake lay in his innocent assumption that it was correct to speak of Christ Church, the Bodleian Library, the Ashmolean Museum *and* the University, to speak, that is, as if 'the University' stood for an extra member of the class of which these other units are members. He was mistakenly allocating the University to the same category as that to which the other institutions belong.

The same mistake would be made by a child witnessing the march-past of a division who, having had pointed out to him such and such battalions, batteries, squadrons, etc., asked when the division was going to appear. He would be supposing that a division was a counterpart to the units already seen, partly similar to them and partly unlike them. He would be shown his mistake by being told that in watching the battalions, batteries and squadrons marching past he had been watching the division marching past. The march-past was not a parade of battalions, batteries, squadrons *and* a division; it was a parade of the battalions, batteries and squadrons *of* a division. . . .

My destructive purpose is to show that a family of radical category-mistakes is the source of the double-life theory. The representation of a person as a ghost mysteriously ensconced in a machine derives from this argument. Because, as is true, a person's thinking, feeling and purposive doing cannot be described solely in the idioms of physics, chemistry and physiology, therefore they must be described in counterpart idioms. As the human body is a complex organized unit, so the human mind must be another complex organized unit, though one made of a different sort of stuff and with a different sort of structure. Or, again, as the human body, like any other parcel of matter, is a field of causes and effects, so the mind must be another field of causes and effects, though not (Heaven be praised) mechanical causes and effects.

The Origin of the Category-mistake
One of the chief intellectual origins of what I have yet to prove to be the Cartesian category-mistake seems to be this. When Galileo showed that his methods of scientific discovery were competent to prove a mechanical theory which should cover every occupant of space, Descartes found in himself two conflicting motives. As a man of scientific genius he could not but endorse the claims of mechanics, yet as a religious and moral man he could not accept, as Hobbes accepted, the discouraging rider to those claims, namely that human nature differs only in degree of complexity from clockwork. The mental could not be just a variety of the mechanical.

He and the subsequent philosophers naturally but erroneously availed themselves of the following escape-route. Since mental-conduct words are not to be construed as signifying the occurrence of mechanical processes, they must be construed as signifying the occurrence of non-mechanical processes; since mechanical laws explain movements in space as the effects of other movements in space, other laws must explain some of the non-spatial workings of minds as the effects of other non-spatial workings of minds. The difference between the human behaviours which we describe as intelligent and those which we describe as unintelligent must be a difference in their causation; so, while some movements of human tongues and limbs are the effects of mechanical causes, others must be the effects of non-mechanical causes, i.e. some issue from movements of particles of matter, others from workings of the mind.

The differences between the physical and the mental were thus represented as differences inside the common framework of the categories of 'thing', 'stuff', 'attribute', 'state', 'process', 'change', 'cause' and 'effect'. Minds are things, but different sorts of things from bodies; mental processes are causes and effects, but different sorts of causes and effects from bodily movements. And so on. Somewhat as the foreigner expected the University to be an extra edifice, rather like a college but also considerably different, so the repudiators of mechanism represented minds as extra centres of causal processes, rather like machines but also considerably different from them. Their theory was a para-mechanical hypothesis.

That this assumption was at the heart of the doctrine is shown by the fact that there was from the beginning felt to be a major theoretical difficulty in explaining how minds can influence and be influenced by bodies. How can a mental process, such as willing, cause spatial movements like the movements of the tongue? How can a physical change in the optic nerve have among its effects a mind's perception of a flash of light? . . .

When two terms belong to the same category, it is proper to construct conjunctive propositions embodying them. Thus a purchaser may say that he bought a left-hand glove and a right-hand glove, but not that he bought a left-hand glove, a right-hand glove and a pair of gloves. 'She came home in a flood of tears and a sedan-chair' is a well-known joke based on the absurdity of conjoining terms of different types. It would have been equally ridiculous to construct the disjunction 'She came home either in a flood of tears or else in a sedan-chair'. Now the dogma of the Ghost in the Machine does just this. It maintains that there exist both bodies and minds; that there occur physical processes and mental processes; that there are mechanical causes of corporeal movements and mental causes of corporeal movements. I shall argue that these and other analogous conjunctions are absurd; but it must be noticed, the argument will not show that either of the illegitimately conjoined propositions is absurd in itself. I am not, for example, denying that there occur mental processes. Doing long division is a mental process and so is making a joke. But I am saying that the phrase 'there occur mental processes' does not mean the same sort of thing as 'there occur physical processes', and, therefore, that it makes no sense to conjoin or disjoin the two.

If my argument is successful, there will follow some interesting consequences. First, the hallowed contrast between Mind and Matter will be dissipated, but dissipated not by either the equally hallowed absorptions of Mind by Matter, or of Matter by Mind, but in quite a different way. For the seeming contrast of the two will be shown to be as illegitimate as would be the contrast of 'she came home in a flood of tears' and 'she came home in a sedan-chair'. The belief that there is a polar opposition between

Mind and Matter is the belief that they are terms of the same logical type.

It will also follow that both Idealism and Materialism are answers to an improper question. The 'reduction' of the material world to mental states and processes, as well as the 'reduction' of mental states and processes to physical states and processes, presuppose the legitimacy of the disjunction 'Either there exist minds or there exist bodies (but not both)'. It would be like saying, 'Either she bought a left-hand and a right-hand glove or she bought a pair of gloves (but not both)'.

It is perfectly proper to say, in one logical tone of voice, that there exist minds and to say, in another logical tone of voice, that there exist bodies. But these expressions do not indicate two different species of existence, for 'existence' is not a generic word like 'coloured' or 'sexed'. They indicate two different senses of 'exist', somewhat as 'rising' has different senses in 'the tide is rising', 'hopes are rising', and 'the average age of death is rising'. A man would be thought to be making a poor joke who said that three things are now rising, namely the tide, hopes and the average age of death. It would be just as good or bad a joke to say that there exist prime numbers and Wednesdays and public opinions and navies; or that there exist both minds and bodies.

II. DILEMMAS (1953)

As anatomy, physiology and, later, psychology have developed into more or less well-organized sciences, they have necessarily and rightly come to incorporate the study of, among other things, the structures, mechanisms, and functionings of animal and human bodies *qua* percipient. Answers are looked for and found to questions of the general pattern With what organs in our bodies do we see, hear, taste and feel things? and What lesions, diseases and fatigues in these organs diminish or destroy our capacity to see, hear, smell, taste and feel things? Harm need not result, though it can result from formulating the general programme of these inquiries in the question-patterns 'How do we perceive?' and 'Of what is seeing the effect?'

I say that harm can result from so formulating the programme of these inquiries. For these questions, so formulated, easily lend themselves to being construed after the pattern of other familiar and well-behaved questions; and when so construed they worry us by behaving extremely badly. I mean this. The questions 'How do we digest our food?' and 'What happens in us when we drink milk or alcohol?' have discoverable and largely discovered answers. The experts know well enough what happens to the milk or alcohol after we have consumed it and what differences the absorption of them make to our blood-streams, our reaction-times and so on. Doubtless there is more to be found out, but we can think what it will be like to have this extra knowledge. We know where it will fit in.

So when we ask 'How do we see trees?' or 'What happens in us when we see trees?' we are predisposed to expect the same sorts of answers, namely reports of modifications in some of our internal states and processes. Further than that, we are predisposed to think that these reports will tell us not only what happens in us when we perceive but what perceiving is, in the way in which the answer to the question 'What happens in us when we eat poison?' does tell us what being poisoned is. As eating results in nourishment and as haemorrhage results, sometimes, in fainting or in death, so, we fancy, some other external happenings result *via* some other complex internal happenings in the special internal happening of seeing a tree.

Yet, however, its details may be filled in, this sort of story leaves us uneasy. When asked whether I do or do not see a tree, I do not dream of postponing my reply until an anatomist or physiologist has probed my insides, any more than he, when asked whether he has seen the zigzag lines on his encephalogram, postpones replying until some other anatomist or physiologist has tested him by a second encephalogram. The question whether I have or have not seen a tree is not itself a question about the occurrence or non-occurrence of experimentally discoverable processes or states some way behind my eyelids, else no one could even make sense of the question whether he had seen a tree until he had been taught complicated lessons about what exists and occurs behind the eyelids.

'No,' it might be said, 'of course seeing a tree is not just a physiological state or a physiological process. Such states and processes can indeed occur without their owner knowing anything at all about them, whereas seeing, hearing and smelling belong where remembering, yearning and wondering belong, namely to the field or stream of consciousness. A person can suffer from a vitamin-deficiency without knowing what vitamins are, much less that he is short of them. But he cannot see or remember or wonder without knowing both that he is doing so and what it is that he is doing. These are not bodily states or processes but mental states or processes, and the questions "How do we see trees?" and "What takes place in us when we see trees?" need not anatomical or physiological answers but psychological answers or, perhaps, a conjunction of psychological with physiological answers.'

It is the regular lament of physiologists from Sydenham to Sherrington, not merely that they cannot trace but, worse, that they cannot think how they even might trace the whole chain of processes from the arrival of the initial external physical impulse at the ear-drum, say, the whole way through to the subject detecting the note of a flute. But, the suggestion is, the lament is gratuitous, for somehow, we do not yet know how, the chain of processes at a certain point changes over from having its links in the body to having its latest link or links in the mind. That is where the terminal process has its seat.

There are, I think, a number of objections to this way of retaining our seeings and hearings as the concluding stages of chain-processes while rendering them inaccessible to observation and experimentation in laboratories. But I do not want to go into them here. What I do hope to do is to show that there is something which is drastically wrong with the whole programme of trying to schedule my seeing a tree either as a physio-logical or as a psychological end-stage of processes. It is not a question of my seeing the tree evading observation and experiment, but of its not being the sort of thing that can be found *or* missed in either the one place or the other. It is not an intractably shy phenomenon, even an introspec-tive phenomenon, because it is not a phenomenon at all. Neither the physiologist nor the psychologist nor I myself can catch me in the act of seeing a tree—for seeing a tree is not the sort of thing in which I can be caught. When I report, perhaps to an oculist, that at a certain moment I saw something, what I report does not qualify to be the filling of any statement of the pattern 'The needle gave me a twinge of pain' or 'His haemorrhage caused him to faint'. To put the point much too crudely, seeing a tree is not an effect—but this is not because it is an eccentric sort of state or process which happens to be exempt from causal explanations but because it is not a state or process at all.

In this one negative respect seeing and hearing are like enjoying. It was partly for this reason that on a former occasion I discussed the notion of enjoyment at such a length, namely to familiarize you with the idea that well understood autobiographical verbs can still be grossly misclassified. I argued that some theorists had tried to fit the notions of liking and disliking into the conceptual harness which suits such terms as 'pain' and 'tickle'. They had misclassified *liking* and *disliking* with sensations or feelings. In somewhat the same way, many theorists have tried to subju-gate the notions of seeing, hearing and the rest to marching in step either with such notions as *pain* and *tickle*, or else with such notions as *inflamma-tion* or *knee-jerk*. It is tacitly assumed that seeing and hearing must be what stimuli stimulate, only, unfortunately, we have not yet found the way to correlate with these stimuli the perceptions which they stimulate.

I want to satisfy you that verbs like 'see' and 'hear' are not verbs of those sorts. Their functions are quite unlike the functions of verbs like 'tingle', 'wince', 'turn pale' or 'faint'; and answerable questions like 'What made him faint or flinch?' become unaskable questions when 'see' or 'taste' replace 'faint' and 'flinch'.

To begin with, seeing and hearing are not processes. Aristotle points out, quite correctly (Met. ix. vi. 7-10) that I can say 'I have seen it' as soon as I can say 'I see it'. To generalize the point that I think he is making, there are many verbs part of the business of which is to declare a terminus. To find something puts 'Finis' to searching for it; to win a race brings the race to an end. Other verbs are verbs of starting. To launch a boat is to inaugurate its career on the water; to found a college is to get it to exist from then on. Now starting and stopping cannot themselves have starts or stops, or, *a fortiori*, middles either. Noon does not begin, go on and finish. It is itself the end of the morning, the beginning of the afternoon and the half-way point of the day. It cannot itself go on for a time, however short. It is not a process or a state. Similarly though we can ask how long a poem is, we cannot ask how long its beginning and end are. They are not sub-stretches of the poem.

We can ask how long it was before the team scored its first goal; or how long the centre-forward spent in manœuvring the ball towards the goal; and even how long the ball was in flight between his kicking it and its going between the goal-posts. But we cannot ask how many seconds were occupied in the scoring of the goal. Up to a certain moment the team was goal-less; from that moment it had scored a goal. But there was no interim moment at which it had half-scored, or scored half of its first goal. Scoring a goal is not a process, but the termination of one and the beginning of another condition of the game. The beginning of a process, such as the start of the motion of an avalanche, is not the cause of that motion; the end of a process, such as the going out of a fire, is the termination but not an effect of the combustion.

It will, I think, be apparent why, with certain reservations, verbs which in this way declare termini cannot be used and are in fact not used in the continuous present or past tenses. The judge may say that he has been trying a man all the morning but not that he has spent the morning or any stretch of the morning in convicting him. I can say that I am occupied in searching for a pencil or trying to solve an anagram, but not that I am occupied in finding the pencil or getting the solution of the anagram. In the same way I can be looking for or looking at something, but I cannot be seeing it. At any given moment either I have not yet seen it or I have now seen it. The verb 'to see' does not signify an experience, i.e., something that I go through, am engaged in. It does not signify a sub-stretch of my life-story.

For safety, let me just mention the reservations. I could certainly say that I was finding misprints all the morning, though not that I was finding some one misprint for any part of that morning. If I found one misprint after another, and the sequence of discoveries went on from breakfast to lunch, then I was finding misprints all the morning. Or, when asked what I am busy about, I could reply that I am occupied in solving anagrams. I have solved some and I have some more which I hope to solve. But I could not say 'I am at present solving this anagram'. Either I have now got the solution or I have not yet got it. In short, a lot of biographical verbs like 'find', 'see', 'detect', and 'solve' share with a lot of other verbs of starting and stopping, which have no special biographical connotations, the negative property of not standing for processes taking place in or to things, or for states in which things remain. The programme, therefore, of locating, inspecting and measuring the process or state of seeing, and of correlating it with other states and processes, is a hopeless programme—hopeless not because the quarry wears seven-leagued boots or a cloak of invisibility, but because the idea that there was such a quarry was the product, almost, of inattention to grammar.

To say that verbs of perceptual detection, unlike those of perceptual exploration, have this resemblance to verbs of stopping and starting is, of course, not to say very much about their business. Checkmating also resembles midnight in this one respect, but a person who knew only this would not know much about checkmating. Let us consider a half-way-house pair of cases. Reaching the end of the measured mile of a race-track takes no time. The runner was running for some five minutes before he reached this point, but his reaching this point did not prolong his running-time. His reaching it is not something with its own beginning, middle and termination. The same is true of winning a mile race. Yet winning involves much more than reaching the end of the measured mile. To win a mile-race, the winner must have been running in competition with at least one other runner; he must not have started before the gun or taken a short-cut or used a bicycle or tripped up his opponent; and he must have reached the end of the measured mile ahead of any opponent. His winning the race comes with his reaching the end of the mile, but to be a victory, it has to satisfy quite a lot of additional requirements. Both are attainings, but they are not homogeneous with one another.

Suppose a man, flying in terror from a bull, crossed the start-line of a race-track as the gun was fired, and in his terror reached the tape ahead of the racers. Should we say that he had won the race? or that as he did not know that there was a race on, or anyhow had no intention of matching his speed against anybody save the bull, therefore he was not in the race and so did not win it? Has the careless chess-player whose cuff accidentally pushes his Queen into a square which puts his opponent's King in checkmate, defeated his opponent? We are inclined to require some intention or purpose of a runner or player before we will use the heavily loaded terminus-verbs 'win' and 'checkmate'.

We may imagine an athletics coach with a scientific training researching into the physiology and the psychology of runners. He finds out how men of different bodily builds and different temperaments race over different distances. He finds out the effects of fatigue, of alcohol, of tobacco, of lumbago and of depression upon their performances. He finds out about muscular co-ordination, rhythm, length of stride, and rates of breathing. He finds out about adrenalin, reaction-times, and electrical impulses in nerve-fibres. But then he laments that he can find no physiological phenomenon answering to his subject's winning a race, or losing it. Between his terminal output of energy and his victory or defeat there is a mysterious crevasse. Physiology is baffled. Then for a moment our experimentally minded coach cheers up. Perhaps winning and losing are not physiological states or processes having their being under the athlete's skin; perhaps they are mental states or processes, experiences which the athlete himself can unearth by careful introspection. Indeed this looks very plausible, since runners, who know nothing of what goes on under their own skins, seem often to have no difficulty in discovering that they have won or lost a race. So presumably they discover these facts by introspection upon their mental states and processes. But then, alas, it turns out that this hypothesis will not do either. A runner's victory, though it is tied up, in lots of important ways, with his muscles, nerves and frame of mind, with his early training and the briefing received just before the race, still refuses to be listed among these or kindred phases of his private career. However fast, resolutely and cleverly he has run, he has not won the race unless he had at least one rival, did not cheat and got to the tape first. That these conditions were satisfied cannot be ascertained by probing still further into him. Winning is not a physiological phenomenon, like perspiring or panting, nor yet is it a psychological phenomenon, e.g. an experience like a surge of confidence or a spasm of annoyance. It happens, but, to put it in a way which is not my way, it does not happen in either of those two places, for all that its happening has a great deal to do with what happened in those two places.

In some respects, though certainly not in very many, the verbs 'see' and 'hear' function like the verb 'win'. They do not stand for bodily or psychological states, processes or conditions. They do not stand for anything that goes on, i.e. has a beginning, a middle and an end. The assertion that a subject has seen a misprint carries with it the assertion that there was a misprint for him to see, somewhat as the assertion that a runner has been victorious or defeated carries with it the assertion that there was at least one other runner. The fact that he has seen a misprint has a great deal to do with facts about the light, the condition and position of his eyes and their distance from the page and the absence of screens, the condition of his retina, nerves, etc., the nature of his early education and his present interests, mood and so on. But his seeing or missing the misprint is not itself among the facts about him which can be established in the ways in which these physiological and psychological facts are established. It is not a fact of any of those sorts. None the less, it is not a mysterious fact, any more than winning or losing a race is rendered a mysterious fact by the failure of experiments upon the runner to establish it.

This partial analogy between the business of the verb 'win' and the business of verbs like 'see' and 'hear' of course breaks down quickly and in a number of places. I want to draw attention to two of these collapses, which are, I think, especially illuminating. First, no one would in fact ever suppose that 'winning' stood for a physiological or psychological condition or process, whereas all of us are under strong pressure to assimilate seeing and hearing to having pangs and twinges. Our immunity from the ludicrous blunder which I have invented is partly due to the fact that we know not merely implicitly and in practice, but explicitly and in theory what are the connotations of the verb 'to win'. We were taught the rules of racing when we were taught to race. We not only knew but could say what constituted cheating and not cheating, what constituted competing and what constituted the finish of a race. Even more conspicuously, we had been explicitly taught the rules of chess before we began to use the word 'checkmate'. But verbs of perceiving, though they also carry complex connotations, partly similar to those of 'win' and 'checkmate', were not and could not have been taught to us in this way. We picked up the ways of handling them without being told what these ways were, much as we picked up the pronunciation of the words of our native tongue without any lessons in phonetic theory.

Secondly, whereas the question whether I have won the race, checkmated my opponent or scored a bull's-eye can be decided at least not worse and often·better by someone else than by myself, the question whether I have seen or heard something does not ordinarily get or need an umpire. In the vast majority of every-day situations, the person who claims to have found or detected something is excellently placed for upholding that claim. He is as expert an umpire and as favourably situated an umpire as anyone could be. But, and it is an important 'but', not always. The reader who claims to have found a misprint or alternatively to have found a passage correctly printed is not to be trusted if he is a bad speller or not well versed in the language of the passage; the child who claims to see the railway lines meeting just beyond the signal-box is not the person to adjudicate on his claim; and the question whether or not the spectators saw the doves emerging from the conjuror's pocket is for him, not them, to decide. Notice that the conjuror is in a position to reject the claim of the spectators that they saw something happen, if he knows that it did not happen. But if they claim to have seen something happen which did happen, then he cannot, on this score alone, concede their claim. If the thing happened, but happened behind a screen, then their claim to have seen it must be rejected. They could not have seen it unless it happened, and unless it happened in such a place, and at such a distance and in such a light that it was visible to them and unless their eyes were open, properly directed and focused and so on. But·when he has conceded that they could have seen it happen, the question whether they did see it happen is not one which he can decide without interrogating them.

What sorts of questions will be put to them? He will not ask them to describe, in retrospect, what experiences they had had, for example what feelings they had felt, what ideas had crossed their minds or what after-images, if any, interfered with their subsequent vision; and of course he will not ask them intricate questions of physiological or psychological sorts, to which they are in no position to give any answers. No answers to such questions would go any way towards deciding whether they had seen what they claimed to have seen. No, he will ask them questions about what they claim to have witnessed happening. If they can tell him facts about the happening which they could not have found out without seeing it happen, their possession of this knowledge is what will satisfy him that they did see it. But sometimes they will not be able to satisfy him in this way, and the question whether they did see what they claimed to see remains undecidable for him. It may also remain undecidable for them too. The anxious mother, listening for the doctor's car, is not sure whether or not she faintly hears the noise of the car a few moments before it does in fact arrive. Perhaps it is imagination—it often is. Perhaps she does just hear it—we often do. But there need be no way of deciding the question after the event.

But in general it is true—we could even say that *of course* in general it is true—that an observer has seen or heard what he says that he has seen or heard. Sometimes he is deceived, for example, by the quickness of the conjuror's hand; but he can be deceived in this abnormal situation only because he is not deceived when witnessing the relatively slow motions of the hands of the people with whom he has ordinarily to do. The child, on his first visit to a skyscraper, may mistakenly judge the vehicles in the street below to be the size of beetles—but for this misestimate to be possible he must have learned to get right, in ordinary situations, the sizes of cars and beetles. The point is that where winning is the scoring of an athletic success, perceiving is the scoring of an investigational success. We find things out or come to know them by seeing and hearing. Of course we know what we have discovered, since to discover that something is the case is to come to know that it is the case. Normally, too, though not necessarily, we know how we discovered it, e.g., by sight and not by smell, or by touch and not by ear; though there are fringe-cases in which we are in doubt whether we found out that she was angry from the look on her face or from the tone of her voice; or whether we detected the proximity of the tree-trunk in the dark from a sort of sudden thickening in the sounds of things or from a sort of nameless hint given by the skin of our faces.

34

J. N. FINDLAY

LINGUISTIC APPROACH TO PSYCHO-PHYSICS (1949–50)

I

I want this evening to discuss the time-honoured question as to whether or not we should credit ourselves (and our human and animal associates) with two distinct 'lives', one consisting in the gross movements of the parts and particles of our bodies, and the other consisting of much more impalpable, ghostly and secret changes, which not only elude outside observers, but also prove somewhat elusive even to those to whom they acctually happen, and are with some difficulty circumscribed in language. I also want to consider how, if we admit two such lives, we should conceive them as related to each other, whether as the histories of distinct agents, or of the same agent differently regarded, and whether we should separate them rigorously or credit them with overlapping phases, and to what extent, finally, we should conceive of them as impinging on each other and modifying each other's course of development. It is this second set of questions rather than the first in which I am principally interested.

My questions are, as I said, time-honoured, but it is not easy to discuss them at the present moment, nor to count on a tolerant hearing. For the whole subject has become hedged about with a large number of prohibitions and warning pronouncements, and ghosts have been laid with such ceremonious finality that one dreads to raise them even for the most wholesome reasons. There used to be a *Verbot*, now happily breaking down, against talking about anything that one couldn't hope to show to other people, in the same sense in which one could show them a pen-wiper or an inkwell, and there also has been a *Verbot* against mixing up different kinds of talk, so that one shouldn't refer to a sensation in the same breath in which one talked about a physical object, there has been a general discouragement, practically amounting to a *Verbot*, against any deviation from the plainest, first-order speech, and latterly there has been a threat, not wholly intelligible to me, that if we say there is anything ghostly under the smooth surface of our outward saying and doing, we shall be then forced to locate a second ghostly process under the first, and so on indefinitely. Now I react very unkindly to any *Verbot* unless it is backed up by reasons that I find conclusively persuasive, and I shall therefore not scruple to consider whether or not we should be said to have a ghostly side to our nature, and how it should be said to be related to our grosser manifestations.

I shall, however, try to say at the outset what sort of inquiry I believe myself to be embarking on, and how I think it ought to be conducted. I should call our inquiry predominantly 'metaphysical', in that its main purport wasn't to discover new facts, but to decide upon a satisfactory way of speaking about the familiar or recondite facts which are laid before us in our common experience or by science. But I should also say that our inquiry was, to a subsidiary extent, empirical, in that our final choice to speak in one manner rather than another, would depend upon the character of the facts to be spoken of (many of them as yet undiscovered) as well as upon pure considerations of linguistic fitness.

In saying all this, I am of course giving an unconventional account of what is involved in metaphysical inquiry, and one that would require more expansion and more justification than I can give it this evening. I am suggesting, first of all, that we can be said to have a certain number of common, impersonal aims in speaking, and that speech can be evaluated as good or bad, as it fulfils or falls short of such aims. And I am also suggesting that, by describing metaphysics in this manner, one isn't giving too warped or too misleading an account of the activities of actual philosophers, who could be classed as metaphysicians, but that one covers those activities fairly and squarely, and throws light upon their detailed procedure.

Now I think good arguments could be advanced for both of these contentions: I could point out that, as beings concerned to communicate and remember, we can't help demanding clarity and definiteness at all points in our discourse, and that, as being concerned to make penetrating references to vast masses of detail we must necessarily seek for simple formulations from which such detail follows smoothly, and with a minimum of clumsiness. And while our ordinary interest in clarity and smoothness may be limited by the occasion or by the subject-matter on hand, yet we can't help experiencing an unpractical, almost aesthetic prolongation of this interest, which leads us to pursue smoothness and clarity to the limit, and to tolerate no mode of speech in which anything is left indefinite, or apparently conflicting, or merely juxtaposed.

That these linguistic aims operate in the work of actual metaphysicians might be shown by examining their books, in which connection one could find no better illustration than the careful masterpieces of C. D. Broad. For though these books are written for the most part, in what has been called the 'material mode of speech', yet they suffer remarkably little

M

if translated into the formal mode, and most of the arguments which are put up in justification of a 'theory' will provide good reasons for preferring some way of speaking. Thus Broad's long weighing of the merits and demerits of the 'sensum' and the 'multiple-relations' theory of the relation of percipients to perceived objects, gain greatly in clearness, and can be freed from many senseless complications, if we regard them not as theories, but as essays in improved speech about familiar facts in ordinary experience.

In regarding our inquiry as one concerned mainly with ways of speaking I am not, of course, regarding it as trivial: it remains exactly what it always was, and to me, at least, the question 'What shall I say to speak well?' is as solemn and important as the old question: 'What shall I do to be saved?' While I disapprove of philosophy by pronouncement or philosophy by prohibition (as also of philosophy by ignoring or not understanding) I am as unfriendly to that facile tolerance which readily agrees to differ. To me philosophical preferences should be based upon good reasons and good reasons are by definition those which can't help wringing some measure of recognition from others, even if those others aren't ultimately moved by them.

II

I turn now to consider, first of all, whether we ought or ought not to split up a person's history into two separate 'stories', that we may roughly distinguish as gross, outward and material, and inward, subtle and spiritual. Now this question I propose to consider with some brevity, both because I have written and spoken on it several times recently, and am rather tired of it, and also because I want to pass on to other questions that I find more interesting. Now it seems to me, that there nearly always are, in a very plain sense, two separate stories about a man involved in certain situations, and engaged in certain activities, and those are, on the one hand, the story which tells us what the man did or underwent, or what he was about to do or undergo, or what he would have done or undergone (in the ordinary sense in which we don't do or undergo anything when we merely 'sit and think'), and the quite different story which tells us how things *felt* or *seemed* to the man in question, when he was involved in this situation or engaged in these activities.

These are distinct stories in the quite obvious sense of being made up of quite different sets of words, quite differently arranged, and they are also distinct in requiring quite a different background and preparation in an understanding auditor. For the experience, the sympathy and the interpretative capacity that are necessary for the understanding of the one story, are quite superfluous in the understanding of the other. And while the one story can be set down in words that bear a plain meaning and can be readily connected with features of our common environment, the other story abounds in phrases involving a 'sort of', a 'rather as if', a 'rather like', a 'just as if', and so forth, which require quite a different training and effort if we are to interpret them properly. Even if there *is* a strained, sophisticated sense in which the one story can be regarded as a 'translation' of the other, it is only when we have understood both stories in the ordinary manner, that we can come to say that this is possible.

I shall now illustrate my meaning by considering a case very carefully dealt with by Professor Ryle, that of a man doing something with a great deal of attention or conscious 'heed'. Now I think that Professor Ryle has told us *one* of the stories concerning this man, the one, namely, that would ordinarily be called 'outward', with very great accuracy and beauty: he has told us how a man doing something in a heedful manner is always able and ready to tell us what he has been doing, and what he is about to do, that he can report on it accurately afterwards, that he becomes tired by his activity in a way in which heedless actions do not tire him, that his activity can be touched off or finely regulated by general orders issued by himself or other persons, that it may be based on past learning, but adjusts itself neatly to the novel features of the situation, and so on and so forth.

This is, as I say, an admirable account of the heedful activity, and one that discriminates many features not previously noted. But it none the less altogether fails to tell us how this heedful activity *feels* to the heeder, except to the extent of telling us that it *doesn't* consist of murmuring to oneself, uttering comments, strictures, encouragements or diagnoses to oneself, which are obviously not at all of the essence of heeding. But how heeding feels to the heedful person is surely something of immense interest and importance, and it isn't something that presents insuperable obstacles to description.

For quite obviously, when we heed something carefully, an extraordinary phenomenon occurs—it is only extraordinary since we so seldom heed our heeding—which we are wont to describe by a number of more or less suitable metaphors: it is as if all we were not heeding faded away into the background, or vanished altogether, however powerfully it might be assaulting our physical sense-organs, or impressing their more sensitive portions. And it is as if certain objects, or, strange to say, even abstract phases of objects, were set in brilliant light, while everything else passed into penumbra or was totally obscured. The phenomenon in fact appears more saliently and impressively, whenever one keeps one's fleshly eyes and ears fixed and immobile, and lets what I may call one's ghostly eyes and ears rove over their deliverances, dwelling as heedfully on the dim and marginal as upon the vivid and central, and *then* notes restrospectively— as one can do without difficulty—how various features in the picture appeared and disappeared, and were at times in a curious manner, half-apparent. To note all this is certainly to become aware of a 'light' and a 'clarity' that are in many ways deeply different from anything else that goes by these names.

We are, of course, bound to describe our phenomenon metaphorically, since the whole process of looking back with descriptive intent on one's just past experience is a trifle unusual. Yet it isn't by any means a difficult proceeding, nor need it be described in terms of that contemporary 'phosphorescence' which some have found so dubious and objectionable. For while the more absorbed passages in our inner life take place, as it were, *in camera*, yet we have but to interrupt their session to receive at once a full, circumstantial, wholly confident report, embracing much queerly worded detail that would never otherwise have been released. While we may quarrel about metaphors, and particularly so when they have been frozen into technicalities, yet the very fact that we *do* quarrel about them, could be said to indicate that we understand them.

Not only does the heedful experience show the quasi-luminous effects I have mentioned, but it also frequently involves what one can only call an accumulated sense of what one has accomplished, as well as a concentrated sense of what one is about to do, both of which 'senses' disappear entirely whenever we can carry out activities in a less heedful and more routine manner. And one could, in the same manner, furnish two distinct stories for any of the other activities that one wouldn't call entirely 'unconscious', though some, doubtless, would present more difficulties than others. But we find, curiously enough, that those stories which are most exciting on the level of saying and doing, often correspond to the poorest stories on the level of seeming and feeling, while those which involve the most vivid appearances and feelings, correspond to the dullest tales upon the level of action.

All this being as tritely obvious as it is, what possible ground could anyone have for saying that there is only *one* story covering every type of human activity, and that proposals to bifurcate it are due to the confusions of philosophers? One might, I think, say so because one thought no clear line could, or should be drawn between the two stories: certainly the same things and persons may occur in both of them, and certainly there is a sense in which the one may be said frequently to carry on what has been started in the other. There are, plainly, quite as many likenesses as differences between solving some problem on paper, and turning it over in one's head.

If one wants to consider what is logically possible, though with small empirical warrant, one can certainly conceive of situations and senses, in which the one story could be said to have become *as* public as the other.

If experiences of a foreign flavour, yet manifesting a characteristic, independent pattern, and seeming to refer back and forth to other experiences similar to themselves, haunted us on occasion or beset us recurrently, we should doubtless feel a strong temptation to say that they were experiences of some other person, that had temporarily strayed among our own. This inclination would be strengthened if we could find affinities and affiliations between such experiences and those that we attributed to the fleshly persons about us, whom we could meet and talk to in the ordinary manner. Wittgenstein, too, has taken great trouble to imagine what it *might* mean to feel another's pain.

Those who would adhere, even in such cases, to that strict convention which makes it nonsense to say that anyone could enjoy the experiences of another, seem to me to be shaping their language too much to suit the circumstances and the communications of this transitory life. They remind me, also, of those determined Euclideans, who on being transported from London to London by way of the whole circuit of spherical space, still said that this couldn't possibly be London, but was only a town exactly like it, since one couldn't return to one's point of origin by going away from it in a straight line.

But though I have the greatest sympathy with the line of objection I am considering, and though I certainly don't want to set up any rigid barriers between an inner and outer, or between the 'public' and the 'private', still the two tales in question do seem to me to mention *some* rather different matters, e.g. the 'light' of attention that we just considered, and they also seem to me (in this life at least) to require to be understood in a somewhat different manner, so that we still have the best of reasons for keeping them separate.

Some might object to speaking about the two stories for a different reason: because they thought the one story, the supposedly 'inner' one, wasn't really a story, because they held it 'hadn't any separate sense', that it told us nothing that couldn't have been better put in the other story, that it merely expressed certain passages in that story in a set of startling 'pictures', which might have an illustrative or a regulative value, but whose usefulness was outweighed by their quite misleading suggestion that they were conveying important and peculiar information. Now this line of objection seems to me to be very strange, and it also seems to me to make use of words in a manner that would need much justification.

For it is surely odd to say that one isn't communicating anything different when one says how things look or feel to a person, and when one says how that person would behave in certain circumstances. The strangeness wouldn't vanish even if one limited this behaviour to such as would provide evidence for the fact that things actually did feel or look in this manner to the person in question. It also seems strange to say that our whole difficult activity of putting ourselves into someone else's position, whether in fancy or fact, subjecting oneself to similar influences and provocations, trying to feel oneself into someone's action and descriptions and then testing and retesting one's readings by a further study of those actions and descriptions—all of which things would be said to be helpful in the understanding of another person's experiences—it would be strange to say that all this activity could result in nothing but the construction of an irrelevant 'picture', which couldn't by itself convey the slightest degree of information or knowledge.

Now all this may be said—one can certainly use the words 'information', 'knowledge', 'communication', 'picture', 'sense', 'different' and so forth in this manner—and to speak in this way may have the merit of stressing that the techniques we use to obtain insight into other people's experiences do not, in this life at least, operate independently of their utterances and actions, but are always prompted and tested by the latter. But it seems, at the same time, gravely misleading to speak in such a way, since it suggests that the 'picture' we are forming is idle and superfluous, that we might readily dispense with it, that we could easily replace it by some wholly lucid, 'outward' story. Whereas it is only by keeping such a 'picture' before us, that we can work out all the innumerable, highly indirect, surprising ways in which some of a man's more retiring attitudes *might* manifest themselves. We can also obviously never give a final outward rendering of this 'picture', but can at best come indefinitely nearer to doing so. For all these reasons I can see no good ground for departing from that ordinary mode of speech which talks in terms *both* of an inward and an outward story.

III

Having decided to say, therefore, that there nearly always are two stories about a man's activity at a given moment, we must now decide how we shall say that these two stories are related to each other. And here we must decide, at the outset, whether to attribute them both to a single agent or person, or whether to consider them as tales about distinct agents, a man's mind or spirit, on the one hand, and his body on the other. Now the mere fact that our common speech follows the former pattern more frequently than the latter, as well as the fact that some philosophers have spoken in the latter manner, would suffice for some to settle the whole issue: we, however, must give better reasons for our preferences.

What then are the circumstances in which it would be reasonable to say that our inward story was descriptive of *one* agent, and our outward story of another? I shall answer this question on principles that I think we actually do follow in such matters, and which require only a little further elaboration and development to be the principles we ought to follow. It would, I think, be reasonable to speak of two agents in a situation like this, if we could work out, on the basis of our actual data, two hypothetical courses of development, each following its own independent and unbroken line, the one representing how our inner story *would* develop (from a given point onwards) if it were unaccompanied by an outward story, and the other representing how our outward story would develop if it were unaccompanied by an inward story. Both these lines of hypothetical development should have their own characteristic pattern, their own natural *nisus*, they should proceed without gaps, and they should *not* follow each other slavishly in their curves and windings.

Not only should it be then possible for us to work out two such lines, but we should also be able to light upon principles which connected deviations in the one pattern of development with certain features in the other, so that the one line could be looked upon as *interfering* with, modifying the direction of, the other. And if the deviations that we had to account for were extremely *sharp* and *notable*, we should have *stronger* reason for speaking in terms of a plurality of agents than if they were trivial and gradual. For, in the latter case, we could perhaps more reasonably say that our single agent had altered, or that it was really different from what we had originally supposed, whereas it wouldn't be so reasonable to say this in the case of marked and sharp changes. Quite plainly we regard a magnet as one agent, and a piece of iron as another, because we think we know how each would behave in the absence of the other, and also because we can see how the behaviour of the one alters in spectacular fashion when the two are brought together.

We may even say that talk in terms of two distinct agents would be reasonable, if we knew *no* way of isolating one of these agents, or subjecting it to a separate examination. If my pen suddenly rose from my desk and pirouetted in the air, plunged itself in my inkwell and wrote madly on the paper, before relapsing into its customary quiescence, it would be not unreasonable to say that it was 'possessed' by some foreign agent, even if we didn't go so far as to call this agent an 'entelechy' or a poltergeist. And this reasonableness would increase if the disturbances followed a regular pattern and also passed regularly from one region to another.

All this has been put in somewhat homely fashion, and could doubtless be developed into long, difficult technicalities in which great play was made with the philosophical notion of 'causality'. We have done no more than make a certain steady consecutiveness and 'belonging together' into a mark of unitary thinghood, while lack of coherence, accompanied by casual interference, were a mark of substantial separateness, a decision based upon tendencies in our language that we have only made definite and explicit.

We hold, therefore, that if each of our stories had its own distinct inner unity and continuity, in which certain marked and sharp 'dints' and deviations could be connected with passages in the other story, we should have reason to adopt that dualistic mind-and-body account that some philosophers have favoured. And this, be it noted, would be so, even if we were only dealing with two *outward* stories, even, for instance, if we found we were in a position to treat men's accounts of their inner experience as irrelevances of behaviour like the queer conduct of the bewitched pen mentioned above. For there is nothing in the mere difference of 'inward' and 'outward' which should as such point to a difference of agents: were the two as slavishly 'parallel' as certain traditional accounts suppose them to be, it would be extremely queer and perverse to attribute them to different agents.

What then shall we say on this matter, having regard not only to the principles of speaking we have laid down, but also to the empirical facts we went to cover? Plainly our inner story wouldn't *seem* to have that inner unity and completeness which would make it reasonable to credit it to a separate agent: it seems to proceed in fits and snatches, to be punctuated by gaps, to require an indefinite amount of supplementation by *something* before it could figure as an agent's history. Nor do we find anything like the sharp, brave *step-up* between such activities as are held to have no inner inspiration (or no relevant one) and such activities as are said to have one, and only such a sharp step-up could lend colour to our manner of speaking.

We find, instead, something quite different: that processes *without* an inner inspiration, that would, in fact, be called 'merely physical' or 'merely physiological' *lead up* unbrokenly to many of our more significant inner experiences, and that the latter likewise *lead down* smoothly to the former. And we find, further, that while there may be many deep descriptive differences between our spread-out, piece-meal outward living, and our fused, concentrated inner changes, there is none the less a sense in which processes beginning in the one are constantly being carried over into the other, and continued, as it were, in another manner and medium.

Now I need not give many examples of this very interesting, wholly familiar *lead-up* and *lead-down*: it is indeed strange that experimentation should have been needed to reveal facts so obvious. I shall illustrate *lead-up*, first of all, by the extremely plain fact that it is, for the most part, our unconscious 'bodies' that do all the sorting out and the 'interpreting' of the influences impinging on us from without, thereby giving rise to those 'percepts' which emerge full-fledged before our 'minds'. It isn't, for instance, because a noise in my right ear *seems* louder than a noise in my left ear, or because it *seems* to arrive there earlier, that it seems to me to come from my right: but it is because it *is* physically louder and earlier, that it seems to come from the direction in question. It isn't, likewise, because a paper first seems grey in some shadowy setting that it then—the setting being recognized and discounted—gets taken for white, but it is because our experienced and accomplished body has sized up the whole situation, and has discounted whatever was abnormal and distorting in it, that the paper comes before us as authentically white. It is likewise the unconscious, merely bodily mother of the psychology textbooks, who responds to her baby's slightest whimper (while ignoring the tram-cars), and starts making appropriate movements at the moment that she also wakes up her slumbering 'mind'. It is likewise not because our whole past history has paraded before us, that we have, after some hesitation, picked out the right word or the appropriate action, but it is probably right to attribute this to an obscure massing and shifting of bodily factors such as that which precedes our suddenly acquired, triumphant ability to deal with some hitherto baffling collar-stud.

In all these cases our 'mind' can surely be said to behave like a high-born lady that consumes all sorts of viands in her dining-room, that have come from a kitchen she has never visited, and are handed to her by a 'slavey' that she never notices. And if one wants a good example of *lead down* one has but to point to the universal fact of silent intent, or, as the psychologists call it, 'mental set': the fact that decisions or instructions consciously entertained lead down insensibly to serene executions, quite undisturbed by any consciousness of purpose, yet not by any means stupid for all that, which go on until some hindrance or some counter-attraction demands that the whole matter should be 'looked into' and our intent consciously reaffirmed.

All these facts could be said to show, with the greatest plainness, that pursuit of goals and intelligent self-adjustment are as much present in what we unconsciously do, as in what consciously appears before us, or is felt within us, even if the higher and more difficult forms of self-direction have need of that 'light' of heedfulness that I previously mentioned. And what goes for intelligence and purpose goes also for their absence (or relative absence) for, as Professor Ryle has made plain, things 'done in our heads' may be as aimless and as unintelligent as things done blindly by our hands.

We may note further that what I have called *lead-up* and *lead-down* are evident, also, in the fact that even in our wholly untutored descriptions of our inward states, we still use the idiom of external action in a setting of circumstances. It is, we say, *as if* we were in this or that position, or before this or that object, and were dealing with it in this or that manner. We may, in fact, say that the characterization of our inner story as 'ghostly' is *doubly* valuable and illuminating: for while it brings out all the deep differences between our outward and our inward manner of being—at least in their extreme phases—the hardness and fullness of the one, and the attenuation and fusion of the other, it none the less also emphasizes that the one is, as it were, nothing but a queer replica and continuation of the other. To sprain one's ankle on a ship's gangway, to live through the vivid appearances and feelings involved in this happening, to imagine vividly what it was like to live through these, to live afterwards through the unillustrated 'nutshell' sense of all that was involved in this: here surely is a ladder leading from the grossly physical to phases more and more 'phantasmal'. I think Professor Ryle manages to strike this spectral note very happily (though he would no doubt detest my 'spectral' language) when he says of our silent soliloquies that they are nothing but 'a flow of pregnant non-sayings'.

The empirical facts being what they are, it would be obviously strained to speak in terms of two agents, a mind and a body, in somewhat casual and external relation to each other. None of the conditions that would justify such a mode of speaking are present. We must, in fact, endorse that perfectly ordinary manner of speaking which treats *a person* as an amphibious being, combining both a fleshly and a ghostly 'side'. It is, in fact, neither proper to confound our lives, nor to divide our person.

Not only must we, therefore, conceive of this single person as straddling two realms, but we must also conceive of him as shifting his weight regularly from one foot to the other, since the arrest of our fleshly performance generally leads to an intensification of our ghostly activities, whereas the perfection of outward performance (we may say after Heraclitus) is generally purchased at the price of 'soul'. But whether a wiser science will ever find a notion of 'energy' capable of accommodating and accounting for these facts, is something that I leave aside as too difficult for me. The facts don't, however, encourage us to give what is ghostly any uniform priority over the bulky, or the latter over the former. If movements are, at times, merely the overflowing expressions of important inner changes, the latter, likewise, at times merely echo and applaud the former, as when we listen in quiet passive astonishment to our own brilliant utterances.

To speak in terms of something two-sided and amphibious may of course prove fruitful of puzzles. We may be led to look for a mysterious *tertium quid*, endowed with undiscoverable properties, which will hold the two lives or sides together. Or we may begin to search after some 'deeper bond' that will render their connection 'intelligible'. These searchings are metaphysical in the worst sense of the word. We can only be freed from such difficulties by dwelling carefully on those actual connections which lead us to attribute certain outward and inward changes to a single person, by noting how our inner life may be said to carry on, to anticipate, to do duty for and to supplement our outward living, and then realizing clearly that it is only through a confusion that we have been led to look for bonds or binders that would make this unity closer or more genuine. We may, in fact, say that the *lead-up*, the *lead-down* and the 'phantasmal' continuation we have mentioned, simply *are* the relationship between our bodies and our souls.

I have, of course, vastly simplified the issue before me by turning my back deliberately on the whole possibility of saying that those purposive, intelligent outward acts which *don't* seem to have an inner inspiration, really have one, although this latter is of an undiscoverable, 'unconscious' kind. This mode of speaking has, of course, been applied to those preparations, those rummagings, those continuations and those hoardings that I previously dealt with, in which *lead-up* and *lead-down* can be said to consist. Everywhere, if we like, we can see the small, peering eyes and the furrowed brows of vigilant brownies, who, unlike men, never let the matter drop, never acquire skill, never learn to do anything automatically and silently, for this would unfortunately mean that they relegated part of their duties to another set of brownies, who might in their turn practise other relegations, and so on indefinitely. And, since brownies have been postulated, we can make them work hard: we can extend their responsibilities to the whole running of the living organism, so that our old dualism will return with novel force, our 'body' being credited with nothing but our most lumpish tendencies, while all order and adjustment spring from the meddling of these unseen 'intelligences'.

Now I don't object on principle to this whole approach, should it really prove better capable of dealing with our facts than any other. I don't abhor the undiscoverable as such, nor do I feel a strong urge to say that all significant talk about it must necessarily be translatable into talk about something else. Provided that the circuit via such undiscoverables really represents a shortening of our theoretical path, I am content to let it be. But it appears to me that the theoretical circuit *via these* brownies is lengthy and unprofitable: it does no more than complicate what is already quite intelligible in itself. For, on reflection, we can see no reason why intelligence and purpose should be more closely associated with a ghostly performance than a fleshly one, or why the latter should *derive* its inspiration from the former.

We may, in fact, say of intelligence and purpose that they are radically amphibious: they lie, after all, in the *way* in which we cope with things and situations, and hence can be equally exhibited on the fleshly and spiritual planes. And if we needed to explain our fleshly purpose and intelligence, by postulating a set of ghostly acts behind them, then, as Professor Ryle has convincingly pointed out, we should require another set of ghostly acts behind these latter, to explain their purpose and intelligence, and so on indefinitely. If we can perhaps be most highly intelligent when we operate 'in our heads', in that we can then deal simultaneously with a large number of issues, stripped of all concrete irrelevances, yet there are none the less grave perils of confusion in these ghostly dealings, which become apparent when we work them out in practice.

We may note, further, that the only inner life of which we have experience is one that is always agreeably padded by relaxed, unvigilant performances, out of which it emerges and into which it relapses. We can form no conception of that Argus-like scrutiny, that everlasting burrowing and fussing, that we should have to attribute to our brownies. We may point, finally, to that ever accumulating body of facts and observations which points to much the same sort of gradual lead-up and lead-down between the living and the lifeless, that we have already seen between the living and the conscious. For all these reasons I adhere to my amphibious 'person' in preference to an 'entelechy' operating from without, which crowds the interstices of our conscious living with a large number of 'unconscious experiences'.

IV

I see no reason, therefore, for saying anything but that I am a single but two-sided person, having an outward and an inward history: I only hope this meagre mouse will not seem too ridiculous. I, at least, have found it interesting to give birth to it. There are, however, two further issues that I ought to consider, connected with less commonplace facts and possibilities than those I have dealt with, and which may have a bearing on our final decision. I must, on the one hand, say something about the feasibility of talking of a 'disembodied' mode of existence, a notion that has been found profitable in dealing with abnormal facts. And I must say something, also, as to the bearings on our recommendations of facts that have been, or that may be yet discovered in regard to our brain, an organ that I haven't yet mentioned, but which is generally regarded as important in the matters now under discussion.

Now in regard to talk about 'disembodied existence', I am sure that very good sense can be given to it, if for no other reason than that Dr Lewy (to say nothing of Professors Moore and Schlick) has thought so. And though we have said that our personal existence reveals itself *both* in the acts and changes of a body, *and* in the way things look and feel from and in that body, still we haven't precluded ourselves from saying that a personal existence of this sort might cease altogether to be an affair of *that* body, or indeed of any body whatever, but might none the less linger on in forms more or less vaguely and dispersedly corporeal, or more purely inward.

I confess, however, that I am not at all clear what I ought to mean by this 'disembodied existence', merely because I *could* mean so many things by it. To live through a long series of cogitative flashes, in which nothing whatever was illustrated or symbolized, and in which one communed with others by a sort of mystical seepage, temporarily extending oneself to embrace portions of their mental history, would be the most truly 'disembodied' manner of being that I can conceive of, though some might question whether I really can conceive of it. And since we know of no *noesis* that isn't, in some fashion, an attenuation of our ordinary dealings with the things around us, it is no doubt possible that something of our concrete personal style of living might be carried over into this disembodied state.

But to move among dissolving Swedenborgian landscapes, clothed in some dream-shape alterable at will, and to converse with other phantasms similarly attired, who shared some but not all of one's visionary environment, would be a manner of existence that one might or might not care to call a 'disembodied' one. Whereas to see one's own funeral from a given point in space, though not with actual eyes, or to fling furniture about, though not with actual hands, would be a manner of being differing remarkably little from our present state of 'embodiment'. Quite obviously, our present ways of speaking are ill-suited to conditions in the after-life: all that we can therefore sensibly do is to avoid speaking so rigorously as to make nonsense of modes of speech which may very well prove to have an explanatory or anticipatory value.

I turn, finally, to consider how, if at all, we should let our psychophysical talk be affected by facts about the happenings in our brains, of which we now only know enough to confuse us, but concerning which we may have better knowledge in the future. Now there is a view concerning our brains according to which they may be compared to perfect, secret *faces*, on which is written, for the eyes of anyone with a key to the cipher, the whole history of our inward feelings and our preparations for action, which are expressed so partially and ambiguously on our fleshly faces. The veil of privacy and secrecy hanging over our inner life is, in fact, on this view, no thicker than our skulls. Not only are we to be thus credited with these perfect, secret faces, but it is also held that everything recorded on them can be explained on principles which obtain elsewhere in the material world, or in the unconscious segment of its living portion, so that *no* reference to what they may be expressing is necessary to explain their changes.

Now this doesn't seem to me at all a plausible theory, and I regard it merely as a product of the verbal difficulties occasioned by our amphibious manner of being, and of the consequent desire to make our outward story self-explanatory and complete, just as the parallel doctrine of 'unconscious states of mind' tries to do the same for our inward story. But the view in question is, without a doubt, an empirical hypothesis, which may in the future have a great deal of factual confirmation, and it is therefore necessary for us to consider how such confirmation should affect our talk about our twofold personal life.

Now *one* way in which this hypothesis has historically affected speakers has been to make them say that while various unconscious bodily activities may genuinely lead up to important inner states, yet the latter don't genuinely lead on to the former. They are merely idle offshoots of our brain-configurations, which make no difference to our subsequent lines of outward action. This theory-cum-way-of-speaking has seemed to some to derogate deeply from our spiritual dignity, though others might find it exhilarating to conceive of their minds as mirrors in which their own irremediable follies may be passively contemplated, much after the manner of the *Manchester Guardian* looking on at the 'notable spectacle of our public death'.

But I really can't see that this supposed situation would make it reasonable to speak in this manner, and to be either humbled or exhilarated thereby: the situation in question might make the use of our inner story *superfluous* in explaining what we outwardly did, but it couldn't, in a significant way, make its use either *illegitimate* or *improper*. We should, in fact, in such a situation, be *as* justified in regarding our brain states as idle epiphenomena of our inward spiritual condition, as the latter of the former and we could, if we liked, make that inner spiritual condition bear the whole responsibility for what we subsequently did. The fantastic situation we have imagined would, in fact, put us in a Buridan's ass position, in which it would be *just* as reasonable to take a purely inward, or a purely outward line of explanation, or in which we might proceed along both lines conjointly. The traditional 'parallelists' and 'epiphenomenalists' were in fact being metaphysical in the worst sense of the word, in preferring one manner of speaking to the other, after they had ruled out all possibility of a deciding difference.

I don't myself think so ill of this world as to think it capable of landing me in such embarrassment. I confess that I think that our brain will prove itself, on careful examination, to abound in as many half-formed gestures and ambiguous expressions as our outward countenances. But should we really carry such ideally expressive faces hidden in our skulls, I don't think that this curious fact should be allowed to affect what we say about the relations of our inner and our outer life.

I have now completed my treatment of the psycho-physical issue. My results have been ordinary, since this seems to me to be genuinely a case in which the course of philosophical reflection leads us only from the familiar to the familiar. But we *might* have been led by such reflection to a manner of speech differing widely from the ordinary. I think it good, anyhow, to concern ourselves at times with old, large issues, since it is only in their context that we can profitably crawl like beetles over smaller bits of canvas. Just as the old issue of truth, after having been shelved for a decade, came back to us unexpectedly in the relation of a language to another language that talks about it, so will most metaphysical issues return in the guise of questions of linguistic preferability. But they will return with a difference, and perhaps I have been successful in illustrating what this difference is.

35

JOHN WISDOM

THE CONCEPT OF MIND (1950–51)

This paper is not a review of Professor Ryle's book *The Concept of Mind*, but it is an attempt to criticize and at the same time to continue it. Before coming to the criticism, may I say how much I admire the power, the simplicity and the grace of Ryle's work. It is an achievement and a part of the progress of philosophy.

Wittgenstein said that we have the idea that the soul is a little man within, and also that we have the idea that within us is a mental mechanism. Ryle says that he will be concerned with the dogma of the ghost in the machine. He has assembled a thousand instances to illustrate the influence and demonstrate the menace of the myth, the myths, of the hidden stream, the concealed mirrors, the private pictures, the invisible incidents, the flames of passion fanned by the winds of fancy.

I am not suggesting that Wittgenstein's treatment of the metaphysics of mind is not very different from Ryle's. He did not neglect what Ryle never adequately recognizes, the difference between the method of verification of statements about thoughts and feelings and the method of verification of statements about the movements of wheels, levers, limbs, electricity and the wind that bloweth where it listeth, visible to none though we hear the sound of it. . . .

The peculiarity of the soul is not that it is visible to none but that it is visible only to one. Unless we understand this we cannot understand why people have so persistently clung to the model for the logic of the soul which gives rise to scepticism not only about the mental acts of others but also about their aches and pains, feelings of quickened heart beats, sensations as of voices, daggers, snakes.

Ryle rightly stresses the fact that pictures in the mind are not like pictures in a gallery, that statements about what is in or on the mirror of the mind have a different logic from those about what is in the mirror on the mantlepiece and that sensation, or the 'observation of the presentational continuum', has a different logic from the observation of a film, and that knowledge that one is observing the presentational continuum or this or that in it, for example, knowledge that one is seeing as it were snakes, has a different logic from knowledge that one is observing a film or this or that in it. He rightly insists that if we talk of sensations as observations and then of these observations as reasons, everything falls into confusion if we expect the same of these reasons as we expect of the reasons garnered from the observation of the scenes of a show.

I don't think he explains clearly *how* things fall into confusion and how solipsism and subjectivism are born, but that is not my point. My point is that, though the sources of solipsism are also sources of doubt about the minds of others, there is also a source of this doubt other than those sources of it which also lead to solipsism. And this source lies in the facts covered by the words 'The soul is visible only to one'.

What are these facts? They are the facts which lead people to say that a person has a way of knowing how he feels which no one else has, has a right to say what he does about how he feels which no one else has ever had or ever will have.

But what are the facts which have led them to say this? And do these facts justify the Sceptic in saying 'No one but Bill really knows how Bill feels. No one but Bill has any real reason for saying anything about how Bill feels'?

First, what are the facts which have led people to say that a man can know himself in a way others can't? They are the same as those which have led people to say that other people have a peculiar difficulty in knowing how a man feels.

One might think that the special facility and the special difficulty lie in the fact that while Bill, if he is in pain, has every right to say that Bill is in pain, Arabella has not because she is in pain the right to say Bill is in pain. Bill, when he feels a choking in his throat has a reason for saying he is angry, while Arabella has not because she has a choking in her throat a reason for saying that Bill is angry.

But isn't this an accident? Suppose Arabella, having a pain or a choking feeling, says with confidence 'Bill is in pain' or 'Bill is angry' and suppose that she is again and again right. We should say 'Extraordinary thing, she knows from her own feelings that Bill is in pain or angry—as if she were Bill himself'. Were she never to learn of the success of her telepathy we should not say that her confidence was reasoned and hardly that it was reasonable, any more than we say this of the young antelope who instinctively knows that lions are dangerous. But we should say that she had every reason for her confidence once she had learned of the unvaried correctness of her claims, like the antelope that has been repeatedly clawed. Again, from a sensation of snakes in blue or in a monogram B, I, L, Arabella might know that Bill was having a sensation as of snakes or was in for the horrors.

Under such circumstances we would say that Arabella has an extraordinary knowledge of Bill's mind, that she can see into his mind, that while the rest of us have to guess from external signs at what is in his mind, she can know what is in his mind as well as he can himself and in the way he does himself. Like Bill, because she has a sensation as of snakes, she has a right to say 'Bill sees as it were snakes'; a choking feeling in her throat, angry words coming to her mind, give her the right to say 'Bill is angry' as they do Bill himself; other pictures, other feelings, give her the right to say 'Bill's in love'.

But the philosophical sceptic says 'Do they *as* they do Bill himself?' No doubt some people do, much more than others, know how another person is feeling by 'feeling themselves into' the other person, and the connection between this and telepathy deserves attention. But the question at the moment is 'Does the philosophical sceptic when he says that a person, A, never really knows how another, B, feels refer to the fact that it seldom or never happens that one person knows the mind of another as we have imagined Arabella to know Bill's mind, that is altogether from feeling as she feels Bill feels?'

And the answer is No. For in so far as a person is referring to this fact, whether or no he is right is to be settled by investigation and experiment, not by philosophical reflection. If someone says philosophically 'One can never really know the mind of another, only the way he lays back his ears and frowns' and we say to him 'That is upon the whole true but it is said that sometimes a person knows the mind of another without at all relying upon external signs and for good or ill this sort of thing may become more common', then the philosopher will reply 'I don't think you quite understand. I am not denying that there occur the most striking instances of telepathy, of a person knowing from his or her own feelings the mind of another. But such a person wouldn't be really and directly knowing the mind of another. Even one with such insight as Arabella's would not because she saw as it were snakes have that right to say that Bill sees as it were snakes which Bill has because he sees as it were snakes'.

It might now be thought that what the philosopher refers to is the fact that while what gives Bill the right to say that he sees as it were snakes or is in for the horrors is *his* sensation of as it were snakes, what gives a telepathic person the right to say that Bill sees as it were snakes or is in for the horrors is *her* sensation of as it were snakes. I am sure that some sceptics about the minds of others would seek to prove their point this way. But this proof proves that no one really knows there's a snake in the grass just as much as it proves that no one really knows that there's a snake in Bill's mind. And therefore let us now ignore this proof; for we are concerned with a Sceptic who finds in some feature of our knowledge of the mind of others a reason for saying that we never know the minds of others, which reason does not plunge him into Solipsism and make him say we can never know whether or no there's a snake in the grass.

We must now again try to say what that feature is. It is this: while one can from one's own sensation as of a snake have a right to say that there is a snake in the grass *in the way any*one can, one cannot from one's own sensation as of a snake have a right to say that there is a snake in someone else's mind *in the way he* can because of his sensation as of a snake. And the familiar but complicated facts to which this refers are the following: Suppose that a certain person, Arabella, upon seeing as it were snakes, says 'Bill sees as it were snakes'. Upon being asked, Bill says he sees no such thing. Arabella is impressed by this but doesn't regard it as proving her wrong; instead she asks the rest of us whether we can see snakes, and when we say 'Yes, we can', she says 'There you are, Bill sees them'. 'But', we say, 'look, he has blundered into them.' 'Ah,' she says, 'he saw them all right. I can see them, you can see them, the camera can see them. That settles it.' In this story we have indeed arranged that Arabella shall know as well as Bill what Bill sees and that the rest of us can do so too. And with this we have arranged too much. For if Arabella uses the words 'Bill sees as it were snakes' in the way described, then with them she makes a statement of a well-known sort, a statement whose familiar features now begin to show through its disguise, the statement 'Snakes, real, live, snakes'.

We must tell a different story if we are to tell one of how Arabella knows as well as Bill the snakes in his mind. We must tell a story in which it doesn't turn out that what she is talking about are real snakes. And we can easily do this. Suppose that Arabella, elated by many proofs of her telepathic powers, now on a new occasion says 'Bill sees snakes'. We ask Bill and he says he does not see snakes. We may, because of Arabella's past successes as a telepathist, suspect that Bill is lying and that later he will say he did see snakes. But if he does not and this happens again and again and Arabella pays no more attention to the evidence we offer against her statements than she would have done had she made them of herself, then we say 'When Arabella says "Bill sees snakes", although she uses Bill's name, what she says amounts to "I see snakes" or "I see snakes and have a feeling about Bill". She has lost her power of insight into Bill's mind and conceals this from us and from herself by using still the words "Bill sees snakes" while using them in such a way that all that counts in a dispute as to whether he does is just the same as what counts in a dispute as to whether she does.'

If we talk about Bill as Arabella does and ignore or treat lightly Bill's protests, then, of course, we may say, as she, perhaps, does, that she knows better than Bill how he feels or what he fancies.

'Exactly so,' says the Sceptic, 'when Arabella's statement becomes really one about herself she knows better than anyone else whether it is right, but while it is still about Bill she doesn't know it to be right like she would were it about herself, that is, like Bill does.'

It is true that the circumstances which make us say of a statement, S, made by A that A has a right to make it just like B has a right to make a statement about how things seem to him, are also the circumstances which make us say that S is not about how things seem to B but about how things seem to A. It thus appears that it is perfectly true that A cannot make a statement about how things seem to B and have a right to say it just like B has.

Now it is not unnatural to express this by saying that A never has that reason for a statement about how things seem to B which B has. And it is not unnatural to express this by saying that when one person makes a statement about the mind of another than he never has all the reason one could have for such a statement.

And this leads to 'No one ever knows anything about the mind of another'. For though we often speak of a person knowing something even when he hasn't all the reason he could have for what he says—for example, we say that a man knows that a stream is flowing because he sees the mill wheel turning—in these cases we speak of knowledge only because, though on the particular occasion in question the person of whom we speak hasn't all those reasons one could have for what he says, on other occasions he has been better placed and has had, not only the reasons he has on this occasion, but also those which one better placed would have—seen beneath the wheel the water. Further, it is only because one who sees a mill wheel turning has on other occasions had other reason to say that the water is high today that we allow that now seeing the mill wheel turning, he has a right to say 'The water's high today'.

Now we have said that no one who makes a statement about the mind of another *ever* has the right to make it which that other has, that therefore he never has had all the reason one could have for the statement he makes.

It is tempting to infer that no one ever knows anything about the mind of another and even that no one ever has any right to assert anything about the mind of another, since it is not true of him that on some other occasion he has been better placed and had then the reason, the ground, the data, the premiss, he now lacks.

But we must notice that if we express the facts referred to by the soul is visible only to one by saying that a person, A, never has all the right, all the reason, one could have for a statement about the mind of B, then we are using these words here very differently from the way we use them when we say of one who sees only a mill wheel that he hasn't on this occasion all the reason one could have for what he says about the mill stream. One who sees only the mill wheel could have all the reason one could have for what he says about the stream and could have all the reason he could have for what he says about the stream. One, A, who has all the reason one ever has for a statement about the mind of another, B, couldn't have all the reason one could have for what he says—not in the sense of 'has all the reason one could have' which requires that he should have the reason B has, in the sense which requires that, like B, he need not look to the face of another for confirmation of what he says. For such a requirement guarantees that what he says is not about another but about himself. When we say of one who sees only the mill wheel that he hasn't all the reason one could have for what he says about the stream one contrasts him with someone better placed. But if because of the facts about statements about the minds of others of which the Sceptic reminds us we say that no one ever has all the right one could have, all the reason one could have, for a statement about the mind of another, then we contrast ourselves with no one, in earth or heaven. If we use 'has all the right he could have' in the way the Sceptic does, then 'A has all the right he could have for a statement about the mind of B' becomes self-contradictory. And if we wed in the usual way 'has all the reason he could have' to 'has all the right he could have' then 'A has all the reason he could have for a statement about the mind of B' becomes self-contradictory. And if we then wed in the usual way 'knowledge' to 'sometimes has all the reason he could have', then 'A has knowledge of the mind of B' becomes self-contradictory and the paradox that no one ever knows the mind of another a necessary truth.

It is not unnatural to describe the facts about the usage of statements about people, particularly about what is in their minds as opposed to what is in their stomachs, by saying that the person the statement is about can have a right to make it which no one else has. It is tempting then to say that the person the statement is about can have reason to make it which no one else can have. It is tempting then to say that he can know the statement to be true in a way no one else can and then to say that no one else can really know it to be true. But we do not in fact in connection with statements about thoughts and feelings use the expression 'has all the right a person could have' like we use 'has just the sort of right some person could have, including the person it is about'; still less do we use 'has all the right *one* could have' in this way; still less do we use 'has all the right *he* could have' in this sense in which no one could have all the right he could have. Nor do we use 'has all the reason one could have' in this way. Still less do we use 'one knows how he feels' in this way, that is, in such a way that one could not, because one could not without having reason for saying it in that sense in which it is senseless to say that one could. That is, we do not use these expressions in such a way that 'No one has real right, real reason, to make, real knowledge of, statements about the minds of others' is a necessary truth. In other words, when in the course of life we say 'Arabella knows how Bill feels, Clarissa does not' we do not mean to deny that, were Arabella to make a statement about how Bill feels according to how *she* feels just as Bill does according to how *he* feels then she would be making a statement not about Bill but about herself. So if we express the fact that it is ridiculous to speak of her doing this by saying that Arabella must always lack reason Bill could have and therefore reason one could have, for statements about the mind of Bill, we must remember that this form of words means the facts it refers to and no more, and that these are not facts from which it follows that she never knows the thoughts and feelings in Bill's mind. When we claim that someone knows the thoughts and feelings of another we do not deny any of those facts about what ultimately gives a right to make statements about thoughts and feelings to which the Sceptic draws our attention. And therefore what the Sceptic says does not show that what we claim could not be true nor that what we claim is false.

This does not show that what we claim is true, it does not settle the question whether sometimes we do know what is in the mind of another. This is a question of fact and not of philosophy. But the fact is we do.

36

C. A. CAMPBELL

ON SELFHOOD AND GODHOOD (1953-5)

The Self's Relation to its Body

The problem that will engage us in the greater part of this lecture is the very old one of the relation of the self to its body. It is common ground that selves, as we know them in experience, in *some* sense have (or perhaps are) bodies as well as minds. The question is, in *what* sense? Over this question the history of modern philosophy records a great clash of opinion.

Among the many problems which the mind-body relationship raises, however, there is one that is peculiarly fundamental for the purpose of these lectures, which is to discover the general nature and structure of the human self. It is this. Is the union of body and mind within the self a merely *de facto* union, so that their separation is at least conceivable? Or is it an *essential* union, so that a self which is not body and mind in one, a self which is not an 'embodied mind', is not a thinkable conception at all? Since at this stage in our total argument it can (I hope) be taken for granted that mind at any rate belongs to the essence of the self, we may pose the question in the form, 'Does or does not body also belong to the essence of the self?'

It has sometimes been claimed that Common Sense opinion, for what it is worth, comes down heavily on the side of those who declare the self to be essentially body as well as mind. But I suggest that this claim is ill-founded. It is true that to the question 'Is a physical body essential to a self?' the plain man may be tempted to reply in the affirmative, under the impression that the 'self' that is being referred to in the question is the self in this earthly existence of ours. But the affirmative answer in that case comes near to being a mere tautology, since the very notion of 'earthly' existence carries with it an implication of 'bodily' existence. It is quite evident, on the other hand, that the plain man is by no means prepared to limit the possible existence of the self to earthly existence. He talks freely about the possibility of a 'future life', of the self's 'survival of bodily death'. This is manifestly incompatible with his conceiving the self as essentially body as well as mind; unless, indeed, he is assuming (which seems unlikely) that some new kind of astral body will accrue to the self after it has lost its fleshly body.

And here we may notice a very significant point. Almost everyone—even those to whom a negative answer seems virtually certain—takes it to be in principle intelligible to ask whether the self can survive the destruction of its *body*. But it is taken by no one to be in principle intelligible to ask whether the self can survive the destruction of its *mind*. This can only mean, I suggest, that for our ordinary opinions a mind is conceived as belonging to the essence of the self in a sense in which a body is not. For it is implied that what survives might be a self even if it had lost its body, but that it could not conceivably be a self if it were deprived of its mind.

It is necessary, of course, to keep clear the question of the essential nature of the self from the question of the essential nature of *man*. Undoubtedly we think of body as belonging to the essential nature of man; since by 'man' we mean a certain biological species into whose definition (as into the definition of all biological species) an organic body enters as a constituent. But when we are thinking of 'selves' we are not thinking of a biological species, and the assertion that every self has a body is not, like the assertion that every man has a body, an analytic proposition.

The views of the ordinary intelligent man on such matters as the self-body relationship are not, I think, wholly devoid of value. He has considerable experience of, and may well have reflected seriously upon, the entities which are under discussion; and he is entitled, accordingly, to have an attention paid to his views here which he could not sensibly claim if he were offering his opinions on, say, the constitution of the atom. But although he does here, in a real if limited sense, 'know what he is talking about', he may of course have arrived at a wrong conclusion: just as he often does, e.g. in the field of ethical controversy, where he also, in a real if limited sense, 'knows what he is talking about'. It may be that, if he reflected more deeply and more consistently upon what it means to be a self, he would come to take the view that it is, after all, unthinkable without a bodily component.

And that is, in fact, the conclusion to which certain modern philosophers of great distinction have come; notably the late Professor G. F. Stout, whose views, always entitled to respect, carry exceptional weight on those problems on the border-line between philosophy and psychology. According to Stout, 'What self-consciousness reveals is not mere mind or "mental phenomena", but mind and body together in the inseparable unity of the embodied self'.[1] We must consider this contention at some length, for it has implications of the most far-reaching kind.

The doctrine that there is no self but the 'embodied' self rests, if I

[1] *Mind and Matter*, p. 308.

understand it aright, upon two main premises. The first is that in every self-conscious experience, even in those cases where we should find it most natural to say that what we are aware of is a purely mental functioning of the self, it is possible by careful introspection to detect the presence of 'organic sensations' (under which general term we may here include 'kinaesthetic' sensations). The second premise is that in experiencing organic sensations we directly locate them in, or refer them to our 'body' —they are, as it were, experiences of the self *qua* body.

Given these two premises, the doctrine of the embodied self follows, I think, cogently enough. For it would then appear that we just do not have the kind of experience which would enable us to attach meaning to a self that is not body as well as mind. There is no such thing as an experience of a *merely* mental state. Descartes was wrong, on this view, in supposing that any greater certitude attaches to the existence of our mind than to the existence of our body. In point of fact (it is alleged) the 'I think' carries with it an assurance of our bodily existence every bit as indubitable as the assurance of our mental existence.

The doctrine fails to follow if *either* of these two premises is invalid. And it is my opinion that, in fact, *both* premises are invalid. I propose to concentrate, however, upon the second of them—i.e. the contention that in experiencing organic sensations we are directly aware of them as bodily —because the first, in the nature of the case, lends itself much less readily to demonstrative argument one way or the other.

Let us begin by getting quite clear about that which is common ground to our opponents and ourselves. I agree with the advocates of the embodied self that there are two radically distinct ways in which we apprehend our own bodies. The body is apprehended, first, in the same way as any other physical object is apprehended by the self, through external perception; chiefly, though not of course solely, visual and tactual perception. But it is apprehended, secondly, in a way in which *no* other physical object is apprehended, through what Stout calls 'internal perception'. The crucial feature of the latter mode of perception, as contrasted with the former, is that in it the body is not apprehended as *object* to, and in that sense *external* to, the subject, but as *itself subjective*, as actually *constituent of* the apprehending subject. Suppose, e.g. I want to examine some minute part of my own body, and require, because of its minuteness, a special focusing of my eyes in order to get the image as clearly defined as possible. In so focusing I have, or may have, certain organic and kinaesthetic sensations which I identify with movement of my eyes. I shall in that case be apparently apprehending the bodily process of focusing my eyes, as well as apprehending the bodily state upon which they are focused. But whereas in the *latter* my body is apprehended as *object* to my subject self, in the *former* my body is apprehended as participating in the process of apprehending, and as therefore a *constituent of* my *subject self.* This is one route along which we come to the recognition that our body and our mind are (in Descartes' phrase) 'so closely intermixed' with one another as to 'compose a certain unity'.

So much, then, is common ground. What I am going to deny is that this location of organic sensations in one's body is something that is intrinsic to the having of the organic sensations. If it is not, then, even should it be true that all our 'mental' experiences involve organic sensations, it will not follow that our 'mental' experiences necessarily involve a reference to our body.

It seems to me that this premise of the 'embodied mind' proponents is wrecked upon one simple fact; the fact, namely, that young children experience organic sensations long before they are aware that they *have* a body—long before, therefore, they could possibly 'locate' them in their bodies. No one denies that for adult experience organic sensations carry with them this reference to one's body, and normally to some specific part of it. Nor is it to be denied that this reference, as we now make it, shows no trace of conscious inference. What has got to be maintained, however, if the premise is to be adequate to the 'embodied mind' conclusion, is that the reference to the body is *intrinsic* to organic sensation in the sense that we cannot have an organic sensation *without* referring it to our body And this seems to be just false; unless, indeed, it be denied—as, so far as I am aware, no psychologist denies—that the child's discovery that it has a body is a gradual achievement, long ante-dated by its experience of organic sensations. If this latter proposition be admitted, then the reference of organic sensations to the body cannot be intrinsic. It must presumably be an *interpretation*, based ultimately on some sort of inference; though an interpretation, admittedly, which habit has rendered automatic at a comparatively early period in our lives.

Nor does it seem to me particularly difficult to understand how such an inference comes about. We need not attempt a detailed account of how the young child gradually comes to isolate a specifically bounded portion of what is at first the externally observed world as belonging to its *self* in that peculiarly intimate sense involved in the recognition of it as 'its body'. It is clearly an elaborate and complicated process, involving primarily, I think, the correlation of certain external perceptions of occurrences in this particular bit of the physical world with certain feeling and motor experiences. The infant discovers, e.g. that when *this* particular bit of the physical world, and *only* this particular bit of the physical world, undergoes certain observed physical effects from other bits of the physical world, *it* (the infant) experiences in *its self* certain feelings—predominantly of pleasure and pain. It discovers, further, that this particular bit of the physical world, in sharp contradistinction to all *other* bits of the physical world, is in a measure responsive to *its* (the infant's) wishes; moving, within limits, under *its* control. In such ways as these the young child comes to realize that there is a definitive portion of the physical world with which its self is uniquely and intimately identified, and to think of that portion of body as *its own* 'body'. And it is to be especially noted that these ways, and I think all other ways, through which the child can come to identify a particular portion of body with itself, presuppose in the child a consciousness of the self which is, up till then, *not* a 'bodily' self.

Now once one has become aware of one's body as *one's* own body, the interpretation of organic sensations as being located in one's body seems to me in principle easily intelligible. Intrinsically, organic sensations are simply sensations with a certain *quale*. What gives rise to the interpretation of them as feelings 'of one's body' is the fact that the *quale* of certain organic sensations has for the subject of them a recognizable likeness to the *quale* of certain feelings which are excited in him by *externally observed* affections of parts of his body, feelings which he has therefore quite naturally come to identify as 'body-feelings'. For example, an externally observed punch in the solar plexus excites, besides mere pain, a certain qualitative feeling; and it is natural (in view of its observed origin) to think of that feeling as a 'body-feeling'. Now when an organic sensation which has a similar *quale* occurs—as in the case of an ordinary stomach-ache—it would be odd if we did not interpret this qualitatively similar feeling as a 'body-feeling' likewise, even though we have not *here* observed that our body is affected in any way. Which specific feeling-*qualia* represent which specific parts of the body can of course be learned by experience alone. But in view of the great multitude of external affections of one's body that are open to one's inspection and are attended by feelings of distinctive *qualia*, it is not in the least surprising that a wide and fairly accurate knowledge of such correlations is built up in a comparatively short time.

We may note in passing that there are certain well-known facts concerning the apprehension of our bodies through organic sensation which seem much easier to account for on the view that the body-reference is an interpretation based on analogical inference than on the view that it is direct. I refer to the phenomena of mislocation. There are any number of instances in which our organic sensations are referred by us to the wrong part of our body—not to speak of the familiar case in which a person who has suffered amputation of a member refers his sensation to a part of his body that no longer exists. There is nothing in the least infallible about the body-reference of organic sensations. Now such mislocation presents no special difficulty if the reference to the body is an interpretation of a felt *quale* based on inference. Suppose that after the surgeon has removed my foot I have a sensation which I identify as an itch in my big toe. If the ultimate ground of that identification is my past experience of correlation between this kind of sensation and observed affections of my big toe, I may feel perhaps, some surprise, but no serious intellectual shock, to discover that in the present case my judgment is mistaken. For I am perfectly well aware of the fallibility of all inductive inferences from particular cases to general laws. If on the other hand the reference of the sensation to my body is supposed to rest, not on inference, but upon some sort of direct apprehension of my body, as is suggested by the doctrine that organic sensation carries with it an *intrinsic* reference to my body, then my apprehension of a bit of my body that isn't there seems to be distinctly more puzzling.

To summarize—my contention is that while we do of course directly experience organic sensations, we do *not* directly experience them as *bodily*. The apprehension of them as body-feelings is an interpretation based on analogical inference. But the practice of so interpreting them speedily becomes habitual, so that the body-reference speedily acquires what F. R. Tennant has called a 'psychical' as distinct from a 'psychological' immediacy[1]—very much as in the case of our adult apprehension of spatial perspectives, where we seem to ourselves to apprehend directly what genetic psychology shows to have become a possible object of our present apprehension only through past inferential processes.

If I am right in this account of the matter, it follows that it is untrue that we have no experience of ourselves save as embodied; untrue that the self has the same direct assurance of its bodily as of its mental existence; and untrue, therefore, that we must regard the body no less than the mind as belonging to the 'essence' of the self. It will *not* follow, of course, that the self does ever as a matter of fact engage in activities in which the body plays no part. This may or may not be the case for all that we have shown. All that we claim here is that self-consciousness does not, as has often been confidently alleged, reveal 'body' to be an intrinsic necessity of selfhood.

It seems to me, therefore, that Common Sense is correct in regarding it as at least an *intelligible* question whether the self can survive the destruction of its body. It may be the case that it is not possible to conceive of states of the conscious self that do not include organic sensations. But if what has been said above is sound, we can perfectly well conceive a self which has organic sensations but does *not* refer them to a body, or again a self which has such sensations and *mistakenly* refers them to a body.

And after all, is it quite certain that we cannot conceive a self which has

[1] *Philosophical Theology*, Vol. I, p. 46.

no organic sensations at all? That in all self-conscious experience organic sensations are detectable was, it will be remembered, the first premise of the argument for the embodied self. But there seems to be some evidence of pathological conditions in which there is total suspension of organic sensation and in which the patient *is* self-conscious.[1] For the patient, apparently, then regards his body as a 'foreign object', and he clearly could not do that if he had no consciousness of self. Hence, if the facts are as reported, it is not true that the only self of which we can be aware is an embodied self. But the facts of the situation are elusive, and perhaps insufficiently established to constitute a firm basis for theory.

The problem of the immortality of the soul is not one that will be systematically debated in these lectures. The significance for it, however, of the point I have just been trying to make is obvious. If it be granted that the self, as known to itself, is not in essential, but only in *de facto* union with its body, then the continued existence of the self after the destruction of its body falls at least into the category of abstract possibilities. Admittedly an 'abstract possibility' does not take us very far. But it leaves the way open for discussing on their merits the various ethical and religious considerations bearing upon the problem of immortality, which, so far as I can see, we should be obliged to rule out of court *a priori* if it were indeed the case that any self to *be* a self must be an *embodied* self.

Self-activity and its Modes

'Activity' and its synonyms—agency, initiation, striving and the like— along with its correlative 'passivity' and its synonyms, are expressions that we use every day of our lives. How, first of all, do we get the idea to which these expressions correspond?

On at least the general provenance of the idea we are fortunately able to count upon a very large measure of agreement. It is almost a philosophical common-place that we do not get the idea from observation of anything in the external world. There we may observe changes of various sorts, but nothing that could of itself even suggest the notion of an agency or activity that brings about the changes. We do come, indeed, rightly or wrongly, to ascribe agency to certain external things. But this ascription, it is agreed, is not based on direct observation of the things. What happens is that we read into these things a character derived from experience of our selves. It is from perception of the inner world of the mind, not from perception of the outer world of matter, that the notion of activity arises for us.

---

[1] Dr F. R. Tennant tells us, though unfortunately without quoting authority, that 'when, through disease, coenaesthesis is in abeyance, a patient will regard his body as a strange and inimical thing, not belonging to him' (*Philosophical Theology*, Vol. I, p. 71).

So much is more or less common ground. Immediately, however, we have to take notice of the fact than many philosophers declare that this idea is a 'fiction'.

Now this is, on the face of it, a somewhat puzzling pronouncement. Evidently it cannot be meant, in calling it a fiction, that there just *is* no idea for which the term 'activity' stands. That there is such an idea is a datum of the whole discussion. What then is meant when people tell us that the idea of activity is a fiction?

It seems to me that there are, in principle, only two things that can with any plausibility be meant in calling the idea of activity a fiction. I shall deal with each in turn.

The first, and less important, is as follows. It may be urged that when we analyse the idea of activity with care, observing what precisely it is that we actually experience in those experiences which we are accustomed to speak of as experiences of 'activity', the constituents that are then disclosed turn out to be of such a character that we are no longer prepared, on reflection, to label the experience one of 'activity' at all. Our analysis reveals, perhaps, a certain complex of ideas and images and body-feelings —of cephalic tension, muscular innervation, and the like. But when we reflect upon this product of our analysis we realize that, if, as seems to us to be the case, there is nothing *else* present in our experiences of 'activity' so-called, we have been deluded in supposing that such experiences have anything in them which entitles us to call them experiences of 'activity'.

I think that this is, at least sometimes, what is meant by calling 'activity' a fictitious idea. But if so, surely the critics' logic is curiously perverse? For how can he judge that the constituents disclosed by his analysis of the experience are such that he is not really entitled to call the experience an experience of 'activity', except in the light of some *different* idea of activity already in his possession which he takes to be a *genuine* idea of activity, an idea of 'activity proper'? Otherwise he is using words without meaning when he says that the experience of these constituents (in conjunction) is not really an experience of 'activity'. And he will be in no better case if, belatedly discovering this implication of his procedure, he should now try to show that his 'different' idea of activity, which he had been using as criterion, is *itself* analysable into constituents which we can see not to warrant us in regarding it as 'really' activity. For he will only be able to condemn this *second* idea of activity in the light of a *further* idea of it in his possession which he takes to be genuine. And so on *ad infinitum*. The attempt to explain away the idea of activity as fictitious always presupposes some other idea of activity which is assumed *not* to be fictitious. The idea of activity, it would seem, cannot be shown to be a fiction along these lines at any rate.

Nevertheless we can, I think, cordially agree with the critic of activity at least to this extent, that none of the sets of constituents into which analysts have so far resolved the experience of it does in fact give us any-thing that we feel satisfied, on reflection, to call 'activity'. Why should this be? Is it just that the analyses are bad analyses? In a sense, yes, and in another sense, no. They are (or may be) excellent analyses of what we *objectively* experience when we experience activity. But they are all of them very bad analyses, or rather they are not analyses at all, of what we *subjectively* experience when we experience activity. Herein, I suggest, lies the real root of the trouble. The critic cannot find anything deserving of the name of 'activity', because he seeks for it where it cannot possibly be found. For activity, if it is anything, is a function of the subject *qua* subject. It cannot be 'objectified'. To attempt to analyse the experience of activity from the standpoint of the external observer, ignoring the stand-point of the subject *qua* subject, the subject in its subjective functioning, is—if I may borrow Stout's apt adaptation of Berkeley's phrase—to blindfold ourselves and then complain that we cannot see. If the critic pursued what I suggest is the proper course of *re-enacting, re-living,* the subjective experience to which the name of 'activity' is commonly ascribed, he would, I think, find what he is looking for: and, by the same token, he would find that which he is himself unwittingly using as a criterion, when he condemns as inadequate to anything one can properly mean by 'activity' the constituents he has analysed out from the standpoint of the external observer.

There are not, perhaps, many errors that bring in their train so extensive a series of philosophical disasters as that of supposing that 'experience' is reducible without remainder to consciousness of something before the mind, something presented to the subject. The error is in part explicable, no doubt, by the fact that it is not his subjective activity, but the objects to which it is directed, that commonly interests the experiencing subject, and that thus lies in the focus of his attention. The subject's consciousness of his own subjective functioning is, as a rule, very faint and inexplicit by comparison with his consciousness of his object. Yet it is a little surprising that the strenuous efforts of notable thinkers like Main de Biran in the nineteenth century, and Alexander, Pringle-Pattison, and Bowman in our own day, who have laboured to show that awareness of the subjective side is in some degree present in all experience, should have borne so very little fruit. Even if we are a little hesitant about endorsing their thesis in its full universality, still there do seem to be at least some experiences, for example that of effortful willing, in which the direct awareness of sub-jective functioning can hardly be missed save by those who are determined on *a priori* grounds not to find it. When we have collated with meticulous care all the items 'objectively' apprehended in an experience of effortful volition, it remains perfectly clear that these items in their totality do not add up to what we in fact experience in making the volition. There is missing what one might call, in Bradley's phrase, 'the felt out-going of the self from the self', the inner experience of the subject in its subjective functioning. To this experience we can at least attach a meaning; for we can reproduce it whenever we set ourselves to re-live a volition, although in the nature of the case it cannot be presented to us as an 'object'. It is thus, and thus alone, that activity in general is to be known: and I ought perhaps to give warning that a good deal of what I have to say in this lecture will be incomprehensible to anyone unable to discover in his experience anything more than the presentation of 'objects' to a 'subject'.

I pass on to the second thing that might, I think, be meant by calling 'activity' a fictitious idea. Even if it be granted that there is an unique kind of experience which is called experience of 'activity', an experience not amenable to any internal analysis which might incline us, on reflection, to wish to withhold from it the name of 'activity' after all; still, it may be urged, there are certain *external* facts which ought to persuade us that we are mistaken in calling it an experience of 'activity'. For a man cannot in strictness be said to be experiencing activity if he is not *really* active. If there are facts which show that, in the given situation, he is not really active, then his 'experience' or 'feeling' of activity must be a delusion. And there *are* facts (it is alleged) which very strongly suggest that a man may feel active and yet not really be active. The man who wills to move his arm feels active in so doing, even if in fact (as might occur through sudden paralysis) his arm remains stationary. Is it not evident that here at any rate his feeling of activity is illusory? His willing does not in fact bring about anything. But if the feeling of activity is illusory here, it is possible in principle that it is illusory everywhere. Perhaps even in normal cases where the bodily movement does follow on the willing the man is deceived in supposing that it is his activity in willing that brings this about. And has not David Hume produced a formidable battery of arguments to show that he *is* so deceived, and that there is no intrinsic connection whatsoever discoverable between the act of willing on the one hand, and, on the other hand, the bodily movement which does in the ordinary run of things ensue?

Hume's arguments do not in fact seem to me so very formidable; but as it is far from evident where one is to find better ones to the same purport, and as they have certainly exerted a great deal of influence upon subsequent philosophy, we shall be obliged to consider them at some length. There is, however, one thing that can be said about them quite briefly, and at once. In so far as they are directed to showing that activity of *any* kind is unreal, they are invalid. The fact that the paralysed man's arm does not move when he wills it to move does not in the least entail that he was wrong in his conviction that he was really active. All that it entails is that he was wrong in his expectation that his 'spiritual' activity in willing *would produce a certain bodily result*—an entirely different thing. The failure to achieve the end to which his activity was directed has no tendency to disprove that he *was* active—spritually active—*in trying to achieve* that end. That the activity will achieve its objective (though only—if we may anticipate a little—in co-operation with other factors not under our control) is in the case of certain bodily movements our normal expectation. But even if this expectation were never fulfilled, the correct implication would be, not that our activity is unreal, but, at most, that it is futile.

In other words, on the question whether one is really active, in the sense of 'spiritually' active, the evidence of the subject's own direct experience is conclusive. Another man may *suggest* to me that I am not 'trying'—say, to move my palsied leg. But I, the subject, *know* whether or not I am trying. And if I do directly experience myself as trying, there can be no more point in asking whether I am *really* active, in the sense of 'spiritually' active, than there would be in asking whether, when I directly experience myself as in pain, I really am in pain.

It must be frankly admitted, however, that what we have gained so far (if we have gained it) against Hume is of only limited importance. Spiritual activity—'trying', 'willing'—is always directed to some objective. If there should be good reason to believe that this spiritual activity has no intrinsic connection with the coming to be of its objective, then even though its reality as such is established, it can hardly be regarded as a very valuable human possession. It is obviously something a great deal poorer that what we commonly mean when we think of ourselves as 'active' beings. We commonly think of our activity as an active *power*, capable of producing effects beyond itself. If in fact this supposed power is a myth, those who insist that 'activity' is a myth will not be so very far wrong after all.

And it is, of course, against activity in this sense of active power that Hume in his famous chapter in the *Enquiry*[1] chiefly directs his attack. His discussion is conducted within the ambit of his search for the original of our idea of necessary connection. The suggestion naturally arises that perhaps the original is to be found in our experience of volition, where we seem to be directly aware of ourselves as actively producing that which we will; e.g. the movement of a limb. Is there is fact this *intrinsic* connection between the act of willing and the movement of the limb, or are we deceived in supposing that we directly discern it? Hume takes the latter

[1] *An Enquiry concerning the Human Understanding*, Section VII (Selby-Bigge's edn.).

N

view. 'We learn the influence of our will from experience alone.'[1] We have no 'internal impression' of our will producing the bodily movement to which it is directed. And Hume thinks he can explain how the illusion that we do have such an impression comes about. What happens is that, after observing repeated instances of acts of will being followed by the bodily movements to which they are directed, 'the mind is caused by habit, upon appearance of the one event, to expect its usual attendant'. Hence 'a new sentiment or impression', a custom-bred expectation, that when we will a bodily movement that bodily movement will take place. This felt compulsion in our minds to pass from the one idea to the other is misinterpreted by us as a necessary connection between the things to which the ideas relate—here the act of will and the bodily movement. Hence on the occasion of willing a bodily movement, we mistakenly suppose that we directly apprehend our volition bringing the bodily movement about.

That (very summarily stated) is how Hume thinks that the illusion comes about. But why is he so sure in the first place that it *is* an illusion?— so sure that we do *not* in volition discern an active power in ourselves? Hume advances a number of arguments. But it will suffice for reasons that will appear shortly, if we concentrate upon one of them. I shall select the argument which is perhaps generally regarded as the most powerful.[2] The specific proposition which Hume is here out to disprove is that in willing a bodily movement we are directly conscious of our will actively producing the bodily movement. His disproof is based upon certain admitted physiological facts. It has been firmly established that when we will to move our leg (and succeed in doing so), the movement of the leg does not follow *immediately* upon our willing. What immediately follow are certain physiological changes. Intervening between our act of will and the bodily movement to which it is directed lies a whole series of cerebral, neural, and muscular movements. Now, in the act of volition we have, normally, no consciousness whatsoever of these intermediary processes. We cannot, therefore, as we commonly suppose, directly discern the power of our will to move our leg, since this power, if it exists at all, is exercised only through intermediaries of which we are totally unaware. The causal relation, if any, between the act of willing and the movement of the leg is a *mediate* relation; and as we are unaware of the mediation, we clearly cannot be directly discerning the mediate relation. The causal relation as we *suppose* it to be, on the other hand, just isn't there; so we must be deluded in thinking that we directly discern it.

This argument of Hume's has often been attacked; and along very

---

[1] *An Enquiry concerning the Human Understanding*, Section VII (Selby-Bigge's edn.) p. 66.
[2] Ibid., pp. 66–7.

divergent lines. It seems to me, however, that none of the criticisms go quite to the heart of the matter. For, in my opinion, Hume and his critics alike assume a basic premise which, while it looks self-evident, is in fact false. This premise is that when, as we say, we 'will to move our leg', the *immediate* object of our will is the moving of our leg.

What I want to suggest is that the expression 'willing to move our leg' is in fact elliptical. If we attend carefully to what is actually in our minds when we 'will to move our leg' we find, it seems to me, that the immediate object of our willing is not the movement of our leg but certain kinaesthetic and other sensations upon which, we have learned from experience, the movement of our leg normally supervenes. No doubt this will appear at first sight a highly paradoxical suggestion; but I am inclined to think that anyone who makes the required introspective experiment with care will discover that it is none the less true. The ulterior object of my willing is the movement of my leg, but the proximate or immediate object is the producing of the appropriate sensations.

Perhaps the easiest way to satisfy oneself that this is the case is as follows. Everyone would agree, I take it, that there are certain sensations associated with the moving of one's leg, and also that, normally, we can produce an image of them at will. But now let us suppose that we have somehow *forgotten* what these specific sensations are—how far this is factually possible is beside the point. Can we, in such a predicament, *will* to move our leg? It seems clear to me that we can *not*—we just don't know how to set about it. We may, of course, *wish* to move our leg. But this is no more the willing to move our leg than the wish to move, say, our appendix is the willing to move our appendix. 'Willing' is always directed to something we conceive to be in our power. If we have forgotten the appropriate sensations, the wish to move our leg must remain a *mere* wish, totally impotent, incapable of passing into a 'willing' of the movement.

It might be objected, indeed, that our inability to will the bodily movement in the absence from our mind of the appropriate sensations does not formally establish the *priority* of the sensations to the bodily movement as object of our willing. Abstractly considered, it might be the case that the bodily movement and the kinaesthetic sensations are inseparable for us, so that we cannot will the one without the other. But a very little reflection shows that this will not do. It seems perfectly possible to think of, and to will the occurrence of, the kinaesthetic sensations by themselves. In fact one can easily enough imagine a case in which, if a man wills the occurrence of the kinaesthetic sensations at all, he *must* will them by themselves. If a man has a foot amputated but still retains the sensations associated with its movement, then, provided he knows his foot is missing, he cannot *will* (though he may of course *visualize*, and *want*) the movement of it; yet he surely may (possibly from sheer curiosity about an interesting psycho-physiological phenomenon) will to produce the appropriate sensations.

I submit, then, that when we will a bodily movement the proximate or immediate object of our willing is the producing of the appropriate sensations, in the conviction—based ultimately on experience—that the ulterior object we have in view, the bodily movement, will thereby come to pass. But since it is only in abnormal situations, where the customary connection of sensations with bodily movement fails us, that the intermediary condition of the achievement of the latter tends to force itself upon our notice, we readily lose sight of this intermediary, and both speak and think as though the bodily movement were the immediate, and indeed the only, object of our willing.

Now when the basic premise of Hume and his critics is re-stated in this way, it puts a very different complexion on the whole matter.

We may readily admit, first of all, that between the movement of the limb and the appropriate sensations we discern no necessary connection. The connection is something that we learn solely from experience. We learn in infancy or in very early childhood, through what are at first instinctive or merely random movements of our body, that as a matter of brute fact certain sensations are usually associated with certain bodily movements. This purely factual information is the pre-condition of the stage at which we can *will* a body-movement. Hume is thus perfectly correct in so far as all that he wants to maintain is that we do not in willing directly discern a necessary connection between our willing and the bodily movement willed. The contingent relationship between the (intermediate) kinaesthetic sensations and the bodily movement rules that out conclusively.

But what Hume requires to show, in order to prove that we do not directly discern real agency, active power, in our willing of a bodily movement is, if our re-statement of the basic premise is sound, something very different. He has to show not just that there is no necessary connection discernible between our willing and the bodily movement, but that there is none discernible between our willing and the appropriate kinaesthetic sensations. He has to show that the *latter* connection is one that we *also* learn from experience. Hume, naturally enough, makes no attempt to show this. Nor, so far as I can see, is it possible to adapt any of the arguments he advances against the necessary connection of the volition with the bodily movement willed to support the different thesis that there is no necessary connection between the volition and the kinaesthetic sensations willed. Thus we could not, e.g. adapt the particular Humean argument with which we have been dealing, by pointing to unperceived intermediaries between the act of will and the occurrence of the kinaesthetic sensations willed. There is no psychological evidence of psychical intermediaries corresponding to the anatomical and physiological evidence of physical intermediaries that seems so decisive in the other case.

We have agreed that it is only by experience that we learn that specific kinaesthetic sensations are associated with specific movements of our body. The question at the moment is whether a plausible case can be made for the view that it is also from experience that we learn that there is a connection between willing these kinaesthetic sensations and their occurrence. I do not think that it can. Any such view presupposes that there is a stage at which we will these sensations without any expectations whatsoever that they will ensue. What, then, could possibly induce us to will them in the first instance? Do we, as it were, say to ourselves 'I should like to move my leg, and I have reason to believe from experience that if certain sensations occurred my leg would move. I should very much like, therefore, that these sensations would occur. What am I to do about it? Let's see whether "willing" them is any use—good gracious! Here they come.' This seems to me implausible in the last degree. I do not see how the 'experiment' of willing a thing with a view to its coming into being could ever suggest itself to a mind which did not already regard willing as an act which tends to bring about that to which it is directed. Or do we perhaps discover the connection by sheer *accident*—happening to will these sensations, and then finding, to our surprise, that the sensations occur? But surely 'happening to will', or 'accidental willing', contradicts the very notion of willing. Willing is not the sort of thing we can do by accident; for the very essence of it is its aim to bring about a definite something. The earlier question therefore recurs, 'What makes us suppose that the act of willing will tend to bring the thing about if we do not already believe in the connection?' The notion that we could conceivably be surprised to find that willing produces what it aims to produce—a notion implied in the suggestion that we learn the connection from experience— seems really absurd. When we will X, we will it because, and only because, we believe that willing X tends to bring X about.

There is one further point that must be dealt with, however, if our answer to Hume is to be reasonably complete.

It is clear enough that if the active power of which we are directly conscious in willing to move a limb relates to the production of certain sensations, not to the movement of the limb, the mere fact that the limb may not be there does not raise any difficulty about accepting the reality of this active power. But suppose, now, a case in which, though the limb may be there, there is total anaesthesia with respect to it. If we are still able to image the kinaesthetic sensations, we can seek by willing to produce them; but they will fail in fact to ensue. Now there can be no doubt that in such a case, just as much as in 'successful' volition, we would seem to ourselves in the volition to be exerting an active power. But is it not evident that here at any rate we should be deceived, since nothing whatever is produced—not even the kinaesthetic sensations? And if we are deceived in supposing that we directly discern an active power in these unsuccessful volitions, must that not reflect back a doubt upon our supposed discernment of an active power in successful volitions?

The difficulty is an instructive one; for the solution of it serves to bring out an important point about the nature of activity which we have not yet had occasion to notice.

It is undeniable, I think, that in the case cited we are deceived on one matter. We are deceived in our expectation that certain kinaesthetic sensations will ensue. But the fact that these sensations do not ensue does not imply that we are deceived in our belief that we are exerting an active power in relation to their production. For it is enough, in order for the volition to be an active *power*, that the exercise of it intrinsically *tends* to bring about the sensations willed; even though the co-operation of other factors, which may or may not be present, is required to ensure a successful issue. The lack of a successful issue is thus perfectly compatible with our being correct in supposing that we directly discern in the volition an active power in relation to the issue. The significance of these unsuccessful cases of volition is to bring home to us that the co-operation of other factors *is* required if the end to which the active power of volition is directed is to be in fact achieved. Our being deceived in our expectation, in the case cited, is due simply to our being unaware that certain of the necessary co-operating factors are absent. Strictly speaking, the active power of volition seems best described in the terms used by Stout—'a tendency towards its own fulfilment'.[1] But no more than this is needed to enable us to maintain, as against Hume, that there is an intrinsic or necessary connection between volition and its 'object'.

But if volitional activity is no more than a tendency to its own fulfilment, is it really justifiable (it may be asked) to speak of a 'necessary' connection between volition and its object? When we speak of a 'necessary' connection between A and B, we usually mean that, given A, we *must* have B. Yet in the case before us it is admitted that, given the volition, we may not get its object.

It seems to me, however, that the point at issue here is at bottom verbal. The expression 'necessary connection' is no doubt most commonly used in the sense just mentioned. But it is also used on occasion merely to mark the contrast with *de facto* connection. It is in that wider sense of the term

[1] *Mind and Matter*, p. 24.

that we are claiming that the connection of volition with its immediate object is necessary. And this is the sense specially relevant within the Humean context. For Hume, seeking to undermine the credentials of the idea of necessary connection, has been arguing that we do not really discern in volition an active power exerting influence upon the coming to be of the object; that the connection is purely *de facto*, not necessary. This is the position we were concerned to refute. Nevertheless I should agree that the common associations of the expression 'necessary connection' make it somewhat misleading in the present case, and that it would be preferable to speak of the connection between volition and its (immediate) object as 'intrinsic' only. There can, I think, be no objection on linguistic grounds to describing this connection as 'intrinsic', if it be true that the volition even 'tends' to bring about its object.

37

D. M. MACKAY

The Classical debate

Everyone admits that some human actions may sometimes be determined by the physical state of the brain. No one doubts that the convulsions of epilepsy or the tremors of Parkinson's disease have, as we say, a physical cause; and most of us would admit that many of our less spectacular actions could probably also be traced back continuously to the physical action of our central nervous system. At least it would not worry us if it were so.

It worries nobody, as long as the actions concerned are not of a kind to which we attach moral significance. But as soon as we come to acts of choice in which questions of responsibility might arise, we find ourselves in the middle of a well-trodden battlefield. On the one hand, there are those who believe that if my choice is to be morally valid, the physical activity of my brain must at some point 'change its course' in a way which is not determined by purely physical factors. They do not mean only that the change would be too complicated to work out in practice—though in fact it probably would be. They believe that even with unlimited powers of calculation, and complete physical information about every part of the brain, it would be impossible to know the change in advance, because, they would say, the change does not depend only on physical factors. If it did, then the choice would not be a morally valid one.

According to this view, then, the brain is to be thought of as an instrument often likened to a pianoforte, with at least a few controlling keys open to influences of a non-physical kind. I shall refer to it, for short, as the 'open-system' view.

Over against this view we have a strong body of opinion, particularly among scientists, which maintains that even when I make a moral choice, the physical changes in my brain depend entirely on the physical events that lead up to them. On this view there would be no discontinuity in the chain of physical cause and effect. A complete knowledge of the immediately preceding state, it is believed, would always be sufficient in principle to indicate beforehand which choice would be made. No openings are admitted for any non-physical influences to disrupt the expected pattern. We may refer to this as the 'closed-system' view of the brain.

On both sides there are plenty of varieties of opinion. Some who hold the 'open-system' view would maintain that each morally valid choice—each choice for which I may properly be held responsible—requires a miraculous physical change to take place in the brain. Others, such as Dr E. L. Mascall in his recent Bampton Lectures, hold that the well-known indeterminacy of small-scale physical events, first formulated by Heisenberg, could allow the brain to respond to non-physical influences without disobeying physical laws.

In the 'closed-system' camp there are even more varieties of opinion about the 'mental' aspect. Some robustly deny that there are any morally valid choices. They agree with the 'open-system' people that a choice could not be valid unless it falsified or went beyond what was indicated beforehand by the state of the brain—but they do not believe that human choices do so. Others, again, would argue that questions of moral validity are 'meaningless'; and so we could go on.

A Prior Question

But I am not concerned here to come down on one side or the other of this traditional fence. I simply do not know—nobody knows—to what extent the processes going on in the brain are physically determined. We are gradually accumulating evidence which suggests that brain tissue does behave according to the same physical principles as the rest of the body; and we now know also that no behaviour-pattern which we can observe and specify is beyond the capabilities of a physical mechanism. On the other hand, it is undeniable that some processes in the brain might occasionally be affected by physically indeterminate events of the sort which Heisenberg's Principle allows.

No, what I want to do is to undercut all discussion of this kind by raising a group of prior questions which might profitably have been asked before sides were picked on the traditional ground. The central question is: Could I be *excused* from responsibility if a choice of mine did *not* involve any physically indeterminate changes in my brain?

At first sight the answer may seem obvious. 'Surely,' you may say, 'a choice which is uniquely indicated beforehand by the state of the brain cannot be called a "free" choice? If you could in principle predict how I shall choose before I make my choice, surely my choosing has no moral validity?' In one sense this *is* obvious. We should all agree that if we could be given a description of our action beforehand, and had no power to help or hinder its fulfilment, then we should have to admit that this action was not 'free' but involuntary. A sneeze, for example, at a sufficiently advanced stage, might be judged involuntary by this criterion. So would a simple reflex action like a knee-jerk or an eye-blink.

But—and this is the point—even supposing that the necessary brain-processes were determined only by physical factors, are we sure that what we normally call a 'free choice' could be described to us in advance? I think not. In fact I believe that whether the brain-mechanism is physically determinate or not, the activity which we call 'making a free choice' is of a special kind which could never be described to us with certainty before-hand. Suppose we are asked to choose between porridge and prunes for breakfast. We think: 'Let's see: I've had prunes all last week; I'm sick of prunes; I'll have porridge.' We would normally claim now to have made a 'free choice'. But suppose that some super-physiologist has been observing our brain-workings all this time, and suppose he declares that our brain went through nothing but physically determinate actions. Does this mean that you could have told us in advance that we would certainly choose porridge? Of course not. However carefully calculated his proffered description of our choice, we would know—and he would know—that we still had power to alter it.

Logical Indeterminacy

No matter how much he tried to allow in advance for the effects of his telling us, we could still defy him to give us a guaranteed description of what our choice would be. This is our plain everyday experience of what most people mean by a free choice: a choice which nobody could (even in principle) describe to us with certainty in advance. My point is that this vital criterion of freedom of choice, which we shall see later can be extended and strengthened, would apply equally well whether the brain were physically determinate in its workings or not. In either case, the state of our brain after receiving his description would not (and could not) be the state on which he based his calculations. If he were to try to allow beforehand for the effects of his description upon us, he would be doomed to an endless regression—logically chasing his own tail in an effort to allow for the effects of allowing for the effects of allowing . . . indefinitely. This sort of logical situation was analysed some years ago by Professor Karl Popper, and the conclusion I think is watertight. Any proffered prediction of our choice would automatically be self-invalidating if its validity depended upon our not knowing it.

It is necessary, however, to carry the argument a stage further. One might get the impression from what I have said that our choice could not be proved free in this sense unless we succeeded in actually falsifying a would-be description of it. But this is not so. If we are supposing that our super-physiologist has access to all our brain-workings, then our freedom to nullify predictions of our choices can in principle be established simply by examining the structure—the blueprint, so to speak—of those brain-workings. It is not necessary actually to make the experiment of presenting us with an alleged 'prediction', in order to verify that the basis of the prediction would be invalidated. The point is simply that the brain is always altered by receiving information; so that the brain which has received a description of itself cannot possibly to be in the state described. Provided that the parts of your brain concerned with receiving and understanding the information are linked up with the mechanisms concerned with your taking the decision (and nobody doubts this even on the 'closed-system' view), then it is logically impossible to give us a guaranteed prediction of a decision we are still deliberating, whether based on advance observation or anything else. It is not that we are unable to ascertain the true description. It is that for us *there is no true description to ascertain*. For us the decision is something not to be ascertained but to be *made*. In fact, any description of our decision as already certain to be of a stated form would be for us *logically indeterminate* (neither true nor false) because it would be self-referring, rather like the statement: 'This sentence I am now uttering is false'.

It is this *logical* indeterminacy, of statements predicting our decisions, which has tended in the past to be confused with *physical* indeterminacy, as something which was thought to be necessary if a choice were to be morally valid. We all feel intuitively that there is something queerly 'undetermined' about the decisions we take—that there is something absurd and self-contradictory in trying to believe or even consider as 'true now' any advance description of them. I hope I have shown that this intuitive feeling is entirely justified—but on grounds which have nothing to do with physical indeterminacy in the matter of our brains. We appear to be so constructed that any would-be prediction of our voluntary actions becomes for us merely an invitation to choose how to act. This is not only theory, but also empirical fact. If anyone tries to predict to us that we are about to choose porridge rather than prunes, no matter how scientific the basis of this statement, we can easily verify that he is simply giving us a fresh opportunity to make up our minds. Whether we decide in the end to fall in with his would-be prediction or to contradict it, we know—and he knows—that it has lost any scientific finality by being offered to us.

'I Knew You'd Choose That'

But, we may well ask, what if our super-physiologist does *not* tell me of this prediction? What if he just keeps his mouth shut and watches how I choose, and then says, 'Aha, I knew you'd choose that'? We must admit straight away that we should feel rather upset if anybody could do that to us every time we made a choice; and I must agree that I do not believe it could ever be done consistently in practice. Consistent success would be possible only if our brains *were* physically determinate, and if the super-physiologist could know the whole of our brain-workings, together with all the influences which would act on them from the outside world. The first supposition is doubtful and the second is certainly impossible on practical grounds of sheer complexity; and between them I think these considerations are enough to account for—and justify—our feeling of incredulity.

But suppose for the sake of argument that it *were* so: that although we can defy anyone to tell us how we are going to choose, yet a successful prediction of our choice could in principle be made by someone who keeps quiet about it. What then? Could we excuse ourselves from responsibility for our choice on these grounds? I do not think so. If we had no power to falsify his prediction, we might indeed excuse ourselves. But in this case there is no doubt that we have the power. Our silent observer is only denying us the opportunity to demonstrate it. He knows, as well as we, that in fact his prediction is only conditionally 'certain': certain just so long as we do not know it; it is rather an odd sort of 'certainty' that you have to hide from someone in case it turns false! Clearly even when he kept quiet the sense in which his prediction was 'certain' would be a rather limited one.

As a matter of fact, the great majority of our choices day by day could be predicted with great success without even opening our heads, by anyone who knows us sufficiently well; but it never occurs to us to question our responsibility for them on these grounds. At least if it does I do not think it ought to, for all it means is that we make most of our choices 'in character'; not that we could not have chosen otherwise (if confronted with the allegedly 'certain' prediction), but simply that we were not inclined to—and might not have felt so inclined even if the prediction had been offered to us.

In short, the super-physiologist's knowledge, if our brain-workings accurately reflected what we were thinking, would do no more than enable him to make predictions as if he knew what was going on in our minds. In that case it would be surprising if he were not successful, so long as he kept quiet; but we could never appeal to his evidence in order to excuse ourselves from responsibility for such choices, for at most it could only offer *confirmatory*—and not contradictory—evidence of the mental processes in terms of which our moral responsibility would be judged.

To sum up thus far, I believe that brain-processes may well include some events which are physically indeterminate as well as many which are not. But I am suggesting that our responsibility for moral choices rests not on any physical indeterminateness of our brains, but on the logical indeterminateness to us of any advance description of our decisions. It is the unique organization of our brains which gives this peculiar status to our decisions—not anything physically queer about their workings. If there is any physical indeterminacy, its effects will be entirely different, as we shall now see.

Heisenberg's Principle

It is just over thirty years since Heisenberg enunciated his principle of indeterminacy, asserting that the motions of atomic particles can never be predicted exactly from the physical data available to us. Laplace's dream of a clockwork universe was gone; in fact, according to Eddington, just half of the data which you would require for a complete prediction of the universe are not available until after the change which we want to predict. But if this came as a blow to the classical physicists it was welcomed with open arms in other quarters. To those who felt that the dignity of man was being threatened by the creeping spread of physical causality to the very mechanism of the brain, Heisenberg's principle seemed a God-send. Here, surely, was the solution to the problem of free will. 'If atomic particles are physically indeterminate in their movements, then, since my brain is made up of atomic particles, its activity is not physically determined, and my will is free'—so the argument ran.

I have been arguing that the kind of 'freedom' which physical indeterminacy would give us is not required in order to establish moral responsibility: that on the contrary, whether my brain were *physically* determinate or not, my choosing is a unique and *logically* indeterminate activity for which I could not escape full moral responsibility. We must now take a look at the other side of the picture; for I have no wish to deny that physically indeterminate events may sometimes take place in our brains; and it is interesting I think to see what kind of effects these events could have upon the delicate and complex processes going on in our heads.

The first thing to keep in mind is that the degree of physical indeterminancy allowed by Heisenberg's principle becomes more and more negligible, the bigger and heavier the objects we are studying. Indeed it is only with the smallest objects of all—electrons, for example—that it is really serious. A nerve cell may be a tiny object by everyday standards, but it is roughly a million million million times heavier than an electron; so the chances of its suffering appreciably from Heisenberg indeterminacy are small indeed. Even if we suppose that the controlling part of a nerve cell weighs only one-millionth of the whole, we are still thinking on a scale a million million times larger than that of the electron.

There are about 10,000,000,000 nerve cells in each of our brains; so the chance that some *one* of these should be disturbed by a physically indeterminate event is correspondingly greater. But this brings me to the second point. The brain is not like a wireless set, in which a single valve-failure is enough to upset the whole performance. The nerve cells in the brain seem to be organized on a principle of team-work, often with hundreds or even thousands of cells working together on any one job—rather like the individual strands in a rope. Even if one of your brain-cells were put out of action altogether, the chances are that it would make no significant difference. Only a most unusual combination of circumstances could allow the behaviour of your brain as a whole to be affected.

One further point needs to be made before we discuss the implications of all this. The brain has to carry on its business in the face of all manner of physical disturbances besides those which Heisenberg has discussed. There are random vibrations due to the heat of the brain-tissue for example, random fluctuations in blood supply, and random disturbances reaching the brain from the outside world. These are not indeterminate influences in principle, but in practice they are far too complex to be predictable; and their effects are much larger than those due to Heisenberg indeterminacy, though similar in other respects. Yet, surprisingly enough, in spite of all those unpredictable influences, the brain still manages to work. It is in fact marvellously designed to be unaffected by disturbances of this kind. It follows that if the brain *is* at all affected appreciably by the physically indeterminate 'Heisenberg' variety of disturbance, this ought to be a much rarer occurrence than the other sorts, which are not absolutely unpredictable. Hardly any of the disturbances which do have significant effects are likely to be of the feeble Heisenberg type.

Effects of Physical Indeterminacy

What, then, could we expect to be the effects of such unpredictable disturbances? In the first place, they would undeniably introduce a certain kind of 'freedom' into the brain's activity. But I suggest that this would not be the freedom characteristic of rational moral choice and responsibility, which we have seen to be something different. It would rather be of the kind we should call 'spontaneity' or even sometimes 'mental aberration'—according to the part of the brain affected by it. In most cases it would mean the interruption of a normal train of thought by an 'unbidden idea', as we would say, or by some 'unaccountable lapse'. Perhaps this really does happen on occasions. If it does, it raises the interesting question whether the person concerned could properly be held responsible for what has happened. So far from enhancing his responsibility, such undetermined events would seem if anything to lessen it. We may be reminded of the fact that great composers and artists have often disclaimed responsibility for their inspirations, saying that they 'received them unbidden' though I am far from suggesting that originality is only a matter of random disturbances in the brain. I only want to emphasize that in most cases the unpredictability produced in this way would not seem to enhance responsibility for the resulting action.

But now, it may be asked, what if I were deliberating a choice between two possibilities which was so finely balanced that I could find no reason for favouring one rather than the other—like Buridan's donkey, which starved to death, we remember, because it could not choose between two equally tempting bundles of hay: might not the outcome ultimately be settled by one of these unpredictable disturbances? I think this might well be so, and that the resulting choice might be unpredictable even to a super-physiologist who knew all that was going on in your head—and kept his mouth shut. But what would be our own view of such a choice? Would we want to give it a higher moral status than one in which the right issue was clear to us and we decided unwaveringly on principle? I doubt it. Indeed I think that to such a finely balanced choice I would attach if anything a lower moral significance—rather as if I had settled it by mentally tossing a coin.

There are, however, more subtle effects which unpredictable disturbances could have. When we make a choice, we take into account all the pros and cons we can think of, weigh them up, and decide accordingly. All of this, I believe, requires physical activity in our brains, which in a sense indicates or represents what we are thinking. Suppose that I make some choice which seems to me straightforward on the evidence I have considered. I see no reason to doubt that the corresponding physical activity in my brain might be equally 'straight-forward'—in other words, it might well have nothing physically discontinuous or 'queer' about it. But now, how did I come to consider the evidence I did? Obviously, I could never think of all the factors that might conceivably be relevant. There is an unconscious selection of evidence, which I believe also involves a physical brain-process; and if this process were to suffer one of these unpredictable disturbances, I might well have no conscious awareness of it at all. It would mean simply that some factor, affecting my decision, would come to mind, or fail to come to mind, as a result. There would be nothing to indicate to me that anything unusual had occurred. And yet, in consequence of this disturbance, the different selection of factors might now lead me just as clearly to the opposite decision.

In either case, I think I would be fully responsible for my decision. But in the second case it would have an unexpectedness, from the observer's angle, which it would lack if there had been no disturbance of the process by which the evidence was brought to my conscious attention. To sum it up, I am suggesting that although physical indeterminacy in the brain is not necessary for moral responsibility, there is some evidence that occasional brain disturbances may be physically unpredictable, and that a small minority of these could be physically indeterminate. Such discontinuities, however, would show themselves more as a kind of originality or spontaneity, than in connection with a deliberate moral choice; and it is only if they affected the unconscious selection of evidence that they might be said to play any significant part in such a choice. Their general effect would be, if anything, to weaken rather than strengthen responsibility for any action which resulted.

From all this you will gather that I have not much hope of Heisenberg's indeterminacy as a gateway through which the mind acts on the brain. Perhaps it would be only fair to try to indicate how I think the two are related, for I believe most seriously in both the spiritual and the physical aspects of our human nature.

'Subject-language' and 'Object-language'

The trouble here, I believe, is that we have two different and entirely legitimate languages which we use about human activity, but that these tend to get mixed up in illegitimate ways. On the one hand there is what we might call 'subject-language,' to which belong words describing mental activity, like thinking, choosing, loving, hating, and so forth. All of these are words defined from the standpoint of myself as the actor in the situation. From the standpoint of an observer of the situation, on the other hand, we can define an entirely different vocabulary, making up what we might call 'object-language'. To this belong words like 'brain', 'nerve-cell', 'glandular secretion', 'electric current', and so forth.

The problem is to discover how descriptions in these two languages can be related. I think out some decision, let us say, and at the same time you observe certain physical events in my brain. Are we to say that my decision causes the physical events, or that the physical events cause my decision, or is there some different way of relating the two? My own view, for what it is worth, is that my decision neither causes nor is caused by its immediate physical concomitants. For we can only say 'A causes B' when A and B are two activities (two separate events or sets of events). And my suggestion is that the mental activity I describe in 'subject-language' and the corresponding brain-activity you describe in 'object-language' are not two activities but two aspects of one and the same activity, which in its full nature is richer—has more significance—than can be expressed in either language alone, or even in both together.

I am not suggesting that mental activity is 'nothing but' an aspect of brain-activity: this would be the attitude which I call 'nothing buttery', and one might equally fallaciously maintain the converse. The idea is rather that each is a descriptive projection, so to say, of a single complex unity which we can call simply my-activity. An observer can describe my-activity under the aspect of brain-activity; I myself can describe it under the aspect of mental-activity; but each, and any, descriptive projection, however exhaustive in its own language, can do only partial justice to the complex and mysterious reality that is my activity as a human being.

As a crude illustration of what I mean by 'doing partial justice', imagine the two descriptions which a physicist and a telegraphist might give of a morse signal, sent by flash-lamp from ship to shore. The physicist might exhaustively record the duration and intensity of every light flash, without ever mentioning the message. The telegraphist might exhaustively record every word of the message without ever mentioning the intensity of the light. Each description, exhaustive though it is, requires to be complemented by the other in order to do justice to the significance of what took place. The two, as we say, are logically complementary. We do not debunk the one by claiming that the other is exhaustive, nor do we justify the one by trying to find discontinuities or gaps in the other.

The Unity of Mental and Physical

It would follow from this view that there is no need—indeed it would be fallacious—to look for a causal mechanism by which mental and physical activity could act on one another. Their unity is already a closer (and a more mysterious) one than if they were pictured as separate activities in quasi-mechanical interaction, one of them visible and the other invisible. Yet it is a unity which safeguards rather than threatens my responsibility for my choosings; for it makes nonsense of any suggestion that my body, rather than I myself, could be held responsible for them. This would be simply to muddle up the two languages—rather like asserting, or denying, that when a man feels in love, his brain-cells feel in love. Such a statement is neither true nor false, but meaningless, because feeling in love is an activity of subjects, not of objects; and when a man is feeling in love, his brain-cells are presumably fully occupied doing something physically describable in 'object-language' as the correlate of his mental condition.

I would suggest indeed that the theory of mental activity as an 'extra' which interacts with the brain, is not only unnecessary, but also open to two serious objections. First, it hangs the whole of morality on an unsupported physical hypothesis—namely, that brain activity shows discontinuities, in the right places, which would require non-physical influences for their explanation. Even in the present primitive state of our knowledge this hypothesis now looks more improbable with every advance in the science of the brain. Secondly, the theory would deny my responsibility for any choices which did not entail physical discontinuity in my brain, even although I made them deliberately, and could defy anyone to describe them to me beforehand. This I believe to be flatly immoral, and a menace to a human being's right, as we say, to 'know his own mind'. If there were any question that someone's brain were disordered—prevented from functioning properly—then it might be legitimate to deny his responsibility. This could in principle be settled by examining the structure of his brain; but it would be fallacious to describe a brain as disordered merely because it failed to show any physical discontinuities, or because one could discern some of the pattern of physical cause-and-effect which was the necessary correlate of the man's mental activity. I believe that this represents a fallacy to be guarded against particularly in much of our contemporary thinking about the penal code. If I am right, there is need for a radical rethinking of the role of psychiatric evidence especially, in the assessing of moral, if not legal, responsibility.

But to follow this now would take us too far. I would just repeat once more the main contention of this paper—that to hang moral responsibility on theories of physical indeterminacy in the brain is both misguided and immoral: misguided, because my responsibility is adequately nailed to my door if my choice is *logically* indeterminate until I make it—which could be true even if my brain showed no physical discontinuities; immoral, because a reliance on physical indeterminacy would deny responsibility for choices (whether good or bad) for which I think a man has a right to claim responsibility. This is no less distressing because those who hold such views do so in the name of human dignity. But I believe that our true dignity lies in having the humility to see ourselves for what we are: and I am convinced that the Christian doctrine of man at any rate, in all its fullness, requires no licence for his brain to suffer non-physical disturbances. There is, as I have said, a profound mystery in our human nature; but it stands wholly apart from any scientific puzzles that we may find in the brain. It will be in our wisdom to avoid any temptation to confound the two.

38

P. F. STRAWSON

PERSONS (1958)

I

In the *Tractus* (5.631–5.641), Wittgenstein writes of the I which occurs in philosophy, of the philosophical idea of the subject of experiences. He says first: 'The thinking, presenting subject—there is no such thing.' Then, a little later: '*In an important sense* there is no subject.' This is followed by: 'The subject does not belong to the world, but is a limit of the world.' And a little later comes the following paragraph: 'There is (therefore) really a sense in which in philosophy we can talk non-psychologically of the I. The I occurs in philosophy through the fact that the "world is my world". The philosophical I is not the man, not the human body, or the human soul of which psychology treats, but the metaphysical subject, the limit—not a part of the world.' These remarks are impressive, but also puzzling and obscure. Reading them, one might think: Well, let's settle for the human body and the human soul of which psychology treats, and which is a part of the world, and let the metaphysical subject go. But again we might think: No, when I talk of myself, I do after all talk of that which has all of my experiences, I do talk of the subject of my experiences—and yet also of something that is part of the world in that it, but not the world, comes to an end when I die. The limit of *my* world is not—and is not so thought of by me—the limit of *the* world. It may be difficult to explain the idea of something which is both a subject of experiences and a part of the world. But it is an idea we have: it should be an idea we can explain.

Let us think of some of the ways in which we ordinarily talk of ourselves, of some of the things which we ordinarily ascribe to ourselves. They are of many kinds. We ascribe to ourselves *actions* and *intentions* (I am doing, did, shall do this); sensations (I am warm, in pain); *thoughts* and *feelings* (I think, wonder, want this, am angry, disappointed, contented); perceptions and memories (I see this, hear the other, remember that). We ascribe to ourselves, in two senses, position: *location* (I am on the sofa), and *attitude* (I am lying down). And of course we ascribe to ourselves not only temporary conditions, states, and situations, like most of these, but also enduring characteristics, including such physical characteristics as height, colouring, shape, and weight. That is to say, among the things we ascribe to ourselves are things of a kind that we also ascribe to material bodies to which we would not dream of ascribing others of the things that we ascribe to ourselves. Now there seems nothing needing explanation in the fact that the particular height, colouring, and physical position which we ascribe to ourselves, should be ascribed to *something or other*; for that which one calls one's body is, at least, a body, a material thing. It can be picked out from others, identified by ordinary physical criteria and described in ordinary physical terms. But it can seem, and has seemed, to need explanation that one's states of consciousness, one's thoughts and sensations, are ascribed *to the very same thing* as that to which these physical characteristics, this physical situation, is ascribed. Why are one's states of consciousness ascribed to the very same thing as certain corporeal characteristics, a certain physical situation, etc.? And once this question is raised, another question follows it, viz.: Why are one's states of consciousness ascribed to (said to be of, or to belong to) anything at all? It is not to be supposed that the answers to these questions will be independent of one another.

It might indeed be thought that an answer to both of them could be found in the unique role which each person's body plays in his experience, particularly his perceptual experience. All philosophers who have concerned themselves with these questions have referred to the uniqueness of this role. (Descartes was well enough aware of its uniqueness: 'I am *not* lodged in my body like a pilot in a vessel.') In what does this uniqueness consist? Well, of course, in a great many facts. We may summarize some of these facts by saying that for each person there is one body which occupies a certain *causal* position in relation to that person's perceptual experience, a causal position which is in various ways unique in relation to each of the various kinds of perceptual experience he has; and—as a further consequence—that this body is also unique for him as an *object* of the various kinds of perceptual experience which he has. This complex uniqueness of the single body appears, moreover, to be a contingent matter, or rather a cluster of contingent matters; we can, or it seems that we can, imagine many peculiar combinations of dependence and independence of aspects of our perceptual experience on the physical states or situation of more than one body.

Now I must say, straightaway, that this cluster of apparently contingent facts about the unique role which each person's body plays in his experience does not seem to me to provide, *by itself*, an answer to our questions. Of course these facts explain *something*. They provide a very good reason why a subject of experience should have a *very special regard* for just one body, why he should think of it as unique and perhaps more important than any other. They explain—if I may be permitted to put it so—why I feel *peculiarly attached* to what in fact I call my own body; they even might be said to explain why, granted that I am going to speak of one body as *mine*, I should speak of this body (the body that I do speak of as mine) as mine. But they do not explain why I should have the concept of *myself* at all, why I should ascribe my thoughts and experiences to *anything*. Moreover, even if we were satisfied with some other explanation of why one's states of consciousness (thoughts and feelings and perceptions) were ascribed to *something*, and satisfied that the facts in question sufficed to explain why the 'possession' of a particular body should be ascribed to the *same* thing (i.e., to explain why a particular body should be spoken of as standing in some special relation, called 'being possessed by' to that thing), yet the facts in question still do not explain why we should, as we do, ascribe certain corporeal characteristics not simply to the body standing in this special relation to the thing to which we ascribe thoughts, feelings, etc., but to the thing itself to which we ascribe those thoughts and feelings. (For we say 'I am bald', as well as 'I am cold', 'I am lying on the hearthrug' as well as 'I see a spider on the ceiling'.) Briefly, the facts in question explain why a subject of experience should pick out one body from others, give it, perhaps, an honoured name and ascribe to it whatever characteristics it has; but they do not explain why the experiences should be ascribed to any subject at all; and they do not explain why, if the experiences are to be ascribed to something, they *and* the corporeal characteristics which might be truly ascribed to the favoured body, should be ascribed to the same thing. So the facts in question do not explain the use that we make of the word 'I', or how any word has the use that word has. They do not explain the concept we have of a person.

II

A possible reaction at this point is to say that the concept we have is wrong or confused, or, if we make it a rule not to say that the concepts we have are confused, that the usage we have, whereby we ascribe, or seem to ascribe, such different kinds of predicate to one and the same thing, is confusing, that it conceals the true nature of the concepts involved, or something of this sort. This reaction can be found in two very important types of view about these matters. The first type of view is Cartesian, the view of Descartes and of others who think like him. Over the attribution of the second type of view I am more hesitant; but there is some evidence that it was held, at one period, by Wittgenstein and possibly also by Schlick. On both of these views, one of the questions we are considering, namely: 'Why do we ascribe our states of consciousness to the very same thing as certain corporeal characteristics, etc.?' is a question which does not arise; for on both views it is only a linguistic illusion that both kinds of predicate are properly ascribed to one and the same thing, that there is a common owner, or subject of both types of predicate. And on the second of these views, the other question we are considering, namely 'Why do we ascribe our states of consciousness to anything at all?' is also a question which does not arise; for on this view, it is only a linguistic illusion that one ascribes one's states of consciousness at all, that there is any proper subject of these apparent ascriptions, that states of consciousness belong to, or are states of anything.

That Descartes held the first of these views is well enough known. When we speak of a person, we are really referring to one or both of two distinct substances (two substances of different types), each of which has its own appropriate type of states and properties; and none of the properties or states of either can be a property or state of the other. States of consciousness belong to one of these substances, and not to the other. I shall say no more about the Cartesian view at the moment—what I have to say about it will emerge later on—except to note again that while it escapes one of our questions, it does not escape, but indeed invites, the other: 'Why are one's states of consciousness *ascribed* at all, to *any* subject?'

The second of these views I shall call the 'no-ownership' or 'no-subject' doctrine of the self. Whether or not anyone has explicitly held this view, it is worth reconstructing, or constructing, in outline.[1] For the errors into which it falls are instructive. The 'no-ownership' theorist may be pre-

---

[1] The evidence that Wittgenstein at one time held such a view is to be found in the third of Moore's articles in *Mind* on 'Wittgenstein's Lectures in 1930–3' (*Mind*, 1955, especially pp. 13–14). He is reported to have held that the use of 'I' was utterly different in the case of 'I have a tooth-ache' or 'I see a red patch' from its use in the case of 'I've got a bad tooth' or 'I've got a matchbox'. He thought that there were two uses of 'I' and that in one of them 'I' was replaceable by 'this body'. So far the view might be Cartesian, but he also said that in the other use (the use exemplified by 'I have a tooth-ache' as opposed to 'I have a bad tooth'), 'I' *does not denote a possessor*, and that no ego is involved in thinking or in having a tooth-ache; and referred with apparent approval to Lichtenberg's dictum that, instead of saying 'I think', we (or Descartes!) ought to say 'There is a thought' (i.e., 'Es denkt').

The attribution of such a view to Schlick would have to rest on his article 'Meaning and Verification,' Pt. V (*Readings in Philosophical Analysis*, H. Feigl and W. Sellars, eds.). Like Wittgenstein, Schlick quotes Lichtenberg, and then goes on to say: 'Thus we see that unless we choose to call our body the owner or bearer of the data (the data of immediate experience) —which seems to be a rather misleading expression—we have to say that the data have no owner or bearer.' The full import of Schlick's article is, however, obscure to me, and it is quite likely that a false impression is given by the quotation of a single sentence. I shall say merely that I have drawn on Schlick's article in constructing the case of my hypothetical 'no-subject' theorist; but shall not claim to be representing his views.

Lichtenberg's anti-Cartesian dictum is, as the subsequent argument will show, one that I endorse, if properly used. But it seems to have been repeated, without being understood, by many of Descartes' critics.

The evidence that Wittgenstein and Schlick ever held a 'no-subject' view seems indecisive, since it is possible that the relevant remarks are intended as criticisms of a Cartesian view rather than as expositions of the true view.

sumed to start his explanations with facts of the sort which illustrate the unique causal position of a certain material body in a person's experience. The theorist maintains that the uniqueness of this body is sufficient to give rise to the idea that one's experiences can be ascribed to some particular individual thing, can be said to be possessed by, or owned by, that thing. This idea, he thinks, though infelicitously and misleadingly expressed in terms of ownership, would have some validity, would make some sort of sense, so long as we thought of this individual thing, the possessor of the experiences, as the body itself. So long as we thought in this way, then to ascribe a particular state of consciousness to this body, this individual thing, would at least be to say something contingent, something that might be, or might have been, false. It might have been a misascription; for the experience in question might be, or might have been, causally dependent on the state of some other body; in the present admissible, though infelicitous, sense of 'belong', it might have belonged to some other individual thing. But now, the theorist suggests, one becomes confused: one slides from this admissible, though infelicitous, sense in which one's experiences may be said to belong to, or be possessed by, some particular thing, to a wholly inadmissible and empty sense of these expressions, and in this new and inadmissible sense, the particular thing which is supposed to possess the experiences is not thought of as a body, but as something else, say an ego.

Suppose we call the first type of possession, which is really a certain kind of causal dependence, 'having$_1$'; and the second type of possession, 'having$_2$'; and call the individual of the first type 'B' and the supposed individual of the second type 'E'. Then the difference is that while it is genuinely a contingent matter that *all my experiences are had$_1$ by B*, it appears as a necessary truth that *all my experiences are had$_2$ by E*. But the belief in E and in having$_2$ by E is an illusion. Only those things whose ownership is logically transferable can be owned at all. So experiences are not owned by anything except in the dubious sense of being causally dependent on the state of a particular body. This is at least a genuine relationship to a thing, in that they might have stood in it to another thing. Since the whole function of E was to own experiences in a logically non-transferable sense of 'own', and since experiences are not owned by anything in this sense, for there is no such sense of 'own', E must be eliminated from the picture altogether. It only came in because of a confusion.

I think it must be clear that this account of the matter, though it contains *some* of the facts, is not coherent. It is not coherent, in that one who holds it is forced to make use of that sense of possession of which he denies the existence, in presenting his case for the denial. When he tries to state the contingent fact, which he thinks gives rise to the illusion of the 'ego', he has to state it in some such form as 'All *my* experiences are had$_1$ by (uniquely dependent on the state of) body B.' For any attempt to eliminate the 'my', or some other expression with a similar possessive force, would yield something that was not a contingent fact at all. The proposition that *all* experiences are causally dependent on the state of a single body B, for example, is just false. The theorist means to speak of all the experiences *had by a certain person* being contingently so dependent. And the theorist cannot consistently argue that 'all the experiences of person P' *means the same thing* as 'all experiences contingently dependent on a certain body B'; for then his proposition would not be contingent, as his theory requires, but analytic. He must mean to be speaking of some classs of experiences of the members of which it is in fact contingently true that they are all dependent on body B. And the defining characteristic of this class is in fact that they are '*my* experiences' or 'the experiences *of* some person', where the sense of 'possession' is the one he calls into question.

This internal incoherence is a serious matter when it is a question of denying what prima facie is the case; that is, that one does genuinely ascribe one's states of consciousness to something, viz., oneself, and that this kind of ascription is precisely such as the theorist finds unsatisfactory, i.e., is such that it does not seem to make sense to suggest, for example, that the identical pain which was in fact one's own might have been another's. We do not have to seek far in order to understand the place of this logically non-transferable kind of ownership in our general scheme of thought. For if we think of the requirements of identifying reference, in speech, to *particular* states of consciousness, or private experiences, we see that such particulars cannot be thus identifyingly referred to except as the states or experiences *of* some identified *person*. States, or experiences, one might say, *owe* their identity as particulars to the identity of the person whose states or experiences they are. And from this it follows immediately that if they can be identified as particular states or experiences at all, they must be possessed or ascribable in just that way which the no-ownership theorist ridicules, i.e. in such a way that it is logically impossible that a particular state or experience in fact possessed by someone should have been possessed by anyone else. The requirements of identity rule out logical transferability of ownership. So the theorist could maintain his position only by denying that we could ever refer to particular states or experiences at all. And *this* position is ridiculous.

We may notice, even now, a possible connection between the no-ownership doctrine and the Cartesian position. The latter is, straightforwardly enough, a dualism of two subjects (two types of subject). The former could, a little paradoxically, be called a dualism too; a dualism of one subject (the body) and one non-subject. We might surmise that the second dualism, paradoxically so called, arises out of the first dualism, nonparadoxically so called; in other words, that if we try to think of that to which one's states of consciousness are ascribed as something utterly different from that to which certain corporeal characteristics are ascribed, then indeed it becomes difficult to see why states of consciousness should be ascribed, thought of as belonging to, anything at all. And when we think of this possibility, we may also think of another: viz., that both the Cartesian and the no-ownership theorist are profoundly wrong in holding, as each must, that there are two uses of 'I' in one of which it denotes something which it does not denote in the other.

III

The no-ownership theorist fails to take account of all the facts. He takes account of some of them. He implies, correctly, that the unique position or role of a single body in one's experience is not a sufficient explanation of the fact that one's experiences, or states of consciousness, are ascribed to something which *has* them, with that peculiar non-transferable kind of possession which is here in question. It may be a necessary part of the explanation, but it is not, by itself, a sufficient explanation. The theorist, as we have seen, goes on to suggest that it is perhaps a sufficient explanation of something else: viz., of our confusedly and mistakenly *thinking* that states of consciousness are to be ascribed to something in this special way. And this suggestion, as we have seen, is incoherent: for it involves the denial that someone's states of consciousness are anyone's. We avoid the incoherence of this denial, while agreeing that the special role of a single body in someone's experience does not suffice to explain why that experience should be ascribed to anybody. The fact that there is this special role does not, by itself, give a sufficient reason why what we think of as a subject of experience should have any use for the conception of himself as such a subject.

When I say that the no-ownership theorist's account fails through not reckoning with all the facts, I have in mind a very simple but, in this question, a very central, thought: viz., that it is a necessary condition of one's ascribing states of consciousness, experiences, to oneself, in the way one does, that one should also ascribe them (or be prepared to ascribe them) to others who are not oneself.[1] This means not less than it says. It

---

[1] I can imagine an objection to the unqualified form of this statement, an objection which might be put as follows. Surely the idea of a uniquely applicable predicate (a predicate which *in fact* belongs to only one individual) is not absurd. And, if it is not, then surely the most that can be claimed is that a necessary condition of one's ascribing predicates of a certain class to one individual (oneself) is that one should be prepared, or ready, on appropriate occasions, to

means, for example, that the ascribing phrases should be used in just the same sense when the subject is another, as when the subject is one self. Of course the thought that this is so gives no trouble to the non-philosopher: the thought, for example, that 'in pain' means the same whether one says 'I am in pain' or 'He is in pain'. The dictionaries do not give two sets of meanings for every expression which describes a state of consciousness: a first-person meaning and a second- and third-person meaning. But to the philosopher this thought has given trouble; indeed it has. How could the sense be the same when the method of verification was so different in the two cases—or, rather, when there was a method of verification in the one case (the case of others) and not, properly speaking, in the other case (the case of oneself)? Or, again, how can it be right to talk of *ascribing* in the case of oneself? For surely there can be a question of ascribing only if there is or could be a question of identifying that to which the ascription is made? And though there may be a question of identifying the one who is in pain when that one is another, how can there be such a question when that one is oneself? But this last query answers itself as soon as we remember that we speak primarily to others, for the information of others. In one sense, indeed, there is no question of my having to *tell who it is* who is in pain, when I am. In another sense I may have to *tell who it is*, i.e., to let others know who it is.

What I have just said explains, perhaps, how one may properly be said to ascribe states of consciousness to oneself, given that one ascribes them to others. But how is it that one can ascribe them to others? Well, one thing is certain: that *if* the things one ascribes states of consciousness to, in ascribing them to others, are thought of as a set of Cartesian egoes to which *only* private experiences can, in correct logical grammar, be ascribed, *then* this question is unanswerable and this problem insoluble. If, in identifying the things to which states of consciousness are to be ascribed, private experiences are to be all one has to go on, then, just for the very

ascribe them to other individuals, and hence that one should have a conception of what those appropriate occasions for ascribing them would be; but not, necessarily, that one should actually do so on any occasion.

The shortest way with the objection is to admit it, or at least to refrain from disputing it; for the lesser claim is all that the argument strictly requires, though it is slightly simpler to conduct it on the basis of the larger claim. But it is well to point out further that we are not speaking of a single predicate, or merely of some group or other of predicates, but of the whole of an enormous class of predicates such that the applicability of those predicates or their negations determines a major logical type or category of individuals. To insist, at this level, on the distinction between the lesser and the larger claims is to carry the distinction over from a level at which it is clearly correct to a level at which it may well appear idle or, possibly, senseless.

The main point here is a purely logical one: the idea of a predicate is correlative with that of a range of distinguishable individuals of which the predicate can be significantly, though not necessarily truly, affirmed.

same reason as that for which there is, from one's own point of view, no question of telling that a private experience is one's own, there is also no question of telling that a private experience is another's. All private experiences, all states of consciousness, will be mine, i.e., no one's. To put it briefly: one can ascribe states of consciousness to oneself only if one can ascribe them to others; one can ascribe them to others only if one can identify other subjects of experience; and one cannot identify others if one can identify them *only* as subjects of experience, possessors of states of consciousness.

It might be objected that this way with Cartesianism is too short. After all, there is no difficulty about distinguishing bodies from one another, no difficulty about identifying bodies. And does not this give us an indirect way of identifying subjects of experience, while preserving the Cartesian mode? Can we not identify such a subject as, for example, 'the subject that stands to that body in the same special relation as I stand to this one'; or, in other words, 'the subject of those experiences which stand in the same unique causal relation to body N as *my* experiences stand to body M'? But this suggestion is useless. It requires me to have noted that *my* experiences stand in a special relation to body M, when it is just the right to speak of *my* experiences at all that is in question. (It requires me to have noted that *my* experiences stand in a special relation to body M; but it requires me to have noted this as a condition of being able to identify other subjects of experience, i.e., as a condition of having the idea of myself as a subject of experience, i.e., as a condition of thinking of any experience as *mine*.) So long as we persist in talking, in the mode of this explanation, of experiences on the one hand, and bodies on the other, the most I may be allowed to have noted is that experiences, *all* experiences, stand in a special relation to body M, that body M is unique in just this way, that this is what makes body M unique among bodies. (This 'most' is, perhaps, too much—because of the presence of the word 'experiences'.) The proferred explanation runs: 'Another subject of experience is distinguished and identified as the subject of those experiences which stand in the same unique causal relationship to body N as my experiences stand to body M.' And the objection is: 'But what is the word "my" doing in this explanation? (It could not get on without it.)'

What we have to acknowledge, in order to begin to free ourselves from these difficulties, is the *primitiveness* of the concept of a person. What I mean by the concept of a person is the concept of a type of entity such that *both* predicates ascribing states of consciousness *and* predicates ascribing corporeal characteristics, a physical situation, etc. are equally applicable to a single individual of that single type. And what I mean by saying that this concept is primitive can be put in a number of ways. One way is to return to those two questions I asked earlier: viz., (1) why are states of consciousness ascribed to anything at all? and (2) why are they ascribed to the very same thing as certain corporeal characteristics, a certain physical situation, etc.? I remarked at the beginning that it was not to be supposed that the answers to these questions were independent of each other. And now I shall say that they are connected in this way: that a necessary condition of states of consciousness being ascribed at all is that they should be ascribed to the *very same things* as certain corporeal characteristics, a certain physical situation, etc. That is to say, states of consciousness could not be ascribed at all, *unless* they were ascribed to persons, in the sense I have claimed for this word. We are tempted to think of a person as a sort of compound of two kinds of subject—a subject of experiences (a pure consciousness, an ego), on the one hand, and a subject of corporeal attributes on the other.

Many questions arise when we think in this way. But, in particular, when we ask ourselves how we come to frame, to get a use for, the concept of this compound of two subjects, the picture—if we are honest and careful—is apt to change from the picture of two subjects to the picture of one subject and one non-subject. For it becomes impossible to see how we could come by the idea of different, distinguishable, identifiable subjects of experiences—different consciousnesses—*if this idea is thought of as logically primitive*, as a logical ingredient in the compound idea of a person, the latter being composed of two subjects. For there could never be any question of assigning an experience, as such, to any subject other than oneself; and therefore never any question of assigning it to oneself either, never any question of ascribing it to a subject at all. So the concept of the pure individual consciousness—the pure ego—is a concept that cannot exist; or, at least, cannot exist as a primary concept in terms of which the concept of a person can be explained or analysed. It can only exist, if at all, as a secondary, non-primitive concept, which itself is to be explained, analysed, in terms of the concept of a person. It was the entity corresponding to this illusory primary concept of the pure consciousness, the ego-substance, for which Hume was seeking, or ironically pretending to seek, when he looked into himself, and complained that he could never discover himself without a perception and could never discover anything but the perception. More seriously—and this time there was no irony, but a confusion, a Nemesis of confusion for Hume—it was this entity of which Hume vainly sought for the principle of unity, confessing himself perplexed and defeated; sought vainly because there is no principle of unity where there is no principle of differentiation. It was this, too, to which Kant, more perspicacious here than Hume, accorded a purely formal ('analytic') unity: the unity of the 'I think' that accompanies all my perceptions and therefore might just as well accompany none. And finally it is this, perhaps, of which Wittgenstein spoke when he said of the subject, first, that there is no such thing, and second, that it is not a part of the world, but its limit.

So, then, the word 'I' never refers to this, the pure subject. But this does not mean, as the no-ownership theorist must think and as Wittgenstein, at least at one period, seemed to think, that 'I' in some cases does not refer at all. It refers, because I am a person among others. And the predicates which would, *per impossible*, belong to the pure subject if it could be referred to, belong properly to the person to which 'I' does refer.

The concept of a person is logically prior to that of an individual consciousness. The concept of a person is not to be analysed as that of an animated body or of an embodied anima. This is not to say that the concept of a pure individual consciousness might not have a logically secondary existence, if one thinks, or finds, it desirable. We speak of a dead person—a body—and in the same secondary way we might at least think of a disembodied person, retaining the logical benefit of individuality from having been a person.[1]

IV

It is important to realize the full extent of the acknowledgment one is making in acknowledging the logical primitiveness of the concept of a person. Let me rehearse briefly the stages of the argument. There would be no question of ascribing one's own states of consciousness, or experiences, to anything, unless one also ascribed states of consciousness, or experiences, to other individual entities of the same logical type as that thing to which one ascribes one's own states of consciousness. The condition of reckoning oneself as a subject of such predicates is that one should also reckon others as subjects of such predicates. The condition, in turn, of this being possible, is that one should be able to distinguish from one another (pick out, identify) different subjects of such predicates, i.e., different individuals of the type concerned. And the condition, in turn, of this being possible is that the individuals concerned, including oneself, should be of a certain unique type: of a type, namely, such that to each individual of that type there *must* be ascribed, or ascribable, *both* states of consciousness *and* corporeal characteristics. But this characterization of the type is still very opaque and does not at all clearly bring out what is involved. To bring this out, I must make a rough division, into two, of the kinds of predicates properly applied to individuals of this type. The

---

[1] A little further thought will show how limited this concession is. But I shall not discuss the question now.

first kind of predicate consists of those which are also properly applied to material bodies to which we would not dream of applying predicates ascribing states of consciousness. I will call this first kind M-predicates: and they include things like 'weighs 10 stone', 'is in the drawing room', and so on. The second kind consists of all the other predicates we apply to persons. These I shall call P-predicates. And P-predicates, of course, will be very various. They will include things like 'is smiling', 'is going for a walk', as well as things like 'is in pain', 'is thinking hard', 'believes in God', and so on.

So far I have said that the concept of a person is to be understood as the concept of a type of entity such that *both* predicates ascribing states of consciousness *and* predicates ascribing corporeal characteristics, a physical situation, etc., are equally applicable to an individual entity of that type. And all I have said about the meaning of saying that this concept is primitive is that it is not to be analysed in a certain way or ways. We are not, for example, to think of it as a secondary kind of entity in relation to two primary kinds, viz., a particular consciousness and a particular human body. I implied also that the Cartesian error is just a special case of a more general error, present in a different form in theories of the no-ownership type, of thinking of the designations, or apparent designations, of persons as not denoting precisely the same thing, or entity, for all kinds of predicate ascribed to the entity designated. That is, if we are to avoid the general form of this error we must *not* think of 'I' or 'Smith' as suffering from type-ambiguity. (If we want to locate type-ambiguity somewhere, we would do better to locate it in certain predicates like 'is in the drawing room', 'was hit by a stone', etc., and say they mean one thing when applied to material objects and another when applied to persons.)

This is all I have so far said or implied about the meaning of saying that the concept of a person is primitive. What has to be brought out further is what the implications of saying this are as regards the logical character of those predicates in which we ascribe states of consciousness. And for this purpose we may well consider P-predicates in general. For though not all P-predicates are what we should call 'predicates ascribing states of consciousness' (for example, 'going for a walk' is not), they may be said to have this in common, that they imply the possession of consciousness on the part of that to which they are ascribed.

What then are the consequences of this view as regards the character of P-predicates? I think they are these. Clearly there is no sense in talking of identifiable individuals of a special type, a type, namely, such that they possess both M-predicates and P-predicates, unless there is in principle some way of telling, with regard to any individual of that type, and any P-predicate, whether that individual possesses that P-predicate. And, in the case of at least some P-predicates, the ways of telling must constitute in some sense logically adequate kinds of criteria for the ascription of the P-predicate. For suppose in no case did these ways of telling constitute logically adequate kinds of criteria. Then we should have to think of the relation between the ways of telling and what the P-predicate ascribes (or a part of what it ascribes) always in the following way: we should have to think of the ways of telling as *signs* of the presence, in the individual concerned, of this different thing (the state of consciousness). But then we could only know that the way of telling was a sign of the presence of the different thing ascribed by the P-predicate, by the observation of correlations between the two. But this observation we could each make only in one case, namely, our own. And now we are back in the position of the defender of Cartesianism, who thought our way with it was too short. For what, now, does 'our own case' mean? There is no sense in the idea of ascribing states of consciousness to oneself, or at all, unless the ascriber already knows how to ascribe at least some states of consciousness to others. So he cannot (or cannot generally) argue 'from his own case' to conclusions about how to do this; for unless he already knows how to do this, he has no conception of *his own case*, or any *case* (i.e., any subject of experiences). Instead, he just has evidence that pain, etc. may be expected when a certain body is affected in certain ways and not when others are.

The conclusion here is, of course, not new. What I have said is that one ascribes P-predicates to others on the strength of observation of their behaviour; and that the behaviour criteria one goes on are not just signs of the presence of what is meant by the P-predicate, but are criteria of a logically adequate kind for the ascription of the P-predicate. On behalf of this conclusion, however, I am claiming that it follows from a consideration of the conditions necessary for any ascription of states of consciousness to anything. The point is not that we must accept this conclusion in order to avoid scepticism, but that we must accept it in order to explain the existence of the conceptual scheme in terms of which the sceptical problem is stated. But once the conclusion is accepted, the sceptical problem does not arise. (And so with the generality of sceptical problems: their statement involves the pretended acceptance of a conceptual scheme and at the same time the silent repudiation of one of the conditions of its existence. This is why they are, in the terms in which they are stated, insoluble.) But this is only half the picture about P-predicates.

Now let us turn to the other half. For of course it is true, at least of some important classes of P-predicates, that when one ascribes them to oneself, one does not do so on the strength of observation of those behaviour criteria on the strength of which one ascribes them to others. This is not true of all P-predicates. It is not, in general, true of those which carry assessments of character and capability: these, when self-ascribed, are in general ascribed on the same kind of basis as that on which they are ascribed to others. And of those P-predicates of which it is true that one does not generally ascribe them to oneself on the basis of the criteria on the strength of which one ascribes them to others, there are many of which it is also true that their ascription is liable to correction by the self-ascriber on this basis. But there remain many cases in which one has an entirely adequate basis for ascribing a P-predicate to oneself, and yet in which this basis is quite distinct from those on which one ascribes the predicate to another. (Thus one says, reporting a present state of mind or feeling: 'I feel tired, am depressed, am in pain'). How can this fact be reconciled with the doctrine that the criteria on the strength of which one ascribes P-predicates to others are criteria of a logically adequate kind for this ascription?

The apparent difficulty of bringing about this reconciliation may tempt us in many directions. It may tempt us, for example, to deny that these self-ascriptions are really ascriptions at all; to *assimilate* first-person ascriptions of states of consciousness to those other forms of behaviour which constitute criteria on the basis of which one person ascribes P-predicates to another. This device seems to avoid the difficulty; it is not, in all cases, entirely inappropriate. But it obscures the facts, and is needless. It is merely a sophisticated form of failure to recognize the special character of P-predicates (or at least of a crucial class of P-predicates). For just as there is not (in general) one primary process of learning, or teaching oneself, an inner private meaning for predicates of this class, then another process of learning to apply such predicates to others on the strength of a correlation, noted in one's own case, with certain forms of behaviour, so—and equally—there is not (in general) one primary process of learning to apply such predicates to others on the strength of behaviour criteria, and then another process of acquiring the secondary technique of exhibiting a new form of behaviour, viz., first-person P-utterances. Both these pictures are refusals to acknowledge the unique logical character of the predicates concerned.

Suppose we write 'Px' as the general form of propositional function of such a predicate. Then according to the first picture, the expression which primarily replaces 'x' in this form is 'I', the first-person singular pronoun; its uses with other replacements are secondary, derivative, and shaky. According to the second picture, on the other hand, the primary replacements of 'x' in this form are 'he', 'that person', etc., and its use with 'I' is secondary, peculiar, not a true ascriptive use. But it is essential to the character of these predicates that they have both first and third-person ascriptive uses, that they are both self-ascribable otherwise than on the basis of observation of the behaviour of the subject of them, and other-ascribable on the basis of behaviour criteria. To learn their use is to learn both aspects of their use. In order to *have* this type of concept, one must be both a self-ascriber and other-ascriber of such predicates, and must see every other as a self-ascriber. And in order to *understand* this type of concept, one must acknowledge that there is a kind of predicate which is unambiguously and adequately ascribable *both* on the basis of observation of the subject of the predicate *and* not on this basis (independently of observation of the subject): the second case is the case where the ascriber is also the subject. If there were no concepts answering to the characterization I have just given, we should indeed have no philosophical problem about the soul; but equally we should not have *our* concept of a person.

To put the point—with a certain unavoidable crudity—in terms of one particular concept of this class, say, that of depression, we speak of behaving in a depressed way (of depressed behaviour) and also of feeling depressed (of a feeling of depression). One is inclined to argue that feelings can be felt, but not observed, and behaviour can be observed, but not felt, and that therefore there must be room here to drive in a logical wedge. But the concept of depression spans the place where one wants to drive it in. We might say, in order for there to be such a concept as that of X's depression, the depression which X has, the concept must cover both what is felt, but not observed, by X and what may be observed, but not felt, by others than X (for all values of X). But it is perhaps better to say: X's depression *is* something, one and the same thing, which is felt but not observed by X and observed but not felt by others than X. (And, of course, what can be observed can also be faked or disguised.) To refuse to accept this is to refuse to accept the structure of the language in which we talk about depression. That is, in a sense, all right. One might give up talking; or devise, perhaps a different structure in terms of which to soliloquize. What is not all right is simultaneously to pretend to accept that structure and to refuse to accept it; i.e., to couch one's rejection in the language of that structure.

It is in this light that we must see some of the familiar philosophical difficulties in the topic of the mind. For some of them spring from just such a failure to admit, or fully appreciate, the character which I have been claiming for at least some P-predicates. It is not seen that these predicates could not have either aspect of their use (the self-ascriptive and the non-self-ascriptive) without having the other aspect. Instead, one aspect of their use is taken as self-sufficient, which it could not be, and then the other aspect appears as problematical. And so we oscillate between philosophical scepticism and philosophical behaviourism. When we take the self-ascriptive aspect of the use of some P-predicate (say, 'depressed') as

o

primary, then a logical gap seems to open between the criteria on the strength of which we say that another is depressed, and the actual state of depression. What we do not realize is that if this logical gap is allowed to open, then it swallows not only his depression, but our depression as well. For if the logical gap exists, then depressed behaviour, however much there is of it, is not more than a sign of depression. And it can become a sign of depression only because of an observed correlation between it and depression. But whose depression? Only mine, one is tempted to say. But if *only* mine, then *not* mine at all. The sceptical position customarily represents the crossing of the logical gap as at best a shaky inference. But the point is that not even the syntax of the premises of the inference exists if the gap exists.

If, on the other hand, we take the other-ascriptive uses of these predicates as self-sufficient, we may come to think that all there is in the meaning of these predicates, as predicates, is the criteria on the strength of which we ascribe them to others. Does this not follow from the denial of the logical gap? It does not follow. To think that it does is to forget the self-ascriptive use of these predicates, to forget that we have to do with a class of predicates to the meaning of which it is essential that they should be both self-ascribable and other-ascribable to the same individual, when self-ascriptions are not made on the observational basis on which other ascriptions are made, but on another basis. It is not that these predicates have two kinds of meaning. Rather, it is essential to the single kind of meaning that they do have that both ways of ascribing them should be perfectly in order.

If one is playing a game of cards, the distinctive markings of a certain card constitute a logically adequate criterion for calling it, say, the Queen of Hearts, but, in calling it this, in the context of the game, one is also ascribing to it properties over and above the possession of those markings. The predicate gets its meaning from the whole structure of the game. So it is with the language which ascribes P-predicates. To say that the criteria on the strength of which we ascribe P-predicates to others are of a logically adequate kind for this ascription is not to say that all there is to the ascriptive meaning of these predicates is these criteria. To say this is to forget that they are P-predicates, to forget the rest of the language-structure to which they belong.

v

Now our perplexities may take a different form, the form of the question, 'But how can one ascribe to oneself, not on the basis of observation, *the very same thing* that others may have, on the basis of observation, a logically adequate reason for ascribing to one?' And this question may be absorbed in a wider one, which might be phrased: 'How are P-predicates possible?' or 'How is the concept of a person possible?' This is the question by which we replace those two earlier questions, viz.: 'Why are states of consciousness ascribed at all, ascribed to anything?' and 'Why are they ascribed to the very same thing as certain corporeal characteristics, etc.?' For the answer to these two initial questions is to be found nowhere else but in the admission of the primitiveness of the concept of a person, and hence of the unique character of P-predicates. So residual perplexities have to frame themselves in this new way. For when we have acknowledged the primitiveness of the concept of a person and, with it, the unique character of P-predicates, we may still want to ask what it is in the natural facts that makes it intelligible that we should have this concept, and to ask this in the hope of a non-trivial answer.[1] I do not pretend to be able to satisfy this demand at all fully. But I may mention two very different things which might count as beginnings or fragments of an answer.

And, first, I think a beginning can be made by moving a certain class of P-predicates to a central position in the picture. They are predicates, roughly, which involve doing something, which clearly imply intention or a state of mind or at least consciousness in general, and which indicate a characteristic pattern, or range of patterns, of bodily movement, while not indicating at all precisely any very definite sensation or experience. I mean such things as 'going for a walk', 'furling a rope', 'playing ball', 'writing a letter'. Such predicates have the interesting characteristic of many P-predicates that one does not, in general, ascribe them to oneself on the strength of observation, whereas one does ascribe them to others on the strength of observation. But, in case of these predicates, one feels minimal reluctance to concede that what is ascribed in these two different ways is the same. And this is because of the marked dominance of a fairly definite pattern of bodily movement in what they ascribe, and the marked absence of any distinctive experience. They release us from the idea that the only things we can know about without observation, or inference, or both, are private experiences; we can know also, without telling by either of these means, about the present and future movements of a body. Yet bodily movements are certainly also things we can know about by observation and inference.

Among the things that we observe, as opposed to the things we know without observation, are the movements of bodies similar to that about which we have knowledge not based on observation. It is important that we understand such observed movements; they bear on and condition our

---

[1] I mean, in the hope of an answer which does not *merely* say: 'Well, there are people in the world'.

own. And in fact we understand them, we interpret them, only by seeing them as elements in just such plans or schemes of action as those of which we know the present course and future development without observation of the relevant present movements. But this is to say that we see such movements (the observed movements of others) as *actions*, that we interpret them in terms of intention, that we see them as movements of individuals of a type to which also belongs that individual whose present and future movements we know about without observation; that we see others, as self-ascribers, not on the basis of observations, of what we ascribe to them on this basis.

Of course these remarks are not intended to suggest how the 'problem of other minds' could be solved, or our beliefs about others given a general philosophical 'justification.' I have already argued that such a 'solution' or 'justification' is impossible, that the demand for it cannot be coherently stated. Nor are these remarks intended as *a priori* genetic psychology. They are simply intended to help to make it seem intelligible to us, at this stage in the history of the philosophy of this subject, that we have the conceptual scheme we have. What I am suggesting is that it is easier to understand how we can see each other (and ourselves) as persons, if we think first of the fact that we act, and act on each other, and act in accordance with a common human nature. 'To see each other as persons' is a lot of things; but not a lot of separate and unconnected things. The class of P-predicates that I have moved into the centre of the picture are not unconnectedly there, detached from others irrelevant to them. On the contrary they are inextricably bound up with the others, interwoven with them. The topic of the mind does not divide into unconnected subjects.

I spoke just now of a common human nature. But there is also a sense in which a condition of the existence of the conceptual scheme we have is that human nature should not be common, should not be, that is, a community nature. Philosophers used to discuss the question of whether there was, or could be, such a thing as a 'group mind'. And for some the idea had a peculiar fascination, while to others it seemed utterly absurd and nonsensical and at the same time, curiously enough, pernicious. It is easy to see why these last found it pernicious: they found something horrible in the thought that people should cease to have toward individual persons the kind of attitudes that they did have and instead have attitudes in some way analogous to those toward groups; and that they might cease to decide individual courses of action for themselves and instead merely participate in corporate activities. But their finding it pernicious showed that they understood the idea they claimed to be absurd only too well. The fact that we find it natural to individuate as persons the members of a certain class of what might also be individuated as organic bodies does not mean that such a conceptual scheme is inevitable for any class of beings not utterly unlike ourselves.

Might we not construct the idea of a special kind of social world in which the concept of an individual person has no employment, whereas an analogous concept for groups does have employment? Think, to begin with, of certain aspects of actual human existence. Think, for example, of two groups of human beings engaged in some competitive but corporate activity, such as battle, for which they have been exceedingly well trained. We may even suppose that orders are superfluous, though information is passed. It is easy to imagine that, while absorbed in such activity, the members of the groups make no references to individual persons at all, have no use for personal names or pronouns. They do, however, refer to the groups and apply to them predicates analogous to those predicates ascribing purposive activity which we normally apply to individual persons. They may, *in fact*, use in such circumstances the plural forms 'we' and 'they'; but these are not genuine plurals, they are plurals without a singular, such as we use in sentences like these: 'We have taken the citadel', 'We have lost the game'. They may also refer to elements in the group, to members of the group, but exclusively in terms which get their sense from the parts played by these elements in the corporate activity. (Thus we sometimes refer to what are in fact persons as 'stroke' or 'tackle'.)

When we think of such cases, we see that we ourselves, over a part of our social lives—not, I am thankful to say, a very large part—do operate conceptual schemes in which the idea of the individual person has no place, in which its place is taken, so to speak, by that of a group. But might we not think of communities or groups such that this part of the lives of their members was the dominant part—or was the whole? It sometimes happens, with groups of human beings that, as we say, their members think, feel, and act 'as one'. The point I wish to make is that a condition for the existence, the use, of the concept of an individual person is that this should happen only sometimes.

It is absolutely useless to say, at this point: But all the same, even if this happened all the time, every member of the group would have an individual consciousness, would be an individual subject of experience. The point is, once more, that there is no sense in speaking of the individual consciousness just as such, of the individual subject of experience just as such: for there is no way of identifying such pure entities.[1] It is true, of course, that suggesting this fantasy, I have taken our concept of an individual person as a starting point. It is this fact which makes the useless reaction a natural one. But suppose, instead, I had made the following

[1] More accurately: their identification is necessarily secondary to the identification of persons.

suggestion: that each part of the human body, each organ and each member, had an individual consciousness, was a separate centre of experiences. This, in the same way, but more obviously, would be a useless suggestion. Then imagine all the intermediate cases, for instance these. There is a class of moving natural objects, divided into groups, each group exhibiting the same characteristic pattern of activity. Within each group there are certain differentiations of appearance accompanying differentiations of function, and in particular there is one member of each group with a distinctive appearance. Cannot one imagine different sets of observations which might lead us, in the one case, to think of the particular member as the spokesman of the group, as its mouthpiece; and in the other case to think of him as its mouth, to think of the group as a single *scattered* body? The point is that as soon as we adopt the latter way of thinking then we want to drop the former; we are no longer influenced by the human analogy in its first form, but only its second; and we no longer want to say: 'Perhaps the members have consciousness'. To understand the movement of our thought here, we need only remember the startling ambiguity of the phrase 'a body and its members'.

VI

I shall not pursue this attempt at explanation any further. What I have been mainly arguing for is that we should acknowledge the logical primitiveness of the concept of a person and, with this, the unique logical character of certain predicates. Once this is acknowledged, certain traditional philosophical problems are seen not to be problems at all. In particular, the problem that seems to have perplexed Hume[1] does not exist—the problem of the principle of unity, of identity, of the particular consciousness, of the particular subject of 'perceptions' (experiences) considered as a primary particular. There is no such problem and no such principle. If there were such a principle, then each of us would have to apply it in order to decide whether any contemporary experience of his was his or someone else's; and there is no sense in this suggestion. (This is not to deny, of course, that one *person* may be unsure of his own identity in some way, may be unsure, for example, whether some particular action, or series of actions, had been performed by him. Then he uses the same methods (the same in principle) to resolve the doubt about himself as anyone else uses to resolve the same doubt about him. And these methods simply involve the application of the ordinary criteria for *personal* identity. (There remains the question of what exactly these criteria are, what their relative weights are, etc.; but, once disentangled from spurious questions, this is one of the easier problems in philosophy.)

[1] Cf. the Appendix to the *Treatise of Human Nature*.

Where Hume erred, or seemed to have erred, both Kant and Wittgenstein had the better insight. Perhaps neither always expressed it in the happiest way. For Kant's doctrine that the 'analytic unity of consciousness' neither requires nor entails any principle of unity is not as clear as one could wish. And Wittgenstein's remarks (at one time) to the effect that the data of consciousness are not owned, that 'I' as used by Jones, in speaking of his own feelings, etc., does not refer to what 'Jones' as used by another refers to, seem needlessly to flout the conceptual scheme we actually employ. It is needlessly paradoxical to deny, or seem to deny, that when Smith says 'Jones has a pain' and Jones says 'I have a pain', they are talking about the same entity and saying the same thing about it, needlessly paradoxical to deny that Jones can confirm that he has a pain. Instead of denying that self-ascribed states of consciousness are really ascribed at all, it is more in harmony with our actual ways of talking to say: For each user of the language, there is just one person in ascribing to whom states of consciousness he does not need to use the criteria of the observed behaviour of that person (though he does not necessarily not do so); and that person is himself. This remark at least respects the structure of the conceptual scheme we employ, without precluding further examination of it.

39

J. J. C. SMART

SENSATIONS AND BRAIN PROCESSES (1959)

This paper[1] takes its departure from arguments to be found in U. T. Place's 'Is Consciousness a Brain Process'.[2] I have had the benefit of discussing Place's thesis in a good many universities in the United States and Australia, and I hope that the present paper answers objections to his thesis which Place has not considered and that it presents his thesis in a more nearly unobjectionable form. This paper is meant also to supplement the paper 'The "Mental" and the "Physical",' by H. Feigl,[3] which in part argues for a similar thesis to Place's.

Suppose that I report that I have at this moment a roundish, blurry-edged after-image which is yellowish towards its edge and is orange towards its centre. What is it that I am reporting? One answer to this question might be that I am not reporting anything, that when I say that it looks to me as though there is a roundish yellowy-orange patch of light on the wall I am expressing some sort of *temptation*, the temptation to say that there *is* a roundish yellowy-orange patch on the wall (though I may know that there is not such a patch on the wall). This is perhaps Wittgenstein's view in the *Philosophical Investigations* (see §§367, 370). Similarly, when I 'report' a pain, I am not really reporting anything (or, if you like, I am reporting in a queer sense of 'reporting'), but am doing a sophisticated sort of wince. (See §244: 'The verbal expression of pain replaces crying and does not describe it.' Nor does it describe anything else?).[4] I prefer

---

[1] This is a very slightly revised version of a paper which was first published in the *Philosophical Review*, LXVIII (1959), 141–56. Since that date there have been criticisms of my paper by J. T. Stevenson, *Philosophical Review*, LXIX (1960), 505–10, to which I have replied in *Philosophical Review*, LXX (1961), 406–7, and by G. Pitcher and by W. D. Joske, *Australasian Journal of Philosophy*, XXXVIII (1960), 150–60, to which I have replied in the same volume of that journal, pp. 252–4.

[2] *British Journal of Psychology*, XLVII (1956), 44–50.

[3] *Minnesota Studies in the Philosophy of Science*, Vol. II (Minneapolis: University of Minnesota Press, 1958), pp. 370–497.

[4] Some philosophers of my acquaintance, who have the advantage over me in having known Wittgenstein, would say that this interpretation of him is too behaviouristic. However, it seems to me a very natural interpretation of his printed words, and whether or not it is Wittgenstein's real view it is certainly an interesting and important one. I wish to consider it here as a possible rival both to the 'brain-process' thesis and to straight-out old-fashioned dualism.

most of the time to discuss an after-image rather than a pain, because the word 'pain' brings in something which is irrelevant to my purpose: the notion of 'distress'. I think that 'he is in pain' entails 'he is in distress', that is, that he is in a certain agitation-condition.[1] Similarly, to say 'I am in pain' may be to do more than 'replace pain behaviour': it may be partly to report something, though this something is quite non-mysterious, being an agitation-condition, and so susceptible of behaviouristic analysis. The suggestion I wish if possible to avoid is a different one, namely that 'I am in pain' is a genuine report, and that what it reports is an irreducibly psychical something. And similarly the suggestion I wish to resist is also that to say 'I have a yellowish-orange after-image' is to report something irreducibly psychical.

Why do I wish to resist this suggestion? Mainly because of Occam's razor. It seems to me that science is increasingly giving us a viewpoint whereby organisms are able to be seen as physiochemical mechanisms[2]: it seems that even the behaviour of man himself will one day be explicable in mechanistic terms. There does seem to be, so far as science is concerned, nothing in the world but increasingly complex arrangements of physical constituents. All except for one place: in consciousness. That is, for a full description of what is going on in a man you would have to mention not only the physical processes in his tissues, glands, nervous system, and so forth, but also his states of consciousness: his visual, auditory, and tactual sensations, his aches and pains. That these should be *correlated* with brain processes does not help, for to say that they are *correlated* is to say that they are something 'over and above'. You cannot correlate something with itself. You correlate footprints with burglars, but not Bill Sykes the burglar with Bill Sykes the burglar. So sensations, states of consciousness, do seem to be the one sort of thing left outside the physicalist picture, and for various reasons I just cannot believe that this can be so. That everything should be explicable in terms of physics (together of course with descriptions of the ways in which the parts are put together—roughly, biology is to physics as radio-engineering is to electromagnetism) except the occurrence of sensations seems to me to be frankly unbelievable. Such sensations would be 'nomological danglers', to use Feigl's expression.[3] It is not often realized how odd would be the laws whereby these nomological danglers would dangle. It is sometimes asked, 'Why can't there be psychophysical

[1] See Ryle, *The Concept of Mind* (London: Hutchinsons's University Library, 1949), p. 93.
[2] On this point see Paul Oppenheim and Hilary Putnam, "Unity of Science as a Working Hypothesis,' in *Minnesota Studies in the Philosophy of Science*, Vol. II (Minneapolis: University of Minnesota Press, 1958), pp. 3–36.
[3] Feigl, op. cit., p. 428. Feigl uses the expression 'nomological danglers' for the laws whereby the entities dangle: I have used the expression to refer to the dangling entities themselves.

laws which are of a novel sort, just as the laws of electricity and magnetism were novelties from the standpoint of Newtonian mechanics?' Certainly we are pretty sure in the future to come across new ultimate laws of a novel type, but I expect them to relate simple constituents: for example, whatever ultimate particles are then in vogue. I cannot believe that ultimate laws of nature could relate simple constituents to configurations consisting of perhaps billions of neurons (and goodness knows how many billion billions of ultimate particles) all put together for all the world as though their main purpose in life was to be a negative feedback mechanism of a complicated sort. Such ultimate laws would be like nothing so far known in science. They have a queer 'smell' to them. I am just unable to believe in the nomological danglers themselves, or in the laws whereby they would dangle. If any philosophical arguments seemed to compel us to believe in such things, I would suspect a catch in the argument. In any case it is the object of this paper to show that there are no philosophical arguments which compel us to be dualists.

The above is largely a confession of faith, but it explains why I find Wittgenstein's position (as I construe it) so congenial. For on this view there are, in a sense, no sensations. A man is a vast arrangement of physical particles, but there are not, over and above this, sensations or states of consciousness. There are just behavioural facts about this vast mechanism such as that it expresses a temptation (behaviour disposition) to say 'there is a yellowish-red patch on the wall' or that it goes through a sophisticated sort of wince, that is, says 'I am in pain'. Admittedly Wittgenstein says that though the sensation 'is not a something', it is nevertheless 'not a nothing either' (§304), but this need only mean that the word 'ache' has a use. An ache is a thing, but only in the innocuous sense in which the plain man, in the first paragraph of Frege's *Foundations of Arithmetic*, answers the question 'What is the number one?' by 'a thing'. It should be noted that when I assert that to say 'I have a yellowish-orange after-image' is to express a temptation to assert the physical-object statement 'There is a yellowish-orange patch on the wall', I mean that saying 'I have a yellowish-orange after-image' is (partly) the exercise of the disposition[1] which is the temptation. It is not to *report* that I have the temptation, any more than is 'I love you' normally a report that I love someone. Saying 'I love you' is just part of the behaviour which is the exercise of the disposition of loving someone.

[1] Wittgenstein did not like the word 'disposition'. I am using it to put in a nutshell (and perhaps inaccurately) the view which I am attributing to Wittgenstein. I should like to repeat that I do not wish to claim that my interpretation of Wittgenstein is correct. Some of those who knew him do not interpret him in this way. It is merely a view which I find myself extracting from his printed words and which I think is important and worth discussing for its own sake.

Though for the reasons given above, I am very receptive to the above 'expressive' account of sensation statements, I do not feel that it will quite do the trick. Maybe this is because I have not thought it out sufficiently, but it does seem to me as though, when a person says 'I have an after-image', he *is* making a genuine report, and that when he says 'I have a pain', he *is* doing more than 'replace pain behaviour', and that 'this more' is not just to say that he is in distress. I am not so sure, however, that to admit this is to admit that there are non-physical correlates of brain processes. Why should not sensations just be brain processes of a certain sort? There are, of course, well-known (as well as lesser-known) philosophical objections to the view that reports of sensations are reports of brain-processes, but I shall try to argue that these arguments are by no means as cogent as is commonly thought to be the case.

Let me first try to state more accurately the thesis that sensations are brain-processes. It is not the thesis that, for example, 'after-image' or 'ache' means the same as 'brain process of sort X' (where 'X' is replaced by a description of a certain sort of brain process). It is that, in so far as 'after-image' or 'ache' is a report of a process, it is a report of a process that *happens to be* a brain process. It follows that the thesis does not claim that sensation statements can be *translated* into statements about brain processes.[1] Nor does it claim that the logic of a sensation statement is the same as that of a brain-process statement. All it claims is that in so far as a sensation statement is a report of something, that something is in fact a brain process. Sensations are nothing over and above brain processes. Nations are nothing 'over and above' citizens, but this does not prevent the logic of nation statements being very different from the logic of citizen statements, nor does it insure the translatability of nation statements into citizen statements. (I do not, however, wish to assert that the relation of sensation statements to brain-process statements is very like that of nation statements to citizen statements. Nations do not just *happen to be* nothing over and above citizens, for example. I bring in the 'nations' example merely to make a negative point: that the fact that the logic of A-statements is different from that of B-statements does not insure that A's are anything over and above B's.)

Remarks on Identity

When I say that a sensation is a brain process or that lightning is an electric discharge, I am using 'is' in the sense of strict identity. (Just as in the—in this case necessary—proposition '7 is identical with the smallest prime number greater than 5'.) When I say that a sensation is a brain process or that lightning is an electric discharge I do not mean just that the sensation

[1] See Place; and Feigl, op. cit., p. 390, near top.

is somehow spatially or temporally continuous with the brain process or that the lightning is just spatially or temporally continuous with the discharge. When on the other hand I say that the successful general is the same person as the small boy who stole the apples I mean only that the successful general I see before me is a time slice[1] of the same four-dimensional object of which the small boy stealing apples is an earlier time slice. However, the four dimensional object which has the general-I-see-before-me for its late time slice is identical in the strict sense with the four-dimensional object which has the small-boy-stealing-apples for an early time slice. I distinguish these two senses of 'is identical with' because I wish to make it clear that the brain-process doctrine asserts identity in the *strict* sense.

I shall now discuss various possible objections to the view that the processes reported in sensation statements are in fact processes in the brain. Most of us have met some of these objections in our first year as philosophy students. All the more reason to take a good look at them. Others of the objections will be more recondite and subtle.

Objection 1. Any illiterate peasant can talk perfectly well about his after-images, or how things look or feel to him, or about his aches and pains, and yet he may know nothing whatever about neurophysiology. A man may, like Aristotle, believe that the brain is an organ for cooling the body without any impairment of his ability to make true statements about his sensations. Hence the things we are talking about when we describe our sensations cannot be processes in the brain.

Reply. You might as well say that a nation of slugabeds, who never saw the Morning Star or knew of its existence, or who had never thought of the expression 'the Morning Star', but who used the expression 'the Evening Star' perfectly well, could not use this expression to refer to the same entity as we refer to (and describe as) 'the Morning Star'.[2]

You may object that the Morning Star is in a sense not the very same thing as the Evening Star, but only something spatiotemporally continuous with it. That is, you may say that the Morning Star is not the Evening Star in the strict sense of 'identity' that I distinguished earlier.

There is, however, a more plausible example. Consider lightning.[3] Modern physical science tells us that lightning is a certain kind of electrical discharge due to ionization of clouds of water vapour in the atmosphere. This, it is now believed, is what the true nature of lightning is. Note that

---

[1] See J. H. Woodger, *Theory Construction*, International Encyclopedia of Unified Science, II, No. 5 (Chicago: University of Chicago Press, 1939), 38. I here permit myself to speak loosely. For warnings against possible ways of going wrong with this sort of talk, see my note 'Spatialising Time', *Mind*, LXIV (1955), 239–41.

[2] Cf. Feigl, op. cit., p. 439.

[3] See Place; also Feigl, op. cit., p. 438.

there are not two things: a flash of lightning and an electrical discharge. There is one thing, a flash of lightning, which is described scientifically as an electrical discharge to the earth from a cloud of ionized water molecules. The case is not at all like that of explaining a footprint by reference to a burglar. We say that what lightning really is, what its true nature as revealed by science is, is an electrical discharge. (It is not the true nature of a footprint to be a burglar.)

To forestall irrelevant objections, I should like to make it clear that by 'lightning' I mean the publicly observable physical object, lightning, not a visual sense-datum of lightning. I say that the publicly observable physical object lightning is in fact the electrical discharge, not just a correlate of it. The sense-datum, or rather the having of the sense-datum, the 'look' of lightning, may well in my view be a correlate of the electrical discharge. For in my view it is a brain state *caused* by the lightning. But we should no more confuse sensations of lightning with lightning than we confuse sensations of a table with the table.

In short, the reply to Objection 1 is that there can be contingent statements of the form 'A is identical with B', and a person may well know that something is an A without knowing that it is a B. An illiterate peasant might well be able to talk about his sensations without knowing about brain processes, just as he can talk about lightning though he knows nothing of electricity.

Objection 2. It is only a contingent fact (if it is a fact) that when we have a certain kind of sensation there is a certain kind of process in our brain. Indeed it is possible, though perhaps in the highest degree unlikely, that our present physiological theories will be as out of date as the ancient theory connecting mental processes with goings on in the heart. It follows that when we report a sensation we are not reporting a brain-process.

Reply. The objection certainly proves that when we say 'I have an after-image' we cannot *mean* something of the form 'I have such and such a brain-process'. But this does not show that what we report (having an after-image) is not *in fact* a brain process. 'I see lightning' does not *mean* 'I see an electrical discharge'. Indeed, it is logically possible (though highly unlikely) that the electrical discharge account of lightning might one day be given up. Again, 'I see the Evening Star' does not *mean* the same as 'I see the Morning Star', and yet 'The Evening Star and the Morning Star are one and the same thing' is a contingent proposition. Possibly Objection 2 derives some of its apparent strength from a 'Fido'-Fido theory of meaning. If the meaning of an expression were what the expression named, then, of course, it *would* follow from the fact that 'sensation' and 'brain process' have different meanings that they cannot name one and the same thing.

Objection 3.[1] Even if Objections 1 and 2 do not prove that sensations are something over and above brain-processes, they do prove that the qualities of sensations are something over and above the qualities of brain-processes. That is, it may be possible to get out of asserting the existence of irreducibly psychic processes, but not out of asserting the existence of irreducibly psychic *properties*. For suppose we identify the Morning Star with the Evening Star. Then there must be some properties which logically imply that of being the Morning Star, and quite distinct properties which entail that of being the Evening Star. Again, there must be some properties (for example, that of being a yellow flash) which are logically distinct from those in the physicalist story.

Indeed, it might be thought that the objection succeeds at one jump. For consider the property of 'being a yellow flash'. It might seem that this property lies inevitably outside the physicalist framework within which I am trying to work (either by 'yellow' being an objective emergent property of physical objects, or else by being a power to produce yellow sense-data, where 'yellow', in this second instantiation of the word, refers to a purely phenomenal or introspectible quality). I must therefore digress for a moment and indicate how I deal with secondary qualities. I shall concentrate on colour.

First of all, let me introduce the concept of a normal percipient. One person is more a normal percipient than another if he can make colour discriminations that the other cannot. For example, if A can pick a lettuce leaf out of a heap of cabbage leaves, whereas B cannot though he can pick a lettuce leaf out of a heap of beetroot leaves, then A is more normal than B. (I am assuming that A and B are not given time to distinguish the leaves by their slight difference in shape and so forth.) From the concept of 'more normal than' it is easy to see how we can introduce the concept of 'normal'. Of course, Eskimos may make the finest discriminations at the blue end of the spectrum, Hottentots at the red end. In this case the concept of a normal percipient is a slightly idealized one, rather like that of 'the mean sun' in astronomical chronology. There is no need to go into such subtleties now. I say that 'This is red' means something roughly like 'A normal percipient would not easily pick this out of a clump of geranium petals though he would pick it out of a clump of lettuce leaves'. Of course it does not exactly mean this: a person might know the meaning of 'red' without knowing anything about geraniums, or even about normal percipients. But the point is that a person can be *trained* to say 'This is red' of objects which would not easily be picked out of geranium petals by a

---

[1] I think this objection was first put to me by Professor Max Black. I think it is the most subtle of any of those I have considered, and the one which I am least confident of having satisfactorily met.

normal percipient, and so on. (Note that even a colour-blind person can reasonably assert that something is red, though of course he needs to use another human being, not just himself, as his 'colour meter'.) This account of secondary qualities explains their unimportance in physics. For obviously the discriminations and lack of discriminations made by a very complex neurophysiological mechanism are hardly likely to correspond to simple and nonarbitrary distinctions in nature.

I therefore elucidate colours as powers, in Locke's sense, to evoke certain sorts of discriminatory responses in human beings. They are also, of course, powers to cause sensations in human beings (an account still nearer Locke's). But these sensations, I am arguing, are identifiable with brain processes.

Now how do I get over the objection that a sensation can be identified with a brain process only if it has some phenomenal property, not possessed by brain processes, whereby one-half of the identification may be, so to speak, pinned down?

Reply. My suggestion is as follows. When a person says, 'I see a yellowish-orange after-image', he is saying something like this: '*There is something going on which is like what is going on when* I have my eyes open, am awake, and there is an orange illuminated in good light in front of me, that is, when I really see an orange'. (And there is no reason why a person should not say the same thing when he is having a veridical sense-datum, so long as we construe 'like' in the last sentence in such a sense that something can be like itself.) Notice that the italicized words, namely 'there is something going on which is like what is going on when,' are all quasi-logical or topic-neutral words. This explains why the ancient Greek peasant's reports about his sensations can be neutral between dualistic metaphysics or my materialistic metaphysics. It explains how sensations can be brain-processes and yet how a man who reports them need know nothing about brain-processes. For he reports them only very abstractly as 'something going on which is like what is going on when. . . .'. Similarly, a person may say 'someone is in the room', thus reporting truly that the doctor is in the room, even though he has never heard of doctors. (There are not two people in the room: 'someone' *and* the doctor.) This account of sensation statements also explains the singular elusiveness of 'raw feels' —why no one seems to be able to pin any properties on them.[1] Raw feels, in my view, are colourless for the very same reason that *something* is colourless. This does not mean that sensations do not have plenty of properties, for if they are brain-processes they certainly have lots of neurological properties. It only means that in speaking of them as being like or unlike one another we need not know or mention these properties.

[1] See B. A. Farrell, 'Experience', *Mind*, LIX (1950), 170–98.

This, then, is how I would reply to Objection 3. The strength of my reply depends on the possibility of our being able to report that one thing is like another without being able to state the respect in which it is like. I do not see why this should not be so. If we think cybernetically about the nervous system we can envisage it as able to respond to certain likenesses of its internal processes without being able to do more. It would be easier to build a machine which would tell us, say on a punched tape, whether or not two objects were similar, than it would be to build a machine which would report wherein the similarities consisted.

Objection 4. The after-image is not in physical space. The brain-process is. So the after-image is not a brain-process.

Reply. This is an *ignoratio elenchi*. I am not arguing that the after-image is a brain-process, but that the experience of having an after-image is a brain-process. It is the *experience* which is reported in the introspective report. Similarly, if it is objected that the after-image is yellowy-orange, my reply is that it is the experience of seeing yellowy-orange that is being described, and this experience is not a yellowy-orange something. So to say that a brain-process cannot be yellowy-orange is not to say that a brain-process cannot in fact be the experience of having a yellowy-orange after-image. There is, in a sense, no such thing as an after-image or a sense-datum, though there is such a thing as the experience of having an image, and this experience is described indirectly in material object language, not in phenomenal language, for there is no such thing.[1] We describe the experience by saying in effect, that it is like the experience we have when, for example, we really see a yellowy-orange patch on the wall. Trees and wallpaper can be green, but not the experience of seeing or imagining a tree or wallpaper. (Or if they are described as green or yellow this can only be in a derived sense.)

Objection 5. It would make sense to say of a molecular movement in the brain that it is swift or slow, straight or circular, but it makes no sense to say this of the experience of seeing something yellow.

Reply. So far we have not given sense to talk of experience as swift or slow, straight or circular. But I am not claiming that 'experience' and 'brain-process' mean the same or even that they have the same logic. 'Somebody' and 'the doctor' do not have the same logic, but this does not lead us to suppose that talking about somebody telephoning is talking

---

[1] Dr J. R. Smythies claims that a sense-datum language could be taught independently of the material object language ('A Note on the Fallacy of the "Phenomenological Fallacy,"' *British Journal of Psychology*, XLVIII (1957), 141–4). I am not so sure of this: there must be some public criteria for a person having got a rule wrong before we can teach him the rule. I suppose someone might *accidentally* learn colour words by Dr Smythies' procedure. I am not, of course, denying that we can learn a sense-datum language in the sense that we can learn to report our experience. Nor would Place deny it.

about someone over and above, say, the doctor. The ordinary man, when he reports an experience is reporting that something is going on, but he leaves it open as to what sort of thing is going on, whether in a material solid medium or perhaps in some sort of gaseous medium, or even perhaps in some sort of nonspatial medium (if this makes sense). All that I am saying is that 'experience' and 'brain-process' may in fact refer to the same thing, and if so we may easily adopt a convention (which is not a change in our present rules for the use of experience words but an addition to them) whereby it would make sense to talk of an experience in terms appropriate to physical processes.

Objection 6. Sensations are private, brain processes are *public*. If I sincerely say, 'I see a yellowish-orange after-image', and I am not making a verbal mistake, then I cannot be wrong. But I can be wrong about a brain-process. The scientist looking into my brain might be having an illusion. Moreover, it makes sense to say that two or more people are observing the same brain-process but not that two or more people are reporting the same inner experience.

Reply. This shows that the language of introspective reports has a different logic from the language of material processes. It is obvious that until the brain-process theory is much improved and widely accepted there will be no *criteria* for saying 'Smith has an experience of such-and-such a sort' *except* Smith's introspective reports. So we have adopted a rule of language that (normally) what Smith says goes.

Objection 7. I can imagine myself turned to stone and yet having images, aches, pains, and so on.

Reply. I can imagine that the electrical theory of lightning is false, that lightning is some sort of purely optical phenomenon. I can imagine that lightning is not an electrical discharge. I can imagine that the Evening Star is not the Morning Star. But it is. All the objection shows is that 'experience' and 'brain-process' do not have the same meaning. It does not show that an experience is not in fact a brain process.

This objection is perhaps much the same as one which can be summed up by the slogan: 'What can be composed of nothing cannot be composed of anything'.[1] The argument goes as follows: on the brain-process thesis the identity between the brain-process and the experience is a contingent one. So it is logically possible that there should be no brain-process, and no process of any other sort either (no heart process, no kidney process, no liver process). There would be the experience but no 'corresponding' physiological process with which we might be able to identify it empirically.

[1] I owe this objection to Dr C. B. Martin. I gather that he no longer wishes to maintain this objection, at any rate in its present form.

I suspect that the objector is thinking of the experience as a ghostly entity. So it is composed of something, not of nothing, after all. On his view it is composed of ghost stuff, and on mine it is composed of brain stuff. Perhaps the counter-reply will be[1] that the experience is simple and uncompounded, and so it is not composed of anything after all. This seems to be a quibble, for, if it were taken seriously, the remark 'What can be composed of nothing cannot be composed of anything' could be recast as an a priori argument against Democritus and atomism and for Descartes and infinite divisibility. And it seems odd that a question of this sort could be settled a priori. We must therefore construe the word 'composed' in a very weak sense, which would allow us to say that even an indivisible atom is composed of something (namely, itself). The dualist cannot really say that an experience can be composed of nothing. For he holds that experiences are something over and above material processes, that is, that they are a sort of ghost stuff. I say that the dualist's hypothesis is a perfectly intelligible one. But I say that experiences are not to be identified with ghost stuff but with brain stuff. This is another hypothesis, and in my view a very plausible one. The present argument cannot knock it down a priori.

Objection 8. The 'beetle in the box' objection (see Wittgenstein, *Philosophical Investigations*, §293). How could descriptions of experiences, if these are genuine reports, get a foothold in language? For any rule of language must have public criteria for its correct application.

Reply. The change from describing how things are to describing how we feel is just a change from uninhibitedly saying 'this is so' by saying 'this looks so'. That is, when the naive person might be tempted to say, 'There is a patch of light on the wall which moves whenever I move my eyes' or 'A pin is being stuck into me', we have learned how to resist this temptation and say 'It *looks as though* there is a patch of light on the wall-paper' or 'It *feels as though* someone were sticking a pin into me'. The introspective account tells us about the individual's state of consciousness in the same way as does 'I see a patch of light' or 'I feel a pin being stuck into me': it differs from the corresponding perception statement in so far as it withdraws any claim about what is actually going on in the external world. From the point of view of the psychologist, the change from talking about the environment to talking about one's perceptual sensations is simply a matter of disinhibiting certain reactions. These are reactions which one normally suppresses because one has learned that in the prevailing circumstances they are unlikely to provide a good indication of the state of the environment.[2] To say that something looks green to me is

---

[1] Martin did not make this reply, but one of his students did.
[2] I owe this point to Place, in correspondence.

simply to say that my experience is like the experience I get when I see something that really is green. In my reply to Objection 3, I pointed out the extreme openness or generality of statements which report experiences. This explains why there is no language of private qualities. (Just as 'someone', unlike 'the doctor', is a colourless word.)[1]

If it is asked what is the difference between those brain processes which, in my view, are experiences and those brain processes which are not, I can only reply that it is at present unknown. I have been tempted to conjecture that the difference may in part be that between perception and reception (in D. M. MacKay's terminology) and that the type of brain process which is an experience might be identifiable with MacKay's active 'matching response.'[2] This, however, cannot be the whole story, because sometimes I can perceive something unconsciously, as when I take a handkerchief out of a drawer without being aware that I am doing so. But at the very least, we can classify the brain processes which are experiences as those brain processes which are, or might have been, causal conditions of those pieces of verbal behaviour which we call reports of immediate experience.

I have now considered a number of objections to the brain-process thesis. I wish now to conclude with some remarks on the logical status of the thesis itself. U. T. Place seems to hold that it is a straight-out scientific hypothesis.[3] If so, he is partly right and partly wrong. If the issue is between (say) a brain-process thesis and a heart thesis, or a liver thesis, or a kidney thesis, then the issue is a purely empirical one, and the verdict is overwhelmingly in favour of the brain. The right sorts of things don't go on in the heart, liver, or kidney, nor do these organs possess the right sort of complexity of structure. On the other hand, if the issue is between a brain-or-liver-or-kidney thesis (that is, some form of materialism) on the one hand and epiphenomenalism on the other hand, then the issue is not an empirical one. For there is no conceivable experiment which could decide between materialism and epiphenomenalism. This latter issue is not like the average straight-out empirical issue in science, but like the issue between the nineteenth-century English naturalist Philip Gosse,[4] and the

---

[1] The 'beetle in the box' objection is, *if it is sound*, an objection to *any* view, and in particular the Cartesian one, that introspective reports are genuine reports. So it is no objection to a weaker thesis that I would be concerned to uphold, namely, that if introspective reports of 'experiences' are genuinely reports, then the things they are reports of are in fact brain processes.

[2] See his article 'Towards an Information-Flow Model of Human Behaviour,' *British Journal of Psychology*, XLVII (1956), 30–43.

[3] Op. cit. For a further discussion of this, in reply to the original version of the present paper, see Place's note 'Materialism as a Scientific Hypothesis', *Philosophical Review*, LXIX (1960), 101–4.

[4] See the entertaining account of Gosse's book *Omphalos* by Martin Gardner in *Fads and Fallacies in the Name of Science*, 2nd ed. (New York: Dover, 1957), pp. 124–7.

orthodox geologists and palæontologists of his day. According to Gosse, the earth was created about 4000 BC exactly as described in *Genesis*, with twisted rock strata, 'evidence' of erosion, and so forth, and all sorts of fossils, all in their appropriate strata, just as if the usual evolutionist story had been true. Clearly this theory is in a sense irrefutable: no evidence can possibly tell against it. Let us ignore the theological setting in which Philip Gosse's hypothesis had been placed, thus ruling out objections of a theological kind, such as 'what a queer God who would go to such elaborate lengths to deceive us'. Let us suppose that it is held that the universe just *began* in 4004 BC with the initial conditions just everywhere as they were in 4004 BC, and in particular that our own planet began with sediment in the rivers, eroded cliffs, fossils in the rocks, and so on. No scientist would ever entertain this as a serious hypothesis, consistent though it is with all possible evidence. The hypothesis offends against the principles of parsimony and simplicity. There would be far too many brute and inexplicable facts. Why are pterodactyl bones just as they are? No explanation in terms of the evolution of pterodactyls from earlier forms of life would any longer be possible. We would have millions of facts about the world as it was in 4004 BC that just have to be *accepted*.

The issue between the brain-process theory and epiphenomenalism seems to be of the above sort. (Assuming that a behaviouristic reduction of introspective reports is not possible.) If it be agreed that there are no cogent philosophical arguments which force us into accepting dualism, and if the brain process theory and dualism are equally consistent with the facts, then the principles of parsimony and simplicity seem to me to decide overwhelmingly in favour of the brain-process theory. As I pointed out earlier, dualism involves a large number of irreducible psycho-physical laws (whereby the 'nomological danglers' dangle) of a queer sort, that just have to be taken on trust, and are just as difficult to swallow as the irreducible facts about the palæontology of the earth with which we are faced on Philip Gosse's theory.

40

G. N. A. VESEY

VOLITION (1961)

I

'Let us not forget this: when "I raise my arm", my arm goes up. And the problem arises: what is left over if I subtract the fact that my arm goes up from the fact that I raise my arm?'[1]

This is a question which would arise very naturally in trying to describe some of the effects of anaesthesia. William James[2] reports that if a patient who has lost sensation in one arm is asked to put the affected hand on top of his head while his eyes are closed, and is at the same time prevented from doing so, he will be very surprised on opening his eyes to find that the movement has not taken place. This, James says, is the rule rather than the exception in anaesthetic cases. Confirmation of this is to be found in case-histories reported in the medical journals.[3]

If one were to consider only such cases as these one might say that what is left over, if I subtract the fact that my arm goes up from the fact that I raise my arm, is: (a) 'It seems to me that I have raised my arm'.

But this is inadequate, since it invites the question, 'Why does it seem to you that you raised your arm? It was not from anything you saw or felt. What gave you the idea that you had raised it?' One feels this to be a meaningful question, even if one cannot find words to answer it.

Furthermore, it may be simply false that it seems to the person that he has raised his arm. He may be well aware that it has not moved. He may even know himself to have lost the arm in question. It is in this connection that physiologists talk of 'phantom limbs'. A 'phantom limb' is not, of course, what we ordinarily mean by 'a phantom'; it is not an apparition, or a spectre. When medical people talk of a 'phantom limb' they are using the word 'phantom' in a technical sense, to refer to 'the seeming persistence of a part that was known to be gone, and the continued possession of many of its original attributes of form, position, and even voluntary

---

[1] Wittgenstein, *Philosophical Investigations*, I, 621.

[2] *Principles of Psychology*, Vol. II, p. 105.

[3] For instance, J. D. Spillane, *Lancet*, 1942, i, p. 42, and J. Purdon Martin, *Lancet*, 1949, i, p. 51.

movement'.[1] The point of using the word 'phantom' is that the limb seems to persist only to the person whose limb it was, and that it does not seem to persist even to him so far as what are usually referred to as 'the five senses' are concerned. Phantom limbs may be either painless or painful. Attempts to move painful phantom limbs usually result in an increase of the pain, but voluntary movement of painless phantom limbs 'is usually possible and often considerable'[2].

Should we say that what is left over, if I subtract the fact that my arm goes up from the fact that I raise my arm, is: (b) 'I raised my phantom arm'?

The term 'phantom' in this phrase having been tailored to fit precisely the sort of cases we have been considering, there can be no question as to its being true that what is left over is a movement of a phantom arm. And there seems no reason (other than the practical one, that the present usage serves to distinguish cases in which there is no actual movement from normal cases) why we should not extend our use of this phrase so that in normal cases also there can be said to be the movement of a phantom arm. In normal cases the movement of the phantom arm will be materialized, so to speak, in the movement of a real arm. In abnormal cases this materialization will be lacking.

But what would we achieve in answering the question thus? Have we, with talk of the movement of phantom arms, reached a point at which we can say 'Now I understand'? Or do we not, rather, feel the need to inquire further, 'But what is it to move a phantom arm?'? For my own part I do not find talk of the movement of phantom arms a satisfactory way of answering the question, if only because the word 'phantom' has associations which are obviously out of place in this context.

One might well say of the patient mentioned by James, who had been prevented from moving his hand, that he had at least *tried* to move it. And hence that what is left over is: (c) 'I tried to move my arm'.

But this is unsatisfactory in that the patient may be unaware of any difficulty in moving his hand. Because of his anaesthesia it is not as if he could feel his hand being held down. From the patient's point of view it is not as if he had to try to move his hand, but as if he could actually, and easily, move it—or, at least, it is like this to him until he opens his eyes.

In short, 'He tried to move his hand' describes not so much what the patient did as what he did not do: he failed to qualify for the description 'He moved his hand'.

Suppose James' patient, when he found that his hand had not in fact moved, were to say: (d) 'I did whatever would ordinarily have produced the movement.'

[1] George Riddoch, *Brain*, 1941, Vol. 64, p. 197.
[2] Riddoch, ibid, p. 218.

What he would mean by this is not immediately obvious. To make a piece of chalk fall to the floor I have to do something else, namely open my fingers, but (one feels like saying) to open my fingers there is not something else I have to do first. After all, they are my fingers, part of me. As Wittgenstein remarks,[1] 'When I raise my arm "voluntarily" I do not use any instrument to bring the movement about'.

It might be said that whether the movement takes place or not there occurs an outgoing of energy from the brain along one or other of the efferent nerves, and that this is what the patient really does.[2] This is 'what would ordinarily have produced the movement'. The objection to this is not that there are no such outgoings of energy (for there are), nor that the agent is not conscious of them (certain psychologists[3] have held that the agent *is* conscious of them, as so-called 'feelings of innervation') but that any such outgoings of energy are not something the agent *does*. If, when asked what he was doing, a person were to reply, 'I am busy discharging energy into my efferent nerves', he would be making what Professor Ryle might call 'a category mistake joke'.

Let us now consider what might be called the 'traditional' answer to our question. It is, at the same time, another meaning which might be given to 'I did whatever would ordinarily have produced the movement'. It is: (e) 'I willed the movement to occur'.

Let us distinguish, first, two fairly common senses of the word 'will' in which it does not seem to be true to say that a person who moves his arm voluntarily, always 'wills' it to move.

The word 'will' is sometimes used in such expressions as 'He willed the waitress to look in his direction', and 'He willed the dice to fall with sixes uppermost'. A characteristic of this use of the word 'will' is that it makes no sense to talk of the person who does the willing, himself doing whatever it is he wills to happen. There is no 'doing' which fulfils 'He willed the waitress to look in his direction': he is not the waitress. In this sense of 'will' one only wills what one cannot do. So one does not, in this sense of 'will', will one's arm to move; one simply moves it.[4]

---

[1] *Philosophical Investigations*, I, 614.

[2] Thus John Ladd, in 'Freewill and Voluntary Action', *Philosophy and Phenomenological Research*, 1951–52, writes: 'A person who has had a limb amputated may unsuccessfully will to move the absent limb. Still he has *done* something, if it only be having had the appropriate imagery and discharging nervous energy into the formerly appropriate nerves'.

[3] See William James, ibid., p. 493.

[4] If this sort of willing were to have effect it would constitute a case of what paranormal psychologists call 'psycho-kinesis'. It has been maintained by Professor J. C. Eccles, in *Nature*, 1951, pp. 53–7, and *The Neurophysiological Basis of Mind*, pp. 284–5, that such psycho-kinesis may well be the explanation of the effect of mind on brain in voluntary action. For a discussion of the idea that voluntary action is like willing other people to do things, see B. O'Shaughnessy, 'The Limits of the Will', *Philosophical Review*, 1956.

The word 'will' is also used when a perosn finds doing something very hard. We talk of a person willing himself to keep hold of a cliff edge, although the pain in his fingers is almost unbearable. And we talk of a person willing himself to appear cool and collected at an important interview. His 'willing himself' is largely a matter of encouraging himself not to give in, not to release his grasp or give way to worrying about the impression he is making. When there is no difficulty the person does not have to will himself.

It is not, or not only, a consideration of these two fairly common uses of the word 'will' which has led to its being said that what a person *really* does in moving some part of his body is to will that part of his body to move. The attraction of the 'I willed the movement to occur' answer does not lie in its being in accord with common usage. The point of giving this answer, and its meaning, is rather to be found in a certain philosophical argument purporting to show that voluntary movement is not at all what we ordinarily take it to be. To this argument, which might be called the 'causal' argument, we must now turn our attention.

II

To facilitate discussion of it, the causal argument[1] may be divided into three steps.

(1) It is a fact that when a person, as we say, 'moves his arm', the actual movement is caused by certain muscles contracting or expanding, which contractions or expansions are caused by impulses in the efferent nerves, which impulses are caused by certain physiological changes in the brain. Therefore what the agent *really* does is not to move his arm. But nor can it be held that what he *really* does is to make those physiological changes in his brain which are the starting point of the physical causal chain, since he is not even conscious of the nature of these changes. Therefore what he *really* does cannot be anything physical at all, but must be something of an altogether different kind, namely mental.

(2) Why it is that a certain mental state should produce, as it seems to, a certain physiological change in the brain, is wholly beyond our comprehension. (For the Cartesian philosopher, Arnold Geulincx, the idea of mind and body interacting was so unintelligible that he found it necessary to invoke God to supply the means of connection, by Himself willing the appropriate bodily changes on the occasion of the mental states. On this

---

[1] My formulation of the argument is based mainly on David Hume, *Enquiries*, Sections 51–3, and *Treatise*, Appendix (Selby-Bigge edition, p. 632); William James, *Principles of Psychology*, II, pp. 524–6; F. H. Bradley, *Collected Essays*, I, pp. 272–83, and *Mind*, N.S. xi, 1902, p. 441; and *Mind*, N.S. xiii, 1904, p. 1; and G. Dawes Hicks, *Proc. Arist. Soc.*, 1912–13, 'The nature of willing' (containing a translation of a passage from Hermann Lotze, *Medicinische Psychologie*, p. 288).

theory the mental states are only the occasional causes of the bodily changes, and the theory is accordingly known as 'occasionalism'. Bradley substituted in place of God a variety of special dispositions to provide the connection. With reference to Bradley's use of the word 'disposition' Dawes Hicks remarked, 'I suspect that too often the notion of disposition does not serve the familiar device of providing a *tertium quid* between two modes of being that seem otherwise to resist the attempt to think of them as intelligibly connected'. Hume contented himself with remarking, 'So far from perceiving the connection between an act of volition, and a movement of the body, it is allowed that no effect is more inexplicable from the powers and essence of thought and matter'.) That is, we have no insight into why a certain mental state should be associated with a certain physiological change in the brain. For all we know, the mental states could have been what they are now and the bodily changes quite different. Consequently 'however manifest it may appear to us that in none of our bodily activities are we consciously so thoroughly at home as in regard to our own movements, however readily we may believe that we are self-acting, even down to the smallest details of such movements, yet in all this we are the victims of illusion'.[1]

(3) Why did we ever suppose ourselves to be 'at home' in our movements? Why are we 'the victims of the illusion that we are self-acting'? Why is it not immediately obvious to everyone that we do something of quite a different kind from a movement, namely something mental, which, by the grace of God (Geulincx), or of special dispositions (Bradley), results in a movement? The answer is that what characterizes the mental state which results in, say, a movement of one's arm, is precisely that it is an uninhibited thought *of the arm moving*. It is this happy coincidence that accounts for the idea we have that we really do move our arms. If, in order to induce those physiological changes in the brain which are appropriate for the arms to move, we had to have an idea, not of the desired arm-movements, but of the necessary brain-changes, then we would never have supposed ourselves to be 'at home' in the movements of our arms: the arm-movements would always have seemed at a remove from us. Confirmation that the mental state of willing consists in having an idea of the movement desired, which somehow triggers off the causal chain ending in the movement (the so-called 'ideo-motor' theory) is to be found in such facts as that 'if an individual merely thinks intently of falling forward, swaying forward begins'.[2] Voluntarily controlled actions are

---

[1] Lotze, *Medicinische Psychologie*, p. 288, as translated by Dawes Hicks. The Humean equivalent to the illusion that we are 'self-acting' would be the illusion that the immediate object of power in voluntary movement is the limb which is moved.
[2] J. P. Guilford, *General Psychology*, pp. 265–9.

thus 'responses to autosuggestions, either in the form of words or imagined actions or ideas of other kinds. In any determined voluntary action we stimulate ourselves verbally with commands to do or not to do an act'.[1]

III

Before attempting a reply to the first two steps of this argument it may be helpful to comment on, and expose some of the implications of, the final step.

Perhaps the most startling consequence of accepting the final step of the argument is that one is thereby involved in denying the validity of the customary distinction between voluntary and involuntary movements. This comes out most clearly in Bradley's treatment of the topic. Accepting, as he does, the ideo-motor theory, he writes[2]: 'An idea of a state of my salivary glands or sexual organs will produce its existence in fact. We hear of those who can blush, shiver, sweat, or shed tears if their mind is set on it. And if we think of various sensations in parts of our bodies, we can produce them at will, and can induce at our pleasure other bodily alterations through emotional excitement. Now on the one hand, I believe, the view could not be sustained that our striped or voluntary muscles are here the necessary agents; and on the other hand to deny that these changes are volitional would be to confess oneself refuted. With the nature of the process, considered physiologically, I am not concerned; but, as will, it is merely a case of our law. Where we have had a bodily state A_1 with a psychical state B_1, then, when B_2 comes in, A_2 tends to appear; and, if an idea of A is what produces the result, that result is volition. . . . This is the essence of volition.'

In the light of this consequence of the ideo-motor theory it is hardly surprising that there have been attempts to disprove it, either by argument or by experiment. It may suffice to mention two such attempts, and an experiment of my own.

William McDougall writes[3]:–

The doctrine of 'ideo-motor action' is an exaggeration and distortion of the truth that every cycle of mental activity tends naturally and primitively to express itself in bodily movement. The 'ideo-motor theory' has been widely accepted and may be found dogmatically stated in many recent books. It asserts that every 'idea' is not only a state or act of knowing but also a tendency to movement; and this is made the basis of a widely

---

[1] J. P. Guilford, *General Psychology*, pp. 265–9.
[2] *Collected Essays*, I, pp. 275–6.
[3] *Outline of Psychology*, pp. 290–1.

accepted general theory of action, the 'ideo-motor theory'. The ideo-motor theory is most plausible in the case of 'ideas' of bodily movement. It has frequently been alleged that, if we think of a movement, that movement inevitably occurs, unless we somehow inhibit it. And one theory of volition asserts that volition is essentially the inhibition of 'ideas' which inhibit the 'idea' of movement. I cannot discover any substantial foundation for such assertions. It is clearly possible to think of such a movement as raising the hand, either as a movement to be made or as a movement not to be made. And I can find no truth in the assertion that, when I think of such a movement, my limb fairly tingles with the tendency to move, and that it is necessary to exert some inhibitory power in order to prevent its movement. To merely think of a movement and to intend or to will a movement are entirely distinct. . . . The relation of our impulses, intentions and volitions to the action movements of our limbs remains entirely obscure, a part of the larger mystery of the relation between experience and bodily processes. The ideo-motor theory is a mistaken attempt to resolve this mystery.

McDougall does not say what he would regard as the proper way of going about resolving the 'mystery of the relation between experience and bodily processes'. But his use of the word 'mystery' suggests that he may think that it is not the sort of problem for scientists *qua* scientists to solve.

Professor C. T. Morgan approaches the problem from the point of view of a physiological psychologist. He writes[1]:

What do we have to do in order to gain voluntary control of a response? It was at one time supposed that, if we could call to mind how the muscles would feel when moved in a certain way—in other words, if we had a clear memory of the proprioceptive sensations produced by the movement—we could then move those muscles appropriately. It was even sometimes supposed that such a memory of a movement must necessarily precede the movement which we desire to make.[2]

Not only, however, is this anticipatory proprioception not necessary, but research has also shown that proprioception alone—or even when combined with a visual image of what the movement should be—is not

[1] 'Voluntary Control of Movement', in Boring, Langfeld, and Weld, *Foundations of Psychology*, p. 50.

[2] For a revival of this theory see Professor C. A. Campbell, 'Self-activity and its modes', in *Contemporary British Philosophy*, *Third Series*, p. 93. Campbell holds that if a person has somehow forgotten what are the specific sensations associated with moving his leg, he cannot will to move it. His ground for this belief is his conviction, based on introspection, 'that the *immediate* object of our willing is not the movement of our leg but certain kinaesthetic and other sensations upon which, we have learned from experience, the movement of our leg normally supervenes'.

a sufficient preliminary process to produce 'at will' a movement never before voluntarily initiated.

In certain experiments, persons who could not move their ears voluntarily had their ear muscles stimulated electrically so as to produce the movement. These persons felt the movement and saw it in a mirror. Still they could not move their ears voluntarily. In attempting to move them, they had the same sense of helplessness which they had experienced before the electrical stimulation. In their attempts, however, they moved the voluntarily controlled muscles of the brow, jaw, and cheek, in such a way that the muscles of the ear were accidentally moved with them. Thus the ear muscles were brought into the reaction pattern, with the result that there occurred both efferent impulses to the muscles and proprioception from their contraction. It was only then that the proprioception, by becoming a link in a reflex circle, helped to develop full voluntary control of the ears.

These facts give us a picture of the origin and development of voluntary movement. It is clear from them that the *first movement* of our muscle groups are unconscious and *involuntary*, and that they come under conscious voluntary control only later, after the muscles have been 'accidentally' innervated.

An experiment of which I have not found any mention in the psychology books, which illustrates Morgan's thesis, is the following. The subject is asked to bare his right arm, and to hold it, fully extended, palm downwards, horizontally in front of him. He is then asked to move his elbow anti-clockwise about 45 degrees *without moving his hand*. In all probability he will report the 'sense of helplessness' to which Morgan refers. He knows what is required, in the sense that he can imagine the movement occurring. He may even be able to imagine how it would feel. But he *cannot* obey the instruction.

Next he is asked to rest his hand flat on a table in front of him. He will find that he can now obey the instruction to move his elbow without moving his hand. He is no longer helpless. But once he takes his hand off the table he is likely to be as helpless as before. And remembering what it felt like to move his elbow without moving his hand is of no assistance.

If, however, he very gradually reduces the pressure of his hand on the table at the same time as he moves his elbow, he will be able to acquire the capacity to move his elbow, without moving his hand, when his hand is *not* resting on the table.

Someone might describe the situation by saying that the subject has learnt *how* to move his elbow without moving his hand. But if we ask the subject how he does it, what the secret is, there is nothing he can say. He can tell us how he acquired the capacity, and he can, while exercising it, say, 'This is how I do it'. Of course, if he is a neurologist, he may be able to explain how it is that he acquired the capacity by doing what he did. *But there is nothing he can say, about what is going on in his mind at the time he does it, which will enable someone else to make this sort of movement.* There is no 'secret' of voluntary action. If a person cannot raise one eyebrow without raising the other, then he cannot. But if he can, then there is nothing to it: he simply does it.

IV

Let us return now to the first two steps in the causal argument, the steps which lead to the conclusion, in Lotze's words, that the appearance of our being 'at home' in our own movements is an illusion.

What are we to make of the very first assertion in the argument, the assertion that arm movements are caused by muscles contracting and expanding, these in turn by nervous impulses, and so on? In the argument this is taken to imply that we are not 'at home' in our bodily movements, that the relation between the mental and the bodily sides of a voluntary movement is no more intimate than that between, say, thinking of something very frightening and sweating.

One way of responding to this would be to dismiss the causal account as irrelevant, and to refuse to countenance talk of what a person *really* does.

But if we dismiss the causal account as irrelevant it seems that we may also be involved in dismissing the question with which we began as meaningless. The patient who was asked to put his hand on top of his head did not do so—his hand did not move. But it was not as if he had simply ignored the request. On the contrary, he was surprised on opening his eyes to find that the movement had not taken place. Are we simply to say that he did not do anything, and leave it at that?

But this reconsideration of the question with which we began itself suggests an alternative to dismissing the causal account as irrelevant. We can say: its relevance has been over-played, as not only providing the reason for talking of what a person *really* does, but also as indicating what the content of such talk must be. We have taken the dose twice, so to speak. We have taken it once in accepting the necessity of introducing a terminology which is such that the truth or falsity of the statements in it is not dependent on the truth or falsity of statements about the body and how it is functioning. (That is, we recognize that we would never have occasion to say of anybody 'He is moving his arm' were it not for the fact that nervous impulses *do* cause muscles to contract, etc.; and we look for a way of describing what a person does—what he *really* does—which is truth-functionally independent of such facts.)

And we have taken the dose a second time in supposing that we are dictated in our choice of a terminology to describe what a person *really* does not only by the requirements (1) that it can truthfully be said of him that he does it no matter what happens in his body, what movements do or do not take place, etc., and (2) that it is something he is aware of doing, but also by the requirement (3) that it shall be whatever has been found to be the first link in the causal chain.

One might think that once the incompatibility of the second requirement and this additional one was seen—for a person is not aware of making physiological changes in his brain—it would be realized that one must have misunderstood the relevance of the causal account in adding this requirement. But such is the strength of the impulse (an impulse which finds expression in a most explicit manner in the works of J. C. Eccles, to which reference has already been made) to assimilate all explanation to explanation in terms of space and energy, that this objection is overcome by thinking of the mind (the events in which we are aware of, by definition) as a sort of energy-system, which is located either in the head itself, or in a higher dimensional space than the physical world,[1] and saying that what we *really* do are events in this energy-system which 'influence' the brain.

The situation may be made somewhat clearer by comparing it with a parallel situation in the case of perception.

It may be pointed out that what colour a carpet looks to someone depends on the state of his nervous system. If he took certain drugs it might look quite different to him. His awareness of the carpet is thus subject to certain conditions—there being light, his having eyes, an optic nerve, etc. Here, just as in the case of voluntary action, a causal account can be given of a person's perception of a carpet as being, say, blue. And in the light of this causal account we may be invited to talk of what the person is *immediately* aware of.

Here again the relevance of the causal account can be over-played. We can regard it as not only providing the reason for talking of what a person is *immediately* aware of, but also as indicating what the content of such talk must be. It provides us with a reason for introducing, if there is not one already, a terminology which is such that the statements in it are *not* subject to verification or falsification by reference to conditions under which we are observing something. And it is taken as indicating what the content of such talk must be, by those who say that what we are immediately aware of is a 'picture' which is somehow aroused in our minds as a result of certain physiological changes in our brains.[2] (If it were not too

---

[1] J. R. Smythies, 'The Extension of Mind', *J. Soc. Psych. Res.*, 1951, pp. 477–502.
[2] J. A. V. Butler, 'Pictures in the Mind', *Science News 22*.

silly for words it would be said that what one was *immediately* aware of was the state of one's brain.)

Now in the case of perception we already have a terminology which is such that statements in it are not subject to verification or falsification by reference to conditions under which we are observing something. We can say, 'What he is *immediately* aware of is *how the carpet looks to him*'. In using this phrase, 'how it looks to him', the conditions under which he observes the carpet are made truth-functionally irrelevant. He can always be mistaken about what he is aware of—the conditions under which he is observing may not be what he takes them to be—but he cannot be mistaken about how whatever he is aware of looks to him.

In saying 'He is *immediately* aware of how the carpet looks to him', we are not debarred from saying, concurrently, that he is *aware* of the carpet. We are not debarred from saying this because 'how it looks to him' is not another *thing*. And so it does not 'come between' the observer and the carpet. He is *aware* of the carpet *and* he is *immediately aware* of how it looks to him.

What we want, it seems, is an account of what a person *really* does, which is like the 'how the thing looks to him' account of what the person is *immediately* aware of. We want an account of what we *really* do which does not put something else in the place of what we *do*, which does not come between us and our bodily movements. (This, I take it, is the point of the remark Wittgenstein quotes, in *Philosophical Investigations*, I, 615, 'Willing, if it is not to be a sort of wishing, must be the action itself. It cannot be allowed to stop anywhere short of the action'.)

The account we are led to give by treating the causal facts as indicating what the content of such an account must be, is one which does put something else in the place of what we do. According to it the connection of mental state and bodily movement is purely contingent. 'For all we know the mental states could have been what they are now and the bodily changes quite different.' From this, the assimilation of voluntary movements to those involuntary ones which are the effect of, say, emotional excitement, follows quite naturally. I may be able to think of something so frightening that I start to sweat. I cannot tell, without experience of the connection, that thinking of something very frightening will ordinarily lead to sweating. That is, I can give a full description of what it is to think of something very frightening without it being evident that it leads to sweating. Similarly, according to this account, a full description of what a person *really* does in moving his arms could be given without it being evident that it ordinarily leads to his arms moving. It is as a consequence of *this* that we are said to be not at home in our movements, not self-acting in them. What one *really* does, on this account, would presumably be something one could do without ever having moved one's arms.

It is as if, in the case of perception, something could look to a person like a carpet without his knowing what it would be like to see a carpet.

V

The two requirements for a description of what a person *really* does in voluntary movement, if the causal account is taken only as providing a reason for such talk, are (1) that it can truthfully be said of him that he does it regardless of what happens in his body, what movements do or do not take place, etc., and (2) that it is something he is aware of doing.

In our language as it stands there simply is no short description which satisfies these requirements. There is no description of what a person *really* does which is as much a part of our everyday language as is the description, 'he moved his arm', of what he does. But there is no reason why we should not introduce some new expression, such as 'So far as he, but not necessarily his arm, was concerned, he moved his arm', or 'So far as the mental side of him as an agent is concerned, he moved his arm'; at the same time stipulating that it is to work like 'He moved his arm', *except that it can be true even when 'His arm moved' is false.*

And thus is the question with which we began answered.

VI

I have tried to characterize the sort of thinking which often lies behind the use of the word 'will'. Any brief characterization of this sort of thinking is bound to be open to misinterpretation. But if I had to put it briefly I would say that what lies behind the use of the word 'will' is the thought that the mind is only accidentally embodied. Its embodiment is an extrinsic not an intrinsic, feature of it. Perhaps the clearest expression of this thought is to be found in the article by Dawes Hicks[1]: 'Seeing that for the realization of a resolve or a purpose the conscious subject is at the mercy of an extraordinarily intricate conjunction of factors lying beyond the range of his inner life, seeing that the mechanism by means of which volition finds expression in the external world is completely hidden from him, the conclusion seems forced upon us that what specifically characterizes volition as a fact of mind must be, to a large extent, at least, independent of the execution which is normally its consequent. The scope of willing, the content of the inner state which we call an act of will, would doubtless be enormously affected if execution habitually happened in a way other than that in which, as a matter of fact, it does happen, but the peculiar characteristic of willing as a state of mind might still be the same as it is now.'

[1] G. Dawes Hicks, *Proc. Arist. Soc.*, 1912–13, p. 40.

What lies behind the preference for such an account of what a person *really* does in voluntary movement, as 'So far as he, but not necessarily his arm, was concerned, he moved his arm', is the thought that 'the scope of willing' and 'the peculiar characteristic of willing as a state of mind', so far from being independent of the movements a person actually makes, are conceptually parasitic on them. The mind, in its origins at least, is *necessarily* an embodied one.

It has been suggested[1] that an examination of the nature of voluntary activity may throw light on the freewill problem. Whether or not this is so depends on what one takes this problem to be.

One thing that can be said is this. Whereas any account on the lines of the ideo-motor theory readily lends itself to an interpretation of the action of mind on body in voluntary movements as causal (even if the cause is only an 'occasional' one), an account such as I have given does not readily lend itself to this interpretation. For if one knows that a person has moved his arm so far as the mental side of him as an agent is concerned, and one knows that his body is functioning properly, then one knows what part of his body will have moved. Hence (if one accepts the Humean thesis that if C is the cause of E then one cannot say, prior to experience of their conjunction, anything about E from a consideration of C alone) the action of mind on body in voluntary movement is not causal action.

Now the freewill problem may be taken to be the problem of explaining how a bodily movement can be accounted for in two different ways—in the 'physical' and the 'personal' ways—with each way seeming to give a complete accounting. This is how the freewill problem has been understood by, for example, those who see a solution in the 'physical' accounting not being as complete as had been thought.[2]

If this is taken to be the freewill problem then what has been said about volition *is* relevant. For if the 'personal' accounting is *not* a causal accounting then it does not conflict with the 'physical' accounting, which *is* causal. The problem is solved, not by denying either determinism or freewill but by showing there not to be a conflict between them.

---

[1] Campbell, *Contemporary British Philosophy, Third Series*, pp. 85–6.

[2] For example, J. C. Eccles, *The Neurophysiological Basis of Mind*, p. 272: 'The principal grounds for the theoretical belief that voluntary control of actions is an illusion are derived from the assumptions that science gives a deterministic explanation of all natural phenomena and that we are entirely within this deterministic scheme. In this context reference may be made to the recent discussion by Popper (*Brit. Journ. Phil. Sci.*, 1950, pp. 117–33, 173–95), in which he concludes that not only quantum physics but even 'classical mechanics is not deterministic, but must admit the existence of unpredictable events'. There are thus no sound scientific grounds for denying the freedom of the will, which virtually must be assumed if we are to act as scientific investigators.'

41

JEROME SHAFFER

COULD MENTAL STATES BE BRAIN PROCESSES? (1961)

In recent discussions of the relation between mental states and brain processes, a view that has received much support is the Identity theory. Its adherents[1] allow that expressions that refer to mental states differ in their meaning from expressions that refer to brain processes, but they claim that the actual existents picked out by the former expressions turn out, as a matter of empirical fact, to be identical with those picked out by the latter expressions. I wish to examine this theory. For convenience, I shall refer to mental states, e.g., feeling pain, having an after-image, thinking about a problem, considering some proposition, etc., as C-states, and I shall refer to whatever brain process may be going on at the same time that some mental state is occurring as a B-process. My main contentions will be (1) that C-states cannot be identical with B-processes because they do not occur in the same place, (2) that there is nothing to stop us from making the Identity theory correct by adopting a convention for locating C-states, and (3) that the question whether it would be useful to adopt such a convention depends upon empirical facts which are at present unknown.

I

Before pointing out why the Identity theory is incorrect, I wish to defend it against some standard objections. These objections arise from the failure to see that it is *de facto* identity, not identity of meaning, that is intended. Descartes, for example, concluded that the mental and the physical could not be identical, had to be separate and distinct substances, because of such facts as these: (1) that the concept of the mental is a quite different concept from the concept of the physical, (2) that someone might be sure of the existence of his mental process while raising doubts about the existence of his body, and (3) that God could make the mind exist in separation from

[1] Cf. U. T. Place, '*Is Consciousness a Brain Process?*' Brit. Jnl. of Psychology, 47 (1956); Herbert Feigl, '*The "Mental" and the "Physical"*,' in H. Feigl, G. Maxwell, and M. Scriven, eds., *Concepts, Theories, and the Mind Body Problem* (Minneapolis: Univ. of Minn. Press, 1958); J. J. C. Smart, 'Sensations and Brain Processes', *The Philosophical Review*, 68 (1959); Hilary Putnam, 'Minds and Machines', in Sidney Hook, ed., *Dimensions of Mind* (New York, 1960).

the body. But none of these facts supports Descartes' conclusion that mental things cannot be identical with physical things. They show only, what is admitted by Identity theorists, that we cannot know *a priori* that the mental and physical are identical. Compare the case of the expressions, 'human being' and 'featherless biped'. The same facts hold, namely (1) that the concept of a human being is a quite different concept from the concept of a featherless biped, (2) that someone might be sure of the existence of human beings while raising doubts about the existence of featherless bipeds, and (3) that God could have made human beings exist as separate things from featherless bipeds. Yet none of these considerations rules out the possibility that, as a matter of pure empirical fact, human beings turn out to be identical with featherless bipeds, in the sense that the two classes are co-extensional, such that anything which is a member of the one class turns out to be a member of the other, also. The same goes for C-states and B-processes. Identity theorists claim only that anything which is a C-state turns out, in fact, to be a B-process also. To put the thesis in Cartesian language, it is claimed that there is only one set of substances, physical substances, and this one set has some members that can be referred to by both physical and mental expressions. None of Descartes' considerations rules out this possibility.

Nor is it a legitimate objection to the Identity theory that where one expression is used we cannot always substitute the other and preserve the truth-value. For it is a necessary consequence of the fact that C-state expressions and B-process expressions differ in meaning that in at least two familiar cases what we can assert about the one we may not be able to assert about the other. First there is the case of the so-called verbs of intentionality: it may be true that a particular C-state is remembered or expected, for example, but false that a particular B-process is remembered or expected. Secondly there is the case of modal statements: it is true that C-states are necessarily C-states but false that B-processes are necessarily C-states. Thus that two things are *de facto* identical does not imply that any truth about the one will be a truth about the other.

II

Are C-states in fact identical with B-processes? There are a number of criteria that must be met if we wish to show that they are. For one thing, we must show that the two exist during the same time interval, for if there were some time in which one existed but the other did not, that would settle conclusively that they were not identical. For example, if we had reason to think that the object referred to by the expression 'the Evening Star' did not exist in the morning, then we would have reason to think that the Evening Star was not identical with the Morning Star. This co-existence requirement seems to be met in the case of C-states and their correlated B-processes. If future discoveries in neurology and psychology were to lead us to think that they occurred at somewhat different times, then we could certainly rule out the Identity theory.

A further condition to be met for identifying C-states with B-processes is that, at any given time, both must be located in the same place. If it can be shown that one is not found in the place where the other is found, then it has been shown that they are not identical. It would be just like showing that the object referred to by the expression, 'The Evening Star,' was not, in the morning, in the place where the object referred to by the expression, 'the Morning Star,' was located; that would show they were not identical.

Is the spatial requirement met by C-states and B-processes? Do they occur in the same place? No. B-processes are, in a perfectly clear sense, located where the brain is, in a particular region of physical space. But it is not true that C-states occur tin he brain, or inside the body at all, for that matter. To be sure, I may have a pain in my leg or in my head; we do locate sensations in the body. But that is not to say that we give location to the *state of consciousness* that I have when I am having a sensation. The pain is in my leg, but it is not the case that my state of being-aware-of-a-pain-in-my-leg is also in my leg. Neither is it in my head. In the case of thoughts, there is no temptation to give them location, nor to give location to the mental state of being aware of a thought. In fact, it makes no sense at all to talk about C-states as being located somewhere in the body. We would not understand someone who pointed to a place in his body and claimed that it was there that his entertaining of a thought or having of an after-image was located. It would make no more sense than to claim that his entertaining of a thought was cubical or a micrometer in diameter.

The fact that it makes no sense to speak of C-states occurring in a volume occupied by a brain means that the Identity theory cannot be correct. For it is a necessary condition for saying that something is identical with some particular physical object, state, or process that the thing be located in the place where the particular physical object state or process is. If it is not there, it cannot be identical with what is there. Here we have something that distinguishes the mind-body case from such examples of identity as men with featherless bipeds, Morning Star with Evening Star, water with H_2O, lightning with electrical discharge, etc. To consider another example, it has been discovered that light rays are electromagnetic radiations of certain wavelengths. The Identity theorist would claim that '*every* argument for *or against* identification would apply equally in the mind-body case and in the light-electromagnetism case'.[1] But this is

---

[1] Putnam, op. cit., p. 171.

incorrect. There are ways of locating rays of light and ways of locating electromagnetic radiations, and it turns out that wherever one is located the other is also. But this cannot be said in the mind-body case.

To do justice to the Identity theory, however, we cannot let the matter rest here. For it is not entirely correct to say that C-states are not located in the brain. That would give the false impression that they were not in the brain because they were somewhere else. Furthermore, how would one show that they were not in the brain? Do we even understand the claim that they are not in the brain? If it makes no sense to speak of C-states as in the brain, then it makes no sense to speak of them as not in the brain either. The fact of the matter is that we have no rules in our language either for asserting that C-states have a particular location or for denying that they have a particular location. So we have here a case in which it is senseless to apply the criterion of same location. But the Identity theory still will not do, because if it is senseless to apply one of the criteria for identity then it is also senseless to claim that there is identity.

III

At this point the Identity theorist may make the following suggestion:

We may easily adopt a convention (which is not a change in our present rules for the use of experience words but an addition to them) whereby it would make sense to talk of an experience in terms appropriate to physical process.[1]

A convention we might adopt would be something like this: for any C-state, if it has a corresponding B-process, it will be said to be located in that place where its corresponding B-process is located. Given this convention, it then becomes a matter for empirical investigation whether any C-state has location in space and where that location, if any, is. The outcome of such an investigation could be settled, at least in principle, with as much exactness as we like.

If we were to adopt such a convention, we should run into the following difficulty, raised by Richard B. Brandt:

Even if one does decide to locate them in the brain it is possible to hold that the brain-volume contains *both* physical events *and* these other events, and to deny that they are one and the same thing.[2]

Brandt does not give examples, but it is easy to do so. Suppose we set up a magnetic field and then put a physical object into it. Then one and the same volume would contain two different things, a physical object and a

[1] Smart, op. cit., p. 152.
[2] Richard B. Brandt, 'Doubts about the Identity Theory', in *Dimensions of Mind*, p. 66.

magnetic field. Why should we say there are two things there, rather than one, a physical object with a particular magnetic property or in a particular magnetic state? Here we need a further necessary condition for identity, in addition to being in the same place at the same time. The presence of the one must be an (empirically) necessary condition for the presence of the other. In the case of the physical object and the magnetic field it is clear that neither one is an empirically necessary condition for the other; take away one and the other would still remain. In the case of C-states and B-processes we have assumed that investigations will show that you cannot have one without the other. If that turns out to be the case, then the third necessary condition of identity will have been met.

The three conditions for identity so far discussed are jointly sufficient. If all three are met, then B-processes and C-states are identical; if it is likely that all three are met, then it is likely that B-processes and C-states are identical. There is no room for any alternative. If B-processes and C-states did not exist at the same time or did not exist at the same place, then a case could be made for saying that they were functionally dependent but different. But if we assume that it will turn out to be the case that they must exist in the same place at the same time, we should be unreasonable to hold out for some other theory—a Causal theory, a Parallelist theory, or the like.

The crucial question, then, is whether we are free simply to adopt a convention for locating C-states in space. Compare the case of adopting a convention for locating fictional characters in space. Suppose we said that since it makes no sense at present to ask where, for example, Snow White is in physical space right now, we shall adopt a convention for assigning location. For any fictional character, it will be correct to say that it is, was, and always will be located in the place where its creator was when he first thought of the character. We could now point to a place and say, 'There is where the fictional character, Snow White, is'. But it is obvious that this could not be a way of locating an object, but only an elliptical way of saying that this is where his creator was. The reason that this could not be a convention for locating fictional objects in space does not depend upon the particular convention we might choose. Any convention of this sort would be absurd because there is no room in the concept of fictional characters for such a convention. This is because it is self-contradictory to speak of a non-existent thing like a fictional character as having some actual location in physical space. The very meaning of 'fictional character' depends upon the contrast with things that actually do have spatial location. Hence we are not free, in this case, simply to adopt a convention for locating, which we can add to our present rules governing expressions that refer to fictional characters.

In the case of C-states it seems to me that room does exist for the adoption of such a convention. There is nothing in the way we teach the use of C-state expressions that rules out their having spatial location, no direct contrast with things that actually do have spatial location. So we can adopt an additional rule that would allow us to locate C-states in space. This is, of course, to change the meanings of expressions that refer to C-states, to change our concept of C-states. It is a change that is consistent with our present rules and that allows us to keep the rest of the concept intact, but it is still a change in the concept. There is, however, no change in the extension of the terms; everything that is a C-state as it is ordinarily conceived will also be a C-state as the concept has been modified, and vice versa. The only difference is that it will now make sense to ask about the physical location of C-states.

Given this modified concept of C-states, the criteria for *de facto* identity of C-states and B-processes have been met. Those things and just those things referred to by C-state expressions will be referred to by B-process expressions. It would be as unreasonable to hold that the world contains C-states in addition to B-processes as it would be to hold that the world contains featherless bipeds in addition to human beings (assuming the two classes are co-extensive) or water in addition to H_2O. Of course it is logically possible that there be disembodied C-states, with no corresponding B-processes. That is to say, an Identity theory that uses the modified concept of C-states is a genuine empirical hypothesis, like the hypotheses that human beings are featherless bipeds and that water is H_2O.

IV

In this section I wish to discuss the objection that nothing at all would be gained by so altering our concept of C-states that the identity would hold. This objection is referred to by Smart as 'the strongest with which I have to deal' (p. 150) and 'the one I am least confident of having satisfactorily met' (p. 148, footnote). The objection may be put in the following way. For it to be a factual discovery that C-states and B-processes are identical, each must have some feature peculiar to itself by which it may be identified as a C-state or as a B-process; but then are we not at least committed to 'the existence of irreducibly psychic *properties*'? (p. 148).

In trying to deal with this objection, Smart thinks he must show that psychic properties must be *defined* in terms of physical properties. He attempts to define C-states in the following way. He maintains that when a person reports the occurrence of a C-state, say the having of a yellowish-orange after-image:—

... he is saying something like this: '*There is something going on which is like what is going on when* I have my eyes open, am awake, and there is an orange illuminated in good light in front of me, that is, when I really see an orange' (p. 149).

Thus Smart attempts to represent the special features of first-person present-tense reports as nothing but rather indefinite assertions which, if made definite (although the speaker may not know enough physiology to make them definite himself), would turn out to be ordinary assertions about B-processes.

The difficulty with such a definition is that it leaves no room for the fact that we are sometimes justified in the reports we make about our own C-states although we have no information at all about B-processes, not even indefinite information. How could one report even the minimal something going on unless one noticed something? And since it obviously is the case that we can notice something even when we notice nothing in our nervous system, it obviously is the case that some other feature must be noticed which entitles us to say that something similar is going on.

In general, it is hopeless to expect to be able to *define* psychic properties in terms of physical properties, and still hold, as Identity theorists do, that it is a factual discovery that C-states and B-processes are identical. Unless there are special features that allow us independently to identify C-states, we can never be in a position to discover their *de facto* identity with B-processes.

I see no reason why the Identity theorist should be disconcerted by admitting that psychic properties are different from physical properties. For to say that psychic properties are different from physical properties is simply a way of saying that mentalistic expressions have different meanings and different conditions for ascription from physicalistic expressions. It is a fact about the world that both sets of expressions have application (how could that be denied?), but this is a fact from which the Identity theory begins, not a fact that destroys it. Furthermore, that psychic and physical properties are different does not in any way imply that they are 'irreducibly' different. To take a classic case, the property of having a certain temperature must be different from the property of having a certain mean kinetic energy, or else it could never have been discovered that they were related in particular ways, ways which we indicate when we say that temperature has been reduced to mean kinetic energy. In general, for one property to be reducible to another, they must be different; something cannot be reducible to itself.

But still one might ask what is to be gained by altering our concept of C-states so as to be able to assert their *de facto* identity with B-processes?

It does seem to me that one now does have a simpler conceptual scheme. The traditional Dualistic theories admitted two distinct classes of entities and events, physical entities and physical events on the one hand and mental entities and events on the other. On the Identity theory there is only one set of entities and events, the physical, and it is just these entities and events which turn out to be what is referred to when people use mentalistic expressions. This is analogous to the discovery that water and steam are not different substances but the same substance in different states. It is perfectly true that not all physical processes will be identical with C-states, only neural processes of a particular sort. And that subset of physical processes will have special features, those which are the logically necessary features of C-states. For example, (1) there will be one and only one person in the world who would know of the existence of a particular C-state even if he lacked any of the grounds that anyone else might have for knowing of the existence of that state, and (2) the one and only privileged person could not fail to know of its existence, if it occurred at all. These are features of C-states and, if C-states turn out to be identical with B-processes then they will be features of B-processes. Thus the simplification presented by the Identity theory has its price. One class of physical events will have the familiar and undeniable features of C-states. These features may be, in some sense, reducible to physicalistic features, but they are not thereby eliminated from the scheme of things. Only extra entities are eliminated.

V

The question whether the conceptual revision proposed by Identity theorists should be accepted or not cannot be determined solely by philosophers. It is in part an empirical question, to be judged in terms of future discoveries in neurology and psychology. Take the similar case of water and H_2O. Imagine the debates that must have raged when it was discovered that water could be replaced by definite proportions of hydrogen and oxygen. Were the water, on the one hand, and the two gases, on the other, merely successive states of some further, underlying thing (cf. Double Aspect theory)? Did the one produce the other (cf. Interaction theories)? Was the one a mere shadowy appearance of the other (cf. Epiphenomenalism)? Was there mere correlation of the one disappearing as the other appeared (cf. Parallelism)? Or was the water *identical* with the combination of the two? The adoption of new uses for such terms as 'element', 'compound', and 'analysis' did not amount merely to trivial solution that simply begged the question in favour of the claim of identity. For it was an empirical discovery that certain substances are 'compounds' of specific 'elements', the discovery that a particular set of terms can be used to represent and describe these substances in such a way as to tie together a large range of phenomena, yield predictions, and furnish explanations. From a knowledge of the chemical constituents and their proportions we can predict and explain many features of the compound–mass, density, spectral patterns, radioactive properties, and frequently much of its physical and chemical behaviour. It is such fruits as these that make plausible the identification of substances with the chemical combination of their constituents.

In the case of the Identity theory, the linguistic innovation consists in modifying our concept of C-states by giving criteria for the spatial location of C-states. Only future discoveries in neuro-physiology can tell us how fruitful this innovation might be. If, for example, we never get beyond the point of having gross, brute correlations between C-states and B-processes, then I can see no advantages in the claim that they are identical. But suppose we can, some day, discover certain physical features which distinguish the physical processes that are identical with C-states from those which are not; suppose we can break down B-processes into structures that correspond to the internal structures of C-states; suppose that detailed theories could be worked out for showing that, given the particular neural variables, we get one C-state rather than another and we can infer new C-states from novel configurations of B-processes. If these developments occur, then, as in the example from chemistry, it would be unreasonable to hold out against the Identity theory. For we would have not merely gross correlations of C-states and B-processes but precisely the detailed kind of point-for-point correlations that entitles us in other cases to say that one property, state, or thing has been reduced to another. The value of thinking of C-states in this new way, as having location in the brain, would have been shown by empirical discoveries. But this is not to say that it would have been an empirical discovery that C-states were located in the brain.

If we were to accept the Identity theory with its new concept of C-states, the question would still remain of what the exact relation is between C-states and B-processes. One possibility, although not the only one, is that of a macro-micro relation. Even here there are alternatives. One would be that C-states were composed of neural components analogous to the physicist's particles or the chemist's elements. If it seems strange to think that C-states might be made up of physical components, remember that even the claim that water is 'composed' of hydrogen and oxygen or of a swarm of subatomic particles requires new concepts of composition and components. A different macro-micro relation might be used, such that C-states consisted of B-processes without being composed of them; such would be the case if a field theory of neural behaviour were adopted. This would be analogous to the claim that a ray of light consists of wave-motion, that a bolt of lightning consists of an electrical discharge. A half-way house, here, might be a claim analogous to the claim that temperature consists of the mean kinetic energy of the molecules. I suspect that none of these details could be settled until we had a good deal more information about the brain.

If someone were to insist on knowing what the relation is between B-processes and C-states as we conceive them now (in contrast to how we might, some day, more usefully conceive them), then part of the answer is that they are not identical, since the spatial criterion is not met. Another part of the answer is that, if present information is a reliable guide, they occur simultaneously and are conjoined in a regular, law-like way. Another part of the answer consists in seeing in detail how this case is like and unlike other cases, e.g., two independent mechanisms, two objects interacting in the same system, a process and its by-products, looking at something from inside of it and from the outside, etc. I doubt if more than this can be done.

NAME INDEX

ANALYTICAL INDEX

ACTIVITY (POWER, FORCE), IDEA OF: not derived from external objects as they appear to the senses, 100, 381; not derived from reflecting on volition, 100-2; criticism of arguments that the idea is fictitious, 382-91; derived from reflecting on our power to produce (images of) kinaesthetic sensations, 387-91

AGENT/SPECTATOR DISTINCTION: 256, 317, 324-9, 383, 400-1; see also DOUBLE ASPECT THEORY, and SUBJECTIVE/OBJECTIVE DISTINCTION

AMPUTATION: see PHANTOM LIMBS

ASPECTS: see DOUBLE ASPECT THEORY

AUTOMATA: theory that man is a conscious automaton, 11, 141-2, 180, 185

BEASTS: criticism of Descartes' view that they are unconscious, 138-9

BODIES, THE THEORY THAT THEY ARE THE SUBJECTS OF MENTAL ACTIVITIES: contended for, as against the Cartesian view that the subjects are immaterial substances, 36-42; possibility that God has given to matter a faculty of thinking, 95; nothing conclusive against this view, 244; it has the advantage of positing no unobserved entities, 308-9; the theory is to be distinguished from theories about the mental phenomena themselves, 333-4

BODILY SENSATIONS: as evidence of body and mind being united, 30, 45-6, 258; their being a source of deception, not contrary to the power and goodness of God, 34-6; the Local Sign theory (that there is something about a bodily sensation that serves as a sign to us of the location of its cause) 16, 197-200, 375-81; the distinction, in sensual feelings of pleasure and pain, between the physical phenomena of sensory quality and the accompanying mental phenomena of feeling, 145-8; the view that there is a bodily location of sensations but not of the states of consciousness we have when we have sensations, 452

BODY: the two ways of its being apprehended, 121-2, 258-63, 377-8

BRAIN: the seat of the mind, 118-19, 313-14; compared to telephone exchange, 212-13, 294, 317-18; the manner of brain-mind liaison, a riddle pressing to be read, 314; brain states not known by direct acquaintance,

contrasted with dualism of one subject and one non-subject, 408–9; *see also* SUBSTANCE

MINDS: entirely indivisible, 33; united to all portions of the body conjointly, 46; in space, 321; capable of motion in space, 93–4; not in space, 295, 338, 452; consist of collections of mental acts, 243; that they exist, as immaterial entities, an hypothesis, 308; by their nature not accessible to sense, 323; not such that one could have an idea of them, 97; possibility that in the dim future we may obtain objective acquaintance with them, 217; not subsumable under the concept of energy, 319–20, 322–3, 326; they are energy-systems located either in the head or in a higher dimensional space than the physical world, 446; they are not mechanical systems, 310, 341; teleological explanation not exclusively applicable to them, 310; *see also* MIND, CONCEPT OF

MIND-STUFF: the reality which we perceive as matter, 169–70, 194; the doctrine of, originated in Kant and Wundt, 171; the doctrine may be true, 238–9; the doctrine fails to account for individual selves, 265

MYSTICAL SEEPAGE: the manner of communion of disembodied spirits, 365

NEUTRAL MONISM: the theory that bodies and minds are different groupings of the same elements, expounded by Mach, James and Russell, 172–9, 202–8, 266–71; likened to subjective idealism, 234–5

OCCASIONALISM: not satisfactory because it introduces a sort of continuous miracle, 66; no other bond in the union of body and soul than the efficacy of divine decrees, 76, 78; a theory based on objections to interactionism, 109; the union of body and mind a stumbling-block which occasionalism fails to surmount, 224; a view held among the disciples of Descartes, 248; not appreciably different from psycho-physical parallelism, 270; an element in the causal argument for the Ideo-motor theory, 440–2

OTHER MINDS: ejects, 165–6, 215–7; belief in them reached by drawing conclusions by analogy, 175, 215, 304; cannot be apprehended by me as they are, but only through their effects, sensations in my mind, 195; conceivability of my being able to recognize your consciousness as a direct sense-impression, 216–7; individuality consists in the impossibility of one person having access to another's presentations, 227; belief on other minds likened to belief in electrons, 337; parochialism of the convention which makes it nonsense to say that anyone could enjoy the experiences of another, 357; the soul's being visible only to one, the source of doubts about the minds of others, 368–74; impossibility of philosophical doubts about the minds of others being coherently stated, 420; God known as certainly and immediately as other minds, 99; *see also* MINDS, and VERIFICATION

PAIN: felt in one's own body but not in other bodies, 27; a teaching of nature that from a painful sensation there follows sadness of mind, 27; possibility of doubt as to whether a limb pains me although I feel pain in it, 27–8; explanation of how one may feel pain in a foot without the foot being hurt, 34–5; pain and sadness entirely different, 74; may justly be termed a sensation, 177; pains differ in quality depending on the place of the disturbance which causes them, 198–9; is the way we experience thwarted active tendency, 264; possibly not a state which has essential reference to an object, 268; not like disliking, 345; what it might mean to feel another's pain, 357; in what way it is not an irreducibly psychical something, 424–7; *see also* BODILY SENSATIONS

PERSON, PRIORITY OF THE CONCEPT OF: the notion which everybody has, that there is one single person who has at once body and consciousness, 52; the perfectly ordinary manner of speaking which treats a person as an amphibious being combining both a fleshly and a ghostly side, 362, 364; argument for, from the requirements for identification, 405–23

PHANTOM LIMBS: phenomena of, inconsistent with the theory that the experiencing subject must be present at the place of the injured limb in which a painful phenomenon is localized, 147; phenomena of, evidence for the Local Sign theory, 380; consciousness of power to command movement of palsied or amputated limbs proof that consciousness of power is illusory, 101–2; impossibility of willing the movement of an amputated limb, 387–8; possibility of voluntary movement of phantom limbs, 437–8

PINEAL GLAND: how it is known to be the main seat of the soul, 46–7; an hypothesis more occult than the most occult quality, 59–61, 326–7

PREDICTION: distinction between 'necessary to predict', 'sufficient to predict', 'necessary to produce', 'sufficient to produce', 250–1; logical impossibility of giving a person a guaranteed prediction of a decision he is still deliberating, 394–7

PRE-ESTABLISHED HARMONY: the connection between the soul and the body inexplicable in any other way, 66; a theory based on objections to interactionism, 109; the answer to a question arising from a completely false position, 300

PRIVATE/PUBLIC DISTINCTION: no mental phenomenon perceived by more than a single individual, 151; there is for each but one experience, his own, 224; the mind essentially private, 331; that the workings of one mind are not witnessable by other observers, part of the official doctrine, 338; the soul visible only to one, 368; that sensations are private but brain

is mind-stuff, 169-71; a monstrous notion, 173; it is consciousness, 192-6; the unknown cause of sensations, 281

THINKING: the essence of mind, 22-6, 28, 36-42, 44, 70; how related to its physical accompaniments, 213-5

TWO-AGENTS ACCOUNT: merely restates the problem in other terms, 157; obviously strained, 358-62

UNCONSCIOUS INTELLIGENCES: unprofitability of postulating them to explain seemingly purposive acts, 363-4

UNION OF BODY AND MIND: proved by the sensations of pain, hunger, thirst, 30, 43; compatible with their being distinct substances, 45; the explanation of the soul's power to move the body and of the body's power to act on the soul and cause sensations, 49; something which the human mind is incapable of conceiving along with the distinction between body and soul, 52; criticism of Descartes' account of the union, 61; the word 'union' ambiguous, 81; nothing more mysterious in all nature, 101; explicable only if the seeming duality of body and mind is relative to our modes of apprehension, 182-3; only a *de facto* union, 375-81

VERIFICATION: other minds unverifiable entities if mentality is not interpreted in terms of behaviour or of brain functions, 336; the difference between the method of verification of statements about thoughts and feelings and that of statements about the movements of wheels, levers, limbs, electricity, and the wind that bloweth where it listeth, visible to none though we hear the sound of it, 368; a method of verification in the case of others but not in the case of oneself, 410

VIBRATION: both vibrations and sounds, modes of feeling, 158; vibrations of nerve cells in the brain, 181; a vibration of nerve strings and a process of thought differ as do the seeing and the hearing of a vibration of violin strings, 183-4; to you my idea might appear as a vibration, 194-6; definition by description of pitch in terms of rate of vibration, 335

VOLITION (WILLING): the power of it over the body not known or felt, 100-2, 288-9; an emotion indicative of physical changes, not a cause of such changes, 140-2, 163; as truly a cause of bodily movement as is the physical activity of the brain, 184; possibly determines which of several possible transitions a given atom in the brain will undergo, 274: its immediate object not a movement but certain kinaesthetic and other sensations, 387-91; not something one can do accidentally, 389; what is left over if I subtract the fact that my arm goes up from the fact that I raise my arm, 437-49